Behavioral Simulation Methods in Tax Policy Analysis

A National Bureau
of Economic Research
Project Report

Behavioral Simulation Methods in Tax Policy Analysis

Edited by Martin Feldstein

The University of Chicago Press

Chicago and London

MARTIN FELDSTEIN is professor of economics, Harvard University (on leave). He was formerly president of the National Bureau of Economic Research and is currently chairman, Council of Economic Advisers.

The University of Chicago Press, Chicago 60637
The University of Chicago Press, Ltd., London

Library of Congress Cataloging in Publication Data

Main entry under title:

Behavioral simulation methods in tax policy analysis.

(A National Bureau of Economic Research project report)
Includes indexes.
1.Taxation—United States—Simulation methods—Addresses, essays, lectures. 2. Fiscal policy—United States—Simulation methods—Addresses, essays, lectures. I. Feldstein, Martin S.
II. Series: Project report (National Bureau of Economic Research)
HJ2381.B4   1983   339.5'25'0724   82-21766
ISBN 0-226-24084-3

Relation of the Directors to the
Work and Publications of the
National Bureau of Economic Research

1. The object of the National Bureau of Economic Research is to ascertain and to present to the public important economic facts and their interpretation in a scientific and impartial manner. The Board of Directors is charged with the responsibility of ensuring that the work of the National Bureau is carried on in strict conformity with this object.

2. The President of the National Bureau shall submit to the Board of Directors, or to its Executive Committee, for their formal adoption all specific proposals for research to be instituted.

3. No research report shall be published by the National Bureau until the President has sent each member of the Board a notice that a manuscript is recommended for publication and that in the President's opinion it is suitable for publication in accordance with the principles of the National Bureau. Such notification will include an abstract or summary of the manuscript's content and a response form for use by those Directors who desire a copy of the manuscript for review. Each manuscript shall contain a summary drawing attention to the nature and treatment of the problem studied, the character of the data and their utilization in the report, and the main conclusions reached.

4. For each manuscript so submitted, a special committee of the Directors (including Directors Emeriti) shall be appointed by majority agreement of the President and Vice Presidents (or by the Executive Committee in case of inability to decide on the part of the President and Vice Presidents), consisting of three Directors selected as nearly as may be one from each general division of the Board. The names of the special manuscript committee shall be stated to each Director when notice of the proposed publication is submitted to him. It shall be the duty of each member of the special manuscript committee to read the manuscript. If each member of the manuscript committee signifies his approval within thirty days of the transmittal of the manuscript, the report may be published. If at the end of that period any member of the manuscript committee withholds his approval, the President shall then notify each member of the Board, requesting approval or disapproval of publication, and thirty days additional shall be granted for this purpose. The manuscript shall then not be published unless at least a majority of the entire Board who shall have voted on the proposal within the time fixed for the receipt of votes shall have approved.

5. No manuscript may be published, though approved by each member of the special manuscript committee, until forty-five days have elapsed from the transmittal of the report in manuscript form. The interval is allowed for the receipt of any memorandum of dissent or reservation, together with a brief statement of his reasons, that any member may wish to express; and such memorandum of dissent or reservation shall be published with the manuscript if he so desires. Publication does not, however, imply that each member of the Board has read the manuscript, or that either members of the Board in general or the special committee have passed on its validity in every detail.

6. Publications of the National Bureau issued for informational purposes concerning the work of the Bureau and its staff, or issued to inform the public of activities of Bureau staff, and volumes issued as a result of various conferences involving the National Bureau shall contain a specific disclaimer noting that such publication has not passed through the normal review procedures required in this resolution. The Executive Committee of the Board is charged with review of all such publications from time to time to ensure that they do not take on the character of formal research reports of the National Bureau, requiring formal Board approval.

7. Unless otherwise determined by the Board or exempted by the terms of paragraph 6, a copy of this resolution shall be printed in each National Bureau publication.

(Resolution adopted October 25, 1926, as revised through September 30, 1974)

Contents

Preface

The papers in this volume represent the initial results of a National Bureau of Economic Research project to develop better methods of simulating the effects of alternative tax policies. In keeping with the NBER tradition, the papers do not offer policy advice but emphasize the empirical findings and methodological aspects of the research.

The research project, which has involved more than a dozen NBER research associates and other economists, began two and a half years ago. Although the researchers are located in universities all across the country (and in Canada and England as well), the project represents a collaborative effort and not just a conference of researchers interested in similar questions. Several of the studies are based on a common set of data and computer programs. Others are closely related in the framework that the researchers have adopted and in the tax proposals that are studied.

Research plans and preliminary research results were discussed at meetings of the NBER Taxation Program and at the NBER's 1980 Summer Institute. A preconference in October 1980 brought all the researchers together to discuss preliminary drafts of these papers. The project was supervised by a committee of which I was chairman and on which David Bradford, Charles McLure, and John Shoven served.

The final papers were then represented at a general conference in January 1981 and revised in subsequent months. The present volume includes the revised papers and the remarks of the conference discussants for each paper.

We are grateful to the National Science Foundation for providing the basic financial support for this project. Support for some of the individual studies was also provided by the NBER Study of Capital Formation and by separate National Science Foundation grants to individual researchers.

Martin Feldstein

Introduction

Martin Feldstein

Because tax rules affect economic behavior, the analysis of any proposed change in tax policy should quantify the effects of that change on economic behavior and on the economy as a whole. Although this advice is clear in principle, it is difficult to apply in practice. As a result, nearly all analyses of tax proposals have ignored the impact of the proposed change on economic behavior. The resulting calculations are therefore uninformative about the economic effects of the proposed tax policy and incorrect about its impact on tax revenue.

The purpose of the National Bureau of Economic Research Project on Behavioral Simulation Methods in Tax Policy Analysis is to begin correcting this situation. Toward that end, our research has concentrated on developing simulation models that incorporate the behavioral responses of individuals and businesses to alternative tax rules and tax rates. We have also worked on extending the computational general equilibrium models that analyze the long-run impact of tax changes on the economy as a whole.

Although several different simulation approaches are therefore included in this volume, the principal focus of the project has been on the microsimulation of individual behavior. The basic data for these simulations are stratified random samples of more than one hundred thousand individual tax reforms that the Internal Revenue Service prepares each year. Our behavioral microsimulations are an extension of the computer simulation approach that the United States Treasury and the Congressional Joint Committee on Taxation have used for over a decade to prepare detailed estimates of the revenue effects of proposed changes in the tax law. The Treasury and Joint Committee calculations take each

Martin Feldstein is professor of economics, Harvard University (on leave). He was formerly president of the National Bureau of Economic Research and is currently chairman, Council of Economic Advisers.

individual's pretax income and expenditures as fixed and calculate how changes in the tax rules would alter the resulting tax liabilities. This same practice of assuming no behavioral response to changes in tax rules has also been common in a number of studies by individual researchers. Although these analyses have played a valuable role in indicating both the aggregate effect of the proposed changes on the government budget and the distribution of the revenue change among income groups, their relevance is limited by their implicit assumption that the proposed tax changes would not alter the economic behavior of individual taxpayers.

In fact, many of the potential changes in tax laws would be expected to have significant effects on individual behavior. For example, a different method of taxing the income of working wives would alter the amount of work that they do.[1] Several studies of the tax treatment of charitable giving indicate that the tax law has a substantial effect on giving and therefore on the corresponding tax deduction.[2] A long list of behavior affected by tax policy could easily be constructed.

Ignoring the effect of a tax change on individual behavior obviously distorts the estimated impact of the proposed tax change on tax revenue. If a lower rate of tax would increase the labor supply of married women, the conventional method of analysis, which ignores this behavioral response, overstates the revenue cost of such a reduction. Similarly, because the deductibility of charitable gifts increases giving, the conventional method of analysis misstates the revenue effect of proposals to alter the deductibility of charitable gifts. The first advantage of incorporating behavioral equations is therefore to improve the accuracy of the estimated revenue effects of proposed tax changes.

The second, and I believe more important, advantage of incorporating behavioral equations is that this permits studying how alternative tax rules would affect the economic behavior itself. Since the purpose of many proposed tax changes is to alter economic behavior (or to reduce distortions that are already present), estimating the behavioral impact should be central to the simulation analysis.

During several years before the beginning of the NBER project reported here, I applied the behavioral simulation approach to studies of the effect of alternative tax policies on charitable giving and on the sale of corporate stock and the realization of capital gains. In these studies, Daniel Frisch, Joel Slemrod, Shlomo Yitzhaki, and I developed the TAXSIM computer program that uses the large IRS samples of individual tax returns to calculate changes in individuals' tax liabilities and behavior and to provide statistical summaries under the existing tax law

1. See chapter 1 by Feenberg and Rosen in the current volume and the earlier studies that they cite.
2. Chapter 5, by Feldstein and Lindsey, summarizes the previous research on the subject.

and alternative proposals. This experience convinced me that it would be both desirable and feasible to extend this approach to a number of other areas.

During 1980 and 1981, a group of NBER research associates collaborated on a variety of methodological and substantive studies of behavioral simulation. Daniel Feenberg had the primary responsibility for extending and updating the TAXSIM program. In the form in which it was used, the program included the Internal Revenue Service samples of individual tax returns for 1972, 1975, and 1977, the most recent data then available. The income tax laws of all of these years as well as the law prevailing in 1980 are available in the overall TAXSIM model.

Although the individual tax return contains a great deal of useful information, there are some important facts that are missing. For example, while information about the separate earnings of husbands and wives is available for the 1975 sample of tax returns, there is of course no information on the tax return about the number of hours that either spouse worked. To study the effect of alternative tax rules on the labor supply of married women, Daniel Feenberg and Harvey Rosen (chapter 1) therefore developed a method of imputing to each tax return the number of hours worked by the wife on the basis of the joint distribution of hours, earnings, and other variables estimated from survey data. Jerry Hausman (chapter 2) also studied the problem of imputing a distribution of working hours on the basis of a separate set of survey data.

A different problem of imputation occurs because taxpayers who do not itemize their deductions do not provide information about such things as charitable contributions and interest expenses. Lawrence Lindsey and I (chapter 5) developed a procedure for imputing an amount of giving to nonitemizers that reflects previous econometric research on the price and income elasticities of charitable giving, the observed distribution of giving among itemizers, and the tax rules that govern itemization.

The basic TAXSIM program, as augmented with the relevant imputed values, provides the framework within which estimated behavioral models can be introduced. The relevant models must ultimately rest on good econometric research. But even the best econometric research is likely to leave a significant margin of uncertainty because the parameter estimates are conditioned on a model specification that represents a substantial simplification of reality. Because all econometric specifications represent "false models" in this sense, simulating a particular tax change with different parameter values and model specifications can provide a useful indication of the range of uncertainty and the confidence that any conclusion deserves. Simulations of this type can also indicate the parameters to which the conclusions are most sensitive and therefore the type of additional econometric work that would be most useful in reducing uncertainty.

Six different microsimulation studies of individual responses to tax policies were completed and are reported in this volume. The most general tax change, an overall reduction in tax rates, was studied by Hausman (chapter 2). Lindsey (chapter 3) focuses on changes in the highest tax rates, examining in particular some alternatives to the maximum tax provision, which was intended to set a ceiling of 50% on the marginal tax rate on earned income but which, as Lindsey shows, rarely succeeds in achieving that limit. Feenberg and Rosen (chapter 1) consider alternative tax treatments of the family, including credits and exemptions for the earnings of a family's second earner. The other three simulations focus on more specific aspects of household behavior: Mervyn King (chapter 4) studies the tax treatment of home ownership, Lindsey and I (chapter 5) examine charitable contributions, while Feenberg and I (chapter 6) study individual saving behavior.

Michael Boskin, Marcy Avrin, and Kenneth Cone (chapter 7) use data derived from Social Security Administration records and the Current Population Survey to estimate the effects of alternative policies on the long-run financial status of the social security program. They explicitly recognize that changes in social security rules induce changes in retirement behavior.

A microsimulation approach can also be used to study the effects of changes in corporate taxation. Although the Internal Revenue Service does not prepare a sample of corporate tax returns for analysis by outside researchers, some problems can be studied with the information provided by corporations in annual reports and 10-K statements. Michael Salinger and Lawrence Summers (chapter 8) use this information to analyze how alternative tax rules would influence share prices and thus corporate investment in plant and equipment. Daniel Frisch (chapter 9) investigates the likely impact of alternative tax treatment of foreign source income on overseas investment by American firms. By working closely with the United States Treasury, Frisch was able to use special tabulations that maintained corporate confidentiality but provided the necessary detailed information on United States overseas investment and income by industry and host country.

In contrast to these eight microsimulation studies of particular aspects of economic behavior, three of the studies presented in this volume are based on computational general equilibrium models of the effects of taxes on the economy as a whole. Lawrence Goulder, John Shoven, and John Whalley (chapter 10) examine the implications of alternative specifications of international trade and capital flows for the response of the domestic economy to domestic tax rules. In all of their analyses, that response is very sensitive to the extent of international capital mobility. Don Fullerton and Roger Gordon (chapter 11) use a closed-economy general equilibrium model to study the effects of changes in capital taxation but emphasize the importance of recognizing benefits that accompany some taxes and measuring effective marginal tax rates instead of the conventional average tax rates. Joel Slemrod (chapter 12) presents a new general equilibrium simulation model that recognizes that individuals and firms adjust their financial behavior in response to changes in the taxation of capital income and uses this model to examine the effects of switching to an inflation-indexed tax system.

The final paper in the volume, by Alan Auerbach and Laurence Kotlikoff (chapter 13), provides a theoretical simulation of the effects of tax rules on personal saving. Their simulation uses a life-cycle model, in which individuals choose the saving rate in each year that maximizes a measure of total lifetime utility subject to the intertemporal budget constraint implied by the interest rate and the structure of tax rates. The analysis emphasizes that the rate of saving in any year therefore depends not only on current tax rules but on the past history of tax rules and on the tax rules that are expected for the future.

The research project has helped us identify several areas for future research. Developing empirical simulation models based on intertemporal optimization is one of the tasks on this agenda. The availability of longitudinal data files like the Retirement History Survey and the Treasury's multiyear tax return file may provide the parameter estimates required to make such modeling a picture of reality. A multiyear approach to tax simulation is also the right way to analyze changes in social security taxes and benefits. As a minimum, the difference between the social security payroll tax per se and the excess of that tax over the induced marginal benefit increases should be examined.

The state income tax rules should be incorporated into the TAXSIM model and used for the analysis of individual behavior. Some preliminary work by Daniel Feenberg suggests that this will be a valuable addition to existing studies.

A link between the corporate tax simulations and the individual tax returns is necessary to examine the consequences of corporate tax integration proposals that do not have the same effect on all types of firms. Daniel Frisch and I have done some work along these lines that we intend to pursue.

Each of the microsimulation studies in this volume focuses on a single type of behavioral response. Some changes in tax rules would, however, be expected to affect several kinds of behavior. The future development of microsimulation analysis should incorporate such multiple responses where appropriate.

A long-run goal for behavioral simulation analysis should be the linking of microsimulations based on individual tax returns and corporate financial statements with the computable general equilibrium models of the entire economy. The prerequisite of this link is an expansion of the financial side of the general equilibrium models and a development of portfolio equations for individual taxpayers.

We regard the work presented in this volume as the first stage in an ongoing research process. Some of the subjects for future research are already being examined. We hope that our preliminary efforts will encourage others to devote more attention to the behavioral aspects of alternative tax rules.

1 Alternative Tax Treatments of the Family: Simulation Methodology and Results

Daniel R. Feenberg and Harvey S. Rosen

> It is hard to grapple with an existing social order, but harder still to have to posit one that does not exist.
>
> Hugo von Hofmannsthal

1.1 Introduction

The choice of a unit of taxation is a fundamental one in any tax system. In most cases, this boils down to whether the tax schedule will be applied to the income of the individual or that of the family. Since the personal income tax was introduced into the United States in 1913, the selection of the taxable unit has been a source of controversy.[1] The choice has fluctuated over time, and even now there is no strong societal consensus.

Currently, single and married people face different tax schedules, with the tax liability of married individuals being based upon the couple's joint income.[2] Consequently, tax burdens change with marital status, although one cannot predict a priori whether tax liabilities will increase or decrease when an individual marries. The answer depends in part upon the closeness of the incomes of the spouses. The general tendency is that the closer

Daniel R. Feenberg is a postdoctoral research economist at the National Bureau of Economic Research. Harvey S. Rosen is with the Department of Economics, Princeton University, and the National Bureau of Economic Research.

This work was supported in part by a grant from the National Science Foundation. The authors are indebted to Donald Fullerton, Christopher Sims, and members of the NBER's research program in taxation and project in tax simulation for useful suggestions. Any opinions expressed are those of the authors and not those of the institutions with which they are affiliated.

1. The pros and cons of various choices are discussed by Rosen (1977), Brazer (1980), and Munnell (1980).
2. The family was established by statute as the principal unit of taxation in 1948. The system of separate schedules for singles and marrieds was introduced in 1969.

the incomes, the more likely that tax liabilities will increase (Munnell 1980).

This state of affairs has been criticized for a number of reasons. Some observers, noting that the tax system often provides financial disincentives for marriage, have argued that the current regime encourages immorality (*Washington Post* 1979). Economists have tended to focus on possible inefficiencies induced when tax liability is based upon family income ("joint filing"). As Boskin and Sheshinski (1979) note, since the labor supply elasticities of husbands and wives differ, economic efficiency would be enhanced if their earned incomes were taxed at different rates. Yet under a system of joint filing, spouses face the same marginal tax rate on the last dollar. A closely related criticism is that the current tax regime tends to discourage married women from entering the marketplace. This is because under joint filing, the wife's marginal tax rate is a function of the husband's earnings.[3]

In the light of these and other criticisms, a number of suggestions have been made to reform the tax treatment of the family. None of these proposals has been accompanied by careful estimates of their effects on income distribution, revenue collections, and labor supply. The purpose of the present paper is to provide this information.

The vehicle for our analysis is the TAXSIM file of the National Bureau of Economic Research.[4] TAXSIM contains virtually all the information from a sample of 2,339 tax returns filed in 1974.[5] (The returns, however, are "aged" so that all magnitudes reported are in 1979 levels.)[6] The file includes information on the taxable earnings of both spouses, interest, dividends, capital gains, rents, etc. Our basic plan is to simulate the effects of alternative tax regimes by computing for each the associated tax liabilities. In this way, one can determine the gainers and losers as the tax system is modified.

An important complication arises because much economic behavior depends upon the tax system, so that *pretax* values of (say) earnings may be a function of the tax regime. More specifically, a number of econometric studies have indicated that although husbands' hours of work are independent of the tax system, the labor force behavior of married

---

3. This argument implicitly assumes that a husband's labor supply is not sensitive to tax rate changes generated by his wife's earnings.

4. TAXSIM is described in detail in Feldstein and Frisch (1977). In the version used here, neither state and local nor social security taxes are taken into account.

5. The file is a stratified sample from the Treasury Tax Model; it includes one return in eighty for returns showing no wife's labor income and one return in twenty with positive wife's labor income. The Tax Model is itself stratified with weights ranging from one to several thousand.

6. In order to bring all figures to 1979 levels we increase all dollar amounts by the proportional change in taxable income from 1974 to 1979, and to increase the number of returns according to the growth of population.

women is quite responsive to the net wage (see e.g. Rosen 1976 or Hall 1973).[7] Thus, ignoring the labor supply response of married women is likely to lead to biased estimates of the effects of tax reform proposals. Our simulations explicitly incorporate endogenous work decisions for wives.

Unfortunately, even a complete set of variables relating to a household's tax situation does not include all of the information needed to predict the effects of taxes on labor supply. For example, standard theoretical considerations suggest that an important determinant of labor supply is the wage rate, but since it is not entered on the tax return, the wage is absent from TAXSIM. Section 1.2 of this paper consists of a careful discussion of the statistical issues surrounding the problem of imputing such missing data. The reader who lacks interest in this methodological question may wish to skip to section 1.3, which explains the behavioral assumptions built into the simulations. Section 1.4 contains the results. The alternative tax regimes considered run the gamut from eliminating joint filing altogether, to retaining joint filing but granting tax subsidies to secondary workers. A concluding section includes some caveats and suggestions for future research.

1.2   Methodological Issues

A behavioral simulation requires data on individuals' tax situations and on their economic and demographic characteristics. The tax information is required to make careful predictions of the revenue implications of alternative tax regimes. The economic and demographic information is needed to estimate the impact of tax changes upon economic behavior.

The fundamental methodological problems of this study are consequences of the fact that no publicly available data set has all this information. The sources typically used by economists to estimate behavioral equations have virtually no federal income tax data (see e.g. Institute for Social Research 1974). On the other hand, data sets that are rich in tax information tend to tell us little else about the members of the sample. For example, because individuals do not report wage rates and hours of work on their federal income tax returns, TAXSIM has no information on these crucial magnitudes. Clearly, then, one must bring together information from (at least) two different data sources in order to perform tax simulations with endogenous labor supply responses.

A popular technique for combining information is statistical matching.[8] The first step in this procedure is to isolate a set of variables that is common to both data sets. Then a search is made to determine which

---

7. The evidence is reviewed more carefully in section 1.3 below.
8. It has been used, for example, to create the Brookings MERGE file. See Pechman and Okner (1974).

observations of each data set are "close" on the basis of these variables.[9] The close observations are pooled in order to form a "synthetic" observation, which is then treated as if it were generated by a single behavioral unit.

In addition to suffering from statistical problems,[10] the matching procedure is enormously expensive in computer time for data sets of even moderate size. In this section we develop an imputation procedure that we think dominates matching on both statistical and cost grounds. We begin by discussing the general problem of predicting tax revenue collections in a simulation model with endogenous behavior. This turns out to provide a useful framework for generating a rigorous data imputation technique, which is done in the second part of this section. In the third part, the procedure is applied to the problem of estimating missing wage data.

1.2.1 Predicting Tax Revenues

Let y be a vector of variables endogenous to the tax system. Included are items such as taxable income, which depends directly upon provisions of the tax code, as well as variables like pretax earnings, which depend upon the tax system only to the extent that the latter influences economic behavior. Let x be a vector of exogenous variables such as age and wealth. If the tax code at a given time is represented by the parameter B, then we can think of the tax system as a function $t(x, y, B)$ which determines the amount of taxes owed by an individual given both the relevant exogenous and endogenous variables. Our problem is to determine how revenues change when there is a change from the current tax regime, denoted B', to some new tax regime, B''.

Call the joint distribution of the exogenous and endogenous variables in the population $f(x, y | B')$. Then total tax revenue under the current regime B' is

$$(2.1) \qquad T(B') = N \int_x \int_y t(x, y, B') f(x, y | B') dy \, dx \, ,$$

where N is the total number of taxpaying units.

The analytic integration implied by (2.1) cannot in practice be performed. An obvious alternative to (2.1) is its discrete analogue,

$$(2.2) \qquad \hat{T}(B') = \sum_{i=1}^{I} t(x_i, y_i, B') P_i \, ,$$

where y_i and x_i ($i = 1, \ldots, I$) are I sample observations from the universe of N taxpaying units and P_i is the sample weight of the ith observation. (In the absence of deliberate stratification, $P_i = N/I$ for all i.)

Under the tax regime B'' tax revenues are

---

9. Criteria for doing the matching are discussed by Kadane (1978) and Barr and Turner (1978).

10. These are explained by Sims (1978).

(2.3) $T(B'') = N \int_x \int_y t(x,y,B'') f(x,y|B'') dy\ dx$.

Unfortunately, even knowledge of $f(x,y|B')$ does not in general give us $f(x,y|B'')$, the joint distribution of x and y under the new regime. Only with the restrictive assumption that y is inelastic with respect to the change in tax regimes can we estimate new tax revenues as

(2.4) $\hat{T}(B'') = \sum_{i=1}^{I} t(x,y,B'') P_i$.

For changes in tax regimes of the sort being analyzed in this paper, the exogeneity assumption is untenable.

In order to predict taxes under B'', the first step is to specify a behavioral relation that gives y as some function of x, the tax code, and an error term independent of x:

(2.5a) $y_i' = y(x_i, B') + u_i'$,

(2.5b) $y_i'' = y(x_i, B'') + u_i''$,

where u_i' is the random error for the ith individual under regime B' and u_i'' is defined analogously. (The errors have means of zero.) Note that independence between u_i' and u_i'' is *not* assumed; indeed, one expects that typically they will conceal a substantial individual "fixed effect" and hence be correlated.

If we substitute equation (2.5b) into (2.3), we find

(2.6) $T(B'') = N \int_x \int_y \left[\int_{u_i''} t(x, y(x,B'') + u_i'', B'') \phi(u_i'') du_i \right]$

                $\times f(x,y|B') dy\ dx$,

where $\phi(u_i'')$ is the density of u_i''. The discrete analogue to (2.6) is

(2.7) $\hat{T}(B'') = N \sum_{i=1}^{I} \left[\int_{u_i''} t(x_i, y(x_i, B'') + u_i'', B'') \phi(u'') du_i'' \right] P_i$.

If the distribution of u_i'' is known,[11] then (2.7) consists entirely of observables. It turns out, however, that both defining $\phi(u_i'')$ and integrating over u_i'' can be avoided by taking advantage of a simple trick. Define

(2.8) $\hat{y}_i'' = y(x_i, B'') + (y_i' - y(x_i, B'))$.

In words, $\hat{y}_i''$ is the expected value of y under the B'' regime plus the error term associated with regime B'. If, as might reasonably be expected, u_i' and u_i'' are highly correlated, then $\hat{y}_i''$ should be a better estimator of y_i'' than $y(x_i, B'')$, because the latter ignores the error in the behavioral equation. More precisely, $\hat{y}_i''$ and y_i'' have identical distributions under the assumption that u_i' is drawn from the same distribution as u_i'', a fairly mild condition. These considerations suggest the following estimator:

11. For example, u_i'' might be the normal error from a regression, whose mean and variance are computed along with the regression coefficients.

(2.9) $$\hat{T}(B'') = N \sum_{i=1}^{I} t(x_i, \hat{y}_i'') P_i ,$$

which can also be written (using the definition of $\hat{y}_i''$) as

(2.10) $$\hat{T}(B'') = N \sum_{i=1}^{I} t(x_i, y(x_i, B'') + u_i', B'') P_i .$$

Since y_i'' and $\hat{y}_i''$ have the same distribution, $\hat{T}(B'')$ is an unbiased estimator of total revenue.

It is useful to compare (2.10) with (2.7). In effect, the integral over u_i'' of (2.7) has been replaced in (2.10) by a sample mean from an identical distribution. (Of course, the sample mean is calculated with one observation, but it is nevertheless an unbiased estimator, and hence performs the same function as a mean calculated over several observations.)

$\hat{T}(B'')$ should be contrasted with an estimator which uses only the predicted value of y_i'' for each observation,

(2.11) $$\tilde{T}(B'') = N \sum_{i=1}^{I} t(x_i, y(x_i, B''), B'')_i .$$

One expects that $\tilde{T}(B'')$ will be less satisfactory than $\hat{T}(B'')$ because in general the distribution of the expectation of a random variable differs from the distribution of the variable itself, if only in having a smaller variance. Only if the tax code and labor supply functions are linear will (2.11) be equivalent to (2.10).

To summarize: We have carefully developed a method for estimating tax revenues under alternative tax regimes. Similar procedures have been used before (see e.g. Feldstein and Taylor 1976), but with a more intuitive statistical justification. Of course, the discussion so far has ignored the possibility that some variables in the x or y vectors may be missing from the TAXSIM file. The theory we have developed in this section, however, turns out to provide a useful framework for thinking about data information problems.

1.2.2   Imputing Baseline Data: Theory

Most of the plausible theories of labor supply suggest that it is necessary to know something about individuals' wage rates and hours of work in order to predict how alternative tax regimes affect revenues. But federal tax returns include only the product of hours and the wage rate, that is, earnings. In this section we show how external information concerning the joint distribution of earnings and hours can be used in conjunction with tax return data to impute the missing variables.

For expositional purposes, we specialize the model developed in section 1.2.1 above. Let the vector y of endogenous variables have two elements, e (earnings) and m (total taxable income).[12] Let the vector x of

---

12. We ignore for the moment the fact that the household may have more than one earner.

exogenous variables consist of one element, w, the pretax wage rate. The tax calculator is then $t(e,m,w,B)$.

Although TAXSIM has e and m, it does not have w. A number of data sets have information on e and w, but not m. Because there is no data set which includes e, m, and w, $f(e,y,w|B')$ cannot be inferred straightforwardly. But if we are willing to make some additional assumptions, $f(\cdot)$ is estimable.

The key assumption is that m and w, *conditional* on e and B, are independent. This seems quite reasonable in that once we know earnings, knowledge of the wage probably contributes little to predicting taxable income. Of course, the independence assumption is not *necessarily* true. It might be the case, for example, that high nonlabor incomes are associated with high reservation wages, ceteris paribus. This would generate conditional dependence of m and w, even given e. In this context, it should also be noted that in actual application there are several variables common to both data sets. Increasing the number of variables upon which independence is conditioned makes the assumption even more reasonable.

Rewriting equation (2.1) for our special case, we have

$$(2.12) \qquad T(B') = N\int_w\int_m\int_e t(e,m,w,B')f(e,m,w|B')de\ dm\ dw\ .$$

Taking advantage of the usual identities concerning the distributions of independent variables,[13] (2.12) can be rewritten as

$$(2.13) \qquad T(B') = N\int_w\int_m\int_e t(e,m,w,B)$$

$$\times \left[\int_w f(\cdot|B)dw \frac{\int_m f(\cdot|B)dm}{\int_m\int_w f(\cdot|B)\,dw\ dm} \right] de\ dm\ dw\ .$$

Now, $\int_w f(\cdot|B)dw$ is the distribution of earnings and taxable income, and is estimable from the TAXSIM file. $\int_m f(\cdot|B)dm$ is the distribution of wages and earnings, and may be estimated from any data set with information on both w and e. Finally,

$$\int_m\int_w f(\cdot|B)dw\ dm$$

is the distribution of earnings and may be estimated from either or both files. Therefore $T(B)$ is identified by the existing unmatched files.

There still remains, of course, the problem of estimating the relevant distribution functions. As noted above, it is impractical to find closed-form expressions for $f(\cdot|B)$ and its marginal distributions. Sims (1978) has suggested that e, m, and w space be partitioned into a large number of cells, and that the marginal cell counts be used as estimated of the three integrals over $f(\cdot|B)$. However, given that in our problem we are dealing

---

13. See, for example, DeGroot (1975, p. 119).

with a number of continuous variables, this approach does not seem operational.

We therefore propose the following alternative. Let $(e_i, m_i; i = 1, \ldots, I)$ be a set of I observations from TAXSIM. Then the discrete probability analogue to equation (2.13) is

$$(2.14) \qquad \hat{T}(B') = \sum_{i=1}^{I} \left[\int_w t(e_i, m_i, w, B') \, \frac{\int_m f(\cdot|B')dm}{\int_m \int_w f(\cdot|B')dw \, dm} \, dw \right] P_i,$$

where the term enclosed in brackets is the expected value of taxes owed by the ith taxpayer, given the joint distribution of wage rates with the other variables. (Note that P_i plays the role that $\int_w f(\cdot|B')dw$ had in (2.13).)

The ratio
$$\frac{\int_m f(\cdot|B')dm}{\int_m \int_w f(\cdot|B')dm \, dw}$$

that appears in (2.14) is just the distribution of wage rates conditioned on earnings and B'. As noted above, it can be estimated from a number of available data sets. It appears, then, that the only stumbling block to evaluating (2.14) is integrating over w. A Monte Carlo approach seems promising here.[14] Essentially, this procedure involves the replacement of the integral over w with a sample mean.

We proceed more formally by defining

$$q_i(w) \equiv t(e_i, m_i, w, B') \, \frac{\int_m f(\cdot|B')dm}{\int_m \int_w f(\cdot|B')dw \, dm} \, P_i \, .$$

Then (2.14) can be rewritten

$$(2.15) \qquad \hat{T}(B') = N \int_w \sum_{i=1}^{I} q_i(w)dw \, .$$

For *any* density function $g(w)$, (2.15) is

$$(2.16) \qquad \hat{T}(B') = N \int_w \sum_{i=1}^{I} \frac{q_i(w)}{g(w)} g(w)dw \, .$$

Observe that *if* w is distributed as $g(w)$, then (2.16) is the expected value of $\sum_{i=1}^{I} (q_i(w)/g(w))$.

Suppose that we have available a device for producing random numbers with distribution $g(w)$. Let $\hat{w}_{ij}$ be the jth such random number generated for the ith individual. Then the basic Monte Carlo strategy suggests replacing integral (2.16) with

14. For a general discussion of Monte Carlo techniques, see Shreider (1966).

(2.17) $$\hat{\hat{T}}(B') = \frac{N}{J} \sum_{j=1}^{J} \sum_{i=1}^{I} \frac{q_i(\hat{w}_{ij})}{g(\hat{w}_{ij})},$$

where J is the number of random drawings.

Suppose now that we let $g(w)$ be the conditional distribution of wages given earnings. Then (2.17) becomes

(2.18) $$\hat{\hat{T}}(B') = \frac{N}{J} \sum_{j=1}^{J} \sum_{i=1}^{I} t(e_i, m_i, \hat{w}_{ij}, B')$$

$$\times \frac{\int_m f(\cdot|B')dm}{g(w_{ij})\int_m\int_w f(\cdot|B')dw\ dm} P_i .$$

When the definition of $g(\cdot)$ is substituted into (2.18), it collapses

(2.18') $$\hat{\hat{T}}(B') = \frac{N}{J} \sum_{j=1}^{J} \sum_{i=1}^{I} t(e_i, m_i, E(\hat{w}_{ij}, B')) P_i .$$

To appreciate the meaning of (2.18') it is useful to contrast it to the alternative expression

(2.19) $$S(B') = N \sum_{i=1}^{I} t(e_i, m_i, E(w_i|e_i, m_i)) P_i ,$$

where $E(w_i|e_i, m_i)$ is the conditional expectation of w_i. To compute $\hat{\hat{T}}(B')$, we must take the average of J values drawn from the conditional distribution of w, while for $S(B')$, w is imputed using simply the conditional mean. To the extent that $t(\cdot)$ is nonlinear, $S(B')$ yields biased estimates.

The only remaining question is how to choose J, the number of random drawings from the distribution. A careful examination of this question would require optimally trading off the (substantial) computational costs of increasing J against the efficiency gains from doing so. Such an exercise is beyond the scope of this paper. We settle upon $J = 1$ as an inexpensive solution that has all the desirable statistical properties of (2.18').

We have come by a rather indirect route, then, to a rigorous yet straightforward solution to the problem of imputing wage rates to the TAXSIM file. Using a separate data file, estimate a regression of the form $w = g(Z) + \epsilon$, where Z is a vector of variables in common between TAXSIM and the data set and ϵ is a random error. Then for the ith observation in TAXSIM, impute the wage as $g(Z_i) + \epsilon_i$, where ϵ_i is a random drawing from the distribution of ϵ.

1.2.3   Imputing Baseline Data: Application to the Wife's Wage

We now apply our statistical theory to the problem of imputing wives' wages.[15] The first task is to select a suitable data set that includes the wage

---

15. Husbands' wages are not required for reasons given in section 1.3 below.

rate. The University of Michigan Panel Study of Income Dynamics (PSID) was chosen because it was the only data set we could locate which included both wage rate and annual income data for a sample from the general population. The much larger Current Population Survey (United States Department of Labor) asks for income in March and the wage rate in May; while these could in principle be matched, we did not attempt to do so. The National Longitudinal Survey (United States Department of Labor 1970) covers only specific age-groups. The major disadvantage of the PSID is the absence of any families with very large incomes. While these families are relatively rare in the population, they are an important source of tax revenue. It would have been useful to have a recent data set in which the rich are oversampled, but none exists.

The next step is to estimate with the PSID data a regression of the wife's wage on some function of those variables that are common to the PSID and TAXSIM. The set of common variables consists of: wife's earnings, husband's earnings, a dummy to indicate whether the wife is over sixty-five, and the number of exemptions. A regression of the wife's wage rate on a set of variables that includes her earnings may at first seem rather strange. After all, since earnings is just the product of wage rate and hours worked, it is an endogenous variable. This observation, although correct, is quite beside the point. The statistical theory developed in the preceding section dictates only that we describe the joint distribution of the wage rate and the common variables, *not* that we estimate a valid structural equation.

After some experimentation, we selected a function second-order in both husband's and wife's earnings. The results are presented in the column (1) of table 1-1. A glance at the table indicates that the standard errors of the earnings variables are somewhat large relative to the size of the coefficients. This is a consequence of multicollinearity among the five earnings variables and is not a cause for concern, because it does not render the predictions biased.

The possibility remains that even given the common variables, other factors significantly influence the wife's wage. In order to see whether this was the case, we augmented the list of regressors with the following variables from the PSID: wife's education, wife's labor market experience, wife's race, and wife's age.

As can be seen from the results given in column (2) of table 1.1, except for years of education none of the variables adds significantly to the explanatory power of the equation. Will, then, the fact that education is not available for the imputation process lead to an important bias in our calculations? We think that any such bias will be minimal. Education is, after all, not available in the tax model precisely because it is not required to calculate taxes. To the extent that education is correlated with some

Table 1.1   **Wife's Wage Regressions**

	(1)	(2)
Constant	1.883	−.2926
	(.1725)	(.3415)
Wife's earnings	.2007	.1840
	(.03188)	(.03174)
(Wife's earnings)^2	.01194	.009699
	(2.295×10^{-3})	(2.278×10^{-3})
Husband's earnings	.03551	.02049
	(.01400)	(.01399)
(Husband's earnings)^2	1.144×10^{-4}	7.0706×10^{-5}
	(2.787×10^{-4})	(2.7699×10^{-4})
Wife's earnings ×	1.734×10^{-5}	.001016
husband's earnings	(1.488×10^{-3})	(.001478)
Wife over 65*	.1389	−.1363
	(.3269)	(.3488)
Number of children	7.843×10^{-4}	.02593
	(.03203)	(.03226)
Wife's education		.1668
	...	(.02077)
Black*		−.09957
	...	(.1610)
Wife's age		.00786
	...	(.004138)
Wife's years of labor		.002968
market experience	...	(.003302)
S.E.E.	10.24	10.06
N	1808	1791

Note: Wage regressions are estimated from PSID. Earnings variables are measured in thousands of dollars. Variables in parentheses are standard errors.
*Dichotomous variables.

variable in TAXSIM that is not in the PSID, there will be some bias, but it is reasonable to expect such correlations to be small.

There turned out to be a problem with the first regression of table 1.1 that led us to reject it as a basis for our wage imputations: the residuals were not homoscedastic. It was therefore difficult to specify the distribution of the residuals, a step which is required in order to assign the random component of the imputed wage. To remedy this difficulty we estimated separate regressions for each of three earnings categories. (We did not investigate the possibility that the error variance might depend upon variables other than income.) These results, which are reported in table 1.2, provided a considerably more homogeneous set of residuals within groups, although not of an identifiable distribution. Therefore the random component of the wage imputation was found by making a random selection from the set of estimated residuals. The imputed wage,

Table 1.2	Wife's Wage Regressions by Earnings Class		
	$0 < e < 2,500$	$2,500 < e < 7,500$	$7,500 < e$
Constant	1.939	2.5599	−3.743
	(.3485)	(.7340)	(1.695)
Wife's earnings	.8703	−.1721	1.055
	(.4363)	(.2937)	(.2542)
(Wife's earnings)^2	−.3306	.0502	−.01547
	(.1618)	(.02883)	(.01050)
Husband's earnings	.001795	.07768	.1943
	(.02599)	(.03021)	(.06958)
(Husband's earnings)^2	-2.482×10^{-4}	.001348	−.001079
	(3.886×10^{-4})	(3.7431×10^{-4})	(.001529)
Wife's earnings ×	.03098	−.01612	−.009877
husband's earnings	(.01484)	(.005626)	(.006135)
Wife over 65	−.1699	.8497	−.5405
	(.4563)	(.4739)	(1.2119)
Number of children	−.02310	.06594	−.1034
	(.05126)	(.03865)	(.1073)
S.E.E.	10.69	7.95	13.03
N	703	810	295

Note: See footnotes to table 1.1.

then, is the sum of this residual and the conditional expected mean estimated from the appropriate equation from table 1.2.

Of course, for nonworking wives this procedure could not be implemented because of the absence of a wage variable to serve the dependent variable. Instead, a procedure was followed similar to that suggested by Hall (1973). We estimated for the sample of working wives a regression of the wage rate on husband's income, number of dependents, and an over sixty-five dummy variable, and used the results to impute wages to the nonworkers. As is well known, this procedure does not correct for the possible effects of selectivity bias (see e.g. Heckman 1980). Given our paucity of explanatory variables, it seemed to us pretentious to attempt this rather subtle correction. Moreover, Hausman (1980, pp. 47, 48) has pointed out that in cases like ours, the correction usually makes no practical difference anyway.

1.3 Behavioral Assumptions

We now turn to the question of how, given our figures on wages rates and hours of work, we can simulate the effects of various tax changes on work effort and the distribution of family income. In effect, our task is to specify the function $y(\cdot)$ of equation (2.5) that relates hours of work to exogenous variables and the tax code. The framework used is the stan-

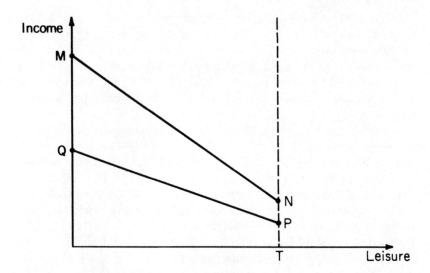

Fig. 1.1

dard microeconomic theory of the leisure-income choice.[16] The theory views the hours-of-work decision as an outcome when the individual maximizes a utility function subject to a budget constraint. This suggests an obvious way to organize our exposition: in section 1.3.1 we discuss the budget constraint generated by the personal income tax system, and in section 1.3.2 we explain how preferences are modeled.

1.3.1 The Budget Constraint

Consider first the budget constraint faced by an untaxed individual with a wage ω and unearned income I. The constraint can be represented graphically on a diagram with income plotted on the vertical axis and hours of leisure on the horizontal. In figure 1.1, if the individual's time endowment is $0T$ hours, then the budget constraint is a straight line MN with slope $-\omega$ and vertical intercept $I(= TN)$. Behind the linear budget constraint are the assumptions that the fixed costs associated with working are negligible and that the gross wage does not vary with hours of work. These assumptions are common to most studies of labor supply. Although the consequences of relaxing them have been discussed,[17] there is no agreement on whether they are important empirically. In this study we retain the conventional assumption that the pretax budget constraint can be represented as a straight line.

16. For a comprehensive discussion of the theory, the reader is referred to Heckman, Killingsworth, and MaCurdy (1979).
17. Hausman (1980) analyzes a model with fixed costs of work, and Rosen (1976) discusses a model in which full- and part-time workers receive different hourly wages.

Assume now that the individual is subject to a proportional tax on both earned and unearned income. Then the effective budget constraint facing the individual in figure 1.1 is PQ, with the tax rate being NP/NT. Note that even with such a simple tax system, one would have to know both the uncompensated elasticity of hours with respect to the wage and the income elasticity in order to predict the impact of taxes upon hours of work.

Of course, the United States tax system is progressive with respect to taxable income, not proportional. As an individual's income bracket changes, she generally faces a discrete increase in the marginal tax rate. This leads to a kinked budget constraint like $RSUVW$ in figure 1.2. Observe that if the individual's optimum is along (say) segment US, then she behaves *exactly* as if optimizing along a linear budget constraint with the same slope as US but with intercept TR'. This fact, which has been observed by Hall (1973) and others, is extremely useful, because it allows us to characterize the individual's opportunities as a series of straight lines. The distance TR' will be referred to as "effective" nonlabor income.

Included in the tax code are a complicated set of exemptions, deductions, and credits. Conceptually, it is not difficult to include their effects in the budget constraint—all that is required is that we be able to compute net income at any given number of hours of work. It should be noted, however, that some tax provisions, such as the earned income credit,

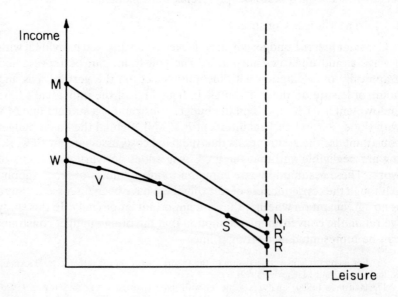

Fig. 1.2

actually lead to nonconvexities in the budget constraint. An important consequence of nonconvexities is that there may be several points at which indifference curves are tangent to the budget constraint. In theory, then, the utility function must be evaluated along each segment of the budget constraint in order to find a global maximum. The specification of a complete utility function—not just a labor supply curve—thus becomes a necessity.

1.3.2   The Utility Function

In order to model preferences we must select both a functional form and specific numerical values for its parameters. One possibility is to choose a reasonable functional form and then estimate the parameters ourselves. The most obvious problem with this approach is that in the TAXSIM model, there are simply not enough data to estimate a convincing labor supply function. As we have already noted, many of the important demographic and economic variables are absent.

Another option is for us to do the estimation using a more appropriate data base and then assign the parameter values to the members of the TAXSIM sample. After considerable thought, this option was rejected. The evidence indicates that the substantive results of labor supply studies are quite sensitive to functional specification and econometric technique.[18] It is therefore unlikely that anyone would have viewed our results as definitive.

Instead, we choose to cull from the literature "consensus" estimates of the wage and unearned income elasticities. Then, assuming some specific form for the utility function and taking advantage of duality theory, we work backward to find the implied utility function parameters. Instead of confining ourselves to one set of parameters, we use several in order to determine the impact upon our substantive results. We first discuss the functional form selected to characterize preferences and then explain how its parameter values are set.

Functional Form

The standard static theory of labor supply behavior starts with a family utility function which depends upon family income and the amounts of leisure time consumed by each spouse. The labor supply of each spouse depends upon the net wages of *both* spouses and effective unearned income. Using several fairly reasonable assumptions, however, one can specify a family utility function with only two arguments: wife's leisure and net family income. This simplification is permissible if the husband's labor supply is perfectly inelastic. In fact, many econometric studies of the labor supply behavior of married men have tended to show that both

---

18. See the excellent survey by Heckman et al.

wage[19] and income effects are small in absolute value.[20] We therefore adopt the simpler model as a reasonable first approximation of reality.

Now that we have decided upon the arguments for the utility function, we turn to the question of its functional form. In making a selection, two criteria are important: (i) it should be simple, both to limit computational costs and to facilitate intuitive understanding of the results; and (ii) it should be broadly consistent with econometric estimates of the labor supply.

Recently, Hausman (1980) suggested that one way to satisfy these criteria is to start with a labor function that fits the data fairly well and then take advantage of duality theory to find the underlying (indirect) utility function. More specifically, Hausman observes that the linear labor supply function has proved very useful in explaining labor supply behavior:

$$(3.1) \qquad H = a\omega + bA + s \, ,$$

where H is annual hours of work, ω is the net wage, A is effective income, and a, b, and s are parameters. Using Roy's identity, which relates various derivatives of the indirect utility function to H, Hausman shows that the indirect utility function $v(w,A)$ underlying (3.1) is

$$(3.2) \qquad v(w,A) = \left(A + \frac{a}{b}w - \frac{a}{b^2} + \frac{s}{b} \right) e^{b\omega} \, .$$

Given the ranges over which a particular individual's ω and A will vary in our simulations, equations (3.1) and (3.2) seem to be adequate approximations, and they are adopted for use in this paper. We assign each family a set of utility function parameters calculated so that current behavior is perfectly predicted by equation (3.1). Specifically, assume that the hours elasticity with respect to the wage for the ith family is η_i^ω and the unearned income elasticity is η_i^A. Then a_i, b_i, and s_i are the solutions to the system:[21]

$$(3.3a) \qquad \eta_i^w = \frac{\omega_i}{H_i} \, a_i \, ,$$

$$(3.3b) \qquad \eta_i^A = \frac{\omega_i}{A_i} \, b_i \, ,$$

19. This includes own *and* cross wage effects. For households in which the wife is the primary earner, i.e. her earnings exceed the husband's, the wife's labor supply is assumed to be perfectly inelastic, as is the husband's.

20. See, for example, Heckman et al. (1979, pp. II.28, II.34). Hausman (1980) also finds a small wage effect but a fairly substantial income effect.

21. Clearly, this procedure cannot be implemented for nonworkers. For these individuals, the following ad hoc procedure is used: calculate the average H, w, and A members of the individual's AGI group who work between 0 and 100 hours per year. Substitute these means into system (3), and use the implied values of a, b, and s for the nonworkers.

(3.3c) $s_i = H_i - a_i \omega_i - b_i A_i$.

Up to this point we have discussed only the behavior of married couples. There are, of course, a substantial number of households headed by men and women without a spouse present. Not a great deal is known about the labor supply patterns of such people.[22] We assume in our simulations that the work behavior of these individuals is unaffected by the income tax. This assumption enables us to focus upon problems in the tax treatment of married couples. It also builds a conservative bias into our estimates of the aggregate behavioral response to change in the economic environment.

Elasticity Estimates

In order to solve equations (3.3), estimates of wage and unearned income elasticities for married women are required. The literature suggests fairly high values for the wage elasticity. The studies reviewed by Heckman, Killingsworth, and MaCurdy (1979) report values between 0.2 and 1.35 (pp. II.28, IV.3), and some investigators have proposed even larger estimates (see e.g. Bloch 1973 or Rosen 1976). There is virtually no guidance with respect to how the wage elasticity varies with income level. Indeed, because of the thinness of all statistical samples in very high income groups (i.e. family income greater than \$35,000 in 1974), essentially *nothing* is known about the labor supply response of the women at the top end of the income scale.

Since we do not know with any confidence how η_i^ω varies with income, in a given simulation we simply assign all wives the same value. One set of simulations is performed with a value of 0.5 and another with 1.0. The results are contrasted to those which emerge when it is assumed that there is no behavioral response whatsoever to the tax system.

Turning now to the setting of values for η_i^A, we find that here also the literature provides less than firm guidance. This is due in part to the problems involved in correctly measuring unearned family income. (Difficulties arise from underreporting, estimating imputed incomes from durable goods, etc.) In addition, unearned income is usually treated as an exogenous variable in hours equations, although theoretical considerations suggest that in a life-cycle context, it is endogenous. Heckman, Killingsworth, and MaCurdy (1979) report that most investigators have found values of η_i^A between -0.002 and -0.2. We use a value of -0.1 in our simulations.

1.4   Results

In this section we simulate the effects of four alternative approaches to the tax treatment of the family: (*a*) an exemption from taxation of 25% of

22. Hausman (1980, p. 53) reports one study in which female heads of households have a substantial labor supply response and another in which the labor response is nil.

the first $10,000 of secondary workers' earnings, (*b*) a tax credit of 10% on the first $10,000 of secondary workers' earnings, (*c*) taxation of the husband and wife as single individuals, with the tax base of each being half of total family income ("income splitting"), (*d*) choice between (i) taxation of the husband and wife as single individuals, with the tax base of each spouse being his or her own earnings plus one-half of family unearned income, or (ii) the status quo.

Regimes *a* and *b* maintain the existing general framework for taxation of the family. They can be viewed as attempts to ameliorate what some observers consider to be an unduly high tax burden on secondary earners.[23] Regimes *c* and *d* represent more serious departures from the status quo. Under regime *c*, the tax unit is the individual, but tax liability is half of family income. In effect, then, all family income is split. Regime *d* represents a substantial attempt to make individuals rather than families the units of taxation, because only unearned income is split.

There are, of course, an essentially unlimited number of ways in which the tax treatment of the family could be changed. We think that these four are of considerable interest both for policy purposes and for demonstrating the capabilities of our simulation model.

Because there appears to be considerable concern about the impact of alternative tax regimes on wives' labor supplies, the simulations of this section focus only on the population of married couples. Appendix B contains results for simulations with married and single people together. In order to keep the number of tables manageable, we present in this appendix only results for the case where η^{ω}, the uncompensated supply elasticity for wives, is 1.0. Appendix C has results for the more conservative estimate of 0.5.

Each tax regime naturally induces a change in revenue collections. It is possible that in practice legislators might want to introduce additional adjustments to keep tax revenues constant. However, one cannot know what form these adjustments would take—changes in the rate schedules, deductions, and/or tax credits are all possibilities. Indeed, at recent congressional hearings, it was suggested that revenue shortfalls generated by changing the tax treatment of families be made up by a "windfall profits" tax on oil. In addition, there is no assurance that there would be a desire to maintain the tax collections associated with the status quo. Legislators might want to accompany the tax reform with a general increase or decrease in revenues. In the light of this ambiguity, we decided not to attempt here any revenue adjustments, although in future work we hope to develop some constant tax revenue estimates.

The current tax regime provides the benchmark to which the various tax reform proposals are compared. The key information is given in table 1.3. For each adjusted gross income (AGI) class, the table shows

23. See, for example, Munnell (1980).

Table 1.3   The Status Quo, 1979

AGI Class (× $1,000)	Number of Returns	Average AGI	Tax Liability	Marginal Tax Rate	Hours Worked per Year	Fraction of Married Women Earning over $1,000 per Year
<5	1,177,081	2,973	−49	−.03	235	.22
5–10	4,441,634	7,669	41	.15	481	.36
10–15	8,431,342	12,424	965	.17	568	.34
15–20	8,446,110	17,469	1,818	.26	613	.43
20–30	15,239,496	24,329	3,055	.26	829	.51
30–50	8,915,744	36,548	6,424	.34	1,037	.64
50–100	1,662,893	66,211	16,480	.41	658	.45
>100	66,002	178,427	68,729	.55	833	.17
Means	...	24,184	3,831	.241	732	.45
Totals	48,780,302	1.180×10^{12}	1.869×10^{11}	...	3.573×10^{10}	

Table 1.4   Exemption of 25% of First $10,000 of
                  Secondary Worker's Earnings

AGI Class (× $1,000)	Tax Liability (exogenous behavior)	Tax Liability ($\eta^\omega = 1.0$)	Marginal Tax Rate	Hours Worked per Year
<5	−49	−49	−.03	235
5–10	17	20	.14	488
10–15	919	920	.16	572
15–20	1,705	1,717	.23	637
20–30	2,776	2,817	.22	874
30–50	5,877	5,992	.29	1,100
50–100	15,922	16,114	.36	712
>100	68,539	68,647	.52	853
Means	3,594	3,637	.20	766
Totals	1.753×10^{11}	1.774×10^{11}	...	3.737×10^{10}

averages[24] of adjusted gross incomes, federal income tax liabilities, marginal tax rates, and hours of work per year supplied by wives, and their labor force participation rates. (Negative tax liabilities and marginal tax rates can arise because the 10% earned income credit is refundable.) As we expect, average and marginal tax rates tend to rise with AGI class. The number of hours worked tends to rise with income, but the relation is not strictly increasing. As other family income increases, there is an income effect which tends to decrease the number of hours that wives work.[25] However, there is also a tendency for the wife's pretax wage to be positively correlated with other family income, which encourages work in the market (assuming a positively sloped supply of hours schedule). One cannot say a priori which effect will dominate.

We now examine how each proposal would change the status quo.

1.4.1   Exemption of 25% of Secondary Worker's Earnings

Table 1.4 shows the effects of allowing the family to deduct 25% of the first $10,000 of the wife's earnings.[26] In order to allow comparability with table 1.3, the adjusted gross income classes are those associated with the status quo.

The exemption has a substantial impact on labor supply. As comparison of the last column with table 1.3 suggests, on average wives supply thirty-four more hours per year than they do under the current system.

24. Sample population weights are used to compute these and all other averages.
25. This is under the assumption that leisure is a normal good, which is consistent with both casual observation and econometric evidence.
26. This is similar in spirit to the Conable bill, H.R. 6822, which gives a 10% exemption to the first $20,000 of the lower earner's income but only if the couple is subject to the marriage penalty. See Sunley (1980).

The increases are most marked in the higher-income brackets. For example, in the $50,000–$100,000 AGI class, annual hours increase by slightly more than fifty. This is because the wives in the higher tax brackets experience the greatest increase in the net wage, ceteris paribus.

On average, tax collections from couples fall by about 5%. In the middle-income ranges there is a tendency for the percentages decrease in tax liability to increase with income. For the sake of comparison, we have noted in the second column of table 1.4 what the revenue predictions would have been had we postulated perfectly inelastic labor supplies for wives. The figures suggest that about one-fifth of the shortfall in tax revenues is restored as a consequence of the increased tax base associated with higher labor supply. Although this is a far cry from the claims of some that tax reductions on earned income will be self-financing, it is enough of a difference to demonstrate the importance of allowing for endogenous behavioral responses.

1.4.2 Tax Credit for 10% of Secondary Workers' Earnings

Under this regime, the family can deduct from its tax bill an amount equal to 10% of the secondary worker's earnings up to a maximum of $10,000. The results are shown in table 1.5. The overall increase in labor supply induced by the credit is greater than that of the 25% exemption. However, this result does not hold for each AGI class. In the two highest groups, work effort is less than under the exemption. The main reason for this is that at the top of the income distribution, marginal tax rates are sufficiently high that one-fourth the marginal tax rate gives a greater work incentive than the 10% tax credit. The cost of generating the greater labor supply is a somewhat lower level of tax revenues.

Table 1.5   **Tax Credit of 10% on First $10,000 of Secondary Worker's Earnings**

AGI Class (× $1,000)	Tax Liability (exogenous behavior)	Tax Liability ($\eta^\omega = 1.0$)	Marginal Tax Rate	Hours Worked per Year
<5	−61	−61	−.046	243
5–10	−8	−7	.12	516
10–15	876	901	.15	612
15–20	1,649	1,679	.21	673
20–30	2,719	2,786	.23	911
30–50	5,940	6,030	.31	1,103
50–100	16,139	16,210	.38	690
>100	68,631	68,670	.52	840
Means	3,576	3,626	.22	793
Totals	1.744×10^{11}	1.768×10^{11}	...	3.867×10^{11}

Table 1.6   Splitting All Income

AGI Class (× $1,000)	Tax Liability (exogenous behavior)	Tax Liability ($\eta^\omega = 1.0$)	Marginal Tax Rate	Hours Worked per Year
<5	−54	−54	−.03	235
5–10	−338	−319	.00	575
10–15	312	290	.20	539
15–20	1,459	1,449	.25	619
20–30	2,714	2,799	.22	910
30–50	5,583	5,663	.29	1,066
50–100	13,875	14,202	.33	751
>100	62,192	62,195	.53	840
Means	3,210	3,258	.214	771
Totals	1.566×10^{11}	1.589×10^{11}	...	3.761×10^{10}

1.4.3   Complete Income Splitting

As we noted earlier, there is now considerable sentiment for the view that, at least for income tax purposes, married people should be treated as much as possible like single people. In this and the succeeding section, we consider the effects when both spouses face the tax schedule that is currently faced by single individuals. In this section, we assume that the tax base for each spouse is one-half of total family income, both earned and unearned. Although we characterize this as "income splitting," note that it differs from the conventional use of that term, because we not only divide income but apply a different rate schedule as well (i.e. the schedule that single persons currently face). In section 1.4.4 we assume that only unearned income is split.

The income splitting results are shown in table 1.6. As one would expect, tax revenues go down compared to the status quo—the shortfall for couples is about $28 billion. On the average, hours of work by secondary workers increase by about forty, but interestingly, for some income groups work effort actually falls. Despite the fact that income splitting generally leads to a substitution effect that increases labor supply, there is also an income effect which tends to reduce it. Apparently, the substitution effect dominates in the upper-income groups, while in some of the lower-income groups the income effect dominates. Even given very simple assumptions on the structure of preference, it is not safe to assume that labor supplies for different groups will change in the same direction.

Because the current tax system tends to benefit married couples with only one earner, it is of some interest to examine how the tax burdens of one- versus two-earner families[27] would change under this tax regime.

27. To make this distinction operational, we define a single earner as one in which the minimum of the earnings of the two spouses is less than $1,000.

The results are shown in table 1.7. Columns (2) and (3) show how income taxes change for two-earner families, and (6) and (7) give the same information for one-earner families. On average, tax liabilities for one-earner families fall by a slightly greater proportion than those for two-earner families. This somewhat surprising result occurs because the one-earner families benefit especially from the splitting of nonlabor income.

1.4.4   Optional Single Filing

This regime gives married couples two options. The first is for each spouse to file as an individual and face the same rate schedule as a single person. Each spouse's tax base is the sum of his or her earned income, plus one-half of unearned family income. Deductions and exemptions are allocated in proportion to income.[28] In principle, proponents of individual taxation would probably want to include in a given spouse's tax base only the income deriving from his or her property. This would be impractical, however, because (*a*) much property is jointly owned and (*b*) spouses might transfer property to each other in order to minimize the family tax burden. It seems to us that imposing equal division of unearned income is a reasonable way to proceed.[29]

The family's second option is to continue filing jointly as it does under the current regime. The simulation program computes the utility level associated with each option (using equation [3.2]). The family is assumed to choose whichever option maximizes utility.

The outcomes are shown in table 1.8. What is most striking about this regime is the increase in labor supply generated, an average increase of about eighty hours per year. At the same time, tax revenues from couples fall by more than 10% as approximately half the families take advantage of individual filing to lower their tax liabilities.

Again, it is of some interest to compare the effects of this tax regime on one- versus two-earner families. This can be done by consulting table 1.7. Columns (2) and (4) indicate that tax liabilities for two-earner families fall by about 13%; columns (6) and (8) suggest that tax liabilities for one-earner families fall by only 8%. Although one-earner families gain to some extent by the ability to split unearned income, the major advantages go to those couples who no longer have to pay the "marriage tax."

Another way to interpret table 1.7 is in terms of the proportionate reductions in tax burdens for one- versus two-earner families. Under regime *c*, 58% of the tax cut goes to one-earner families. Regime *d*, on the other hand, gives only 42% of the reduction to these families. One expects, then, that if confronted with the choice between complete

28. The Fenwick bill (H.R. 3609) would allocate each itemized deduction to the spouse who actually makes the payment. As Sunley (1980) points out, this would lead to great complications in tax planning.

29. In contrast, the Fenwick bill would allocate unearned income on the basis of ownership (see Sunley 1980).

Table 1.7   One- versus Two-Earner Families under Regimes c and d

AGI Class (× $1,000)	Two-Earner Families				One-Earner Families			
	Average AGI (1)	Status Quo Taxes (2)	Taxes: Regime c (3)	Taxes: Regime d (4)	Average AGI (5)	Status Quo Taxes (6)	Taxes: Regime c (7)	Taxes: Regime d (8)
<5	4,150	−269	−269	−269	2,649	12	5	12
5–10	8,079	224	−139	112	7,434	−64	−422	−69
10–15	12,039	799	117	548	12,627	1,051	380	997
15–20	17,646	1,798	1,347	1,449	17,333	1,834	1,528	1,673
20–30	24,531	3,230	3,008	2,764	24,116	2,872	2,580	2,743
30–50	35,555	6,121	5,422	5,447	38,300	6,959	6,087	6,685
50–100	62,154	14,714	12,999	12,602	69,525	17,924	15,186	14,668
>100	169,465	62,532	56,280	55,795	180,285	70,013	63,422	63,105
Means	24,928	3,744	3,229	3,226	23,533	3,908	3,284	3,579
Totals	5.678×10^{11}	8.527×10^{10}	7.355×10^{10}	7.349×10^{10}	6.119×10^{11}	1.016×10^{11}	8.539×10^{10}	9.305×10^{10}

Note: Regime c is complete income splitting. Regime d is optional single filing.

Table 1.8   **Optional Single Filing**

AGI Class ($\times$ \$1,000)	Tax Liability (exogenous behavior)	Tax Liability ($\eta^\omega = 1.0$)	Marginal Tax Rate	Hours Worked per Year
<5	−49	−49	−.03	235
5–10	−29	−3	.13	522
10–15	826	843	.15	592
15–20	1,554	1,576	.19	692
20–30	2,662	2,754	.22	932
30–50	5,708	5,895	.28	1,162
50–100	13,392	13,739	.29	829
>100	61,480	61,850	.47	872
Means	3,327	3,414	.206	815
Totals	1.623×10^{11}	1.665×10^{11}	...	3.978×10^{10}

income splitting and optional single filing, one-earner families would tend to support the former, ceteris paribus.

1.5   Concluding Remarks

In this paper we simulated the effects of alternative tax treatments of the family using a model which allows for the possibility of tax-induced changes in labor supply behavior. In order to do so, several methodological problems had to be solved. It was especially important to develop a statistical procedure for imputing values to missing variables. We hope that our "random imputation" technique will be useful to other investigators in a wide variety of applications.

Using the statistical methodology, we examined tax reform proposals that represented both minor and major departures from the current regime. These included various types of preferential treatment for the earnings of secondary workers as well as new rules governing the impact of marriage upon filing status. In a number of cases, we found that failure to allow for an endogenous labor supply response would have led to substantial errors in the revenue estimates. This was true even though the behavioral elasticities we postulated were rather modest in size.

We were often surprised about the directions and magnitudes of the behavioral responses to tax changes. Despite the very simple preference structure that we postulated, "back of the envelope" estimates about what would happen in a given simulation often turned out to be wrong. In a complicated tax structure with discretely changing marginal tax rates, income effects can induce unexpected responses.

In order to point out directions for future research, it is useful to consider some questions that a skeptical reader might raise.

1. *What about the labor supply response of husbands?* We have assumed that the labor supply of husbands is perfectly inelastic. As noted in section 1.3, this assumption is broadly consistent with the econometric literature. However, the possibility remains that for both sexes other dimensions of labor supply—human capital decisions, time of retirement, choice of occupation—might be affected by the tax system. Unfortunately, practically nothing is known about whether such effects exist.[30] As evidence on these issues begins to accumulate, presumably it can be incorporated into TAXSIM.

2. *What about life-cycle effects?* The foundation of this paper has been the standard static model of leisure-income choice. In theory, it would probably be better to examine labor supply decisions in a life-cycle context. To do so, however, would complicate the analysis immensely, as well as increase our data requirements—longitudinal data would be required. If a life-cycle analysis were successfully undertaken, it would allow us to account for changes in the demographic structure of the population, as well as to show how various tax policies affect individuals according to lifetime, rather than current, income classes. Although the lack of a life-cycle perspective clearly limits the usefulness of our results for analyzing very long run effects, a shorter horizon is probably more relevant for the current policy discussion.

3. *What about general equilibrium considerations?* Our simulations assume that pretax wages and interest rates remain constant despite the presence of some substantial changes in labor supply. It would clearly be desirable to make gross factor returns endogenous. Unfortunately, if we want detailed and careful information on tax burdens by income class, marital status, or virtually any other characteristic, a very large micro-data set is necessary. Setting up a useful general equilibrium model in this context currently appears infeasible. It should be noted that existing general equilibrium models of tax incidence assume a relatively small number of classes of individuals (see e.g. Fullerton, Shoven, and Whalley 1978).

4. *What about macroeconomic considerations?* The previous question concerned how much the gross wage might change if people desired to work more hours; here it is asked whether the hours could be absorbed by the economy at all. It is beyond the scope of this paper to develop a complete macroeconomic model of the employment effects associated with tax reform. We merely note that a case can be made that with proper monetary and fiscal policies, additional labor supply could be absorbed by the economy.[31] Similarly, we have made no attempt to assess how the macroeconomic feedbacks due to changing tax revenues might affect our substantive results.

---

30. See Rosen (1980).
31. See, for example, Feldstein (1972).

Thus, although we believe that the simulations in this paper are sufficiently careful to be considered seriously in the debate on tax policy, a good deal of work remains to be done.

Appendix A

About 70% of taxpayers in 1974 did not itemize their personal deductions (medical and dental expenses, interest payments, local taxes paid, etc.) but accepted instead the standard deduction. The standard deduction was then 15% of adjusted gross income with a minimum of $1,300 and a maximum of $2,000. Because some of the tax code changes we study would affect the decision to itemize deductions, it is important that this decision be endogenous to the model. Hence we must make an estimate of deductible expenses incurred by nonitemizers. The purpose of this appendix is to explain how deductible expenses were imputed to non-itemized returns.

Rather than use some extraneous data source, we have simply assumed that the distribution of deductible expenses follows a lognormal distribution (conditional on income) and that the parameters of this function may be inferred from the truncated sample. With these parameters known, random deviates with the correct conditional distribution may be used as proxies for the unknown expenses. If the distribution is correctly modeled and reflects the influence of all the variables on the tax return, then our estimates of tax rate (or any other functions of items on the tax return) will be unbiased.

This procedure ignores possible price effects of itemization on expenditure. This is permissible because we require only an estimate of deductible expenses at the prices associated with itemization rather than an estimate of actual deductible expenditures by nonitemizers.

The probability of a joint return showing itemized deductions depends strongly on income, ranging from less than 1% at incomes less than $5,000 to more than 99% at incomes over $1 million, but it does not seem to relate to any other available variables. For example, our regressions indicated that the number of dependents living at home, which might plausibly influence mortgage interest and medical bills, did not significantly influence either the decision to itemize or the amount of itemized deductions for those who did itemize. This result appeared in both ordinary least squares and Tobit equations.

The sample was divided into nine income categories. It was assumed that for each category except the first (AGI less than $5,000) a truncated lognormal distribution characterized the observed distribution of deductions. Two alternative means were used to recover the parameters of the untruncated distribution:

1. Where the point of truncation is known, Cohen (1951)[32] provides formulas for estimating the mean and variance of an underlying distribution from the first three moments of an observed truncated distribution. (Remarkably, these are in closed form.) If v_i is the ith moment of the observed distribution and c is the truncation point, then

$$u = c + (2v_1v_2 - v_3)/(2v_1^2 - v_2)$$

and

$$s = (v_1v_3 - v_2^2)/(2v_1 - v_2)$$

are the estimates of the mean and standard deviation of the underlying normal distribution. Estimates are presented in table 1.A.1, in the columns labeled "Cohen."

2. The second approach to estimate u and s as parameters of the regression

$$\ln D_j = u + \frac{1}{s} [F^{-1}(P_j)] + e,$$

where D_j is the amount deducted by the jth household, $F^{-1}(\cdot)$ is the inverse of the cumulative normal distribution, and P_j is the observed sample probability that $D < D_j$. These results are given in table 1.A.1 under the headings "regression."

It is comforting to note that at least in the middle-income categories where there is a nearly even split between itemizing and not itemizing, there is reasonable agreement between the results generated by the two procedures. However, neither procedure produced (or was really expected to produce) reasonable results in the lowest-income category, and here the values of $u = 6.5$ and $s = 0.5$ were imposed.

With the parameters u and s in hand, the actual imputations are quite straightforward. Let c equal the log of the standard deduction. Then the probability of not itemizing is $F[(c - u)/s]$. Now let x be a random variable distributed uniformly on the interval [0,1]. Then $\{F^{-1}(x)s + u\}$ is a normal random deviate with mean u and standard deviation s, and $\{F^{-1}(xF[(c - u)/s]) + u\}$ is a random deviate from the truncated distribution below the point of truncation. The imputations are found, then, by having the computer generate values for x, and substituting values of u and s from table 1.A.1. It turned out that the imputations using the parameters from procedure 2 seemed more reasonable than those from Cohen's method, so the former were used.

---

32. The formula for the mean given here differs from that given in Cohen's paper because of a typographical error in that paper. This error is unfortunately perpetuated by Johnson and Kotz (1970).

Table 1.A.1   The Distribution of Deductible Expenses by Income Class

Income (× $1,000)	Estimated Mean (μ)		Estimated Standard Deviation(s)		Median Itemized Deductions*	Mean AGI
	Cohen	Regression	Cohen	Regression		
5	...	...	...	...	0	3,795
5–10	8.01	7.28	.167	.596	0	8,199
10–15	8.10	7.75	.34	.527	0	12,706
15–20	8.31	8.21	.2	.373	8.03	17,456
20–50	8.53	8.40	.133	.497	8.43	27,503
50–100	9.24	9.18	.602	.655	9.22	66,562
100–500	9.89	9.89	.804	.910	9.88	154,225
500–1,000	11.51	11.28	1.24	1.27	11.53	674,093
1,000	12.19	12.32	.616	1.38	12.27	1,952,799

*Median of log of itemized deductions for each income class, computed directly from the data. The value of zero is assigned for classes in which less than half the sample itemized deductions.

Appendix B

In the text, we report simulation results only for the subsample consisting of married couples. This is in order to focus attention on the impact of taxation on wives' labor supply. Of course, for revenue projection purposes, the entire sample is relevant, and these results are presented here. Table 1.A.2 has information for the current system. Table 1.A.3 shows how tax revenues vary by adjusted gross income class for each of the tax regimes described in section 1.4. We show revenues assuming both (a) no behavioral response and (b) wage and income elasticities of 1.0 and -0.1, respectively, for married women.

Appendix C

We argued in the text that for married women's hours of work, values of 1.0 and -0.1 are reasonable estimates of the wage and income elasticities, respectively. Nevertheless, it seems worthwhile to redo the simulations assuming a more conservative value of 0.5 for the wage elasticity. The results are reported in tables 1.A.4–1.A.7. There is an exact correspondence between these tables and tables 1.4–1.8 of the text. Both sets of tables look at the same tax regimes as they affect the subsample of married couples. The only difference is in the assumed value of the wage elasticity.

For regimes a and b, the results barely differ from their counterparts in section 1.4. Because these regimes do not induce major changes in marginal tax rates, the particular value of the wage elasticity of supply is not of major importance. On the other hand, regimes c and d are much

Table 1.A.2   **The Status Quo, 1979 (marrieds and singles)**

AGI Class ($\times$ \$1,100)	Returns	Average AGI	Tax Liability	Marginal Tax Rate
<5	6,323,365	2,173	-18	$-.01$
5–10	13,520,001	7,595	379	.18
10–15	17,197,557	12,431	1,278	.21
15–20	11,502,705	17,420	1,983	.27
20–30	17,500,605	24,117	3,192	.27
30–50	9,899,335	36,829	6,719	.35
50–100	1,800,712	66,166	16,795	.42
>100	510,856	180,072	69,576	.55
Means	...	19,530	3,042	.235
Totals	78,255,136	1.528×10^{12}	2.380×10^{11}	

Table 1.A.3   Tax Revenues under Alternative Tax Regimes (marrieds and singles)

AGI Class (× $1,000)	Regime a*		Regime b*		Regime c*		Regime d*	
	Tax Liability (exogenous behavior)	Tax Liability ($\eta^\omega = 1.0$)	Tax Liability (exogenous behavior)	Tax Liability ($\eta^\omega = 1.0$)	Tax Liability (exogenous behavior)	Tax Liability ($\eta^\omega = 1.0$)	Tax Liability (exogenous behavior)	Tax Liability ($\eta^\omega = 1.0$)
<5	−18	−18	−18	−20	−19	−19	−18	−18
5–10	372	373	380	364	255	262	357	366
10–15	1,257	1,255	1,279	1,236	959	948	1,211	1,219
15–20	1,900	1,909	1,983	1,859	1,720	1,712	1,790	1,805
20–30	2,949	2,985	3,193	2,900	2,895	2,970	2,850	2,930
30–50	6,227	6,330	6,720	6,284	5,962	6,034	6,075	6,243
50–100	16,279	16,452	16,794	16,479	14,388	14,691	13,942	14,263
>100	69,403	69,502	69,576	69,487	63,613	63,617	62,964	63,301
Means	2,893	2,920	3,042	2,882	2,654	2,684	2,727	2,781
Totals	2.264×10^{11}	2.285×10^{11}	2.380×10^{11}	2.255×10^{11}	2.077×10^{11}	2.101×10^{11}	2.134×10^{11}	2.177×10^{11}

*Regime a: Exemption of 25% of first $10,000 of secondary worker's earnings. Regime b: Tax credit of 10% on the first 10% of secondary worker's earnings. Regime c: Complete income splitting. Regime d: Optional individual filing.

more effective at reducing tax rates, and the wage elasticity becomes more relevant.

By construction, the behavioral responses in this appendix are muted compared to their counterparts in section 1.4. However, it is striking that allowing for even a very mild behavioral response has significant effects on both tax revenues and hours of work.

Table 1.A.4   **Exemption of 25% of First $10,000 of Secondary Worker's Earnings**

AGI Class (× $1,000)	Tax Liability (exogenous behavior)	Tax Liability ($\eta^\omega = .5$)	Marginal Tax Rate	Hours Worked per Year
<5	−48	−48	−.03	235
5–10	17	20	.14	488
10–15	919	920	.16	572
15–20	1,705	1,717	.23	637
20–30	2,776	2,816	.22	875
30–50	5,877	5,992	.29	1,100
50–100	15,923	16,115	.36	712
>100	68,539	68,647	.52	853
Means	3,593	3,637	.220	766
Totals	1.753×10^{11}	1.774×10^{11}	...	3.737×10^{10}

Table 1.A.5   **Tax Credit of 10% on First $10,000 of Secondary Worker's Earnings**

AGI Class (× $1,000)	Tax Liability (exogenous behavior)	Tax Liability ($\eta^\omega = .5$)	Marginal Tax Rate	Hours Worked per Year
<5	−61	−61	−.046	239
5–10	−8	−3	.12	495
10–15	876	892	.14	591
15–20	1,649	1,664	.21	643
20–30	2,719	2,750	.22	869
30–50	5,941	5,989	.31	1,072
50–100	16,140	16,180	.37	675
>100	68,631	68,650	.52	837
Means	3,576	3,601	.22	762
Totals	1.744×10^{11}	1.756×10^{11}	...	3.72×10^{10}

Table 1.A.6   **Splitting All Income**

AGI Class (× $1,000)	Tax Liability (exogenous behavior)	Tax Liability ($\eta^\omega = .5$)	Marginal Tax Rate	Hours Worked per Year
<5	−54	−54	−.03	235
5–10	−338	−333	−.01	528
10–15	312	295	.20	551
15–20	1,459	1,452	.25	614
20–30	2,714	2,759	.22	874
30–50	5,583	5,621	.29	1,051
50–100	13,876	14,038	.33	704
>100	62,191	62,191	.53	835
Means	3,210	3,233	.214	752
Totals	1.566×10^{11}	1.577×10^{11}	...	3.670×10^{10}

Table 1.A.7   **Optional Single Filing**

AGI Class (× $1,000)	Tax Liability (exogenous behavior)	Tax Liability ($\eta^\omega = .5$)	Marginal Tax Rate	Hours Worked per Year
<5	−49	−49	−.03	235
5–10	−29	−13	.13	503
10–15	826	838	.15	585
15–20	1,555	1,568	.18	659
20–30	2,662	2,713	.22	884
30–50	5,708	5,805	.27	1,102
50–100	13,392	13,563	.28	753
>100	61,480	61,670	.47	852
Means	3,327	3,374	.202	778
Totals	1.623×10^{11}	1.646×10^{11}	...	3.796×10^{10}

References

Barr, B., and J. Turner. 1978. A new linear programming approach to microdata file merging. In United States Treasury Office of Tax Analysis, *1978 compendium of tax research*, pp. 131–50.

Bloch, F. 1973. The allocation of time to market and non-market work within a family unit. Stanford University: Institute for Mathematical Studies in the Social Sciences.

Boskin, M. J., and E. Sheshinski. 1979. Optimal tax treatment of the family: Married couples. NBER Working Paper no. 368.

Brazer, H. 1980. Income tax treatment of the family. In H. Aaron and M. Boskin, eds., *The economics of taxation*. Washington, D.C.: Brookings Institution.

Cohen, A. C. 1951. On estimating the mean and variance of singly truncated normal frequency distributions from the first three moments. *Annals of the Institute of Statistical Mathematics* 3, no. 1 (January): 37–44.

DeGroot, M. H. 1975. *Probability and statistics*. Reading, Massachusetts: Addison-Wesley.

Feldstein, M. S. 1972. Reducing unemployment to 2 percent. Washington, D.C.: Government Printing Office.

Feldstein, M. S., and D. Frisch. 1977. Corporate tax integration—estimated effects on capital accumulation. *National Tax Journal* 30, no. 1 (January): 37–51.

Feldstein, M. S., and A. K. Taylor. 1976. The income tax and charitable contributions. *Econometrica* 44: 1201–22.

Fullerton, D.; J. B. Shoven; and J. Whalley. 1978. General equilibrium analysis of U.S. taxation policy. In United States Treasury Office of Tax Analysis, *1978 compendium of tax research*.

Hall, R. E. 1973. Wages, income, and hours of work in the U.S. labor force. In E. Cain and H. Watts, eds., *Income maintenance and labor supply*. Chicago: Rand McNally.

Hausman, J. A. 1980. The effects of taxes on labor supply. Mimeo, MIT.

Heckman, J. 1980. Sample selection bias as a specification error. In J. Smith, ed., *Female labor supply*, pp. 206–48. Princeton: Princeton University Press.

Heckman, J.; M. Killingsworth; and T. McCurdy. 1979. Recent theoretical and empirical studies of labor supply: A partial survey. Mimeo, University of Chicago.

Institute for Social Research, Survey Research Center. 1974. *A panel study of income dynamics; procedures and tape codes, 1974 interviewing year; wave VII*, a supplement. Ann Arbor.

Johnson, N., and S. Kotz. 1970. *Continuous univariate distributions*. Boston: Houghton Mifflin.

Kadane, J. B. 1978. Some statistical problems in merging data files. In United States Treasury Office of Tax Analysis, *1978 compendium of tax research*, pp. 1201–22.

Munnell, A. 1980. The couple versus the individual under the federal personal income tax. In H. Aaron and M. Boskin, eds., *The economics of taxation*. Washington, D.C.: Brookings Institution.

Pechman, J. A., and B. Okner. 1974. *Who bears the tax burden?* Washington, D.C.: Brookings Institution.

Rosen, H. S. 1976. Taxes in a labor supply model with joint wage-hours determination. *Econometrica* 44, no. 3 (May): 485–507.

————. 1977. Is it time to abandon joint filing? *National Tax Journal* 30, no. 4 (December): 423–28.

————. 1980. What is labor supply and do taxes affect it? *American Economic Review*, papers and proceedings, 70, no. 2 (May): 171–76.

Shreider, Y. A. 1966. *The Monte Carlo method.* Pergamon Press.

Sims, C. 1978. Comment. In United States Treasury Office of Tax Analysis, *1978 compendium of tax research*, pp. 172–77.

Sunley, E. M. 1980. Statement before the House Ways and Means Committee on the tax treatment of married and single taxpayers. Mimeo, United States Treasury, April.

United States Department of Labor. 1970. *Dual careers*, vol. 1. Manpower Research Monograph, no. 21. Washington, D.C.

United States Department of Labor, Bureau of Labor Statistics. Various dates. Unpublished codebooks for Current Population Survey.

Washington Post. 1979. Sintax. 26 July.

Comment   David A. Wise

Feenberg and Rosen have presented an approach to simulating the effects that changes in the tax code would have on tax revenue and women's labor supply. I say women's labor supply because the authors assume in this paper that husbands are not affected by the changes they analyze. Those aspects of their procedure that are interesting also provoke questions about the preferred procedure to use in making inferences like theirs, an issue to which I will return later. The authors have chosen to use as a base for their analysis a sample of tax returns. Thus they begin with good information on earnings. But they do not have information on the components of earnings: wage rates and hours worked. Their problem is to describe the budget constraint faced by the family, assuming that the husband's earnings are exogenous. To do this, they must predict the wife's wage rate and then use the tax code—or a hypothetical one—to "predict" the budget constraint faced by the family.

I shall first present a simple outline of the Feenberg-Rosen procedure and use it as a framework within which to make specific comments. I shall then make more general remarks and comment on the simulation results.

The procedure with respect to a family *i* may be described as follows:

1. Assume husband's earnings given.
2. Predict wife's wage rate

David A. Wise is Stambaugh Professor of Political Economy at the John F. Kennedy School of Government at Harvard University and a research associate at the National Bureau of Economic Research.

$$\hat{w}_i = f \begin{pmatrix} \text{variables common to} \\ \text{TAXSIM and PSID} \end{pmatrix} + \begin{pmatrix} \text{random draw from} \\ \text{empirical residual} \\ \text{distribution} \end{pmatrix}.$$

3. Predict wife's hours

$$\hat{H}_i = (\text{earnings from TAXSIM})_i \div \hat{w}_i .$$

4. Describe baseline family budget constraint using tax code and husband's earnings.
5. Assume parametric form of labor supply and associated utility functions

$$H = aw + bA + s, \quad v(w, A)$$

$$= (A + \frac{a}{b} w - \frac{a}{b^2} + \frac{s}{b})e^{bw} .$$

6. Assume "representative" wage and income elasticities η^w and η^A from the literature and choose values of a, b, s to satisfy

$$\eta^w = \frac{\hat{w}_i}{\hat{H}_i} a_i, \quad \eta^A = \frac{\hat{w}_i}{A_i} b_i, \quad s_i = \hat{H}_i - a_i\hat{w}_i - b_iA_i .$$

7. Predict baseline tax revenue t'_i using model and tax code.
8. Use actual tax revenue t_i^0 given in TAXSIM.
9. Define residual

$$u'_i = t'_i - t_i^0 .$$

10. Predict tax revenue t''_i under new regime using model and "new" tax code.
11. Take tax revenue under new regime to be

$$\hat{t}_{i''} = t''_i + u'_i .$$

12. Aggregate over i's.

To assume no response by husbands (step 1) seems to me to be defensible in an initial analysis of the problem. But given the relatively small behavioral impact on the simulation results, I am not confident that the effect of husbands' behavioral responses could ultimately be treated as a small part of the total. The income maintenance experiments, for example, identified a significant labor supply response by heads of families to changes in tax codes, especially changes in unearned income (to which the authors' results are not directed).

Steps 2 through 4 randomly assign a budget constraint to the family, with the randomness coming from the predicted wage rate in step 2. Step 2 is one of the interesting aspects of their procedure, although I found their long discussion of it unnecessary. The explicit treatment of the disturbance term is important because the tax-imposed budget constraint is nonlinear. Without the addition to the expected wage rate of a draw from the disturbance distribution, the range of budget constraints would be narrower than the empirically observed range and, concomitantly, high and low marginal tax rates would be underrepresented.

Whether it is important to draw from the empirical residual distribution depends on its shape. If the distribution is nonsymmetric, it may be important; if not, simply using the estimated variance (from a regression package, for example) would probably do quite well.

Then the authors suppose that $\hat{H}_i$ results from optimizing a utility function of the form set forth in step 5.

A weak link in the authors' procedure I believe is the method they use to assign values to the parameters in the utility function. They choose estimated wage and income elasticities (η^w and η^A) from the literature and then used the relations in step 6 to determine the utility function (and labor supply function) parameters for the family. The problem with this process it seems to me is that the pieces are basically not compatible.

The utility function is one used by Hausman. But he allows b_i to be random across individuals and assumes a_i to be constant; his procedure estimates the parameter a_i and a mean and variance for b_i. With nonlinear budget constraints, elasticities are ill defined because they depend on which segment of the budget constraint one is on. Thus, under the assumptions to this point, there would be no single η^w and η^a. Nonetheless, Feenberg and Rosen choose values for them and using the previously estimated $\hat{w}$ and $\hat{H}$ assign to each individual both an a_i and a b_i; both become random across individuals. Also, Hausman's use of the functional form in step 5 assumes that w is the net wage and A is "as if" or "virtual" income. Elasticities from the literature are normally not consistent with these definitions. Thus the Feenberg-Rosen process seems to be trying to fit together pieces that are at odds with one another. It is hard to know how to interpret their results.

In addition, if one is going to use the functional form in step 5, then one should use parameter estimates for a_i and b_i that "fit" the data, given this functional form. An alternative to step 6 that may be more consistent with step 5 would be to use an estimate of a_i and a choice of b_i from its estimated distribution—based on estimates using this functional form— to assign a utility function to each person. This would be more appealing if the simulations were based on the data used for estimation. Here they are not.

The authors, of course, have no information on women who do not work. For this group, they assign the same utility function parameters that they assign to persons working 0 to 100 hours. I believe that this assumption is likely to be quite far from reality because much of the labor supply response to a tax change may come through its effect on participation. Because there are likely to be substantial fixed costs connected with working, persons who do not work may on average be quite different from those who work even a little. In particular, with the parameters assumed to be random across persons, those who do not work are concentrated among persons with parameter values at the tails of the distributions. On average, those who work a little are likely to have values that differ substantially from the tail average.

Having selected a budget constraint (steps 2 through 4) and having selected a utility function (steps 5 and 6), the authors in step 7 predict—on the basis of the budget constraint, the utility function, and the tax code—the baseline tax revenue, observed in the tax file. The difference between the observed and the predicted baseline revenue yields a residual u_i' (steps 8 and 9). The residual is due entirely to error in the prediction of the wife's earnings, since the husband's earnings are taken as given. The tax revenue under a new hypothesized regime (step 11) is taken to be the predicted revenue—based on the model and the new tax code—plus a term equal to the error u_i' in prediction of the baseline revenue. Although the authors take this to be an unbiased estimate, it is unbiased only if the entire residual is taken to represent a fixed effect with respect to alternative tax regimes. This may be a reasonable assumption to make as long as the time period is presumed to be unchanged. Otherwise, under a new regime in a different time period, the large transitory component of earnings would substantially reduce the correlation between the two residuals.

I have also a few general comments with respect to the procedure. The prediction of wage rates using the residual distribution (although not necessarily the empirical one) is certainly necessary in this context. But this is only an intermediate stage in the process; it does not represent a distribution over possible final outcomes—tax revenue in particular. It is bothersome because the error in this step interacts with the error in the choice of utility function parameters and in the prediction of tax revenue, but in an ill-defined way. This is particularly true with respect to the choice of utility function parameters, which seems unconvincing to me. It is troublesome because the pieces here do not fit together in a way that allows easy understanding of the effects of the assumptions on the outcome, a property that would be appealing in a simulation paper. The simulations themselves do not address the issue.

These problems of course arise from the need to splice together two data sources. Feenberg and Rosen must choose the parameters of a utility function, but are not able to select parameters that fit the data. Thus a general question that comes to mind is whether it is best to follow the authors' route or to base estimation and simulations on the same data source. The Feenberg-Rosen approach has the distinct advantage of

Table C1.1 Tabulation from Feenberg-Rosen Results

Regime		Status Quo (1)	No Behavioral Response (2)	With Behavioral Response (3)
(a) 25% exemption of 1st $10,000 of wife's earnings	R: $\eta=1$	1.869	1.753 (-6.2% re 1)	1.774 ($+18.1\%$ re 1–2)
	$\eta=.5$			1.774
	H: $\eta=1$	732		766
	$\eta=.5$			766
(b) 10% credit on 1st $10,000 of wife's earnings	R: $\eta=1$	1.869	1.744 (-6.7% re 1)	1.768 ($+1.6\%$ re 1–2)
	$\eta=.5$			1.756
	H: $\eta=1$	732		793
	$\eta=.5$			762
(c) Income splitting	R: $\eta=1$	1.869	1.566 (-16.2% re 1)	1.589 ($+7.6\%$ re 1–2)
	$\eta=.5$			1.577
	H: $\eta=1$	732		771
	$\eta=.5$			752
(d) Single individual taxation or status quo	R: $\eta=1$	1.869	1.623 (-13.2% re 1)	1.665 ($+17.1\%$ re 1–2)
	$\eta=.5$			1.646
	H: $\eta=1$	732		815
	$\eta=.5$			778

Source: Feenberg and Rosen's tables 1.3–1.8 and 1.A.4–1.A.7.

Notes: R = total tax revenue; H = wife's annual hours worked; η = life's wage elasticity; re = with respect to. The actual revenue figures are the amount shown times 10^{11}.

accurate baseline tax data. It is difficult to evaluate the estimation of labor supply response in the model, however. I suspect the possible error here could be very substantial. (This is especially troublesome since the simulated behavioral responses are relatively small and the reported simulations based on different wage elasticities lead to very similar results. Whether this reflects reality or only their model is unclear.)

An alternative approach is to fit a utility function (like that in step 5) to data on wage rates and hours worked—determining the budget constraint by the tax code—and then to simulate outcomes under a new code, based on that sample and the utility function parameters that fit it best. This is the procedure followed by Hausman, for example. This procedure has the advantage of internal consistency, and it is easy to check the effect of a different parameter assumption on the simulated outcomes. Its shortcoming is that such data that are available do not represent a random sample of tax files and it may not be straightforward to weight them so that they do. In addition, these data sets do not contain tax payments, so that accurate baseline tax revenue data are not available. More experimentation would help determine the ultimate accuracy of the two approaches.

Finally, I have a few comments on the simulation results themselves. From the Feenberg-Rosen results I have put together a summary tabulation (table C1.1). According to these results, of the four regimes simulated, if there were no behavioral response, tax revenue would be reduced by 6 to 16%. Of these amounts, from 2 to 18% is accounted for by the estimated labor supply response.

The change in wage elasticity from 1 to 0.5 has what to me is a surprisingly small effect on the results. It has *no* effect under regime *a*. Under regime *b* it reduces hours of work by 3.9%. The authors explain the result by arguing that their hypothetical regimes do not change marginal tax rates very much, but income splitting presumably would. However, under their regime *c*, the change in wage elasticity from 1 to 0.5 reduces simulated hours of work by only 2.5%.

Given the tenuous nature of the assumptions of the model, I would like to see many more simulations that would allow some evaluation of how sensitive the results are to the assumptions. I would also like to see some sensitivity analysis with respect to the assumed income elasticity. At least in the income maintenance experiments, the income effect of tax changes was in general more important than the wage effect.

2   Stochastic Problems in the Simulation of Labor Supply

Jerry A. Hausman

Suppose that we have successfully estimated a structural model of labor supply. Given the large amount of public interest in the question of income tax reform, an important use of the estimated model would be to assess the possible effects of proposed reforms on the labor supply, tax revenues, and individual welfare. These evaluations are sometimes performed using local elasticity estimates. However, such a simplified analysis may not be very accurate for the rather large changes contemplated in many tax reform proposals. Another problem with simplified elasticity calculations is that they often ignore the considerable heterogeneity of the population response. A better approach would seem to be to use the estimated structural model to predict the effect of the tax changes. Thus we would need to derive analytically the statistical expectation of the population response under the proposed changes; or if analytical derivation proves to be mathematically intractable, a Monte Carlo approach would provide the results.

But an important potential problem arises when such simulations are conducted. This problem arises because of the nonlinear, and often nonconvex, budget sets which are a consequence of progressive income taxation as well as other tax and transfer policies. In a nonlinear econometric model with nonlinearities of this type, it is not necessarily the case that the sources of stochastic variation have an additive zero expectation term within a simulation exercise. Nor is it the case that such effects are necessarily small, since R^2 values in labor supply models are typically not that high; i.e. much unexplained residual variation remains after the

Jerry A. Hausman is with the Department of Economics, Massachusetts Institute of Technology, and the National Bureau of Economic Research.

Research support has been provided by HHS, NSF, and the NBER. Paul Ruud and Ken West have given excellent research assistance.

model has been specified and estimated. Thus for a particular individual we might well expect that careful treatment of the stochastic specification in calculating the appropriate expectation would be quite important. Yet for the population at large, or, equivalently, a very large sample, the importance of the stochastic components is unclear. In the sample, if the variation of the exogenous variable is sufficiently large and the fit of the equation sufficiently good, the effect of the stochastic component may be small. Perhaps a more promising approach is to realize that extremely accurate computation for each individual may not be needed, because a law-of-large-numbers type of result may hold for the entire sample. That is, rather crude computational techniques may be used for each individual, but the sample mean values can still be quite accurate. Significant computational savings occur because say only one Monte Carlo draw is done for each individual. While the variance of the predicted response of that given individual may be large, in the complete sample the large variance may not be important, because of a large-number type of averaging. This sort of technical question is the major focus of this paper.

The plan of the paper is as follows. In section 2.1, we outline the problem of labor supply with nonlinear budget constraints. We also specify and use estimates of a linear supply model. This section and the estimates within it follow from Hausman (1981*b*). In section 2.2, the stochastic problems which arise in simulation of nonlinear budget set models are studied. Both analytical and Monte Carlo approaches are considered. Comparative statistics for computer times are given to indicate potential savings from the use of simple computational techniques. Then, in section 2.3, we consider tax reform proposals. The type of tax reform proposal considered is a reduction of tax rates by 10% to 30%. Here not only do we consider labor supply effects and welfare effects, but also we look at tax revenue considerations. It is important to emphasize at the outset that all analysis takes place within a partial equilibrium framework. Thus general equilibrium effects which might be quite important, especially in long-run response, are not treated.

2.1   The Econometrics of Labor Supply with Taxes

The essential feature which distinguishes econometric models of labor supply with taxes from traditional demand models is the nonconstancy of the net, after-tax wage. Except for the case of a proportional tax system, the net wage depends on hours worked because of the operation of the tax system. Also, the marginal net wage depends on the specific budget segment that the individual's indifference curve is tangent to. Thus econometric techniques need to be devised which can treat the nonlinearity of the budget set. An econometric model needs to take the exogenous nonlinear budget set and explain the individual choice of desired hours.

We first describe such a model for convex and nonconvex budget sets. As expected, the convex case is simpler to deal with. We then consider other issues of model specification such as variation in tastes and fixed costs to working.

Econometric estimation is quite straightforward in the case of a convex budget set. Convex budget sets arise from the operation of a progressive tax system. Let us first analyze the simplest case, that of a progressive tax on labor income so that the marginal tax rate is nondecreasing. In figure 2.1 three marginal tax rates are considered, t_1, t_2, t_3, which lead to three after-tax net wages, w_1, w_2, w_3, where $w_i = w(1 - t_i)$. y_1 denotes nonlabor income. H_1 and H_2 correspond to kink point hours which occur at the intersection of two tax brackets. But an important addition to the diagram are the "virtual" incomes y_2 and y_3, which follow from extension of a given budget segment to the vertical axis. They are denoted as virtual income because if the individual faced the linear budget set $B_2 = (w_2, y_2)$, he would still choose hours of work h^* as in figure 2.1. An important property of such convex budget sets in the presence of strictly quasi-concave preferences is that only one tangency (at most) will exist between the individual indifference curves and the budget set. Hausman (1979) uses this result to demonstrate that only a specification of the labor supply

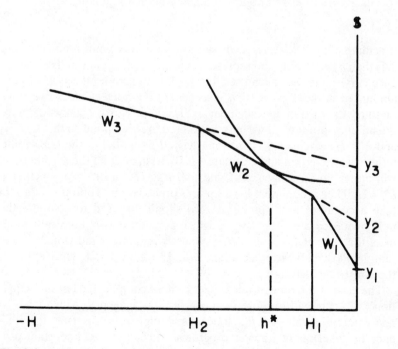

Fig. 2.1

function is necessary for estimation. The form of the underlying utility function is not necessary.

Since a unique tangency or a corner solution at zero hours will determine desired hours of work, we need only determine where the tangency occurs. To do so we begin with a slight generalization of the usual type of labor supply specification:

$$(1.1) \qquad h = \tilde{g}(w,y,z,\beta) + \epsilon = h^* + \epsilon \ ,$$

where w is a vector of net wages, y is a vector of virtual incomes, z are individual socioeconomic variables, β is the unknown vector of coefficients assumed fixed over the population, and ϵ is a stochastic term which represents the divergence between desired hours h^* and actual hours. The typical specification that has been used in $\tilde{g}(\ )$ is linear or log linear and scalar w and y corresponding to the market wage and nonlabor income. The stochastic term is assumed to have classical properties so that no quantity constraints on hours worked exists. However, $0 \le h \le \bar{H}$, where H is a physical maximum to hours worked. We also assume that when the β are estimated the Slutsky conditions are satisfied so that $\tilde{g}(\ )$ arises from concave preferences.

The problem to be solved is to find h^* when the individual is faced with the convex budget set B for $i = 1, \ldots, m$. To find h^* we take the specification of desired hours on a given budget segment B_i:

$$(1.2) \qquad h_i^* = g(w_i, y_i, z, \beta) \ .$$

Calculate h_1^*; if $0 \le h_1^* \le H_1$, where the H_i are kink point hours in figure 2.1, then h_1^* is feasible and represents the unique tangency of the indifference curves and the budget set. If $h_1^* \le 0$, then zero hours is the desired amount of work. However, if h^* exceeds H_1, it is not feasible, so we move on to try the next budget segment. If $H_1 \le h_2^* \le H_2$, we again would have the unique optimum. If we have bracketed the kink point so that $h_1^* > H_1$ and $h_2^* < H_1$, then $h^* = H_1$ so that desired hours fall at the kink point. Otherwise we go on and calculate h_3^*. By trying out all the segments we will either find a tangency of find that $h_i^* > H_i^*$ for all i, in which case $h^* = \bar{H}$. Then a nonlinear least squares procedure or Tobit procedure to take account of a minimum at zero should be used to compute the unknown β parameters. The statistical procedure would basically minimize the sum of $\Sigma_{j=1}^{N} (h_j - h_j^*)^2$, where j represents individuals in the sample. Perhaps a better technique would be to use Tobit, which enforces the constraint that $h_j \ge 0$.

The case of the nonconvex budget is more complicated because equation (1.2) can lead to more than one feasible tangency, which leads to many potential values of h_i^*. Nonconvex budget sets arise from the presence of government transfer programs. The four most important programs of this type are low-income tax credit, Aid for Dependent Children

(AFDC), social security benefits, and a negative income tax (NIT) program. In figure 2.2, in which we indicate a common type of nonconvex budget set, we have two tangencies of the indifference curves with the budget set.

How can we decide which of these feasible h_i^* is the global optimum? Burtless and Hausman (1978) initially demonstrated the technique of working backward from the labor supply specification of equation (1.2) to the underlying preferences, which can be represented by a utility function. The basic idea was to make use of Roy's identity, which generated the labor supply function from the indirect utility function $v(w_i, y_i)$:

$$(1.3) \qquad \frac{\partial v(w_i, y_i)}{\partial w_i} \bigg/ \frac{\partial v(w_i, y_i)}{\partial y_i} = h_i^* = g(w_i, y_i, z, \beta)$$

along a given budget segment. So long as the Slutsky condition holds, $v(w_i, y_i)$ can be recovered by solving the differential equation (1.3). In fact, $v(\ )$ often has a quite simple closed form for commonly used labor supply specifications.

For the linear supply specification $h_i^* = \alpha w_i + \beta y_i + z \gamma$ which is used in this paper, Hausman (1980) solved for the indirect utility function:

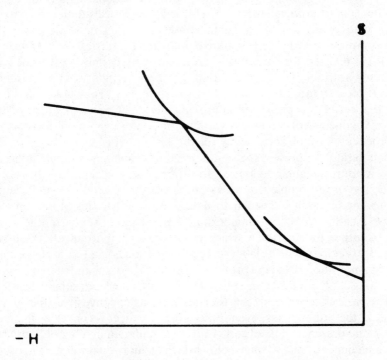

– H

Fig. 2.2

$$(1.4) \qquad v(w_i, y_i) = e^{\beta w_i} \left(y + \frac{\alpha}{\beta} w_i - \frac{\alpha}{\beta^2} + \frac{z\gamma}{\beta} \right) .$$

Given the indirect utility function, all of the feasible tangencies can be compared, and the tangency with highest utility is chosen as the preferred hours of work h^*. Then, as with the convex budget set case, we can use either nonlinear least squares or a Tobit procedure to estimate the unknown coefficients. While using a specific parameterization of the utility function is upsetting to some people, it should be realized that setting down a labor supply function as in equation (1.2) is equivalent to setting down a utility function under the assumption of utility maximization. To the extent that the labor supply specification yields a robust approximation to the data, the associated utility function will also provide a good approximation to the underlying preferences. The utility function allows us to make the global comparisons to determine the preferred hours of labor supply. The convex case needs only local comparisons, but the nonconvex case requires global comparisons because of the possibility of multiple tangencies of indifference curves with the budget set.

We next introduce the possibility of variation in tastes. In the labor supply specification of equation (1.1), all individuals are assumed to have identical values of β so that variation of observationally equivalent individuals must arise solely from ϵ. However, empirical studies seem to do an inadequate job of explaining observed hours of work under the assumption of the representative individual. Burtless and Hausman (1978) allowed for variation in preferences by permitting β to be randomly distributed in the population. Their results indicated that variation in β seemed more important than variation in α. They also found that variation in β represented approximately eight times as much of the unexplained variance as did variation in ϵ. An even more satisfactory procedure would be to allow all the taste coefficients to vary in the population. At present the requirement of evaluating multiple integrals over nonrectangular regions for the more general specification has led to the use of the simple case of variation of one or two taste coefficients. Further research is needed to determine whether this more complex specification would be an important improvement over current models.

Another consideration which can have an important effect on the budget set for women's labor force participation is fixed costs of working. Transportation costs, the presence of young children, and search costs of finding a job can lead to a fixed cost element in the labor supply decision. The basic effect of fixed costs is to introduce a nonconvexity in the budget set at the origin. Thus, even if the original budget is convex as in figure 2.1, the presence of fixed costs leads to a minimum number of hours H_0, which depends on the wage below which an individual will not choose to work. In figure 2.3 nonlabor income is y_1, with the original convex budget set denoted by the dotted line. However, the presence of fixed costs

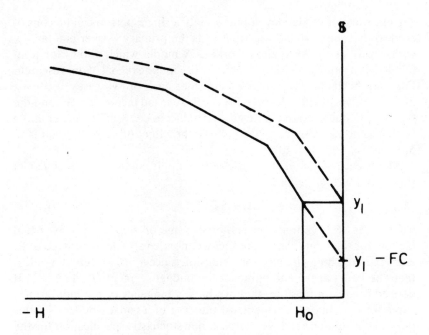

Fig. 2.3

lowers the effective budget set to the point y_1 − FC. The individual would
not choose to work fewer than H_0 hours because she would be better off
at zero hours. This nonconvexity invalidates the simple reservation wage
theory of labor force participation since hours also need to be accounted
for. Hausman (1980) in a labor force participation study of welfare
mothers found average fixed costs to be on the order of $100 per month.
The importance of fixed costs could explain the often noted empirical fact
that very few individuals are observed working fewer than ten or fifteen
hours per week.

We estimated a model of labor supply (Hausman 1981*b*) which takes
full account of the effect of taxation for two groups in the population. The
labor supply of husbands and wives is considered for 1975 for a sample
from the Michigan Income Dynamics Data. Budget sets were constructed
using both federal and state tax regulations (cf. Hausman 1981*b*). It is
important to note that we did not have access to actual tax return data.
Instead, we imputed deductions beyond the standard deduction using
population averages. At present no data source has both all the necessary
labor supply data and actual income tax return information.[1] At the

1. Sample selection criteria and budget set assumptions are discussed in Hausman
(1981*b*). We note that farmers, the self-employed, and severely disabled individuals are
excluded from the sample. Potential problems of tax evasion and tax avoidance should be
decreased by our sample selection procedures. Also, for families with incomes which place

current stage of model development only a single person can be considered so that the husband was treated as the primary worker in a family, with a wife as the secondary worker. A model which allows for joint family labor supply decisions seems the obvious next goal of our research. For both husbands and wives we consider each of two cases: a convex budget set where the effects of FICA, the earned income credit, and the standard deduction are averaged to produce a convex budget set and a complete nonconvex budget set where the effect of each program is to introduce a nonconvexity.

Along each segment the basic labor supply model used is linear in wages and virtual income:

$$(1.5) \qquad h_i^* = \alpha w_i + \beta y_i + z\gamma ,$$

where h_i^* is desired hours, w_i is the net wage on segment i, y_i is virtual income for segment i, and z are socioeconomic variables. For fixed α, β, and γ, desired hours h_i^* may not be feasible since h_i^* may be greater or less than the hours at the end points of the budget segment H_{i-1} and H_i. If desired hours are feasible, then we have a tangency of the indifference curve and the budget segment. In the case of a convex budget set this tangency is unique, and we then use our stochastic specification for the deviation of actual hours from desired hours for person j as

$$(1.6) \qquad h_j = h_{ij}^* + \eta_j .$$

Since observed hours $h_j \geq 0$, the stochastic term η_j is assumed to be independent and truncated normal across individuals in the population. Thus we have a Tobit specification for the hours worked variable. However, if $h_j^* = 0$, we assume that the individuals do not choose to work and so set $h_j = 0$ also. Since the final model has two sources of stochastic variation, the interpretation of η_j differs from standard models. Here we picture the individual faced by a choice among a set of jobs that differ in normal (long-run) hours worked. He chooses that job closest to his h_j^*. But observed h_j may differ because of unexpected layoffs, short time, overtime, or poor health. As an empirical matter we find the standard deviation of η_j to be reasonably small, which indicates that individuals are successful in matching jobs to their desired hours of work.[2]

---

them above the range of the standard deduction, we used data from the *Statistics of Income* which should capture a large proportion of tax avoidance procedures. But data problems will nevertheless remain. It certainly seems preferable, however, to account for taxes rather than to ignore them as is the typical tradition in the labor supply literature, e.g. Smith (1980), in which only one of seven papers recognizes the existence of income taxation.

2. I disagree with my discussant's (Heckman's) remarks about his evidence on the piling up of labor supply at kink points for two reasons. First, the presence of η_i reduces to zero the probability that anyone is *observed* at a kink point. We should still observe a dispersion of individuals over the budget set. Second, since the kink points differ for each individual, I do not see how a casual look at the data can give us more evidence. Last, he is incorrect in his claim that the econometric procedures depend critically on exact knowledge of the location of the kink points.

If the budget set is nonconvex, h_j^* is not necessarily unique, because multiple tangencies can occur between the indifference curves and the budget set. Then h_{ij}^* is chosen as the tangency leading to maximum utility, which is determined by use of the corresponding indirect utility function from equation (1.4). We again use the stochastic specification of equation (1.6) to express the deviation of actual hours from desired hours of work. It is interesting to note that, although certain interior kink points in figure 2.2 in the nonconvex case cannot correspond to desired hours, we might still observe them as actual hours of work due to the stochastic term η_j in the model.

The second source of stochastic variation in the model arises from a distribution of tastes in the population. In line with our previous research we specify β to be a truncated normal random variable which falls in the interval $(-\infty, 0)$. An upper limit of zero is specified since we assume that leisure is a normal good. Thus, as β ranges over the permissible interval, there is a certain probability that any amount of hours corresponds to desired hours. As an empirical matter β turns out to be the major source of stochastic variation in the model, which confirms our previous findings reported in Burtless and Hausman (1978).[3]

The estimated results for husbands are presented along with asymptotic standard errors in table 2.1. The coefficients are generally estimated quite precisely, especially the wage and nonlabor income coefficients. The socioeconomic variables have coefficients of reasonable magnitude except the house equity, which perhaps reflects factors in the mortgage credit market and the special tax treatment of houses. We first note that the uncompensated wage coefficient is essentially zero. Not only is the estimate close to zero, but the estimated standard error is quite small. In the extreme case of two standard deviations from the estimate for the nonconvex case, a change in the net wage of $1.00 along a budget segment leads to an expected increase in annual hours worked of 32.5, which is less than 2% of the sample mean. The expected change in hours

---

3. This specification of different tastes for leisure is perhaps the most controversial part of the model since it represents the most marked departure from usual labor supply models where coefficients are assumed identical across individuals. There, all population heterogeneity arises through the additive disturbance term η_j, e.g. the labor supply models contained in Smith (1980). A further discussion is contained in Hausman (1981b). To test for robustness of the specification, I tried different functional forms for the probability distribution in Hausman (1980). Also, Burtless and Hausman (1978) and Hausman (1981b) used instrumental variable techniques which do not depend on normality assumptions. Nor do they depend on the normal good assumption for leisure. The results were quite similar to the full maximum likelihood model estimates. I disagree with my discussant's remarks on the robustness of the procedure. My investigations lead me to believe that the procedures I use are considerably *more robust* than the reservation wage model of labor supply with its unsupported proportionality assumption. For instance, in his latest estimates, which ignore the existence of taxes (Heckman 1980, p. 229), the estimate of the uncompensated labor supply elasticity for wives changes from 2.1 to 4.8, with only a minor change in econometric specification. Both estimates are quite high, with the latter estimate absurdly so. My estimates are considerably more robust to econometric specification, as the labor supply elasticities for the three different budget sets of table 2.2 indicates.

Table 2.1   Husbands' Annual Hours of Work ($\times$ 1,000)

Variable	Convex	Nonconvex
μ_β – nonlabor income (1,000s)	2.037	1.061
	(.0729)	(.245)
σ_β	.6242	.4541
	(.0234)	(.0570)
Wage	.0002	.0113
	(.0090)	(.0106)
Constant	2.4195	2.366
	(.0589)	(.153)
Children < 6	– .0039	.0113
	(.0255)	(.0635)
Family size	.0341	.0657
	(.0170)	(.0310)
(Age – 45,0)	– .0011	– .0055
	(.0108)	(.0235)
House equity	.0026	.0036
	(.0009)	(.0008)
Bad health	– .1387	– .0520
	(.1436)	(.564)
σ_η	.2794	.2862
	(.0178)	(.0540)
Mean β	– .166	– .153
Standard deviation of β	.156	.141
Median of β	– .120	– .113

Note: Asymptotic standard errors are presented in parentheses below each estimated coefficient.

is only 11.3, while in the convex case the expected change in annual hours is 0.2. The finding of an extremely small uncompensated wage effect is in accord with the previous empirical findings. Thus the direct effect of income taxation that reduces the net wage has almost no effect on hours worked among husbands.

However, our results do differ from previous studies in indicating a significant income effect. Remember that we allow a distribution of preferences in the population. The estimated probability density for the nonconvex case is shown in figure 2.4. The distribution has substantial skewness since it is the extreme left tail of the truncated normal distribution with the standard deviation approximately equal to the mean in magnitude. My previous work has also found this general form even when different probability densities are used, e.g. Hausman (1980), where a Weibull density is used. The underlying parameters of the preference distribution are estimated quite precisely so that the finding is not likely to be an accidental occurence.

Next we present the empirical results for a sample of married women. Our sample consists of the wives of the males used in the previous section.

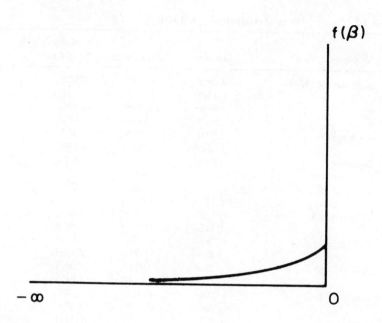

$f(\beta)$

$-\infty$

O

Fig. 2.4

Previous research has indicated that married women's labor supply decisions are sensitive to the net wage so that we would expect to find that taxes create both an important uncompensated wage effect and an income effect, as they do for husbands. As previously stated, we treat wives' labor supply decisions conditional on husbands' earned income. Thus wives are considered to be secondary workers, which may not be a proper assumption. Since in our sample labor force participation of husbands is near 100% while that of wives is near 50%, perhaps treating wives' earnings conditional on husbands' earnings is not a particularly bad assumption. However, the crucial question is whether husbands' earnings should enter the wives' labor supply decision as exogenous nonlabor income. It is probable that some jointness in decision making takes place when the husband adjusts his hours of work to his wife's earnings. A family labor supply model would be able to treat these problems better, but here we only provide estimates for the conditional model.

We turn now to the estimates of the labor supply equations which are presented in table 2.2. We present estimates for a convexified budget set, for the complete nonconvex budget set, and for a nonconvex budget set with fixed costs included. First, note that we find substantial uncompensated wage and income elasticities. For the average woman who is working full time we find the uncompensated wage elasticity to be 0.995 for the

Table 2.2   **Wives' Annual Hours (× 1,000)**

Variables	Convex	Nonconvex	Nonconvex with Fixed Costs
μ_β – income (1,000s)	2.0958	1.7519	2.0216
	(.1389)	(.1475)	(.1186)
σ_β	.5390	.4836	.5262
	(.0460)	(.0490)	(.0711)
α – wage	.4951	.5058	.4608
	(.2310)	(.0932)	(.1062)
Intercept	.5790	.3501	.6234
	(.9517)	(.4907)	(.5766)
Family size	.2387	.2202	.2144
	(.1270)	(.0773)	(.1259)
Children < 6	− .1695	− .1123	.1472
	(.3426)	(.2239)	(.1576)
College education	− .7851	− .7205	− .6903
	(.4216)	(.2390)	(.4389)
Age (35–45)	.2328	.0733	.0824
	(.1102)	(.0349)	(.0436)
Age (45 +)	− .1066	− .1043	− .1989
	(.0644)	(.0539)	(.0660)
Health	− .4771	− .3139	− .3581
	(.7274)	(.4753)	(.4647)
Equity	− .0221	− .0150	− .0210
	(.0172)	(.0039)	(.0113)
Fixed costs: intercept	...	...	1.2125
			(.3570)
Fixed costs: kids < 6	...	...	.1720
			(.9541)
Fixed costs: family size	...	...	− .2118
			(1.6106)
σ_η	.3086	.2907	.2801
	(.2388)	(.2099)	(.2386)
Mean of β	− .125	− .118	− .123
Standard deviation of β	.112	.109	.113
Median of β	− .089	− .085	− .088

nonconvex results, and a similar magnitude for the convex results, 0.978, is found. When fixed costs are added, the uncompensated wage elasticity falls to 0.9065. Thus all three estimates indicate that the effect of the income tax in decreasing the net, after-tax wage is important in determining wives' labor supply. Since wives' net wage is lowered substantially by the presence of the "marriage tax," the tax effect may be much greater than if wives' earnings were not added to husbands' earnings for tax purposes. On the other hand, we also find an important effect of nonlabor income (and actual income). The elasticity at the means is approximately − 0.2. This effect causes more wives to go to work, because their husbands' earnings are reduced by taxes. The two effects have opposite signs so that a simulation is needed to evaluate the net effect of the marriage tax.

In this section we have presented our specification of the labor supply in the presence of nonlinear convex budget sets and nonconvex budget sets. The stochastic specification has been emphasized since it will play an important role in the simulation results. We now consider how the results can be used to simulate the effects of tax reform. We emphasize computational considerations so that the simulations can be conducted at low or moderate costs of computer time.

2.2   Tax Change Evaluation

In this section we develop formulas for expected hours of work, expected tax revenue, and expected deadweight loss given our model of labor supply and the estimates of the previous section. The main question that we attempt to answer is how much attention must be paid to the stochastic components of the specification to obtain accurate estimates. We consider both analytical and Monte Carlo approaches to the problem. We want to find accurate and low-cost computational techniques which permit the use of simulation methodology. At the same time keep in mind the typically large samples which are involved in a simulation. These large samples make computational techniques an important consideration. But the large samples may also allow possible simplifications in computational techniques because of the averaging process used in the calculation of simulation results.

For a given person j the desired hours of work on budget segment i is specified to be

$$(2.1) \qquad h_{ij} = \alpha w_{ij} + \beta y_{ij} + Z_j \gamma + \eta_j = h_{ij}^* + \eta_j \,,$$

where w_{ij} is the net, after-tax wage on segment i and y_{ij} is virtual income for segment i, i.e. the intercept of segment i extended back to the vertical axis in figure 2.1. The vector z_j represents socioeconomic characteristics of individual j. Now if w_{ij} and y_{ij} were determined exogenously and α, β, and γ were fixed coefficients, then we could use the standard linear expectation rules to derive $Eh_{ij} = \alpha w_{ij} + \beta y_{ij} + Z_j \gamma$. Of course, we specify β to be distributed randomly in the population in the intervals $(-\infty, 0)$. But the extension to stochastic β does not create much difficulty because again, given exogenous w_{ij} and y_{ij},

$$(2.2) \qquad Eh_{ij} = \alpha w_{ij} + y_{ij} E\beta + Z_j \gamma$$

$$= \alpha w_{ij} + \left(\mu_\beta - \sigma_\beta \left[\frac{\phi(\mu_\beta/\sigma_\beta)}{1 - \Phi(\mu_\beta/\sigma_\beta)} \right] \right) y_{ij} + Z_j \gamma$$

$$= \alpha w_{ij} + \bar{\beta} y_{ij} + Z_j \gamma \,,$$

where μ_β and σ_β are the underlying parameters of the nontruncated distribution for β, respectively, while ϕ and Φ are the standard normal density function and distribution function, respectively. The problem to be faced, then, is that w_{ij} and y_{ij} are determined by the budget segment B_{ij}, which depends on two stochastic components, η_j and $v_j = \beta_j - \bar{\beta}$. Thus we have the problem that the variables on the right-hand side are not determined exogenously. Nor do we have a simple formula for their expectation as we would in the linear simultaneous equations case. Thus, not unexpectedly, we need to consider the complete budget set when calculating the conditional expectation of hours worked, tax revenue paid, or deadweight loss and account for the "endogeneity" of w_{ij} and y_{ij}. It turns out to be the nonlinearity of the budget set together with the distribution of preferences specification which cause the significant costs of labor supply simulations. As we indicate below, the solution for that part of the β distribution which corresponds to a given budget segment is a nontrivial calculation.

We first consider the analytical conditional expectation for hours worked. The expectation is

$$(2.3) \qquad Eh_j = \sum_{i=1}^{m} \left[\int_{\beta_{i-1,j}}^{\beta_{ij}} \int_{q_{ij}(\beta)}^{\infty} (h_{ij}^*(\beta) + n_j) f(\eta_j) f(\beta) d\eta_j \, d\beta \right]$$
$$+ \sum_{i=1}^{m-1} \left[\int_{r_{i,j}}^{\infty} (h_{ij}^* + \eta_j)(F(\beta_{ij}) - F(\beta_{i-1,j})) f(\eta_j) d\eta_j \right].$$

As we discussed in the last section for $\beta < \beta_j^*$, the minimum β which causes desired hours to be positive ($h_{ij}^* > 0$), we assume that actual hours $h_j = 0$. Thus equation (2.3) calculates the expectation of actual hours h_j over the range for which desired hours h_{ij}^* are positive. The first sum in the equation corresponds to the case where desired hours fall along a budget segment $i = 1, m$. The range of β values which causes this to happen is denoted $(\beta_{i-1,j}, \beta_{ij})$. Note that in the nonconvex case some segments may have the intergral end points equal, which means that desired hours will not fall anywhere on the segment. It is basically this calculation which leads to the greatest expense in simulation since calculation of the univariate and bivariate integrals is not that costly. The nonconvex budget set of figure 2.2 indicates the possibility of an indifference curve that is tangent to two budget segments simultaneously. Thus in the nonconvex case there are portions of the budget segment which cannot correspond to desired hours. For this possibility to happen, the indirect utility function of equation (1.4) is equal for a given β for two sets of values of w_i and y_i. Calculation of these β values for each nonconvexity in the budget set requires the iterative solution of a nonlinear equation. Given the further facts that the points of mutual tangency are unknown and that complete budget segments may be skipped over, the computation of the $(\beta_{i-1,j}, \beta_{ij})$ for all budget segments $i = 1, m$ is a rather complicated task. Thus we look for possible simplifications in simulation to reduce both the computer costs and the required programming time.

The outer integral in equation (2.3) determines desired hours $h_{ij}^*(\beta)$. But actual hours $h_{ij} = h_{ij}^*(\beta) + \eta_j$. The inner integral accounts for this second source of stochastic variation. Note that for large negative values of η_j we have $h_{ij} < 0$. Thus $q_{ij}(\beta) = h_{ij}^*(\beta)$, the minimum value of η which keeps actual hours positive. The second sum in equation (2.3) corresponds to desired hours falling at one of the $m - 1$ curves, or kink points, of the budget set. The lower limit to the integral, r_{ij}, again determines the range for positive h_{ij}.

Evaluation of the integrals in equation (2.3) is not especially difficult, even given the bivariate integrals. Conditioning formulas can be used, and known partial fraction expansions for univariate integrals lead to quick evaluation. These simplifications follow basically from the linear specifications of h_{ij} in equation (2.1). Unfortunately, because of the nonlinearity of the expenditure function, the computation of integrals becomes considerably more complicated for calculating deadweight loss. The expenditure function which corresponds to the indirect utility function of equation (1.4) is

$$(2.4) \qquad e(w_{ij}, U_j) = \exp(-\beta w_{ij})\, U_j - \frac{\alpha}{\beta}\, w_i + \frac{\alpha}{\beta^2} - \frac{Z_j \gamma}{\beta}.$$

The nonlinearity arises from β appearing in both the exponential and the denominators of the coefficients. For a given β, deadweight loss is measured by calculating either the compensated or equivalent variation via the expenditure function of equation (2.4) and then subtracting off compensated taxes paid, using the definition of Diamond and McFadden (1974).[4] Hausman (1981a) has demonstrated the necessity of doing the correct Hicksian measure of consumer surplus because use of the incorrect Marshallian measure can lead to very large errors in calculation of the deadweight loss. For calculation of deadweight loss, equation (2.3) is altered to account for the deadweight loss for β values which correspond to zero hours of work. Otherwise, the general formula remains the same, with the main difference that the nonlinear calculation required for deadweight loss makes computation considerably more slow than in the case of hours worked, which is a linear function of β. Conditioning formulas for the integrals are no longer applicable, and quadrature methods to evaluate the univariate and bivariate integrals are now required.

---

4. Other definitions are discussed in Auerbach and Rosen (1980).

To evaluate computation techniques we tried four approaches listed in order of decreasing computational burden on a sample of men in 1975 from the Panel Study of Income Dynamics (PSID) data base:

1. Analytical evaluation, via the computer, of the integrals in equation (2.3). For the nonlinear deadweight loss calculation we took the $\tilde{\beta}_{ij}$ corresponding to the mean β on the interval $(\beta_{i-1,j}, \beta_{ij})$ so that complete quadrature methods were not necessary to evaluate the integrals.

2. The distribution of β was still integrated over, but one Monte Carlo draw from a normal distribution was done for η_j.

3. The distribution of β was integrated over, and η_j was set to zero.[5]

4. β was taken at its mean value $\bar{\beta} = \mu_\beta - \sigma_\beta\phi(\mu_\beta/\sigma_\beta)/[1 - \Phi(\mu_\beta/\sigma_\beta)]$. Corresponding to $\bar{\beta}$ we find $h_{ij}^*(\beta)$, and η_j is set to zero. This technique also removes any need for integration for taxes paid or calculation of deadweight loss.

Note that the second approach leads to unbiased (or consistent) estimates of the expectation. Such estimates will have more variance than the actual expectations of the first approach because of the variance created by the Monte Carlo draws. However, we consider a sample of 200 men to see whether the appropriate law of large numbers works fast enough for this consideration not to be important. Potential bias is created by approach (3) since the expectation of η_j is positive and decreases along each segment as β_j increases. Last, approach (4) creates additional bias because it runs afoul of the rule that the expectation of a nonlinear function is not equal, in general, to the function of the expectation. Potential problems arise here for both hours of work and deadweight loss because of the nonlinearity of the budget set.

In table 2.3 we consider the four techniques on the first five men in our simulation file to see what happens at the individual level. The column labeled "hours" gives actual hours, while the next four columns calculate the expectation of hours corresponding to methods (1)–(4). The next two sets of columns correspond to the expectation of taxes paid and the expectation of deadweight loss using the equivalent variation measure.

Since method (1) leads to the correct evaluation of the expectation, it provides the standard of comparison for methods (2)–(4). For labor supply we see that method (2) leads to considerable variance, as expected. Method (3), which sets $\eta = 0$, gives identical results to method (1). Method (4), which takes the mean $\bar{\beta}$, leads to some bias, although only a small amount. For expected taxes paid, methods (3) and (4) again have a bias which is somewhat larger in this case. Last, deadweight loss seems most sensitive to the technique used. Techniques (3) and (4) are off

---

5. The women's sample might be better than the men's sample for testing this option because the sensitivity around zero hours for a man is probably quite small. Thus biases are not apt to be important for men. However, subsequent simulations have indicated that, while the bias is slightly larger for women, it is still probably small enough to be ignored.

Table 2.3   Individual Evaluation Methods (× 1,000)

Indi-vidual	Actual Hours	Expected Hours				Expected Taxes Paid				Expected Deadweight Loss			
		H(1)	H(2)	H(3)	H(4)	T(1)	T(2)	T(3)	T(4)	DWL(1)	DWL(2)	DWL(3)	DWL(4)
1	2.708	2.393	2.136	2.393	2.389	1.105	.883	1.104	1.100	.162	.395	.151	.156
2	1.928	2.097	2.679	2.097	2.101	5.208	7.661	5.165	5.058	2.971	.993	2.784	2.848
3	1.994	1.900	2.114	1.900	1.887	2.560	2.934	2.543	2.455	.449	.401	.401	.496
4	2.310	2.233	2.559	2.223	2.245	3.082	3.857	3.061	3.063	1.081	.337	1.022	1.015
5	2.121	2.201	1.455	2.201	2.142	1.713	.814	1.704	1.602	.314	1.974	.287	.382
Means	2.212	2.163	2.189	2.163	2.153	2.734	3.230	2.715	2.656	.995	.820	.929	.997

by about 7% in these calculations. Thus our tentative conclusion for individual calculations is that for labor supply and taxes paid method (3) is probably an appropriate technique to use.[6] However, for deadweight loss, full analytical evaluation of the integrals seems necessary for accurate calculation of the expectation.

We now turn to the major use of simulation for tax changes. We simulate over a file of approximately 225 men from the PSID file to see what happens to accuracy for mean changes. This file was found large enough to capture the limiting behavior of the different evaluation methods. Note that a substantial amount of computer processing time is involved here.[7] Taking the amount of time to do method (1) as unity, we find that method (2) takes 0.560 while method (3) takes 0.500 and method (4) takes 0.360 as long. Where many simulations are done over tax files that have thousands of entries, these time considerations can become quite important. Given the nonlinearity of the problem, the simulations can take up large amounts of computer time.

Simulation results are given in table 2.4. We now find that method (2) gives almost identical results to method (1) for hours and taxes. This result is as expected since the Monte Carlo method should give accurate computations once the law of large numbers has had time to take effect. Method (3) is fine for hours, but it is note quite as good for taxes. Moreover, it offers only a very slight savings over method (2). Method (4) probably can be rated as unsatisfactory given the size of tax changes that we are usually interested in evaluating. For deadweight loss calculations, method (2) is off by about 4%. The other two methods are off by double that amount. Here we might conclude that larger samples are probably needed for method (2) to be sufficiently accurate. Methods (3) and (4) might be rejected as too inaccurate to evaluate proposed tax changes. Thus we may conclude this section with the finding that methods (2) and (3) are both appropriate for use in the evaluation of tax change on labor supply and taxes. For computation of deadweight loss, where nonlinearities become important, only method (2) is approximately accurate. However, for samples of the size we are considering, method (1), which involves calculation of all the integrals involved in the expectation, provides the only truly accurate method. The appropriate next step in this line of research is to develop formulas for the (asymptotic) standard errors which correspond to the results in table 2.4. Given the nonlinearities inherent in the calculation of hours, taxes, and deadweight loss, asymptotic expansions would be used to account for the uncertainty in the parameter estimates. But the accuracy of these techniques might be

---

6. Method (4) may also be satisfactory for a first approximation.

7. While relative computer costs are difficult to compare, a simulation on the full sample of 1,000 families on the Massachusetts Institute of Technology IBM 370 computer costs around $60.

Table 2.4   **Full Sample Evaluation Methods: Mean Response ($\times$ 1,000)**

Method	Hours	Taxes	DWL
1	2.169	2.268	.652
2	2.165	2.267	.676
3	2.169	2.251	.608
4	2.138	2.153	.709

questionable here. Evaluation of the accuracy of the expansions would require a full-scale Monte Carlo study in itself. Yet such information might be very helpful, especially if the standard errors for the calculations in table 2.4 turn out to be sizable. We need to remember that "parameter uncertainty" does not average out by a large-numbers type of result in simulations because of perfect correlation across sample draws in the use of parameter values. This area seems to be an important aspect of future research in the field. We now turn to evaluation of some proposed tax changes. Method (3) is used for expected hours and expected taxes, while we use method (1) to evaluate expected changes in deadweight loss.

2.3 Simulation Results

In this section we consider the effect of two different types of tax systems. The first type of tax is the current federal tax on labor income including both the income and payroll tax. We compare it to a no-tax situation. To measure the change in labor supply we calculate the change in expected hours of work using equation (2.3). The appropriate choice for the change in individual welfare is not quite as clear. We use the equivalent variation calculated from the expenditure function of equation (2.4). Choice of the equivalent variation as the measure of deadweight loss, or the excess burden of taxation, seems appropriate since we later consider changes from the current system to an altered tax system. Since in the altered tax system individual welfare may be higher, we want to know the cost (in utility) of staying with the current system. But two possible objections to our measure is that we aggregate across individuals, giving each individual the same weight in the implicit social welfare function, and that different individuals are allowed different coefficients in their expenditure functions. The problems created for analysis of vertical equity considerations by these choices are discussed in Atkinson and Stiglitz (1976). The latter problem may not be especially serious since parameter differences arise from a distribution of preferences which is common to the entire population.

The other type of tax system that we consider involves a cut in tax rates of a given percentage. We consider the expected change in labor supply, the expected change in tax revenue, and the expected change in dead-

Table 2.5   **Mean Tax Results for Husbands**

Market Wage	DWL	DWL/Tax Revenue	DWL/Net Income	Change in Labor Supply
$3.15	$ 66	9.4%	.8%	−4.5%
$4.72	$ 204	14.4%	2.0%	−6.5%
$5.87	$ 387	19.0%	3.1%	−8.5%
$7.06	$ 633	23.7%	4.5%	−10.1%
$10.01	$1,749	39.5%	9.9%	−12.8%

weight loss from the current system. Much recent attention has focused on the revenue effects of a change in the income tax rates. It is important to note that our analysis is wholly *partial equilibrium* in nature. We look only at changes in expected labor supply. Thus potentially important factors such as changes in market wages and changes in inputs of other factors of production are not considered. A more complex general equilibrium model is needed to answer these questions. Also, since tax revenues will be decreasing, the problem of compensation arises. The problem of potential versus actual compensation was the basis of the Kaldor-Hicks-Scitovsky-Samuelson-Little debate of the 1940s. Without the choice of an explicit social welfare function we cannot resolve this problem. But we assume no posttax redistribution of income among individuals, since such actual (rather than potential) compensation is unlikely to take place.

In table 2.5 we look at the effect of the current tax system for five categories of husbands defined by their market wage.[8] Overall, we find that the tax system decreases the labor supply by 8.5% and that the mean deadweight loss as a proportion of tax revenue raised is 28.7%. We note important differences among the five categories. First, we see that deadweight loss rises rapidly with the market wage as expected. In terms of the welfare cost of the tax we see that the ratio of deadweight loss to tax revenue raised starts at 9.4% and rises to 39.5% by the time we reach the highest wage category. We see that the cost of raising revenue via the income and payroll taxes is not negligible. In terms of a distributional measure we see that the ratio of deadweight loss to net income also rises rapidly. In fact, this measure indicates that individuals in the highest wage category bear a cost about ten times the lowest category while individuals in the second highest category bear a cost five times as high. Without a specific social welfare measure, we cannot decide whether the

8. When we refer to the current tax system, we are actually using the 1975 data, which the model was estimated with. However, except for the rise in social security contributions, the taxation of labor income has not changed significantly since 1975. Of course, individuals on average have moved into higher marginal tax brackets because of the lack of indexation of the income tax.

current tax system has too much, too little, or about the right amount of progressiveness. But the measures of table 2.5 seem important in thinking about the problem. Last, note that the change in labor supply from the no-tax situation again rises with the wage category. The high marginal tax brackets have a significantly greater effect on labor supply than do the low tax brackets.

We now do a similar set of calculations for our sample of wives. While we found both significant deadweight loss and an important effect on labor supply for husbands compared to the no-tax situation, the situation is more complicated for wives. First, about half of all wives do not work. In the absence of an income tax, the net wage would rise, causing some of them to decide to work and others to increase their labor supply. But at the same time their husbands' after-tax earnings would also rise, which has the opposite effect on labor force participation. Thus both effects must be accounted for in considering the effects of the income tax. Overall for wives, (in table 2.6), we find the ratio of deadweight loss to tax revenue to be 18.4%. But it should be remembered that this ratio understates the effect on labor force participants alone. For labor supply, we find that taxes serve to increase the labor supply in the lowest wage category but decrease the labor supply as the wage rises. Overall, they decrease the labor supply by 18.2%. Thus, again for wives we see that the current income tax system both has an important labor supply effect and imposes a significant cost in welfare terms for raising tax revenue.

We now turn to a consideration of tax proposals of the Kemp-Roth type. We will consider two levels of tax cuts, 10% and 30%. The question which has been focused on most is what effect these tax cuts would have on tax revenues. Our results are partial equilibrium so that general equilibrium effects are not accounted for. The main effect here arises from the change in labor supply. But increased hours also move some individuals into higher tax brackets. Both effects need to be accounted for. In table 2.7 we present two Kemp-Roth simulation results. For the 10% tax deduction the mean hours of labor supply for husbands rise 22.5 hours, or 1.1%. Tax revenues fall by 7.4%. Even given the fact that our

Table 2.6   **Mean Tax Results for Wives**

Market Wage	DWL	DWL/Tax Revenue	DWL/Net Income	Change in Labor Supply
$2.11	$ 23	4.6%	.3%	+31.2%
$2.50	$ 119	15.3%	1.3%	−14.2%
$3.03	$ 142	15.9%	1.5%	−20.3%
$3.63	$ 184	16.5%	1.7%	−23.8%
$5.79	$1,283	35.7%	8.6%	−22.9%

Table 2.7   **Kemp-Roth Tax Cut Proposals for Husbands**

	10% Tax Cut			30% Tax Cut		
Market Wage	DWL/Tax Revenue	DWL/Net Income	Change in Labor Supply	DWL/Tax Revenue	DWL/Net Income	Change in Labor Supply
$3.15	8.5%	.7%	+.4%	6.8%	.4%	+1.3%
$4.72	13.3%	1.7%	+.5%	10.9%	1.1%	+1.6%
$5.87	17.4%	2.6%	+.9%	14.5%	1.8%	+2.7%
$7.06	21.8%	3.8%	+1.1%	17.9%	2.5%	+3.1%
$10.01	36.1%	8.2%	+1.4%	29.5%	5.3%	+4.6%

model is partial equilibrium, rudimentary calculations demonstrate that general equilibrium effects are very unlikely to be large enough to cause tax revenues from decreasing significantly in the short run, as our results show. In terms of the welfare cost of the tax we see that the deadweight loss falls significantly. The ratio of mean deadweight loss to tax revenue falls from 22.1% under the current system to 19.0% under the 10% tax cut plan. For the 30% tax cut labor supply increases by 2.7% while tax revenue falls by 22.6%. Again, we see that deadweight loss decreases significantly and the ratio of deadweight loss to tax revenues raised decreases to 15.4%. In terms of distributional changes the top quintile has the greatest increase in utility as a ratio to net income. Thus, as expected, decreasing taxes by a constant percentage reduces deadweight loss but does so in a manner most beneficial to those individuals who face the highest tax rates. Kemp-Roth type tax cuts have large effects both in terms of decreasing deadweight loss and in decreasing government revenue. Without knowledge of marginal government expenditure, it is difficult to evaluate the trade-off. But we cannot recommend Kemp-Roth cuts on welfare grounds alone, given the substantial fall in government revenue.

For wives we do not present detailed quintile results because the overall pattern is similar to the results for husbands. The mean results are given in table 2.8. Overall, we see that the labor supply response to a tax cut is greater for wives than for husbands. We expect this since the wage

Table 2.8   **Overall Kemp-Roth Tax Cut for Wives**

	Tax Cut	Change in Tax Revenue	Change in DWL	Change in Supply (hours)
	10%	−3.8%	−10.6%	+50.2
	30%	−16.2%	−17.4%	+117.0

elasticity is about twice the income elasticity, so we should have a net increase in labor supply. Furthermore, the difference in the elasticities is about four times that of husbands, and we do observe a significantly larger response. For the 10% tax cut case, labor supply increases by 4.1% and tax revenues fall by 3.8%. For the 30% tax cut case, labor supply increases by 9.4% and tax revenues fall by 16.2%.

Our overall evaluation of the Kemp-Roth tax proposals is that while tax revenues will decrease by significantly less than the tax cut, overall government revenue from the income and payroll tax will decline. An argument might be made that general equilibrium results may be large enough to reverse this conclusion, but I doubt that it is a valid argument, especially in the short run. Thus, unless a strong argument can be made for reducing government expenditures with little welfare loss from the recipients, the Kemp-Roth tax cut proposals cannot be supported on the basis of our results alone. They certainly do not have the "free lunch" properties claimed by some of their supporters.

References

Atkinson, A., and J. Stiglitz. 1976. The design of tax structure: Direct versus indirect taxation. *Journal of Public Economics* 6: 55–76.

Auerbach, A., and H. Rosen. 1980. Will the real excess burden stand up? Mimeo, NBER.

Burtless, G., and J. Hausman. 1978. The effect of taxation on labor supply: Evaluating the Gary negative income tax experiment. *Journal of Political Economy* 86, no. 6 (December): 1103–30.

Diamond, P., and D. McFadden. 1974. Some uses of the expenditure function in public finance. *Journal of Public Economics* 3: 3–22.

Hausman, J. 1979. The econometrics of labor supply on convex budget sets. *Economic Letters* 3: 171–74.

———. 1980. The effect of wages, taxes, and fixed costs on women's labor force participation. *Journal of Public Economics* 14: 161–94.

———. 1981a. Exact consumers' surplus and deadweight loss. *American Economic Review* 71: 662–76.

———. 1981b. The effect of taxes on labor supply. In H. Aaron and J. Pechman, eds., *The effect of taxes on economic activity*. Washington: Brookings Institution.

Heckman, J. 1980. Sample bias as a specification error. In. J. P. Smith, ed., *Female labor supply: Theory and estimation*. Princeton, New Jersey: Princeton University Press.

Smith, J. P. 1980. *Female labor supply: Theory and estimation*. Princeton, New Jersey: Princeton University Press.

Comment   James J. Heckman

In his paper Hausman applies econometric methods developed in the literature on sample selection bias and censored samples to estimate labor supply behavior in response to various forms of tax policies. "Kinked" convex and nonconvex budget constraints receive the lion's share of the attention in the analysis. Various methods of simulating the estimates are then proposed and implemented.

I have little to say about Hausman's simulation procedures. To discuss simulation of the estimates before discussing the quality of the estimates puts the cart before the horse. I have reservations about the input used in the simulation procedures and feel that it is premature to use the estimates offered by Hausman as a serious guide to assessing the impact of alternative tax policies on labor supply.

My principal reservations about his estimates focus on the specification of the budget set confronting individuals that is used in the empirical work and on the econometric specification of the labor supply equations. Before turning to these issues, however, it is useful to place the current work in context.

Kosters's (1967) pioneering work on labor supply was based on the following key assumptions: (a) taxes are proportional, (b) a worker is free to choose any hours of work at "his" wage, (c) the income of one spouse is predetermined in the labor supply of the other (for married workers). Boskin (1973) and Hall (1973) relaxed (a) and (c) while retaining (b). The standard tax deduction formula is used to compute effective marginal tax rates. Tax schedule "kinks" are ignored as a first approximation, and the linearization device employed in the Hausman paper for a kinked constraint (section 2.1) was used to parameterize the effective after-tax wage confronting the worker. Both Boskin and Hall replace the income of the spouse (where appropriate) with the theoretically more correct wage. The main empirical findings reported in these and other papers done at the same time suggested a backward-bending male labor supply function (for hours worked for most groups) and strong positive wage effects for most female groups (both hours worked and participation). A persistent empirical problem in this literature is the often statistically insignificant and sometimes positive effect of measures of "exogenous income" on labor supply. The range of male labor supply estimates is 0.19 to 0.07 for the uncompensated substitution effect, but this range is by no means universally accepted. (For a survey see Heckman, Killingsworth, and MaCurdy 1981.)

James J. Heckman is with the Department of Economics at the University of Chicago, and the National Bureau of Economic Research.

Rosen (1976) relaxed (*b*) using a hedonic model that arises from explicit consideration of employer interests in employee hours of work. His empirical findings on the wage-hours locus have been confirmed in later work. Rosen also utilizes a variant of the Boskin-Hall procedure to compute effective taxes facing individuals.

Hausman follows in the tradition of Boskin and Hall but focuses on several important problems overlooked in their work. First, Boskin and Hall both ignore the simultaneity problem that arises in using computed marginal and average tax rates. The point here is simple but empirically important. Given a nonproportional tax, the computed tax rate depends on the error in the labor supply equation. Putting tax-adjusted wage rates and virtual income levels on the right-hand side of a labor supply equation (as do Boskin and Hall) creates a standard simultaneous bias problem. Hausman's procedure attempts to avoid this sort of bias.[1] Second, Boskin and Hall both ignore the kinks at various levels of adjusted gross income in the official tax tables. In a progressive system there should be bunching at the kinks. Individuals at these kinks are at a corner equilibrium in their labor supply so that the textbook theory of labor supply must be modified, albeit in a straightforward way. Because of these kinks, the standard instrumental variable solution to the first problem does not work. Besides addressing these issues, Hausman also explicitly allows for individual heterogeneity in preferences following up on the work of Hall (1975) and Heckman (1974). He demonstrates, as had the papers cited, that there is considerable dispersion in preferences for work in the population. Finally, Hausman follows Cogan (1980, 1981) in introducing fixed costs into the analysis of labor supply.

There are few original ideas contained in this paper. However, the synthesis of the work of others is interesting. The main contribution of the paper is the development of computational algorithms. Hausman takes the textbook one-period labor supply model and imposes it onto his data in order to secure estimates and generate policy simulations. In doing so he ignores a considerable body of accumulated empirical evidence that casts doubt on the validity of the textbook model. Hausman's procedures critically depend on access to data that he does not have and that economists are unlikely to have in the near future.

This paper is a microeconometric counterpart of the standard macroeconometric exercise that was conducted in the 1960s when the consensus view was that the remaining research agenda in that field was a matter of "fine tuning." Hausman adopts the view that was assumed then, that

---

1. Rosen also discusses this point, but his solution—evaluating tax rates at a standard hours of work position—trades a simultaneous equation bias for an induced measurement error bias that is likely to be very sizable. This general problem in the Boskin-Hall procedure has been noted by many analysts. See the survey in Heckman, Killingsworth, and MaCurdy (1981) for a discussion of this point.

there is agreement on the validity of the simple theory, that the basic empirical facts are well known, and that all that is required to produce policy forecasts is a simply computed algorithm. Would that it were so.

My comments on this paper are directed toward the general research strategy and the specific procedures used to achieve the estimates reported in Hausman's paper. In particular, I discuss the following topics: (1) The specification of the choice set facing individuals. (2) The arbitrary, and sometimes very controversial, functional forms and distributional assumptions that are imposed onto the data in order to secure estimates. (3) The economic interpretation of consumer surplus measures and deadweight losses in the presence of heterogeneity in consumer preferences.

The Choice Set

There is no question that kinks appear in adjusted gross income tax schedules if they are properly measured. Kinked nonconvex constraints characterize many social programs and social experiments.

I am surprised to find so much discussion of the econometrics of kinks in the Hausman paper without empirical demonstration of the importance of the problem. Specifically, I refer to the bunching that one expects to find in the presence of convex preferences and kinks. There should be some piling up of labor supply at kink points. I know of no such evidence, and in looking casually at the CES data for 1972 I find no evidence of such bunching. Of course one reason for finding no bunching is that it is very difficult to compute the correct kink points for a consumer unless we known itemizations and deductions. Hausman's econometric procedures rely critically on the assumption that kink points are known to the econometrician, a point I elaborate below. I question, in practice, whether they are in fact known. Another "reason" for the absence of evidence on the importance of kinks is the ad hoc assumption built into Hausman's model that workers are forced off their preferred labor supply curve by exogenous shocks that are independent of the preferences and resources of workers.

I am also surprised to find so little attention devoted in this paper and in the literature in general to the problem of tax avoidance and labor supply. The problem strikes me as more important than the problem of kinks. Rational economic behavior suggests that individuals will devote resources to avoid taxes and that they will take advantage of tax subsidies on goods such as housing. Tax rates computed from standard tables (as Hausman computes his tax rates) will overstate the true tax rate paid. Dollar taxes paid will understate the true cost of the tax by the direct avoidance costs (even abstracting from labor supply adjustments). Dollar taxes estimated from a tax schedule will overestimate true taxes paid (including avoidance costs). In the appendix I sketch a very simple model to demonstrate these points.

There I demonstrate that for a plausible tax avoidance function, estimates, such as Hausman's, that ignore tax avoidance behavior understate true income and overstate estimated income effects, leading to an overestimate of welfare losses. The true kink point confronting consumers varies in a manner that depends on consumer preferences for goods that are subsidized by the tax system (e.g. housing) and resources available to the consumer. This means that Hausman's econometric procedures, which require the econometrician to compute individual taxes, are inappropriate in the absence of detailed information about consumption behavior.

There is the additional complication that, because some goods are subsidized by the tax system, the simple two-dimensional labor supply analysis utilized by Hausman is inappropriate. It is appropriate to analyze labor supply and a composite good "consumption" only if the tax system does not subsidize the consumption of specific items such as housing. But it does. Numerical estimates of the bias from this source are not yet possible. The Hausman model is misspecified because it omits such relative price effects induced by the tax system. This point helps to explain the apparently (perverse) positive effect of home equity on labor supply reported in table 2.1.

In the appendix, I present a model for incorporating tax avoidance effects into the analysis of labor supply and offer some rough estimates of the empirical importance of the phenomenon. If my numbers hold up in further investigation, the bias from neglecting tax avoidance is considerable.

I next turn to a point to which I have alluded several times: *that Hausman's econometric procedures require that the budget set confronting the consumer be known to the econometrician.*[2] Because of considerable unobserved variability in deductions and exemptions that is not accounted for in Hausman's tax computation algorithm, and because for some groups of workers (primarily females) wages must be estimated, the true position of the budget set is not known to the econometrician. Hausman only allows two types of variability in the model (in the income coefficient β and in the discrepancy between actual and desired hours of work). Measurement error in specifying the budget set introduces a third type of variability that cannot be represented as either of the first two types. Thus *his maximum likelihood procedure*, which requires a full accounting for all sources of variability in order to deliver consistent estimates of the structural parameters of the model, *does not produce*

---

2. Hausman claims that this is not so in his footnote 2, but there is no demonstration of this claim there or in any of his papers because the claim is false.

consistent estimates. This is so because the after-tax wages used in his formula (1.4) are measured with error as are the segments on the labor supply axis that purport to correspond to the after-tax wages. Using imputed after-tax wages from his procedure, one computes the wrong probability that an individual desires to be on a given branch of a budget set if the budget set is not correctly specified. As a consequence, Hausman's estimators are inconsistent.

These problems are not insurmountable, but they are not addressed, much less solved, in any of Hausman's papers. An exact analysis of the magnitude of the bias that results from this source is difficult. Roughly speaking, in a group of otherwise identical individuals those with more taste for work have greater incentive to avoid taxes. Under Hausman's imputation scheme, such people are allocated to a higher tax bracket than they actually face. Substitution effects are overstated, leading to an overestimate of computed welfare losses. Neglecting dispersion in wage rates by assigning average wages to individuals tends to lead to a downward bias (in absolute value) in estimated substitution effects. This second effect would be most pronounced for women (for whom wages are more likely to be imputed), perhaps accounting in part for Hausman's relatively low estimated substitution elasticity for women. (See Heckman, Killingsworth, and MaCurdy 1981 for a survey of recent results on the labor supply of women.)

For more detailed discussion of this topic, see Heckman and MaCurdy (1981, pp. 88–95, especially pp. 92–93). The essential point made there is that errors in variables problems in general nonlinear models, such as Hausman's, require more careful analysis than has been accorded to them in the literature. In light of this point, I cannot help but speculate that previous empirical procedures such as those of Boskin and Hall that incorporate less (false) information into the estimation procedure may be more robust than procedures such as Hausman's which assume information that does not exist and which produce inconsistent estimators if the information is false.

The Imposition of Functional Forms and Prior "Information"

In light of the long-standing empirical controversy surrounding the sign of the income effect (β), I feel that it is inappropriate to impose negativity onto the estimates as Hausman does. This point is particularly important in the estimates of the male labor supply equation. Hausman's estimated substitution effect (α) is essentially zero. By imposing a negative income effect onto the data by his econometric procedure, Hausman guarantees that his procedure will produce a larger compensated substitution effect—and hence a larger welfare loss—than other studies have. At a minimum, I think that unrestricted estimates should be reported and a test of Hausman's assumptions that the mean of β and the largest population value of β are negative should be performed. This point is especially relevant in light of previous published results by Burtless and Hausman (1978, p. 1124), who report that when β is permitted to become positive, the estimated mean value of β is not statistically significantly different from zero.

Hausman justifies the imposition of a nonpositive value of β by appealing to the argument that leisure is a normal good. Much previous research indicates that when β is not restricted, it frequently is estimated to be positive (as in fact is the coefficient on house equity in Hausman's table 2.1—which coefficient can be interpreted as estimating β multiplied by the rate of return on housing stock). There are two reasons for this (Heckman 1971; Greenberg and Kosters 1973; Smith 1980): (*a*) the endogeneity of assets in a life-cycle model of labor supply, and (*b*) the correlation between preferences for work and savings. These papers indicate that the standard one-period model of labor supply as used by Hausman must be modified to produce useful results. Hausman chooses to ignore all of this research and decides the matter by fiat. For this reason his estimates, which ignore life-cycle phenomena and the endogeneity of assets, are not to be taken as serious guides to policy.

A similar remark applies to the use of functional forms to secure estimates of fixed costs and other unobservables. The new game in labor supply, pioneered by Cogan (1980, 1981), is to interpret departures of estimated labor supply functions from a simple functional form as evidence for the presence of fixed costs and the dispersion of preferences. In the appendix, I indicate how this game can be played to produce estimates of tax avoidance parameters.

There is much accumulating evidence (Heckman and Singer 1982; Goldberger 1981; Duncan 1981) that parameter estimates of nonlinear models of the sort estimated by Hausman are very sensitive to the choice of functional form of the model and the distributions of unobservables. In light of this recent work, I am very uneasy that so much mileage is obtained from imposing arbitrary, and intrinsically untestable, nonlinearities and distributional assumptions onto the data in order to secure labor supply estimates. I am not as negative as Hausman on the more modest empirical procedures used by previous analysts who make less grandiose claims about the validity of their models and use less "information" in securing labor supply estimates. Given our current state of knowledge about labor supply, there should be less "fine tuning" and more insight if the sort of bold claims made in the Hausman paper are to be taken seriously. Much more evidence on the robustness of the estimates reported in this paper to departures from the assumptions of the model is required.

The Implications of Heterogeneity on the
Calculation of Welfare Losses

In light of Hausman's finding (and that of previous analysts Hall 1975 and Heckman 1974) that there is considerable heterogeneity in consumer marginal rates of substitution between goods and leisure, the interpretation to be placed on the reported estimates of welfare loss is not clear. Hausman notes this point in his paper, but does not discuss it in any detail. His estimates *overstate* the true amount of compensation that the society must be paid to be just as well off as before a tax change because the society can redistribute income among heterogeneous consumers, and Hausman's estimates assume that no redistribution occurs.

Miscellaneous Comments and a Summary

I agree with Hausman's conclusion that the Kemp-Roth tax cut proposals will not produce a free lunch. A reading of the estimates derived in the pre-Hausman literature on labor supply supports this conclusion. Hausman's numerical results offer another shred of evidence that supports the view held by most economists that the Laffer curve has no empirical foundation in the labor supply literature.

I am less convinced by the estimates of welfare losses due to income taxes that are presented in his paper. For reasons already advanced, Hausman's procedures tend to produce inflated estimates of welfare losses.

Appendix   *A Simple, Econometrically Tractable Model
of Tax Avoidance and Labor Supply*

Let $U(X,L)$ be the preference function of the consumer. X is goods consumption, and L is leisure. $0 \leq L \leq 1$. Let the tax function facing the consumer be proportional. The after-tax fraction of income received is $\theta(A)$, where A is dollar avoidance costs, $\theta'(A) \geq 0$, $\theta''(A) \leq 0$, $\lim_{A \to \infty} \theta(A) \leq 1$. For simplicity, avoidance is assumed to be nondeductible and nonutility bearing.[3] The wage is W, and the consumer can freely choose his hours of work. R is his unearned income.

3. The specification of the tax avoidance function warrants some discussion. A more general analysis would write taxes paid after avoidance $\tilde{T}$ as a function of taxes paid with no avoidance T and avoidance expenditure A: $\tilde{T} = F(T,A)$ with $F_A < 0$ and $F(T,0) = T$. The consumer's problem is to maximize tax saving less avoidance cost $(T - \tilde{T}) - A$. A sufficient condition for an interior solution is $F_{AA} > 0$ and $\partial F/\partial A < -1$ for $A = 0$ and all $T > 0$.

Specializing F so that $\tilde{T} = T\varphi(A)$ with $\varphi(0) = 1$, $\varphi' < 0$, $\varphi'' > 0$, for a strictly proportional income tax t, the θ function adopted in the text is $\theta(A) = 1 - t\,\varphi(A)$.

For a kinked tax schedule expressed in terms of total income Y,

$$Y = R + W(1 - L) \,,$$
$$T = t_1 Y \quad Y \leq Y_1 \,,$$
$$T = t_1 Y_1 + t_2(Y - Y_1) \quad Y > Y_1 \,,$$

we define the fraction of income retained after taxes as

The consumer's problem is

$$\max U(X,L) \text{ s.t. } \theta(A)(R + W(1-L)) - PX - A = 0 \ .$$

There is a prior maximization problem: First choose A. The first-order condition is

$$\theta'(A)(R + W(1-L)) = 1 \ .$$

For $R > 0$, $\theta''(A) < 0$ is sufficient. As income increases, avoidance expenditures increase. The standard tax table reveals $\theta(0)$. The computed marginal tax rate, as a function of income, is $\theta(A)$, which is always less than $\theta(0)$. $1 - \theta(A)$ is the effective marginal tax rate.

The effect of tax avoidance is to make the true tax function more concave. A progressive tax table may appear as regressive after tax avoidance occurs. Consider a proportional tax. Figure C2.A.1 displays the table after-tax income after avoidance for the case $\theta''' < 0$. Figure C2.A.2 demonstrates the apparent budget set confronting the consumer, the tax table schedule, and the true constraint (inclusive of tax avoidance). In investigating the labor force participation decision using a constraint computed from the standard table, we understate true income and overstate estimated income effects. Using the apparent schedule (ignoring A) underestimates income effects. Substitution effects are overestimated. The effect on computed welfare losses (ignoring A) of estimates computed from the standard tables is to overstate the true welfare loss for two reasons: (a) the estimated compensated substitution effect is overestimated and (b) the true tax change of any computed tax change is smaller. Including A, this effect is partially but never completely offset. Below, I present preliminary estimates that suggest that these effects may be empirically quite strong.

Analogous results hold for the case of a kinked progressive standard tax table. The true constraint has a kink, and in the neighborhood of each kink point the slope of the true schedule to the right of the kink exceeds the slope of the true schedule to the left of the kink (see footnote 3). For sufficiently high after-tax income, the true marginal tax rate to the left of the kink may be *less* than the true marginal tax rate to the right of the

---

$$\theta(A,Y) = 1 - t_1\varphi(A), \quad Y \leq Y_1 \ ,$$

$$\theta(A,Y) = 1 - \left[t_2 + (t_1 - t_2)\frac{Y_1}{Y}\right]\phi(A), \quad Y > Y_1 \ .$$

For optimal values of A, θ is a continuous function of Y but is not a continuously differentiable function of Y. In the neighborhood of Y_1, the derivative of income after taxes and avoidance cost to the left of Y_1 exceeds the derivative of income after taxes and avoidance cost to the right of Y_1. To see this, note that optimal A is a continuous function of Y and to the right of Y, using the envelope theorem, income after taxes and avoidance cost $E(= Y - \bar{T} - A)$ has the derivative $\partial E/\partial Y = 1 - t_2\phi(A)$, $Y > Y_1$, while the derivative of E with respect to Y to the left of Y_1 is $\partial E/\partial Y = 1 - t_1\phi(A)$.

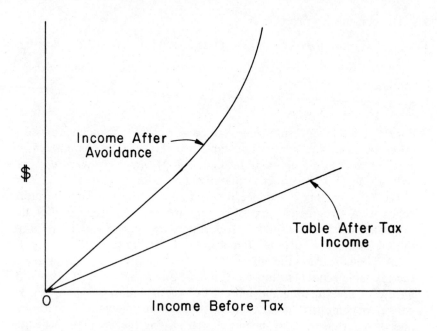

Fig. C2.A.1   Income after avoidance and table after-tax income as functions of income before tax.

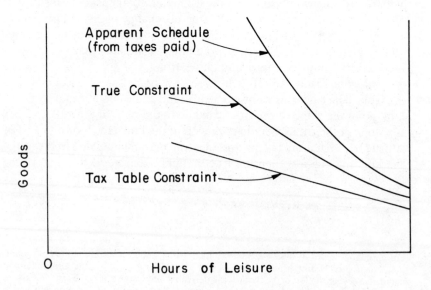

Fig. C2.A.2   Apparent constraint, true constraint, and tax table constraint for $R > 0$.

kink. This case is illustrated for a one-kink standard tax table in figure C2.A.3. There is a further complication that may be empirically quite important and which may cause the kink to disappear from the data. If tax avoidance costs can be written off in part and we cannot observe A, we may not be able to locate the abscissa of the kink in the figure. The same is true if avoidance is broadened to consider a variety of purchases and deductions not directly observed that affect adjusted gross income. The true kink point may vary in a population of consumers with the same wage and unearned income.

If A has a utility-bearing aspect (e.g. the subsidy on owned homes versus rented homes), a slightly more complicated analysis is required. The price of A depends on income. In a multigood world, the Hicks composite commodity theorem no longer applies so that the simple composite good used to derive indifference curves (or labor supply functions) and to specify the constraint set no longer holds. The after-tax price of A belongs in the labor supply function, and the computation of welfare loss requires a multidimensional analysis.

Is any of this empirically important? Since A cannot be observed, it may be argued that the preceding analysis is of little empirical relevance. This argument is incorrect. If the sort of strong functional form assumptions used by Hausman and Cogan to estimate unobservable fixed costs are adopted, it is also possible to estimate A. For the sake of brevity we only consider an apparent proportional tax case.

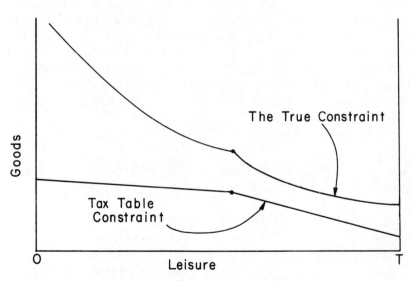

Fig. C2.A.3   True constraint and tax table constraint for the case of a one-kink progressive tax and $R > 0$.

Let $\theta(A) = k - b/(A + 1)$, so the apparent tax rate is $k - b$ (for $A = 0$). Then income after taxes and tax avoidance is (letting $h = 1 - L$)

$$[Wh + R][k] - b^{1/2}[Wh + R]^{1/2} + 1 .$$

Adopt a linear labor supply specification as a maintained assumption. Then, linearizing the true budget constraint in the fashion suggested by Hall and Boskin, the true marginal wage is

$$W\left[k - \frac{1}{2} b^{1/2}[Wh + R]^{-1/2}\right]$$

and virtual income is

$$1 + Rk - b^{1/2}[Wh + R]^{1/2} + Whb^{1/2}\frac{1}{2}[Wh + R]^{-1/2} ,$$

so the following labor supply equation may be fitted:

$$h = \alpha W\left[k - \frac{1}{2} b^{1/2}[Wh + R]^{-1/2}\right]$$
$$+ \beta\left[Rk - b^{1/2}[Wh + R]^{1/2} + Whb^{1/2}\right.$$
$$\left. \times \frac{1}{2}[Wh + R]^{-1/2} + 1\right] + Z\gamma + \epsilon .$$

Since we know $k - b$, we can estimate α, b, k, and β. Thus we can compute welfare losses. Because of the nonlinearity of the reduced form h function, we may use polynomials in Z as instruments. Modification of the analysis to a kinked convex case is a trivial extension.

If we have access to reported taxes, a simpler procedure is available so that it is not necessary to resort to arbitrary functional form restrictions on labor supply functions to estimate tax avoidance. Reported taxes are

$$[Wh + R]\left[1 - k + \frac{b}{A + 1}\right] .$$

Since $A + 1 = b^{1/2}[Wh + R]^{1/2}$ from the first-order condition for optimal tax avoidance, observed income after taxes is

$$[Wh + R]\left[1 - k + \frac{b^{1/2}}{[Wh + R]^{1/2}}\right].$$

Since we know $k - b = \phi$, substitute in the tax function to reach

$$[Wh + R][1 - \phi - b] + b^{1/2}[Wh + R]^{1/2} .$$

Regressing reported taxes on income generates estimates of $b^{1/2}$. This procedure can be used for the kinked constraint case.

How important is this problem? Without a serious analysis of the data on reported taxes versus taxes computed from standard tables, it is impossible to say. A very rough estimate obtained from the 1972 CES data in which taxes paid are reported suggests that b is roughly 10. This implies that a person earning $16,000 in adjusted gross income in 1972 spent about $400 on tax avoidance. This implies that the true marginal tax rate for this person is 25.5% rather than the quoted 28% and that true taxes paid (including avoidance) come to about $500 less than what is estimated from the standard form. If these results hold up in a thorough study, they suggest that the effect of ignoring tax avoidance may be empirically quite important.

It is interesting to note that the effect of ignoring tax avoidance behavior is to overstate estimated welfare losses. Moreover, a more comprehensive view of the tax system suggests that more effort might profitably be devoted to specifying the correct choice set for consumers and that econometric methods, such as those advocated by Hausman, that require exact information on the constraint set will generate biased estimates of tax response.

It is important to point out that different conclusions would be produced by other functional forms for the after-tax fraction of income function $\theta(A)$. Much further empirical and theoretical work is required before we can be sure that tax avoidance behavior is of any empirical importance.

References

Boskin, M. 1973. The economics of labor supply. In G. Cain and H. Watts, eds., *Income maintenance and labor supply*. Chicago: Markham.

Burtless, G., and J. Hausman. 1978. The effect of taxation on labor supply: Evaluating the Gary negative income tax experiment. *Journal of Political Economy* 86, no. 6 (December): 1103–30.

Cogan, J. 1980. Labor supply with fixed costs of market entry. In J. P. Smith, ed., *Female labor supply: Theory and estimation*. Princeton, New Jersey: Princeton University Press.

———. 1981. Female labor supply with time and money costs of participation. *Econometrica* 49, no. 4: 945–64.

Duncan, G. 1981. A relatively distribution-robust censored regression estimator. Mimeo, Department of Economics, Washington State University, May.

Goldberger, A. 1981. Abnormal selection bias. Mimeo, University of Wisconsin, March.

Greenberg, D., and M. Kosters. 1973. Income guarantees and the working poor. In G. Cain and H. Watts, eds., *Income maintenance and labor supply*. Chicago: Markham.

Hall, R. 1973. Wages, income, and hours of work in the U.S. labor force. In G. Cain and H. Watts, eds., *Income maintenance and labor supply*. Chicago: Markham.

――――. 1975. The effects of experimental negative income tax on labor supply. In J. A. Pechman and P. M. Timpane. eds. *Work incentives and income guarantees*. Washington: Brookings Institution.

Heckman, J. 1971. Three essays in the supply of labor and the demand for market goods. Princeton, New Jersey: Princeton University Press.

――――. 1974. The effects of childcare programs on women's work effort. *Journal of Political Economy*, March, pp. 136–63.

Heckman, J.; M. Killingsworth; and T. MaCurdy. 1981. Empirical evidence on static labour supply models. In *The economics of the labour market*, pp. 75–122. HMSD, British Treasury.

Heckman, J., and T. MaCurdy. 1981. New methods for estimating labor supply functions: A survey. NORC Discussion Paper 80-5. In R. Ehrenberg, ed., *Research in labor economics*, vol. 4. Greenwich, Connecticut: JAI Press.

Heckman, J., and B. Singer. 1982. The identification problem in econometric models for duration data. Paper presented at World Congress of the Econometric Society, Aix-en-Provence, France (September 1980). Forthcoming in *Advances in econometrics*. Cambridge: Cambridge University Press.

Kosters, M. 1967. Effects of an income tax on labor supply. In A. Harberger and M. Bailey, eds., *The taxation of income from capital*. Washington: Brookings Institution.

Rosen, H. 1976. Taxes in a labor supply model with joint wage-hours determination. *Econometrica* 44, no. 3 (May): 485–508.

Smith, J. P. 1980. Assets and labor supply. In J. P. Smith, ed., *Female labor supply: Theory and estimation*. Princeton, New Jersey: Princeton University Press.

3 Alternatives to the Current Maximum Tax on Earned Income

Lawrence B. Lindsey

The Maximum Tax on Personal Service Income, passed as a part of the Tax Reform Act of 1969, provides a tax reduction to taxpayers with substantial earned income. However, it does not, as is widely assumed, place a 50% limit on the rate at which earned income is taxed. In an earlier paper (Lindsey 1981) I showed that the vast majority of high-income taxpayers still face marginal tax rates on earned income in excess of 50%.

This paper considers alternatives to the current maximum tax rules which would be more effective at setting a 50% ceiling on the rate at which earned income is taxed. Particular attention is paid to the behavioral response of taxpayers faced with a change in the tax rules.

The simulations contained in this paper are made with the National Bureau of Economic Research TAXSIM model. This model bases its calculations on the 1977 Tax Model File provided by the Internal Revenue Service. This data file contains a stratified random sample of individual tax returns; a random sample of 7,703 of these returns was used for this paper.

The data have been aged to reflect 1981 dollar amounts. TAXSIM does this automatically by increasing all dollar items by the percent increase in personal income between the two years. A further adjustment is made to the number of returns in each income class. The TAXSIM estimates of total revenue are within 2% of Department of Treasury revenue estimates for any given tax year.

Lawrence B. Lindsey is tax economist at the Council of Economic Advisers. He is on leave from Harvard University and the National Bureau of Economic Research.

The author is deeply grateful to Martin Feldstein, Richard Musgrave, and Daniel Feenberg, whose comments and criticisms were invaluable. He is also thankful to Jerry Hausman for his suggestions on functional form.

83

Four alternatives to the present law are considered. Two of these involve a rewriting of the existing maximum tax rules to more effectively limit the top earned income tax rate to 50%. These alterations as well as existing law create complicated nonlinearities in the tax schedule. The TAXSIM model is designed to generate precise marginal tax rates for both earned and unearned income to take account of these complexities. The third alternative involves a change in the existing statutory rate schedule to make the top tax rate 50% on all income. The fourth alternative considered is abolition of the existing maximum tax altogether and application of the current rate schedule to all income regardless of source.

The methodological emphasis of this paper is on simulating the behavioral response of taxpayers to changes in the tax law. Two types of behavior are considered: changes in effort and changes in tax avoidance. Although a well-established literature exists on the effect of tax rates on labor supply, most of the studies do not include the affluent, the people affected by the reforms considered in this paper. Therefore a range of parameter values for the effects of price and income on effort has been used. The literature on tax avoidance behavior is not well established. I present an empirical estimation of this behavior and am conducting further research on this topic. I use this estimated value as well as a value half as great as that estimated and a parameter value implying no avoidance behavior. The reader is free to make judgments based upon his or her expectations of the actual parameters.

Section 3.1 examines the current maximum tax law and the reasons for its failure to set a top rate on earned income of 50%. Section 3.2 considers alternative tax rules and their revenue cost in the absence of a behavioral response. The excess burden placed on earned income by the different rules is also presented in this section. Section 3.3 discusses the techniques used in simulating taxpayer response to alternative tax rules. Section 3.4 presents the results based on a range of parameter values for the behavioral model.

3.1   The Existing Maximum Tax Provision

Under existing law a taxpayer qualifying[1] for the maximum tax provision is allowed to subtract from what his or her tax liability otherwise would have been the difference between the ordinary tax liability on earned taxable income and what that liability would have been if a 50% top rate had been imposed. Figure 3.1 illustrates the provision. Without

1. Taxpayers who are married filing separately or who average their income are ineligible for the maximum tax. Furthermore, in order to qualify, the taxpayer must have earned taxable income at least as great as the 50% bracket amount, $60,000 for married taxpayers, $41,700 for single taxpayers.

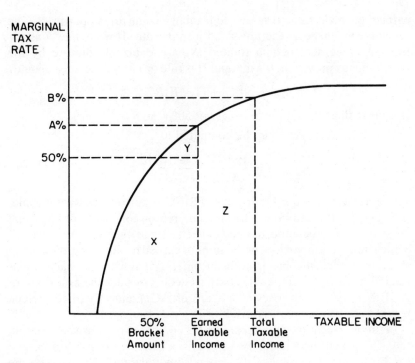

Fig. 3.1

the maximum tax the taxpayer's liability would have been the sum of areas X, Y, and Z. The taxpayer is allowed to subtract the difference between the ordinary liability on earned taxable income (areas X and Y) and what the liability would have been if a 50% rate had been imposed (area X). In short, the taxpayer receives a tax reduction equal to area Y and pays tax equal to areas X and Z. The tax due on unearned income (area Z) is unaffected by this rule.

However, this is not equivalent to a maximum rate on earned income of 50%. Consider what happens if the taxpayer earns another dollar of taxable income. Without the maximum tax provision he or she would pay $B\%$ on this dollar. The maximum tax provision reduces the tax rate by the difference between what it would have been if the taxpayer had only earned income, $A\%$, and 50%, or a tax rate reduction of $(A - 50)\%$. Therefore even with the maximum tax, the tax rate on earned income is $(B - A + 50)\%$. This rate will exceed 50% unless $B\%$ equals $A\%$. Only taxpayers with very large earned income, so that both B and A equal the statutory limit of 70%, and taxpayers with little or no unearned income are in this situation.

A second complication in the maximum tax law which increases the marginal tax rate on earned income above 50% is that only a fraction of earned income is treated as earned taxable income for tax purposes. The remainder is taxed at the unearned income rate. If we define F as the fraction of earned income treated as earned taxable income by the maximum tax provision, the marginal tax rate on earned income becomes

$$F(B - A + 50)\% + (1 - F)B\% \ .$$

It is clear that this rate is in excess of 50%, as $B > A > 50$.

Under existing law F can be computed as

$$\frac{\text{TAXINC}}{\text{AGI}} + \frac{\text{PSINC}}{\text{AGI}} - \frac{\text{TAXINC}}{\text{AGI}} \times \frac{\text{PSINC}}{\text{AGI}} \ ,$$

where TAXINC is taxable income, PSINC is personal service income, and AGI is adjusted gross income. The reason for this fraction is that deductions must be apportioned between earned and unearned income. The current law apportions deductions to earned income according to the share of earned income in total income. The fraction of each dollar treated as earned income rises both as deductions decline as a share of AGI (taxable income rises as a share of AGI) and as earned income becomes a greater share of AGI.

In summary, the current maximum tax law fails to establish a maximum rate on earned income for two reasons. First, the tax rate on earned taxable income $(B - A + 50)\%$ depends upon the tax rate levied on the total amount of income received $(B\%)$. Second, only a fraction of earned income is treated as earned for tax purposes. In order to achieve a maximum tax rate of 50%, the tax rate on earned taxable income must be independent of B and thus independent of the total amount of income received, and the fraction of earned income treated as earned taxable income must be set at unity.

3.2   Alternative Tax Rules

As noted in the preceding section an effective 50% ceiling on the tax rate on earned income requires two features: a tax rate on earned income independent of total income received and full treatment of earned income as earned taxable income. Figures 3.2 and 3.3 show how the first feature may be achieved.

Figure 3.2 shows the tax rate for a taxpayer with unearned income in excess of the 50% bracket amount. His or her tax liability (shown by the shaded area) would be equal to what would ordinarily be owed on unearned income if that were all the income received plus 50% of earned income. Note that the tax rate on earned income (50%) would be independent of the amount of earned or unearned income received, unlike present law.

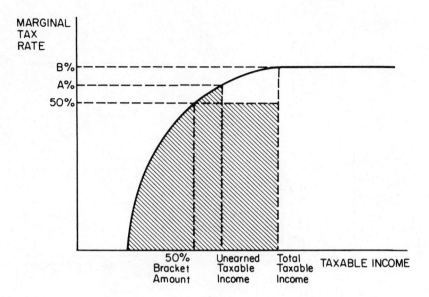

Fig. 3.2

Figure 3.3 shows the tax rate for a taxpayer with unearned income less than the 50% bracket amount. The shaded region shows the tax liability would be equal to what would be owed if a 50% top bracket were in effect. Again, the tax rate on earned income would be 50% regardless of the amount of earned or unearned income received.

The change in tax rules represented by figures 3.2 and 3.3 might be termed a reversal of the "stacking" order. In figure 3.1, unearned income is stacked on top of earned income for the maximum tax provision. In figures 3.2 and 3.3 earned income is stacked on top of unearned income. It is essential that the type of income subject to a maximum rate be stacked on top if the top rate is to be effective. Otherwise the tax rate on the favored income source is dependent on the total amount of income received.

It should be noted that the reversal of the stacking order also lowers the marginal tax rate on unearned income. This is because the unearned tax rate is also independent of the total amount of income received. Reductions in both the earned and unearned rates must be considered when evaluating the behavioral effects of a change in the law.

The second feature which must be changed in order to have an effective 50% maximum tax rate is the allocation of deductions from adjusted gross income. The current apportionment based on the share of AGI which is earned causes only a portion of additional earned income to be

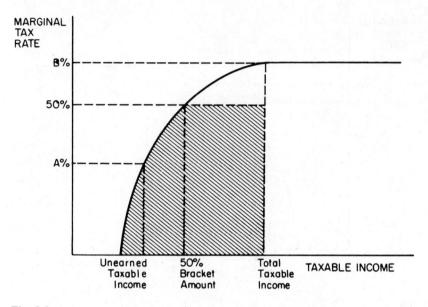

Fig. 3.3

treated as earned for tax purposes.[2] In order for all earned income to be treated as earned for tax purposes, deductions must be subtracted either entirely from earned income or entirely from unearned income. Of course the alternative chosen will affect the after-tax cost of the deduction since the earned and unearned rates may be different. Applying all deductions to unearned income reduces their cost by the rate applicable to unearned income. As this rate is at least as great as the rate applied to earned income, the cost of this option in revenue is greater. Similarly, the behavioral response to such a change will be different. If any tax avoidance takes place, it will reduce the tax liability by the higher unearned income tax rate for each dollar of taxable income avoided. This will be considered in section 3.3.

The alternative of applying all deductions to earned income effectively levies a tax equal to the difference between the unearned and earned rates on all deductions made. While it is clear that this will cost less in revenue, it also raises the price of many "merit" goods to maximum tax payers.

The options of applying deductions to earned income (REFORM-E) and applying deductions to unearned income (REFORM-U) are com-

2. The definition of earned taxable income is

$$ETI = \frac{PSINC}{AGI} \times TAXINC - PREF .$$

pared with abolishing the maximum tax and lowering the maximum rate to 50% on all income in the tables accompanying this chapter.

Table 3.1 shows the distribution of marginal tax rates on earned income under the five different sets of tax rules. The percentages shown are of the estimated 2.72 million taxpayers who would have faced marginal tax rates on earned income of 50% or greater had there been no maximum tax. Note that the current maximum tax provision lowers the earned income rate to 50% or less for only 7% of these taxpayers. One-third of these taxpayers have a marginal tax rate on earned income greater than 54%. On the other hand, reducing the top bracket to 50% will lower all marginal rates to under 52%; the same will be accomplished for 95% of these taxpayers by implementing REFORM-U. REFORM-E will lower the tax rate on earned income to 52% or less for 92% of these taxpayers.

The reason that tax rates may be above 50% even if that is the top tax bracket involves some of the income constraints of the tax code. For example, the medical deduction is allowed only for expenses in excess of 3% of adjusted gross income. As earning another dollar will lower deductions by 3 cents, taxable income will rise by $1.03. At a 50% marginal tax rate, the extra dollar earned will increase tax liabilities by 51.5 cents. The marginal tax rates on earned income may be lower than 50% because of the personal income constraint on retirement contributions.

Table 3.2 shows the distribution of the changes in revenue resulting from a change in the maximum tax provision. The current maximum tax rule gives about 60% of the tax reduction to taxpayers with adjusted gross

Table 3.1   **Distribution of Marginal Tax Rates on Earned Income**

Marginal Rate (× $1,000)	Abolish Max Tax	Current Max Tax	50% Top Bracket	REFORM-U	REFORM-E
Under 50	. . .	.5	5.9	4.8	1.9
Exact 50	. . .	6.2	27.0	25.1	24.3
50–51	39.2	47.4	38.5	38.6	39.0
51–52	1.2	12.1	28.6	26.8	25.9
52–54	. . .	.8	. . .	. . .	. . .
54–56	31.0	19.2	. . .	2.6	3.6
56–60	7.5	4.9	. . .	.7	1.4
60–65	11.7	5.6	. . .	.8	1.9
65–70	5.1	2.2	. . .	.3	1.2
Over 70	4.3	1.1	. . .	.3	.8

Note: Percentages reflect the share of 2.72 million taxpayers who would have had marginal tax rates on earned income of 50% or greater if there had been no maximum tax.

Table 3.2   **Distribution of Benefits/Costs of Tax Changes**
                     (number of beneficiaries/losers)

AGI Class (× $1,000)	Abolish Max Tax	50% Top Bracket	REFORM-U	REFORM-E
Under 50	4,000	53,000	8,000	3,800
50–100	403,000	780,000	729,000	673,000
100–200	349,000	494,000	474,000	407,000
200–500	79,000	105,000	100,000	75,000
500–1,000	7,000	10,500	10,000	6,500
Over 1,000	1,600	3,400	3,000	1,500
Average Tax Change				
Under 50	+270	−90	−810	−1,030
50–100	+440	−450	−500	−470
100–200	+3,210	−2,680	−2,030	−1,800
200–500	+16,600	−14,500	−9,200	−6,900
500–1,000	+51,700	−54,300	−22,000	−11,000
Over 1,000	+151,200	−246,000	−46,000	−5,500
Total Tax Change (millions)				
Under 50	+1	−5	−6	−4
50–100	+177	−351	−365	−316
100–200	+1,120	−1,324	−962	−733
200–500	+1,311	−1,523	−920	−518
500–1,000	+354	−570	−220	−72
Over 1,000	+238	−836	−138	−8

income above $200,000. This compares with 62% for a complete reduction in rates to 50%, 49% for REFORM-U, and 36% for REFORM-E.

Table 3.3 compares the excess burden imposed by different tax regimes. The excess burden measure I use is explained in Yitzhaki (1975). This measure contrasts the taxes actually collected via a labor income tax with what could have been collected via a lump-sum tax and left the taxpayer at the same level of utility. The result takes the familiar form

$$\text{excess burden} = \frac{1}{2}e_i t i^2 W_i \, ,$$

where e_i represents the individual elasticity of labor supply, t_i his or her marginal tax rate on earned income, and W_i labor income. The excess burden is an increasing quadratic function of tax revenue collected. If contrasted with the revenue collected, this measure provides a relative efficiency cost of various tax rules. The measure also takes no account of any excess burden placed on capital income. The W_i term reflects only personal service income.

Table 3.3   **Relative Efficiency of Various Tax Changes**

Proposal	Change in Taxes (billions)	Change in Excess Burden (billions)	Efficiency
50% Max bracket	−4.599	−.380	.08
Abolish max tax	+3.202	+1.246	.39
REFORM-E	−1.645	−.289	.18
REFORM-U	−2.608	−.368	.14

The calculations assume a labor supply elasticity of 0.1 for all individuals. The reader may choose to substitute a different elasticity for this estimate of e_i to get a measure of the efficiency of any one tax regime. However, the relative efficiencies of each of the tax changes is unaffected by the choice of elasticity.

As the calculation is a function of the square of the tax rate, a 70% rate will level twice the excess burden of a 50% rate. Abolishing the maximum tax would involve an increase in revenue with twice the efficiency cost of the next highest alternative. REFORM-E involves a reduction in tax revenue of $1.651 billion, but would be the most efficient reduction from the view of the excess burden on labor income. As a reduction to 50% of the top bracket would apply in large part to capital income, the efficiency loss is relatively low.

3.3 Simulation Methods

This paper concentrates on simulating two different kinds of responses by taxpayers to changes in the maximum tax rules: changes in the degree of sacrifice made to work and save, and changes in the avoidance of income tax. Well-established parameter values for these responses do not exist. The taxpayer makes his or her decisions based upon a number of separate yet interrelated margins: work and leisure, savings and consumption, and receipt of taxable income and avoidance of taxable income.

3.3.1 The Effect of Tax Rules on Effort

The effect of a change in tax rules on work effort is the combined result of a substitution or compensated price effect and an income effect. A reduction in marginal tax rates induces greater effort by raising the after-tax wage. However, the resulting tax reduction increases the taxpayer's disposable income, producing a countervailing income effect.

Using the Slutsky equation, this may be expressed as

$$\frac{\delta h}{\delta w} = S_{ww} + h \frac{\delta h}{\delta y},$$

where h represents labor effort, w the after-tax wage, and y income. The compensated price effect S_{ww} is constrained to be nonnegative, and $\delta h/\delta y$ is presumed to be negative.

The labor supply function for individual i can be expressed as

$$h_i = k_i w_i^\alpha y_i^\beta ,$$

where α represents the uncompensated wage elasticity of labor supply and β the income elasticity of labor supply; k_i represents the individual's tastes. The constant elasticity formulation may be defended for changes of the magnitude concerned here, although this specification is not plausible for extreme values.

The Slutsky relation may be expressed in terms of elasticities:

$$S_{ww} = h \;\frac{\alpha}{w} - \frac{\beta h}{y} .$$

Further manipulation produces an expression in terms of the compensated wage elasticity ϵ_c:

$$\epsilon_c = \alpha - \beta \;\frac{wh}{y} .$$

The taxpayers subject to the options considered in this paper often have substantial nonlabor income. The compensated elasticity therefore varies substantially across the sample. The quantity wh/y represents the share of labor income in total income. This has a mean value of roughly 0.75 for current maximum taxpayers.

Nonlabor income affects the labor supply decision by altering the budget constraint between consumption and leisure:

$$(1 - t)L + M = C + (1 - t)(L - h) .$$

L represents the taxpayer's endowment and is enumerated in before-tax consumption units. C represents consumption and $L - h$ leisure. M is a lump-sum term which includes both capital income and the lump-sum payment implied by the progressive income tax. Hausman (1981) has termed this latter component "virtual income."

Figure 3.4 illustrates how a progressive tax system yields a lump-sum term. A worker sacrificing l_1 hours of leisure works l_0 hours tax free and pays a tax t_1 on all labor income in excess of l_0. The taxpayer's marginal decision is based on a price of leisure of $1 - t_1$ but not the full income reduction this would imply if he or she paid tax on the total labor supplied. The taxpayer receives an income transfer of $M_1 = tl_0$ aside from the tax paid $t_1 l_1$. The income transfer M_2 represents $(t_2 - t_1)(l_2 - l_0) + t_2 l_1$; this is the difference between the tax rate paid on the last unit of labor supplied and the tax rate actually paid on inframarginal units. Note that if the tax rate schedule is known, the income term M

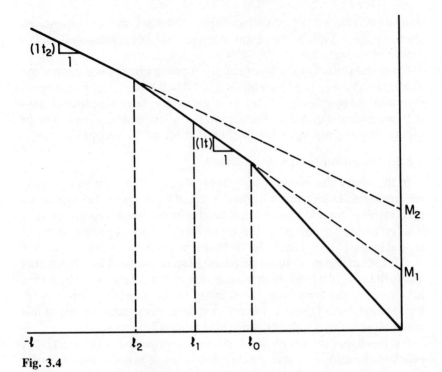

Fig. 3.4

is uniquely defined by the taxpayer's last dollar marginal tax rate. Variations of labor supply along any segment, or between any two kinks, do not alter the income term M.

The maximum tax creates a further complication. The marginal tax rates on earned and unearned income are different, and are altered by different amounts in each of the options considered in this paper. The taxpayer faces a consumption-savings choice as well as a consumption-leisure trade-off. The change in the tax rate on capital income might well alter this decision. However, the combined price and income effects of the change produce an ambiguous result on a priori grounds. I assume that aggregate capital income is unaffected by the change in the tax rate on either labor or nonlabor income. However, the reduction in the tax rate on capital income does increase the taxpayer's virtual income. This will tend to depress the supply of labor by the household.

With the exception of abolishing the existing maximum tax, all of the options considered here have a greater effect on the return to capital income than on the return to labor income. The assumption of zero elasticity of capital income to changes in the tax rate is probably an understatement of the response of taxpayers to lower rates and was chosen to minimize predicted revenue changes. Similarly, values which suggest a highly inelastic supply of labor have been chosen for this simulation. Four sets of values have been used; the implied compensated elasticity for a typical maximum taxpayer has been computed and is indicated by table 3.4.

Empirical studies of the labor supply of prime age males suggest wage elasticities of zero. The households studied in this paper are overwhelmingly married couples and therefore likely to have labor supplies substantially more elastic than this. The parameter values used here imply a labor supply only slightly more elastic than that for prime age males.

3.3.2   The Effect of Tax Avoidance

In the above discussion it was assumed that all income was actually subject to tax. In fact, much income received is not taxed. Tax avoidance may involve donation of income to charitable organizations. It may involve taking advantage of the exclusions available to some forms of capital income. Avoidance also includes tax preferences granted to particular uses of capital or to the purchase of state and local bonds. The tax on much farm, rent, and small business income may be avoided by taking advantage of the separately taxed entity for consumption purposes. A formal model of all these avoidance decisions is beyond the scope of this paper. It remains a topic of continuing research, however.

For this paper the avoidance decision is approached at the margin. A utility-maximizing taxpayer would allocate his or her resources in order to equate the marginal after-tax benefits from each purchase. The marginal dollar expended on avoidance brings benefits equal to the marginal dollar less tax used for ordinary consumption purposes. As a result, the price p used above to compute effort is unaffected by the level of tax avoidance. The marginal cost of avoidance also is p.

Because of the maximum tax, taxpayers face different prices for avoiding labor and nonlabor income. The price of some forms of avoidance, in particular preference items, is also increased by the maximum tax. This is due to the "poisoning" provision of the maximum tax law, which treats one dollar of labor income as capital income for each dollar of preference income received. In effect the preferences are taxed at the difference between the unearned income and earned income marginal tax rates, a

Table 3.4   **Parameter Values Used in Simulation**

Wage Elasticity	Income Elasticity	Implied Compensated Elasticity
0	0	0
0	−.1	.075
.075	−.1	.15
.1	−.2	.30

difference which may be as high as 20%. However, preference income constitutes only a small portion of income which avoids tax. I therefore have taken the price of avoidance as a simple weighted average of the earned (t_e) and unearned (t_u) marginal tax rates, where the weight depends on the share of labor income in total income τ:

$$p = \tau(1 - t_e) + (1 - \tau)(1 - t_u) \ .$$

It is also possible that inframarginal dollars of avoidance cost less than the marginal dollars. This would affect the virtual income of the taxpayer in the same way as the nonlinear tax schedule affected it. A reduction in marginal tax rates would lower the inframarginal income taxpayers receive from low-cost avoidance items and therefore raise labor supply. In order to err on the side of conservatism I have ignored the inframarginal transfer on untaxed income by assuming that all avoidance costs the marginal price.

While the marginal price of avoidance is known, the quantity of income which avoids tax is unknown. I have considered the following relation:

$$\text{avoidance} = A(\text{price, income, tastes}) \ .$$

I used a sample of 7,703 returns from the 1977 Individual Tax Model File, the same sample used in the simulations reported in section 3.4. The taxpayer's total income was estimated as his or her potentially taxable income reported in the file. Potential income was calculated by adding retirement contributions, capital gains deductions, the dividend exclusion, and reported preference income to adjusted gross income. If the taxpayer reported any Schedule E loss, it was excluded. Schedule E gains were unaffected. The standard deduction and personal exemptions for the 1977 tax year were then subtracted as they involve no avoidance behavior by the taxpayer.

Avoidance is calculated as the difference between potentially taxable income and income which is actually taxed. Neither the author nor any reader should consider this a definitive measure. The definition of what should constitute taxable income has concerned such noted economists as Musgrave and Pechman. I do not wish to enter the debate. If anything, this estimate probably understates "true" potential income. Interest from state and local bonds is excluded as are unrealized capital gains, imputed rental income, and the imputed value of household services. No effort has been made to estimate tax evasion. On the other hand, some might argue that the inclusion of state and local taxes and charitable contributions is inappropriate. As the taxpayers in this study are liable to have substantial capital assets which are not observed, the relation I estimate probably understates the true effect of price on avoidance.

However, some might argue that much of the estimated avoidance is actually the realization of long-term capital gains. I have therefore defined an alternative income concept which excludes the capital gains deduction from both the income and the avoidance terms. Four relations were estimated:

(1) $$\text{RATIO}_i = \alpha + \beta\ \text{FDARAT}_i + \epsilon_i\ ,$$

(2) $$\text{RATIO}_i = \alpha + \beta\ \text{FDARAT}_i + \lambda\ \ln(\text{INCOME})_i + \epsilon_i\ ,$$

(3) $$\text{RATIO}^*_i = \alpha + \beta\ \text{FDARAT}^*_i + \epsilon_i\ ,$$

(4) $$\text{RATIO}^*_i = \alpha + \beta\ \text{FDARAT}^*_i + \lambda\ \ln(\text{INCOME}^*)_i + \epsilon_i\ .$$

RATIO_i is the share of potential income which avoids tax, FDARAT_i is the taxpayer's weighted average of first-dollar tax rates on earned and unearned income, and INCOME_i is the taxpayer's potential income. The asterisk denotes the alternative concept of avoidance, which excludes the capital gains deduction. A first-dollar rate was used to minimize possible simultaneity problems. That is, the rate used was the rate which would have applied had the taxpayer avoided tax on only one dollar of income.

There seems no a priori reason why the share of income which avoids tax should vary systematically with income. Inclusion of an income term in equations (2) and (4) is done to test for possible scale economies in avoidance or for the possibility that, aside from the higher marginal tax rates, tax avoidance behavior is associated with being rich. The results suggest that income is not an important factor:

(1) $\text{RATIO} = -0.086 + 0.742\ \text{FDARAT}$,
                    (0.006)   (0.012)

(2) $\text{RATIO} = -0.084 + 0.748\ \text{FDARAT}$
                    (0.009)   (0.026)
                    $-\ 0.0004\ \ln(\text{INCOME})$,
                    (0.0016)

(3) $\text{RATIO}^* = -0.074 + 0.686\ \text{FDARAT}^*$,
                    (0.006)   (0.011)

(4) $\text{RATIO}^* = -0.067 + 0.708\ \text{FDARAT}^*$
                    (0.009)   (0.024)
                    $-\ 0.0016\ \ln(\text{INCOME})$.
                    (0.0015)

Standard errors are reported below the coefficient. The income coefficient is both small and insignificant. The price term has a highly significant t statistic, and all four equations are significant to the 0.9999 level using an F test. The R-square terms range from 0.329 to 0.341, which is quite reasonable for cross-section data. The exclusion of long-term capital gains deductions has little effect on the coefficient.

The usual collinearity of income and the tax rate is substantially reduced by the maximum tax. Taxpayers earning from $60,000 to $10 million may have marginal tax rates of 50%, while taxpayers within this range may have rates as high as 70%. In fact, the marginal tax rate on earned income falls as earned income rises for maximum taxpayers and the rate on unearned income may also fall as unearned income rises (see Lindsey 1981). The maximum tax provision therefore permits substantial enough variation between rate and income to make estimation possible.

This estimated response of taxpayers to changes in marginal tax rates suggests that 0.7% less income will avoid tax for each 1% reduction in the marginal tax rate. This paper also presents estimates using a simulated response only half as great; that is, an additional 0.35% of potential income is subject to tax for each 1% reduction in the tax rate.

As an example of this effect, consider a married couple with potential income of $100,000 of which $20,000 is capital income. Their current avoidance price is 44 cents on the dollar (an average marginal tax rate on earned and unearned income of 56%). They avoid taxes on roughly 31% of their income. A tax rate reduction to 50% would mean an increase in their taxable income of $4,200, from $69,000 to $73,200. This is certainly a plausible order of magnitude. The actual simulation procedure uses the taxpayer's actual ratio of taxable income to potential income and adjusts the ratio by the avoidance parameter value times the change in the marginal tax rate.

3.3.3   Combining Behavioral Effects

This behavioral model assumes the taxpayer responds simultaneously to prices on two margins. The share of the taxpayer's income which avoids tax is determined by a first-dollar price based upon his or her potential income. The amount of potential income is determined by a constant elasticity type of response of labor income to the last-dollar tax rate on earned income and its corresponding virtual income. But these terms are determined by the share of potential income which avoids tax.

The simultaneous optimization of potential income and share which avoids tax is computed in the following manner: first, the taxpayer's current first- and last-dollar prices are computed by TAXSIM. Then the first- and last-dollar prices are computed given the alternative set of maximum tax rules assuming no behavioral response by the taxpayer. The difference between the first-dollar prices under current law and the alternative law is used to compute a new percentage of potential income which avoids tax.

This new percentage of avoidance is applied to an unchanged level of potential income to generate a measure of taxable income assuming only the avoidance response. This measure of taxable income is equivalent to assuming that the taxpayer has a zero price and income elasticity of labor supply. Marginal tax rates on earned and unearned income are computed given this new level of taxable income. If these tax rates are the same as the tax rates under current law, no increase in labor supply can be expected. If these new tax rates are different from current law, a new level of virtual income is computed and a new level of effort results. This new level of effort or potential income may lead to a new level of avoidance if the higher potential income produces a new first-dollar tax rate. If not, the old level of avoidance is retained.

The new avoidance measure is used with the new potential income to produce a new level of taxable income. If the marginal tax rates at this level of taxable income equal the earlier tax rates, a stable preference decision has been reached. If not, the iteration procedure continues until the new set of tax rates equals an old set of tax rates.

A possible problem with this iterative procedure is the kinked nature of the budget set. Iteration may produce a result alternatively at a high and a low price. Figure 3.5 shows such a possibility. The true utility-maximizing value for the taxpayer is to be on the kink. But the iterative procedure evaluated at p_1 will place the taxpayer at l_2 on the p_2 segment, and evaluation at p_2 will place the taxpayer at l_1 on the p_1 segment. If this result occurs, the kink between the two segments is automatically chosen. The price and virtual income corresponding to the higher segment, in effect a "next"-dollar price, is used for evaluation.

3.3.4   Simulation Procedure Differences among the Options

The two relevant prices, one applying to extra sacrifice, the other to avoidance behavior, depend upon the option considered. For example, the abolition of the maximum tax, or the alternative option of cutting the maximum statutory rate to 50%, involves equal tax rates on earned and capital income. On the other hand, the existing maximum tax and the two reform options may involve different marginal tax rates on earned and unearned income. For these latter two options a weighted average of the earned and unearned tax rates is used to estimate the last-dollar price.

The first-dollar price, the price of avoidance, is different for the two reform options than for the former options mentioned. If all deductions are applied to earned income, then the price of avoiding a dollar of taxable income is determined by the earned income tax rate. If the deductions are applied to unearned income, then the price is determined by the unearned income tax rate. The present price of avoidance is a weighted average of the first-dollar earned and unearned tax rates.

If deductions are applied to unearned income, then some taxpayers may see a decrease in the price of avoidance. This will lower the share of income which is reported and reduce tax revenue. If, on the other hand, deductions are applied to earned income, an unambiguous increase in the

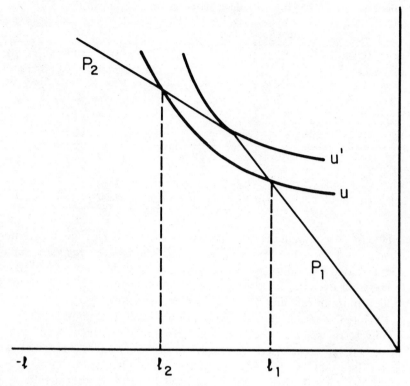

Fig. 3.5

price of avoidance will result. This will lower the share of potential income which avoids tax and will tend to produce higher revenues.

Lowering the maximum rate to 50% on all income also unambiguously increases the price of avoidance, thereby increasing taxable income. On the other hand, increases in avoidance will occur among taxpayers currently benefiting from the maximum tax if it is abolished. The next section examines the effect of these behavioral changes on income tax revenues.

3.4   Results

The results of the simulations are presented in tables 3.5–3.8. The surprising conclusion one can draw is that it is possible to reduce marginal tax rates and still increase tax revenue. Table 3.5 suggests that the existing maximum tax provisions are probably a revenue raiser in that abolishing the maximum tax will lead to a decrease in tax revenue. Even at half the estimated value of the avoidance response, tax revenues are simulated as decreasing when the rates are increased. Table 3.5 gives the best picture of a labor supply response, as the current maximum tax

Table 3.5   **Effects of Abolishing Maximum Tax**
Taxpayers Affected = 843,000
Current Tax Liability = 38.840 billion

Behavioral Assumption		Avoidance No Response	No Response	Half Estimated Response (.35)	Estimated Response (.70)
Labor Supply					
Price	Income				
0	0		+3.202	-.112	-3.378
0	-.1		+1.373	-1.738	-4.926
.075	-.1		+.618	-2.563	-5.581
.1	-.2		-1.480	-4.342	-7.320

yielded a reduction in the marginal tax rate on earned income far greater than any of the other options considered. The greatest response simulated yielded $4.7 billion more in tax revenue from the labor supply effect alone while even the most modest labor supply response yielded nearly $2 billion more in revenue than the no-response case.

Even in this case the avoidance response is likely to dominate the labor supply response. If no labor supply response is assumed, $6.6 billion more in revenues is raised due to less avoidance. The avoidance response is not the usual "supply side" response commonly discussed today. No additional factors of production are brought forth. Rather it reflects a transfer of resources from favored activities to the taxpayer and the government. The actual welfare change is ambiguous.

Table 3.6 shows that a further reduction of tax rates to a statutory limit of 50% will be a revenue raiser if the full avoidance response occurs. The labor supply response is relatively small. In the no-avoidance case an

Table 3.6   **Effects of Establishing a Maximum Bracket**
Taxpayers Affected = 1,446,000
Current Tax Liability = 59.369 billion

Behavioral Assumption		Avoidance No Response	No Response	Half Estimated Response (.35)	Estimated Response (.70)
Labor Supply					
Price	Income				
0	0		-4.559	-1.338	+1.817
0	-.1		-4.500	-1.285	+1.944
.075	-.1		-4.225	-.988	+2.225
.1	-.2		-3.995	-.827	+2.474

Table 3.7   **Effects of Applying Deductions to Unearned Income**
Taxpayers Affected = 1,323,000
Current Tax Liability = 59.447 billion

Behavioral Assumption		Avoidance	No Response	Half Estimated Response (.35)	Estimated Response (.70)
Labor Supply					
Price	Income				
0	0		−2.608	−2.246	−1.856
0	−.1		−2.546	−2.228	−1.783
.075	−.1		−2.289	−1.991	−1.538
.1	−.2		−2.099	−1.867	−1.357

additional $600 million may be raised, or $1.2 billion additional earned. The reduction in the top rate to 50% will largely affect nonlabor income. A negative income effect on labor supply will therefore substantially offset the extra effort produced by the reduction in the earned income rate. If a capital income response is also included, an additional revenue increase of roughly one-third the order of magnitude of the current maximum tax will result. The revenue cost of a 50% maximum rate is therefore overstated by this simulation by $1 to $2 billion if one assumes that capital income will respond like labor income.

Applying deductions to unearned income is likely to be a revenue loser. As the unearned tax rate may well be higher than the current average of earned and unearned rates, avoidance may well be even more attractive under this reform for many taxpayers. Even the maximum avoidance response will produce only $750 million as a revenue offset.

Applying deductions to earned income has two benefits from a revenue

Table 3.8   **Effects of Applying Deductions to Earned Income**
Taxpayers Affected = 1,168,000
Current Tax Liability = 47.596 billion

Behavioral Assumption		Avoidance	No Response	Half Estimated Response (.35)	Estimated Response (.70)
Labor Supply					
Price	Income				
0	0		−1.645	−.070	+1.399
0	−.1		−1.552	−.023	+1.499
.075	−.1		−1.340	+.193	+1.730
.1	−.2		−1.145	+.309	+1.941

point of view. First, it is a less costly option even assuming no response. This is because current avoidance partially offsets nonlabor income under current rules. Under this option avoidance would reduce the tax liability by only the earned income marginal rate. Second, the behavioral response to avoidance would be greatest, as the price of avoidance has been increased to 50 cents on the dollar. This will mean that a higher fraction of income will be subject to tax.

In conclusion, it is likely that a reduction or reform of the upper brackets of the tax rate schedule would be relatively costless or might even increase tax revenues. However, a majority of the revenue offset from a behavioral response does not come from an increase in factor supply. Rather it is a pecuniary gain to the government and taxpayers as a result of less expenditure on tax avoidance. The high labor supply elasticities used in many supply side models of the economy may exaggerate the benefits of a tax rate reduction. However, the neglect of the avoidance response by any model produces a serious overestimate of the revenue cost of marginal rate reductions.

References

Auerbach, A. J., and H. S. Rosen. 1980. Will the real excess burden please stand up? NBER Working Paper no. 495. June.

Burtless, G., and J. Hausman. 1978. The effect of taxation on labor supply: Evaluating the Gary negative income tax experiment. *Journal of Political Economy*, vol. 86, no. 6.

Fullerton, D. 1980. On the possibility of an inverse relationship between tax rates and government revenues. NBER Working Paper no. 467. April.

Hausman, J. 1981. Labor supply. *How taxes affect economic behavior*. Washington: Brookings Institution.

Kahn, H. 1960. *Personal deductions in federal income tax*. NBER Fiscal Studies, no. 6. Princeton, New Jersey: Princeton University Press.

Lindsey, L. 1981. Is the maximum tax on earned income effective? *National Tax Journal*, June.

Yitzhaki. 1975. Personal taxation incentives and tax reform. Mimeo, University of Jerusalem, Israel.

Comment   Joseph J. Minarik

The first part of Lindsey's paper, dealing with marginal tax rates on earned income of over 50%, is not controversial. This basic finding was stated in 1974 by Emil M. Sunley, Jr., in his paper "The Maximum Tax on Earned Income" (*National Tax Journal* 27: 543–52, especially 545–46), which is not cited in Lindsey's paper.

There are also no basic problems with the second part of the paper, the static revenue estimates. Lindsey's results are in close agreement with similar tabulations using the Brookings tax calculator. There are, however, two points of interpretation that should be discussed.

Lindsey correctly states that there are over 2.5 million taxpayers who would be subject to marginal tax rates on earned income of over 50% at 1981 income levels and without the current law's maximum tax provision in place. What Lindsey noted in an earlier draft of the paper but (in my view unfortunately) omitted from the conference version is that this group is quite heterogeneous. In fact, it can be subdivided into three distinct parts. First, there are those taxpayers who are categorically ineligible to use the maximum tax because they use income averaging or file separate returns. These taxpayers constitute 36% of the larger group. The second category includes those taxpayers with too little earned income to qualify for the maximum tax under the present stacking rules; in other words, their earned income alone is not enough to reach beyond the 50% tax bracket. This category includes 34% of the larger group. The remainder of the roughly 2.5 million taxpayers use the maximum tax provision.

My understanding is that Lindsey's proposed changes to the maximum tax provision would not remove the categorical restrictions on its use. However, taxpayers who have insufficient earned income to qualify under current law would be provided substantial tax relief: $0.6 billion if deductions were applied to earned income. Only $1.1 billion of the total static revenue losses would accrue to those currently using the maximum tax provision. When the maximum tax was suggested in 1969, the House was very conscious of revenue constraints and sought to target the provision as carefully as possible (House Ways and Means Report, pp. 208–9). The Senate deleted the provision, again largely for revenue reasons (Senate Finance Report, pp. 309–10). The revenue loss question is at least as important now as it was in 1969, and targeting is again relevant. The Brookings tax calculator projected that the category of returns with

Joseph J. Minarik is a research associate in the Economic Studies Program, the Brookings Institution, Washington.

Tim Cohn and Ed Shephard provided their usual stellar research assistance. Susan Woollen typed the manuscript against all odds; any errors that appear are the author's. Research funds were provided by the National Science Foundation.

too little earned income to qualify for the current maximum tax provision would average only $22,000 of earned income per return in 1981; this group is composed substantially of investors and rentiers whose labor income is a distinctly secondary source of support. Whether their labor supply is at all elastic to wage rates is, at least in my opinion, highly questionable; and the deadweight revenue loss (and thus the counteracting income effect) of their inframarginal labor supply is clearly substantial.

A second question of interpretation is the relative success of the current maximum tax provision in reducing marginal tax rates. To phrase Lindsey's verbal evaluation just a bit differently, the current provision reduces the marginal tax rate on earned income to 52% or less for 66% of those now facing rates over 50%; his earned and unearned deduction allocation regimes achieve 52% rates or lower for 92 and 95% of the taxpayers, respectively. The margin of performance may not be as great as a first reading of the paper would suggest. And, of course, part of the reduction in rates that Lindsey's changes achieve is due only to the inclusion of taxpayers with low earned income who are ineligible under current law. If we restrict our view to those currently using the maximum tax provision, 77% achieve rates of 52% or lower under current law, more than the 66% for the entire universe. Here again, a substantial portion of the effect of Lindsey's law changes relates not to the problems with the current code, which he did discuss, but rather to the inclusion or exclusion of particular taxpayers within the current provision, which he did not discuss.

This leaves for discussion only the behavioral revenue estimates. The most important question is how Lindsey arrives at his surprising finding that liberalizing the maximum tax provision will raise revenue.

Lindsey's labor supply responses are based on a simple application of wage and income elasticities chosen to represent the range of estimates in the literature. My own judgment is that the compensated wage elasticities of 0.0 and 0.075 are quite adequate to bracket the feasible range, even though Lindsey presents two larger response estimates. My pessimism is based partly on the likely inelasticity of the labor supply in hours of individual high-wage workers, who probably already work full time and bear considerable responsibility in their present jobs. Another cause for skepticism is that Lindsey is implicitly using in the simulations not a wage rate elasticity of *hours worked* but a wage rate elasticity of *earnings*. It seems by no means certain that additional hours of effort will command the same wage as the inframarginal hours, especially for the married couples on whom Lindsey so heavily hangs his hat. For an extreme example, one might concede that a 30% reduction in the marginal tax rate on earnings might induce the heretofore idle spouse of the chief executive officer of a major corporation to increase the family's hours worked by 10%, but one would be hard pressed to imagine that he or she could find work at the spouse's hourly wage rate.

Nevertheless, the labor supply response is a largely academic issue, because it accounts for only a small fraction of the projected revenue response—about $500 million at the very outside, or more likely only about $100 million, of the static revenue losses of about $1.5 and $2.5 billion due to the proposed liberalizations of the maximum tax. Thus the real revenue raiser is the anticipated response of reduced "tax avoidance," the most speculative part of Lindsey's work.

It seems to me unlikely that the stronger taxpayer response to a cut in taxes on earned income will come through reduced tax avoidance rather than greater earnings. On careful consideration, I must conclude that Lindsey's estimates of reduced tax avoidance are extremely shaky and represent overstatements of the likely effects.

The most basic problem with Lindsey's estimates of tax avoidance behavior is his measure of tax avoidance itself. He defines avoidance as the difference between taxable income and "potential taxable income," which is equal to the sum of adjusted gross income and a list of additional items: the excluded portion of long-term capital gains, retirement contributions, the dividend exclusion, reported preference income, and Schedule E losses. This definition is replete with problems. Are state and local tax liabilities "avoidance"? Are medical expenses? Casualty losses? Implicitly, Lindsey is assuming that a reduction in the marginal tax rate on earned income will cause an increase in taxable income equal to a proportion of this potential income concept, which includes (at least in my opinion) many income items that are quite irrelevant for this purpose.

Nor is Lindsey's disclaimer that the "definition of what should constitute taxable income has concerned . . . noted economists . . . I do not wish to enter the debate" in any way satisfactory. After Lindsey has fitted regression equations to his concept of potential taxable income and projected that proportions of it will be added to actual taxable income, given his proposed changes in the tax law, he cannot avoid the debate. He has dived into it headfirst, like it or not.

Finally, Lindsey's assertion that "[if] anything this estimate probably understates true 'potential'" is no comfort whatsoever. If the measure of potential income is conceptually wrong, be it too high or too low, then its correlation with tax rates yields no information on true tax avoidance behavior.

The second major problem with Lindsey's measure of tax avoidance behavior is his estimation procedure. He fits a very simple linear regression equation to data on tax rates and the ratio of taxable income to his potential income, and finds a positive correlation between tax rates and his concept of tax avoidance. This procedure can be faulted on several counts. First and most fundamentally, if the concept of potential income is not a good representation of tax avoidance behavior, as was suggested above, then the entire exercise is irrelevant.

But even if the present concept of tax avoidance is accepted, the model seems much too simplistic to capture anything approaching the full complexity of taxpayer behavior with respect to the items added into Lindsey's potential income. Such important and omitted variables as the taxpayers' ages, wealth, split of income between property and labor sources, etc., surely render the equation a victim of misspecification.

Lindsey's inclusion of a potential income variable in two of his equations does not solve this specification problem. For much the same reason as was mentioned above, if the potential income concept has no meaning in this context, adding a potential income variable to the equation cannot make it meaningful.

Lindsey cites the similarity of the tax rate coefficients in the two versions of his equation, one including and one not including the capital gains exclusion as a tax avoidance item, as an indication that his estimates are sound. At least in my opinion, that similarity is the best indication that his estimates are not well founded. Figure C3.1 shows that the capital gains exclusion accounts for a large share of what Lindsey originally defined as tax avoidance and that the share increases rapidly as income increases. It is hard to understand how the share of potential income that avoids tax could remain almost the same when such a large part of tax avoidance is defined out of the game. To see this, consider Lindsey's results from the equation that does not cover the excluded half (using 1977 law) of long-term gains. Suppose that the top bracket rate were reduced from 70 to 50%. Then, using Lindsey's coefficient, the 78.5% of all taxpayers with adjusted gross income of $500,000 and up who now face a 70% top rate (exclusive of the maximum tax) would reduce their tax avoidance according to Lindsey's definition by 49%—which is equivalent to totally suspending the use of all tax preferences under the minimum tax, forswearing all net losses on Schedule E, not claiming the dividend exclusion, making no tax exempt retirement contributions, and giving up half of all itemized deductions exclusive of state and local taxes paid. This seems an unreasonable result to me.

In any event, even though the coefficients of the two versions of the equations are virtually the same, the tax avoidance behavior will be drastically different depending on whether the capital gains exclusion is included in or excluded from the tax avoidance base. Unfortunately, Lindsey never tells us whether his simulations include or exclude a capital gains tax avoidance effect.

Summary

Lindsey's assessment of marginal tax rates under the maximum tax is well founded and agrees with a discussion of the subject published much

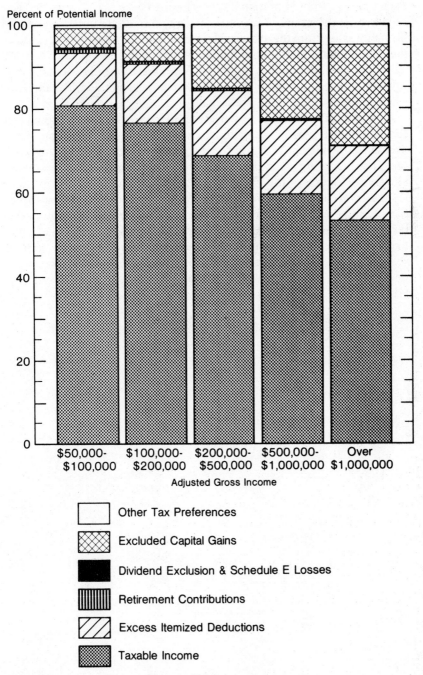

Fig. C3.1   Tax avoidance of high-income taxpayers.

earlier. His measures of the static revenue loss from modifications to the maximum tax to hold marginal rates closer to 50% are reasonable. His estimates of the range of revenue recovery due to greater labor supply probably exaggerate the actual response somewhat, especially because of the use of numbers approximating the elasticity of the supply of *hours* for what is in the simulation really an elasticity of *earnings*. However, Lindsey's middle-range parameters probably show something like the true supply response, and it is quite small.

It is in a "tax avoidance" response that Lindsey finds the jet propulsion for his revenue-raising simulations. He downplays his definition of tax avoidance, saying he "[does] not wish to enter the debate," but then goes on to use his definition to simulate a behavioral response anyway. In my view the definition of tax avoidance is faulty, the estimates of behavioral responses are too simplistic to embrace the complexity of taxpayer behavior, and the forecasts are unrealistic. Until we learn a lot more about tax avoidance behavior than we now know, Lindsey's claim that "it is likely that a reduction or reform of the upper brackets of the tax rate schedule would be relatively costless or might even increase tax revenues" must be considered an assertion, not a demonstrated fact.

4 The Distribution of Gains and Losses from Changes in the Tax Treatment of Housing

Mervyn A. King

4.1 Introduction

Economists have long debated the merits of changes in the tax treatment of housing, and reform of housing policy has been a perennial topic of discussion both within and outside government in the United Kingdom. Given the size of government subsidies and the importance of housing in both the budgets and balance sheets of households, this interest is not surprising. Public subsidies (regardless of the precise definition of an economic subsidy) run to many billions[1] of dollars per annum, and investment in housing now accounts for 50% of the net worth of the United Kingdom personal sector.

Among the frequent suggestions for reform are the reintroduction of a tax on the imputed income of owner-occupiers (such a tax existed in the United Kingdom until 1963 and was known as Schedule A) and, as an alternative, the abolition of tax relief on mortgage interest. In the public sector the Conservative government elected in 1979 has proposed changes in the level of subsidies which would have a direct impact on the level of rents charged to local authority tenants. In assessing the effects of such policies it is clearly important to assess the distribution of gains and losses from any potential reform. Decision makers are naturally reluctant to commit themselves to change without detailed knowledge about who gains and who loses.

Mervyn A. King is the Esmée Fairbairn Professor of Investment at the University of Birmingham, England, and a research associate at the National Bureau of Economic Research.

The research for this paper was supported by Social Science Research Council Programme Grant no. HR 4652 and the NBER. The author is very grateful to Paul Ramsay for programming the calculations, and to A. B. Atkinson, R. H. Gordon, P. H. Hendershott, N. H. Stern, and L. Summers for valuable comments on an earlier draft.

1. 1 billion = 10^9.

The usual approach to such questions is to estimate the overall efficiency gain by an approximation formula (for example, the "triangle" measure of Harberger 1974) and to examine the distributional consequences only in rather aggregative terms or for hypothetical households (the well-known married couple with two children on average earnings). When individual household data are available, this is an inefficient and inaccurate method of calculating both the efficiency effects of a reform and the distributional consequences of a change. Even if it were possible to argue persuasively that a particular reform would lead to an increase in efficiency in the economy as a whole, policymakers should, and almost certainly would, demand from the economist information on the distribution of gains and losses from the reform. In this paper we present a method for computing the gains and losses from changes in housing policy by simulating the effects of different reforms using a data set for 5,895 individual households in England and Wales constructed from the Family Expenditure Survey. The aim of the paper is primarily methodological, and is to illustrate the calculation of gains and losses with reference to one particular reform, namely the reintroduction of a tax on imputed income from owner occupation. It should not be assumed that such a change is the most probable direction for reform in Britain (more likely, perhaps, is a continuation of the present trend toward phasing out mortgage interest deductibility), but it has been widely discussed and presents a good example for the methodology outlined here.

Calculations of gains and losses are carried out under two assumptions. First, we assume that behavior is unchanged, which is the kind of calculation performed by government departments. This figure is useful for purposes of comparison and corresponds to the "first-round" effect of the change. The second case is where we allow explicitly for behavioral responses using econometric estimates of the demand for housing derived from the same data set as we use for simulation. Incorporating behavioral responses enables us to compute exact measures of the welfare gain or loss for each household in the sample, and to examine not only the overall efficiency gains but also the distributive effects of a reform. We show that it is important not to view the distributive effects simply in terms of an average gain or loss for each decile, say, of the original distribution, but to examine the variation within each decile. We also examine some summary statistics which show the value a decision maker will attach to a reform corresponding to different sets of attitudes on his part toward vertical and horizontal equity. This enables us to evaluate a proposed reform in terms of the trade-offs between its effect on the average level of welfare (the efficiency gain), the distribution of welfare levels, and the ranking of households within the distribution. A diagram is used to show the trade-offs between these three effects.

Section 4.2 of the paper discusses the measurement of welfare gains and losses, section 4.3 discusses the government's revenue constraint, section 4.4 analyzes the valuation of a reform in terms of a social welfare function, section 4.5 describes some of the relevant features of the United Kingdom housing market and the measurement of housing costs, and section 4.6 presents the results of simulating a reform of the tax treatment of owner-occupied housing which removes the subsidies to owner occupation and distributes the proceeds as an equal lump sum to all households.

4.2   The Measurement of Gains and Losses

We wish to exploit econometric estimates of the demand for housing in our measurement of gains and losses from reform. To do this we assume that a household's preferences are defined over two commodities, housing services (H) and a composite commodity of other goods and services (C). These preferences may be represented by either a direct or an indirect utility function. For household h the two functions are given by

(1) $$u_h = u(x_{Hh}, x_{Ch}) \ ,$$

(2) $$v_h = v(y_h, p_{Hh}, p_{Ch}) \ ,$$

where

x_{Hh} = the quantity of housing services consumed,
x_{Ch} = the quantity of the composite commodity consumed,
y_h = posttax household income (assumed to be exogenous),
p_{Hh} = the tax-inclusive price of housing services,
P_{Ch} = the tax-inclusive price of the composite commodity.

Note that in general prices are household-specific. It is important to allow for price variation within the sample when analyzing housing policy because the price of housing services varies from household to household depending upon factors such as marginal tax rates and income-related subsidies. The form of the utility function we shall use in the simulations will be discussed below. First, we define what we mean by a reform.

In the supposed initial, or original, position, household h has exogenous income y_h^0 and faces prices p_{Hh}^0 and p_{Ch}^0. After the reform the household faces a new vector of postreform income y_h^p and prices p_{Hh}^p and p_{Ch}^p. A reform is defined as the mapping from the original to the postreform vector

(3) $$\{y^0, p_H^0, p_C^0\} \rightarrow \{y^p, p_H^p, p_C^p\} \ .$$

Several issues arise in the definition of a reform. First, the postreform levels of incomes and prices cannot be chosen independently without considering their effect on the government's budget constraint. We shall consider revenue-neutral reforms, and the implications of this for the definition of the postreform variables are discussed below in section 4.4. Second, a reform which alters the prices facing consumers will change the aggregate demand for housing services, and in turn this may lead to a partially offsetting change in producer prices. The magnitude of this effect will depend upon the elasticity of supply of housing services. In the first simulations we shall ignore supply effects and assume that producer prices are fixed (i.e. an infinite supply elasticity). But we shall also examine an alternative assumption about the elasticity of supply. Finally, the effect of the change in the price of housing services on tenure choice will be ignored. In principle this can easily be allowed for in the analysis by letting the relevant price facing a household be that of the preferred tenure, owner occupation or rental (see Rosen and Small 1981), but in the United Kingdom rationing is the major determinant of housing tenure because of constraints in the capital market and the lack of a free market in rental housing (King 1980). Hence we have assumed that tenure choice is given. Future work will investigate the interaction between rationing and price, and their effects on tenure choice.

The reform we shall simulate is the removal of tax concessions to owner-occupied housing, with the additional revenue thus generated being distributed as a lump-sum subsidy. We shall assume that this is achieved by the introduction of a new tax on the imputed income from owner occupation (for further discussion of this see Atkinson and King 1980; Hughes 1980). The price index of other consumption will remain unchanged.

For each household in the sample we shall define two measures of the gain or loss resulting from the reform. The first is the impact or "first-round" effect of the reform, which is the effect on the household's cash flow assuming that the household does not change its behavior. We shall call this the *cash gain* (CG). It is the sort of statistic which government departments compute, and, although open to obvious objections, it is a natural first step in the analysis of any reform. It is independent of any assumptions about the form of the utility function (i.e. about household preferences). Cash gain is defined by

$$(4) \qquad \text{CG} = \hat{y}^p - y^0 - (p_H^p - p_H^0)x_h^0 \,,$$

where x_h^0 is the original quantity of housing services consumed and $\hat{y}^p$ is an estimate of the postreform income consistent with a revenue-neutral reform given unchanged behavior. The true y^p will differ from $\hat{y}^p$ because of changes in household behavior. For a revenue-neutral reform

$$(5) \qquad \sum_h (\hat{y}_h^p - y_h^0) = \sum_h (p_{Hh}^p - p_{Hh}^0)x_{Hh}^0 \,.$$

It is clear from (4) and (5) that by definition the mean value of cash gain is zero. Because it ignores behavioral responses, the cash gain measure provides no information about the efficiency aspects of the reform, but it does indicate the immediate distributional consequences of the reform before households have had time to adjust their behavior.

In the long run, behavioral responses to the changes in prices and incomes will invalidate the use of cash gain as a measure of the change in a household's welfare. Our second measure of the cash value of the reform to a household allows for behavioral responses. This is defined as the sum of money the household would have accepted in the initial position as equivalent to the impact of the reform. We call this the *equivalent gain* (EG). In other words, carrying out the reform is equivalent to giving each household a sum of money equal to the value of its equivalent gain. It is defined in terms of the indirect utility function by

$$(6) \qquad v(y^0 + \text{EG}, p_H^0, p_C) = v(y^p, p_H^p, p_C) \ .$$

These two measures of the gain to a household provide exact measures of the welfare gain from a reform and its distribution among households. Cash gain measures the impact effect of a reform; equivalent gain measures its long-term effect.

In addition to the distributional effect of the reform, we shall wish to compute the efficiency gains, and this raises the question of the relation between our measure of the equivalent gain and conventional measures of the excess burden or deadweight loss from distortionary taxes. Exact measures of excess burden based on explicit utility functions are discussed by Mohring (1971), Diamond and McFadden (1974), Rosen (1978), Hausman (1981), Auerbach and Rosen (1980), and Kay (1980). The concept of equivalent gain offers a particularly simple and appealing way of computing an exact measure of deadweight loss because, for revenue-neutral reforms, the efficiency gain to the economy as a whole is simply equal to the sum of equivalent gains over households.

The reason for this is clear. A reform which is self-financing satisfies the overall production constraint of the economy (provided that the effect of the reform on prices and exogenous incomes has been correctly specified). Hence a revenue-neutral reform which produces a positive average equivalent gain is equivalent to a Pareto improvement combined with a set of lump-sum redistributions among households. In other words, if the mean value of equivalent gain is positive, then there exists a set of lump-sum transfers in the original position such that the reform makes each household better off by an amount equal to the mean value of EG. The sum of the equivalent gains is therefore an exact measure of the efficiency gain (or reduction in deadweight loss) from the reform.

In order to compute a value for the equivalent gain of each household we must specify both a functional form and parameter values for the indirect utility function. In this study we shall use estimates of the homothetic translog indirect utility function used to generate equations for the demand for housing services reported by King (1980). The indirect utility function takes the form

$$
(7) \qquad \log v = \log \left(\frac{y}{p_C} \right) - \beta_1 \log \left(\frac{p_H}{p_C} \right) - \beta_2 \left[\log \left(\frac{p_H}{p_C} \right) \right]^2 .
$$

Using the Roy-Ville identity we obtain the demand function

$$
(8) \qquad x_H = \frac{y}{p_H} \left[\beta_1 + 2\beta_2 \log \left(\frac{p_H}{p_C} \right) \right] .
$$

Since the price of housing services varies across households, the demand equation given by (8) may be estimated using cross-section data. The following parameter estimates were obtained using household data in England and Wales from the Family Expenditure Survey for the tax year 1973/74 (King 1980; standard errors in parentheses):

$$
\beta_1 = \underset{(0.0008)}{0.1022} ,
$$

$$
\beta_2 = \underset{(0.0009)}{0.0238} .
$$

Although this specification assumes unitary income elasticities of demand, such an assumption may not be unreasonable given the results of Clark and Jones (1971) for the United Kingdom and Rosen (1979) for the United States, and also of other studies when viewed in the light of the biases discussed by Polinsky (1977) (for an elaboration of this point see King 1980).

From (6) and (7), and noting that in the reform simulated $p_C^0 = p_C^p = p_C$, we may solve for the equivalent gain to give

$$
(9) \qquad \mathrm{EG} = y^p \left\{ \left[\frac{p_H^0}{p_H^p} \right]^{(\beta_1 + \beta_2 \log z)} \right\} - y^0 ,
$$

where

$$
z = \frac{p_H^0 p_H^p}{p_C^2} .
$$

For those households whose housing costs do not alter (namely renters) the value of their equivalent gain is equal to the lump-sum transfers they receive. For homeowners, however, the equivalent gain depends on the change in the price of housing services and the preference parameters.

4.3 Self-Financing Reforms

A reform is defined by specifying for each household a set of postreform prices and an income level. These values cannot be chosen independently but must satisfy an overall revenue constraint to ensure feasibility. A self-financing reform must yield the same level of total revenue as in the initial position, and we shall assume that revenue raised by reducing housing subsidies is returned to households in the form of a flat-rate lump-sum subsidy denoted by l. In practice this could be achieved by a combination of a rise in the tax threshold and an increase in cash benefits (principally unemployment benefit and basic retirement pensions) to those below the tax threshold. This is a good approximation to a lump-sum subsidy because the marginal rate of income tax in the United Kingdom is a constant for a very large fraction of the population (Kay and King 1980).

Preferences are assumed to be defined over housing services and a composite commodity of other goods and services. If the tax rate on the composite commodity is held constant, then

$$(10) \qquad Nl = \sum_h (t_{Hh}^p p_{Hh}^p x_{Hh}^p - t_{Hh}^0 p_{Hh}^0 x_{Hh}^0 + t_C p_C (x_{Ch}^p - x_{Ch}^0)) \ ,$$

where t_H and t_C are the tax-inclusive commodity tax rates on housing services and on other consumption, respectively, and where the former is household-specific.

From households' budget constraints we have that

$$(11) \qquad p_C(x_{Ch}^p - x_{Ch}^0) = l + p_{Hh}^0 x_{Hh}^0 - p_{Hh}^p x_{Hh}^p \ .$$

Combining these two equations we have

$$(12) \qquad l = \frac{1}{(1 - t_C)N} \sum_h \{p_{Hh}^p x_{Hh}^p (t_{Hh}^p - t_C) - p_{Hh}^0 x_{Hh}^0 (t_{Hh}^0 - t_C)\} \ .$$

If the composite commodity tax rate varies across households, then in the above equation t_c is replaced by the unweighted average of the household-specific composite commodity tax rates. The only unobservable variable in this expression is the demand for housing in the postreform equilibrium. Given the demand function in (8), it is possible to solve explicitly for l, in which case

$$(13) \qquad l = \frac{\dfrac{1}{N} \sum_h \{\alpha_h y_h^0 - p_{Hh}^0 x_{Hh}^0 (t_{Hh}^0 - t_C)\}}{1 - t_C - \dfrac{1}{N} \sum_h \alpha_h} \ ,$$

where

$$\alpha_h = \left\{ (t_{Hh}^p - t_C) \left(\beta_1 + 2\beta_2 \log \left(\frac{p_{Hh}^p}{p_C} \right) \right) \right\} \ .$$

4.4 The Social Value of a Reform

In addition to information about the distribution of CG and EG among households, we shall also compute several measures of the "social value" of a reform. By this we mean any measure which requires some assumption about the cardinality of individual utility functions, so that we may construct a social welfare function. To derive CG and EG requires only an ordinal measure of utility.

The first set of calculations is for various indices of inequality of both the original and the postreform distributions. It is conventional to examine the distribution of "income," but this presupposes an unidimensional measure of a household's welfare. Since prices differ between households and also between the original and postreform positions, the level of income is an inadequate measure of a household's welfare. The problem arises, of course, only when preferences are defined over more than one commodity. The obvious unidimensional measure is the value of the indirect utility function. But this requires a suitable normalization and does not avoid the problem of choosing a reference price vector at which welfare comparisons can be made. The normalization we shall choose is to define the concept of "equivalent income" (King 1983b). A household's equivalent income y_E is defined as that level of income which, at the reference price vector, gives the same level of utility as that which the household enjoys at the actual level of income and prices it faces. Formally,

$$(14) \qquad v(y_{Eh}, p_{HR}, p_{CR}) = v(y_h, p_{Hh}, p_{Ch}) \, ,$$

where p_R is the reference price vector.

From (7) we have that

$$(15) \qquad y_{Eh} = y_h \left(\frac{p_{HR}}{p_{Hh}}\right)^{\beta_1} \left(\frac{p_{CR}}{p_{Ch}}\right)^{1-\beta_1}$$
$$\times \exp\left\{\beta_2 \left(\left[\log\left(\frac{p_{HR}}{p_{CR}}\right)\right]^2 - \left[\log\left(\frac{p_{Hh}}{p_{Ch}}\right)\right]^2\right)\right\} .$$

With this expression for equivalent income we may compute values for both original and postreform equivalent income for each household in the sample. The choice of the reference price level is arbitrary, but the most sensible choice is to use the average level of prices in the original position. It is much easier to ask policymakers to provide relative valuations of increments to equivalent income at different levels of equivalent income (a measure of inequality aversion on the part of the policymaker) for the current (original) price level than for some other hypothetical price level. It is clear from (14) that with this choice of reference price level, if there were no differences between the prices faced by different households, then the original level of equivalent income would be equal to the level of original income and the postreform level of equivalent income would equal original income plus the value of the household's equivalent gain (King 1983).

A measure of inequality may now be defined over the distribution of household equivalent incomes, both before and after the reform. The inequality measure on which we shall concentrate is the Atkinson (1970) index, which imposes the condition that the inequality index should be independent of the mean of the distribution. This in turn implies a social welfare function which exhibits constant relative-inequality aversion. We compute this index for the two pairs of distributions which are the analogues to the two measures of household gain defined above. The first is a rather simpleminded comparison between the distribution of original income y^0 and the distribution of $y^0 + CG$. This measure requires no assumption about individual preferences orderings and ignores behavioral responses. The second comparison is between y_E^0 and y_E^p. This describes the distribution of (suitably normalized) utility levels in the original and postreform positions.

For each of these comparisons we also compute the index of "horizontal inequality" proposed by King (1983a), which is a function of a variable d_h, where d_h is the absolute value of the difference between the equivalent income of household h in the postreform distribution and the level of equivalent income in the postreform distribution which corresponds to the rank of household h in the original distribution (normalized by mean postreform income). The Atkinson index of vertical inequality (I_v) and the index of horizontal inequity (I_H) are related to the index of overall inequality (I) by the simple relation

$$(16) \qquad 1 - I = (1 - I_H)(1 - I_v) \, ,$$

$$(17) \qquad I = 1 - \left[\frac{1}{N} \sum_{h=1}^{N} \left(\frac{y_{Eh}}{\bar{y}_E} \exp(-\eta d_h) \right)^{1-\epsilon} \right] \quad \epsilon \neq 1$$

$$\qquad\qquad = 1 - \exp \left[\frac{1}{N} \sum_{h=1}^{N} \left(\log \frac{y_{Eh}}{\bar{y}_E} - \eta d_h \right) \right] \quad \epsilon = 1$$

for the distribution $\{y_{Eh}\}$, where ϵ and η are, respectively, the vertical and horizontal inequality aversion parameters. Both inequality aversion parameters vary from zero to infinity. When they are zero, the social welfare function is concerned solely with the efficiency gains from the reform. When ϵ and η are positive, the social welfare function takes into account not only efficiency gains but also changes in the shape both of the distribution and of the ranking within the distribution. The calibration of the parameters may be explained as follows. If the same social value is attached to a marginal dollar in the hands of a household with equivalent income y as to x dollars for a household with equivalent income ρy, then $x = \rho^\epsilon$. For example, when $\epsilon = 0.5$, one dollar taken from a household with twice average income has the same social value as 50 cents given to a household with one-half the average income. The social value of the equivalent income of a household which has changed positions in the distribution is equal to the social value of an income $ye^{-\eta d}$. When $\eta = 0.5$ a change in ranking equivalent to 10% of mean income ($d_h = 0.1$) is regarded as equivalent to a reduction in income of about 5%, and when $\eta = 5$ the corresponding reduction is approximately 40%.

Finally, we compute an exact measure of the social value of a reform which parallels our measure of the value of the reform to an individual household and which may be termed the "social equivalent gain." We assume a social welfare function of the form which underlies the inequality indexes given by (17). The social equivalent gain is the sum of money which, if distributed in such a way as to produce an equal increment in original equivalent income, would produce a level of social welfare equal to that derived from the postreform equilibrium. The social equivalent gain is denoted by SG and is defined by

$$(18) \qquad \sum_h (y_{Eh}^0 + \text{SG})^{1-\epsilon} = \sum_h (y_{Eh}^p \exp(-\eta d_h))^{1-\epsilon}.$$

This equation gives the social gain as a function of the two inequality aversion parameters. When they are both zero, only the efficiency aspects of the reform are taken into consideration. In general, however, positive values of ϵ and η mean that the distributional benefits of the reform are valued as well as the efficiency gains, and the total effect is expressed in terms of a money measure.

The social equivalent gain implicitly trades off efficiency versus distributional benefits, and this may be shown explicitly in terms of a diagram. If we set SG = 0, then (18) is a functional relation between ϵ and η which gives pairs of values of the two inequality aversion parameters for which the policymaker is indifferent between the original and postreform positions. This locus may be plotted on a diagram with ϵ on the vertical axis and η on the horizontal axis. If the reform results in an efficiency gain then the curve will cut the horizontal axis in the positive quadrant, whereas if there is an efficiency loss it will cut the vertical axis. Any point in the positive quadrant represents a particular social welfare function, and thus the diagram shows for which social welfare functions the reform will be approved and for which the status quo will be preferred to the reform.

4.5   Housing Costs and the United Kingdom Housing Market

4.5.1   Basic Assumptions

The most significant feature of the United Kingdom housing market is the variance of prices for housing services faced by different households.

This arises mainly within the rental sector (both public and private) in which the coefficient of variation of the price of housing services exceeds 0.4 (King 1980). The variance of housing costs within the owner-occupied sector is much less because the source of variation here derives mainly from differences in marginal tax rates. As mentioned earlier, the United Kingdom system closely approximates a linear tax schedule.

Nevertheless, there is substantial variation in housing costs between the different tenures. Owner occupation has grown rapidly and now accounts for about 60% of all dwellings. As in the United States, no tax is levied on the imputed rental income from owner occupation and interest on mortgages is tax deductible. In addition, no capital gains tax is charged on principal residences. These provisions provide a subsidy to owner occupation relative to the level of rents in the uncontrolled rental sector. About 30% of dwellings are rented public (local authority) housing, and only 10% are privately rented. Of the latter, in the sample period of 1973/74 most had controlled rents but some (furnished rental units) were uncontrolled. The combination of government subsidies and rent control led to rents in the subsidized rental sector well below the level of rents in the uncontrolled furnished rental sector.

The data set we shall use consists of the 5,895 households in England and Wales with positive housing costs which participated in the Family Expenditure Survey (FES) during the tax year 1973/74. (We have excluded households living in rent-free accommodation provided by employers.) The FES is a continuous stratified sample survey of household incomes and expenditures. Of the 5,895 households, 3,143 were in owner occupation, 1,752 in local authority housing, 765 in controlled private rental dwellings, and 235 in uncontrolled rental accommodation. Since 1973 the share of owner occupation has risen from 53% to almost 60%, with a corresponding decline in the private rental sector.

Household income is defined as "normal" gross household income plus income in kind (including imputed income from owner occupation) minus tax and national insurance contributions. Capital gains are excluded because they are not recorded in the FES. Estimates of "normal" income are provided by individuals in response to interview questions designed to elicit information about such factors as overtime earnings and short-time working. Consumption of housing services is measured by a dwelling's "gross rateable value." In the United Kingdom an official assessor assigns to each dwelling an estimate of its rental value known as the gross rateable value. Revaluations for all dwellings in England and Wales were made immediately prior to the survey period. The price index of housing costs for tenants is defined as expenditure (the sum of rent and rates [property taxes] minus any rebates) divided by gross rateable value. For owner-occupiers the price index of housing services is the "effective rental" plus rates (net of rebates) divided by gross rateable value. The "effective rental" of owner-occupied housing is the product of its rental value (which we measure by gross rateable value) and a factor denoted by μ, which allows for the tax subsidy to owner occupation. The value of μ may under certain assumptions be written as (Rosen 1979; King 1980)

$$(19) \qquad \mu = 1 - a\tau \, ,$$

where τ is the homeowner's marginal tax rate and $(1 - a)$ is the fraction of rental value accounted for by depreciation and maintenance. The value of a may be represented by the ratio of net to gross rateable value, both of which are recorded in the FES. This measure of housing costs does allow for inflation, and the reader is referred to King (1980). The price of the composite commodity varied among households because they were sampled at different dates during the year. The retail price index for consumption other than housing services was computed for each month and the appropriate index used for each household.

The reform we shall simulate is the introduction of a tax on imputed rental income. This is equivalent to setting the value of μ equal to unity. No change is made either in the level of subsidies to rental housing or to the price index of the composite commodity. Given these changes to the prices facing each household, the lump sum which is paid out of the additional revenue generated is computed from equation (13). Postreform income of each household is given by

$$(20) \qquad y_h^p = y_h^0 + l \, .$$

It remains only to define the tax rates for each household. For owner-occupiers and local authority tenants the tax rate on housing services is defined by

$$(21) \qquad t_H = \frac{p_H - 1}{p_H} \, .$$

For other private tenants the discrepancy between housing costs and rental value is not due solely to taxes but to factors such as rent control as well. In these cases the tax rate is equal to rates (net of rebates) divided by absolute expenditure (the product of p_H and x_H). The value of the tax rate on the composite commodity was taken to be the ratio of taxes on consumers' expenditure (other than housing) minus subsidies to consumers' expenditure at market prices in 1973 (tables 4.6 and 4.8, *National Income and Expenditure 1980*). This gives a tax rate of 15.6%.

The reform is now fully defined, and statistics on the efficiency and distributional effects of the reform described in sections 4.2 and 4.4 may now be calculated. The results are discussed below in section 4.6.

4.5.2 Alternative Assumptions

As set out above, our definition of the reform implicitly assumes an infinite elasticity of supply of housing services because we ignored any change in the producer price of housing services which might result from the changes in consumption. We take the producer price of the composite commodity q_C as *numéraire*. The supply of housing services is related to the relative producer price of the two commodities, and for purposes of simulation we shall consider the case in which there is a constant elasticity of supply of housing services. This is consistent with the following specification of the economy's production possibility frontier. Let this be denoted by the function

$$(22) \qquad F(X_H, X_C) = 0 \ ,$$

where

$$X_H = \sum_h x_{Hh} \ ,$$

$$X_C = \sum_h x_{Ch} \ .$$

In competitive equilibrium we have that

$$(23) \qquad \frac{q_H}{q_C} = \frac{F_H}{F_C} \ ,$$

where F_H and F_C denote the partial derivatives of F with respect to its two arguments. Assume that the production possibility frontier is described by

$$(24) \qquad \frac{\alpha}{1+s} X_H^{1+s} + X_C = 0 \ ,$$

where α and s are constants. Then from (23) and (24)

$$(25) \qquad \frac{q_H}{q_C} = \alpha X_H^s \ .$$

The value of s is the inverse of the price elasticity of supply of housing services. Since q_C is taken as the *numéraire*,

$$(26) \qquad q_H^p = \lambda q_H^0 \ ,$$

where

$$(27) \qquad \lambda = \left(\frac{X_H^p}{X_H^0} \right)^s \ .$$

For a finite supply elasticity the postreform values of the price of housing services are (for owner-occupiers and uncontrolled tenants) equal to the values given above by the definition of the reform multiplied by λ.

One consequence of a finite supply elasticity is that the market values of homes will be lower in the postreform equilibrium than in the original position. This reduces the wealth of homeowners and landlords. Since almost all rental accommodation in the United Kingdom is subject to rent control with security of tenure for tenants, the effect on the net worth of landlords is likely to be small and we shall ignore this. To convert the fall in house prices to an equivalent reduction in permanent income we multiply by an appropriate real interest r. Hence equation (20) becomes

$$(28) \qquad y_h^p = y_h^0 + l - Dr(1 - \lambda)V_{Hh}^0 ,$$

where $D = 1$ for owner-occupiers and zero otherwise, and V_{Hh}^0 = preform market value of home.

We assume a value for r of 2.5% per annum, which is clearly an arbitrary choice; but in the absence of a model of portfolio behavior an assumption of this kind is necessary. No data on house prices are collected by the FES. Values of house prices were therefore imputed to each dwelling by using the estimated relation between house prices and rateable values found by Hughes (1981) using data from building societies. The fitted equation is quadratic with regionally varying coefficients (over the ten standard regions of England and Wales). Hughes's estimates refer to 1976, and these were adjusted to 1973 by an index of house prices (table V1.18, *Housing Policy Review Technical Volume*, part 2). We shall present results for two different assumptions about the supply elasticity. First, we take as the base case an infinite elasticity of supply ($s = 0$), which might be defended as a not unreasonable assumption in the very long run. Second, we consider an elasticity of 2.0 ($s = 0.5$), which is in line with empirical estimates for the United States (Huang 1973; Poterba 1980).

Since the postreform demand for housing depends upon both λ and l, equations (27) and (28) are two nonlinear simultaneous equations in λ and l, which are solved by iterative methods. Given equilibrium values for λ and l, postreform values of prices, incomes, and consumption may be computed, and the reform is completely defined.

If the desired lump-sum transfers are infeasible, then an additional dollar raised by the elimination of subsidies will have a social value of more than one dollar. This reflects the gains which could be obtained by using the extra revenue to reduce other distortionary taxes rather than using it, as assumed here, to make lump-sum payments to households. In principle, this alternative use of the revenue should be modeled directly in order to gauge accurately both its efficiency and distributional consequences. But since there are many alternatives, we will illustrate the possible outcome by regarding the effective lump-sum transfer made possible by the reform as equal to γl, where γ is the value of an extra dollar generated by the tax system. We shall consider two values of γ: 1.0 and 1.2, respectively. Two amendments to the equations defining a reform are necessary to incorporate γ. These are

(29) $$y_h^p = y_h^0 + \gamma l - Dr(1 - \lambda)V_{Hh}^0 \; ,$$

(30) $$l = \frac{\dfrac{1}{N} \sum_h \left\{ \alpha_h y_h^0 - p_H^0 x_H^0 (t_H^0 - t_C) \right\}}{1 - \gamma(t_C + \dfrac{1}{N} \sum_h \alpha_h)} \; .$$

4.6 Results

In this section we present the results of simulating the introduction of a tax on imputed rental income. The reform was defined in section 4.5. Table 4.1 shows some summary statistics of the effect of this reform for the base case with an infinite supply elasticity and $\gamma = 1$. The price of housing services is unchanged for tenants but is increased for owner-occupiers. The price of other consumption goods is unchanged, and income is increased on average because the proceeds of the new tax are distributed to households as a lump-sum subsidy. The values of prices and incomes before and after the reform are shown in table 4.1 together with the values of pre- and postreform equivalent incomes, the values of housing consumption, and the values of both cash and equivalent gain. All monetary values are in £ per week.

The lump-sum subsidy which can be financed is 83.3 pence per week in 1973 prices (from [20] this is the difference between mean y^0 and mean y^p), which corresponds to £2.42 per week at 1980 prices. The efficiency gains of the reform (which equal the mean value of equivalent gain per household) amount to 16.5p per week at 1973 prices, 48.2p per week at 1980 prices. This is almost exactly 20% of the value of the lump-sum subsidy and is equal to 0.4 of 1% of mean household income.

Even the summary results in table 4.1 show that in addition to the positive efficiency gain from the reform, the distributional effects are substantial. The maximum gain to a household is equal to the additional lump-sum payment, and this is exactly equal to the gain experienced by tenants. Some owner-occupied households, however, lose markedly. The maximum gain is much smaller than the maximum loss (comparing the figures in the "maximum" and "minimum" columns for the measures of gain). In the main this reflects the distribution of the tax receipts in the form of a lump-sum subsidy. If the revenue had been distributed in proportion to consumption or income in the original position, then the disparity between maximum gains and losses would have been much less. Nevertheless, even with the lump-sum subsidy more people gain from the reform than lose (see the columns "number positive" and "number negative"). Looking first at the value of cash gain, which measures the impact effect of the reform, we see that 54.3% of households gain from

Table 4.1 Summary Statistics of Reform, All Tenures

	Minimum	Average	Maximum	No. Positive	No. Negative	Standard Deviation	Coefficient of Variation
y^0	3.415	44.233	618.876	5,895	0	29.070	.657
p_H^0	.150	.982	7.572	5,895	0	.396	.403
p_C^0	1.000	1.034	1.064	5,895	0	.022	.021
y^P	4.248	45.065	619.709	5,895	0	29.070	.645
p_H^P	.150	1.117	7.572	5,895	0	.416	.372
p_C^P	1.000	1.034	1.064	5,895	0	.022	.021
y_E^0	2.948	44.188	601.890	5,895	0	28.846	.653
y_E^P	3.667	44.357	602.699	5,895	0	28.254	.637
CG	−12.551	.000	.739	3,199	2,696	.845	4.981
EG	−10.497	.165	.833	3,622	2,273	.824	.477
x^0	.353	4.912	53.496	5,895	0	2.342	.477
x^P	.221	4.239	61.406	5,895	0	2.650	.625

the reform and the balance lose. These figures underestimate the proportion of households which benefit from the reform, because they ignore behavioral responses. Incorporating behavioral responses into the calculation of gains, we find that the proportion of households which gain from the reform (have a positive value of equivalent gain) rises to 61.4%. In other words, ignoring behavioral responses leads to an underestimate of the number of households which would gain from the reform of 11.7%.

Table 4.2 shows the same set of summary statistics for owner-occupiers only. The mean value of equivalent gain is − 41.9p per week, whereas for households in rented accommodations the figure is + 83.4p per week. The price of housing services to owner-occupiers rises by 25.8%. As with the full sample, the mean value of equivalent gain is only a partial view of the effects of the reform. The distribution of the values of equivalent gain around the mean seems at least as significant as the value of the mean itself. This is illustrated by table 4.3, which shows the mean values of both cash and equivalent gain for deciles of the original income distribution. We also show for each decile the numbers of households which gain and lose from the reform. The mean value of equivalent and cash gain declines as we move up through the income distribution, and from the sixth decile upward the number of people who lose exceeds the number who gain from the reform. In the bottom three deciles all households gain from a reform, but in the top six deciles there are significant numbers of households who both gain and lose. In the fifth decile, for example, the mean value of equivalent gain is positive, but there are almost equal numbers of households who gain and lose. Clearly, when assessing the effects of a reform, one should not overlook the distribution of gains and losses within subgroups (such as deciles of the income distribution or tenure groups).

Summary measures of the effects of the reform on vertical and horizontal inequality are shown in tables 4.4 and 4.5. These show inequality measures as defined in section 4.3 for two comparisons of the distributions of (1) initial income and initial income plus cash gain, and (2) initial equivalent income and postreform equivalent income. In both cases it can be seen that the distributional effects of the reform are significant and that this particular reform reduces the measure of vertical inequality for all values of the vertical inequality aversion parameter. The effects of the reform on horizontal inequity are such that the index of overall inequality is higher in the postreform distribution than in the original distribution for low values of the vertical inequality aversion parameter, whereas for egalitarian social preferences the index of overall inequality is lower in the postreform distribution.

The value of the social gain is shown in table 4.6. The entries in this table measure the social valuation of the reform for different values of the vertical and horizontal inequality aversion parameters in £ per week.

Table 4.2   Summary Statistics of Reform, Owner-Occupiers

	Minimum	Average	Maximum	No. Positive	No. Negative	Standard Deviation	Coefficient of Variation
y^0	5.468	51.782	472.821	3,143	0	31.047	.600
p_H^0	.743	.982	1.363	3,143	0	.057	.058
p_C^0	1.000	1.033	1.064	3,143	0	.022	.021
y^P	6.301	52.615	473.654	3,143	0	31.047	.590
p_H^P	1.013	1.235	1.609	3,143	0	.057	.046
p_C^P	1.000	1.033	1.064	3,143	0	.022	.021
y_E^0	5.590	51.760	482.533	3,143	0	30.928	.598
y_E^P	6.293	51.342	471.821	3,143	0	30.196	.588
CG	−12.551	−.647	.648	447	2,696	.664	−1.027
EG	−10.497	−.419	.688	870	2,273	.735	−1.755
x^0	.353	5.483	53.496	3,143	0	2.637	.481
x^P	.577	4.717	42.666	3,143	0	2.766	.586

Table 4.3   **The Distribution of Gains by Deciles**
                       of Original Income (£ per week, 1973 prices)

Decile	Mean Income	Mean CG	Mean EG	No. Gainers[†]	No. Losers[†]	% Gainers
1	10.77	.52	.76	589	0	100
2	17.13	.34	.67	590	0	100
3	24.34	.28	.58	589	0	100
4	31.39	.24	.48	556	34	94
5	37.64	.13	.36	305	284	52
6	43.65	.05	.24	260	330	44
7	49.43	− .05	.14	246	343	42
8	57.07	− .24	− .09	193	397	33
9	67.64	− .40	− .32	173	416	29
10	103.20	− .87	− 1.15	121	469	20
Overall	44.23	0	.17	3,622	2,273	61

[†]The "no. gainers" is the number of households with a positive value for equivalent gain, and the "no. losers" refers to households with negative equivalent gain.

When both parameters are zero, social preferences are defined only over the efficiency benefits of the reform, and the entry in the top left-hand corner of the table measures the average efficiency gain. This differs slightly from mean equivalent gain because the two measures of change in deadweight loss are defined with respect to different price vectors, the mean price level in one case and the actual price level for each household in the other. For zero values of the horizontal inequity aversion parameter, the social gain measures only the effect of the reform on vertical inequality, and it is evident from the table that the value of the social gain rises quite sharply as the value of the vertical inequality aversion parameter increases. For example, for an ϵ value of 2.0 the social gain is 63p per week, which is almost four times as large as the pure efficiency gain.

If we consider positive values for the horizontal inequity aversion parameter, then we see that for low values of the vertical inequality aversion parameter the social gain is actually negative. This is because the benefits in terms of a more equal distribution are offset by the social costs of the change in the ordering within the distribution brought about by the reform. This trade-off between the efficiency gains, the change in vertical inequality, and horizontal inequity is shown more explicitly in figure 4.1. In this diagram the line of indifference shows those combinations of the two inequality aversion parameters for which we are indifferent between the original and the postreform position. Any point in the positive quadrant represents a set of social preferences, and for preferences to the northwest of the indifference line the reform is preferred to the original distribution. For preferences to the southeast of the indifference line the original position is preferred to the postreform equilibrium.

Table 4.4   **Inequality Index for the Distributions of y^0 and $y^0 + CG$**

Index of Vertical Inequality

ε	Original Distribution	Final Distribution
.0	.000	.000
.5	.088	.085
1.0	.174	.168
2.0	.337	.324
5.0	.639	.610

Index of Horizontal Inequality

	η			
ε	.500	1.000	2.000	5.000
.0	.008	.015	.030	.072
.5	.007	.014	.029	.070
1.0	.007	.014	.027	.067
2.0	.006	.012	.024	.058
5.0	.003	.007	.014	.035

Index of Overall Inequality

ε	Original Distribution	Final Distribution η				
		.000	.500	1.000	2.000	5.000
.0	.000	.000	.008	.015	.030	.072
.5	.088	.085	.092	.098	.111	.149
1.0	.174	.168	.174	.180	.191	.224
2.0	.337	.324	.328	.332	.340	.364
5.0	.639	.610	.611	.612	.615	.624

The calculations presented so far assume an infinite supply elasticity of housing services. Although estimates of the long-run supply elasticity are hard to come by, it is not implausible to suppose that it is a good deal less than infinite (White and White 1977). We have therefore repeated the calculations for an assumed value of the supply elasticity of 2.0, which seems in line with some of the estimates reported for the United States (Poterba 1980). The supply price of housing services is now endogenous to the model. Changes in the supply price reflect changes in factor prices (mainly in land prices), and these feed through to household incomes in the way described in section 4.5.

Summary statistics of the reform assuming a supply elasticity of 2.0 are shown in table 4.7. After the reform the fall in the producer price of housing services is 5.7% and the lump-sum payment which can be financed is 83.1p per week. The mean equivalent gain rises slightly

Table 4.5   Inequality Index for the Distributions of y_E^0 and y_E^P

Index of Vertical Inequality

ε	Original Distribution	Final Distribution
.0	.000	.000
.5	.087	.082
1.0	.171	.161
2.0	.330	.311
5.0	.635	.596

Index of Horizontal Inequality

ε	η			
	.500	1.000	2.000	5.000
.0	.006	.012	.024	.058
.5	.006	.011	.023	.055
1.0	.005	.010	.020	.050
2.0	.004	.008	.015	.038
5.0	.001	.002	.005	.012

Index of Overall Inequality

ε	Original Distribution	Final Distribution η				
		.000	.500	1.000	2.000	5.000
.0	.000	.000	.006	.012	.024	.058
.5	.087	.082	.087	.092	.103	.133
1.0	.171	.161	.166	.170	.179	.204
2.0	.330	.311	.313	.316	.321	.337
5.0	.635	.596	.597	.597	.598	.601

(compared with table 4.1) to 21.9p per week. No great significance should be read into this, because the fact that producer prices are endogenous does not in itself give rise to any additional reason for an efficiency gain. But since the reform entails moving from one second-best equilibrium to another, it is perfectly possible for the mean value of equivalent gain to rise when supply responses are taken into account. The approximate nature of the imputation of house prices (and the calculation of the implied fall in permanent income) means that there is uncertainty about the precise value of the mean equivalent gain.

Allowing for supply effects illustrates also the phenomenon noted by White and White (1977), namely that removal of the subsidy to owner occupation benefits renters not only because they receive a lump-sum payment financed out of the additional revenue but also because they face lower rents. The mean equivalent gain for tenants in the uncon-

Table 4.6   **Social Gain (£ per week)**

			η		
ε	.000	.5000	1.000	2.000	5.000
.0	.169	− .102	− .369	− .899	− 2.426
.5	.319	.109	− .099	− .509	− 1.699
1.0	.447	.292	.137	− .167	− 1.050
2.0	.269	.552	.475	.323	− .124
5.0	.778	.769	.758	.738	.675

trolled sector is £1.08 per week with a supply elasticity of 2.0 compared
with 83.3p per week for an infinite supply elasticity.

The final calculations refer to the shadow value of increased revenues.
With a value of γ of 1.2 (and ignoring supply responses) the mean
equivalent gain is 36.6p per week compared with 16.5p per week for
$\gamma = 1.0$. The proportions of the sample which gain are, respectively, 68.1
and 61.4% for the two assumptions. Clearly, the efficiency gains are
sensitive to alternative uses of the higher revenue generated by the tax on
imputed income. The introduction of labor supply or other household
decisions into the model would enable these alternative uses to be modeled exactly and will be the subject of future work.

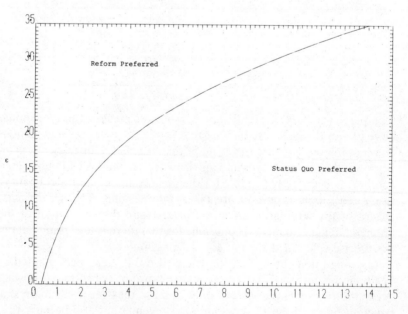

Fig. 4.1   Indifference line for reform.

Table 4.7   **Summary Statistics of Reform, Supply Elasticity = 2.0**

	Minimum	Average	Maximum	No. Positive	No. Negative	Standard Deviation	Coefficient of Variation
y^0	3.415	44.233	618.876	5,895	0	29.070	.657
p_H^0	.150	.982	7.572	5,895	0	.396	.403
p_C^0	1.000	1.034	1.064	5,895	0	.022	.021
y^P	4.246	44.928	619.707	5,895	0	29.002	.646
p_H^P	.150	1.075	7.138	5,895	0	.389	.362
p_C^P	1.000	1.034	1.064	5,895	0	.022	.021
y_E^0	2.948	44.188	601.890	5,895	0	28.846	.653
y_E^P	3.699	44.409	602.698	5,895	0	28.345	.638
CG	−12.551	.000	.739	3,199	2,696	.845	
EG	−7.869	.219	2.027	3,648	2,247	.742	3.388
x^0	.353	4.912	53.496	5,895	0	2.342	.477
x^P	.230	4.313	61.405	5,895	0	2.710	.628

4.7 Conclusions

We have presented a methodology for computing the gains and losses from tax reform which provides information on both the efficiency and distributional effects of reform. The figures refer to both the impact effect of the reform and the long-run consequences once households have adjusted their behavior. Behavioral responses were incorporated by using econometric estimates of the parameters of an indirect utility function. The efficiency and distributional aspects were linked by the concept of "equivalent gain."

The aim of this paper has been to illustrate a methodology that can be used for general tax reform analysis using large data sets so that the calculations described here become a more routine task than is usually the case in policy analysis, especially in government. The question of who gains and who loses from a reform is of economic and political interest, and with the growing use of microdata sets the economist will be able to provide to policymakers information relevant to this question.

References

Atkinson, A. B. 1970. On the measurement of inequality. *Journal of Economic Theory* 2: 244–63.

Atkinson, A. B., and M. A. King. 1980. Housing policy, taxation, and Reform. *Midland Bank Review*, spring, pp. 7–15.

Auerbach, A. J., and H. S. Rosen. 1980. Will the real excess burden please stand up? (Or, Seven measures in search of a concept). Working Paper no. 495.

Clark, C., and G. T. Jones. 1971. The demand for housing. Centre for Environmental Studies Working Paper no. 11. London.

Diamond, P. A., and D. L. McFadden. 1974. Some uses of the expenditure function in public finance. *Journal of Public Economics* 3: 3–21.

Harberger, A. C. 1974. *Taxation and welfare*, Boston: Little, Brown.

Hausman, J. A. 1981. Exact consumer's surplus and deadweight loss. *American Economic Review* 71, no. 4: 662–76.

Huang, D. S. 1973. "Short-run instability in single family starts. *Journal of the American Statistical Association* 68: 788–92.

Hughes, G. A. 1980. Housing and the tax system. In G. A. Hughes and G. M. and Heal, eds., *Public policy and the tax system*. London: Allen & Unwin.

———. 1981. The taxation of housing: Some analytical and simulation results. Mimeo, Cambridge University, Cambridge, England.

Kay, J. A. 1980. The deadweight loss from a tax system. *Journal of Public Economics* 13: 111–19.

Kay, J. A., and M. A. King. 1980. *The British tax system*. 2d ed. Oxford: Oxford University Press.

King, M. A. 1980. An econometric model of tenure choice and the demand for housing as a joint decision. *Journal of Public Economics* 14: 137–59.

———. 1983a. An index of inequality: With applications to horizontal equity and social mobility. *Econometrica*, vol. 51.

———. 1983b. Welfare analysis of tax reforms using household data. Forthcoming in *Journal of Public Economics*.

Mohring, H. 1971. Alternative gain and loss measures. *Western Economic Journal* 9: 349–68.

Polinsky, A. M. 1977. The demand for housing: A study in specification and grouping. *Econometrica* 45: 447–61.

Poterba, J. M. 1980. Inflation, income, taxes, and owner-occupied housing. NBER Working Paper no. 553.

Rosen, H. S. 1978. The measurement of excess burden with explicit utility functions. *Journal of Political Economy* 86 (supplement): S121–35.

———. 1979. Housing decisions and the US income tax: An econometric analysis. *Journal of Public Economics* 11: 1–24.

Rosen, H. S., and K. A. Small. 1981. Applied welfare economics with discrete choice models. *Econometrica*, vol. 49.

White, M. H., and L. J. White. 1977. The tax subsidy to owner-occupied housing: Who benefits? *Journal of Public Economics* 7: 111–26.

Comment   Patric H. Hendershott

King calculates the impact of the reintroduction in the United Kingdom of a tax on the imputed rental income of owner-occupiers. This tax was in place prior to 1963, and it may be a viable policy option in the United Kingdom, in contrast to the United States. The calculated impacts of this tax reform, computed using data for nearly 6,000 households in 1973–74, include (*a*) the total efficiency gain; (*b*) the distributive effects by and within income deciles; (*c*) the distributive effects in terms of indexes of vertical and horizontal inequality; and (*d*) several measures of the social value of the reform. King emphasizes the methodology underlying his calculations rather than the calculations per se.

My remarks are divided into three parts. The first part is a summary of the calculation of individual household gains and losses and the total efficiency gain of the reform when the supply of housing services is infinitely price elastic. This calculation is a model of clarity and can serve as an excellent methodological guide for the analysis of the impact of a wide range of government programs. The second part of my discussion relates to the analysis when the supply price of housing services has a finite elasticity. I conclude with a critique of the use of the indexes of horizontal and vertical inequality in the measurement of the social value of the reform.

Gains and Losses of Individual Households

In a simple two-commodity model, housing (H) and a nonhousing composite commodity (C), King's "equivalent gain" (EG) (positive or negative) from the reform for a given household is the change in income that, at prereform prices, provides the household with the same utility that it would receive with the reform. That is, EG is calculated from King's equation (6):

$$(1) \qquad v(y^0 + \text{EG}, p_H^0, p_C^0) = v(y^p, p_H^p, p_C^p) \ ,$$

where the subscripted variables are household-specific and are inclusive of good-specific net (of subsidy) taxes, y is nominal income less nonconsumption net taxes, and the superscripts denote original (0) and postreform (p) values. Implementation of this procedure requires (1) specification of an indirect utility function and the price and output adjustment mechanism of the economy, (2) a description of the government use of the additional tax revenues, and (3) an analysis of the direct impact of the tax reform on the household-specific price of housing services.

Patric H. Hendershott is a professor of finance at The Ohio State University and a research associate of the National Bureau of Economic Research.

King's specification takes the following form: a translog indirect utility function is hypothesized and employed to derive a demand function for housing services. Estimation of the demand function fully specifies both the utility function and the demand for the composite commodity. The two demands, in turn, fully determine the quantities of the two goods because infinite supply price elasticities are assumed. The revenue raised from the new tax are assumed to be returned to households in equal amounts as a rebate. The value of the rebate per household is computed and added to the original income of the household to determine the postreform nominal income.

For the aggregate economy, King assumes that money expenditures net of all taxes and inclusive of all subsidies are constant. That is,

$$(2) \qquad p_C^A X_{CT} + p_H^A X_{HT} = K ,$$

where the A superscript denotes average net of tax prices, the T superscript refers to total economy-wide quantities, and K is a constant. The reform-induced change in the quantity of the composite commodity is thus related to the change in housing consumed by

$$(3) \qquad \Delta X_{CT} = - (p_H^A/p_C^A)\Delta X_{HT} .$$

After a careful analysis of the current subsidy to individual home-owners, King meticulously computes the direct impact of the reform on the price of housing services for each homeowner and calculates its equivalent gain. The mean equivalent gains for households in different income deciles, as well the proportions in each that gain, are reported in his table 4.3. The bottom seven deciles gain on net, the rebates outweighing the additional taxes, although over half the households in the sixth and seventh deciles lose. Possibly because no households in the lowest three deciles are homeowners, all of them gain. One-fifth of the total tax imposed (the subsidy removed) constitutes an efficiency gain. Of course, if the increased government revenue were returned to households in a different manner, then the distributive effect could be much different. In fact, it would be a useful exercise to determine which method of returning the revenue—a general income tax cut that would benefit upper income households, for example—would minimize the distributive effect while maintaining the overall efficiency gain. This analysis is clearly written, internally consistent, and of wide applicability.

The Case of a Finite House Price Elasticity

In an extension of this analysis, King replaces the assumption of infinite housing supply price elasticity with an elasticity of 2. Thus the tax-induced decline in the demand for housing lowers the price of housing, and this cushions the rise in the price of housing services. Owners benefit from the latter but lose from the decline in the asset value of their houses.

With the finite supply elasticity for housing, the total efficiency gain increases by a third.

The source of the increased efficiency gain is likely the assumed constancy of the price of the composite (nonhousing) commodity. The tax-induced change in relative prices raises the demand for the composite commodity at the expense of housing. As a result, the supply price of the composite commodity would be expected to rise, just as the supply price of housing falls. The importance of the constancy of the composite commodity price can be seen most clearly by considering renters. Their postreform nominal income is assumed to equal their original nominal income plus the lump-sum rebate financed by the tax on implicit rents of owners. With the price of housing declining, renters gain further in addition to the lump-sum transfer. Their loss owing to the rise in the price of other goods is ignored; the assumption of constant nominal income when the aggregate price level is falling is inappropriate.

In this analysis King accounts for a decline in the market value of houses on homeowners. Although he does not present results by tenure mode or income decile, this effect would obviously magnify the redistribution from higher-income homeowners to lower-income renters. However, a full accounting of the impact of the rise in the price of the composite good might more than offset this redistribution. An increase in the real price of nonhousing capital will raise wealth both directly and indirectly via the market value of equities, and this gain will be sharply skewed toward higher-income households.

Calculation of the Social Gain

In his most ambitious undertaking, King calculates some measures of the social value of the reform. These measures depend on changes in equivalent income (y_E) and the utility or disutility that society or the individuals in it derive from the particular pattern of changes that evolve. Equivalent income is defined analogously to the sum of original income plus the equivalent gain (see equation [1]), except that the average values of original prices, rather than the household-specific prices, are employed. Why King shifts to average prices is not entirely clear, but I expect that this shift has little impact on the calculated social gain because the gain depends on the change in equivalent income where original equivalent income is the level that, evaluated at original average prices, gives the same utility as individual households earned prior to the reform. More specifically, the social gain (SG) is calculated from

$$(4) \qquad \sum_{h=1}^{N} (y_{Eh}^0 + SG)^{1-\epsilon} = \sum_{h=1}^{N} (y_{Eh}^p \exp(-\eta d_h))^{1-\epsilon},$$

where the h subscript denotes individual households and ϵ, η, and d are "inequality" parameters. When $\epsilon = \eta = 0$, the social gain is simply the sum over all households of their changes in equivalent income. This gain ought to be the same as the efficiency gain of the earlier analysis.[1]

King views the efficiency gain as an inadequate measure of the social gain for two reasons. First, society is averse to inequality in income. Thus a reform that leads to a more equal distribution of income—such as the taxation of housing—provides a social gain beyond the efficiency gain. Second, households attach disutility to a drop in their ranking in the income distribution, even if their own income is unchanged. Moreover, this disutility is apparently greater than the utility gain of households who rise equally in the ranking. Thus any reform will cause a social loss to the extent that it alters the ranking of households in the income distribution.

I have some difficulty with King's treatment of each of these concepts. Insofar as society is averse to income inequality and there are no costs to removing it, income inequality will be eliminated. The fact that inequality exists suggests that it plays a useful role and that its removal would entail costs. Generally, it is felt that removal of income inequality would reduce incentives to work, and thus equity considerations are traded off against efficiency considerations. In this view, a reform that increases equality by definition worsens efficiency and, if the equity-efficiency trade-off is initially in balance, society will lose on net. King accounts for the equity gain but ignores the efficiency loss. While one can throw this loss into the category of "general equilibrium considerations to be dealt with later," it seems rather misleading to measure one effect and not another when one has reason to believe that the latter more than offsets the former.

There is substantial plausibility to the notion that a household's utility depends on its relative income (the Jones or Duesenberry effect). Further, increases in relative income seems unlikely to increase utility as much as decreases lower it. My difficulty here is that the indirect utility function underlying King's analysis does not incorporate any relative income effect; i.e. the microeconomic relation in the model is inconsistent with the macroeconomic social utility calculation.

An extremely simple way to include a relative income response would be to add $\log [\phi(R)]$ to King's equation (9), where R is the household's rank in the income distribution and $\partial \phi / \partial R > 0$. If the household housing demand function could be maintained, then the equivalent gain equation (11), which is $EG = y^p z - y^0$, where z depends on relative prices, would become

$$(5) \qquad EG = y^p z \frac{\phi(R^0)}{\phi(R^p)} - y^0 .$$

That is, the equivalent gain (and equivalent income) calculations would be altered (lowered in absolute value). The $\phi(R)$ function is related to

1. The average gain is 16.9p per week rather than 16.5p per week, the difference apparently being due to the use of average prices.

King's η, with $\phi(R) = 0$ when $\eta = 0$. Unfortunately, it is different to envision a ranking function that would not alter the form of the estimated housing demand function, and it would be especially difficult to model a function that captures the asymmetric impact of increases and decreases in household income ranking. But this is required to provide a micro-foundation for the social utility function.

5 Simulating Nonlinear Tax Rules and Nonstandard Behavior: An Application to the Tax Treatment of Charitable Contributions

Martin Feldstein and Lawrence B. Lindsey

The effect of existing tax rules on charitable contributions has been the subject of several econometric studies in recent years.[1] The present paper uses the results of those studies as the basis for examining the potential effects of alternative tax rules that might be applied in extending the charitable deduction to nonitemizers.[2] Our focus is on the effect that such changes in tax rules would have on charitable contributions, on tax liabilities, and on the distribution of these effects by income class.

Our methodological emphasis is on simulating behavioral responses to *nonlinear* tax rules, e.g. a rule that allows nonitemizers to deduct charitable gifts in excess of $300 per year. We examine three types of response to such nonlinear rules. The first is based on conventional demand analysis with a nonlinear budget constraint. The second recognizes that individuals have an incentive to respond to a floor by "bunching" their

Martin Feldstein is professor of economics, Harvard University (on leave). He was formerly president of the National Bureau of Economic Research and is currently chairman, Council of Economic Advisers.

Lawrence B. Lindsey is tax economist at the Council of Economic Advisers. He is on leave from Harvard University and the National Bureau of Economic Research.

The authors are grateful to the members of the Tax Simulation Project and especially to Daniel Feenberg and Daniel Frisch for helpful discussions, to the NBER and National Science Foundation for support of this research, and to Harvey Galper for valuable comments on the previous version. The views expressed here are the authors' and should not be attributed to any organization.

1. See Boskin and Feldstein (1977), Clotfelter (1980), Clotfelter and Steuerle (1979), Feldstein (1975a,b), Feldstein and Clotfelter (1976), Feldstein and Taylor (1976).

2. A variety of proposals to extend the charitable deduction have been made over the years, especially in conjunction with tax change proposals that would reduce the fraction of taxpayers itemizing their personal deductions. One recent proposal is contained in the bill introduced in the House of Representatives by Congressmen Fisher, Moynihan, and Packwood (S. 219, 96th Congress, 2d session). For a copy of the bill and further analysis, see "Hearings before the Subcommittee on Taxation and Debt Management generally and the Committee on Finance, United States Senate, January 30 and 31, 1980."

contributions over time, e.g. by contributing only in alternate years to reduce the fraction of total contributions that are below the floor and therefore that do not receive the tax benefit. The third approach departs from the usual utility maximization model of demand to consider a quite different type of altruistic behavior that may be appropriate for studying charitable contributions. The essential feature of this approach is that it assumes each individual wishes to make charitable gifts with some fixed net-of-tax cost; changes in tax rules alter the gross amount of giving to maintain this net cost.

All three approaches are generally consistent with the available statistical evidence. The behavior of taxpayers under existing rules does not allow a choice among the three models; in statistical terms, the model is underidentified. This underidentification does not affect predictions of the effects of alternative *linear* tax rules, e.g. substituting a credit for the existing deduction. Although the predicted effects of an alternative linear tax rule do not depend on which of the three models is assumed to be correct,[3] with *nonlinear* tax rules the three models can have very different implications. Predictions of the effects of nonlinear tax rules must therefore be regarded as conditional on the model specification, and any user of our analysis must "weight" these conditional predictions by his own subjective probabilities of the appropriateness of the model.

The simulations are all made with the National Bureau of Economic Research TAXSIM model. This computerized model, like the one used by the Treasury and the Joint Committee on Taxation, bases its calculations on the large stratified random sample of individual tax returns that are provided for this purpose by the Internal Revenue Service. But unlike these other models, the NBER TAXSIM model is specifically designed to take into account the response of taxpayer behavior to changes in tax rules.[4] The version of the model used in the present paper is based on the tax law for 1977 and uses a sample of 23,111 individual tax returns for that year.[5]

The first section of the paper summarizes the previous econometric evidence on charitable giving that forms the basis for the parameter values used in the current simulations. Section 5.2 describes the alternative tax rules and the three models of behavior that will be simulated. Some technical aspects of the simulation procedure, including the imputation of contributions to nonitemizers and the calculation of the effective cost of charitable gifts, are discussed in section 5.3. The simulation results are presented in sections 5.4 and 5.5. There is a brief concluding section.

3. The choice between the third model and the first two does have some effect on the estimated response to changes in tax rules, but the size of the effect is relatively small.

4. The economists who have participated in the development of the TAXSIM model are Daniel Feenberg, Martin Feldstein, Daniel Frisch, Larry Lindsey, and Harvey Rosen.

5. These 23,111 returns are a random 25% sample of the 1977 Treasury Tax Model Public Use Sample.

5.1 Econometric Evidence on Charitable Giving

Since this paper will not present any new econometric evidence on charitable giving, it is useful to review the previous research. The current tax law allows any taxpayer who itemizes his deductions to subtract the value of charitable contributions in calculating taxable income. The "price" of one dollar's contribution to a charitable organization in terms of the foregone disposable income of the donor therefore varies inversely with his marginal tax rate. Of course, for anyone who does not itemize his deductions, the price of one dollar's contribution is one dollar of foregone disposable income.[6]

The key parameter that determines the effect of the existing charitable deduction and of alternative linear tax rules is the price elasticity, i.e. the elasticity of the individual's gross (pretax) charitable gift with respect to the price of giving. The appropriate value is of course the *partial* elasticity, holding constant the level of income and such other demographic characteristics that might be associated with the price. Several studies in recent years, based on quite different bodies of data, have concluded that the price elasticity of giving is between -1.0 and -1.5. There is a striking degree of consistency and relative precision in these estimates even though they are based on different years and different types of data.

Feldstein (1975*a*,*b*) used the data published by the Internal Revenue Service on the mean level of charitable giving and the mean level of disposable income in each of twenty-seven adjusted gross income (AGI) classes for the alternate years between 1948 and 1968. These data refer only to individuals who itemized their deductions. A constant elasticity specification was estimated:

$$(1) \qquad \ln G_{it} = b_0 + b_1 \ln P_{it} + b_2 \ln Y_{it} + e_{it} ,$$

where G_{it} is the mean charitable gift of individuals in AGI class i in year t, P_{it} is the price calculated at the mean taxable income in that class, and Y_{it} is the mean disposable income in that class. The changing tax rates as well as the differences in the rates among classes were used to estimate the price elasticity. The basic estimate in this study, with the sample restricted to taxpayers whose AGIs were between \$4,000 and \$100,000 at 1967 prices, was -1.24 with a standard error of 0.10. Including all income classes in the sample raised the elasticity to -1.46 with a standard error of 0.08.

Feldstein and Clotfelter (1976) used individual household data collected by the Census Bureau in 1963 and 1964 for the Federal Reserve Board's Survey of Financial Characteristics of Consumers. Their sample of 1,406 individuals provided information on wealth and demographic

---

6. This ignores the special problem of gifts of appreciated property, a subject to which we return later.

characteristics as well as on income and charitable giving. The data made it possible to estimate for each household the price of charitable giving and a measure of disposable income defined as the total income received minus an estimate of the tax that would be due if no contribution were made. The basic price elasticity estimate in this study was − 1.15 (standard error 0.20). Several variants of the basic equation showed that the estimated price elasticity was not sensitive to the measurement of permanent income or the inclusion of a variety of other demographic and economic characteristics.

Feldstein and Taylor (1976) used a similar specification to study a sample of more than 15,000 taxpayers who itemized their deductions and whose tax returns were included in the 1970 Treasury Tax File, a stratified random sample of individual tax returns. The basic price elasticity estimate was − 1.29 (standard error 0.06). Repeating this calculation for the 1962 Treasury Tax File data showed a price elasticity of − 1.09 (standard error 0.03). A price elasticity estimate based on the change in the tax schedule between 1962 and 1970 was − 1.39 (standard error 0.19).

Similar estimates were obtained in several other studies using different sets of microeconomic data. Reece (1979) used the 1972–73 Consumer Expenditure Survey of the Bureau of Labor Statistics and estimated a price elasticity of − 1.19 using a Tobit procedure. Dye (1977) studied 1974 University of Michigan Survey Research Center data on households with incomes under $50,000 and estimated a price elasticity of − 2.25. Clotfelter and Steuerle (1979), using tax data for 1975, estimated a price elasticity of − 1.25. And Clotfelter (1980), using the unstratified random sample of tax returns for 1972, obtained a price elasticity of − 1.40.

These estimates refer to the entire population or to all taxpayers who itemized and not to any particular income class. The present analysis of the potential effect of extending the charitable deduction to those who do not currently itemize their deductions makes it particularly important to have an estimated price elasticity for middle and lower income households; more than 90% of 1977 nonitemizers had adjusted gross income of less than $20,000. Although separate estimates for each income class cannot be made as precisely as for the sample as a whole, the evidence generally indicates that the relevant elasticity for this group is as high as for the population as a whole.

The pooled data by year and income class (Feldstein 1975a,b) were analyzed in separate regressions for different income groups. For the sixty-four observations with mean real income (in 1967 dollars) between $4,000 and $10,000, the estimated price elasticity was − 1.80 (standard error 0.56). Among taxpayers with real incomes between $10,000 and $20,000, the corresponding estimate was − 1.04 (standard error 0.76, with twenty-seven observations).

Despite the small samples, these data had the advantage of tax schedules that varied over time. When attention is limited to a single cross section of individual data, it is more difficult to estimate separate equations in each income class. This is particularly true in the low and middle income classes, where there is a very high correlation between income and tax rates.[7] It is nevertheless possible to allow the estimated price elasticity to vary with income or marginal tax rate while estimating the other parameters from the entire sample.

The Feldstein and Clotfelter (1976) study found that the price elasticity was greatest for those with the highest "price of giving"; the estimated elasticity was − 1.82 (s.e. 0.64) for those with a price of giving in excess of 0.7 and then fell to − 1.26 (s.e. 0.42) for those with a price between 0.3 and 0.7 and to − 1.16 (s.e. 0.20) for those with a price below 0.3. The differences are not statistically significant but, if anything, provide evidence that the current nonitemizing population has a higher elasticity.

The Feldstein and Taylor (1976) study had a much larger sample and could therefore obtain estimates with smaller standard errors. The estimated price elasticities varied inversely with income, from − 2.26 (s.e. 0.42) for taxpayers with incomes below $10,000 and − 1.82 (s.e. 0.24) for taxpayers with incomes between $10,000 and $20,000 to − 1.17 (s.e. 0.09) for those with incomes between $50,000 and $100,000 and − 1.27 (s.e. 0.06) for those with incomes over $100,000. An analogous equation for 1962 is not reported. Estimates of separate price and income elasticities in each income class give implausible values for the lowest income class (those with AGI between $4,000 and $20,000): − 3.67 (s.e. 0.45) for 1962 and − 0.35 (s.e. 0.52) for 1970.

In a separate study designed to measure the price elasticity for the lower and middle income groups, Boskin and Feldstein (1977) used survey data collected in 1974 by the University of Michigan Survey Research Center on households with incomes below $30,000. Because these are survey data rather than tax return data, they contain information on contributions by nonitemizers as well as itemizers. This provides much more price variation at each income level. The Boskin-Feldstein analysis estimated a price elasticity of − 2.54 (s.e. 0.28) for this group. An additional analysis of these data showed that the difference between itemizers and nonitemizers could be explained completely by the price effect without recourse to a separate "itemization" effect.

Clotfelter and Steuerle (1979) estimated a variety of different specifications for separate income classes using the Treasury Tax Model for 1975. They found that the estimated results in the lower income class were quite

---

7. In higher income classes, there is much more variation in tax rates at each level of adjusted gross income as well as substantial income variation within tax brackets.

sensitive to the particular specification. The basic logarithmic equation implied price elasticities of -0.9 for incomes of $4,000 to $10,000 and -1.3 for incomes of $10,000 to $20,000. Estimating a single equation for all income classes but using a more general functional form implied lower price elasticities; the estimates ranged between -0.4 and -0.7. But constraining the coefficient to be the same for all income classes reverses this effect and implies price elasticities of -2.2 and -1.4. In our view, this sensitivity shows the difficulty of trying to infer separate elasticities for low and middle income groups.

Before turning to the simulations, it is useful to consider the plausibility of a price elasticity between 1 and 2 for a typical nonitemizing family. In 1977, families with adjusted gross incomes between $10,000 and $15,000 who itemized their deductions gave an average of $522. If such a family had a taxable income of $8,000, the price per dollar of giving would be approximately 80 cents. A price elasticity of -1.0 and a price of 0.80 imply that deductibility raises giving by 25%, i.e. by $104 from $418 to $522. Similarly, a price elasticity of -2.0 implies that deductibility raised giving by 56%, or by $188 from $334 to $522. Changes of this magnitude are not contrary to intuition or to any other evidence.

To be conservative, the estimates developed in this paper will generally be based on a price elasticity of -1.3. Some additional estimates using price elasticities of -0.7, -1.0, and -1.6 will also be presented.

5.2   Extending the Contribution Deduction to Nonitemizers

The basic proposal to be analyzed in this paper allows all taxpayers to deduct charitable contributions in the calculation of taxable income. More specifically, taxpayers who itemize other deductions would continue to include charitable contributions as part of their deductions. Taxpayers who do not itemize other deductions would be allowed to subtract their charitable contribution from gross income in the same way that they now subtract an amount for each exemption. In this way, there is no change in adjusted gross income or in any of the amounts that depend on it.

This basic scheme might be modified by limiting the charitable deduction of nonitemizers to the excess over some dollar amount or some percentage of the taxpayer's adjusted gross income. A rationale for such a "floor" is that the standard deduction implicitly recognizes some minimal or typical charitable gift so that individuals should get an explicit deduction only for the excess over that amount.[8] An alternative rationale

---

8. The logic of that argument is hardly compelling. If the charitable deduction is extended nonitemizers, it would be more appropriate to reduce the standard deduction by the currently assumed amount of the "typical" gift and then allow all individuals the full amount of their deduction.

for a floor is that it can reduce the loss of tax revenue and, to the extent that contributions exceed the floor amount, the reduction in revenue loss would have no impact on the marginal incentive to give. For example, in 1977 taxpayers with AGIs between $15,000 and $20,000 who did not itemize made charitable gifts averaging nearly $400. For someone giving an average amount, a $300 floor would have no effect at the margin on the incentive to give. The current paper analyzes two alternative floors: the first is $300, and the alternative is 3% of AGI.

5.2.1   The Conventional Demand Model

The effects of extending the charitable deduction to nonitemizers, and particularly the effects of the floors, depend on the type of individual behavior that is assumed. The most basic behavioral assumption, and the one that underlies the specification of the econometrically estimated equations, is that individual giving responds to a change in price according to the constant elasticity formula:

$$(2.1) \qquad G_1 = G_0(P_1/P_0)^\alpha \, ,$$

where G_1 is the level of annual giving after the "reform," G_0 is the level of annual giving before the reform,[9] P_0 is the price before the reform,[10] P_1 is the price after the reform, and α is the price elasticity of demand. There is no need to adjust separately for the change in disposable income since the estimated price elasticity includes the income effect as well as the substitution effect; i.e. the initial econometric equation defines the disposable income as AGI minus the tax that would be due if the individual made no charitable contribution.

More specifically, equation (2.2) describes what is essentially the response of nonitemizers (i.e. those who under existing law are nonitemizers) when they are allowed to deduct charitable gifts. For most itemizers, the proposal involves no change in behavior. However, about 6% of current itemizers would cease to itemize if they could then deduct their charitable contributions; i.e. their itemized deductions excluding charitable contributions are less than the standard deduction to which they would be entitled.[11] For most of these "switchers" there is no change in marginal tax rate and therefore no change in price. However, since an individual switches only if his tax bill is reduced, there is a small income

---

9. The method of imputing an initial level of giving for nonitemizers is discussed in section 5.3 of this paper.

10. For nonitemizers, P_0 differs from 1 only because of gifts of appreciated property. This difference is discussed in section 5.3. Although as a practical matter the difference from 1 for this group is small enough to ignore completely, our price calculations do reflect for each individual the average percentage of appreciated property in total contributions.

11. In 1977, the standard deduction was $3,200 for a married couple and $2,200 for a single individual.

effect. The giving of a switcher can be calculated according to the equation

(2.2) $$G_1 = G_0(P_1/P_0)^\alpha (Y_1/Y_0)^\beta \, ,$$

where Y_0 is the initial value of total income minus the tax liability if the individual makes no contribution and Y_1 is the corresponding value if the individual stops itemizing and uses the standard deduction.[12] The difference between Y_1 and Y_0 is the tax that the individual saves by switching from itemizing to using the standard deduction, given that the charitable contribution is deductible in any case.

Although the demand behavior implied by equation (2.1) is adequate for estimation and for simulating alternative linear budget constraints, it is inadequate for analyzing alternative nonlinear budget constraints. Figure 5.1 illustrates the nature of this problem in a simple case. The standard deductor initially faces a budget line UVW with a slope of -1 between giving (G) and other spending (C). He chooses point E_1. Allowing standard deductors to take an additional deduction for charitable gifts above a floor (F) puts a kink in the budget line which becomes UVX.

In the case shown in figure 1a, the individual was giving more than the floor even without the deduction. For such an individual, the deductibility with a floor is equivalent to an ordinary price change except for an offsetting negative income effect equal to mF, where m is the individual's marginal tax rate. This case could therefore be analyzed using the demand function of equation (2.2) with appropriate definitions of P_1 and Y_1.

In the case shown in figure 1b, the individual was giving less than the floor. The change in the budget constraint therefore occurs in an irrelevant section of the budget constraint and the individual continues to give at E_1. This could also be analyzed using the demand function, since the price is unchanged for this individual.

But the choice in figure 1c cannot be analyzed with the demand function. The individual initially gives an amount less than the floor F. But the individual's indifference curve cuts the new branch of the budget constraint, implying that the individual's optimum point is on the new branch. This can only be determined by an explicit utility comparison.

In order to be able to deal with situations like figure 1c, we therefore continue the analysis with the help of an explicit utility function that implies the constant elasticity demand structure of equation (2.2). We follow Hausman (1979) and write the indirect utility function of individual i as

(2.3) $$V_i(p,y) = -k_i \frac{p^{1+\alpha}}{1+\alpha} + \frac{y^{1-\beta}}{1-\beta} \, .$$

---

12. An income elasticity of 0.7 is used in the calculations; see Feldstein and Taylor (1976) for supporting evidence. Because the relevant income changes are always very small, the results are *very* insensitive to the choice of this elasticity.

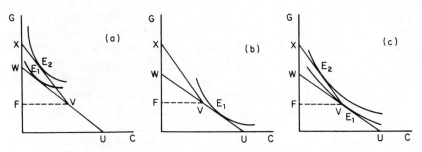

Fig. 5.1   Alternative response to deductibility above a floor.

This indirect utility function implies a demand function with constant price elasticity α and constant income elasticity β. Since existing law provides a linear budget constraint from small changes in giving,[13] we can use the price and income elasticities estimated in previous studies with equation (2.1) to parameterize this utility function. The value of k_i for individual i can then be calculated as the value which causes the demand for giving implied by equation (2.3) for individual i to equal the actual observed amount of giving.

With the help of such a parameterized indirect utility function for each individual, we proceed in the following way to calculate the value that each individual would give if nonitemizers could deduct gifts in excess of floor F. (To simplify the description of our procedure, we now ignore gifts of appreciated property and the possibility that giving causes the individual to change tax brackets.)[14]

First, if the initial giving of individual i (G_{0i}) exceeds the floor (F), we can use equation (2.3) to calculate the new level of giving by reducing the price of 1 to $1 - m_i$ (where m_i is the individual's marginal tax rate) and by lowering the individual's income by m_iF. We then use these values to calculate the new level of giving, G_{1i}. This corresponds to figure 1a.

If G_{0i} is less than the floor, we consider first the potential reaction if the individual faces the reduced price above the floor. If with this price (and the associated income correction) the implied giving is still less than the floor, we know we are in case 1b, in which giving is unchanged. If, however, the implied giving is greater than the floor, we are in case 1c and must choose between the possibilities by comparing the implied utilities. Conditional on the assumption that the individual will not change his giving (i.e. will remain at E_1 in figure 1c because the indifference curve tangent to the new section of the budget line is lower than the indifference

13. There is a nonlinearity for the few individuals whose giving causes them to switch brackets or to move from nonitemizer to itemizer. Ignoring the switch from nonitemizer to itemizer biases the estimated price elasticity toward 0.

14. The full computer program recognizes both of the possibilities. The method of dealing with property gifts is discussed in section 5.3. Changes in tax brackets are reflected by using the new marginal price and changing the initial level of income.

curve tangent at E_1), we evaluate the utility at the initial price ($p_i = 1$)[15] and unchanged income, say V_{0i}. Then, conditional on the assumption that the individual increases his giving (i.e. moves to point E_2 in figure 1c), we take p_i to be the itemized price ($P_i = 1 - m_i$, except for gifts of appreciated property) and reduce income by $m_i F$. This implies an increased value of giving G_{1i} and an associated utility value V_{1i}. The choice between the two points is then made by comparing V_{0i} and V_{1i} for the individual.

An analogous calculation is used to analyze the possibility that an individual who is currently an itemizer might switch to using the standard deduction if he could continue to itemize his charitable gifts. To decide whether to switch, the individual compares his utility level as an itemizer with the utility level that he would achieve as a nonitemizer who can deduct his charitable giving. In practice, about 6% of current itemizers would find that it is desirable to use the standard deductions when charitable gifts become eligible for a separate deduction.

5.2.2   The Bunching of Gifts

The use of a floor provides an incentive for individuals to "bunch" their charitable giving. With a $300 floor, a nonitemizer who gives $300 each year would get no tax reduction. By giving $600 every other year, the individual would also have a $300 tax deduction every other year, or a 50 cent deduction per dollar of contribution. And by giving $900 every third year, the deduction would rise to 67 cents per dollar of gift. Although the "logical" extreme is of course implausible because of the resulting effect on the individuals' marginal tax rates and because individuals and institutions both have reasons to favor a steady flow of giving, the presence of a floor seems very likely to lead to some bunching.

There is, unfortunately, no experience with charitable deduction floors that can be used to estimate their likely effect on bunching. We have, however, constructed two alternative simulation models and tested the parametric sensitivity of the results.

Both models assume that the extent of bunching depends on the potential tax saving from bunching and therefore on both the size of the contribution and the individual's marginal tax rate. In both models the possibility of bunching is limited to a two-year cycle. The first model assumes that each individual bunches either all of his contributions or none. That is, if he is a "buncher," he gives only in alternate years. The probability of being a buncher depends on the tax incentive. The second model assumes that everyone is a "partial buncher"; some fraction of his total giving is bunched (i.e. given only in alternate years) while the rest of

---

15. In the actual calculations, p_1 is lower than 1 because of gifts of appreciated property.

his contribution is given every year. We will now describe these models as they apply to someone who is currently a nonitemizer.[16]

The tax incentive to bunch is a function of the relative cost of giving with and without bunching. Let G_{1i} be the amount that individual i (a nonitemizing taxpayer) would give if charitable gifts in excess of a floor could be deducted.[17] Let CG_{1i} be the net cost to individual i of making this charitable gift in a single year, i.e. without bunching. CG_{1i} is equal to G_{1i} reduced by the tax saving associated with the contribution, i.e. the tax saving that results from deducting the excess of G_{1i} over the floor. Similarly, let BCG_{1i} be the net cost of making this charitable gift by bunching two years' gifts into a single year.[18] We assume that the propensity to bunch depends on the ratio of these net costs: BCG/CG.

More specifically, the first model assumes that the probability that individual i will bunch is given by

$$(2.4) \qquad \text{PROB}_i = 1 - (BCG_{1i}/CG_{1i})^\rho$$

with $\rho > 0$. Note that under current law, with no floor, there is no incentive to bunch:[19] $BCG = CG$ and PROB $= 0$. However, a floor on the charitable deductions implies $BCG < CG$ and therefore PROB > 0. The greater the value of ρ, the more sensitive the probability of bunching to the relative cost. To appreciate the order of magnitude of this effect, consider a taxpayer who would contribute \$400 without bunching ($G_{1i} = 400$) and whose marginal tax rate is 30%. With a \$300 floor, the cost of giving is \$370 with no bunching and \$325 with bunching. Thus PROB $= 1 - (325/370)^\rho = 1 - (0.88)^\rho$. *If* $\rho = 2$, PROB $= 0.23$, while $\rho = 0.5$ implies PROB $= 0.06$ and $\rho = 10$ implies PROB $= 0.73$. Since econometric evidence about ρ is unavailable, the simulations show the sensitivity of the conclusions to alternative values of ρ.

Of course, those individuals who bunch change the amount of their gift because of bunching. If without bunching the individual's gift is below the floor while bunching makes the gift (in the year in which it is given) greater than the floor, there is a reduction in the price of giving and therefore an incentive to give more. Among those whose gift would be

16. For itemizers, the possibility of switching is again evaluated by comparing the tax liability as an itemizer with the tax liability as a nonitemizer, but this time including the effect of bunching.

17. The calculation of G_{1i} was described in section 5.2.1.

18. This is calculated by finding the tax reduction associated with contributing $2G_{1i}$, i.e. the tax saving that results from deducting the excess of $2G_{1i}$ over the floor, and then subtracting *half* of this tax saving from G_{1i}.

19. This assumes that the individual cannot predict year-to-year changes in his marginal tax rate. In fact, there is some predictable variation and therefore some incentive to bunch. Although we believe this is likely to be small, some investigation with the longitudinal tax rule would be worthwhile.

above the floor without bunching, bunching has a positive income effect on the amount of the gift.

In general, a floor reduces the loss of tax revenue that results from extending the deduction to nonitemizers and also reduces the incentive to give associated with such an extension. Bunching increases the revenue loss but, even in the case of complete bunching, still leaves a smaller revenue loss than with no floor. However, even with bunching the incentive to give is not as great as without a floor. Whether the floor raises or lowers the tax-revenue "loss" per dollar of induced extra giving is an empirical question that we will examine in section 5.5 with the help of the simulations.

The alternative "partial bunching" model assumes that *all* taxpayers bunch *some* of their giving if there is a floor and that the extent of bunching depends on the cost ratio BCG/CG. The idea of partial bunching is based on the asymmetry of information between donors and donees. Much giving is done in response to requests for contributions and is done in such a way that the donee organization and others know the amount of the donor's gift. The individual who responds to a request for a contribution by saying "I give every other year and this is my off year" may not be credible. Individuals may also prefer to appear more generous, especially for relatively small amounts, by appearing to ignore tax considerations. And making a contribution may seem better than trying to explain the tax law to the sellers of Girl Scout cookies or Little League decals.

We assume that the specific incentive to partial bunching is of the same form as equation (2.4):

(2.5) $$\text{PROB}_i = 1 - (BCG_{1i}/CG_{1i})^\rho \ ,$$

where PROB_i is the proportion of the charitable gift that individual i bunches. The amounts of the gifts in the "low" and "high" giving years depend on the interaction between bunching, floors, and tax saving. For example, if $(1 - \text{PROB}_i)G_{1i}$ is greater than the floor, bunching does not change the price of giving in either year but does have an income effect that raises giving to (say) G_{2i}. In this case, the individual gives $(1 - \text{PROB}_i)G_{2i}$ in the low year and $(1 + \text{PROB}_i)G_{2i}$ in the high year. Alternatively, if G_{1i} is less than the floor but $(1 + \text{PROB}_i)G_{1i}$ exceeds the floor, there are both price and income effects in the "high" year but only an income effect in the "low" year. We assume that in the "high" year the individual in this case gives

$$(1 + \text{PROB}_i)G_{1i}(P_1/P_0)^\alpha(Y_1/Y_0)^\beta \ ,$$

where P_1 reflects the marginal deductibility and Y_1 differs from Y_0 because of the effects of the floor (which lowers Y_1) and the bunching (which raises Y_1). Although the income-effect adjustments are not precise, they are relatively small and further elaborations or refinements have no significant effects.[20]

There is one further aspect of the partial bunching model that deserves comment. In the case in which giving without bunching substantially exceeds the floor, the equation that describes partial bunching might still leave giving in both years at levels above the floor. Since in that case there is no gain from bunching, we assume that the proportion bunched is actually zero.

The difference between the effects of the two models of bunching depends on the taxpayer's initial situation. There are cases in which partial bunching would save no tax and have no effect on giving while total bunching would do both. There are other cases in which partial bunching would have a larger total effect on both giving and tax receipts. The net balance is examined in section 5.5 with the help of the simulations.

5.2.3   Net Altruism

Although charitable giving can be modeled like other types of consumer spending, it is worth considering the possibility that charitable behavior is actually "different." Individuals may make charitable gifts because of a sense of responsibility, religious devotion, altruism, guilt, or other considerations that *may* cause behavior to differ from traditional utility maximization. We emphasize *may* because, even with these motivations, actual charitable giving might behave just as traditional theory predicts. Certainly the normal price and income elasticities found in the econometric studies are consistent with this.

But individuals might think about charitable giving in terms of their desire to "sacrifice" or to contribute their "fair share" rather than in terms of the benefits that they can achieve for the donee organization. In this case the deductibility of charitable gifts has the effect of reducing the donor's "sacrifice" or "net contribution." To achieve the initial level of sacrifice, the donor must increase the size of his contribution. If the individual wishes to make a fixed sacrifice regardless of the tax law, full deductibility (with no floor) causes the individual to behave as if he had a price elasticity of -1; that is, $G_1 = G_0(P_1/P_0)^{-1}$ since this implies a constant net cost of giving, $P_1 G_1 = P_0 G_0$.

Although the econometric evidence suggests that the price elasticity is absolutely larger than 1, the possibility of a price elasticity of -1 cannot be ruled out. If the observed price elasticity were -1, the available evidence could not be used to distinguish between the traditional demand model and the alternative "net sacrifice" or "net altruism" model. With no floor, the two models are observationally equivalent.

20. See footnote 15.

The presence of a floor causes a substantial difference between the conventional demand model (with a price elasticity of -1) and the "net altruism" model. Consider an individual who, with no deductibility, contributes $400 and whose marginal tax rate is 30%. The net cost to such an individual is $400. Allowing deductibility with no floor causes the contribution to rise to $400(0.7)^{-7} = 571$ dollars. With a $300 floor, the conventional model predicts that giving will fall short of $571 only because of a small income effect; the extra tax of $90 caused by the floor would reduce giving by about $5. But the $300 floor implies that the "net altruist" must give substantially less than $571 to maintain the original $400 net cost. In particular, a total gift of $443 would have a net cost of $400.

The possibility that individuals decide on the basis of *total* net cost rather than *marginal* net cost implies that a floor does not reduce the loss in tax revenue per dollar of induced additional giving. In the example of the previous paragraph, deductibility with no floor would cause giving to rise by $171 and tax revenue to fall by $171 ($0.3 \times 571$). Deductibility with a $300 floor would cause giving to rise by $43 and tax revenue to fall by $43 ($0.3 \times 143$).

The implications of the "net altruism" model will be considered as part of the simulations in section 5.5.

5.3   Some Technical Aspects of the Simulation Procedure

As we noted in the introduction to this paper, our simulations use the NBER TAXSIM model with the 1977 tax law. Our sample of 23,111 returns is a one-in-four random sample from the Treasury's Public Use File of 1977 tax returns. In simulating the effect of any tax change proposal, we use the model to calculate consistent values for each individual of the price of giving under the new law, the amount that that individual gives, and the individual's new tax liability. The entire TAXSIM model with all features of the tax code are used in these calculations. By using the sampling weights provided by the Treasury, we can then aggregate the individual changes in giving and in tax liabilities to obtain estimates for all taxpayers and for taxpayers in each income class.

Two technical issues in the simulation deserve special attention: (1) the calculation of the price of giving, and (2) the estimation of the initial level of giving of nonitemizers.

5.3.1   The Price of Giving

The price of giving is defined as the net cost to the taxpayer of a marginal increase in the charitable contribution. In the simple case of full deductibility, there would be a difference between this "last-dollar price" and the price associated with the first dollar of giving only if the individual gives enough to change his marginal tax rate. For most taxpayers, and especially for those in the income classes that currently do not itemize, the level of giving is low enough that there would be little or no difference between the first- and last-dollar prices. When there is a difference, we use the last-dollar price and adjust the income term for the effect of the difference between the marginal and inframarginal prices.

The difference between the first-dollar price and the last-dollar price is particularly important when there is a floor. In all cases, the simulation algorithm uses a procedure that converges on the marginal price that is consistent with the predicted level of giving.

In calculating the price of giving it is not enough to use the marginal tax rate that the individual faces on additional earnings. There are two reasons for this. First, a one-dollar charitable gift and a one-dollar decrease in earnings can affect the individual's tax liability differently for a number of reasons. The charitable gift can interact with the maximum tax on earned income and the deduction limitation, while a change in earnings alters adjusted gross income and therefore the deductions and limits that depend on AGI. We avoid these problems by using the TAXSIM model to calculate explicitly the effect on the tax liability of a one-dollar charitable gift.[21]

The second problem is that individuals may contribute property as well as cash. When securities or other appreciated property is given to charity, the taxpayer deducts the market value of the assets and pays no tax on the capital gain.[22] To the extent that the taxpayer uses appreciated assets to make his gifts, this provision of the law reduces the cost of giving. Moreover, this aspect applies to nonitemizers as well as to itemizers.

There are three problems involved in reflecting gifts of appreciated property in the price variable: (1) What fraction of total giving takes the form of appreciated property? (2) What fraction of the value of the appreciated property is gain that would otherwise be taxed? (3) What is the relevant effective tax rate? We follow the procedure used in the earlier econometric studies from which the price elasticity was derived. We calculate each taxpayer's price as a weighted average of the price of cash gifts and the price (or cost) of gifts of appreciated property, using as weights the *average* fractions of both types of gifts in the taxpayer's AGI class.[23] If the taxpayer would otherwise have sold the contributed prop-

---

21. To reduce rounding error problems, we actually calculate the effect of a ten-dollar gift.

22. This is consistent with the general proposition that a gift of appreciated property does not constitute "recognition" of the gain and that the recipient of the property has the same basis as the donor. Since a charity is not taxed on its own capital gain, the carryover of the basis is irrelevant.

23. The fraction of total gifts that take the form of property rises from about 3.5% for taxpayers with AGIs below $15,000 to more than 70% for taxpayers with AGIs over $100,000.

erty immediately, the extra tax saving per dollar of gift associated with giving the property to charity is the product of the marginal tax rate on capital gains (mc) and the ratio of "gain" to value in the property that is contributed (g/v). Since the taxpayer also has the option of postponing the sale of the property or giving the property to another individual, the actual tax saving is less than $mc(g/v)$, say $\lambda \times mc \times (g/v)$. Although the capital gains tax rate (mc) can be calculated explicitly for each individual, neither λ nor g/v is directly observable. In the previous econometric work (Feldstein and Clotfelter 1976; Feldstein and Taylor 1976), a maximum likelihood procedure was used to estimate the product $\lambda(g/v)$ on the assumption that this was the same for all individuals. The maximum likelihood value of $\lambda(g/v) = 0.50$ is used in the current calculation. Of course, since our focus in this paper is on the low- and middle-income taxpayers who now do not itemize (or who would stop itemizing if a separate charitable deduction were allowed), gifts of appreciated property are relatively unimportant and any errors introduced by our approximation are likely to be very small.

5.3.2 The Giving of Nonitemizers

Although the tax returns indicate the contributions of all taxpayers who itemized their deductions, no information is available about the contribution of nonitemizers under existing law. An initial value of giving G_{0i} must be imputed to each nonitemizer before any of the calculations can begin. This imputation is done by matching each nonitemizer to an "equivalent" itemizer and then assigning to the nonitemizer the itemizer's gift scaled down to reflect the price difference and any difference in income.

More specifically, our imputation program read in parallel separate computer tapes for the nonitemizers and the itemizers. For each nonitemizer, the program looked at successive itemizers until a record was found with the same adjusted gross income class. The giving and the price of the itemizer, GI and PI, were then used to calculate a trial value of giving for the nonitemizer (GN) according to the formula

$$GN = GI(PI/PNI)^{-\alpha}(YI/YNI)^{-\beta}.$$

This in effect assigns to the nonitemizer the level of giving that the "matched" itemizer would have chosen if he had not been allowed to deduct this contribution, with a further correction for the difference between their disposable incomes.

Of course, some itemizers choose to itemize only because they make large charitable gifts; without their charitable deduction, they would pay less tax as nonitemizers. It would be wrong to include these individuals in the group of itemizers used to impute giving to nonitemizers since the imputed giving would be too high for a nonitemizer. We therefore deleted this group in the imputation process.

Despite this, our procedure can still impute to a nonitemizer a level of giving which is so high that, if he had made that contribution, he would have chosen to itemize. We therefore truncate the imputed giving by imposing the limit that the initial gift of a nonitemizer must not exceed the greater of the standard deduction reduced by 3% of AGI and $500.

5.4 The Basic Simulation Results

This section presents the simulation results based on the traditional demand model of charitable giving. The analysis compares the implications of alternative price elasticities and examines the effects of two different floors below which nonitemized gifts are not deductible.

All of the calculations refer to 1977. The proposed changes are regarded as modifications in the tax law as of 1977, and all dollar amounts are based on the sample of actual tax returns for 1977. The calculations are not forecasts of the short-run effects of a legislative change but simulations of what 1977 might have looked like if the tax rules relating to charitable gifts had "always" been different.[24]

Table 5.1 describes the situation as it actually was in 1977 under the existing tax rules.[25] Approximately 23 million itemizers contributed a total of nearly $19 billion. Since the tax returns contain no information about gifts by nonitemizers, their "actual" behavior in 1977 under existing tax rules must itself be estimated. This estimation procedure has already been described in section 5.3.2. The final four columns of table 5.1 present estimates corresponding to four different price elasticities. It is clear that since most nonitemizers have rather low marginal tax rates, the choice among the price elasticity assumptions has relatively little effect on the estimated total giving by nonitemizers. The range of estimates is from $17.5 billion to $19.7 billion.

Table 5.2 summarizes the aggregate effects of alternative ways of extending the charitable deduction to nonitemizers. These estimates include not only the response of those who were nonitemizers in 1977 but also the changes in taxes and in giving among itemizers who would switch to nonitemizer status if the tax rule were changed.

Consider, for example, the effect of full deductibility with a price

24. See Clotfelter (1980) on the difference between the long-run and the short-run responses to changes in tax rates. The response to a permanent change in tax rules might, however, be more rapid than the response to transitory changes in tax rates.

25. Although these figures do not correspond exactly to published IRS numbers because we have used a sample of returns, the large size of the sample guarantees that errors are very small.

Table 5.1   Actual and Imputed Charitable Contributions

| AGI Class (× 1,000) | Number of Returns (×1,000) | | Mean Charitable Gift | | | | |
| | Itemizers | Non-itemizers | Itemizers | Nonitemizers: α = | | | |
				−.7	−1.0	−1.3	−1.6
Less than $5,000	194	23,261	364	212	209	206	204
$5–$10	1,486	18,249	419	341	334	327	320
$10–$15	3,057	10,488	522	322	307	293	279
$15–$20	4,671	7,247	509	415	391	368	346
$20–$25	4,772	3,017	568	366	336	308	282
$25–$30	3,209	1,191	679	495	416	352	298
$30–$50	4,193	571	917	624	552	485	423
Over $50	1,336	83	4,029	600	550	497	447
All returns	22,916	64,108	819	307	295	283	273
Total ($ billion)	…	…	18,775	19,656	18,881	18,156	17,486

Note: Contributions of itemizers are the actual mean contributions of individuals who itemized their returns in 1977. Contributions of nonitemizers are imputed using the method described in section 5.3 of the text.

Table 5.2   Aggregate Effects of Extending the Deductibility of Charitable Contributions

Proposal	Increase in Giving: α =				Reduction in Tax Revenue: α =				Budgetary Efficiency: α =			
	−.7	−1.0	−1.3	−1.6	−.7	−1.0	−1.3	−1.6	−.7	−1.0	−1.3	−1.6
Full deductibility	2.529	3.506	4.506	5.450	3.991	4.042	4.101	4.160	.63	.87	1.10	1.31
Floor, $300	2.078	2.879	3.608	4.302	2.314	2.368	2.430	2.484	.90	1.22	1.48	1.73
Floor, 3% of AGI	1.729	2.409	3.039	3.610	1.835	1.886	1.943	2.003	.94	1.28	1.56	1.80

Notes: All amounts are in billions of 1977 dollars. These calculations assume conventional demand behavior with no bunching, as described in section 5.7 of the text.

elasticity of -1.0. The simulations imply that this would increase giving by \$3.5 billion and would reduce tax revenue by \$4.0 billion. For the nonitemizers alone, the price elasticity of 1.0 implies that the revenue loss would exactly equal the increase in giving. The excess of the revenue loss over the increased giving reflects the fact that previous itemizers who switch save substantially more in taxes than the increase, if any, in their giving. The "budgetary efficiency" estimate of 0.87 is the ratio of increased giving to reduced taxes implied by extending full deductibility to nonitemizers if the price elasticity is 1.

A more realistic price elasticity, of 1.3, implies a 29% higher level of increased giving but only 2% greater revenue loss. The budgetary efficiency value rises to 1.10, implying that charities receive an additional \$1.10 for each extra dollar of revenue foregone by the Treasury.

Limiting the deduction of gifts by nonitemizers to the excess over \$300 reduces both the revenue loss and the increased giving. With all these elasticities, the increase in giving is reduced by much less than the fall in revenue. With an elasticity of -1.3, for example, the \$300 floor reduces additional giving by \$900 million (from \$4.506 billion to \$3.608 billion) but reduces the tax loss by nearly twice as much (from \$4.101 billion to \$2.430 billion, a decline of \$1.7 billion).

A floor equal to 3% of AGI instead of a flat \$300 has quite similar aggregate effects. With a price elasticity of -1.3, giving falls \$1.5 billion (from \$4.506 billion to \$3.039 billion) while the tax loss is reduced by more than \$2.1 billion (from \$4.101 to \$1.943). Note that increasing the floor from \$300 to 3% of AGI actually reduces giving by more than the saving in taxes; total giving falls an additional \$569 million while the tax loss is cut by only \$487 million. The primary reason for this is that the effect of the percent-of-AGI floor is concentrated more on those taxpayers with high marginal tax rates for whom the relative reductions are large.

Table 5.3 shows the changes in mean giving and tax liabilities in each AGI class and, for reference, the initial levels of giving and tax liabilities. These figures combine itemizers and nonitemizers. All of the calculations are based on a price elasticity of -1.3.

Consider, for example, taxpayers in the \$10,000 to \$15,000 AGI class. Of the 13.5 million taxpayers in this group, 10.5 million were nonitemizers in 1977. Extending full deductibility of charitable gifts to all taxpayers would cause giving to increase by an average of \$74 and taxes to fall by an average of \$63. A \$300 floor would reduce this increase in giving by \$20 but would lower the fall in taxes by \$30. Raising the floor from \$300 to 3% of AGI would reduce giving by an average of \$5 and would save an average of \$4 in taxes.

Note that full deductibility has its maximum effect on the giving and taxes per return at the income levels between \$15,000 and \$20,000. Below

Table 5.3 Distribution of Changes in Mean Contributors and Tax Liabilities by Income Class

| AGI Class (× 1,000) | Number of Returns (× 1,000) | Initial Levels | | Increases in Giving and Reductions in Taxes | | | | | |
| | | | | Full Deductibility | | $300 Floor | | 3% AGI Floor | |
		Giving	Taxes	Giving	Taxes	Giving	Taxes	Giving	Taxes
Less than $5	23,455	208	11	5	5	5	3	4	4
$5–$10	19,735	334	437	61	54	46	32	52	35
$10–$15	13,545	344	1,206	74	63	54	33	49	29
$15–$20	11,918	423	2,078	93	84	80	52	65	38
$20–$25	7,789	467	3,026	61	59	49	32	29	18
$25–$30	4,399	591	4,274	61	57	50	34	26	16
$30–$50	4,763	865	6,879	50	50	46	35	24	15
Over $50	1,419	3,818	29,130	75	70	72	60	40	20
All returns	87,024	424	1,913	52	47	41	28	35	22
Total ($ billion)	87,024	36.931	166.456	4.506	4.101	3.608	2.430	3.039	1.943

Note: All calculations are based on a price elasticity of −1.3 and refer to all taxpayers, including both current itemizers and nonitemizers.

$10,000 the relatively low marginal tax rates provide less incentive while above $20,000 the majority of taxpayers already itemize their deductions.

Imposition of a $300 floor would have virtually no effect on giving by taxpayers with AGIs over $25,000 since most such taxpayers would give more than $300 if deductibility were allowed. The absolute effect of the $300 floor on the mean level of giving is also greatest among taxpayers with incomes between $10,000 and $20,000. By contrast, a floor equal to 3% of AGI has a very substantial effect on the gifts and taxes of relatively high income taxpayers. A 3% floor virtually eliminates any tax saving for those with incomes over $25,000. Although total giving is lower with a 3% of AGI floor than with a $300 floor, giving by the large number of taxpayers with incomes under $10,000 is slightly higher.

Although table 5.2 suggests that a floor would be an "efficient" way of modifying the extension of the charitable deduction to all taxpayers (in the sense that it would save substantially more tax revenue than it would reduce charitable giving), table 5.3 indicates that a floor would also significantly change the distribution among income classes of both the increased giving and the reduced tax liability. Similarly, table 5.3 makes it clear that the choice between a $300 floor and a 3% of AGI floor involves not only aggregate efficiency considerations but also the income class distribution of the changes in giving and in tax liabilities. Of course, differences in the income class distribution of giving have significant effects on the types of charities that benefit.

5.5   Simulating Nonstandard Behavior

All of the calculations in section 5.4 were based on the conventional static utility maximization model of consumer demand for charitable giving. The more dynamic assumption that taxpayers respond to a floor by bunching contributions over time will be examined in the current section. The more radical departure from conventional utility maximization, the net altruism model of charitable giving, will also be considered.

5.5.1   Bunching

Any floor on the charitable deduction would provide taxpayers with an incentive to "bunch" their charitable contributions, giving a high level of contributions in some years and a low level in others. Because the existing law does not contain such a floor, we have no evidence about the likely extent of bunching. This section therefore presents simulation results for a rather broad range of two-year bunching assumptions. The restriction to a two-year cycle is significant and should be borne in mind in considering the results. All of the simulations refer to a price elasticity of -1.3.

When a taxpayer responds to a floor by bunching his contributions, he reduces the amount of his giving that is not deductible and thereby increases the tax saving associated with any level of giving. Moreover, to the extent that annual unbunched giving would be less than the floor while bunched giving exceeds the floor, the process of bunching also reduces the marginal price of giving and thus encourages increased giving. These two effects apply to both the "total bunching" and "partial bunching" models described in section 5.2.

Recall that, with the total bunching model, the probability that individual i will bunch is given by

$$(5.1) \qquad \text{PROB}i = 1 - (BCG_{1i}/CG_{1i})^\rho \ ,$$

where CG_{1i} is the net cost to taxpayer i of giving the amount that he would choose to give in the presence of a floor if he does not bunch and BCG_{1i} is the net cost of giving that amount with bunching. Table 5.4 presents simulation results with four different values of the bunching sensitivity variable.

The striking feature of the results in this table is that bunching appears to have only a very modest effect on both tax revenue and giving. For example, a $300 floor with no bunching reduces giving by $898 million, from $4.506 billion to $3.608 billion. With the bunching described by the moderate sensitivity value of $\rho = 2$, the decline in giving is reduced from $898 million to $861 million. Even with the high sensitivity value of $\rho = 10$, giving is still reduced by $743 million. Indeed, even the limiting case in which everyone who can benefit from bunching does bunch still leaves the extra giving $427 million lower than without a floor.

The effect of bunching on tax revenue is limited in a similar way. Without bunching, the $300 floor reduces the revenue loss by $1.671 billion, from $4.101 billion to $2.430 billion. Even with the high sensitivity value of $\rho = 10$, the $1.671 billion revenue effect on the floor is reduced by only $175 million. This very small effect of bunching on the revenue loss reflects the distribution of gifts by nonitemizers, particularly the large number of relatively small gifts, for which the floor would eliminate all or nearly all deductibility. An individual who gave less than $150 a year without bunching would get no deduction even if she bunched completely. And a taxpayer who gave $400 every other year instead of $200 each year still would get a deduction for only one-fourth of her total giving.

Table 5.5 presents results for the partial bunching model, in which all taxpayers who can benefit from bunching do bunch at least part of their gift. The results are similar to the probabilistic total bunching model of table 5.4 but indicate even smaller effects on giving and tax revenue.[26]

---

26. The figures for full and partial bunching with $\rho = \infty$ would be exactly equal if there were no gifts of appreciated property. The small difference in our calculations reflects differences in the assumed realization of capital gains.

Table 5.4   **The Effect of Bunching on Aggregate Contribution and Tax Liabilities**

Proposal	No Bunching, Changes in		Bunching Sensitivity									
			$\rho = .5$, Changes in		$\rho = 2.0$, Changes in		$\rho = 10.0$, Changes in		$\rho = \infty$, Changes in	
	Giving	Taxes	Giving	Taxes	Giving	Taxes	Giving	Taxes	Giving	Taxes
Full deductibility	4.506	4.101			(NOT RELEVANT)					
$300 floor	3.608	2.430	3.617	2.442	3.645	2.447	3.763	2.605	4.079	2.818
3% of AGI floor	3.039	1.944	3.051	1.955	3.089	1.988	3.246	2.112	3.686	2.347

Note: Changes in giving and taxes are stated in billions of 1977 dollars. See text for definition of bunching sensitivity.

Table 5.5   **The Partial Bunching Model**

| | | | Bunching Sensitivity | | | | | | | |
| | No Bunching, Changes in | | $\rho = .5$, Changes in | | $\rho = 2.0$, Changes in | | $\rho = 10.0$, Changes in | | $\rho = \infty$, Changes in | |
Proposal	Giving	Taxes	Giving	Taxes	Giving	Taxes	Giving	Taxes	Giving	Taxes
					(NOT RELEVANT)					
Full deductibility	4.506	4.101								
$300 floor	3.608	2.430	3.615	2.431	3.616	2.432	3.730	2.498	4.093	2.825
3% of AGI floor	3.039	1.944	3.044	1.945	3.045	1.946	3.164	2.008	3.697	2.354

Note: Changes in giving and taxes are stated in billions of 1977 dollars. See text for definition of bunching sensitivity.

Since there is no experience with floors on which to base empirical estimates of the taxpayers' likely response, it is reassuring that the results of this section are not sensitive to a wide variation in assumptions about the possible extent of bunching. It should, however, be borne in mind that only two-year bunching was considered and that if taxpayers bunched over a longer period the effects would be more substantial.

5.5.2 Net Altruism

The "net altruism" model of charitable giving described in section 5.2.3 implies that individuals choose the amount to contribute to charity to achieve a desired net cost to themselves. Individual differences in the desired net cost reflect differences in income and taste. Alternative tax rules affect charitable giving by altering the amount that individuals can contribute per dollar of net cost. Any loss in tax revenue is matched by an equal increase in charitable giving.

In the simple context of extending the charitable deduction without any floor, net altruism is equivalent to a price elasticity of -1 for the nonitemizers themselves. However, net altruism implies that the taxpayers who switched from itemizing to using the standard deduction will add the resulting tax saving to their charitable gifts. Moreover, where giving causes a reduction in marginal tax rates, the net altruist contributes all of the inframarginal tax saving while traditional demand behavior implies that inframarginal saving has only a small income effect. The difference between the conventional demand model with unitary price elasticity and the net altruism model is shown in the first row of table 5.6.

The contrast between conventional demand and net altruism is much greater where there are floors. Table 5.6 shows that the conventional demand model with a unitary price elasticity implies that a $300 floor causes giving to fall by $600 million and increases tax revenue $1.7 billion. With net altruism, the reduced deductibility has a much greater effect on giving. Giving falls by $1.9 billion, and the tax revenue rises by an equal amount. The results are similar if the floor is stated as a percent of AGI.

If the net altruism model reflects reality, extending the deduction with a floor does not have greater budgetary efficiency than full deductibility. Introducing the floor in itself no longer increases tax revenue by more than it reduces giving. With net altruism, the principal reason for having a floor is to reduce the scale and cost of extending deductibility. The floor would of course also affect the income class distribution of the induced changes in giving and tax payments and therefore the mix of donees that benefit.

The choice between the net altruism model and the conventional demand model cannot be settled decisively with the available evidence. To the extent that the estimated price elasticity is significantly different from -1, the data do support a conventional demand analysis. But it is

Table 5.6   **The Effect of Net Altruism Behavior on Aggregate Contributions and Tax Liabilities**

Proposal	Conventional Demand with $\alpha = -1$			Net Altruism		
	Changes in		Budgetary Efficiency	Changes in		Budgetary Efficiency
	Giving	Taxes		Giving	Taxes	
Full deductibility	3.506	4.042	.867	3.871	3.951	.979
$300 floor	2.879	2.368	1.216	1.963	2.008	.978
3% of AGI floor	2.409	1.886	1.277	1.543	1.573	.980

Note: Changes in giving and taxes are stated in billions of 1977 dollars. See text for definition of bunching sensitivity.

quite possible that some individuals behave according to net altruism principles while the behavior of others is best described by a conventional demand analysis. If so, the observed price elasticity is a misleading guide to what would happen if deductibility with a floor were extended. The results would then be some mix between the net altruism behavior of table 5.6 and the conventional demand response with a price elasticity between -1.3 and -1.6.

5.6 Concluding Remarks

The primary purpose of the present paper is methodological: to examine how tax simulation could be extended to incorporate nonlinear budget constraints and nonstandard economic behavior. We have shown how econometric estimates derived under existing tax rules can be extended to deal with this wider range of simulations. On those issues for which existing evidence is not informative we have presented simulations that indicate the sensitivity of the conclusion to the unknown aspects of behavior.

The specific simulations indicate that the econometric evidence on charitable giving implies that extending the charitable deduction to nonitemizers would raise individual giving by about 12% of the existing total amount, or $4.5 billion at 1977 levels. The extension would reduce tax revenue by slightly less, about $4.1 billion. A floor of $300 or 3% of AGI would reduce the revenue loss by 30 to 40%, even if there were significant bunching. The effect of the floor on increased giving depends critically on whether taxpayers' behavior is guided by conventional demand principles or by the net altruism rule. A reasonable conclusion is that a floor would reduce giving by less than the increased revenue but that the difference between them would not be very large.

In conclusion, it should perhaps be stressed that the appropriate tax treatment of charitable contributions depends on much more than the effects of alternative tax rules on the magnitude and distribution of contributions and taxes. Andrews (1972), for example, has argued that a correct definition of net income requires deducting charitable gifts while Surrey (1973) has argued the opposite. Feldstein (1980) has emphasized that a tax subsidy of individual giving may be preferable to government spending for the same purpose even when a dollar of tax revenue loss induces less than a dollar of additional giving, if individual giving is influenced by the level of government spending on the particular activity. Still others have emphasized the administrative and compliance problems associated with extending the deduction to low income taxpayers, who are rarely audited. All these considerations are important but lie beyond the scope of the current paper.

References

Andrews, W. D. 1972. Personal deductions in an ideal income tax. *Harvard Law Review* 86 (December): 309–85.

Boskin, M. J., and M. Feldstein. 1977. Effects of the charitable deduction on contributions by low-income and middle-income households: Evidence from a national survey of philanthropy. *Review of Economics and Statistics* 59 (August): 351–54.

Clotfelter, C. T. 1980. Tax incentives and charitable giving: Evidence from a panel of taxpayers. *Journal of Public Economics* 13: 319–40.

Clotfelter, C. T., and C. E. Steuerle. 1979. The effect of the federal income tax on charitable giving. Mimeo, Duke University and Office of Tax Analysis, United States.

Dye, R. F. 1977. Personal charitable contributions: Tax effects and other motives. In *Proceedings of the National Tax Association*, pp. 311–18. Columbus Ohio: National Tax Association–Tax Institute of America.

Feldstein, M. 1975a. The income tax and charitable contributions. Part 1. Aggregate and distributional effects. *National Tax Journal* 28: 81–100.

———. 1975b. The income tax and charitable contributions. Part 2. The impact on religious, educational, and other organizations. *National Tax Journal* 28: 209–26.

———. 1980. A contribution to the theory of tax expenditures: The case of charitable giving. In H. Aaron and M. Boskin, eds., *Essays in honor of Joseph Pechman*. Washington: Brookings Institution.

Feldstein, M. and C. Clotfelter. 1976. Tax incentives and charitable contributions in the United States. *Journal of Public Economics* 5: 1–26.

Feldstein, M. and A. Taylor. 1976. The income tax and charitable contributions. *Econometrica* 44: 1201–22.

Hausman, J. A. 1979. Exact consumer's surplus. Massachusetts Institute of Technology. Mimeo.

Reece, W. S. 1979. Charitable contributions: New evidence on household behavior. *American Economic Review* 69: 142–51.

Surrey, S. S. 1973. *Pathways to tax reform*. Cambridge: Harvard University Press.

Comment   Harvey Galper

My general overall evaluation of the Feldstein-Lindsey paper (hereafter F-L) is that it is an ideal illustration of how tax simulation work should

Harvey Galper at the time of this writing was director, Office of Tax Analysis, United States Treasury. He is currently a senior fellow at the Brookings Institution.

proceed methodologically. Modeling behavioral responses to tax changes is not an easy undertaking. The data base one has to deal with may be incomplete in several respects; the particular tax changes which one may want to simulate may not be easily translatable to price and income effects, which economists are accustomed to dealing with; and the empirical literature may not always provide guidance on which price and income elasticities to apply. Yet, as this paper demonstrates, through imaginative solutions simulation results can be provided on various effects of proposed changes in tax law.

I do, however, have some comments to make on this paper, starting with the review of the empirical literature. There has accumulated over the last five years a significant literature on the responsiveness of charitable contributions to the tax price, much of this literature resulting from efforts of one of the current authors. The tax price is defined essentially as 1 minus the marginal tax rate of the donor, although some modifications for appreciated property may also be required. From a review of the literature F-L conclude that the elasticity of giving with respect to the tax price is quite high—on the order of 1.3 in absolute terms—and that this same elasticity can be used to describe the tax behavior of nonitemizers. This is a very key assumption in the analysis in this paper, even though simulations with lower elasticities are also examined to some degree.

I find it quite difficult to accept as the general case an elasticity as high as 1.3 for nonitemizers. On a priori grounds, there are reasons why nonitemizers may be expected to exhibit less sensitivity to tax prices for charitable contributions. In fact, one reason why taxpayers may even take the standard deduction is that they are less sensitive to tax prices.

In the end, of course, the question is an empirical one. And while the literature has demonstrated clearly that individuals with higher marginal tax rates are highly sensitive to the price of giving, the case in my view has not been made for lower-income nonitemizers. In an excellent article that reviews this literature and provides evidence of their own empirical work, Clotfelter and Steuerle conclude that "estimates of the price elasticity tend to vary by income class and are sensitive to the specification of the regression model. The estimates from the *most reasonable cross-sectional specifications* range from −0.4 to −0.9 for low income taxpayers to −1.7 to −1.8 for high income taxpayers."[1]

Other researchers have also found a significant relation between higher absolute elasticity and higher income.[2] It is true that various specifications

1. C. T. Clotfelter and C. E. Steuerle, "Charitable Contributions," in H. J. Aaron and J. A. Pechman, eds., *How Taxes Affect Economic Behavior* (Washington: Brookings Institution, 1981), emphasis added.

2. See, for example, M. Feldstein, "The Income Tax and Charitable Contributions," part 1, "Aggregate and Distributional Effects," *National Tax Journal*, vol. 28 (March 1975); M. Feldstein and A. Taylor, "The Income Tax and Charitable Contributions," *Economet-*

do cause the results to bounce around. But I would interpret the weight of evidence as indicating more modest price elasticities for lower-income taxpayers. Adding a possible lower tax consciousness for nonitemizers, I would conclude that an elasticity of about − 0.7 would be more characteristic of lower-income nonitemizers.

As an aside, it should be noted that the econometric problems with respect to estimating the response of behavior such as charitable giving to tax prices have not been fully resolved. To a degree, the problem of simultaneity between giving and tax price is handled by taking as the measure of tax price the first-dollar price, that is, the price if there were no charitable contributions made at all, rather than the last-dollar price, or the price from the last dollar of contributions made. Indeed, the empirical literature on this subject invoked by F-L in defending the − 1.3 elasticity assumption generally uses the first-dollar price or some variant of it. One obvious problem is that for the actual simulations in this paper, the price elasticity is assumed to be that appropriate for the last-dollar price rather than the first-dollar price. The question here is, Are there any reasons to expect elasticity with respect to the last-dollar price, assuming it can be accurately estimated, to be significantly different from that found from reviewing the literature on the first-dollar price?

Another much more general question is whether the decision to make a charitable contribution can be legitimately examined under the assumption that all other itemized deductions are given. In other words, itemization may be a much more complex simultaneous process than can be modeled by treating each deduction separately. There are obvious statistical problems in attempting to estimate several possible itemized deductions simultaneously all subject to a schedule of rising marginal tax rates. However, there are instances in this paper where implicitly or explicitly this simultaneity issue is raised. For example, some of the elasticity findings from the empirical literature reported in the paper are based on the assumption that itemizers will *continue to itemize* even if, in the absence of charitable giving, they find it advantageous to use the standard deduction. The implicit assumption must be that other deductions can be taken to offset the possible decline in contributions. If this is so, then itemized deductions are indeed interrelated and cannot be examined independently.

Also, the discussion of bunching by F-L implies that a legitimate response to a proposal that allows a deduction only for charitable contributions in excess of a floor amount is to concentrate deductions in particular years, that is, to try to exceed the floor in those years even if this is not possible in every year. However, why cannot this be done for all

rica vol. 44 (November 1976); E. M. Sunley, "Federal and State Tax Policies," in D. W. Breneman and C. E. Finn, Jr., eds., *Public Policy and Private Higher Education* (Washington: Brookings Institution, 1978).

itemized deductions together in order to exceed the standard deduction in some years? That is, a taxpayer could conceivably alter the timing of payment of interest, taxes, and medical bills in addition to charitable contributions. If a taxpayer has such flexibility, there is again the possibility of an interdependence of deductions. Clotfelter especially has emphasized that the interaction between a *particular* itemized deduction and the *decision* to itemize can bias the estimates of elasticities in particular samples.[3]

These comments are offered only in the spirit of encouraging additional work in this area. With our current state of knowledge, there is probably little more that can be done in the way of incorporating such effects into existing tax simulation models.

In the analysis of extending the contribution deduction to nonitemizers, I found very appealing the use of a utility function approach to analyze consumer choices under nonlinear budget constraints. However, I must confess to some disenchantment with the "net altruism" notion. According to this notion, individuals want to make a fixed net, that is, after-tax, contribution to charities regardless of the tax price. It is certainly true algebraically that such an approach is indistinguishable from an elasticity of − 1 in a traditional demand analysis. However, unlike a traditional demand analysis, the net altruism notion implies that the donor derives no utility whatsoever from the funds received, and disbursed, by the philanthropic organization—whether for health research, education, or the cultural enrichment of the community. Only the amount of individual sacrifice is of concern to the donor. Such altruism seems of a strange sort indeed.

The treatment of bunching is an intriguing way of dealing with an unobservable possibility—the concentration of gifts in particular years in response to allowing charitable deductions only in excess of a floor amount. In fact, this is illustrative of the ingenuity required to use and run simulation models in general. Very often, the particular tax proposals to be analyzed do not lend themselves to strictly linear price and income rules. The tax law abounds in floors, phaseout ranges, and complex interactions which not only make the calculation of the tax price itself very difficult but also cause taxpayers to engage in maximizing behavior that may involve intertemporal shifts of income or deductions. The approach must be the one that is followed here: allow a range of possible taxpayer responses and examine the sensitivity of the results.

Before simulations of the effects of allowing nonitemizers to deduct charitable contributions can be performed, it is necessary first to impute current charitable contributions to nonitemizers. I have some reserva-

---

3. C. T. Clotfelter, "Tax Incentives and Charitable Giving: Evidence from a Panel of Taxpayers," *Journal of Public Economics*, vol. 13, no. 3 (June 1980).

tions about the imputation procedure used in the NBER model. One indication of my concern is that the total volume of giving by nonitemizers—on the order of $18.5 billion—seems very high. Total contributions of itemizers and nonitemizers amounted to about $37 billion in 1977 under the F-L imputation procedures. This amount is about one-quarter higher than the most recent estimate for 1977 ($29.3 billion) set forth in *Giving USA*, a publication that reports on trends in American philanthropy.[4] This would result in a ratio of total giving to personal income of 2.4%, 20% greater than the previous peak of 2.0%, reached in 1970. Treasury imputations for 1977 of the giving of nonitemizers are $12.3 billion, about two-thirds of the F-L result. This yields a total contribution figure of $30 billion, quite close to the *Giving USA* estimate.

Since the NBER imputation procedure reflects the assumption that the only difference between nonitemizers and itemizers is that the two groups face different tax prices and incomes, this assumption itself may require reexamination. The imputation procedures in the Treasury model take a somewhat different approach. The Treasury model makes imputations for all itemized deductions simultaneously, subject to the constraint that the sum of all such imputed deductions cannot exceed the zero bracket amount (the standard deduction).

F-L recognizes that imputations cannot be so high as to cause taxpayers to itemize, and they try to control for this in their imputation procedures in two ways. First, nonitemizers are only compared with those itemizers who would continue to itemize even if they made no charitable contributions. That is, those who itemize only because of large charitable contributions are excluded from the reference group. Second, the model truncates imputed giving to reduce the possibility of excessively high imputations. These procedures, however, are not particularly constraining. The first restriction eliminates just the greatest outliers among the itemizers, and the truncation procedure has even less effect. For example, a joint return with AGI of $50,000 is still allowed a maximum imputed gift of $1,700, almost twice the average giving of itemizers in the $30,000 to $50,000 income class. For lower-income taxpayers, the truncation is even less stringent. I would therefore encourage some experimentation with a simultaneous imputation procedure in which all itemizable expenses are imputed to nonitemizers but under the constraint that their sum cannot exceed the standard deduction. (One by-product of this approach is that other itemizable expenses can also be examined to determine their sensitivity to tax prices.)

A few comments on the simulations themselves may be in order. First, since, except for the net altruism variant, floors on deductible contribu-

4. American Association of Fund Raising Journal, *Giving USA*, 25th Annual Issue, New York, 1980, p. 11.

tions serve to reduce the revenue loss considerably without greatly affecting giving, a case could be made for adding a floor to current law—perhaps using the revenue gain for general rate cuts. If the simulations presented are reasonably accurate, the revenue gain is likely to be much greater than the cutback in giving. The results of such a simulation would be quite interesting.

Second, it is now possible to estimate not only the long-run effect of these changes in tax rules, as presented in the F-L paper, but also the short-run effects on a year-to-year basis by applying the work of Clotfelter.[5] Clotfelter finds considerable lags in adjusting to desired long-run behavior and estimates a six-year time period for 90% of the long-run solution to be realized. Furthermore, in the case of allowing nonitemizers to deduct charitable contributions, the lags may be somewhat longer since Clotfelter also finds that new itemizers display less sensitivity to price changes than former itemizers.

As a final comment, a point made by Kenneth Arrow in discussing the use of microeconomic simulation models for public policy analysis is worth emphasizing here. Arrow was critical of the excessive preoccupation with budgetary costs in simulation models to the exclusion of the economist's main concerns—equity and efficiency. In his words, "theoretically, the only justification for even considering budgetary costs as such is that they are financed by taxes which have their own distortionary significance."[6] This comment is applicable to the current paper as well. Even if the revenue loss is less than the increase in giving, the revenue loss still must be made up in some fashion. Why not make fuller use of the considerable effort and ingenuity that have gone into the development of this model by undertaking a more complete analysis of this issue? In particular, the utility functions developed to determine consumer choices are just the tool needed to satisfy Arrow's concern.

It would be possible to examine alternative ways of raising the revenue that is lost by the proposals examined here to see who the gainers and losers are in a *net* sense and also to analyze whether overall social welfare has been improved. This would then provide the framework for an even more general approach in which the increase in tax rates required to finance these proposals affects other aspects of behavior such as the supply of savings and labor. With such an analysis, we will be able to break out of the mold of narrowly comparing the revenue loss and the giving gain as if an elasticity of − 1 really meant something.

5. Clotfelter, "Tax Incentives and Charitable Giving."
6. K. J. Arrow, "Microdata Simulation: Current Status Problems, Prospects," in R. H. Haveman and K. Hollenbeck, eds., *Microeconomic Simulation Models for Public Policy Analysis*, vol. 2 (New York: Academic Press, 1980), p. 264.

6

Alternative Tax Rules and Personal Saving Incentives: Microeconomic Data and Behavioral Simulations

Martin Feldstein and Daniel R. Feenberg

6.1 Introduction

Personal saving has traditionally accounted for more than half of all real net private saving in the United States. Incentives that increase the personal saving rate therefore have a potentially significant effect of the total rate of capital formation.[1] The purpose of the current paper is to present some new microeconomic evidence that is relevant to evaluating alternative changes in the personal tax treatment of savings and of interest and dividends.

There are, of course, many factors in addition to the personal tax rules that contribute to the low rate of saving in the United States, including consumer credit rules, the social security system, the taxation of business income, and the tax treatment of personal interest expenses. Our focus on the personal tax treatment of savings and the income from savings should not be misinterpreted as an indication that we believe that personal tax rules alone are responsible for the low United States saving rates. We do believe, however, that changes in these tax rules are a potentially useful way of increasing saving.

There has nevertheless long been resistance among both economists and government officials to changing the tax rules to encourage saving.[2]

Martin Feldstein is professor of economics, Harvard University (on leave). He was formerly president of the National Bureau of Economic Research and is currently chairman, Council of Economic Advisers. Daniel R. Feenberg is a research associate at the National Bureau of Economic Research.

The views expressed here are the authors' and should not be attributed to any organization.

1. Total capital formation also depends on government saving and international capital flows. Government saving has always been small and, in the majority of years since 1950, has been negative. Feldstein and Horioka (1980) show that United States net international capital flows have averaged less than 1% of saving and, for the OECD as a whole, are not responsive to domestic differences in saving rates.

2. Some would say to "reduce the features that discourage saving." The difference depends on whether one takes "income" or "expenditure" as the appropriate object of taxation. We need not comment on this issue in the current paper.

The opposition to encouraging saving has in part been a vestige of the Keynesian fear that a higher rate of saving might only increase unemployment. Whatever the relevance of this concern in earlier decades, oversaving is no longer regarded as a potential problem. A further source of opposition to modifying the tax rules to encourage saving has been a concern that any such change would thwart the egalitarian thrust of tax policy. This in turn reflected a belief that the incentive effects of tax changes would be negligible, implying that tax policy could encourage saving only by redistributing disposable income from lower income taxpayers with low marginal propensities to save to higher income taxpayers with high marginal propensities to save.

In contrast, there is now strong professional and political interest in tax changes that could encourage personal saving.[3] This reflects in part a reassessment of the earlier studies that had concluded that saving is not sensitive to the rate of return and therefore also not sensitive to the tax treatment of that return. Because those studies used nominal rather than real interest rates, the interest rate coefficient was biased in a way that made it appear to be insignificant or even to have the reverse sign (Feldstein 1970). New studies that relate saving to an estimate of the *real* net rate of return have suggested that savings do respond positively to this more appropriate measure of the return (Boskin 1978). Unfortunately, the problems of measuring the relevant real expected return are such that the econometric evidence is never likely to be compelling. It is important therefore that the general theory of consumer behavior implies directly that a compensated increase in the real net rate of return necessarily induces individuals to postpone consumption. The effect on saving of a change in the taxation of capital income therefore depends on the timing of tax payments and on the response of government spending.[4] If government spending in each year remains unchanged, national savings must rise. If the compensating changes in the tax keep tax liabilities in each year unchanged, private saving must also increase.[5]

Tax changes that reduce the difference between the pretax and posttax returns on capital may be worthwhile even if the saving rate does not respond positively to the net rate of return. A gap between the pretax and posttax rates of return implies a loss of welfare no matter what the uncompensated savings response. Of course, since the revenue lost by reducing the tax on saving could alternatively be used to reduce some other distorting tax, the desirability of reducing the tax on saving is not unambiguous. Nevertheless, recent investigations in the theory of opti-

3. See, for example, chapter 13 of the present volume as well as Becker and Fullerton (1980), Boskin (1978), Bradford (1980a), Feldstein (1977, 1978a), Fullerton et al. (1979), King (1980), McLure (1980), Summers (1978), and von Furstenburg (1980).
4. This sentence and the following two sentences are explained in Feldstein (1978b).
5. The proposed changes in the tax treatment of saving are compensated changes if not reducing the tax on saving would imply that some other tax would be reduced.

mal taxation do not suggest that the tax rate on the income from savings should probably be lower, and perhaps very much lower, than the tax rate on labor income.[6] If the marginal rate of substitution between current consumption and future consumption is independent of the quantities of leisure consumed, the optimal tax rate on the income from savings is zero (Mirrlees 1976). Substantial departures from this separability assumption still leave it optimal to tax capital income less than labor income. Indeed, if subsidizing retirement consumption reduces the distorting effect of the labor income tax on preretirement work effort, it may be optimal to "tax" the income from saving at a negative rate, i.e. to subsidize it. Explicit calculations of a simple model using empirically plausible but conservative parameter values (i.e. assuming that the compensated supply responses of both labor and saving are zero) imply that there may be a substantial potential welfare gain associated with reducing the tax on capital income and making up the lost revenue by an increase in the tax on labor income (Feldstein 1978a; see also Green and Sheshinski 1978 and Summers 1980). More generally, the potential gain from reducing the tax on capital income depends on the extent of the existing wedge between pretax and net-of-tax rates of return. It is significant therefore that in recent years personal, business, and property taxes have taken more than two-thirds of the real pretax return on capital used by nonfinancial corporations (Feldstein and Poterba 1980).

Although economists have generally been concerned with reducing this source of welfare loss, the public and congressional discussion has focused on increasing aggregate saving. Moreover, the recent proposals to encourage saving emphasize the incentive effects of a higher net rate of return and not a redistribution of disposable income from lower income to higher income groups. Indeed, a principal reason for using personal tax changes in addition to changes in business tax rules is to permit a targeting of the tax reduction benefits on middle income taxpayers rather than on all taxpayers in proportion to their existing wealth.

A further reason for directly encouraging an increase in personal saving is to reduce the inflationary pressures that might otherwise accompany a tax-induced increase in the demand for investment. Although the total rate of capital accumulation is constrained by the rate of saving, capital accumulation can be increased without altering the personal tax rules if the corporate tax rules are changed to increase the rate of return after the corporate income tax. This in turn raises the net return to savers and encourages increased saving. If the savings response were rapid enough, the economy would shift to a higher rate of investment with no increase in the rate of inflation. In practice, however, the corporate tax changes would probably raise investment demand more rapidly than the

6. We use the expressions "tax on saving" and "tax on the income from saving" interchangeably.

supply of savings. The result would be an increase in inflationary pressure.[7] Direct tax incentives to save can prevent these inflationary pressures by causing the increase in saving to occur at the same time as the increase in investment demand.

Two dynamic aspects of saving are particularly important. First, because saving represents an adjustment of the stock of wealth, a relatively small change in the desired level of wealth can induce a relatively large increase in the rate of saving. Second, because the desired level of wealth depends on the expected *future* net rates of return, an anticipated reduction in the future rate of tax on investment can induce a rise in current saving. Thus there can be an increase in saving without any concurrent government deficit.[8]

There is surprisingly little econometric evidence about individual saving behavior and the likely magnitude of response to alternative tax rules. In particular, there is no evidence that deals explicitly with such things as the *anticipated* rate of return, the effect of the tax rate per se, or the impact of nonlinear rules like the maximum levels of deductible savings for the current Individual Retirement Accounts. Although we cannot fill these gaps in the current paper, we believe that we can provide some useful information on the current distribution of saving, wealth, and investment income in relation to tax rates and total income. This evidence can be used to evaluate the potential impact and revenue cost of alternative tax rules in a way that is just not possible without detailed microeconomic evidence. In particular, we focus on the conflict between the desire to limit the deductions or exclusions of the individual filer (in order to reduce the total revenue loss and to focus the benefits on middle income taxpayers) and the possibility that such limits would eliminate any *marginal* incentive for most taxpayers.

Our analysis uses two bodies of microeconomic data. The principal data source is the Treasury's public use sample of individual tax returns. We use a stratified random sample of 26,643 individual tax returns for 1972 (a one-in-four random sample of the full public use sample) in conjunction with the NBER TAXSIM model,[9] which computes tax liabilities and tax rates based on the tax law as of 1972 and the alternative modifications. This data set provides detailed information on current interest and dividends, labor income, and total taxable income for each individual. A special advantage of the 1972 data is that the exact age of

7. The inflationary pressure could of course be checked by a tighter monetary policy, allowing the money rate of interest to rise relative to the Wicksellian natural rate of interest during the transition. But such exclusive reliance on monetary policy in the transition is not without substantial real costs in our economy with many long-term fixed interest contracts.

8. These ideas about the timing of tax changes are discussed briefly in Feldstein (1980) and developed more fully in chapter 13 of the present volume.

9. The economists who have participated in the development of TAXSIM are Daniel Feenberg, Martin Feldstein, Daniel Frisch, Larry Lindsey, and Harvey Rosen.

each taxpayer is included (based on IRS examination of Social Security Administration records for each individual). Our second body of data is the 1972 Consumer Expenditure Survey of the Bureau of Labor Statistics. Although the sample of 7,795 observations is inferior to the TAXSIM data in a number of ways,[10] it has the unique advantage of containing information on individual financial saving. Since the TAXSIM sample used in this paper is also for 1972, results obtained with the two data sets are generally comparable.

Although a great many specific proposals to encourage saving have been made, all of them have in common the purpose of increasing the net rate of return on saving or, equivalently, of increasing the amount of future consumption that can be obtained per dollar of current consumption that is foregone. The proposals that are particularly concerned with saving and that form the focus of our analysis can usefully be divided into two types: (1) those that allow the taxpayers to exclude some amount of *saving* from taxable income and (2) those that allow the taxpayer to exclude some amount of *interest and dividend income* from taxable income.[11] Before examining the specific saving proposals, we comment briefly on some more general tax proposals that also might encourage saving.

The most general of these proposals is to replace the income tax with a tax on consumer spending.[12] In comparison to the income tax, a consumption tax in effect allows a deduction for all saving. A more modest partial move in the direction of a consumption tax would be to adopt a value-added tax to replace part of the current tax structure. This again would be like the deduction method because income that is saved would avoid the value-added tax.

Several general proposals that would reduce the effective tax rate on interest and dividends have also been actively discussed. Some form of integration of the corporate and personal taxes (presumably by giving individuals a credit for corporate taxes in proportion to dividends received) would raise the net rate of return on equity investment and

10. The Consumer Expenditure Survey contains fewer observations on high income families, is aggregated into family units rather than taxpayer units, and does not contain a precise measure of taxable income.

11. These two methods can be equivalent in the sense that they define the same lifetime budget constraint for an individual and therefore induce the same consumption choices. This equivalence is violated to the extent that these are bequests or that the individual's marginal tax rate varies over time. Moreover, in practice these proposals would differ for a very long transition period because different cohorts of taxpayers are affected differently; e.g. the benefits of deducting saving have little effect on those who are already retired while an interest and dividend exclusion does; more generally, on the nonequivalence in the transition generation of consumption taxes (that allow a savings deduction) and labor income taxes (that exclude capital income) see Feldstein (1978b).

12. This proposal has a long and venerable pedigree that is discussed in Kaldor (1955) and Musgrave (1959). See also Bradford (1980b), Feldstein (1976), Fisher (1937), Kay and King (1978), the Meade Committee (1978), and the United States Treasury (1977).

therefore encourage equity finance as well as increased saving. The same would be true of a proposal to permit individuals to exclude a limited amount of dividends that are reinvested in new issue corporate stock. Adjusting the measurement of interest income to exclude some or all of the effect of inflation on interest rates would encourage the use of debt as well as increased saving. The proposals to reduce the maximum marginal tax rate to 50% or to tax "personal services income" and "investment income" on two separate schedules would raise the net return on all forms of capital.

Although these general proposals might be useful in encouraging saving, we shall not explore them further in the paper, in order to concentrate on the simpler and more direct deduction and exclusion proposals. Section 6.2 examines the deduction approach and considers the consequences of such a change in both the short-run transition and the longer run. The next section then analyzes the short- and long-run consequences of interest and dividend exclusion proposals. There is a brief concluding section.

6.2 Deductions for Saving

Under existing law, an individual who is not a participant in an employer-sponsored pension plan[13] can establish an Individual Retirement Account (IRA) and contribute up to 10% of his wage and salary, with a limit of $1,500 per year. These contributions are deductible from total income in calculating taxable income, and the earnings on the assets in the IRA are not subject to tax. A penalty is imposed if the funds are withdrawn from the IRA before the individual reaches age fifty-nine. Withdrawals after that age are taxable as ordinary employment income. The IRA is thus similar to a consumption tax with respect to the eligible amount of saving.[14]

The saving incentive provided by the IRA could be increased in three ways: (1) by raising the percentage and/or dollar ceilings on contributions; (2) by extending the IRA option to everyone with wage and salary income and not just to those who are not already participating in a pension plan; and (3) by increasing the liquidity of the IRA accounts by permitting withdrawals after as little as (say) four years. To the extent that IRA participants are effectively constrained by either the 10% or $1,500 limits, the IRA does not provide any marginal incentive to save more. In the present paper we compare some of the implications of 10%

13. A "participant" in such a pension plan need not have or be accruing any vested benefits.
14. Individuals with self-employment income are eligible for a similar program. Anyone can contribute up to 15% of self-employment income to a Keogh Plan, with a maximum of $7,500. The contribution is deductible, and the income of the plan is untaxed. Withdrawals are taxed as ordinary employment income.

and 15% limits with ceilings of $2,000 and $3,000. Because higher limits increase the revenue cost of these plans, we also consider a combination of a higher ceiling and partial deductibility, e.g. allowing an individual to contribute 15% of earnings up to $3,000 but deduct only half of this amount. Such partial deduction plans increase the range of marginal effectiveness although, for previously intramarginal contributions, they reduce the incentive as well as the cost. (Because the 1972 tax return data do not separate the earnings of husbands and wives, all of the proposals are defined in terms of the taxpaying unit rather than the individual.)

The current rule that limits eligibility for an IRA to those who do not participate in employer pension plans eliminates approximately 50% of all employees.[15] Moreover, those employees without pension coverage tend to be those who are least likely to save and least likely to be affected by tax considerations; they have low incomes and are frequently quite young.[16] The current eligibility limit thus eliminates substantially more than 50% of those who would be encouraged by saving deductibility if it were generally available. The current paper examines a savings deduction plan in which all individuals with wage and salary income may participate.[17]

Finally, the restriction that funds must remain in the IRA until the individual reaches age fifty-nine (or be subject to a special withdrawal tax and other penalties) substantially reduces the liquidity of the IRA savings. For many individuals, this reduction in liquidity may outweigh the higher net-of-tax return that the IRA offers. An individual at age forty may be unwilling to commit funds for nineteen years even in exchange for a higher rate of return. This illiquidity could be eliminated by allowing individuals to choose at the end of a short period like four years between withdrawing the funds in the account (and paying tax on the amount) or "rolling over" the funds for another four-year period. In practice, individuals who are reluctant to commit funds for a very long period may decide sequentially to leave the funds in the IRA account rather than pay the tax on the withdrawal. Although we have no way to examine this issue with the existing data, this possibility for making IRA accounts more attractive should be borne in mind when considering the likely responses to extending the IRA option to all individuals.

If the savings deduction is judged as an incentive to a higher rate of saving,[18] there are three potential problems. First, during a transition

15. On the extent of private pension coverage, see President's Commission on Private Pensions (1980).

16. The number of IRA plans indicates that only about 5% of those who are eligible have actually established an IRA; see Lubick (1980), p. 14.

17. The Canadian government introduced such a plan in 1972.

18. As opposed to judging it in terms of removing the tax wedge between the pretax and posttax rates of returns or of switching the tax base to avoid what some regard as an unjust double taxation of income that is saved.

period after the tax law is changed, individuals can reduce their tax liability without any increase in saving by transferring previously accumulated assets into the special account. Under an IRA–type plan with a 10% limit, an individual with assets equal to one year's earnings could obtain the maximum savings deduction for a decade without doing any additional saving. Indeed, for such an individual, the tax change would provide no marginal incentive to save while the tax reduction for previous saving would increase disposable income and therefore presumably cause an increase in consumer spending.[19] The extent to which this is a problem depends on the amount of financial assets (relative to earnings) that individuals have available and on their willingness to sacrifice the liquidity of those assets by committing them to an IRA.[20] We shall examine in detail the amount of financial assets that individuals have and the potential revenue effect if these assets were transferred to a special savings account during a transition period after the introduction of a savings deduction rule.

The second potential problem with a savings deduction plan is that, even after the transition period in which individuals merely transfer preexisting assets into a special savings account, there would be some individuals for whom a savings deduction with dollar and percentage limits would provide either no marginal incentive or a marginal incentive that is small relative to the intramarginal tax reduction. Thus an individual earning $10,000 and saving $900 might increase his saving by $100 to the $1,000 maximum allowed by a 10% ceiling but would receive a tax reduction on the entire $1,000 amount. With even a 20% marginal tax rate, the tax cost would be double the induced saving. We shall investigate the potential importance of the problem by examining the current distribution of savings relative to wage and salary income and the potential savings and revenue effects if individuals respond in different ways to the change in tax rules.

The third problem is that individuals may not be very responsive to the change in the net rate of return implied by the savings deduction. Because we are uncertain about the likely response, we shall present results for several different behavioral assumptions. At one extreme, we assume no behavioral response. At the other, we assume that all individuals take maximum advantage of the potential deduction. We also investigate a

19. This would, of course, be offset by a reduction in other consumer spending caused by the increase (or lack of decrease) in some other tax.

20. Individuals might in principle borrow and use the borrowed funds to finance their IRA contributions, thus earning tax-free interest in the IRA and paying tax-deductible interest on the borrowed funds. We ignore the possibility of borrowing on the assumption that most individuals have little opportunity to borrow without collateral and that the expanded IRA (like the existing IRA and Keogh) could not legally be accepted as collateral for a loan. Individuals might borrow by enlarging their house mortgage, but this would be discouraged by the need to hold most of the proceeds of such borrowing for several years before it could be contributed to the IRA.

response described in terms of the elasticity of current consumption with respect to the marginal rate of transformation between current and future consumption.

Before looking at the specific results, four notes of caution are appropriate. First, our analysis is only a partial equilibrium one. We assume that interest rates and other factor incomes remain unchanged. Second, the only behavioral response that we consider is saving. Since a higher net rate of return improves the trade-off between current work and future consumption, some individuals may respond by working more. Their saving would increase even if their saving rate remained unchanged. Of course, for some individuals the income effect would dominate and work effort would be decreased.[21] We ignore any such change in work effort and labor income. Third, we do not adopt an explicit life-cycle framework for our analysis. This implies that we do not take age explicitly into account in calculating the response to tax rules[22] and that we do not deal separately with the increased saving of the savings cohorts and their subsequent increased dissaving. Analyzing the complex dynamics of explicit intertemporal optimization would require much better data than currently exist. Moreover, there is no agreement on the extent to which individual saving does correspond to such rational life-cycle optimization. Finally, we consider only limited tax consequences; in particular, we ignore the effects of increased accumulation on corporate tax revenue.

6.2.1   Asset Transfers during Transition

We begin our analysis by examining the extent to which individuals could respond to an expanded IRA program by transferring preexisting assets into the special savings accounts. The data we present show that this is a relatively unimportant problem except perhaps for those with relatively high incomes.

Table 6.1 presents the cumulative distribution of gross financial assets in each income class based on the 1972 Tax Model. Although the tax returns do not report financial assets as such, the gross financial assets can be estimated from the reported interest and dividends. For this purpose, we have used a uniform dividend yield of 3% for all taxpayers and a uniform interest rate of 4.5%.[23] It may be useful to bear in mind that in 1972 per capita disposable personal income was $3,837 and by 1980 it had

21. If the change in the saving rule is a compensated change, the income effect could be ignored. Of course, the alternative tax change might also affect current work and thus current saving.

22. In some calculations, however, we assume that taxpayers over the age of sixty-five are not eligible to participate.

23. The 1972 mean dividend price ratio for the Standard and Poor's corporate index of 500 stocks was 2.84%. The maximum interest rate that could be paid on time deposits was 4.5%.

Table 6.1   **Cumulative Distribution of Gross Financial Assets**

Gross Financial Assets	AGI Class (× $1,000)				
	0–10	10–20	20–30	30 +	All
$0	69	38	16	6	55
$1,000	79	54	27	10	66
$2,000	83	63	34	13	72
$5,000	89	75	47	20	80
$10,000	93	84	62	28	87
$20,000	96	91	74	39	92
$40,000	98	96	85	54	95

Source: 1972 Tax Model.

Note: Dividend and interest are capitalized at .03 and .045, respectively. Individuals over age sixty-five are excluded.

somewhat more than doubled (in current prices) to $8,010. The population to which this tabulation refers includes all families and unrelated individuals, except those headed by someone aged sixty-five or older. Note that among those with incomes under $10,000 (approximately $20,000 at 1980 levels), 79% had less than or equal to $1,000 of gross financial assets. Only 11% had as much as $5,000.

Since our concern is with the extent to which individuals could use existing financial assets to contribute to an IRA–type plan without doing any new saving, we have also restated these estimates of gross financial assets in terms of the number of years that they could be used to fund the maximum IRA–type contribution for which the individual is eligible. For example, with an allowable IRA–type contribution equal to 10% of income with a maximum of $2,000, an individual earning $15,000 with $7,000 of gross financial assets would have enough to finance somewhat more than four years of maximum IRA contributions. Table 6.2 shows the cumulative distribution of "potential years" for taxpayers grouped by income class based on IRAs equal to the lesser of $2,000 and 10% of wage and salary income. These data exclude taxpayers over age sixty-five and apply the IRA rule to taxpaying units rather than separately to each individual. Note that in the class with adjusted gross incomes (AGIs) of less than $10,000, 79% did not have enough financial assets to finance even a single year's maximum IRA contribution. Since this under $10,000 group contained 60% of all taxpayers below age sixty-five, it is clear that for the great majority of taxpayers there is little problem of a substantial revenue loss while these individuals finance IRA–type contributions out of previously accumulated assets. Even in the higher income group with 1972 AGIs of $10,000 to $20,000, 60% lacked even one year's worth of IRA contributions at the maximum allowable rate. Only about 15% of taxpayers with AGIs below $10,000 and 20% with AGIs between $10,000

Table 6.2   **Cumulative Distribution of the Number of Years of Transferable Assets**

Years of Trans-ferable Assets	AGI Class (× $1,000)				
	0–10	10–20	20–30	30+	All
1	79	60	39	27	69
2	82	69	47	31	75
3	84	73	54	34	78
4	85	77	60	36	80
5	86	80	64	38	82
6	87	82	68	40	83
7	88	84	70	41	85
8	89	85	73	44	86
9	90	87	74	46	87
10	90	88	76	47	88
11	91	89	79	49	88
12	91	89	79	50	89
13	91	90	81	52	89
14	91	91	82	53	90
15	91	91	82	54	90
16	91	92	82	55	90
17	92	92	83	55	91
18	93	93	84	57	92
19	93	93	85	58	92

Source: 1972 Tax Model.

Note: Cumulative percentage of taxpayers without the indicated number of years' worth of financial assets to finance an IRA equal to 10% of wages, with a ceiling of $2,000, solely from those assets. Individuals over age sixty-five are excluded. Dividends and interest are capitalized at .03 and .045, respectively.

and $20,000 had enough financial assets to finance as much as five years of contributions.

Table 6.3 presents the aggregate implications of this potential asset transfer for a savings deduction plan that allows contributions of 10% of income with a $2,000 annual maximum. The table shows that the maximum contribution that individuals could legally deduct totaled $56.1 billion, or slightly more than $800 per taxpayer. By contrast, the maximum amount that could be financed by transfer from existing assets in the first year was only $26.9 billion. It should be emphasized that this maximum transfer would occur only if all taxpayers were prepared to lose the liquidity of these assets in order to obtain the higher net-of-tax return. (Note that because of the $2,000 ceiling approximately four-fifths of this deduction accrues to those with incomes below $20,000 and nearly all of it to those with incomes below $30,000.)

The distribution of assets in tables 6.1 and 6.2 implies that this first-year transfer would exhaust much of the available assets of most taxpayers.

Table 6.3   Aggregate Effects of Alternative Savings Deduction Plans

AGI Class (× $1,000)	Millions of Returns	Maximum Contribution ($ billions)	Contributions from Assets ($ billions)	
			Year 1	Year 3
0-10	42.2	17.9	5.1	3.1
10–20	22.2	28.6	14.4	8.1
20–30	4.1	7.2	5.2	3.6
30+	1.6	2.4	2.1	1.9
All	70.0	56.1	26.9	16.8

Source: 1972 Tax Model.
Note: Potential reductions in taxable income with the introduction of a universal IRA. The maximum deduction is 10% of wages with a ceiling of $2,000. Individuals over age sixty-five are excluded.

The final column of table 6.3 confirms the importance of this by tabulating the amount of preexisting assets that could be transferred in the third year of such a new tax rule. The total amount of transferable assets is reduced from $32 billion to only $17 billion, or less than one-third of the maximum potential contribution in that year.

In interpreting the revenue losses associated with asset transfers, it is important to bear in mind that they represent a one-time fixed cost of transition to a new system. The true economic cost of this revenue loss is not the revenue loss itself but the much smaller excess burden that would be incurred in making up this lost revenue or that otherwise could have been avoided if the lost revenue had instead been used to reduce some other distorting tax. The corresponding gain is the present value of the perpetual reduction in the excess burden caused by the incorrect mix of taxes on capital and labor incomes. Because this is a comparison of a one-time cost with a perpetual gain in a growing economy, the one-time transition cost is likely to be relatively small.

6.2.2 Marginal and Intramarginal Saving after the Transition

After the transition period, an individual can have a tax deduction only for net saving that actually adds to individual wealth and the national capital stock.[24] Of course, some of this saving would have been done anyway. Moreover, for those individuals who would in any case have saved more than the maximum deductible amount, the deductible saving would be intramarginal and the tax rule would influence saving only by an income effect. For such individuals, since some of the tax reduction would be spent, the net effect would be an increase in consumption. But for those individuals who would otherwise have saved less than the

24. Unless the individual borrows to finance these contributions. See footnote 20 for the reasons why this is not likely to be a significant problem.

deductible amount, the new rule would provide a marginal incentive to save. If, however, the saving would have been close to the limit, the increased saving may be constrained to be less than the tax reduction.

To shed some light on this issue, we have examined the distribution of existing saving rates relative to wage and salary income. For this purpose, we use the 1972 Consumer Expenditure Survey and define saving as the "change in nominal net financial assets, excluding the appreciation of portfolio assets." We use this definition of saving (rather than say the change in net worth) because it defines the kind of saving for which the tax deduction would be allowed. We then use this information to calculate the amount of intramarginal saving and other preexisting saving for which taxpayers would receive deductions and compare this to the potential increases in saving that might be induced under different assumptions about the behavioral response of taxpayers. The effects on tax revenue are also calculated.

Table 6.4 presents the cumulative distributions of the ratio of net financial saving to wage and salary income for four income classes as well as for households as a whole. It is clear that a 10% limit on deductible saving would be a binding constraint for only a small fraction of all households. Among those with income below $10,000, only 14% saved 10% of their income in the form of financial asset accumulation. The fraction is essentially the same for those with incomes between $10,000

Table 6.4   **Cumulative Distribution of the Ratio of Changes in Net Financial Assets to Wage and Salary Income**

Ratio of Change in Financial Assets to Wage and Salary Income	Income Class (× $1,000)				
	0–10	10–20	20–30	30+	All
− .04	15	16	14	12	15
− .02	19	20	18	15	19
< 0	23	26	24	20	24
0	69	57	49	41	61
.02	76	69	59	54	70
.04	80	77	68	63	77
.06	83	81	74	67	80
.08	85	84	77	69	83
.10	86	87	79	72	85
.12	88	88	86	73	87
.15	89	90	86	77	89
.18	90	91	87	78	90
.36	94	96	94	88	95

Source: 1972 Consumer Expenditure Survey.
Note: Tabulations exclude households with no wage or salary income.

and $20,000. Among those with incomes over $20,000, the $2,000 limit on saving deductibility becomes the constraint instead of the 10% limit. This implies that deductibility would be inframarginal for a larger fraction of these taxpayers. But the figures for the $20,000 to $30,000 class imply that only about one in five would otherwise be at or above the deductibility limit.

Another striking feature of table 6.4 is the very high fraction of households who report no change in their gross financial assets. Some 24% of all households indicate some reduction in financial assets during the year, and an additional 37% indicate neither saving nor dissaving. Only 39% report positive saving. A tax rule allowing deductibility of saving would provide an unambiguous incentive to save more to the 60% with zero or negative saving since there would be no offsetting income effect associated with preexisting saving (Feldstein and Tsiang 1968).

We have prepared simulations to compare the effects on saving and tax revenue of four alternative savings deductions and several different possible behavioral responses. The two basic savings deductions are 10% of earnings with a $2,000 limit and 15% of earnings with a $3,000 limit. A more restricted alternative that reduces the revenue loss without changing the set of taxpayers for whom the deduction provides a marginal incentive would limit the tax deduction to only half of the contribution to the saving plan; i.e. a taxpayer with earnings of $15,000 could contribute up to $1,500 but would receive a tax deduction for only $750. The earnings on all the assets in the fund would, however, be untaxed. The final option presented in this table is designed to offset the fact that higher income taxpayers already save a larger fraction of their income than low income taxpayers. For taxpayers with incomes over $10,000, it restricts the deduction to the excess over a "floor" equal to 5% of the earnings over $10,000. For example, a taxpayer with earnings of $20,000 could only deduct savings contributions in excess of $500. Such a taxpayer could contribute an additional $2,000 but would receive a deduction only of $2,000 for the $2,500 contribution. This would have no adverse incentive effect on anyone who would save at least 5% under existing tax rules. Moreover, even the initial 5% has some incentive effect associated with it since the income on all the assets in the fund is untaxed. Indeed, for some high income taxpayers for whom the $2,000 ceiling is a binding limit, the ability to contribute an additional 5% of nondeductible earnings may be an incentive to save.[25]

For each of the four alternative plans, we have calculated the increase in savings and decrease in tax revenue implied by several alternative behavioral response assumptions. The first assumption, that there is no change in saving, provides a reference standard for comparing the tax

---

25. Individuals might, of course, seek to circumvent the floor by bunching their saving into alternate years, but this would be worth doing only if the ceiling were not binding.

revenue implications of alternative behavioral responses. At the opposite extreme would be the assumption that taxpayers increase their saving to the maximum amount of the allowed deduction. It seems very unlikely, however, that individuals who currently do no saving would suddenly switch to this maximum amount. We have therefore examined two alternatives that are much more conservative. The first assumption is that only those who currently have positive saving would switch to the maximum, with no change in the behavior of nonsavers. The alternative assumption is that taxpayers with positive assets would take the maximum deduction while those with no assets would not respond at all. A fourth assumption is an arbitrary intermediate response: each taxpayer who has positive saving increases his saving halfway from his actual 1972 level to the maximum amount. For example, a taxpayer with $15,000 of earnings and $500 of preexisting annual savings would, with the 10% plan, increase his saving to $1,000.

The other three behavioral response calculations reflect the assumption that consumer spending responds to the income and substitution effects of a deduction rule with constant partial price and income elasticities. The basic concept in this calculation is the relative "price" of current consumption in terms of foregone future consumption. Consider an individual who decides between spending a dollar now or saving it and spending the principal and accumulated interest at the end of T years.[26] Let the nominal interest rate be i, the inflation rate be π, and the individual's marginal tax rate be θ. Under current law, the individual chooses between spending one dollar now and spending $(1 + (1 - \theta)i)^T$ dollars in year T. The real value of that Tth year spending is $(1 + (1 - \theta)i)^T/(1 + \pi)^T$, or, ignoring terms that are of second order, $(1 + (1 - \theta)i - \pi)^T$. We shall call this rate of transformation R_0. If the individual could instead deduct the dollar of saving, by foregoing one dollar of current consumption he could add $1/(1 - \theta)$ dollars to his current savings. If the saving accumulates untaxed, this grows to $(1 + i)^T/(1 - \theta)$ dollars at the end of T years. The individual pays tax on this nominal value, although presumably at a lower tax rate ($\theta' < \theta$) because he is then retired. The net of tax accumulation is thus $(1 - \theta')(1 + i)^T/(1 - \theta)$. In real terms this is (again ignoring second-order terms)

$$R_1 = (1 - \theta')(1 + i - \pi)^T/(1 - \theta).^{27}$$

Note that if $\theta' = \theta$, the combination of deductibility and the nontaxation of the interest on the savings account is equivalent to having no

26. In reality, there would not be single year but a probabilistic interval with probabilities that reflected survival probabilities.

27. If only a fraction λ of the contribution is deductible but the subsequent tax is limited to the same fraction of withdrawals, the rate of transformation becomes $R_1 = (1 - \lambda\theta')(1 + i - \pi)^T/(1 - \lambda\theta)$; with a binding level of deductibility, the plan has no effect on marginal saving and therefore $R_1 = R_0$.

deduction and then allowing the savings to accumulate completely untaxed (i.e. with no tax when funds are disbursed from the account). This
is equivalent to consumption tax treatment and removes the distortion in
the individual's choice between early and late consumption. However,
the distortion between leisure and consumption (both present and future)
remains and presumably biases the individual's decision in favor of
leisure. At the alternative extreme, in which withdrawals from the fund at
retirement are untaxed ($\theta' = 0$), the individual chooses between one
dollar of current consumption and $(1 + i - \pi)^T/(1 - \theta)$ dollars of consumption in year T. This represents a more favorable trade-off between
current and future consumption than a consumption tax and thus distorts
consumption in favor of the retirement years. But because it permits the
individual to transform a dollar of pretax earnings into retirement consumption at the real rate of interest, such treatment offsets the bias
against working that is inherent in the consumption tax. Indeed, with
$\theta = 0$ this method is equivalent to no tax at all as far as the trade-off
between current leisure and future consumption is concerned.

For the purpose of the simulations, we approximate the change in
consumption as the sum of a price effect and an income effect:

$$(2.1) \qquad dC = \frac{\partial C}{\partial R} dR + \frac{\partial C}{\partial Y} dY ,$$

where C is consumption, R is the price of current consumption (in terms
of foregone future consumption), and Y is disposable income. From
equation (2.1) it directly follows that

$$(2.2) \qquad \frac{dC}{C} = \frac{R}{C} \frac{\partial C}{\partial R} \frac{dR}{R} + \frac{Y}{C} \frac{\partial C}{\partial Y} \frac{dY}{Y}$$

$$= \alpha_R \frac{dR}{R} + \alpha_Y \frac{dY}{Y} ,$$

where α_R and α_Y are the price and income elasticities. We shall assume
that these partial price and income elasticities are locally constant.

We use this approximation to calculate the level of consumption under
the deduction rule (C_1) as a function of the initial consumption level (C_0),
the two related price values (R_1 and R_0), and the income effect of the tax
change (dY). For simplicity, we shall describe this in the case where the
individual initially has a positive level of saving ($S_0 > 0$) but in which the
deduction limit is never binding (i.e. both S_0 and the level of saving under
the deduction rule, S_1, are less than the limit, L). In this case, the relative
price increase caused by the deduction rule is $dR/R = (R_1 - R_0)/R_0$. The
income effect depends on the change in income caused by the deduction
rule at the initial level of saving. Recall that under current tax law the
individual who saves S_0 "buys" future consumption of $S_0 R_0$. With the

deduction rule, this same level of future consumption can be bought at the lower current cost, R_0S_0/R_1. The difference between these two is the increase in income at the initial consumption pattern. Thus $dY = S_0 - S_0R_0/R_1 = S_0(R_1 - R_0)/R_1$. Substituting these expressions into equation (2.2) we obtain

$$(2.3) \qquad \frac{C_1 - C_0}{C_0} = \alpha_R \frac{R_1 - R_0}{R_0} + \alpha_Y \frac{S_0(R_1 - R_0)}{Y_0R_1} .$$

It is clear that equation (2.3) is only an approximate measure of the change in consumption. We use the linear approximation of equation (2.1) and evaluate it at the initial values of R_0 and S_0. We define consumption to include all uses of income other than financial saving and taxes; in particular, we include mortgage repayments in consumption. Moreover, we look only at a single year in isolation. In a full life-cycle model, the price effects would be more complex, the income change would reflect the discounted value of the price changes in future years as well, and the initial level of income (Y_0) would be replaced by a discounted value of future incomes. (Note, however, that if the individual's saving rate remained relatively constant over a number of years, the use of S_0/Y_0 instead of a ratio of two discounted values would not change the result appreciably.)

The magnitudes of the income and substitution effects determine whether the switch to a deduction rule raises or lowers consumption. The effect on saving can then be calculated from the change in consumption and the change in tax revenue:

$$(2.4) \qquad (S_1 - S_0) + (C_1 - C_0) + (T_1 - T_0) = 0 ,$$

where T_0 is the individual's tax liability under current tax law and T_1 is the tax liability under the deduction rule. For an individual whose final level of saving is below the deduction limit, $T_1 - T_0 = -\theta S_1$; i.e. the individual's tax liability is reduced by the product of his marginal tax rate (θ) and his savings deduction (S_1). Note that equation (2.4) implies that even if the income and substitution effects on consumption balance so that consumption remains unchanged ($C_1 - C_0 = 0$), saving will increase if the tax liability falls ($S_1 - S_0 > 0$ if $T_1 - T_0 < 0$). Of course, the income effect could dominate the price incentive and cause consumption to rise by enough to leave savings lower. To evaluate this in the current case, we need values of α_R and α_Y and the microeconomic distributions of tax rates, savings, and incomes.

Before discussing the values of α_R and α_Y, we may comment briefly on three special cases, where saving is negative, zero, or above the limit. If initial saving is negative ($S_0 < 0$), there is neither an income effect nor a price effect. Both consumption and saving remain unchanged. With zero initial saving, there is a price effect but no income effect; consumption falls and saving rises. For an individual whose initial saving exceeds the deduction limit $(S_0 > L)$, there is no price effect (since $R_1 = R_0$) and an income effect given by $L(R_1 - R_0)/R_1$; consumption rises and saving may rise or fall. Finally, for an individual whose initial level of saving is below the ceiling $(S_0 < L)$ but for whom equations (2.3) and (2.4) imply that S_1 exceeds the ceiling, we take saving to be either the limit or, if it is greater, the value of saving implied by the income effect alone.

In all of our simulations, we assume a unit elasticity of consumption with respect to disposable income: $\alpha_Y = 1$. Since we lack reliable econometric evidence on α_R, we perform simulations for a range of values. At one extreme is the case of $\alpha_R = 0$, i.e. no substitution effect. In this implausible limiting case, the only response to the tax change is the income effect and therefore an increase in consumption. More generally, $\alpha_R < 0$ and the response of consumption depends on the relative strength of substitution and income effects. Since intuition about consumer behavior is in terms of the uncompensated price elasticity rather than the pure price effect, we derive simulation values of α_R from assumptions about the uncompensated response of consumption for a "representive" taxpayer with disposable income of $Y_0 = \$10,000$, savings of $S_0 = \$200$, and a marginal tax rate of $\theta = 0.25$. To calculate the values of R_0 and R_1, let $i = 0.10$ be the nominal interest rate and $\pi = 0.08$ be the rate of inflation. Assume that the time to retirement consumption is $T = 15$ years and that in retirement the individual's marginal tax rate will be half what it is now: $\theta' = 0.50\theta$. Then $R_0 = (1 + (1 - \theta)i - \pi)^T = (1 + 0.075 - 0.08)^{15} = 0.93$ and $R_1 = (1 - \theta)(1 + i - \pi)^T/(1 - \theta) = 0.875\ (1.02)^{15}/0.75 = 1.57$. Thus $R_1/R_0 = 1.69$.

Consider first the case in which a change in the net rate of return has no effect on consumption, i.e. $C_1 = C_0$. Equation (2.3) then implies that

$$(2.5) \qquad 0 = \alpha_R \frac{R_1 - R_0}{R_0} + \alpha_Y \frac{S_0(R_1 - R_0)}{Y_0 R_1}$$

or, with $\alpha_Y = 1$,

$$(2.6) \qquad \alpha_R = -\frac{S_0}{Y_0} \frac{R_0}{R_1}.$$

These specific assumptions for our representative taxpayer then imply $\alpha_R = -0.0118$. Note that although this value of α_R implies that the income and substitution effects balance and leave consumption unchanged for the "representative" taxpayer, someone with a lower initial saving rate will have a smaller income effect and will therefore be induced by the deduction rule to reduce consumption while someone with a higher initial saving rate will be induced to increase consumption.

We also present simulations based on the assumption that an increase in the net rate of return would cause our representative taxpayer's consumption to decrease, i.e. that the substitution effect outweighs the income effect. More specifically, we approximate the consumption response of this type of "representative" taxpayer to deductibility as a 2% decrease in consumption. Equation (2.3) then implies[28]

$$(2.7) \qquad -0.02 = \alpha_R \, \frac{1.57 - 0.93}{0.93} + \frac{0.02(1.57 - 0.93)}{1.57} \, ,$$

or $\alpha_R = -0.041$.

The relation between these responses of a "representative" individual and the aggregate responses that we obtain in the simulations reflects the distribution of initial saving rates and price changes and the effects of the deductibility ceilings. We should again emphasize that these calculations are not precise estimates but are approximations for a broad range of parameter values. A more complete analysis would instead derive each individual's consumption response with the help of an explicit utility function in a life-cycle context. Realistic life-cycle calculations would have to take into account bequests and inheritances as well as family structure, private pension benefits, social security, etc. Liquidity considerations and the possible favorable misunderstanding of the deductibility should also be considered. At this time, there is just not enough information to perform such a calculation.

In the simulations we calculate two different measures of the effect of the deduction on tax revenue. The first of these is the short-run effect that results from the immediate deduction of the savings deposited in the special account. This is approximately equal to the product of the individual's marginal tax rate and the lesser of savings (S_1) and the ceiling on the savings deduction. In fact, we use the Tax Model to calculate more precisely the effect of the savings deduction in a way that takes into account the nonlinearity of the tax schedule and other features of the tax law. Of course, for taxpayers with negative savings, there is no change in tax revenue.

Because withdrawal of funds from the savings account requires paying tax, the initial deduction is in part only a postponement of the tax liability. Indeed, if the tax rate in retirement is equal to the tax rate when working $(\theta' = \theta)$, the initial deduction is fully offset by the subsequent withdrawal tax. The advantage of the deduction account is then only that the income on the assets accrues without tax. More generally, the long-run reduction in tax revenue reflects both the lower tax rate when funds are withdrawn $(\theta' < \theta)$ and the exclusion from taxable income of the interest and dividend income on the amount of saving that would have

---

28. Recall that for the representative taxpayer the real net rate of return rises from -0.005 to 0.020; including the deductibility effect implies that the current opportunity cost of consumption rises from 0.93 to 1.57.

been done under the old law (since the income on the induced saving would not otherwise exist).

We calculate the long-run revenue loss by noting first that the initial level of saving S_0 grows under current law to $R_0 S_0$ before it is consumed while with the deductions it grows to $R_1 S_0$. The entire difference, $(R_1 - R_0)S_0$, is the accumulated value of the lower taxes that the government collects on S_0 and on the resulting interest and dividend income. The present value of that difference as of the initial date, discounting at the real pretax rate of returns, is $(R_1 - R_0)S_0/(1 + i - \pi)^T$. This is the present value of the revenue loss associated with the initial level of saving. The additional saving causes an additional revenue loss to the extent that the tax rate in retirement (θ') is less than the tax rate at the time that the deduction is taken. If S_1 is less than the deduction limit, the initial revenue loss on the induced saving is $\theta(S_1 - S_0)$. The induced saving grows over time to $(S_1 - S_0)(1 + i - \pi)^T$ and yields a tax revenue of $\theta'(S_1 - S_0)(1 + i - \pi)^T/(1 + i - \pi)^T = \theta'(S_1 - S_0)$. The net revenue loss on the induced saving is thus $(\theta - \theta')(S_1 - S_0)$. The full long-run reduction in revenue (associated with the single year's saving) thus has a present value of $(R_1 - R_0)S_0/(1 + i - \pi)^T + (\theta - \theta')(S_1 - S_0)$. The simulations modify this formula in the appropriate way in the cases where initial saving is negative or where the limit on deductibility is binding and use the full tax simulation calculations instead of just the marginal tax rate.[29]

Table 6.5 summarizes the results of these simulations. Consider first the effects of the alternative plans on tax revenue if taxpayers do not adjust their saving at all. A savings deduction limited by 10% of wages and $2,000 would have an immediate revenue cost of $49. The present value of the full long-run tax effect is slightly larger, $60, implying that the exclusion of the interest and dividends outweighs the recouping of part of the initial deduction. Increasing the limits by 50% (to 15% of wages and $3,000) increases the initial cost by proportionally less but increases the long-run deduction by almost 50%. This indicates that the primary value to taxpayers of the higher limits is in the implied interest and dividend exclusion. Finally, note that, while cutting the deduction in half obviously halves the short-run revenue loss, the long-run revenue effect is much less.

Consider now the effects of the alternative saving responses to the 10% deduction limit. If taxpayers who already do some saving increase their saving to take full advantage of the deductions, average saving would rise by $158. The deduction of this saving would increase the revenue loss by $36, from $49 to $85. The present value of the long-run revenue loss would also rise, but by proportionately less since the increase reflects the

29. This measure of revenue loss does not reflect the extra corporate tax revenue that would be collected on the additional capital.

Table 6.5   Simulations of Different Behavioral Responses to Alternative Savings Deduction Rules: Mean Changes in Saving and Taxes

| | 10% Deduction, $2,000 Limit Change In | | | 15% Deduction, $3,000 Limit Change In | | | Partial Deduction: One-Half of 15% Deduction, $3,000 Limit Change In | | | Deduction with Floor: 10% Deduction, $2,000 Limit, Floor of 5% of Income over $10,000 Change In | | |
| | | Tax Revenue | | | Tax Revenue | | | Tax Revenue | | | Tax Revenue | |
	Saving	Short Run	Long Run	Saving	Short Run	Long Run	Saving	Short Run	Long Run	Saving	Short Run	Long Run
Savings unchanged	0	49	60	0	61	86	0	31	67	0	37	24
Savings increase to maximum if saving > 0	158	85	78	298	125	118	289	64	83	97	57	34
Savings increase to maximum if assets > 0	129	79	75	240	116	114	240	61	82	79	53	32
Savings increase halfway to maximum if saving > 0	79	67	69	144	94	102	144	94	99	48	47	29
Representative consumption unchanged ($\alpha_R = .0118$)	58	47	57	57	54	82	28	29	66	26	32	22
Representative consumption increased ($\alpha_R = 0$)	10	37	51	5	43	77	-8	25	64	10	30	21
Representative consumption decreased ($\alpha_R = -0.041$)	157	69	68	168	79	94	111	39	71	68	40	26

Source: Simulations based on 1972 Consumer Expenditure Survey.

Note: All figures are mean annual amounts for the population of household units and are expressed in 1972 dollars.

differences between the initial deduction and the present value of the extra revenue obtained when the funds are withdrawn. The corresponding figures when the response is limited to those who initially had positive assets or when the size of the response is halved are similar although obviously somewhat smaller.

The partial price elasticity associated with unchanged consumption for the representative taxpayer ($\alpha_R = -0.0118$) causes saving to rise by an average of $58 per taxpayer. The immediate revenue loss associated with this is $47, and the long-run revenue loss is $57. Thus, in this case, the increased personal saving exceeds the immediate reduction in personal tax revenue and is approximately equal to the long-run tax reduction. If the incentive to postpone consumption does cause a fall in consumption, the increase in saving exceeds the short-run and long-run loss of tax revenue.

Since all of these figures are means per taxpayer and there were 70 million taxpayers in 1972, these estimates imply that the immediate revenue cost of a 10% deduction plan is a minimum of $3.5 billion (at 1972 levels) with no saving response. Beyond that, each dollar of induced saving reduces revenue by only about 20 cents. With consumption unchanged, the revenue loss is $3.5 billion and the increased saving is $4 billion. With consumption reduced by 2%, the revenue loss is somewhat less than $5 billion and the saving increase is about $10 billion.

Tables 6.6 and 6.7 analyze the effects of a savings deduction by income class. Table 6.6 accepts the conservative assumption of unchanged consumer spending and examines the impact on saving and taxes of alternative deduction plans. It is clear that the basic deduction of 10% of wages with a $2,000 limit induces proportionately more response at each higher level of income. Note that switching from a 10%, $2,000 limit to a 15%, $3,000 limit has virtually no effect except in the highest income group. Table 6.7 focuses just on the 10%, $2,000 deduction limit but examines the responses in each income class associated with different types of behavior. One point worth noting is that the effect of different price elasticities on the amount of saving is proportionately greater for low income taxpayers than for high income taxpayers. Note also that, regardless of the price elasticity, there is little tax reduction below $10,000 and that above $10,000 the tax reduction rises at least in proportion to income.

6.3   Exclusion of Interest and Dividends

Until 1980, an individual taxpayer could exclude the first $100 of dividend income from AGI and therefore from taxable income. A couple could exclude twice that amount. The law was modified in 1980 to double these exclusions and to extend them from dividends to both dividends

Table 6.6   **Distributional Implications of Alternative Savings Deduction with No Change in Consumption: Mean Changes in Saving and Taxes**

Income Class (× $1,000)	10% Deduction, $2,000 Limit Change in			15% Deduction, $3,000 Limit Change in			Partial Deduction: One-Half of 15% Deduction, $3,000 Limit Change in			Deduction with Floor: 10% Deduction, $2,000 Limit, Floor of 5% of Income over $10,000 Change in		
		Tax Revenue			Tax Revenue			Tax Revenue			Tax Revenue	
	Saving	Short Run	Long Run	Saving	Short Run	Long Run	Saving	Short Run	Long Run	Saving	Short Run	Long Run
0–10	13	9	9	11	10	15	6	5	12	12	9	9
10–20	60	53	70	58	61	96	28	33	79	26	38	35
20–30	166	143	168	146	160	273	67	88	221	69	88	38
30+	444	310	329	521	387	427	282	193	291	172	175	16
All	58	47	57	57	54	82	28	29	66	26	32	22

Source: Simulations based on 1972 Consumer Expenditure Survey.
Note: All figures are means and are expressed in 1972 dollars.

Table 6.7   Distributional Aspects of Alternative Behavioral Responses to a 10% Savings Deduction: Mean Changes in Saving and Taxes

	Change in Saving by Income Class (× $1,000)				Short-Term Change in Taxes by Income Class (× $1,000)				Long-Run Changes in Taxes by Income Class (× $1,000)			
	0–10	10–20	20–30	30+	0–10	10–20	20–30	30+	0–10	10–20	20–30	30+
Savings unchanged	0	0	0	0	9	58	155	260	9	73	174	307
Savings increase to maximum if saving > 0	44	251	353	267	16	110	252	371	12	99	223	362
Savings increase to maximum if assets > 0	26	207	320	253	14	101	243	366	11	95	218	360
Savings increase halfway to maximum if saving > 0	22	126	177	134	13	84	204	319	11	86	199	336
Representative consumption unchanged ($\alpha_R = .0118$)	13	61	166	444	9	53	143	310	9	70	168	329
Representative consumption increased ($\alpha_R = 0$)	2	6	41	112	7	43	115	194	8	65	154	272
Representative consumption decreased ($\alpha_R = 0.041$)	39	194	462	691	13	77	210	452	11	82	202	400

Source: Simulations based on 1972 Consumer Expenditure Survey.

and interest. For anyone with interest and dividend income below the limit, the exclusion effectively eliminates the tax on such income at a margin and therefore has the full neutrality of a consumption tax.

The principal problem with the current exclusion is that the limit may be too low. For a couple with more than $400 of interest and dividends, the exclusion is intramarginal and has no effect on the taxation of additions to wealth. With today's interest rates, a couple with as little as $4,000 of wealth could easily find that the income from any additional saving would be fully taxed. This section considers alternative proposals to raise the limit on the exclusion. To reduce the cost of such an increase, we also consider two partial exclusion plans (the first plan excludes 20% of all interest and dividend income while the second plan excludes one-half of the first $1,000 of interest and dividend income)[30] and a plan with a floor (individuals with incomes in excess of $10,000 can only exclude interest and dividend income to the extent that it exceeds 5% of the income over $10,000 and then only up to a limit of $1,000).

From the taxpayers' point of view, the interest and dividend exclusion has two advantages over a savings deduction that implies the same real net rate of return. First, because the interest and dividend exclusion is not restricted to a separate account, there is no loss of liquidity to counterbalance the increase in yield. Second, there are no additional accounting or record-keeping requirements. Both of these features suggest that, all other things being equal, individuals are likely to be more responsive to an exclusion than to a savings deduction. Against this might be balanced the "psychological" effect of the savings deductions in focusing attention on an immediate tax reward for saving. We know of no evidence on the basis of which this can be evaluated.

The dividend and interest exclusion also has the advantage that there is no transition problem comparable to the transfer of existing assets that ocurrs with a savings deduction. Of course, the interest and dividend exclusion has an analogous problem since taxes are reduced immediately on the interest and dividends earned on preexisting wealth. But this problem does not just apply during the transition. Rather, with the interest and dividend exclusion, there is no real distinction between the initial "transition" tax reductions and the subsequent "steady state" reduction in taxes that result from assets that would have existed even without the exclusion.

The principal issue in judging the potential usefulness of the interest and dividend exclusion is the amount of additional saving that is gener-

---

30. Different combinations of the "exclusion limit" and the "exclusion fraction" correspond to the same loss of tax revenue but have different incentive effects. The incentive effect depends on the distribution of existing wealth and on the sensitivity of saving to the net return. It would be interesting to use the information on the distribution of assets and alternative assumptions about the savings response to examine the implication of alternative combinations of the limit and the exclusion fraction.

ated per dollar of foregone tax revenue. Of course, there is no revenue loss directly caused by the *increased* accumulation of wealth induced by the new tax rule. The interest and dividends that go untaxed would not have existed otherwise and therefore obviously would not have been taxed. All of the revenue loss is due to the exclusion of interest and dividends or wealth that would have existed in any case.[31] This revenue loss therefore depends on the distribution of existing interest and dividends, the limit on the exclusion, and the fraction that is excluded if there is less than a full exclusion. Section 6.3.1 presents evidence on this distribution.

In evaluating the likely response to an interest and dividend exclusion, we give particular attention to those who currently have zero interest and dividends. As the data in section 6.2 on the distribution of gross financial assets implied, this is a very sizable group. Among taxpayers as a whole, 46% had no interest and dividends. The concentration of individuals at zero reflects a kink in the intertemporal budget constraint. Even in the absence of taxes, the budget constraint would be kinked at the point of zero saving, reflecting the fact that the borrowing rate exceeds the rate that individuals receive on deposits. Since most taxpayers do not itemize their deductions, the tax rules leave the borrowing rate unchanged but reduce the net lending rate even more.[32]

Because of the kink, individuals with different preferences will have the same behavior. Because the reason that a particular individual has zero interest and dividends in equilibrium cannot be determined from the available data, the likely effect of a tax change is ambiguous as well. Figure 6.1 illustrates this ambiguity in a two-period model of income and consumption. In both parts of this figure, line ABC represents a constant interest rate budget line between current and future consumption. At point B, the individual neither borrows nor lends. The tax on interest income shifts the lending segment of the budget constraint from BC to BE. The higher interest rate on borrowing than on lending shifts the borrowing segment from AB to DB.

In figure 6.1a, the individual faced with the constant interest rate budget line ABC would choose to save and therefore to consume at point X. But with the kinked budget line DBE, the individual chooses point B with no borrowing and lending. In figure 6.1b, the individual faced with

31. At first, this seems to be in sharp contrast to the savings deduction plan where a deduction is given for induced saving as well as for the saving that would have occurred in any case. But the deduction itself is relevant only to the extent that the marginal tax rate of the saver exceeds his marginal tax rate when funds are withdrawn. Even when this is true, it is not a reason for preferring one plan over the other without knowing more about the response of individuals to this aspect since schemes with equal revenue loss could obviously be designed.

32. In 1972, all interest income was taxable. Although a $200 exclusion applied to dividend income, most taxpayers did not have any dividend income.

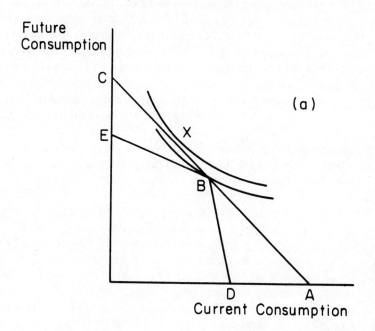

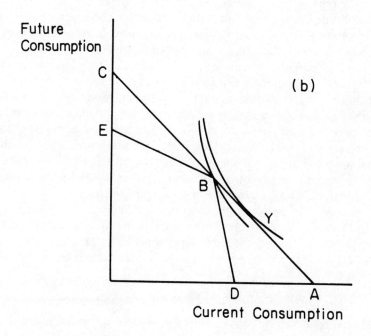

Fig. 6.1   The kinked intertemporal budget constraint.

line ABC would choose to borrow and therefore to consume at point Y. But with the kinked budget line DBE, this individual also chooses point B. The exclusion of interest and dividend income would raise the savings segment of the budget line from BE to BC. In figure 6.1a, this induces the individual to save and shifts the equilibrium from B to X; in contrast, in figure 6.1b this has no effect on the individual's behavior. Because we only observe that the individual is now at point B and cannot distinguish between the 6.1a and 6.1b situations, the effect of the tax change is ambiguous.

We might in principle reduce the uncertainty by distinguishing between those individuals with zero interest and dividends who also borrow and those who do not. The borrowers are in equilibrium on segment BD and would not be influenced by a shift in the lending line from BE to BC. The ambiguity would therefore pertain only to those who were truly at point B with no borrowing as well as no lending. There are two difficulties with this line of reasoning. The first is a practical one: information on borrowing is only available for itemizers and is therefore not available for the majority of taxpayers and for an even larger share of the group without interest and dividends since itemizing of deductions is relatively uncommon in this group. But even if information on borrowing were available, there would be a problem since many individuals both borrow and lend. Since the borrowing is generally at a higher interest rate than the lending (typically consumer credit and savings accounts), the observed behavior reflects considerations of liquidity and convenience and therefore cannot be reconciled with the simpler analysis of figure 6.1.

Since the prospective behavior of those who currently have no interest or dividends is inherently ambiguous, we present simulations based on two alternative assumptions about this group. The first type of simulation makes the very conservative assumption that all individuals would prefer to be borrowing and therefore do not change their saving in response to an interest and dividend exclusion rule. The alternative sets of simulations assume that all individuals respond by increasing their wealth to take at least some advantage of the exclusion; no distinction is made between those who initially have interest and dividend income and those who do not. This behavior is consistent with figure 6.1a (although with the individual switching from B to a point that may induce less saving than at X if the exclusion limit is binding). Further information about the simulation method as well as the simulation results will be presented in section 6.3.2.

6.3.1   The Distribution of Interest and Dividend Income

The current distribution of interest and dividend income determines the tax revenue effects of various exclusion limits and the extent to which changes in the limits can have marginal incentive effects. In considering the data presented in this section, it is important to bear in mind that the 1980 level of per capita income was approximately double the 1972 level and therefore that the typical taxpayer in 1980 had approximately twice the amount of financial assets. Moreover, the level of interest rates and the dividend-price ratio also doubled between 1972 and 1980. Thus a taxpayer who had $200 of interest and dividends in 1972 probably had about $800 in 1980.

Table 6.8 presents the cumulative frequency distribution of interest and dividend income by AGI class. Note that 46% of all taxpayers had no interest and dividend income and that an additional 25% had between $1 and $200 of such income. Introducing a $200 exclusion would thus provide an increase in the *marginal* real net interest rate for 71% of taxpayers while giving a tax reduction with no marginal incentive effect to the remaining 29%. Extending the exclusion from $200 to $400 would add an additional 7% to the number of taxpayers with a higher real net return and would double the intramarginal tax saving for the 22% of taxpayers with more than $400 of interest and dividends.

Since the vast majority of 1972 taxpayers had AGIs below $10,000, the overall pattern also describes the distribution of interest and dividend income in that income class. The pattern is also similar among those with AGIs between $10,000 and $20,000. Only in the very small class of taxpayers with higher incomes (less than 10% of 1972 taxpayers had AGIs over $20,000) did the interest and dividend distribution differ substantially from this pattern. For example, among those with AGIs between $20,000 and $30,000 of income, only 45% had less than $200 of interest and dividend income. For that income class, a $200 exclusion would be intramarginal for 55% of taxpayers.

Table 6.9 shows that the distribution of interest and dividend income also differs substantially by age. While 71% of all taxpayers had less than or equal to $200 of interest and dividends, more than 90% of those less

Table 6.8   **Cumulative Distributions of Interest and Dividend Income by Adjusted Gross Income Class**

Interest and Dividend Income	AGI Class (× $1,000)				
	0–10	10–20	20–30	30+	All
$0	58	37	16	5	46
$200	77	70	45	18	71
$400	82	80	59	26	78
$800	87	87	73	40	85
$1,600	91	93	82	54	90

Source: 1972 Tax Model Data.

Note: Values shown are cumulative percentages of taxpayers with less than the indicated amount of interest and dividend income.

Table 6.9   **Cumulative Distributions of Interest and Dividend Income by Age Class**

Interest and Dividend Income	Age Class				
	22–29	30–49	50–64	64+	All
$0	65	51	34	18	46
$200	91	80	59	32	71
$400	95	87	69	39	78
$800	97	93	78	50	85
$1,600	98	94	89	63	90

Source: 1972 Tax Model.

Note: Values shown are cumulative percentages of taxpayers with less than the indicated amount of interest and dividend income.

than twenty-nine years old and 80% of those aged thirty to forty-nine fell into this category. By contrast, only 32% of those over age sixty-four had as little as $200. These figures indicate that a $200 exclusion in 1972 would have had a marginal incentive effect for a relatively large fraction of preretirement taxpayers and that, for those older than sixty-five, the exclusion would be largely an intramarginal reward for earlier saving.

6.3.2   Simulations of Alternative Exclusion Rules

We now present the results of simulations of alternative exclusion rules. These simulations use the TAXSIM model for 1972; the baseline simulation therefore includes a $200 dividend exclusion. For cost reasons, we have reduced the sample by a one-in-three selection, yielding a simulation sample of 8,881 taxpayers.

The effect of an exclusion rule on tax revenue depends only on the parameters of the exclusion rule and not on the taxpayers' behavioral response. This reflects the fact that no revenue is lost on the induced increase in saving and the resulting increase in interest and dividend income.

Because the exclusion rules refer to the income earned on the stock of financial assets and not to annual savings, we simulate the behavioral response in terms of the stock of financial assets (or "assets" for short). We estimate each taxpayer's initial level of assets by assuming that the interest income reflects an interest rate of 4.5% and that the dividend income reflects a dividend-price ratio of 3.0%. On this basis we estimate an initial average level of gross financial assets of $8,230 for each of the 77.5 million tax returns.

Table 6.10 presents the simulated effects on tax revenue and on assets of the six exclusion plans: (1) exclusion of the first $200 of interest and dividend income; (2) exclusion of the first $400; (3) exclusion of the first $1,000; (4) exclusion of half of the first $1,000; (5) exclusion of interest

Table 6.10   **Simulated Effects of Alternative Dividend and Interest Exclusions with Different Behavioral Responses: Mean Changes in Tax Revenues and Assets**

	$200 Limit	$400 Limit	$1,000 Limit	$1,000 Limit, 50% Exclusion	$1,000 Limit with Floor*	No Limit, 20% Exclusion
1. Decrease in tax revenue	$13	$21	$37	$19	$30	$34
Increase in assets:						
2. Maximum response	$3,284	$7,122	$19,646	$19,646	$14,390	
3. Halfway response	$1,642	$3,561	$9,823	$9,823	$7,195	
4. Maximum response for those with positive initial financial assets only	$727	$2,008	$6,861	$6,861	$4,639	
5. Constant elasticity, $\eta = 1$	$98	$219	$546	$270	$369	$1,539
6. Constant elasticity, $\eta = 2$	$191	$429	$1,089	$543	$733	$3,283

Source: Simulations based on 1972 TAXSIM Data.

*The floor restricts the interest and dividend exclusion to the excess of interest and dividends over 5% of their income over $10,000.

and dividend income in excess of a floor equal to 5% of income over $10,000 subject to a limit of $1,000; and (6) exclusion of 20% of interest and dividend income without limit. These simulations are based on all taxpayers, including those over age sixty-five. The first row shows the effect of each exclusion rule on the mean annual tax liability per taxpayer. Under the existing law, the mean 1972 tax liability was $1,247. Exclusion of the first $200 of interest as well as dividends would reduce this by $13 to $1,234. This very small change in tax revenue reflects the fact that most taxpayers have much less than $200 of interest and dividends. With 77.5 million tax returns, the reduction of $13 per return implies a total revenue loss of $1.0 billion.

Increasing the exclusion from $200 to $400 reduces mean tax revenue by $8 per return; i.e. a doubling of the exclusion raises the revenue loss by about 60%. Similarly, raising the exclusion by 150% from $400 to $1,000 only raises the revenue loss by about 75% or $16 per return. Limiting the exclusion to 50 percent of the first $1,000 cuts the revenue loss in half; i.e. the total revenue loss with this rule is $19 per return or about the same as for a full exclusion of the first $400 of interest and dividends. Limiting the exclusion to the excess over a floor of 5 percent of income over $10,000 cuts the revenue loss from $37 to $30. Finally, the 20% exclusion without limit reduces tax revenue by $34 per return.

Four types of behavioral responses are simulated. The first assumes that each taxpayer increases his assets enough to take full advantage of the exclusion. Thus for the $200 exclusion each taxpayer accumulates a total of $4,445 of assets since we assume an interest rate of 4.5%. Although the average initial value of assets is $8,230 the distribution of these assets is such that most taxpayers have substantially less than $4,000; as table 6.8 indicated, 71% of taxpayers had less than $200 of interest and dividends. The first number in the second row of table 6.10 indicates that the average increase in assets if each taxpayer accumulated enough to take advantage of the full $200 exclusion would be $3,284.

The second simulation reduces the full response in an arbitrary way by assuming that everyone moves half way from his existing assets to the full $4,445. Thus someone who currently has $3,000 of assets increases them by $772. This response is of course equivalent to assuming that half of the taxpayers do not respond at all while half respond fully, or to any other distribution of individual responses that averages a half-way response.

The third simulation makes the very conservative assumption that all those taxpayers with no dividend and interest income in 1972 would not respond at all to the exclusion. All other taxpayers increase their assets to take full advantage of the exclusion. The result, shown in the third row of table 6.10, is an increase in mean assets of $727.

The final simulation also begins with the conservative assumption that those taxpayers who initially have no assets would continue to have no assets. Moreover, those with a relatively small initial amount of assets are assumed to show a correspondingly small increase in wealth. In particular, we assume that their behavior is governed by a constant elasticity response of assets to the relative "costs" of present and future consumption.

$$(3.1) \qquad \frac{A_1}{A_0} = \left(\frac{R_2}{R_0}\right)^{\eta},$$

where A_0 is the actual assets with the existing law, A_1 is the assets with the exclusion, and R_0 and R_2 are the rates of transformation with the current and alternative tax rules. With an exclusion but no deduction, $R_2 = (1 + i - \pi)^T$ an, as before, $R_0 = (1 + (1 - \theta)i - \pi)^T$; for any individual whose interest and dividend income already exceeds the exclusion, $R_2 = R_0$ and there is no change in assets. We are fully aware that this is a very rough model of behavior that does not capture the life-cycle character of the induced change in consumption and that quite arbitrarily assumes that all those who currently have no assets are either myopic or would prefer to be net borrowers even if there were no tax on interest income. We nevertheless illustrate this constant elasticity asset response by simulating with two alternative values: $\eta = 1$ and $\eta = 2$. A unit elasticity implies, for example, that an individual with a marginal tax rate of 20% and initial assets of $2,000 would increase her assets by $692; an elasticity of 2 would imply an increase of $1,623. The results of these simulations are shown in rows 5 and 6. With a $200 limit and a unit elasticity of response, the average increase in assets would be $98; an elasticity of 2 implies a mean asset increase of $191.

Although the results for the other exclusion limits in table 6.10 are self-explanatory, three comments are worth making. Note first that increasing the exclusion limit raises the potential accumulation by more than a proportionate amount even though the revenue effect rises less than proportionately. Second, the floor reduces the revenue cost of a $1,000 limit exclusion by $7 or somewhat less than 20%. In contrast, the increase in assets in every behavioral simulation fell by a greater percentage. Third, the 20% exclusion has by far the largest behavioral effect both absolutely and per dollar of revenue loss.

It is clear from the wide range of possible responses that we have recorded in table 6.10 that our uncertainty about the effect of a dividend and interest exclusion is very substantial. The 1980 legislation, introducing a $400 interest and dividend exclusion, will provide a natural experiment from which we can hope to learn more about the nature of the individual savings response. Of course, the evidence on even the first year's experience will not be available in usable form until about 1984 and policymakers may want to make decisions about savings incentives before then. It is perhaps reassuring therefore that the simulations reported in table 6.10 indicate that the alternative exclusion plans involve quite little revenue loss. Moreover, even these revenue loss figures overstate the net impact of an interest and dividend exclusion to the extent that the additional capital is invested in the corporate sector and results in increased corporate tax revenue.

6.4   Conclusion

The public's increased awareness of the low rate of personal saving in the United States and of the high effective tax rate on the income from personal saving has generated a growing interest in changing the individual income tax rules to stimulate saving. Although there are many specific plans, there are two principal options: (1) deductions from taxable income for savings deposited in special accounts where interest then accrues untaxed until the funds are withdrawn and (2) the exclusion of interest and dividends from taxable income. The revenue loss that would result from such deductions or exclusions can be limited by restrictions on the maximum amount of the deduction or exclusion or by allowing only a partial deduction or exclusion. The problem with any such ceiling or floor, however, is that it may eliminate marginal incentives (for those with savings or investment income above the ceiling or well below the floor) or severely restrict the size of the incentive effect (for those who are near the ceiling). The desirability of any saving plan depends critically on its ability to limit the revenue loss without destroying the marginal incentives.

Analyzing the effects of limits and floors requires microeconomic data on savings, financial assets, and interest and dividend income. The present paper uses such data from individual tax returns and from the Consumer Expenditure Survey to estimate the potential effects of alternative tax rules. Because the likely response of households to new tax rules is not known, we present simulations for a variety of different behavioral assumptions.

Although the savings deduction and the interest exclusion are fundamentally very similar, they are likely to have quite different effects during a rather long period of transition because they treat active savers very differently from those who previously saved and are currently dissaving. Moreover, potential savers may be influenced by the liquidity differences between the two methods or by the appearance that the immediate deduction confers a greater benefit. Because individuals differ in their situations and perceptions, a combination of both plans might be more effective in raising saving than an equal-cost reliance on either plan alone. The paper therefore presents separate analyses of the two types of plans.

The evidence that we present is not adequate for choosing the best combination of these options or even for deciding whether either option should be chosen. We do not have sufficient information about savings behavior to predict the response of capital accumulation to these plans. Moreover, the design of an approximate tax policy involves not only the savings response but more general aspects of excess burden and the fair distribution of the tax burden.

But the analyses in this paper are sufficient to demonstrate that some of the potential problems that have been raised as objections to the savings proposals are not very serious. First, although some of any savings deduction would merely reward saving that would have occurred in any case, even with a deduction limited to 10% of wages and salaries (with a ceiling of $2,000) there would be very few savers for whom the incentive was intramarginal. Similarly, at 1972 levels of wealth and interest rates, a $400 exclusion of interest and dividends would provide a marginal incentive for more than 75% of taxpayers.

The second basic fact that emerges in our study is that the reduction in tax revenue caused by an exclusion or deduction plan would be relatively modest. With the exclusion plans, the revenue loss does not depend on the taxpayers' response to the changed incentive. In 1972, a $400 interest and dividend exclusion would have entailed a revenue loss of only $21 per taxpayer, or an aggregate of less than $2 billion. Increases in the $400 limit involve substantially less than proportionate increases in the revenue loss. The revenue effect of a savings deduction plan does depend on the reaction of savers to the new incentive. Although some preexisting assets would be transferred into the special accounts in the years immediately after a savings deduction plan was introduced, the potential transfer amounts and associated revenue loss are relatively small for the vast majority of taxpayers. After the transition period, if there were no increase in saving, a deduction limited to 10% of wage income (with a ceiling of $2,000) would entail a revenue loss at 1972 levels of only $4 billion.[33] Any actual increase in saving that is induced by the deduction would then substantially exceed the associated loss of tax revenue.[34]

33. This short-run revenue loss is based on the existing savings distribution and excludes asset transfers; see section 6.2.1 for evidence on the modest one-time revenue cost of allowing deductions for asset transfers. The corresponding long-run revenue loss, which also reflects both the loss of the subsequent tax revenues that would have been collected on the interest and dividends on these savings and the gain in tax revenue that would eventually be collected when the funds are withdrawn, would be about $5 billion.

34. Recall that if the revenue loss on this additional saving is measured by the immediate consequence of the deduction, an extra dollar of saving reduces tax revenue by only about 20 cents. This tax reduction is partially recovered (in a present value sense) to the extent that the individual's tax rate is as high when the funds are withdrawn. Although no tax is collected on the interest and dividends earned on the extra capital, this is not a revenue loss since it would not otherwise have existed. Indeed, the corporate income tax on this additional capital could more than offset the loss in personal tax revenue.

References

Becker, C. and D. Fullerton. 1980. Income tax incentives to promote saving. NBER Working Paper no. 487.

Boskin, M. J. 1978. Taxation, saving, and the rate of interest. *Journal of Political Economy* 86: S3–S27.

Bradford, D. F. 1980*a*. The economics of tax policy toward savings. In G. von Furstenburg, ed., *The government and capital formation*. Vol. 2 in the series on capital investment and saving. Cambridge: American Council of Life Insurance.

———. 1980*b*. The case for a personal consumption tax. In J. Pechman, ed., *What should be taxed: Income or expenditure?* pp. 75–113. Washington: Brookings Institution.

Feldstein, M. 1970. Inflation, specification bias, and the impact of interest rates. *Journal of Political Economy* 78: 1325–39.

———. 1976. Compensation in tax reform. *National Tax Journal* 39, no. 2: 123–30.

———. 1977. Does the United States save too little? *American Economic Review* 67, no. 1: 116–21.

———. 1978*a*. The welfare cost of capital income taxation. *Journal of Political Economy* 86, no. 2: S29–S51.

———. 1978*b*. The rate of return, taxation, and personal savings. *Economic Journal* 88: 482–87.

———. 1980. Tax incentive without deficits. *Wall Street Journal*, 25 July.

Feldstein, M., and C. Horioka. 1980. Domestic savings and international capital flows. *Economic Journal* 90: 314–29.

Feldstein M., and J. Poterba. 1980. State and local taxes and the rate of return on nonfinancial corporate capital. NBER Working Paper no. 508R.

Feldstein, M., and S. C. Tsiang. 1968. The interest rate, taxation, and the personal savings incentive. *Quarterly Journal of Economics* 82: 419–34.

Fisher, I. 1937. Income in theory and income taxation in practice. *Econometrica* 5: 1–55.

Fullerton, D. A.; J. B. King; J. B. Shoven; and J. Whalley. 1979. Static and dynamic resource allocation effects of corporate and personal tax integration in the U.S.: A general equilibrium approach. NBER Working Paper no. 337.

Green, J. R., and E. Sheshinski. 1978. Optimal capital-gains taxation under limited information. Harvard Institute of Economic Research Discussion Paper no. 604.

Kaldor, N. 1955. *An expenditure tax*. London: Allen & Unwin.

Kay, J. A., and M. A. King. 1978. The British tax system. Oxford: Oxford University Press.

King, M. 1980. Savings and taxation. NBER Working Paper no. 428.

Lubick, Donald. 1980. Unpublished memo. Office of Tax Policy, U.S. Treasury, Washington.

McLure, C. E., Jr. 1980. Taxes, saving, and welfare: Theory and evidence. NBER Working Paper no. 504.

Meade Committee. 1978. *The structure and reform of direct taxation.* London: Allen & Unwin.

Mirrlees, J. A. 1976. Optimal tax theory: A synthesis. *Journal of Public Economics* 6: 327–58.

Musgrave, R. A. 1959. *The theory of public finance.* New York: McGraw-Hill.

President's Commission on Private Pensions. 1980. *An interim report of the President's Commission on Private Pensions.* Washington: Government Printing Office.

Summers, L. H. 1980. Tax policy in a life cycle model. NBER Working Paper no. 302.

United States Department of the Treasury. 1977. Blueprints for basic tax reform. Washington: Government Printing Office.

von Furstenberg, G. M. 1980. *The government and capital formation.* Cambridge: Ballinger.

Comment   Martin J. Bailey

The paper "Alternative Tax Rules and Personal Saving Incentives," by Martin Feldstein and Daniel R. Feenberg, correctly emphasizes the advantages of a comprehensive reform of the taxation of income from capital, and correctly remarks on the political imperatives that force a piecemeal approach in its place. The quantum leap of a major Pareto improvement in this area is unmistakably out of reach, whereas the time is ripe for third-best proposals such as integrations of corporate and personal income taxes and the limited exclusions considered in this paper. Pragmatically, therefore, the paper is a necessary, valuable exercise. If read with the proper care and selectivity, the results are useful and are superior to the corresponding estimates produced by the Treasury Department and by the Joint Committee on Internal Revenue Taxation.

The estimates can be further improved and narrowed down by better methods. Hence my comments imply restrained enthusiasm for the results as given: I regret that the authors failed to use all the analytical tools they had at their command. The principal tools they neglected are neatly summarized in the following quote from their paper: "The effect on savings of a [reduction] in the taxation of capital income therefore depends on the timing of tax payments and on the response of government

Martin J. Bailey is with the Department of Economics, University of Maryland.

spending. If government spending in each year remains unchanged, national saving must rise. If the compensating changes in the tax keep tax liabilities in each year unchanged, private saving must also increase." These propositions, now well established, were derived from the theory of household maximization subject to budget constraint, a theory regrettably neglected in the balance of the paper. Also omitted was the compensated tax change, whose use would have obviated discussion of the controversy about the Ricardian equivalence theorem and with the related and highly debatable income effects. Without these complications the only possible outcome is a fall in consumption, and the range of cases to be considered would be markedly reduced.

Also, sampling error can be considerably reduced in tax simulations by nonrandom sampling from the Treasury's public use sample of individual tax returns, taking all due care to avoid bias in the selection criteria.

Throughout the paper, purchases of financial assets are considered equivalent to savings, subject to only slight caveat. The authors do explain that taxpayers with eligible assets would use up a savings exclusion for several years by transferring these assets into the special tax-privileged accounts. They also argue that taxpayers would be deterred by the inconvenience from converting an ineligible asset, such as the home, into eligible form by borrowing against it (e.g. by increasing the mortgage.) However, there is no appreciable inconvenience in using the net proceeds of a new, larger mortgage to buy eligible assets and then to transfer them year by year into the special account. Similarly, an increased dividend exclusion would doubtless induce more corporations to specialize in high dividend-payout ratios. Responses like these will reduce and could even nullify the predicted national savings (or consumption) responses.

The reader will note that this comment on taxpayer responses involving no new saving increases the chance of a zero consumption effect, in contrast to my earlier comment suggesting that consumption must decline. Thus the criticisms partly offset each other. However, the fact remains that for compensated tax changes the case of a consumption increase cannot occur (apart from asymmetrical distributional effects). A zero consumption change would be the extreme case among the possibilities.

Careful analysis of taxpayer responses to tax changes is the needed next improvement in the estimation of revenue effects—a step that has been in development in various studies for some time. It is only beginning to affect official estimates, although that picture has lately changed from one extreme to the other in the flamboyant appearance of "supply-side" ideas and claims. The Feldstein and Feenberg paper is a constructive attempt to improve the picture.

7 Modeling Alternative Solutions to the Long-Run Social Security Funding Problem

Michael J. Boskin, Marcy Avrin, and Kenneth Cone

7.1 Introduction

Since its enactment, the Social Security System has enjoyed unique popularity among public income support programs. In the past several years, however, rising payroll taxes, a huge long-term deficit, and concerns over its effects on the economy have led an increasing number of observers to conclude that social security is in urgent need of reform.

This system serves two major goals: to replace income lost at retirement, and to provide minimum income support for the aged. The former, the insurance goal, is based on earned entitlements; the welfare, or transfer, goal aims at social adequacy of support. Each goal enjoys wide public support as well as important policy justifications. For example, imperfections in the private annuities market and imperfect foresight regarding future incomes, inflation, life expectancy, etc., may lead many citizens to "undersave" for retirement, forcing them to become general charges on the public via welfare or other programs in the absence of social security.

Over more than four decades, the Social Security System has helped mitigate these problems in an important way. It has provided substantial income security to the elderly; it has kept many elderly persons out of

Michael J. Boskin is professor of economics at Stanford University and a research associate and director of the Social Insurance Program at the National Bureau of Economic Research. Marcy Avrin is a research associate at the National Bureau of Economic Research. Kenneth Cone, a graduate student at Stanford University at the time this paper was written, is now assistant professor of economics at the University of Chicago.

The authors thank John Shoven and Denny Dennis for valuable advice, and John Wolfe and Joseph Applebaum for helpful suggestions. The National Science Foundation provided partial support for this research under grant SOC 78-07139. Reported here is part of the NBER's research in social insurance. Any opinions expressed are those of the authors and not of any organizations.

extreme poverty; and it has transferred billions of dollars annually from the younger, wealthier generation of workers to the older, poorer generation of retirees. These are significant achievements indeed. However, the system, which was designed decades ago, has not kept up fully with rapidly changing economic, social, and demographic conditions. It is having several substantial and probably unintended adverse effects on the overall economy; and it faces a long-term funding crisis of substantial proportions.

Social security is thought of in several alternative ways: as an actuarially fair pension fund; as a separable system of taxes and transfer payments; and as a pure consumption loan intergenerational transfer program, where each generation transfers a fraction of its labor income to the retired generation with the expectation that the succeeding generation will treat it similarly. In truth, the existing Old Age Survivors Insurance (OASI) System is none of the above, but has components of each (as well as additional complexities).

The current system differs from the private pension fund analogue in several respects. First, it is unfunded in that current payouts are financed by contemporaneous "contributions," or taxes. This had the advantage of allowing retirement benefits to be initiated immediately, making the initial recipients "windfall" beneficiaries. That is, they received retirement income supplements with little or no previous contributions. Income was similarly transferred from the initial working population to the initial retirement generation. This intergenerational transfer has continued as the system has matured, although the percentage of net transfers (the expected value of a participant's receipts less payments) in total benefits has diminished. One drawback of this system is that while people accumulate future claims against the system, no corresponding wealth accumulation occurs for the system as a whole. Thus, while the working population is being forced to "save," no funds are made available for capital formation in the economy. At any point in time, the system is "bankrupt" in that it has massive future retirement obligations and only a relatively trivial amount of assets. A government can operate such a system because of its powers to tax future income in order to finance its obligations.

There are other major differences between social security and the private annuity or pension fund analogue. The benefits are distinctly tilted in favor of the low-income worker, the worker with a short work history, and the retiree with a spouse with an uncovered work history and those with little retirement income. That is, relative to a system where each participant earned a common rate of return on his or her contributions, the current Social Security System involves a set of taxes and transfers. This redistribution within a generation, in contrast to the intergenerational transfer mentioned above, is accomplished by such mechanisms as a progressive benefit formula, a minimum benefit, a uniform dependent's benefit, and an earnings test.

7.2   The Major Problems Confronting Social Security

Three major sets of problems plague social security today. The first is the issue of equity, both inter- and intragenerational. A large proportion of benefits received by retired workers is really an intergenerational transfer. Also, different groups in a given generation of the population are treated differently by the Social Security System. Low-income workers receive a higher fraction of their previous earnings in benefits than do high-income workers, married couples usually receive half again as much as single persons with the same earnings history for the primary earner, those with short-covered earnings histories are favored, etc.

A second set of problems plaguing the Social Security System is the potentially adverse effects that it may have on private incentives to work, save, hire workers, etc.

Probably the most overwhelming problem confronting social security as a pay-as-you-go system is the long-term funding crisis. Even after the 1977 social security amendments, the long-term deficit in the OASI System was well over $600 billion (in 1977 dollars). By 1982 this amount had increased to well over one trillion dollars. This is the amount by which the present value of legislated benefits exceeds the present value of legislated taxes. To put this in perspective, this amount is about the size of the privately held regular national debt. The major cause of this projected deficit is the drastic change in the age structure of the population. Once the post–World War II baby boom retires (around 2010) the ratio of retirees to workers will increase enormously. The best estimate is that the ratio of retirees to workers will increase by over 60%—from slightly less than one to three to about one to two. Given the pay-as-you-go nature of the system, this implies either a huge increase in taxes to maintain the ratio of benefits to before-tax wages or a significant decline in the ratio. Neither prospect is appealing, but there is no avoiding the choice.

In addition to the rapidly changing age structure of the population, the trend to earlier retirement combined with increased life expectancy has increased the average length of retirement considerably. In 1948 one-half of all males over the age of sixty-five were in the labor force; today that figure is only one in five. The average life expectancy of the elderly has increased over two years since 1960. Thus the length of the average retirement period has increased by about one-third since 1950. This has greatly strained the financial resources of the elderly; to achieve any given level of annual consumption, a retiree now needs substantially greater savings, intrafamily transfers, or public support.

What does all this imply for the long-run financial outlook for social security? Even the large tax increases of the 1977 amendments will prove insufficient to finance the program through the first half of the next century. If the current law is maintained until 2025, payroll tax rates would have to increase by more than 8 percentage points to meet benefit payments.[1] This would imply combined employer and employee tax rates of about 23% of payroll! Given the huge outcry against the large (but much smaller) increases legislated in 1977, it is clear that the time has come to reexamine the future course of social security. The alternative is continued unpopular tax increases, which add to costs and prices, reduce net wage rates, redirect the system further from an earned entitlements or annuity basis, and continually erode public support of the Social Security System.

While several short-run "quick fixes" have been proposed, such as bringing into the system those, such as government employees, not currently included, or eliminating the ceiling on taxable earnings, these cannot produce a reduction in the long-term deficit unless they are accomplished in a manner that is actuarially disadvantageous to the groups concerned.[2] For example, bringing government employees under social security would increase current tax revenues but add to future obligations. This could reduce the deficit only if government employees were given a "bad" deal. But we could then expect them to resist such a proposal en masse.

7.3   The Transfer and Annuity Components of Social Security

In order to appreciate the relation between the annuity and the intergenerational transfer components of social security, let us begin by examining the most extreme case: the first cohort of retirees under the United States Social Security System. Consider an individual who was age sixty-two in 1937 and retired in 1940 at age sixty-five.

For a worker making average earnings and investing the sum of employer and employee contributions at interest rates then prevailing, the accumulated retirement principal in 1940 would have been only $68.36, yielding an annuity of $6.59 per year. Clearly, benefits far in excess of contributions would be required if any substantial benefits were to be paid.

The actual average annual benefit paid in 1940 to a male age sixty-five was $270.60. Since an annuity would have yielded only $6.59, $264.01 of the benefits were a pure transfer, or welfare payment.[3] Since the benefits

---

1. See Robertson (1978). The 8 percentage point increase includes that estimated to fund the deficits in hospital and disability insurance as well as OASI.
2. They might be defensible on other grounds.
3. This example is taken from Parsons and Munro (1977).

may and, in fact, did change over the retirement period, it is more convenient to compare capitalized savings and benefits over the expected time span than to compare annuity payments and annual benefits. For the individual in question, the present value of lifetime benefits was $2,962.09, of which $2,893.73 was a transfer. Thus this individual paid for only 2.3% of the benefits received. This percentage has been increasing for individuals over time. Those retiring at age sixty-five in 1970 paid for approximately 32% of the benefits received.

Different indivduals receive vastly different "deals" in the sense of the ratio of benefits received to taxes paid plus interest. This occurs for a number of reasons including the progressive benefit formula, the minimum benefit, the spouse's benefit, the different periods of coverage, etc.

7.4 Separating the Transfer and Insurance Components

Many problems in the Social Security System relate to the conflict between its twin goals of earned benefits and income adequacy. Most critics of the program propose reforming it in the direction of one goal or the other. Separating the transfer and annuity goals would have different effects on individuals depending on their age, income, industry, etc.

The three sets of problems plaguing social security—the long-term funding deficit, the apparent inequities, and the adverse incentives— have generated much interest in reforming the system. One proposed reform is the separation of the transfer and annuity goals of the program. In principle, it may be desirable to separate the financing of these different goals of the system. Separating the transfer and annuity functions of the Social Security System and funding them respectively out of general revenues and earmarked payroll taxes has been recommended for a number of reasons.

First, the current system is so complex as to obscure the relation between contributions and benefits and impede a rationalization by firms and employees of total retirement support, private pension plus social security.

Second, as we shall demonstrate below, many groups in the population are getting a "bad" deal from social security compared to an actuarily fair system. Separating the transfer and annuity goals would provide the *same rate of return for all workers* under social security's annuity program. The inequities which undermine support of the system would be eliminated in this part of the program.

Third, transfers to the elderly poor (beyond Supplemental Security Income) could be financed from general revenues. Many object to financing an income guarantee for the aged poor from a tax which bears so heavily on the low-income workers. The current income tax exemptions, deductions, and low-income allowance, which together exempt the first several thousand dollars of earnings from tax, indicate the general belief that those at the very bottom of the income scale should not have to help finance general income support programs.

The same argument applies to any intergenerational transfers providing earnings-related benefits beyond those provided by pure insurance and the minimum income guarantee. Many object to a system in which current unskilled workers surrender income (beyond their *own* insurance) to subsidize retired professionals beyond what is actuarially fair.

In separating the insurance from the transfer goals, general revenue financing would also require the transfer goals to compete openly with other government priorities, including tax cuts. General revenue financing would permit policymakers and the public openly to determine the value of transfers to the elderly in relation to other social priorities and to promote cost-effective measures for doing so. It will permit differential needs assessment to deal with different circumstances (marital status, etc.) in the context of a transfer program, where many precedents for doing so already exist.

7.5   Toward a Solution

As we begin to grapple with the problems of the Social Security System, from the apparent inequities and inefficiencies to the long-term deficit, serious consideration is being given to two major reforms: separating the dual functions of social security and financing them separately, and raising average retirement ages. Separating the transfer component of the system (and funding it out of general revenues) would encourage more cost-effective transfers and enable us to strengthen the earned entitlement functions, which, in turn, would eliminate many inequities and help restore public confidence in the financial integrity of the system. Raising retirement ages would relieve much of the financial pressure on social security and make much sense in view of other labor force and demographic changes.

In what follows we have analyzed a series of long-run policy alternatives along these lines and have calculated the projected costs and benefits of each for workers of different ages. The age cohorts, cohorts 1 through 5, are ages twenty-five through thirty-four, thirty-five through forty-four, forty-five through fifty-four, fifty-five through sixty-four, and sixty-five and older, respectively. Those who are not yet twenty-five constitute cohort X. We have also calculated the implications of these alternatives with regard to the social security surplus or deficit to the year 2050. Basically, for each alternative, we ask two questions. First, what is the ratio of the present value of benefits an age cohort can expect to receive at age sixty-five to the accumulated value of its lifetime contributions to social security? Second, what is the present value of the resulting social security retirement deficit through 2050?

We have investigated these questions in terms of the following alternative plans:

1. The *Base Case* analyzes the Social Security System as it stands today.[4]
2. The *Trans* alternative reduces benefits to eliminate transfers for cohorts 2–5.
3. The *Trans 80* alternative eliminates transfers and adjusts taxes in 1980 to close the future deficit as of 1980. (Taxes were actually lowered by 1.5% of income.)
4. The *Tax 80* alternative raises taxes by 1.7% of income beginning in 1980 to close the future deficit as of that year.
5. The *Tax 2030* alternative raises taxes by 3.9% of income beginning in 2030 to close the future deficit as of that year.
6. The *Ret* alternative increases retirement ages an average of three years.

Thus these alternatives allow us to determine the effects of decreasing benefits by eliminating transfers, increasing taxes, and increasing the retirement age.

In all of these alternatives we consider only the old age insurance portion of the Social Security System. Thus we exclude taxes and benefits paid for disability, health, and part of survivor insurance. (The model *does* include the increased benefits paid to wives when their husbands die.) We will refer to the retirement insurance system as OASI, to distinguish it from OASDHI, which includes health and disability insurance.

In order to understand the basis of these calculations, it is important to consider the data on which they are based, the method of analysis used, and the assumptions upon which they rely.

7.5.1   Data

The data used in the calculations are the 1975 Social Security Exact Match File that merges individual records from the 1973 Current Population Survey (CPS) with OASI earnings and benefit records. With these data, the pattern of actual OASI benefits, as well as lifetime contributions into the system by all individuals, can be found. These data permit redistribution across cohorts to be separated from the annuity aspects and enable us to estimate values for individual households. Since the data used include only a sample of 5,000 individuals in each cohort, sample

---

4. Sensitivity of the Base Case estimates to various assumptions was also tested.

weights and populations statistics are used to generalize the sample results to the entire population. The weights are present in the file.

The data actually used in the analysis from the social security longitudinal earnings tape include the sum of covered earnings from 1937 to 1950, covered earnings from 1951 to 1975, estimated quarters of coverage from 1937 to 1950, and actual quarters of coverage from 1951 to 1975.

From the 1973 CPS, the following data were used: region, farm residence, age, sex, race, marital status, class of worker, occupation, industry, weeks worked in 1972 as a civilian, industry of longest civilian job in 1972, years of school completed, and wage and salary amount.

7.5.2   Method of Analysis

For cohorts 1–5 we determine the relation between the summation of aggregate contributions and the expected aggregate benefits of all individuals currently in the Social Security System, assuming in all cases but Ret that the retirement age is sixty-five for husbands and singles and that wives retire with their husbands.[5] For an individual, the value of total contributions into the system at the point of retirement is the summation of actual and expected OASI taxes paid both by himself and by his employer compounded by a real rate of interest (3% in the base case). These calculations use actual and forecasted income, historical and forecasted maximum taxable income limits, and historical and forecasted tax rates.

The expected value of OASI benefits over the worker's remaining life is calculated considering the probability of survival and the wage index from *Social Security Bulletin, Annual Statistical Supplement, 1975*.[6] Wives receive benefits based on their own or their husbands' benefits, whichever is larger. The entire analysis is converted to 1977 dollars.[7]

In order to determine the expected contributions for individuals who

5. A fraction of each cohort, those in noncovered industries or with insufficient quarters of coverage, are considered to be ineligible for benefits. Wives who do not qualify on their own or on their husbands' behalf receive no benefits. The retirement pattern can also be simulated by a retirement behavior equation, but these initial estimates are used to compare them with typical Social Security Administration assumptions.

6. The year of death for each individual in cohorts 1–5 was predicted using a random number generator and his or her probability of death at each age, conditional on race and sex. Individuals predicted to have died before reaching the age of sixty-five are excluded from the analysis of average net benefits, although their taxes are included in the general financing calculations. For cohort X, we used "average" men and women for each year-of-birth cohort, and reduced taxes and benefits in each year to account for the cumulative probability of death. We used an average life expectancy assumption to find the number of years that a wife in cohort X will collect widow's benefits. This assumption potentially adds a small bias in our calculations. Year-of-death predictions used *The U.S. Fact Book* (1978) for all ages less than sixty-five and ages sixty-five, seventy, and eighty. For ages not given, year of death was predicted interpolating from the 1969–71 death rates in National Center for Health Statistics (1975).

7. Benefits are increased by 17% for cohort 5 to adjust for the disproportionate number of widows, whose social security entitlements are not captured by the data.

have not yet reached the age of sixty-five, we applied the contribution rates specified in the 1977 amendments to the Social Security Act to known earnings and predicted future earnings for each individual. Earnings were predicted separately for males and females using an estimating equation based on positive 1972 earnings of all individuals in the sample. The predictions, determined from the estimated coefficients of the independent variables in the equation and the characteristics of the individuals, were indexed over time using 7% for inflationary earnings increases and the assumption of a 1.5% per year earnings increase due to productivity for the Base Case.[8] Female income is adjusted for labor force participation.[9]

More formally, we "age" our survey data so that we know both the past work history and the projected future work history and retirement benefits for the sample population. Having done this we calculate the present value of each household's total contribution at retirement (PVC_R^i). These are calculated as

$$PVC_R^i = \sum_{t=1}^{R} C_t^i \frac{1}{(1+r)^{R-t}},$$

where R is a given retirement age and r is the interest rate "credited" to a social security "account" under our pension plan analogue.[10] In fact, all projected contributions and benefits are calculated so that they are the anticipated dollar amount times the probability of the individual surviving to that time.

We calculate the expected retirement benefits at age of retirement (PVB_R^i) as

$$PVB_R^i = \sum_{t=R}^{N} B_t^i \frac{1}{(1+r)^{R-t}},$$

where N is 100, beyond which the survival probability is taken to be zero.

Given that survival probabilities are already embedded in B_t and C_t, an actuarially fair system would be one where $PVC_R^i = PVB_R^i$. We define

8. The actual dependent variable used was the log of earnings. The independent variables include dummy variables for a southern location, rural location, race, the fact of being married, white collar status, service collar status, blue collar status, employment in an industry, self-employment, weeks worked, and level of education.

9. Female labor force participation was assumed to keep the same age distribution as in 1975, but to slowly increase for each age group until 2005. The rate increases 12.5 percentage points for each age group by 2005. (This is based on assumptions of the *1977 Annual Report of the Trustees of the Social Security System.*) Again, this is for comparison only. Future estimates will incorporate a separate female labor force participation equation.

10. We make the usual assumption that the employer component is borne by employees, and hence include the employer part of the payroll tax in estimating total contributions on behalf of a worker. Alternative incidence assumptions could be used, and the data adjusted accordingly. The result, of course, would be to "credit" less tax payment and to increase the size of transfers, as the share of employer contributions assumed paid by someone other than employees increases.

the expected present value of any transfer received by the participant as $T_R^i = PVB_R^i - PVC_R^i$.

The same type of analysis is performed for cohort X, which involves making several assumptions regarding the future.[11]

After performing the analysis of taxes and benefits by cohort for various scenarios, we sum the results in order to determine the budget surplus or deficit that results from each scenario.

7.6 An Overall Comparison of Alternative Social Security Situations

Let us begin by examining some general measures of the overall situation for the OASI system under alternative scenarios. In particular, we consider aggregate taxes, benefits, and the deficit under alternative social security situations and, correspondingly, the total transfers and transfers as a percentage of income for alternative social security situations. The situations to be discussed include the Base Case, i.e. current law, including currently legislated but not yet implemented tax increases; the Base Case with a slightly lower rate of productivity growth; two situations in which the transfer component is eliminated and dealt with separately under general revenues, Trans 80 and Trans; and Ret, which increases the retirement age by three years. Table 7.1 presents estimates of the aggregate taxes, benefits, and resulting present value of the long-term deficit under these alternative scenarios. Recall that we are making *very conservative assumptions* with respect to the projected long-term deficit in considering the Base Case in order to try to maintain comparability, roughly speaking, with the assumptions made by the trustees of the Social Security System.

The Base Case is estimated assuming an annual rate of productivity growth of 1.5% per year and an annual inflation rate of 7% per year, and the total taxes and benefit are discounted at a real rate of 3% with all figures being presented in 1977 dollars. Thus, for the Base Case, we note that the total taxes amount to approximately $3.3 trillion whereas total

11. The assumptions are as follows: (1) In terms of cohort size, actual population statistics are used for individuals born from 1953 to 1977. Estimates of size for 1978 to 2050 were made assuming that birthrates would decline from 1.7 to 1.65 in 1980 and then slowly increase to 2.1 in 2005. (2) Female labor force participation is assumed to keep the same age profile as in 1975 but to slowly increase for each age group until 2005. The rate increases 12.5 percentage points for each group by 2005. (3) Coverage by the Social Security System is assumed constant at 90%. (4) The percentage of women married is assumed constant at 93% on the basis of data from the *Statistical Abstract*. (5) Unemployment is assumed constant at 5%. (6) The mortality rates for each age group are assumed to remain constant. (7) Each couple is assumed to retire together at age sixty-five. (8) The wage is adjusted to account for the fact that *all* income used in the estimates is below the taxable limit since the wage equation and the Social Security Match Tape data are used. The adjustment is based on taxable/total ratio in 1977.

These assumptions are based on those of the *1977 Annual Report of the Trustees of the Social Security Administration*.

Table 7.1   **Aggregate Taxes, Benefits, and the**
              Deficit under Alternative Reforms

Case	Total Taxes[a]	Total Benefits[a]	Deficit[a]
Base	3,336.9	3,968.8	632.0
Base with productivity = 1.0%	2,839.6	3,570.5	731.0
Trans 80	2,798.6	2,656.5	−142.1
Trans	3,336.9	2,656.5	−680.3
Ret	3,500.9	3,345.6	−155.3

[a]All figures are in billions of discounted 1977 dollars.

benefits amount to about $4 trillion. Again, recall that these figures are adjusted for inflation and discounted to 1977. With these assumptions, the estimated long-term deficit amounts to $632 billion. Recall that this does not include the hospital and disability insurance programs, in which case taxes, benefits, and the deficit would all be substantially larger. This enormous deficit occurs primarily because of the changing age structure of the population, as noted above. When the baby boom generation starts to retire, we face the awkward prospect of an extremely large and rapid increase in the ratio of retirees to workers in our society. Even if the actuarial assumptions of the social security trustees are accurate—and we believe they are optimistic—we will have to raise social security taxes or lower social security benefits, or raise other tax revenues, or some combination of these options, by an enormous amount in the years ahead. This combination would have to amount to $632 billion (discounted dollars) in 1977; if we wait for the baby boom generation to retire around the year 2030, the combination necessary will be between $2.5 and $3 trillion in 1977 dollars.

The estimated taxes, benefits, and deficit for the Base Case are very sensitive to the assumptions incorporated in making projections over the long term. Because of the importance of compounding even small differences in growth rates, even so small a difference as one-half of 1% in the rate of productivity growth increases the long-term deficit—holding other assumptions constant—by almost $100 billion in present value terms. Table 7.1 demonstrates that, when the productivity growth assumption is lowered from 1.5% to 1% per annum, the Base Case results in a decreased tax revenue, again in present value discounted dollars of almost $500 billion to $2.8 trillion, and a reduction in total benefits by about $400 billion from slightly under $4 trillion to slightly under $3.6 trillion. The recent behavior of productivity does not give us much cause for optimism for restoring a rapid rate of economic growth in our economy and does not augur well for the long-term deficit of social security.

Another assumption which is extremely important in the calculation of taxes, benefits, and the deficit concerns the length of retirement. As noted above, early forecasts drastically underestimated how rapidly life expectancies would increase. In the 1960s and 1970s, the life expectancy increased about three years for women and one and one-half years for men. Simultaneously, there has been a rapid acceleration in the numbers of people taking early retirement. In 1948, one-half of males over age sixty-five were in the labor force; in 1980, only one-fifth of males over sixty-five are working. If life expectancy rises still further, the long-term deficit in social security will increase drastically. As a rough approximation, *increasing life expectancy and eligibility for social security benefits by an extra year would add about $250 billion to the long-term deficit.* In view of the increased length of retirement periods (because of increased life expectancy and earlier retirement) and in view of the higher fraction of the population attending college and hence which is entering the labor force later and is shifting out of physically demanding and dangerous jobs, one major avenue of reform of social security would be to raise the age at which people could collect social security benefits. We simulated one such scenario: raising the retirement age from sixty-five to sixty-eight, or, more precisely, adding a maximum of three years to work-lives (which is obviously relevant only to those who survive to those ages). Under the assumptions of the Base Case for productivity growth, inflation, etc., such a move would result in a very modest increase in taxes from the additional years of work (about $170 billion) but would result in a $620 billion benefit decrease. *Note that this would be accomplished without decreasing the annual benefit received by any worker once retired.* The reduction in total benefits in discounted 1977 dollars would come about solely because people would be retiring later and hence would be collecting benefits for a shorter period of time. Such a reduction would more than offset the impending enormous social security deficit and the impending enormous tax increases that would be necessary under the current system above and beyond those already voted. Indeed, such a program in conjunction with the other assumptions noted above would leave social security with a surplus of over $150 billion. An alternative scenario, raising the retirement age less rapidly and not quite as high, could still put the Social Security System into long-term balance. This scenario highlights the extreme importance of the length of the retirement period for the total benefits paid out and the long-term deficit of the system.

The long-term benefit payouts and tax collections, especially the former, are also extremely sensitive to the enormous percentage of transfer payments involved in social security benefits, especially for older current workers and retirees. Two other scenarios were simulated to analyze the removal of positive transfer payments: Trans and Trans 80. The Trans alternative removes the transfer component of benefits completely for cohorts 2–5. The negative transfers for cohorts 1 and X are maintained. The transfers are assumed to be shifted to general revenues in a manner to be decided once a genuine earned entitlement system is set up. We must note, however, that setting up a transfer payment system for the elderly to be funded out of general revenues may involve either increases in general revenue taxes or decreases in other projected government expenditures as well as the sharp reductions in payroll taxes and projected future payroll tax increases we are about to describe. Also, part of the reduced payroll tax revenue (about 20%) would be recouped automatically by increased taxes once the employer component of social security used to finance these transfers was no longer deductible from taxable income for other taxes. Under Trans, taxes will not go down at all, but total benefits will go down about one-third, from slightly under $4 trillion to about $2.7 trillion. This totally reverses the deficit picture from a two-thirds of a trillion dollar deficit to a two-thirds of a trillion dollar surplus discounted to 1977. Besides totally eliminating the need for future tax increases, the two-thirds of a trillion dollar surplus obviously could result in further deductions in social security taxes from *present* levels. It could also be used to finance transfer payments if we shifted total transfers into general revenue.

The Trans 80 alternative substantially reduces taxes as well as total benefits. Indeed, the total benefits would be treated exactly as under Trans. The difference is that tax revenues would be reduced substantially from 1980 on, leaving social security itself with a very modest surplus of $140 billion.

This overall version of the total situation with respect to taxes, benefits, and the long-term deficit highlights not only the current extreme long-term deficit of the Social Security System as presently constituted, and the large tax increases above and beyond the 1977 legislated ones impending in view of the long-term deficit, but also the opportunities and possibilities for deriving a solution by separating the benefits paid to achieve the twin goals of social security: earned entitlement and income adequacy during retirement. It also highlights the extreme sensitivity of the long-term deficit, benefit payments, and tax receipts to such things as slower productivity growth and changes in the length of the retirement period. We might conclude this brief discussion by noting that the long-term future of social security is not something to be left to the long term to deal with. Every year we postpone dealing with the problem gives us one less year to generate a smooth transition to a more rational and cost-effective system of providing adequate income support for our elderly population.

To analyze the transfer component involved in social security at the aggregate level in a little more detail, we present in table 7.2 estimates of the total transfers and transfers as a percentage of total national income,

Table 7.2   Total Transfers and Transfers as Percent of Income under Alternative Reforms

Case	Total Transfers to Cohorts 2–5[a]	Transfers as % of National Income
Base	1,818.8	4.7%
Base with productivity = 1.0%	1,746.3	5.3
Trans 80	72.3	.2
Trans	0	0
Ret	1,542.0	3.8

[a]All figures are in billions of discounted 1977 dollars.

under the same scenarios discussed above in conjunction with table 7.1. We estimate here that the total transfers to cohorts 2–5. For the Base Case under the standard (if optimistic) assumptions, total transfers to cohorts 2–5 would be $1.8 trillion and amount to slightly under 5% of total national income! Placed in perspective, this is only slightly less than the share of income being devoted to defense expenditures. Some of the transfers to cohort 5 have been paid; the estimated remaining transfers amount to $1.3 trillion.[12] Under the standard assumptions of the Base Case with our slightly lower rate of productivity growth, transfers decline slightly to $1.75 trillion but increase the percentage of the now smaller income (arising from the lower productivity growth) to slightly over 5%. Obviously, under the Trans alternative total transfers have been eliminated completely and hence are zero in both the total and as a percentage of income; the Trans 80 alternative allows transfers to be paid for several additional years before taxes are adjusted (remember we start from a base year of 1977, since that is when our data end), and transfers would be virtually abolished in this case. Finally, we note that the increase in the retirement age for all cohorts after cohort 5 would substantially reduce transfer payments by about $275 billion to cohorts 2–5 and reduce transfers as a percentage of national income by approximately 1 percentage point. These enormous amounts for total transfers to cohorts 2–5 reveal that fundamental changes in social security toward separating the transfer and annuity goals of the program would allow major changes in the social security tax structure.

7.7 Detailed Results for the Base Case

In order to present disaggregated figures concerning the benefits received, taxes paid, and transfers received by the *average* family of differ-

12. John Wolfe and Joseph Applebaum kindly pointed out our failure to separate out transfers already paid to retirees (from those remaining to be paid) in the earlier versions of this paper.

ent age and income, we will focus on the Base Case assumptions. Recall from the discussion above, however, that these assumptions may be somewhat optimistic and that slower productivity growth or increased retirement periods would add substantially to the taxes necessary to finance "promised" benefits. The Base Case simply ignores the long-term deficit and assumes that, despite the enormous long-term deficit, current workers will not be forced to pay any tax increases above and beyond those already legislated. Were part of the solution to the long-term deficit to *gradually* raise taxes above and beyond those increases already legislated, as discussed in the next section, current workers would have to bear substantially more of the burden than under the Base Case; indeed, younger workers would lose substantially with respect to social security. Under the Base Case, assuming that taxes would not be raised until the baby boom generation retires or later, almost all current workers come out fairly well in terms of their average net benefits above and beyond taxes paid plus interest, but workers under the age of twenty-five will ultimately be forced to finance such benefits.

Table 7.3 analyzes the Base Case for six different age cohorts: for current retirees (for simplicity, persons over sixty-five); for ten-year age groups (twenty-five through thirty-four, thirty-five through forty-four, forty-five through fifty-four, and fifty-five through sixty-four); and for cohort X, persons under the age of twenty-five. (Family age is defined as the age of the husband.) The situation of a family of each age category is depicted in terms of the average tax paid per family, the average benefit received per family (the difference between benefits and taxes), and the

Table 7.3   Base Case

	Cohort 5 (65+)	Cohort 4 (64–55)	Cohort 3 (54–45)	Cohort 2 (44–35)	Cohort 1 (34–25)	Cohort X (<25)
Average tax per family	$7,058	18,345	33,883	53,326	73,843	
Average benefit per family	$49,400	47,639	56,600	66,321	73,577	
Average net benefit per family	$42,343	29,294	22,718	12,994	−267	
Average net benefit as % tax per family	600.0	160.0	67.0	24.4	−.36	
Total taxes paid by cohort (billions)	$172	235	349	389	540	1,500+
Total benefits paid to cohort (billions)	$1,282	629	570	483	503	
Transfers as % of total benefits	86.6	62.7	38.8	19.4	−7.39	

Notes: Assumes 7% inflation, 1.5% productivity growth, 3% discount. For eligible survivors only. Ages of cohorts are given as of 1977.

average net benefit as a percentage of the taxes the family paid. Also tabulated are the total taxes paid by the cohort and the total benefits paid to the cohort when they ultimately retire under current estimates, as well as the transfers as a percentage of total benefits received by the cohort when they ultimately retire.

There are a variety of important points illustrated by the Base Case. First, the average tax per family, adjusted for inflation and discounted to the husband's year of retirement, will increase markedly as time goes by and hence is much higher for younger workers than older workers or current retirees. This occurs for a number of reasons: some of the retirees will not have paid taxes through their entire lives; the tax rates actually paid and taxable ceiling used for each year have been growing through time and hence the annual taxes paid have been growing through time and will continue under current law. The average tax paid in 1977 dollars adjusted for inflation will be 10 times as high for twenty-five through thirty-four year olds as for people currently retired.

Benefit payments increase much less rapidly through time; hence, as we get to younger ages, net transfers become negative. Current retirees and persons soon to retire will receive benefits based not so much on what they paid in taxes but on an estimate of what the current tax revenue will support. Since current tax revenues are levied at a higher rate and on a larger income base than were taxes collected from the current retirees and those soon to be retired, their benefits are obviously much higher than the taxes paid plus interest. Therefore twenty-five through thirty-four year olds will receive only about one-half again as much in the real 1977 value of benefits once they retire as do current beneficiaries (those sixty-five and older). Again, recall the Base Case ignores possible changes in life expectancies or retirement patterns. Differencing the benefits and taxes reveals the very large net benefits, or transfers, received by current retirees and those about to retire. The average current retiree receives about $42,000 as a net transfer from the taxes paid to the Social Security System by current workers. This amounts to 6 times what these people on average paid plus interest. An average family in the next cohort, the fifty-five through sixty-four year olds, will receive back as a transfer payment 1.6 times what they paid in plus interest, a total of slightly over $30,000. The average net benefit, or transfer, declines for progressively younger ages both in absolute amounts and still more rapidly as a percentage of tax paid per family, since the latter will rise rapidly. By the time we get to younger workers (ages twenty-five through thirty-four), they are actually losing in terms of the taxes paid plus interest being less than the average benefits they can expect to receive. Persons under the age of twenty-five will suffer a loss under the current calculation. Because of the untenable state of the long-run deficit, the current calculation is unrealistic for this young cohort and their actual loss will probably be much larger. The total taxes paid and benefits received by each cohort follow the obvious pattern: taxes rise substantially as we pass through time. Again, these tax amounts *do not include any increases* that must be voted if we are to close the long-run deficit by increasing taxes rather than decreasing benefits or by adopting one of the structural reforms suggested below. Transfers as a percentage of total benefits follow a pattern similar to those for the average family. The overwhelming bulk of benefits are transfers for current retirees; for the next cohort about 60% will be transfers; for the forty-five through fifty-four age cohort slightly under 40% will be transfers; transfers will eventually vanish and become negative as we reach the younger cohorts. Obviously, for ages under twenty-five there will be a large negative transfer. Also, the transfers as a percentage of total benefits will decrease for all age cohorts not currently retired if we start to raise taxes now in anticipation of closing the deficit. The time pattern of such tax increases will be reflected in differential rates of reduction of the transfers as a percentage of total benefits for the different age groups. In the extreme, if we wait until the baby boom generation retires, transfers as a percentage of total benefits will be an extremely large negative number for those currently under the age of twenty-five.

Table 7.4 takes a deeper look at the net transfers from social security

Table 7.4   **Net Transfers by Income Class**

	Income Class[a]			
	<6,000	6,000–8,000	8,000–10,800	10,800 +
Cohort 1				
Net benefits[b]	5,972	3,505	2,267	− 1,923
% break[c]	8.1	4.9	3.1	− 2.5
Cohort 2				
Net benefits	15,700	15,586	13,185	11,054
% break	26.7	23.4	20.4	16.3
Cohort 3				
Net benefits	24,519	25,645	24,170	20,733
% break	50.1	46.7	44.5	35.1
Cohort 4				
Net benefits	30,446	30,224	29,432	30,292
% break	69.2	64.3	61.3	57.8
Cohort 5				
Net benefits	39,376	36,587	39,671	42,476
% break	87.6	80.0	81.0	75.3

Note: Base Case with inflation = 7%, productivity = 1.5%, discount rate = 3% net of inflation.

[a]In 1977 dollars, for head of household only.

[b]Net benefits = benefits for average family in income class, where both survive to retirement, in 1977 dollars, discounted to year of retirement, less taxes paid computed analogously.

[c]% break = net benefits ÷ benefits paid.

received by individuals in the different cohorts. We examine net benefits received and the percentage break (net benefits divided by total benefits) for four different income classes. For each cohort, we note that the percentage break declines rapidly as income increases. For example, for the cohort twenty-five through thirty-four years old the percentage break goes from slightly over 8% for families with incomes under $6,000 to − 2.5% for families with incomes above $10,800. Again, for cohort 5, the current retirees, the percentage break declines from 87.6% to 75.3% as we move up the income scale. This particular feature of the relation between the percentage break and income reflects primarily the progressivity of the benefit payment formula, which is tilted heavily toward replacing a larger fraction of preretirement income for low-income workers than for higher-income workers. Of course, the total net benefits may be slightly larger for some cohorts for higher-income people, reflecting the interaction of the larger intergenerational transfer and the larger tax payment which higher-income individuals make.

Finally, in examining the Base Case, we take a look at one other type of transfer as a percentage of benefits paid: disaggregating by industry of employment (table 7.5). Transfers as a percentage of benefits paid vary substantially across industries for a number of reasons: the different average income earned by workers of different industries, the slightly different tax treatment in effective payroll tax rates because of differential proportions of workers above and below the taxable ceiling, etc. It is important to note that once again the substantial net transfer to current retirees and expected net transfers to the oldest cohorts of workers will turn negative for the youngest cohorts. These negative transfers will

Table 7.5	Transfers as Percent of Benefits Paid for Selected Industries by Cohort				
	Cohort				
Industry	1	2	3	4	5
Agriculture	−1.1	14.9	40.9	57.7	80.0
Mining	−42.1	−10.1	5.1	39.5	NA
Construction	−37.9	−18.5	11.3	43.8	70.2
Manufacturing	−27.3	−6.3	17.3	46.8	64.5
Transportation/ communication	−24.1	−16.4	24.4	48.5	69.0
Wholesale	−31.7	−4.2	17.6	38.1	69.4
Retail	−9.2	14.7	41.4	58.4	82.5
Service	3.8	21.4	41.5	62.8	83.5
Banking, insurance, real estate	−19.4	9.3	28.7	51.3	79.3

Note: Estimates are for average individual in each industry.

occur even without considering the large tax increases necessary to finance the impending long-run deficit.

With these insights into the current social security situation in mind, we turn to a brief discussion of the alternative scenarios mentioned above.

7.8   Disaggregated Estimates for Alternative Reform Possibilities

We have calculated, for a series of potential benefit and tax reforms, disaggregated estimates of average taxes per family, average benefits per family, average net benefits per family, average net benefits as a percentage of taxes per family, total taxes paid and benefits received by each cohort, and transfers as a percentage of total benefits for each cohort.

The first alternative considered is that labeled "Trans" (see table 7.6). Recall that this eliminates all transfers to cohorts 2–5 and sets up a situation where transfers would be treated separately under general revenues if so desired. In this scenario, we note the familiar pattern of the average taxes paid per family rising substantially as we move to younger and younger cohorts. We note the same pattern for average benefits. However, now a different pattern emerges for the average net benefits received per family. In this case the average net benefits are virtually zero for all age cohorts. They differ slightly because we have not constrained the transfer to be zero for each cohort in each case, but have reduced the aggregate benefit payout each year to eliminate the transfer. Once again, the total taxes paid and total benefits received by each cohort increase

Table 7.6	Trans					
	Cohort as of 1977					
	5	4	3	2	1	X
Average tax per family[a]	7,058	18,345	33,882	53,326	73,843	
Average benefit per family[a]	6,629	17,793	34,769	53,461	73,576	
Average net benefit per family[a]	−429	−552	886	134.9	−267	
Average net benefit as % tax per family	−6.07	−3.01	2.62	.25	−.36	
Total taxes paid by cohort (billions)[a]	172.1	235.0	349.4	389.0	539.6	1,500+
Total benefits paid to cohort (billions)[a]	172.1	235.0	350.4	389.0	502.5	
Transfers as % of total benefits	.01	−.01	.29	0	−7.39	

[a]In 1977 dollars.

Table 7.7   Trans 80

| | Cohort as of 1977 | | | | | |
	5	4	3	2	1	X
Average tax per family[a]	7,045	17,818	31,368	47,729	64,409	
Average benefit per family[a]	6,629	17,793	34,770	53,461	73,577	
Average net benefit per family[a]	−415	−24.6	3,401	5,732	9,168	
Average net benefit as % tax per family	−5.89	−.14	10.84	12.0	14.23	
Total taxes paid by cohort (billions)[a]	171.6	228.8	324.6	349.0	470.0	
Total benefits paid to cohort (billions)[a]	172.1	234.9	350.4	389.0	502.5	
Transfers as % of total benefits	.25	2.60	7.36	10.28	6.46	

[a]In 1977 dollars.

substantially as we go to younger and younger cohorts and net to approximately zero in the aggregate for each cohort.

Moving from Trans to Trans 80 (table 7.7), which you recall involves a tax cut as well as eliminating the transfers, yields a very similar pattern to that discussed above for Trans; indeed, the benefits received by the average family in each cohort are identical to the situation under Trans, as are the total benefits paid out to each cohort. However, now the taxes differ somewhat to take account of the modest surplus that would result by eliminating all the transfers. In this case the average taxes per family are somewhat lower for each cohort, decreasing progressively more in percentage terms for younger and younger age cohorts. The total taxes paid per cohort follow the same pattern.

Table 7.8 presents the same analysis under the Base Case assumptions for the scenario we label "Ret" to indicate retirement ages raised by three years on average. As noted before, Ret results in a situation in which slightly higher taxes will be paid by the younger cohorts because they will be working slightly longer, and the benefits received, while maintainable at the same annual level, will be paid out over a somewhat shorter period.[13] Therefore the aggregate benefits and the average benefits will decline relative to the Base Case; we present estimates of benefits discounted to the original retirement age and note the decline in absolute

13. A Ret-type reform could be phased in: The retirement age could be increased to sixty-seven or sixty-eight gradually, before the baby boom generation reaches retirement age, by delaying the age of eligibility for benefits a month per year, for example. This would avoid problems of changing the rules abruptly for those soon to retire or just retired.

Table 7.8 **Ret**

	Cohort as of 1977					
	5	4	3	2	1	X
Average tax per family[a]	6,459	20,582	36,885	57,328	77,680	
Average benefit per family[a]	45,208	43,319	51,087	59,284	64,079	
Average % Reduction relative to Base Case	8.5	9.0	9.7	10.6	12.9	
Average net benefit per family[a]	38,750	22,737	14,202	1,956	−13,601	
Average net benefit as % tax per family	600	109.04	38.50	3.41	−17.51	
Total taxes paid by cohort (billions)[a]	172.1	236.6	355.7	382.3	508.4	
Total benefits paid to cohort (billions)[a]	1,282.2	525.7	465.4	395.3	396.7	
Transfers as % of total benefits	86.58	55.0	27.88	3.29	−28.18	

Note: Values listed here are conditional on our standard assumption of the continuation of current life expectancies.
[a]In 1977 dollars.

and percentage terms. For example, the twenty-five through thirty-four year old cohort loses about $9,500, or 13% of average family benefits relative to the Base Case estimates presented in table 7.3. Remember, however, that the benefits calculated in the Ret scenario are *feasible* because the long-term funding deficit has been closed. The Base Case benefit calculations ignore the funding problem and hence are *not feasible* without tax changes. We note again that the average net benefit per family declines with age from $38,000 for current retirees to virtually zero for people now forty to a large negative number for people now around the age of thirty. The same is obviously true of average net benefits as a percentage of taxes per family. We note, however, that the total benefits received by each cohort will decline substantially with the later retirement. This decline becomes progressively more important as we approach younger age cohorts and reflects the importance of doing something about the long-term deficit as soon as possible, before enormous implicit obligations, which are currently unfunded, become cemented in place and we are forced to go to enormous tax increases to fund them.

This point is vividly documented by comparing Ret with the two tax scenarios: Tax 80, a small tax increase now (above those already legislated to take effect in the future), which will totally close the deficit; and Tax 2030, a large tax increase to finance the baby boom generation's

Table 7.9   Tax 80

	Cohort as of 1977				
	5	4	3	2	1
Average tax per family[a]	7,074	18,966	36,839	59,907	84,935
Average benefit per family[a]	49,400	47,640	56,600	63,321	73,576
Average net benefit per family[a]	42,327	28,674	19,761	6,414	−11,358
Average net benefit as % tax per family	598.3	151.2	53.64	10.71	−13.37
Total taxes paid by cohort (billions)[a]	172	237	378	440	605
Total benefits paid to cohort (billions)[a,b]	1,297	614	592	485	516
Transfers as % of total benefits	87	61	36	9	−17

[a]In 1977 dollars.
[b]These values differ slightly from the Base Case because a smaller sample size was used in this calculation.

retirement in the year 2030. Estimates for the latter two alternatives are contained in tables 7.9 and 7.10, respectively. Recall that these refer to the increases necessary to cover the OASI deficit only; the Disability Insurance and Health Insurance deficits would add considerably to the totals. The average tax paid and average benefit received per family look rather similar to the Ret case; the average net benefits differ somewhat. What is most important is the large difference in the total benefits received by each cohort as part of the Social Security System and the total social security taxes paid for each cohort. Under Trans, Trans 80, or Ret, the benefits are reduced in the Social Security System either directly or indirectly, and the total benefits paid to each cohort are much lower than if the implicit unfunded obligation involved is paid. The total benefits paid to younger cohorts differ enormously under the Tax 80 and Tax 2030 programs, as do the taxes paid. For example, while the total benefits paid to each cohort are identical under Tax 80 and Tax 2030, the time patterns and hence aggregate amounts of taxes paid by each age cohort differ substantially. The aggregate taxes paid by current retirees and by workers aged fifty-five through sixty-four are virtually identical under these two scenarios. By the time we get to the thirty-five through forty-four year olds, Tax 80 has this cohort paying $50 billion more in social security taxes than if we wait until after they retire to raise the tax rates in order to finance the unfunded deficit. For those aged twenty-five through thirty-four the difference amounts to $80 billion! This highlights the importance

Table 7.10   **Tax 2030**

	Cohort as of 1977				
	5	4	3	2	1
Average tax per family[a]	7,058	18,346	33,883	53,326	73,843
Average benefit per family[a]	49,401	47,640	56,600	66,321	73,576
Average net benefit per family[a]	42,343	29,294	22,717	12,994	−267
Average net benefit as % tax per family	600	159.68	67.05	24.37	−.36
Total taxes paid by cohort (billions)[a]	167	230	349	393	526
Total benefits paid to cohort (billions)[a,b]	1,297	614	592	486	516
Transfers as % of total benefits	87	63	41	19	−2

[a]In 1977 dollars.
[b]These values differ slightly from the Base Case because a smaller sample size was used in this calculation.

of chosing a time frame for dealing with the long-term funding problems of social security. Chosing to do nothing about this implies that we are trying to stick younger and younger generations with the bill. Will they be willing to finance future retirement payments at much higher tax rates than now exist?

In summary, we may note the variety of potential strategies for disentangling the severe problems that high and rising social security taxes and dual-purpose unrationalized benefits create. We can simply say that we are going to raise taxes by substantially more than those legislated in the 1977 amendments either currently (Tax 80) or in the distant future (Tax 2030), and try to shift around the burden of paying for these increased social security benefits, which are not currently funded, or we can try to rationalize the benefit payments by separating out the transfer and annuity goals of the system, strengthening the earned entitlement function and having a separate transfer payment program funded by general revenues at whatever level is deemed socially desirable. The latter alternatives exist under Trans and Trans 80, and are easily combined with a slight increase in the retirement age as in Ret. These different scenarios suggest not only that there will be an enormous long-run impact on our overall economy depending upon which of these types of avenues we pursue, but that different groups in the population will be taxed and benefited quite differently depending upon which of these alternatives we select. It is time for a fundamental refocusing of social security to rationalize the benefit structure and relieve the long-run burden of the much higher payroll taxes implicit in the unfunded deficit. This paper is the first of our social security simulation model projections. Subsequent work will deal with other issues (e.g. alternative indexing possibilities). We hope to stimulate discussion as well as provide some quantitative estimates of the taxes, benefits, and deficit implied by alternative potential solutions to the long-run social security funding problems.

7.9 Further Work Completed

Since the original version of this paper was written, the Social Security Administration 1980 trustees' annual report was issued with considerably altered assumptions in their intermediate and pessimistic Base Case scenarios. Therefore we have recalculated a variety of the aggregate tax, benefit, and deficit totals, and discounted them back to 1980 under the assumptions used by the Social Security Administration 1980 trustees' annual report. These results are summarized in table 7.11. In all cases, "intermediate" refers to the intermediate assumptions of the trustees and "pessimistic" refers to the pessimistic assumptions of the trustees. The major differences between the 1980 assumptions and those made previously are a slower rate of productivity growth, higher inflation in the pessimistic case, lower fertility rates, higher unemployment in the short term, and a lower discount rate.

The general nature of the results conforms closely with those reported earlier in our paper—obviously, however, updated to 1980 from 1977 dollars. For example, the intermediate base projection reveals a deficit of slightly under $1 trillion in the social security retirement system; the pessimistic assumptions reveal a real 1980 deficit of almost $1.5 trillion. Because the Social Security Administration trustees have chosen to use lower discount rates in reporting results in their 1980 report, we also present in rows 3 and 4 the same estimates using our earlier 3% real discount rate; this reduces the present values of the deficit to about two-thirds of those just reported. The other major findings remain qualitatively unchanged: Raising the retirement age to sixty-eight runs a modest surplus under the intermediate assumptions and nearly eliminates the deficit under the pessimistic one. Eliminating the transfers runs large surpluses, but such a scenario, of course, would have to be supplemented by an expanded income security program for the elderly, which would probably more than make up for the difference. Raising taxes in 1980 or in 2030 to close the deficit over the entire period 1980–2050 would require, in the four cases considered, tax rate increases above and beyond those already legislated of 1.6 and 2.4%, in the intermediate and pessimistic scenarios beginning in 1980; and 7% and 12% under these two scenarios in the year 2030.

Table 7.11 **Aggregate Taxes, Benefits, and the Deficit under Alternative Reforms**

Cases	Total Taxes	Total Benefits	Deficit
Base intermediate	5,125	6,045	920
Base pessimistic	5,231	6,700	1,468
Base intermediate, 3% discount	4,293	4,878	584
Base pessimistic, 3% discount	3,998	4,868	866
Retirement at 68, intermediate	5,394	5,032	− 363
Retirement at 68, pessimistic	5,526	5,571	46
Eliminate transfer, intermediate	5,125	4,741	− 384
Eliminate transfer, pessimistic	5,231	5,168	− 63
Taxes raised 1980, intermediate	6,045	6,045	0
Taxes raised 1980, pessimistic	6,692	6,699	7
Taxes raised 2030, intermediate	6,045	6,045	0
Taxes raised 2030, pessimistic	6,698	6,699	1

Note: All figures are in billions of discounted 1980 dollars.

As can be seen, the assumptions of the Social Security Administration trustees are becoming slightly more pessimistic, and hence the problems discussed in this paper are, if anything, becoming more and more acute.

7.10 Induced Retirement

All the estimates made thus far conform in their assumptions to those usually made by the Social Security Administration trustees, for example, those that pertain to labor force participation, retirement behavior, etc. It is possible, and indeed in some cases desirable, to build *behavioral* simulations into the model that will account for econometric evidence on these decisions. Since the real level of social security benefits is scheduled to increase substantially as time goes on through the use of wage, as opposed to price, indexing of the formula calculating the initial benefits, any response of retirement behavior to increases in real social security benefits should be taken into account in analyses of the type performed above. As a first step in this direction, we have overridden the Social Security Administration's retirement assumption with a series of retirement probability equations taken from Hurd and Boskin (1981). These retirement probability equations were estimated from data which merged the Longitudinal Retirement History Survey with social security earnings histories. The reader is referred to that paper for a detailed discussion of the estimates. The only point we wish to make here is that in that paper substantial evidence is presented for the hypothesis that increases in the real level of social security benefits increase the probability of retirement for persons aged sixty to sixty-five. Using the elasticity of estimates of the probability of retirement in combination with the scheduled increases in real social security benefits, we have made some calculations about the reduction in working years that will probably result from the Social Security benefit increases and therefore about the decreases in tax revenue and increases in benefit payments that might ensue. We have arrived at the following estimates of the deficit including the Hurd and Boskin (1981) induced retirement response (in 1980 dollars):

Intermediate assumptions $1,051 billion
Pessimistic assumptions $1,688 billion

We predict that, in the period 1980–2050, 116 million fewer person years will be worked, an average decline of 1.5 work years between the ages of sixty and sixty-five for a male who becomes sixty in the year 2030. The weighted average elasticity of the *annual* probability of retirement during these age intervals, given that people had not retired previously with respect to real social security wealth (the real present value of expected social security benefits) is slightly over 1. As can be seen from the figures above, the deficit increases by approximately 14% in both the intermediate and pessimistic cases.

While these are not enormous figures, it is clear that substantial increases in social security benefits can lead to substantially earlier retirement, and our figures should really be taken as a lower bound, since they truncate at age sixty. There could also be an induced retirement at still earlier ages, which we have not taken into account.

Our conclusion is simply that behavioral responses for a variety of types of behavior, especially retirement, induced by changes in the social security law, or by intergenerational transfers which are not offset through private means, may well be important enough to include in analyses of social security reform proposals. Certainly, ignoring such induced retirement effects appears to lead to a nontrivial underestimate of the deficit.

Further work, on both retirement and other behavioral decisions, will enrich the model considerably and will be the subject of future research.

References

Hurd, M. D., and M. J. Boskin. 1981. The effect of Social Security on retirement in the early 1970s. Stanford: NBER. Mimeographed.

National Center for Health Statistics. 1975. *U.S. decennial life tables* 1: 1. Washington: Government Printing Office.

Parsons, D., and D. Munro. 1977. Intergenerational transfers in Social Security. In M. Boskin, ed., *The crisis in Social Security.* San Francisco: Institute of Contemporary Studies.

Robertson, A. 1978. Financial state of Social Security programs after the Social Security Amendments of 1977. *Social Security Bulletin,* March.

United States Bureau of the Census. 1975. *Statistical abstract of the United States,* 96th annual ed. Washington: Government Printing Office.

The U.S. Fact Book. 1978. Washington: Government Printing Office.

Comment   Henry Aaron

The paper by Boskin, Avrin, and Cone contains three distinct themes. First, it provides estimates of the aggregate long-run deficit and examines particular modifications in the structure of social security that would, among other things, close the long-run deficit in the system. Second, it simulates how the social security system affects workers belonging to different cohorts and with different earnings. Third, it simulates the distributional differences among various methods of correcting the long-run deficit in the social security system. In all cases the paper focuses on the long-term financial condition of the system; it wholly lays short-run issues to the side. So shall I.

In my comments I shall try to show that the paper does an admirable job of revealing the large differences in how the various proposed changes to the current system will affect different cohorts, but that it does not deal satisfactorily with the first two issues.

Background

I begin my comments with a description of the elements of the social security system, knowledge of which is necessary for reading this paper.

The system is financially self-contained. Revenues come from a proportional tax on earnings below a legislated maximum in covered employment. With the exception of three recent ad hoc adjustments, this max-

Henry Aaron is a senior fellow with the Brookings Institution, Washington, and professor of economics at the University of Maryland.

imum rises at the same rate as do money earnings. The benefit structure is progressive—in the sense that the elasticity of benefits with respect to average earnings at each point in time is less than 1.

As under defined-benefit pensions, workers employed during a period when the system is being liberalized are the beneficiaries of "past service credits" (the Social Security Administration term) or "immaturity benefits" (my term). Boskin, Avrin, and Cone use the term "transfer benefits" to denote any benefits greater than those that could be paid from the accumulation of employee and employer taxes compounded at a real interest rate of 3%. When one is looking at cohorts of workers, transfer benefits are equal to the past service credits or immaturity benefits enjoyed by that cohort. When one is looking at particular workers, transfer benefits include not only immaturity benefits but also additions to or subtractions from benefits attributable to the progressive benefit formula.

The use of the single term "transfer benefits" confuses two distinct analytical and policy questions regarding social security: what to do about the debt resulting from the payment of past service credits to past, present, and future social security beneficiaries, and what to do about the "tilt," or degree of progressivity, in the social security benefit formula. I believe that this confusion, in the end, detracts from the relevance of the paper to debates about how social security should be changed.

In addition to having a progressive benefit formula and awarding past service credits, social security also bases benefits on family circumstances. Extra benefits are paid to certain relatives of entitled decedent, retired, or disabled workers.

The social security system will be in surplus for the next twenty-five years (counting from 1980), balance for the next fifty years, and deficit for the seventy-five year planning horizon which Congress has stipulated for social security.[1] Over the next twenty-five years, according to the latest estimates of the actuaries, the social security system (OASDI) will be in surplus by 1.27% of payroll against an average cost of 10.67% of payroll, a surplus of 11.9% of cost. Over the next fifty years, the social security system will be in surplus by a smaller amount. Over the seventy-five year horizon, the deficit is 0.93% of payroll or 7.1% of the average cost of 13.17%; this deficit clearly is confined during the third twenty-five year period, running from 2030 to 2054, during which time the deficit is 3.39% of payroll on an average cost of 15.79%, for a deficit of 21.5%.[2]

1. The authors correctly disregard the short-term financial problems of social security, because the issues are quite unrelated to the long-term issues.
2. The social security trustees, operating on the premise that if projections based on three sets of assumptions (the practice before 1981) are useful, projections based on five should be marvelous (the practice in the 1981 trustees' reports), have provided a confusing array of alternative projections. The text estimates are projections II-A from the 1981

What the Authors Do

Boskin, Arvin, and Cone take as their starting point the fact that currently legislated payroll taxes are insufficient to pay for currently legislated social security benefits throughout the seventy-five year period over which Congress has determined that the calculations of financial soundness of the social security system shall be evaluated. According to estimates described below, the present value of this deficit is large: $632 billion. The authors note that this deficit can be eliminated by benefit reductions or by increases in taxes dedicated to social security. The bulk of the paper consists of an analysis of the effects on several cohorts of five possible legislative changes in benefits and taxes. The authors calculate the expected present value of taxes and benefits for each of six age cohorts. They use a 3% real interest rate and assume that real wages grow 1.5% per year.[3]

The technique of the simulation is as follows. The authors generate earnings histories for workers of different ages based historically on the 1975 Exact Match between social security records and the Current Population Survey and prospectively from wage regressions. The methods used in estimating future wages are not clearly presented and could not be even approximated from the description contained in the paper.

Then the authors say that they calculate the payroll taxes that would be paid by a worker with such an earnings history and the benefits that such workers could expect to receive taking account of expected mortality. The authors do not state what tax schedule or benefit formula they use. They make a number of simplifying assumptions about relative ages and labor force behavior of husbands and wives. They accumulate payroll taxes at 3% real interest to age sixty-five, discount expected retirement benefits at the same real rate to age sixty-five, and deflate the difference to 1977 dollars. They sum these differences within and across cohorts. They disregard workers who die before age sixty-five, and they ignore all benefits other than retirement benefits paid to workers and spouses or survivors' benefits paid to the spouses of retirees. In other words, they disregard all benefits paid on behalf of workers decedent before age sixty-five and all benefits paid to children and other relatives of retirees except spouses.

The policy alternatives that the authors explore flow from their belief, stated in congressional testimony that the redistribution that occurs

---

trustees' report. Projection II-B, which employs more pessimistic but not implausible assumptions, shows a seventy-five year deficit of 1.82% of payroll on a total cost of 14.07%, a 12.9% deficit.

3. The authors assume that inflation proceeds at 7% per year, but because of the indexing features of social security, the results should be quite insensitive to variations in the assumed rate of inflation.

within the social security system is hidden and excessive and that the increase in life expectancy experienced in recent decades justifies increases in the age at which unreduced benefits may be claimed. I shall return to these judgments later.

The first policy alternative—Trans—would pay benefits to workers age thirty-five or older equal in present value only to the accumulated value of payroll taxes paid by them or by their employers, plus interest. Workers younger than thirty-five would be treated as they are under current law. Thus older workers would be denied past service credits or immaturity benefits to which they are entitled under current law, and the benefit formula would be converted from one that is progressive with respect to average covered earnings into one that is proportional with respect to taxes paid.

It is clear to me that such a change has no practical interest whatsoever as a guide to policy. It changes the rules of the game for older workers, inflicting benefit reductions as large as 87% for workers over age sixty-five and 63% for workers age fifty-five to sixty-four, while leaving benefits of workers under thirty-five unaffected. That would mean reducing the average benefit paid to newly retired workers in August 1980 from its actual level of $361.77 per month to $47.03 for workers sixty-five or older and to $133.85 for workers fifty-five to sixty-four.

Having been confronted by a solid phalanx of fourteen bipartisanly hostile congressmen when I testified on behalf of the comparatively tame proposal to tax half of social security benefits, I would relish sitting in the audience when the authors testified on behalf of *this* proposal—but I would not want my children to witness the carnage.

In fact, I trust, the authors do not really regard such a change as sound policy. Rather, it is an effective device to use in a simulation exercise to illustrate the size and distribution of immaturity benefits. They are the dominant portion of benefits for the oldest cohorts, are a diminishing fraction for younger cohorts, and turn negative for the youngest workers, who are assumed to spend their entire working lives under a single system. The negative value of social security for the youngest cohorts is a frequent, but misleading finding, and I shall comment on it below.

The second policy alternative—Trans 80—is similar and tells much the same story. Under this alternative all workers would be paid benefits equal to the accumulated value of taxes plus interest, and taxes would be raised sufficiently—1.5 percentage points in the authors' calculations— to bring the system into long-term balance. This simulation yields essentially the same results as the preceding one because the major difference is that the system is also changed for the youngest cohorts, but that change matters little because they do not receive immaturity benefits of any size anyway.

Two other alternatives—Tax 80 and Tax 2030—leave benefits unchanged but increase taxes sufficiently to eliminate the long-term deficit.

The first increases payroll taxes by 1.7 percentage points in 1980, the second by 3.9 percentage points in 2030.

The final policy change—Ret—adds a maximum of three years to the working lives of every worker. In contrast to the elimination of immaturity benefits for some or all workers, this change reduces benefits for all classes of workers—by 8.5 to 13% for different cohorts.

Critique

The method of analysis used by Boskin, Avrin, and Cone is an entirely appropriate way to answer a particular question. That question is, Will a particular worker, with a particular assumed earnings history and family arrangements, get cash benefits worth more or less in present value terms than the taxes he and his employer pay? This question is frequently asked, and it is of some interest; but I do not believe that it is the right question to ask about the equity of the social security system, and it is not the question that the authors attempt to answer. The authors ask how social security affects particular cohorts of workers, and for this question their methods are inadequate.

Rates of return. In judging whether social security provides particular workers with a fair or an unfair return, it is important to include the value of insurance protection that does not actually lead to cash payments. We all know that private insurance entails selling costs and profits that together form a wedge between the present value of premiums and the present value of cash benefits actually paid, the so-called load factor. The fact that such a load factor exists and often is sizable does not prove that insurance is a bad buy. In fact, people continue to buy fire and health insurance, despite the fact that such load factors assure them that they will get back less, on the average, than they paid in, because insurance provides valuable protection against risk, even when the feared eventuality does not occur. The individual who never makes a claim under his fire insurance may be very well served, although the present expected value of claims by all people so insured is less than the sum of all premiums (because of the load factor). Furthermore, social security, alone among all assets, provides covered workers full protection against inflation risk and capital market risk caused by variations in interest rates. Thus, in order to calculate whether social security is a good buy or not, one should calculate (*a*) the present expected value of benefits *prospectively* taking account of the probability of various outcomes, and (*b*) the value of the insurance protection, including certain unique features of social security, such as complete protection against both inflation and capital market risk attributable to variations in interest rates. Thus, for the purpose of deciding whether social security is a good or a bad buy for individual workers, a proper calculation must be done prospectively and it must take account of the utility value of reduced risk.

The authors of this paper take a retrospective look, and they disregard the value of social security as insurance. For this reason, their estimates say little about whether social security is a good or a bad buy for individual workers except in those cases where benefits so clearly exceed taxes that there can be no room for quibble.

The authors, however, do not look at individual workers (except briefly, in tables 7.4 and 7.5). Rather they look at cohorts and at the system as a whole. If one is interested in calculating the value of social security for cohorts, however, the same considerations arise as for individuals. The value of social security to today's twenty-five to thirty-four year olds consists of the expected value of benefits that they will receive as retirees or that their dependents or survivors will receive as a result of their retirement or death, plus the utility gain from reduced risk. As noted above, the authors do not attempt such estimates. The value of social security should include the value of protection against inflation and capital market risk and the insurance protection against various contingencies. It has been estimated, for example, that indexed bonds would sell at real interest rates much below those on ordinary bonds of similar maturity. Until such time as we enable other insurers to provide fully indexed benefits by issuing index bonds or by some other device, this important attribute of social security should figure prominently in evaluating whether it is a good or a bad buy for cohorts.

The negative value of social security for the youngest cohorts reported in this study results (disregarding the crudity of the estimates) from the absence of immaturity benefits and use of a 3% real interest rate. The authors do not justify this rate. The Social Security Administration assumes a real interest rate of 2.1% after 1995 and less before. They do not justify that rate. I suspect that relatively few individual investors have earned real net (or even gross) of tax returns of as much as 3% lately on their portfolios. The old natural constant of 3% may reassert itself, but analysts should tell potential social security beneficiaries how they can earn such rates before they use them to discount streams of benefits and taxes.

If we disregard past service credits, we all know from Samuelson that the steady-state rate of return to pay-as-you-go social insurance is the sum of the rates of growth of population and real wages. We are not in a steady state; but all that the negative present value calculations of the authors show is that 3% exceeds the appropriate weighted implicit rate of growth of population and real wages. It is worth comparing the results of Boskin, Avrin, and Cone with those of my colleague Louise Russell. She finds that if taxes are set at whatever rate is necessary to assure payment of retirement benefits promised under current law, the internal rate of return declines but remains positive for all cohorts. Her calculations also exclude insurance and risk avoidance benefits of social security.

The deficit. The most striking statistic in this paper is the estimate of the overall deficit of the social security system, 632 billion 1977 dollars. Or to bring matters more up-to-date, 987 billion 1981 dollars. What does this mean?

In one sense it means nothing because, as noted above, the system simulated in this paper differs in essential ways from the actual social security system. In fact, the estimated deficit measured as a percent of payroll is close to official estimates, and they indicate that presently promised social security benefits will cost more than the taxes we have legislated will support.

The actual deficit as estimated by the social security actuaries and the similar deficit estimated by the authors may be presented in different ways. The officially estimated deficit is equal to .93% of wages subject to payroll over the next seventy-five years (compared to the 1.7% estimate of the authors). It is equal to 0.4% of gross national product over the next seventy-five years. It is equal to 3.39% of covered payroll during the period 2030–54. It is equal to 1.2% of gross national product over the same twenty-five year period.

Six hundred thirty-two billion dollars is a large number. But so is $219,600 billion, the present value of gross national product measured over the next seventy-five years under the assumption that nominal GNP is discounted at the same interest rate by which it grows.

One or two percent of GNP is a large number, but it is worth keeping in mind that in 1978 government expenditures claimed 11.4% more of GNP in France than in the United States, 9.2% more in Germany than in the United States, 25% more in Sweden than in the United States, and 9.9% less in Japan than in the United States. Moreover, the proportion of GNP absorbed by government rose during the eight years from 1970 to 1978 by 8.8 percentage points in France, 9.7 percentage points in Germany, 20 percentage points in Sweden, 9 percentage points in Japan, and 1.8 percentage points in the United States.

It may be that the rest of you are prepared to endorse the authors of this paper in describing a deficit that can be removed by an increase in taxes equal to less than one-half of 1% of gross national product over the next seventy-five years, an increase that both the United States and other nations have undertaken in a couple of years, as "large," "untenable," "extremely large," "overwhelming," "huge," "massive," "immense" or just plain "enormous." One can only admire such rhetorical vigor.

Policy. Instead of argumentation by thesaurus, however, the issue of what changes should be made in the social security system deserves straightforward analysis and discussion, certainly at scholarly meetings. One of the authors of this paper has taken public stands on long-term changes in social security, and the paper endorses some of these positions. The positions are (a) to divide the social security system into two parts, one of which would return to covered retirees an annuity with the same present value as that of taxes paid by the worker and his employers, and one of which would be a negative income tax for the aged; and (b) to increase the number of years of work by three years. In practice, the working-life proposal would be implemented by an increase from sixty-five to sixty-eight in the age at which unreduced benefits are paid. The first proposal would eliminate both immaturity benefits and the "tilt," or redistributive, component of the benefit formula. I regard the elimination of past service credits as so improbable and as such poor policy as not to deserve serious discussion.

The question of whether redistribution to the low-income aged should be carried out through an entitlement program or an income tested program is more serious. To eliminate such redistribution while preserving past service credits, one would establish a benefit formula that paid retirees a benefit related proportionally rather than progressively to average earnings. Such a modification in the social security benefit formula could be used to accomplish two distinct objectives. The first would be to reduce the amount of redistribution from current workers to retirees with low current income. The second would be to improve the accuracy with which a given amount of redistribution is accomplished. The latter objective would be achieved if one established a negative income tax for the low-income aged that provided this group with the same total resources (or possibly even more) than the present system does. Savings would result because payment of benefits to people with low average past earnings, but adequate current income or wealth, would be curtailed. In previous conversations Michael Boskin has told me that he has no interest in reducing the amount of redistribution to the low-income elderly and indeed would increase it by liberalizing the benefits paid under supplemental security income, the present negative income tax for the elderly.

The motivation for moving to a two-tier system, therefore, is in part to eliminate or to reduce the payment of redistributive benefits to workers who have had low covered earnings but have adequate current resources. Another motive, enunciated in this paper, is the clarification for public debate of the degree of redistribution carried out through public programs. Presumably, such clarification would affect the amount or character of redistribution over time.

The elimination of mistargeted benefits is a real gain; and it may be important. Universal coverage by social security of federal, state, and local employees would end much of the present mistargeting by depriving government employees of the privilege of seeming to be low-wage workers when earnings from brief periods of post–civil service covered employment are averaged over their whole working lives. Nevertheless, a two-tier system would provide a residual of improved targeting. I do not know how large it would be nor do the authors nor does anyone else, because the analysis of how much targeting would be improved has not been done.

Moving to a two-tier system would also generate costs. The costs would take two forms. The first entails real resources, not misdirected transfers. The reduction of entitlements would increase the number of people who would apply for means-tested benefits. Means-tested programs cost more to administer than do entitlements, about 10% of the amount transferred under the former compared with 2% under the latter. I do not know what the total increase in costs of administration would be nor do the authors nor does anyone else, because the analysis of how much administrative costs would rise has not been done.

The second kind of cost is a transfer cost. The take-up rate on means-tested programs is much lower than that of entitlements. As a result some fraction of those legally entitled to means-tested benefits would not claim them because of stigma or administrative difficulties. I do not know how many people would fall into this category, nor do I know how this loss (or the losses suffered by those who would apply despite filing costs and stigma) should be weighed nor do the authors of this paper nor does anyone else, because the analysis has not been done.

It may be that the benefits would outweigh the costs; I doubt it. But my real point is that no one has done the analysis necessary to justify the radical change to our most important social program advanced by the authors of this paper and by others. Congress should not be expected to overhaul our largest social program just to fulfill the logically sound principle we all learned in graduate school that full achievement of policy goals requires one independent policy for each independent objective.

I cannot resist observing that if one wishes to sort out redistributional and earnings replacement objectives, one can achieve this objective, without incurring either of the costs I have just described, by means of a double-decker plan: a universal demogrant for the aged and disabled, combined with a benefit proportional to earnings and with suitable changes in the positive tax system.

One of the authors of this paper (Boskin) has also endorsed an increase by three years in the age at which unreduced benefits are paid. He does so because life expectancy has increased, is likely to continue to increase, and may in the author's opinion increase more than demographers project. He and his coauthors conclude that an increase in the age at which unreduced benefits are paid is desirable.

I have supported the enactment now of such an increase, to take effect around the turn of the century, but I am far less certain than the authors about the desirability of such an increase. The increase in the costs of social security that will occur early in the twenty-first century are real and important, even if they do not deserve the rather inflated rhetoric employed by the authors. It is important that decisions be made now that permit the generation that will have to pay those costs to make decisions unencumbered by unbreakable commitments to benefits that will require rising taxes. I strongly suspect that those generations will vote the higher taxes and elect to pay benefits approximating what is promised under current law. All public opinion polls to date support that contention: people of all ages overwhelmingly indicate that they would rather pay higher social security taxes than curtail benefits.

But attitudes do change. And if we want to preserve the option to increase the retirement age at all, it is a political fact that very lengthy notice must be given of such an increase. However, those of us who favor putting on the books an increase in the age of first entitlement for unreduced benefits should keep in mind the comments made by one of our colleagues, William C. Hsaio: "Too frequently those who advocate later retirement policy are armchair theorists. Their jobs require the physical exertion of sitting at a desk, lifting a 3-ounce pencil, in a modern air-conditioned office. The mental exertion consists of reading and writing memorandums and conducting discourse through a telephone line. They have never experienced the exhaustion of lifting 50 pound boxes for 8 hours a day, or continuously operating a pneumatic press. Yet they assume 65-year old workers can continue to lift those weights or operate a heavy machine until they reach age 68."[4]

Unless we are able to design income support to deal with those who retire involuntarily before age sixty-five, who become physically incapable of performing their jobs, or who lose their jobs and cannot find new ones late in their working lives, I submit that no increase in the age at which unreduced benefits are paid will or should come into effect.

I regret that the authors did not choose to analyze the conversion from wage to price indexing of the formula used for computing initial entitlements, a proposal whose immediate adoption Boskin has supported and whose deferred adoption I have supported.

4. Testimony to the Subcommittee on Oversight of the Committee on Ways and Means, House of Representatives, 96th Congress, 2d Session, Serial 96–116, p. 39.

8 Tax Reform and Corporate Investment: A Microeconometric Simulation Study

Michael A. Salinger and Lawrence H. Summers

This paper develops a methodology for simulating the effects of alternative corporate tax reforms on the stock market valuation and investment plans of individual firms. The methods are applied to estimate the effects of alternative corporate tax reforms on the thirty Dow Jones companies. The estimates are all based on extensions of Tobin's q theory of investment to take account of the effects of tax policy. As well as providing the basis for the estimates of the effects of tax policy, the results here provide strong microeconometric support for the q theory of investment. The q theory approach provides a superior method for estimating the effects of investment incentives because it recognizes the effects of changes in the cost of capital on the desired level of output.

A central concern in the design of tax policy is the avoidance of windfall gains or losses. This concern is closely related to the goal of providing incentives only at the margin. A crucial virtue of the q approach employed here is that it provides a clear delineation of the impact of tax policies on the market value of existing capital as well as of new capital. It thus allows an examination of the incidence of tax changes on the holders of different assets. This represents an important extension of the incidence concepts usually used in public finance, which focus only on the rate of return on capital with no consideration of the wealth effects caused by short-run changes in its relative price.

The interaction of inflation and the corporate tax system has received widespread attention in recent years. As is by now well understood, inflation affects the corporate tax system in three important ways. Historic cost depreciation and firms' reluctance to use LIFO inventory accounting cause inflation to raise the tax burden on corporate capital.

Michael A. Salinger and Lawrence H. Summers are with the Massachusetts Institute of Technology and the National Bureau of Economic Research.

This is offset by the deductibility of nominal rather than real interest payments. While the impact of these interactions of inflation and the tax system on aggregate investment and stock market valuation has been discussed extensively, their effect on the behavior of individual firms has been little studied. Even if indexing the tax system had little effect on the level of aggregate investment or the stock market, the results in this paper suggest that it would have a large impact on the composition of investment among firms. Full indexing of the corporate tax system, for example, would raise the Dow Jones average by about 8%. The effects of the investment experience of individual firms would vary substantially.

The first section of the paper outlines the q theory of investment that provides the basis for the simulations reported in this paper. The analysis draws on the work of Hayashi (1982) and Abel (1979) in linking the Tobin q approach to investment with the firm's problem of determining an optimal investment path in the presence of adjustment costs. In particular, it shows how an investment equation relating the level of investment to tax-adjusted q can be used to infer the shape of a firm's adjustment cost function. The q theory provides an improved basis for estimating the effects of tax reform on investment because the process of adjustment is modeled explicitly.

The estimation of q investment equations for the thirty Dow Jones companies is discussed in the second section. These estimates require the estimation of a time series of tax-adjusted q for each company. These are developed using Compustat data. The time series estimates are quite supportive of the q theory. The data confirm the importance of the tax adjustments to q suggested by the theory.

In the third section, the impact of alternative tax returns on q and investment is examined. This requires calculating the present value of the expected change in revenue which would result from alternative reforms. It is also possible to calculate the impact of these policies on the market value of individual firms' equity. The results suggest that some reforms could have potent effects. Complete indexing would raise the Dow Jones average by an estimated 7.6%. The variance among companies is substantial, with the effect ranging from − 13% for Sears to 20% for American Brands.

The fourth section combines the results of the preceding sections to provide evidence on the response of investment to indexing the tax system and to various reforms. The results suggest that, because adjustment costs are very large, tax reforms are likely to have a much larger impact on long-run capital intensity than on investment in the short run. The results of the q theory approach are contrasted with those obtained using other methods.

A fifth (and final) section reviews some limitations of the analysis and suggests directions for future research.

8.1 Taxes in a q Theory of Investment

This section describes the procedure developed in Summers (1981*a*) for using investment equations involving Tobin's q as a basis for estimating the impact of tax policies on both investment and the stock market. Here the focus is on the investment decisions of individual firms. The essential insight underlying Tobin's theory is that in a taxless world, firms will invest so long as each dollar spent purchasing capital raises the market value of the firm by more than one dollar. Tobin goes on to assume that as a good approximation the market value of an additional unit of capital equals the average market value of the existing capital stock. That is, the value of the marginal "q" on an additional dollar of investment is well proxied by average q, which is the ratio of the market value of the capital stock to its replacement cost. It is natural then to assume that the rate of investment is an increasing function of the marginal return to investment as proxied by q.

An approach of this type has several virtues relative to other standard approaches to explaining investment. Perhaps most important, the q theory approach is supply oriented. In the formulation presented below, firms make output and capital intensity decisions simultaneously. This captures the essence of an important channel through which investment stimuli are supposed to work. By reducing the cost of one factor of production, firms are encouraged to supply more output. This channel is obscured in most of the standard econometric approaches to investment decision making, in which the level of output is taken as predetermined. In this section, we show that the q theory of investment can be derived from the assumption that firms face adjustment costs and make investment decisions optimally with the objective of maximizing market value. Output along with investment is treated as a choice variable.

A second virtue of the q theory approach is that it can be used to evaluate a wider menu of policy proposals than standard methods. Almost all of the empirical literature on tax policy and investment neglects entirely taxes levied at the personal level. These are difficult to introduce into investment equations of the flexible accelerator type. Since they do affect stock market values, they are easily handled by the q theory approach. In addition, because the q theory is derivable directly from the assumption of intertemporal optimization, it can be used to evaluate the effects of policy announcements and temporary policies. The approach is forward looking and so can be used to study the effects of future policies on current investment. As Robert Lucas has emphasized, standard econometric investment equations cannot be used to predict the effects of any fundamental changes in policy.[1] The approach developed

---

1. This criticism applies at two levels. First, most standard approaches of the type used in policy evaluation exercises do not include any forward looking variables. Thus there is no

here is immune from this criticism because the only parameters which are estimated are technological and do not depend on the policy rule.

In what follows, the behavior of a representative, competitive firm seeking to maximize the market value of its equity is considered. We begin by examining how individuals value corporate stock and then turn to the firm's decision problem. Throughout, it is assumed that firms neither issue new equity nor repurchase existing shares.[2] Hence share prices are proportional to the outstanding value of a firm's equity. We assume that equity holders require a fixed real after-tax return ρ in order to induce them to hold the outstanding equity. The approach here is partial equilibrium in that the required rate of return is assumed to be unaffected by changes in tax policy. While this assumption is obviously appropriate for an individual firm, its relevance to an economy-wide tax change is less clear. However, Summers (1981a, b) argues that any effects of tax reforms on the required rate of return are likely to be minor and of ambiguous sign. The required return ρ is the sum of the capital gains and dividends net of tax. It follows that

(1) $$(\rho + \pi)V_t = (1 - c)\dot{V}_t + (1 - \theta^D)\text{Div} ,$$

where c represents the effective accrual rate of taxation on capital gains,[3] θ^D the tax rate on dividends, and π the rate of inflation. Differences in the tax rates faced by different investors are ignored. To solve this differential equation it is necessary to impose a transversality condition. We do this by requiring that at time t

(2) $$\lim_{s \to \infty} V_s \exp\left[-\int_t^s \frac{\rho + \pi}{1 - c} \, du \right] = 0 .$$

This condition precludes the possibility of an explosive solution to (1).

With the transversality condition satisfied and the assumption of perfect foresight, the solution to (1) becomes

(3) $$V_t = \int_t^\infty \frac{1 - \theta^D}{1 - c} \, \text{Div} \, \exp\left[-\int_t^s \frac{\rho + \pi}{1 - c} \, du \right] ds .$$

---

way to use them to contemplate the effect of an announced change in policy. Implicitly, they assume that all tax parameters are expected to remain permanently constant. Second, because expected tax changes are an important feature of the historic experience, the equations are misspecified so that parameter estimates are unlikely to be reliable. The substantial importance of these problems is demonstrated by the simulations below.

2. Under the conditions described below, firms would never want to issue new equity. Legal restrictions severely limit firms' ability to repurchase their own shares. A discussion of these restrictions and the limitations of other mechanisms which might seem to be functionally equivalent to repurchasing shares is contained in Auerbach (1979). For the issues considered here the assumption that shares are not repurchased is not likely to have important effects.

3. This corresponds to the statutory rate adjusted for deferral and the lack of constructive realization at death.

In the steady state, where taxes, the price level, and dividends are held constant, this expression reduces to

$$(4) \qquad V = \frac{(1 - \theta^D)\text{Div}}{\rho} \ .$$

In this case capital gains taxes do not matter because there are no capital gains. More generally, as in (3), capital gains taxes raise the discount rate on future dividends as well as affect the valuation of current dividends. Note that equation (3) implies that because of dividend taxes an extra dollar of promised dividends raises share valuation only by $(1 - \theta^D)$.

The firm seeks to choose an investment and financial policy to maximize (3) subject to the constraints it faces. It is constrained by its initial capital stock and by a requirement that sources equal uses of funds. It will also be necessary to assume that credit market constraints do not permit the firm to finance more than a fraction of its investment with debt.[4] This can be thought of as a measure of the firm's debt capacity. In the model presented below, the firm will always choose to borrow as much as possible; we assume that a share b of all new investment comes from debt issues and the remainder is financed through retained earnings. Finally, the firm cannot change its capital stock costlessly. The cost of installing extra capital is assumed to rise with the rate of capital accumulation. For convenience, it is assumed that the cost function is convex and homogeneous in investment and capital. Under these conditions dividends may be derived as after-tax profits less investment expenses.[5] That is,

$$(5) \qquad \text{Div} = [pF(K,L) - wL - pbiK](1 - \tau) - [1 - \text{ITC} - b$$
$$+ (1 - \tau)\phi]pI + \tau D + pbK(\pi - \delta^R) \ ,$$

where K and L refer to factor inputs, p is the overall price level, $F(K,L)$ is the production function, w is the wage rate, i is the nominal interest rate, τ is the corporate tax rate, ITC is the investment tax credit, ϕ is the adjustment cost function, I represents investment, δ^R is the real rate of depreciaton, and D represents the value of currently allowable depreciation allowances. It has been assumed that adjustment costs are expensed and ineligible for the investment tax credit.

The tax law is assumed to allow for exponential depreciation at a rate δ^T that may differ from δ^R but to be based on historical cost. This implies that

4. This is a crude way of modeling the effects of bankruptcy costs on the firm's choice of a debt-equity ratio. As noted below, the assumption of a constant debt-capital ratio is a fairly good representation of recent American experience. McDonald (1980) treats the choice of financial policy in more detail.

5. The assumption here is that all marginal equity finance comes from retained earnings. This follows from the assumption made earlier of a constant number of shares. It accounts for some of the apparently paradoxical results described below. The last term reflects the net receipts from new debt issues (withdrawals) necessary to maintain the debt-capital ratio as the capital stock depreciates and the price level rises.

(6) $\qquad D_s = \int_0^s \delta^T p_u I_u \exp\left[-\delta^T(s-u)\right] du$.

Combining equations (3) and (5), making use of (6), and rearranging yield an expression for the value of a firm's equity at time t:

(7) $\qquad V_t = \int_t^\infty \left[[pF(K,L) - wL - pbKi](1-\tau)\right.$

$\qquad\qquad - [1 - \text{ITC} - Z_s - b$

$\qquad\qquad + (1-\tau)\phi]pI + pbK(\pi - \delta)]$

$$\frac{(1-\theta^D)\mu_s}{(1-c)\mu_t} ds + B_t \ .$$

All the tax parameters can be arbitrary functions of time. For ease of exposition the following symbols have been introduced:

(8a) $\qquad \mu_s = \exp\left[-\int_0^s \frac{\rho + \pi}{1-c} du\right]$,

(8b) $\qquad B_t = \int_t^\infty \tau_s \delta^T \exp\left[-\delta^T(s-t)\right]\frac{\mu_s}{\mu_t}\frac{1-\theta^D}{1-c} p_t K_t ds$,

(8c) $\qquad Z_s = \int_s^\infty \tau \delta^T \exp\left[-\delta^T(u-s)\right]\frac{\mu_u}{\mu_s} du$.

These rather formidable expressions have simple interpretations. B_t represents the present value of depreciation allowances on existing capital. Z_s is the present value, evaluated at the time of the investment, on a dollar of new investment. In maximizing (7) the firm can ignore B_t, since it is independent of any future decisions. The constraint faced by the firm in maximizing (7) is that capital accumulation equals net investment:

(9) $\qquad \dot{K}_s = I_s - \delta^R K_s$.

The first-order conditions for optimality are[6]

(10a) $\qquad F_L = \dfrac{W}{p}$,

(10b) $\qquad [1 - \text{ITC} - Z_s - b + \phi(1-\tau)] = \dfrac{\lambda(1-c)}{p_t(1-\theta^D)}$

$\qquad\qquad - (1-\tau)\dfrac{I}{K}\phi'$,

---

6. Assuming that adjustment expenses were treated as investment under the tax law would not importantly alter the results. If these costs are taken to represent managerial effort, or as interference with concurrent production, the assumption in the text is appropriate. Similar conditions differing because of assumptions about taxation have been derived by Hayashi (1981) and Abel (1982).

(10c)
$$\frac{\dot{\lambda}}{p_t} = \frac{\lambda}{p_t}\left[\frac{\rho + \pi}{(1-c)} - \pi + \delta^R\right] - [(F_K - bi)(1 - \tau)$$
$$+ \left(\frac{I}{K}\right)^2 (1-\tau)\phi' + b(\pi - \delta^R)]\frac{(1 - \theta^D)}{(1-c)}.$$

Equation (10b) characterizes the investment function. It implicitly defines a function linking investment to the shadow price of capital λ/p_t and the tax parameters. The condition for zero investment is that

(11)
$$\frac{\lambda}{p_t} = \frac{(1 - \theta^D)}{(1-c)}[1 - ITC - Z_s - b].$$

This result can be characterized in intuitive terms. It implies that the shadow price of additional capital goods is equated to their marginal cost in after-tax dollars. Equation (11) implies that there will be investment even if the shadow price of new capital goods is less than 1. This is because taxes and debt finance reduce the effective price of new capital goods.

Equation (10b) is of no operational significance as a theory of investment unless an observable counterpart to the shadow price λ/p_t can be developed. Hayashi (1982) has shown in a similar model with a less elaborate tax system how the shadow price is linked to the market valuation of existing capital. The derivation below follows his very closely. Equation (7) implies that

(12)
$$\frac{V_t - B_t}{p_t K_t} = \int_t^\infty \left[\frac{(pF_K K - pbiK)(1 - \tau)}{pK}\right.$$
$$- \frac{(1 - ITC - Z_s - b + (1 - \tau)\phi)I}{K}$$
$$\left. + b(\pi - \delta^R)\right]\frac{(1 - \theta^D)\mu_s pK}{(1-c)\mu_t p_t K_t} ds$$
$$= \int_t^\infty \left[\left[\frac{1 - \theta^D}{1-c}\exp\left[-\int_t^s \left(\frac{\rho+\pi}{1-c} - \pi - \frac{\dot{K}}{K}\right)du\right]ds\right.$$

using the definition of μ. The first-order conditions (10) imply that equation (12) can be rewritten

(13)
$$\frac{V_t - B_t}{p_t K_t} = \int_t^\infty \left[(F_K - bi)(1 - \tau) + b(\pi - \delta^R) - \frac{\lambda I}{p_t K_t}\frac{1 - \theta^D}{1-c}\right.$$
$$+ (1-\tau)\phi'\left[\frac{I}{K}\right]^2 \frac{1 - \theta^D}{1-c}\exp$$
$$\left[-\int_t^s \left(\frac{\rho+\pi}{1-c} - \pi + \frac{\dot{K}}{K}\right)du\right]ds.$$

Now, using the first-order condition for λ, it can be seen that

(14)
$$\frac{V_t - B_t}{p_t - K_t} = \int_t^\infty \left[\frac{\lambda}{p_t} \left(\frac{I}{K} - \frac{\rho + \pi}{1 - c} - \delta^R - \pi \right) - \frac{\dot{\lambda}}{p_t} \right]$$

$$\times \exp \left[- \int_t^s \left(\frac{\rho + \pi}{1 - c} - \pi - \frac{I}{K} + \delta^R \right) du \right]$$

$$ds = \frac{\lambda_t}{p_t} .$$

The shadow price of additional capital may thus be expressed as a function of the firm's market value. The term B_t is subtracted from market value since the depreciation allowances the firm will receive on existing capital provide no inducement to further investment. Substituting equation (14) in equation (10b) yields an investment function expressible entirely in terms of observables:

(15)
$$\frac{I}{K} = \frac{\dot{K}}{K} + \delta^R = h \left(\frac{\dfrac{(V - B)(1 - c)}{pK(1 - \theta^D)} - 1 + b + \text{ITC} + Z}{(1 - \tau)} \right),$$

where $h( ) = (\phi + (I/K) \phi')^{-1}$. Equation (15) is a structural investment function relating investment and stock market valuation.

For simplicity we postulate that up to some level of I/K, adjustment is costless. Above that level, marginal adjustment costs rise linearly with investment. That is, total adjustment costs are

(16)
$$A = \frac{\beta}{2} \left(\frac{I}{K} - \gamma \right)^2 K \qquad \left(\frac{I}{K} - \gamma \right) \geq 0$$

$$= 0 \qquad\qquad \left(\frac{I}{K} - \gamma \right) < 0 .$$

It follows that the function $\phi( )$ is given by

(17)
$$\phi \left(\frac{I}{K} \right) = \frac{\beta \left(\dfrac{I}{K} - \gamma \right)^2}{2 \dfrac{I}{K}},$$

which is homogeneous in I and K as required. This implies that the investment function (15) can be written as

(18)
$$\frac{I}{K} = h(Q) = \gamma + \frac{1}{\beta} Q ,$$

where Q represents tax-adjusted Tobin's q and is given by

$$Q = \frac{\dfrac{(V - B)(1 - c)}{pK(1 - \theta^D)} - 1 + b + \text{ITC} + Z}{(1 - \tau)}.$$

By estimating equation (18) the parameters of the adjustment cost function $\phi(\ )$ can be inferred. This is the approach taken in the next section.

Before turning to the data, it is necessary to highlight the restrictiveness of the assumptions under which the stock market provides a proxy for the marginal q which drives investment decisions. The crucial assumption in the preceding derivation is that capital is both malleable and homogeneous. Only with this technological assumption does the market value of existing capital provide a proxy for the increment to market value arising from new investment. The assumption made here is inconsistent with putty-clay formulations in which existing capital can only be used in fixed proportions while new capital is malleable. It is also inconsistent with the view that the recent energy shocks have reduced the market value of existing energy-intensive capital but raised the incentive to invest in new energy-conserving capital.

A second restrictive assumption is that firms produce with constant returns to scale and earn no rents. If firms earn rents because of decreasing returns, intangible investments, or market power, these will be reflected in their market value and so measured q will not be a satisfactory proxy for the return to investment.

While these limitations are severe, they are in no way unique to the q theoretic approach to investment. Exactly the same issues arise in connection with variants on the flexible accelerator approach.

8.2   Construction of the Tax-adjusted Q Variable

This section presents estimates of the Q investment equations which provide the basis for an estimate of the impact of tax policy. With the early exception of Grunfeld (1960), almost all the empirical work using q has focused on aggregate or industry investment. Little or no account has been taken of tax effects. The construction of the necessary data is described in the appendix. The equations were estimated for the thirty Dow Jones companies.

In table 8.1, estimates of Tobin's q ratio of the market value of the firm to the replacement cost of its capital stock are displayed along with the tax-adjusted variant of Q for the companies included in the sample. Note that Q is the shadow price of capital less its acquisition cost. It is therefore comparable to $q - 1$ rather than q. The magnitudes of the estimates appear plausible. Moreover, companies whose prospects look dim, such as the steel companies, have low values of q whereas companies with rapid growth prospects, such as IBM, have high values of q. In all

Table 8.1   1978 q and Q

Company	q	Q
Allied Chemical	.644	.196
Aluminum Company of America	.658	.296
American Brands	.989	1.543
American Can	.569	−.007
American Telephone & Telegraph	.765	.480
Bethlehem Steel	.303	−.807
E. I. DuPont de Nemours	.964	1.513
Eastman Kodak	1.607	3.906
Exxon	.714	.674
General Electric	1.444	3.501
General Foods	.995	1.523
General Motors	.723	.934
Goodyear Tire	.554	−.181
International Nickel	.622	−.022
International Business Machines	3.083	9.845
International Harvester	.545	−.034
International Paper	.854	.992
Johns-Manville	.933	.728
Merck	3.026	8.829
Minnesota Mining & Manufacturing	2.129	5.850
Owens-Illinois	.599	−.010
Proctor & Gamble	1.783	4.625
Sears	2.010	4.255
Standard Oil of California	.791	.631
Texaco	.670	.177
United States Steel	.362	−.660
Union Carbide	.554	.036
United Technologies	1.170	2.198
Westinghouse	.517	.072
Woolworth	.544	−.222

likelihood, the high values of q for some companies also reflect the market's valuation of intangible assets. Lindenberg and Ross (1981) estimated q in a fashion similar to the estimates in this paper. They report eighteen year averages of q for each company. The correlation between the two sets of estimates of eighteen year averages of q for the twenty-five firms common to both samples is 0.953. On average, however, our estimates of q tend to be higher than theirs. We assume that capital depreciates faster than they do. Their calculations of capital-augmenting technical change only partially offset the difference in the depreciation rates. In estimating q, one needs to make many arbitrary assumptions. The high correlation between the two studies suggests that these assumptions have more of an effect on the level than on the variations in q.

Theory, failing to take account of taxes, suggests that firms should not invest when q is less than 1. This is the case for most of the firms in the sample. Only for a much smaller fraction of the sample is the tax-adjusted measure Q less than zero. The difference is due in large part to the fact that the Q measure takes account of the effects of dividend taxes, which reduce the opportunity cost of corporate retentions. Note, however, that even using this concept, eight companies appear to have no incentive to invest. The reason that these companies actually invest almost certainly involves the failure of the assumption made here that capital is homogeneous and malleable. In a world of heterogeneous capital, even firms with very low market values will find some investment worthwhile.

Estimates of equation (18) for the thirty companies are shown in table 8.2. The equations are all estimated using ordinary least squares. Because the estimates of Q are likely to be less reliable for the earlier years in the sample, we used only the last fifteen observations on each company. Some of the equations do exhibit serial correlation. Rao and Griliches (1969) show that when the error process is first-order autoregressive and the autocorrelation coefficient is relatively high (generally 0.4 or greater), the GLS transformation can improve efficiency even in small samples. If the error process is of higher order, then simply doing a first-order autoregressive transformation can reduce the efficiency of the estimator. With only fifteen data points, making higher-order autocorrelation corrections is not likely to improve efficiency, so we chose not to make any autoregressive transformations. When there is positive serial correlation, however, the t statistics for the OLS estimates will be overstated if we assume that the errors are white noise. Thus the t statistics reported are based on the assumption that the errors follow a first-order autoregressive process.

The results support the Q theory. In twenty-eight of the thirty regressions, the estimated slope coefficient is positive. Nearly half of the estimates are statistically significant. The low R^2 values indicate, however, that much of what affects investment decisions is not captured by the Q variable. The bottom rows of the table report estimates of the equations pooling the company data. Regardless of whether allowance is made for company-specific effects, the coefficient of Q is highly significant. If different firms have the same adjustment cost functions, then both the intercept and slope will be equal across firms. Because we do not do the GLS transformation, we cannot do an F test of this hypothesis. Instead, we do a χ^2 test, which overwhelmingly rejects the null hypotheses that both parameters are equal across firms. We also test for the equality of just the slopes and just the intercepts. In both cases, we reject the null hypothesis.[7]

7. To do a χ^2 test, we run the following regression:

$$\frac{I}{\text{RNPPE} + \text{RLINV}} = a_0 + a_1 Q + a_2 \text{FRMDUM1} + \ldots$$
$$+ a_{30}\text{FRMDUM29} + a_{31}\text{FRMDUM1} \times Q$$
$$+ \ldots + a_{59}\text{FRMDUM29} \times Q,$$

where FRMDUM1 to FRMDUM29 are firm dummies. Let V be the estimated covariance

Table 8.2   **Investment Equations Using Tax-adjusted Q**

Company	Intercept	Slope	
Allied Chemical	.152	.018	$R^2 = .19$
	(5.93)	(1.31)	DW = 1.30
Aluminum Company of America	.115	.020	$R^2 = .34$
	(7.82)	(2.23)	DW = 1.56
American Brands	.101	.059	$R^2 = .55$
	(3.01)	(3.99)	DW = 2.01
American Can	.097	.038	$R^2 = .56$
	(7.07)	(3.75)	DW = 1.77
American Telephone & Telegraph	.157	.008	$R^2 = .26$
	(10.96)	(1.32)	DW = .64
Bethlehem Steel	.150	.073	$R^2 = .53$
	(11.74)	(3.45)	DW = 1.60
E. I. DuPont de Nemours	.206	.004	$R^2 = .12$
	(5.92)	(1.02)	DW = 1.09
Eastman Kodak	.111	.007	$R^2 = .58$
	(2.79)	(3.48)	DW = 1.25
Exxon	.177	−.003	$R^2 = .04$
	(10.05)	(−.55)	DW = 1.06
General Electric	.179	.013	$R^2 = .26$
	(2.81)	(1.77)	DW = 1.03
General Foods	.117	.011	$R^2 = .64$
	(5.39)	(3.45)	DW = 1.02
General Motors	.242	.007	$R^2 = .15$
	(7.26)	(1.41)	DW = 1.74
Goodyear Tire	.134	.037	$R^2 = .74$
	(10.56)	(6.11)	DW = 1.57
International Nickel	.122	.007	$R^2 = .13$
	(2.76)	(.96)	DW = .93
International Business Machines	.316	.006	$R^2 = .11$
	(2.59)	(.945)	DW = .45
International Harvester	.153	.015	$R^2 = .05$
	(5.43)	(.57)	DW = 1.00
International Paper	.151	.012	$R^2 = .02$
	(2.39)	(.46)	DW = 1.27
Johns-Manville	.181	−.009	$R^2 = .06$
	(5.72)	(−.76)	DW = 1.36
Merck	.245	.001	$R^2 = .03$
	(3.04)	(.51)	DW = 1.29
Minnesota Mining & Manufacturing	.193	.005	$R^2 = .18$
	(3.19)	(1.46)	DW = 1.42
Owens-Illinois	.130	.030	$R^2 = .29$
	(2.71)	(1.81)	DW = 1.22
Proctor & Gamble	.163	.002	$R^2 = .01$
	(3.12)	(.33)	DW = .95
Sears	.029	.016	$R^2 = .79$
	(1.07)	(7.28)	DW = 1.91
Standard Oil of California	.120	.020	$R^2 = .53$
	(9.17)	(3.48)	DW = 1.73
Texaco	.136	.009	$R^2 = .37$
	(8.14)	(2.19)	DW = 1.35

Table 8.2 (cont.)

Company	Intercept	Slope	
United States Steel	.090	.010	$R^2 = .04$
	(5.28)	(.85)	DW = .69
Union Carbide	.169	.009	$R^2 = .10$
	(7.37)	(.51)	DW = 1.10
United Technologies	.114	.068	$R^2 = .56$
	(2.25)	(3.18)	DW = 1.15
Westinghouse	.113	.022	$R^2 = .57$
	(4.30)	(3.24)	DW = 1.05
Woolworth	.181	.013	$R^2 = .25$
	(7.31)	(1.41)	DW = .68
All companies with common intercept	.166	.004	$R^2 = .28$
	(21.09)	(4.77)	
All companies with different intercepts	. . .	.006	$R^2 = .54$
		(4.32)	

The theory of investment developed in the preceding section implies that lagged values of q should not have any effect on current investment. It takes no account of delivery lags or lags in implementing investment plans. This is a potentially serious difficulty. The equations in table 8.2 were therefore reestimated including lagged values. While this improved their explanatory power a little bit, lagged Q was rarely significant, so these results are not reported here.

In table 8.3, the relative explanatory power of Q and q is contrasted. If equation (18) were the true investment function, then the coefficient on Q would be positive and significant and the coefficient on q would be insignificant. With only three exceptions, the coefficient of Q is positive; in over half the regressions, it is significant. Nearly all of the coefficients of q are negative, and nearly half are significant. This is not surprising. Because capital is not homogeneous and the stock market is extremely volatile, one would expect the stock market component of q to be a very noisy signal of the marginal return on incremental investment. The tax-adjustment parts of the Q series are much less subject to error. It is therefore reasonable to expect that their effect would be greater than that of the stock market. This is reflected in the negative coefficients on q. This point underscores the importance of making tax adjustments in studying the relation between investment and q.[8]

---

matrix of the regression. Let V be the lower right-hand 58×58 submatrix of V. Let a be the column vector composed of a_2 to a_{59}. Under the null hypothesis that the adjustment cost functions are identical, $a'(V)^{-1} a^A \chi^2_{58}$. The test statistic is 357.8. The statistics for the tests that just the intercepts and just the slopes are equal are, respectively, 95.5 and 120.8. Notice that our estimate of the covariance matrix asymptotically approaches the true covariance matrix only as $t \to \infty$. Even though the pooled regression has 450 data points, T is still 15, so the asymptotic distribution of the test is unlikely to hold.

8. If we had a larger sample, we could handle the errors in variables with an instrumental variables procedure. The tax rates are appropriate instruments because they are measured

Table 8.3   **Investment Equations Using Q and q**

Company	Intercept	Q	q	
Allied Chemical	.407	.144	−.413	$R^2 = .33$
	(2.44)	(1.82)	(−1.57)	DW = 1.30
Aluminum Company of America	.207	.067	−.146	$R^2 = .39$
	(1.98)	(1.26)	(−.89)	DW = 1.56
American Brands	.077	.045	.042	$R^2 = .55$
	(1.07)	(1.15)	(.40)	DW = 1.96
American Can	.306	.147	−.346	$R^2 = .66$
	(2.98)	(2.72)	(−2.04)	DW = 2.22
American Telephone & Telegraph	.002	−.064	.231	$R^2 = .49$
	(.028)	(−1.77)	(2.02)	DW = 1.03
Bethlehem Steel	.561	.274	−.707	$R^2 = .67$
	(3.10)	(3.06)	(−2.27)	DW = 2.04
E. I. DuPont de Nemours	.323	.070	−.221	$R^2 = .35$
	(5.32)	(2.48)	(−2.36)	DW = .98
Eastman Kodak	.195	.032	−.096	$R^2 = .85$
	(6.54)	(5.28)	(−4.25)	DW = 1.63
Exxon	.304	.084	−.258	$R^2 = .39$
	(5.81)	(2.43)	(−2.53)	DW = 1.50
General Electric	.325	.059	−.185	$R^2 = .26$
	(1.77)	(1.06)	(−.84)	DW = 1.04
General Foods	.168	.043	−.100	$R^2 = .74$
	(6.29)	(3.02)	(−2.27)	DW = 1.71
General Motors	.412	.105	−.339	$R^2 = .44$
	(5.48)	(2.61)	(−2.44)	DW = 1.76
Goodyear Tire	.164	.052	−.050	$R^2 = .74$
	(1.46)	(.95)	(−.27)	DW = 1.57
International Nickel	.341	.102	−.340	$R^2 = .13$
	(5.70)	(4.23)	(−3.98)	DW = .93
International Business Machines	.494	.078	−.263	$R^2 = .70$
	(5.88)	(4.47)	(−4.30)	DW = .95
International Harvester	.458	.161	−.493	$R^2 = .29$
	(2.61)	(1.86)	(−1.74)	DW = 1.40
International Paper	.631	.189	−.678	$R^2 = .49$
	(3.94)	(3.15)	(−3.12)	DW = 1.19
Johns-Manville	.172	−.013	.016	$R^2 = .06$
	(1.05)	(−.18)	(.06)	DW = 1.36
Merck	.309	.023	−.082	$R^2 = .44$
	(5.12)	(3.00)	(−2.91)	DW = 1.74
Minnesota Mining & Manufacturing	.260	.028	−.087	$R^2 = .34$
	(3.76)	(1.95)	(−1.64)	DW = 1.60
Owens-Illinois	.517	.201	−.601	$R^2 = .55$
	(3.38)	(3.07)	(−2.64)	DW = 1.47
Proctor & Gamble	.223	.058	−.182	$R^2 = .48$
	(5.81)	(3.25)	(−3.20)	DW = 1.75
Sears	−.019	−.002	.060	$R^2 = .79$
	(−.170)	(−.043)	(.431)	DW = 1.87
Standard Oil of California	.248	.087	−.221	$R^2 = .64$
	(3.84)	(2.57)	(−2.00)	DW = 2.07
Texaco	.238	.063	−.178	$R^2 = .47$
	(3.33)	(1.70)	(−1.47)	DW = 1.48

Table 8.3 (cont.)

Company	Intercept	Q	q	
United States Steel	.196	.070	− .170	$R^2 = .04$
	(3.91)	(2.52)	(− 2.38)	DW = .75
Union Carbide	.419	.142	− .428	$R^2 = .38$
	(1.36)	(.83)	(− .73)	DW = 1.87
United Technologies	.239	.122	− .195	$R^2 = .60$
	(1.90)	(2.37)	(− 1.10)	DW = 1.34
Westinghouse	.122	.028	− .017	$R^2 = .57$
	(1.96)	(.89)	(− .17)	DW = 1.08
Woolworth	.254	.052	− .132	$R^2 = .32$
	(3.45)	(1.36)	(− 1.05)	DW = .99
All companies with common intercept	.226	.031	− 0.90	$R^2 = .33$
	(12.08)	(4.16)	(− 3.48)	
All companies with different intercepts	. . .	.033	− .099	$R^2 = .59$
		(5.15)	(− 4.38)	

The results obtained in this section provide quite strong microeconometric support for the q theory of investment. The results parallel closely those obtained in Summers' (1981a) study of aggregate investment over the entire 1929–78 period. The aggregate results suggest a somewhat larger responsiveness of investment to q than is found here. This is probably because aggregation reduces some of the noise in individual firms' q. Future progress in reconciling micro- and macroestimates of the effects of q, and in improving the explanatory power of these equations, must await the development of methods for taking account of rents and the nonhomogeneity of the capital stock.

8.3 Tax Reform and Corporate Valuation

This section assesses the impact of alternative tax reforms on corporate profitability and on share valuation. The equations estimated in the previous section provide the basis for estimating the impact of a given tax reform on a firm's investment. In order to estimate the effect of a given tax reform on a firm's investment, one must first calculate its effect on Q. The principal difficulty in this calculation comes in estimating the effect of the reform on V, the market value of firm equity. The procedure followed here is to estimate the impact on the market value of equity by calculating the present value of the change in tax liabilities which a reform will cause assuming that the firm's growth is not affected by the tax change.

A proper calculation of this type would require the simultaneous estimation of the entire growth path of the firm. This path is of course

precisely compared with the value and replacement cost of the firm and because they are determined exogenously. In small samples, however, instrumental variable regressions are badly biased.

affected by tax reforms. Deriving the path of investment following a tax change requires the solution of a two-point boundary value problem as described in Summers (1981a). Because the response of investment to change in Q is estimated to be small, the approximation error involved is likely to be very small.

The first step in estimating the change in market value from a tax change is estimating its effect on after-tax profits. In this paper, we consider three alternative tax reforms: indexation of the tax system to adjust for inflation, 25% acceleration of depreciation deductions, and reduction in the statutory corporate tax rate from 46 to 40%.[9] It is easiest to begin by describing how the change in profits arising from the corporate rate reduction was calculated.

In general, reported profits differ from taxable profits. As a result, to estimate the effect of a change in the corporate tax rate, we look at actual taxes paid. With a tax rate of 46%, taxes are given by

$$T = 0.46\pi^T - \text{ITC} - \text{FTC},$$

where T = taxes, π^T = taxable profits, ITC = investment tax credit, and FTC = foreign tax credit. Reducing the corporate tax rate to 0.40 increases profits by $0.6\pi^T$. We assume that all foreign taxes paid can be claimed as a credit.[10] Thus we estimate the change in profits by

(19) $$\Delta\pi(\text{tax reduction}) = \frac{6}{46}(T + \text{ITC} + \text{FTC}).$$

The change in profits from accelerating depreciation and using replacement cost depreciation are, respectively,

$$\Delta\pi(\text{depreciation acceleration})$$

$$= \left(\frac{8}{3L} - \frac{2}{L}\right)\text{NPL}^T \times 0.46,$$

$$\Delta\pi(\text{replacement cost depreciation})$$

$$= \frac{2}{L}(\text{NPL}^R - \text{NPL}^T) \times 0.46.$$

In indexing debt, we allow firms to deduct only real interest payments on the market value of the debt. Using an ARMA procedure based only on prior data, we estimate that at the beginning of 1978 the expected inflation rate over a long horizon was 0.053. We thus deduct from profits:

9. Specifically, we assume that the useful life for tax purposes is reduced by 25%. The reduction results in a 33⅓% increase in δ, the depreciation rate.

10. Firms may claim foreign taxes up to the United States statutory tax rate times foreign pretax profits as a tax credit. The maximum applies to all foreign taxes paid. Thus a firm can offset taxes above the United States corporate tax rate by operating in another country with a tax rate lower than the United States'.

(20) $\Delta\pi(\text{debt indexation}) = 0.053 \times \text{MVDEBT} \times 0.46$.

In general, the inventory adjustment is

(21) $\Delta\pi(\text{inventory indexation}) = 0.46 \times \text{FRFIFO}$
$$\times \text{INV}_{-1} \times \frac{\text{CPI}}{\text{CPI}_{-1}}.$$

When inventories are drawn down, however, an adjustment also has to be made for liquidated LIFO inventories. As in the estimation of real inventories, we assume that the reduction in LIFO inventories comes from goods purchased in the previous year.

To estimate the change in market value, we need to project future values for each firm's taxes, net plant, debt, and inventories. We assume that the real value of these quantities grows at the same rate. We estimated the growth rate of real net property, plant, and equipment from 1964 to 1978. Over that period, some of the firms had growth rates exceeding 10% per year. In general, such growth rates reflect the adjustment to a new equilibrium and we do not expect them to continue. Thus we average the historic growth rate with 3% to get expected future growth.

In the calculations below, it is assumed that investors expect that the rate of inflation will remain permanently at 0.053. It is assumed that potential tax reforms are permanent and unanticipated. When considering, for example, the acceleration of depreciation, we assume that people did not foresee the tax law change. When the change occurs, people expect it to last forever. We assume that a real discount rate of 10% can be applied to all cash flows. This may be misleading, since the risk characteristics of depreciation allowances differ greatly from those of pretax profits.

The formula for the change in V from corporate tax rate reduction, inventory indexation, and debt indexation is

$$\Delta V = \frac{\Delta\pi}{0.1 - g} \frac{1 - \theta^D}{1 - c},$$

where g is the growth rate. To reduce the effect of wide annual fluctuations, we use three year averages of inventories and taxes paid rather than the 1978 values. The averages are calculated in real terms and adjusted for growth.

The change in V from a change in the depreciation tax law is the sum of the changes in the value of depreciation deductions on existing capital and on future additions to capital. The former is simply the change in B. New investment at time t is given by

$$\text{NI}(t) = \left(g + \frac{2}{L}\right)\text{RNPPE}(0)e^{gt},$$

where RNPPE represents the real value of net property, plant, and equipment. The change in the value of the depreciation deduction at time t of investment at time t is the change in Z. Thus the change in the value of depreciation deductions on all future new investment is the change in Z times the discounted stream of investment.

While most recent discussions of corporate tax reforms have focused on the likely impact on investment, issues of equity should be considered as well. Unsophisticated observers focus on the distinction between tax relief for business and for individuals. This is misleading, as corporations should be thought of as conduits. All taxes are ultimately borne by individuals in their role as labor suppliers, consumers, or suppliers of capital. The change in the value of the stock market following a tax change is a direct measure of the present value of the burdens it will impose on the suppliers of equity capital. It thus seems a natural candidate for measuring the incidence of capital tax reforms.

In addition to examining the impact of tax policy on the functional distribution of income, it is instructive to model the effects of tax reforms on the stock market for two other reasons. First, it is widely accepted that a good tax reform should minimize windfall gains and losses. The size of the policy-induced jump in the stock market is a good measure of its windfall effect. If, as available evidence suggests, investors fail to hold diversified portfolios, then differential effects of tax reforms on different securities create windfall gains and losses.

Second, the effect of tax policy on the stock market is of concern to those sensitive to issues of vertical equity. Virtually all corporate equity is owned directly or indirectly by the very wealthy. About 75% is held directly by individuals. Of this, available evidence indicates that about 50% is held by families with incomes in the top 1% of the population. This actually understates the true concentration because much of the remainder of the stock is held by individuals with deceptively low reported incomes due to successful sheltering or life-cycle effects. The remaining stock is mostly held by pension funds, foreigners, and insurance companies. Since almost all pension plans offer defined benefits, the pension's assets are ultimately owned not by the beneficiaries but by the shareowners in the corporations with pension liabilities. Hence this stock also should be assigned primarily to rich households. The distributional consequences of insurance company and foreign ownership are less clear. But the conclusion that any tax-induced change in profitability which shows up in the stock market redounds almost entirely to the very wealthy seems inevitable. Therefore the analysis below focuses on the effects of tax reforms on both investment and the stock market. Recent research suggests the importance of dividend clienteles. This implies that changes in the relative valuation of different firms may have large effects on the distribution of wealth.

In table 8.4 the effects of indexing the tax system are considered. The relative effects of the different components of indexing vary among firms. Indexing debt has a small impact on Kodak, which is almost entirely equity financed, and a large impact on AT&T, which is largely debt financed. Inventory indexation has no effect on firms already using LIFO but a large effect on American Brands, which primarily uses FIFO. With only two exceptions, the effect of total indexation is to increase firm value, thus suggesting that the interaction of inflation and corporate taxes has at least partially contributed to the decline in the real value of the stock market. In some cases, indexation has a significantly larger impact on profits than on firm value. This phenomenon is undoubtedly a result of some firms having unusually low real profits in 1978. In making these calculations, we implicitly assume that a reduction in taxable profits is of value to the firm. The effect of total indexation on firm value ranges from − 13.3% for Sears to 20.4% for American Brands. Typically, indexation leads to an increase in firm value of between 5% and 10%.

This contradicts the results of several earlier studies (e.g. Shoven and Bulow 1975) which suggested that indexing would be approximately neutral or actually increase corporate income tax liabilities. The reason is that our calculation focuses on the long-run impact of increases in inflation rather than their immediate impact on the current income, which includes revaluations of outstanding long-term debt.

These calculations of the impact of indexation on stock market valuations implicitly assume that the market is rational with respect to inflation. This hypothesis is examined explicitly in Summers (1981c), who finds some evidence that at least historically the market has failed to fully recognize the effects of inflation-taxation interactions.

Table 8.5 considers the effect of reducing the corporate tax rate from 0.46 to 0.4 and of accelerating depreciation by 25%. On average, the latter reform increases firm value by 7%. Not surprisingly, the effect on capital-intensive firms is larger. The effect of a reduction in the tax rate ranges from 4.1% for Bethlehem Steel to 34.7% for Exxon. If taxable income equals real income, the tax rate reduction should increase firm value by 11%. Because the interaction of inflation and the tax system cause taxable profits to be higher than real profits, the tax rate reduction should increase firm value by more than 11%. In fact, the average increase in firm value from indexing in table 8.4 is consistent with the 13% average increase in firm value from a tax rate reduction. The variation among firms of the effect of indexing does not, however, explain the variation of the effect of the tax rate reduction. The 34.7% increase in Exxon's value, for example, cannot be explained by the inflation-induced overstatement of profits. In 1978, Exxon's foreign and federal taxes were 65% of its taxable income. A large portion of Exxon's taxes were foreign. Saudi Arabia levies a large "tax" on oil extraction. It is not clear that this

Table 8.4   Effect of Indexation on Profitability and Stock Market Valuation

Company	% Change in V				% Change in Profits			
	Inventories	Depreciation	Debt	Total	Inventories	Depreciation	Debt	Total
Allied Chemical	2.9	14.3	−13.6	3.6	.1	98.7	−78.0	20.9
Aluminum Company of America	4.0	11.3	−13.8	1.5	4.5	16.1	−12.4	8.4
American Brands	41.2	5.9	−26.7	20.4	39.5	5.5	−19.6	25.3
American Can	10.7	10.3	−9.1	11.9	31.6	37.2	−20.2	48.5
American Telephone & Telegraph	.5	18.4	−21.8	−2.9	1.3	47.5	−44.5	4.2
Bethlehem Steel	7.7	32.0	−24.0	15.7	.4	84.9	−33.5	51.9
E. I. DuPont de Nemours	2.9	8.7	−6.1	5.5	3.3	10.3	−5.4	8.2
Eastman Kodak	2.4	5.3	−.6	7.1	2.2	5.0	−.4	6.8
Exxon	.0	10.3	−5.5	4.8	.1	19.2	−7.8	11.5
General Electric	3.0	4.3	−4.3	3.0	4.4	6.5	−4.9	6.1
General Foods	13.3	5.2	−5.2	13.3	22.6	11.0	−7.0	26.5
General Motors	5.1	9.7	−2.5	12.3	3.4	6.0	−1.3	8.1
Goodyear Tire	14.6	18.9	−26.2	7.3	29.8	38.7	−40.9	27.6

International Nickel[a]	25.7	18.0	-28.7	15.0	*	*	*	*
International Business Machines	.8	3.8	-.2	4.4	2.1	9.1	-.6	10.6
International Harvester	16.7	8.4	-22.6	2.5	37.2	20.4	-38.1	19.5
International Paper	21.8	10.6	-12.2	20.2	3.3	16.8	-14.3	5.7
Johns-Manville	.0	10.9	-9.2	1.7	.0	9.6	-6.5	3.2
Merck	8.9	6.6	-5.6	9.9	6.8	3.9	-3.5	7.2
Minnesota Mining & Manufacturing	7.5	5.2	-3.5	9.2	7.2	4.7	-2.8	9.2
Owens-Illinois	7.0	17.3	-19.5	4.8	12.1	32.2	-26.4	17.9
Proctor & Gamble	2.2	3.7	-3.2	2.7	3.8	6.0	-4.2	5.6
Sears	.0	2.8	-16.1	-13.3	.4	4.5	-17.2	-12.2
Standard Oil of California	2.0	9.4	-5.1	6.3	.8	13.6	-4.8	9.6
Texaco	4.0	13.0	-9.3	7.7	2.2	25.3	-12.3	15.2
United States Steel[a]	.0	17.8	-16.3	1.5	*	*	*	*
Union Carbide	6.1	15.8	-15.7	6.2	.2	32.3	-27.0	5.5
United Technologies	12.6	3.7	-3.8	12.5	17.7	6.0	-4.7	19.0
Westinghouse	9.9	11.0	-7.0	13.9	9.9	12.9	-5.5	17.3
Woolworth	20.7	11.7	-17.1	15.3	21.0	13.2	-13.7	20.5

[a]Negative profits in 1978.

Table 8.5   Effect of Tax Changes on Profitability
                 and Stock Market Valuation

Company	% Change in V		% Change in Profits	
	Tax Rate Reduction	Depreciation Acceleration	Tax Rate Reduction	Depreciation Acceleration
Allied Chemical	8.2	9.3	87.0	111.8
Aluminum Company of America	9.0	7.3	10.8	12.6
American Brands	25.5	3.9	21.2	5.7
American Can	11.6	6.6	25.8	27.6
American Telephone & Telegraph	3.8	12.0	11.1	46.1
Bethlehem Steel	2.6	20.7	13.6	55.0
E. I. DuPont de Nemours	8.2	5.7	9.4	12.1
Eastman Kodak	13.8	3.5	11.4	5.4
Exxon	34.7	6.7	46.9	19.0
General Electric	10.0	2.8	11.4	7.5
General Foods	14.1	3.4	19.6	9.1
General Motors	22.9	6.4	11.3	8.0
Goodyear Tire	18.5	12.3	28.8	38.2
International Nickel[a]	12.8	11.5	*	*
International Business Machines	9.1	2.6	20.6	17.2
International Harvester	9.6	5.5	25.1	20.4
International Paper	6.7	6.9	8.4	16.7
Johns-Manville	16.5	7.0	15.4	9.1
Merck	19.4	4.3	11.9	5.9
Minnesota Mining & Manufacturing	13.9	3.4	13.0	6.0
Owens-Illinois	12.3	11.2	15.8	29.8
Proctor & Gamble	10.7	2.4	14.3	5.6
Sears	4.6	1.8	4.8	3.8
Standard Oil of California	11.7	6.1	11.4	11.2
Texaco	15.2	8.4	15.8	21.7
United States Steel[a]	4.3	11.4	*	*
Union Carbide	5.6	10.3	10.1	37.5
United Technologies	13.6	2.5	18.3	7.4
Westinghouse	13.5	7.1	14.6	10.9
Woolworth	20.3	7.7	19.0	13.7

[a]Negative profits in 1978.

tax is an income tax, so it may not qualify for the foreign tax credit. Even if it does, the tax may be large enough to make Exxon's tax rate on foreign profits well above 0.46. In either case, our assumption that all foreign taxes can be claimed as a credit is likely to be violated.

8.4 Tax Reforms, Q, and Investment

In this section we derive estimates of the impact of the tax reform packages considered above on firm investment. The estimates are calculated first by using the estimates of the impact of tax changes on V displayed in tables 8.4 and 8.5 to find the estimated change in Q, and then by multiplying this figure by the coefficient on Q in the firm investment equation.

It should be stressed at the outset that these estimates are subject to very substantial error. Beyond the difficulties of inaccuracy in the data, a major limitation of the analysis is that for some firms the effect of changes in Q is estimated only with a large standard error. Moreover, the effect of tax reforms on V is estimable only approximately due to the somewhat arbitrary assumptions made about the choice of a discount and growth rate, and the neglect of the economy-wide feedback effects of increased capital accumulation. While these conclusions are, to say the least, tentative, they illustrate the potential of this methodology for a much richer analysis of the effects of tax changes.

An additional issue is posed by FIFO inventory accounting. As table 8.4 demonstrates, a substantial fraction of the gains to corporations from indexing arise from the elimination of the taxation of FIFO profits. There exist some reasons to believe that any extra taxes incurred as a result of FIFO inventory accounting do not discourage investment in plant and equipment. It is argued that the taxes are voluntary and so are unlikely to be paid if they impose a burden. In addition it is argued that taxes on inventory holdings should have no impact on the return to plant and equipment investment and so should not affect these investment decisions.

Table 8.6 presents the effects of indexation on Q and on investment. While there is considerable variation among firms, total indexation generally increases investment by less than 5%. Table 8.7 gives the projections of how lowering the corporate tax rate and accelerating depreciation affect Q and investment. Again, the increase in investment by most of the firms is between 0% and 5%. Comparing these results with tables 8.4 and 8.5, it is clear that the tax changes have a larger impact on firm valuation than on investment.

Comparing tables 8.6 and 8.7 with tables 8.4 and 8.5, it can be seen that in the short run the costs of these changes are large compared with their benefits. In many cases, the amendments would have a much greater impact on firm value than on investment. For example, completely indexing the tax system would increase International Paper's market value by 20.2%. At the same time, International Paper would increment its investments by only 0.6%. Similarly, a 15% growth in the value of International Nickel would stimulate additional investment of only 1.5%. While these firms are outliers, market value would increase twice as much as investment for most firms.

The large change in firm value would also have an undesirable impact on the distribution of wealth. These changes in the corporate income tax

Table 8.6   Effect of Indexation on Q and Investment

Company	Change in Q				% Change in Investment			
	Inven-tories	Depreci-ation	Debt	Total	Inven-tories	Depreci-ation	Debt	Total
Allied Chemical	.037	.256	-.176	.117	.4	2.9	-2.0	1.3
Aluminum Company of America	.054	.233	-.184	.103	.9	3.9	-3.0	1.8
American Brands	.830	.441	-.540	.731	26.2	13.9	-16.7	23.4
American Can	.130	.215	-.110	.235	5.2	8.6	-4.4	9.4
American Telephone & Telegraph	.007	.298	-.309	-.004	.0	1.5	-1.5	.0
Bethlehem Steel	.037	.218	-.116	.139	2.9	17.0	-9.0	10.9
E. I. DuPont de Nemours	.076	.353	-.158	.399	.1	.6	-.3	.4
Eastman Kodak	.126	.445	-.030	.541	.6	2.2	-.1	2.7
Exxon[a]	.000	.292	-.110	.182	*	*	*	*
General Electric	.134	.385	-.188	.331	.8	2.2	-1.1	1.9
General Foods	.351	.284	-.136	.499	3.0	2.4	-1.2	4.2
General Motors	.117	.409	-.057	.469	.3	1.2	-.2	1.3
Goodyear Tire	.121	.315	-.218	.218	3.6	9.2	-6.4	6.4

International Nickel	.267	.287	−.297	.257	1.6	1.7	−1.8	1.5
International Business Machines	.087	.498	−.027	.558	.1	.8	−.0	.9
International Harvester	.135	.245	−.183	.197	1.4	2.5	−1.8	2.1
International Paper	.042	.283	−.239	.086	.3	2.1	−1.8	.6
Johns-Manville[a]	.000	.308	−.179	.129	*	*	*	*
Merck	.853	.980	−.537	1.296	.4	.5	−.3	.6
Minnesota Mining & Manufacturing	.514	.584	−.240	.858	1.1	1.2	−.5	1.8
Owens-Illinois	.076	.288	−.210	.154	1.7	6.6	−4.8	3.5
Proctor & Gamble	.128	.352	−.184	.296	.1	.4	−.2	.3
Sears	.000	.323	−.651	−.328	.0	5.5	−11.0	−5.5
Standard Oil of California	.040	.257	−.098	.199	.6	3.9	−1.5	3.0
Texaco	.057	.277	−.133	.201	.4	1.8	−.9	1.3
United States Steel	.000	.170	−.105	.065	.0	1.9	−1.2	.7
Union Carbide	.070	.286	−.179	.177	.4	1.5	−1.0	.9
United Technologies	.400	.292	−.120	.572	10.7	7.8	−3.2	15.3
Westinghouse	.136	.320	−.096	.360	2.7	6.3	−1.9	7.1
Woolworth	.174	.331	−.144	.361	1.3	2.4	−1.0	2.7

[a]Change in investment not projected when estimated coefficient of tax-adjusted Q is negative.

Table 8.7   Effect of Tax Reforms on Q and Investment

Company	Change in Q		% Change in Investment	
	Tax Rate Reduction	Depreciation Acceleration	Tax Rate Reduction	Depreciation Acceleration
Allied Chemical	.065	.167	.7	1.9
Aluminum Company of America	.064	.151	1.1	2.5
American Brands	.286	.287	9.0	9.1
American Can	.109	.140	4.3	5.6
American Telephone & Telegraph	−.006	.193	−.0	1.0
Bethlehem Steel	.076	.141	5.9	11.0
E. I. DuPont de Nemours	.028	.233	.0	.4
Eastman Kodak	.262	.291	1.3	1.4
Exxon[a]	.544	.189	*	*
General Electric	.035	.254	.2	1.5
General Foods	.165	.185	1.4	1.6
General Motors	.356	.270	1.0	.8
Goodyear Tire	.135	.205	3.9	6.0
International Nickel	.110	.184	.7	1.1
International Business Machines	−.052	.333	−.0	.5
International Harvester	.045	.161	.4	1.6
International Paper	.009	.184	.0	1.4
Johns-Manville[a]	.206	.199	*	*
Merck	.811	.641	.4	.3
Minnesota Mining & Manufacturing	.269	.384	.6	.8
Owens-Illinois	.105	.187	2.4	4.3
Proctor & Gamble	.092	.227	.1	.2
Sears	−.269	.211	−4.5	3.6
Standard Oil of California	.129	.167	2.0	2.5
Texaco	.163	.180	1.1	1.2
United States Steel	.076	.109	.9	1.2
Union Carbide	.038	.186	.2	1.0
United Technologies	.151	.192	4.1	5.2
Westinghouse	.137	.208	2.7	4.1
Woolworth	.144	.218	1.0	1.6

[a]Change in investment not projected when estimated coefficient of tax-adjusted Q is negative.

are being considered along with reductions in personal income taxes for people in top income brackets. Combined, these policies may cause a large shift of wealth to those who are already wealthy.

If the government's objective is to increase investment, it should implement the reforms which most directly affect the relative cost of capital. Indexing or accelerating depreciation induces more investment for a given increase in market value than do the other changes. Consider, for example, the effects of indexing inventories and depreciation for

American Can. The two changes have a nearly equal effect on firm valuation, but depreciation indexing has almost twice the effect on investment that inventory indexing does. Similarly, the tax rate reduction would increase the value of Goodyear by 20.4% while the depreciation acceleration would increase it by only 12.3%. The latter change would, however, increase Goodyear's investment more than the former.

Investment studies that use aggregate data miss the effect of policies on the composition of investment. Yet, the results in this study suggest that the impact of tax changes would vary significantly across firms. Since these results are for a small number of firms, it is difficult to say whether most of the variation is across or within industries. Insofar as adjustment costs are part of an industry's technology, one might expect similar results for firms in the same industry. On the other hand, the analysis in section 8.1 assumed a competitive market structure. Especially for the Dow 30, this assumption is tenuous. It is possible that the response to a tax change could depend on a firm's competitive position within an industry. The three chemical firms in the sample show similar responses to all the changes. In contrast, though, Bethlehem Steel's investment is much more sensitive to tax changes than United States Steel's. An important extension of this paper would be to explore more systematically the effect of taxes on the composition of investment.

8.5 Conclusions

This preliminary attempt to examine the impact of alternative tax reforms on the investment decisions of individual firms has yielded promising results. The q theory approach has substantial predictive power at the microlevel. The econometric results suggest that explanatory power is enhanced even further when tax effects are recognized. The simulation results confirm that tax policies can have large effects on both stock market valuations and investment incentives in both the short and the long run. They also indicate that the effects of investment incentives are likely to differ very substantially across firms.

The differences arise from variations both in the magnitude of tax effects on firms' incentives to invest and in the responsiveness of firms' investment to changes in investment incentives. The latter are due, according to the model, to differing adjustment cost functions.

While these results are informative and encouraging, a great deal needs to be done before it will be possible to make accurate predictions of the impact of tax reforms on individual corporate or even industry investment decisions. The most important area for further investigation is the relaxation of the stringent assumptions about the homogeneity of capital and absence of rents that were made here. This will probably necessitate the addition of other variables to Q investment equations. Ultimately, work along these lines promises us a greater understanding not just of tax effects on investment but also of tax effects on the other components of a firm's net worth such as intangibles.

Appendix

The source of the data is the Compustat tapes and spans the years 1959 to 1978. To estimate tax-adjusted Q, we need estimates of the market value of equity, the market value of debt, the replacement value of inventories, the replacement value of the capital stock, and the taxable capital stock. Throughout the analysis, we tried to get these figures for the beginning of each year.

Market Value of Equity

Compustat gives the closing price of a share of stock for each company. The value of common stock at the beginning of the year is estimated as the closing value in year $t - 1$ times the number of shares outstanding at $t - 1$. The value of preferred stock is estimated by dividing preferred dividends by the Standard and Poor's preferred stock yield.

Market Value of Debt

Compustat lists the book value of both long-term and short-term debt. We assume that the market value of short-term debt equals the book value. In principle, to estimate the market value of long-term debt, we need to know the years to maturity, coupon rate, and default characteristics of all debt issues. Compustat does not have this information. Following Brainard, Shoven, and Weiss (1980), we assume: (1) All new issues of long-term debt have a maturity of twenty years. (2) The coupon rate is the BAA rate prevailing in the year of issue, and the default characteristics of the bonds continue to warrant a BAA rating until they reach maturity. (3) In 1959, the maturity distribution of bonds for each firm was proportional to the maturity distribution of aggregate outstanding issues.[11] (4) New issues of long-term debt for the years 1960 to 1978 are given by

$$N_t = \text{LTD}_t - \text{LTD}_{t-1} + N^*_{t-20, t-1}$$
$$\text{if } \text{LTD}_t - \text{LTD}_{t-1} + N^*_{t-20, t} \geq 0,$$
$$N_t = 0 \qquad \text{if } \text{LTD}_t - \text{LTD}_{t-1} + N^*_{t-20, t} < 0,$$

where LTD_t = new issues of long-term debt in year t, $N^*_{i,t}$ = debt issued at time i still outstanding at time t, and LTD_t = long-term debt in year t. We add $N^*_{t-20, t-1}$ because, each period, the debt issued twenty years

---

11. The data on aggregate outstanding issues come from *Historical Statistics of the United States*, series X 499–509, p. 1005.

earlier is retired. (5) If $\text{LTD}_t - \text{LTD}_{t-1} + N^*_{t-20,t-1} < 0$, the issues from each previous year are reduced proportionately. That is,

$$N^*_{i,t} = N^*_{i,t-1} \frac{\text{LTD}_t}{\text{LTD}_{t-1} - N^*_{t-20,t-1}}.$$

Each year the market value of debt issued in year i ($\text{MVN}^*_{i,t}$) is calculated using the familiar formula for the value of a coupon bond:

$$\text{MVN}^*_{i,t} = N^*_{i,t} \left[\frac{\text{BAA}_i}{\text{BAA}_t} \left[1 - \left(\frac{1}{1 + \text{BAA}_t} \right)^{i+20-t} \right] + \left(\frac{1}{1 + \text{BAA}_t} \right)^{i+20-t} \right].$$

The value of all long-term debt outstanding in year t (MVLTD_t) is, then,

$$\text{MVLTD}_t = \sum_{i=t-19}^{t} \text{MVN}^*_{i,t}.$$

The Replacement Value of Inventories

To estimate the replacement value of inventories, one needs to know the method of inventory valuation. For companies using FIFO, the reported level of inventories equals the market value of inventories. For companies using LIFO, the reported level of inventories bears little relation to the market value. Compustat does give the inventory valuation method. In addition to LIFO and FIFO, it allows for specific identification, average cost, retail method, standard cost, and replacement cost inventory valuation. We assume that all methods except for LIFO are identical to FIFO. When companies report more than one method of inventory accounting, Compustat lists them in descending order of importance but gives no estimate of the relative weights. We assume that the first method reported accounts for ⅔ of the real value of inventories and the second method accounts for the remaining ⅓. We make this assumption even when more than two methods are reported. Finally, we assume that the methods reported in 1978 were also used from 1959 to 1977.

We assume that reported LIFO inventories equal the market value of LIFO inventories in 1959. This assumption is plausible because there was a sustained period of price stability before 1959. For a company that uses only LIFO, reported inventories will stay constant if the real value of inventories does not change. To get the new replacement cost of inventories under such circumstances, we multiply the old replacement cost by the inflation rate. Throughout this paper, increases in the consumer price index are used for the inflation rate. Reported inventories increase or decline as the real level of inventories increases or declines. When reported inventories rise, the addition is evaluated at current prices.

When reported inventories fall, the price level at which liquidations are valued is not clear since we do not know when they were purchased. We assume that they were purchased the previous year. Thus, letting INV_t be reported inventories at time t and $RLINV_t$ be real inventories at time t, we calculate real inventories as follows:

$$RLINV_t = RLINV_{t-1} \frac{CPI_t}{CPI_{t-1}}$$
$$+ INV_t - INV_{t-1} \quad \text{if } INV_t \geq INV_{t-1},$$

$$RLINV_t = (RLINV_{t-1} + INV_t$$

$$- INV_{t-1}) \frac{CPI_t}{CPI_{t-1}} \quad \text{if } INV_t < INV_{t-1}.$$

When more than one inventory valuation method is used, we need to decompose inventories into a LIFO and a FIFO component. The calculation is complicated because inflation changes the fraction of reported LIFO and FIFO inventories. For example, consider a firm that in year t has 100 units of LIFO inventories and 100 units of FIFO inventories. Assume that both the LIFO and FIFO inventories are valued at $1 per unit. Thus the fraction of both real and reported inventories for which FIFO is used is ½. In year $t + 1$, the company produces and sells 100 units of both LIFO and FIFO goods. Suppose the price level doubles in year $t + 1$. The firm reports $100 of LIFO inventories and $200 of FIFO inventories. While the fraction of real inventories for which FIFO is used is still ½, reported FIFO inventories are now ⅔ of total reported inventories.

Let $FRFIFO_t$ be the fraction of reported inventories for which FIFO is used in year t. When the real value of inventories is unchanged, reported inventories increase by a factor of $FRFIFO_{t-1} ((CPI_t/CPI_{t-1}) - 1)$. Let

$$\Delta = INV_t - INV_{t-1} \left[1 + FRFIFO \left(\frac{CPI_t}{CPI_{t-1}} \right) \right].$$

The term Δ is the change in reported inventories caused by a change in real inventories. Let $\Delta RLINV_t$ be the change in real inventories, evaluated at prices in time t. We can decompose Δ into LIFO and FIFO components ($\Delta LIFO$ and $\Delta FIFO$, respectively). Similarly, let $\Delta RFIFO$ and $\Delta RLIFO$ be the fractions of the change in real inventories for which FIFO and LIFO are used.

In general,

(A1) $$RLINV_t = \frac{CPI_t}{CPI_{t-1}} \times RLINV_{t-1} + \Delta RLINV_t,$$

(A2) $\qquad$ $\text{FRFIFO}_t = \dfrac{\dfrac{\text{CPI}_t}{\text{CPI}_{t-1}} \times \text{FRFIFO}_{t-1} \times \text{INV}_{t-1} + \Delta\text{FIFO}}{\text{INV}_t}.$

Equation (A1) says that real inventories in year t are real inventories in year $t-1$, evaluated at year t prices, plus the change in real inventories. The numerator on the right-hand side of (A2) is the level of reported FIFO inventories. Thus equation (A2) merely says that the fraction of reported inventories for which FIFO is used is reported FIFO inventories divided by total inventories. Not all of the variables in (A1) and (A2) are observable. In order to calculate RLINV_t and FRFIFO_t, we need to find expressions for ΔRLINV_t and ΔFIFO_t in terms of observable variables.

Consider the case in which $\tfrac{2}{3}$ of real inventories is FIFO and $\tfrac{1}{3}$ is LIFO. When the real valuation of inventories rises (i.e. when $\Delta \geq 0$), the new LIFO inventories are evaluated at current prices. While it is logically possible that they are evaluated at past prices, our assumption is reasonable because inventory-to-sales ratios are much less than 1. Thus

(A3) $\qquad$ $\Delta\text{FIFO}_t = \Delta\text{RFIFO}_t = \tfrac{2}{3}\Delta_t,$

(A4) $\qquad$ $\Delta\text{LIFO}_t = \Delta\text{RLIFO}_t = \tfrac{1}{3}\Delta_t.$

Plugging (A3) and (A4) into (A1) and (A2) yields

$$\text{RLINV}_t = \text{RLINV}_{t-1}\left(\frac{\text{CPI}_t}{\text{CPI}_{t-1}}\right) + \Delta,$$

$$\text{FRFIFO}_t = \frac{\text{INV}_{t-1}\text{FRFIFO}_{t-1}(\text{CPI}_t/\text{CPI}_{t-1}) + 2\Delta/3}{\text{INV}_t}.$$

When Δ is negative, decreases in FIFO inventories must be valued at current prices. As before, decreases in LIFO inventories must be valued at the previous year's prices. Thus

(A5) $\qquad$ $\Delta\text{FIFO}_t = \Delta\text{RFIFO}_t,$

$\qquad\qquad\qquad$ $\Delta\text{LIFO}_t = \Delta\text{RLIFO}_t\,\dfrac{\text{CPI}_{t-1}}{\text{CPI}_t},$

(A6) $\qquad$ $\Delta = \Delta\text{RFIFO} + \dfrac{\text{CPI}_{t-1}}{\text{CPI}_t}\,\Delta\text{RLIFO}.$

Remembering that real LIFO inventories are half of real FIFO inventories, equations (A5) and (A6) imply

(A7) $\qquad$ $\Delta\text{RFIFO}_t\left(1 + \dfrac{1}{2}\dfrac{\text{CPI}_{t-1}}{\text{CPI}_t}\right) = \Delta$

(A8) $\qquad$ $\Delta\text{RLINV}_t = 3\Delta\Big/\left(2 + \dfrac{\text{CPI}_{t-1}}{\text{CPI}_t}\right).$

Finally, putting (A8) into (A1) and putting (A5) and (A7) into (A2) yields

(A9)
$$RLINV_t = RLINV_{t-1} \frac{CPI_t}{CPI_{t-1}}$$

$$+ 3\Delta / \left[2 + \frac{CPI_{t-1}}{CPI_t} \right],$$

(A10)
$$FRFIFO_t = \left[FRFIFO_{t-1} \times INV_{t-1} \times \frac{CPI_t}{CPI_{t-1}} \right.$$

$$\left. + \frac{\Delta}{1 + \frac{1}{2} \frac{CPI_{t-1}}{CPI_t}} \right] / INV_t.$$

Equations (A9) and (A10) have only observable variables on the right-hand side.

When real FIFO inventories are ⅓ of total real inventories, the equations are as follows:

$$\Delta = I_t - I_{t-1} \left[FRFIFO_{t-1} \left(\frac{CPI_t}{CPI_{t-1}} - 1 \right) + 1 \right].$$

If $\Delta > 0$, then

$$RLINV_t = RLINV_{t-1} \frac{CPI_t}{CPI_{t-1}} + \Delta,$$

$$FRFIFO_t = \frac{FRFIFO_{t-1} \times INV_{t-1} \times CPI_t/CPI_{t-1} + \frac{1}{3}\Delta}{INV_t}.$$

If $\Delta < 0$, then

$$RLINV_t = RLINV_{t-1} \frac{CPI_t}{CPI_{t-1}} + \Delta \frac{3CPI_t}{2CPI_{t-1} + CPI_t},$$

$$FRFIFO_t = \left[FRFIFO_{t-1} \frac{CPI_t}{CPI_{t-1}} INV_{t-1} \right.$$

$$\left. + \Delta \frac{CPI_t}{CPI_t + 2CPI_{t-1}} \right] / INV_t.$$

In the model in section 8.2, production and sales occur simultaneously. As a result, the model does not allow for inventories. In estimating the model, however, inventories must be considered because they are reflected in the value of the firm. In the results reported here, inventories are added to the denominator of the expression $(V_t - B_t)/p_t K_t$. An alternative treatment is to subtract them from the numerator. Since inventories are not completely liquid assets, one might choose to subtract only a fraction of the real value of inventories from the numerator. We experimented with all three methods and got virtually identical results.

Capital Stock

In general, reported net property, plant, and equipment (NPPE) differs not only from replacement cost but also from taxable net property, plant, and equipment (RNPPE and TNPPE, respectively). To estimate RNPPE and TNPPE, we construct an investment series and estimate depreciation rates.[12] In doing so, we assume: (1) All of a firm's capital has the same useful life (L). (2) Firms use the straight-line method for book depreciation.[13] (3) Both tax and actual depreciation are exponential with depreciation rate $2/L$. This method is identical to double declining balance depreciation.[14] (4) All investments are made at the beginning of the year, and all depreciation is taken at the end of the year. (5) Investment for years $1959 - L + 1$ to 1978 is proportional to aggregate investment in these years and is consistent with gross property, plant, and equipment in 1959.

Under these assumptions, we can estimate the useful life in any year by

$$L_t^* = \frac{\text{GPPE}_{t-1} + I_t}{\text{DEP}_t},$$

where GPPE_t = book value of gross property, plant, and equipment in year t, I_t = investment in year t, and DEP_t = book depreciation in year t. In practice, L^* fluctuates from year to year, so the L we use is an average of L^* from 1960 to 1978.

Assuming that NPPE is 0 in year $1959 - L$, we estimate TNPPE and RNPPE from $1959 - L + 1$ to 1978 as follows:

$$\text{TNPPE}_t = (\text{TNPPE}_{t-1} + I_t)(1 - 2/L),$$

$$\text{RNPPE}_t = \left(\text{RNPPE}_{t-1} \frac{\text{CPI}_t}{\text{CPI}_{t-1}} + I_t\right)(1 - 2/L).$$

12. In general, there are serious problems with using property, plant, and equipment figures reported by companies. For example, one can go far awry by estimating gross plant in year t by adding gross plant in year $t - 1$ to investment in year t and subtracting estimated retirements. Even if one goes to the annual report and gets actual retirements, the procedure is not foolproof. Depreciation method changes and mergers are the most common causes for the estimates to fail.

13. The Compustat footnotes in principle gave the method of depreciation, but we found it impossible to use information. First, Compustat says whether depreciation is straight-line, accelerated, or a combination of both. Many companies reported a combination of methods. Second, the depreciation method often changes from year to year. Third, the footnote was often out of position on the tape, so we could not use the footnote in a computer program.

14. Companies that use double declining balance depreciation can switch to straight-line depreciation on the remaining balance once during the life of the asset. As a result, exponential depreciation only approximates actual depreciation. See Shoven and Bulow (1975).

The estimates of TNPPE$_t$ and RNPPE$_t$ for the years prior to 1959 use less than $L-1$ years of data. As a result, they are essentially meaningless. Starting with 1959, enough years of investment enter the calculations but the data come almost entirely from aggregate figures. For the years nearer the end of the sample, more firm-specific data are available so the estimates are more reliable.

In estimating μ_s, B_t, and Z_t, we assume that expected inflation and the required return on investments are constant. Specifically, we estimate $\rho + \pi$ by adding 0.06 to the BAA bond rate. The dividend and the capital gains tax rates vary among individuals. We use the effective tax rates estimated by Feldstein and Poterba (1980), who calculated a weighted average of tax rates across taxpayers. In each period, people expect existing tax rates to last forever. Given the assumption that ρ, π, c, θ^D, and τ are constants, the integrals in equation (8a), (8b), and (8c) are easy to estimate:

$$\frac{\mu_s}{\mu_t} = \exp\left[-\frac{\rho + \pi}{1 - c}(s - t)\right],$$

$$B_t = \frac{1}{\delta + \dfrac{\rho + \pi}{1 - c}}\, \tau\delta\, \frac{1 - \theta}{1 - c}\, P_t K_t,$$

$$Z_t = \frac{1}{\delta + \dfrac{\rho + \pi}{1 - c}}\, \tau\delta.$$

References

Abel, A. 1982. Dynamic effects of permanent and temporary tax policies in a q model of investment. *Journal of Monetary Economics* 9: 353–73.

Auerbach, A. 1979. Share valuation and corporate equity policy. *Journal of Public Economics* 2: 291–305.

Brainard, W. C.; J. B. Shoven; and L. Weiss. 1980:2. The financial valuation of the return to capital. *Brookings Papers on Economic Activity*, pp. 453–511.

Eisner, R. 1978. *Factors in business investment*. Cambridge, Massachusetts: Ballinger.

Feldstein, M., and J. Poterba. 1980. State and local taxes and the rate of return on nonfinancial corporate capital. NBER Working Paper no. 508.

Grunfeld, Y. 1960. The determinants of corporate investment. In A. C. Harberger, ed., *The demand for durable goods*, pp. 211–66. Chicago: University of Chicago Press.

Hayashi, F. 1982. Tobin's marginal q and average q: A neoclassical interpretation. *Econometrica* 50 (January): 213–33.

Lindenberg, E. B., and S. A. Ross. 1981. Tobin's q ratio and industrial organization. *Journal of Business* 54 no. 1: 1–32.

McDonald, R. 1980. Corporate financial policy and investment. Mimeo, Massachusetts Institute of Technology, Cambridge, MA.

Rao, P., and Z. Griliches. 1969. Some small sample properties of several two-stage regression methods in the context of autocorrelated errors. *Journal of the American Statistical Association*, March, pp. 253–72.

Shoven, J., and J. Bulow. 1975:3. Inflation accounting and nonfinancial corporate profits: Physical assets. *Brookings Papers on Economic Activity*, pp. 557–98.

Summers, L. H. 1981a:1. Taxation and corporate investment: A Q theory approach. *Brookings Papers on Economic Activity*, pp. 67–127.

———. 1981b. Taxation and the size and composition of the capital stock. NBER Working Paper, forthcoming.

———. 1981c. Inflation and the valuation of corporate equities. NBER Working Paper no. 824.

Comment   Robert J. Shiller

Salinger and Summers here present and estimate a model of firm behavior that is used to evaluate the effects of changes in tax laws on the value of the firm and on the level of investment. The estimation and simulation problems posed by the basic model are very simple when compared to the problems posed by other models currently used to answer the same questions. There is, in fact, only one estimated coefficient whose value influences the results Salinger and Summers present. In contrast, the answers provided by a conventional large-scale macroeconometric model might depend in varying degrees on hundreds of parameters estimated in diverse equations. Moreover, conventional simulations would require additional information, such as the form monetary policy takes after the tax law changes. The simplicity of the Salinger-Summers model is due partly to their merely ignoring effects considered by other models. It is also due, however, to an elegant simplicity of the model itself, which I find quite intriguing.

The basic model presented here was presented in an earlier paper by Summers (1981) and draws on earlier work by Abel (1982) and Hayashi (1982). Two critical assumptions are responsible for the estimated investment function which appears here: the assumption of stable adjustment

Robert J. Shiller is with Yale University and the National Bureau of Economic Research.

cost function of a certain form and the assumption of homogeneity of degree one in both production and demand. Their function does *not* depend on any assumption of a stable production function, demand function, factor supply function, or expectation function. It is entirely consistent with the investment function estimated that these functions may jump around erratically and even that the discount rate used by the market to capitalize dividends may be erratic. The claim that I have made elsewhere that stock prices are too "volatile" to be accounted for entirely in terms of information about future dividends does not, strictly speaking, contradict this model. The investment function derived here is not immediately vulnerable to the rational expectationist criticism that parameters of estimated functions depend on the government policy rule. This criticism would be relevant only if adjustment costs were for some reason a function of the policy rule. It should be added, of course, that if these other functions cannot be modeled, then we will be unable to answer most of the basic questions we are interested in regarding the tax policy. The simulations they do with the model in this paper do depend on such stability assumptions and are vulnerable to rational expectationist criticism.

The reason why the investment function estimated here is so simple is that the model implies that the *price* of the firm's stock (relative to the capital stock) captures all the information relevant to the investment decision if this price is transformed as described in the text to produce tax-adjusted Q. Thus any shifts in the production function, demand function, or factor supply functions as well as information about future shifts are reflected in the price of stock. Earlier investment functions also depended on the price of the firm's stock but for different reasons. For example, in the MIT–Penn SSRC (MPS) model the cost of capital which enters the investment function depends on the dividend price ratio, but this ratio is taken to reflect the rate of discount in the market, not information about future technology or demand, and is ultimately a reflection of the monetary policy in force. Expectations of future demand are modeled by different variables. In practice, the same statistical correlation between investment and stock price may be reflected in the MPS investment function.

The assumption of homogeneity of degree one is crucial for the Salinger-Summers investment function because investment decisions are made at the margin, i.e. with respect to a marginal Q. The observed Q is in effect an average Q. The assumption of constant returns to scale may not be altogether reasonable when one considers some of the individual firms studied here. If we take the model literally, it is assumed that, were it not for costs associated with acquisition of new plant and equipment, General Motors (one of the firms for which the investment function had a poor fit) could at any point of time double its size and expect its value to double. This is inconsistent with the notion that the price of General Motors stock is a reflection of rents accruing because of its monopoly on some popular makes, rents which could rise or fall without engendering any investment opportunities. The model would imply that Exxon (a firm for which the coefficient in the estimated investment function had the wrong sign) would contract its investments after the oil-crisis-induced fall in its share price in 1975. The fact that it increased its capital expenditures then (on new domestic production and exploration facilities) suggests that average and marginal Q moved in opposite directions.

While we may have no clear or hard evidence that many firms do or do not face homogeneous constraints in production and demand and factor supply in the sense required by this model, we have more concrete knowledge about the kind of inhomogeneities imposed by the tax system. That the tax system destroys homogeneity is in itself no problem as long as the tax system does not make it impossible to infer marginal Q from average Q. Unfortunately, there is a problem in inferring marginal Q and this problem reintroduces the well-known problems of modeling expectations into this otherwise simple framework. In order to infer marginal Q, Salinger and Summers make a number of assumptions. Interest on debt is made equal to a constant b times the current nominal interest rate times the nominal value of the current capital stock. They are assuming that debt is issued so that the real value of debt is always b times the real capital stock. Thus new purchases of debt (which must be subtracted from retained earnings in equation [12] to arrive at dividends) is equal to $Pb(I - \pi + \delta^R)$. If the firm were assumed to follow another debt policy or were to finance with long-term debt, then the state of the firm at time t would not be summarized by its capital stock at time t. Additional information would be required about how much debt was outstanding and what interest rates it bore. They might better have handled interest deductibility on debt by assuming new debt was proportional to I, say, was long-term, and distinguishing between interest deductions on past debt and new debt. They did something analogous to this in their separation of the depreciation deduction into two parts, B_t and Z_t. The term Z_t depends on expected future variables, so that expectations must still be modeled.

The other crucial assumption for the analysis is that costs of adjustment are a stable function of investment divided by the capital stock. That adjustment costs depend only on I/K causes the maximization problem to have only one shadow price, which is good since we observe only one price of the firm. Formally, the model also assumes that the function is perfect, although of course the estimated regression involves an error term. The natural interpretation for the error term is that it reflects stochastic variations in the costs of adjustment. It would be good if such variations were explicitly allowed for in the model, though I suspect the resulting changes may not be fundamental. What is required for consistent ordinary least squares estimation of a model which can be used for judging the effects of tax policy or investment, then, is that this error term be uncorrelated with Q. If Q varies primarily because of exogenous changes in tax parameters, this may be reasonable. In fact, the time series behavior of Q depends primarily on behavior of the share price. This share price could be fluctuating because of changes in the cost of adjustment. Consider a firm which produces a commodity whose price follows, say, a sine wave through time. If its cost of adjustment should decline by a multiplicative factor for a while, the value of the firm and hence Q should rise. If this firm were in the sample on the rising portion of its cost of adjustment curve, then this higher Q would coincide with higher investment. This implies, then, an upward bias on the estimated coefficient which would tend to cause an overstatement of the effects of tax changes on investment.

Other sources of fluctuations in the residual might include errors in measurement in Q or I/K, or nonlinearities in the adjustment cost function. Purely unsystematic errors in measuring I/K would cause no bias, while such errors in Q would cause a downward bias in the regression coefficient. Some systematic errors in measurement might also be expected. If their estimates of K (which result from a simple cumulation of investment) were contaminated by unsystematic measurement error, then both I/K and Q would be affected in the same direction by the error, which would tend to cause an upward bias in the regression coefficient. New "information" about future variables ought in itself to cause no residuals in this estimated investment function as it might in conventional investment functions for which such information is not part of the hypothesized expectations mechanism.

By estimating an adjustment cost function rather than a production function, demand function, or the like, Salinger and Summers bring us into unfamiliar territory. Knowing very little about such functions, one feels little reason to doubt that they are stable through time or that they have the form indicated. We should not allow ourselves to be complacent about these assumptions, however, just because we know little about them.

One is tempted to imagine, from the description in the text, that adjustment costs are the costs of paying real estate agents to find new floor space, hiring planners to decide on the layout of new plants, and hiring workers to uncrate and install new machines. In practice, I think such costs are a trivial component of the true costs of adjustment modeled here. These costs represent the real barriers which prevent AT&T or IBM, say, from doubling their size. These firms would need to penetrate new markets in order to do so. We might imagine that these firms have a monopoly, not in the markets for the individual products we associate them with, but on a sort of organizational structure which enables them to aggressively and creatively pursue new product lines and incur "adjustment costs" in doing so. These costs of adjustment are then quite intangible. Should they be made a function of I/K? Why should they not be a function of I/L? It is easy to make this change in the model, which yields an investment function whose dependent variable is I/L rather than I/K. Why should adjustment costs not be a function of H/L, where H is new hires? This would yield a very different model, in which q need not equal one but in which firms would always hold an "optimal" capital stock and I_t would depend on the change in a conventional cost of capital figure. Alternatively, why should adjustment costs not depend on $I/(K -$ inventories)?

The Salinger-Summers model does not distinguish between the price of capital goods and the price of aggregate output. It would certainly be in the spirit of the model and a technical improvement to assume that investment costs are reflected in a new capital goods price index P_K. Then the model would relate Q to $V/(P_K K)$ rather than $V/(PK)$. Such a model would then make Q inversely related to the relative price of capital goods P_K/P. In contrast, the Witte (1963) model would suggest that investment is a *positive* function of P_K/P. The difference is one of demand versus supply. The Witte model is a supply function of producers of capital goods, which we expect to find upward-sloping in P_K and inversely related to the general level of costs for capital goods producers which might be measured by P. If we estimated the Salinger-Summers investment function with Q based on $V/(P_K K)$, we would have to ask what *identifies* the investment function here. For the Salinger-Summers demand for investment function to be identified, it would have to be the case that some other variables influence supply, and for proper consistent estimation of the investment demand function we would need these variables as instruments. Ordinary least squares would be biased, the extent of the bias depending on the relative magnitudes of demand versus supply shocks. The coefficient in the investment function could be so biased as to have the wrong sign, if shocks to the adjustment cost function cause corresponding moves in the price of capital goods and hence opposite moves in Q. In practice, the Salinger-Summers model, which uses P rather than P_K, does not allow this effect.

The regression results for 1964–78 in table 8.2 often look very good when one considers how simple the model is. Of the twenty-eight firms, twenty-five had slope coefficients with the right sign. In most cases, the R^2 is around 0.4. In contrast, in Summers's earlier paper (1981), which used aggregate investment data from 1930 to 1978, the R^2 was only 0.046, while the coefficient of 0.013 is actually larger than the coefficient of 0.010 estimated in this paper in the pooled regression. Perhaps the higher R^2 in the individual firm regression reflects a much higher variance in the independent variable Q. Some firms do very badly (e.g. Chrysler stock had a nearly steady decline over the period 1964–78), and others do very well (IBM stock rose dramatically).

The coefficients in the regression have a simple interpretation. The time variation in Q is due primarily to time variation in the price of the firm (which is why the table 8.3 regressions cannot tell whether Q or q belongs, since the two variables are fairly collinear). In the absence of taxes, $Q = q - 1$, where q is Tobin's q. In the presence of taxes, aggregate Q is roughly equal to $2q - 1$ (though this approximation works poorly in explaining the cross-firm variation in Q shown in table 8.1). Suppose Q moves from 0 to 1 because the price of the firm, which had been equal to ½ the value of the capital, had doubled. Then the predicted change in I/K is equal to the coefficient in the regression. Thus an estimated coefficient of 0.02 implies that the firm whose price doubled will increase in size by only 2% per year. Inverting the investment cost function, we find that marginal adjustment costs as a function of I increase by a factor of 50 when I doubles.

Why are the estimated coefficients so small? The first explanation which comes to mind is that there are really decreasing returns to scale for the individual firms. Other sources of estimation bias may be involved. I am also inclined to imagine that stock prices may be vulnerable to "fads" or the like, and that firm managers who decide on earnings retention do not see their true shadow price of capital in the market price.

The paper performs simulations of the effects on the value of the firm V and on investment I of several tax reforms: indexation, reduction in the corporate tax rate, and acceleration of depreciation. As the authors acknowledge, the "procedure cannot be justified within the model." The model implies that in order to predict the impact on V the authors must return to making stability assumptions of the kind which the investment function approach here obviated. They must make some assumption about the effect on macroeconomic variables, the discount rate, the level of demand, and the wage rate. In turn, they would then have to make assumptions about firm production functions and solve the intertemporal optimization problem after the tax reform to get the new V. Summers discussed such simulations in his earlier paper. In this paper they are less ambitious or more realistic. A key feature of their argument is their claim that, since the coefficient in the investment function is small, the effect on future revenues is small. For the purpose of the simulation, future pretax profits are assumed to continue on a growth path, unchanged by the reform, discount rates are assumed to be constant, and tax policy changes are assumed to be permanent. These simulations are in the nature of simple "back of the envelope" calculations. While the avowed purpose here is to simulate the effects of tax changes which are permanent and presumably announced to be permanent, any shorter-run tax policy simulation would be vulnerable to a rational expectationist criticism. If tax changes are perceived as temporary i.e. are generated by a policy rule, the impact on V and I could be greatly misstated. In contrast, the advantage of the investment function studied here is that investment depends only on *current* tax parameters and V regardless of expectations about future taxes because information about these future taxes is incorporated in V. In the simulation methodology used here, such information would not be incorporated in V.

References

Abel, A. B. 1982. Dynamic effects of permanent and temporary tax policies in a q model of investment. *Journal of Monetary Economics* 19, no. 3 (May): 353–73.

Hayashi, F. 1982. Tobin's marginal q and average q: A neoclassical interpretation. *Econometrica* 50, no. 1 (January): 213–24.

Summers, L. H. 1981. Inflation, taxation, and corporate investment: A Q theory approach. Mimeo, MIT.

Witte, J. G. 1963. The microfoundations of the social investment function. *Journal of Political Economy* 71, no. 5 (October): 441–56.

9   Issues in the Taxation of Foreign Source Income

Daniel J. Frisch

This paper is a simulation study of the international aspects of United States corporate taxation. In the late 1970s, international operations of United States corporations accounted for a fifth of total profits and a quarter of total investments.[1] Taxes on these activities can have important effects on the international and domestic investment decisions of the firms. For these reasons, analysis of the taxation of United States corporations is incomplete unless international aspects are considered.

Attempts in the late 1970s to reform the United States tax structure did not ignore international aspects. President Carter's 1978 proposals included some major changes in this area. Although these suggestions went the way of most of the other elements in his package, the issues they raised are likely to reappear in future calls for reform. For example, President Carter's package called for the ending of "deferral," an aspect of United States tax law that is discussed below.

In 1977, the IRS issued a set of regulations that made a potentially important change in the way overseas income is to be defined for tax purposes.[2] These "861 regulations," which are also discussed below, have been the subject of considerable controversy, since they may affect investment decisions in a number of important ways. A major goal of this

Daniel J. Frisch is with the Department of Economics, University of Washington, Seattle, and the National Bureau of Economic Research.

The author is indebted to Martin Feldstein, David Hartman, and Thomas Horst for invaluable criticism and comments. The United States Treasury Department, Office of International Tax Affairs, provided financial assistance and was most cooperative in providing data. The National Bureau of Economic Research also provided financial and logistical support.

1. Bergsten, Horst, and Moran (1978, p. vii).
2. Treas. Reg. 1.861-8, T.D. 7456, 1977-G, I.R.S. 6.

study is to analyze methods of defining foreign taxable income, especially methods for deciding what part of total profits are to be taxed as domestic income, and what part as foreign income. The issues raised by the "861 regulations" are discussed in this context.

This study extends previous work in three ways.[3] The analysis of methods for allocating income between domestic and foreign sources is the first extension. Although a previous work did consider the 861 regulations in isolation, no general treatment of the revenue impact of these methods seems to exist.[4]

The second extension involves the level of aggregation of the analysis. This study uses data which contain information cross-tabulated by industry of the United States firm and by country where the income was earned. The impact of many aspects of international tax law turns on the precise alignment of United States and foreign tax parameters. Therefore the availability of data from a number of countries is potentially of great value, since a range of foreign tax situations may be included.

Previous studies in contrast have had to rely on information tabulated by the industry of the United States firm, with totals of domestic and overseas income reported for each industry. Aggregating across countries in this way may obscure important effects, since firms operating in one set of countries may be affected in one way by a tax change while firms in other countries may be affected not at all or in the opposite direction.

The third extension concerns responses that the firms might make to changes in tax law. Any such change will in general alter the structure of investment incentives, and the firms' investment decisions can be expected to change. Responses of this kind may have sizable consequences for the firms and for evaluation of tax policies toward them.

Section 9.1 lays out the issues to be considered. First, issues involving the current United States tax structure, given the measures of taxable income, are discussed. Then the issues involving definition of domestic and foreign income are described. A list of nine reform proposals that illustrate these issues is formulated.

The next section describes the development of INTERSIM, the tax calculator used in performing the simulations. Data used by it and techniques used to calibrate it are discussed.

Section 9.3 presents the simulations of changes in tax revenues, given that the firms do not change their behavior. First, a baseline simulation is defined and results for it are displayed. Then, the results of simulating each of the nine proposals are presented.

3. Recent simulation studies of international taxation include Bergsten, Horst, and Moran (1978, chapter 6 and appendix B) and Hufbauer and Foster (1976).
4. The 861 regulations are examined in Bergsten, Horst, and Moran (1978, chapter 6). Musgrave (1973) and Surrey (1978) discuss more general questions but do not conduct revenue simulations.

Section 9.4 extends the analysis to cover behavioral responses by the firms. Responses that can and cannot be included are outlined. Methods to implement those than can be included, and assumptions required by those that cannot, are discussed.

The next section discusses the effects of each of the reform proposals on behavior in more detail. It also presents the results of rerunning the simulations with behavioral responses built in.

There is a brief concluding section.

9.1   Issues to Be Considered

9.1.1   The Foreign Tax Credit Mechanism

By convention, each country is given the primary right to tax income earned within its borders. The United States, like many other countries, claims the further right to tax the income of its "persons," including corporations, earned abroad. United States law recognizes the primary right of the host countries through the foreign tax credit mechanism.

The first step in this mechanism is to define the total income of United States corporations, including income earned abroad, and tax it at a standard rate (now 46%). Then, a credit is allowed for foreign taxes paid, except that if the foreign tax rate is greater, credits only up to the domestic rate may be claimed. In effect, if the foreign government taxes at the United States rate or higher, then income earned there is not taxed further at home. But if the foreign government chooses to tax at less than the standard rate, the United States collects a tax equal to the difference. Of course, this describes a simple foreign tax credit mechanism; actual practice in the United States is subject to several compromises and difficulties.[5]

It should be noted that even a pure foreign tax credit mechanism may not be the tax structure that maximizes welfare. It would ensure that United States firms would not have a tax incentive to invest in low-tax countries rather than in the United States, since low tax rates would be brought up to the United States level. In this sense it would bring the world closer to "capital export neutrality," defined as the situation where United States owned capital pays the same corporate tax rate no matter where employed. The incentive to avoid high-tax countries would still exist, however, unless an unlimited credit for foreign taxes were allowed. But then the pernicious incentive would exist for foreign governments to raise their tax rates on United States firms almost without limit, since the revenue would be at the expense of the United States Treasury. A further point is that "capital export neutrality" may improve worldwide welfare

---

5. This description is, of course, highly oversimplified. McDaniel and Ault (1977) provides an overview of these issues.

by removing distortions in the location of capital, but United States welfare may not be improved. Still further, the presence of other taxes, including the taxes on domestic capital, makes the question of taxes on foreign source income a second-best one. For these reasons, welfare evaluation of the tax schemes is beyond the scope of this study.[6]

One departure of current United States practice from a pure foreign tax credit mechanism concerns pooling the tax situations of several countries. A United States firm may operate in two other countries, one with a tax rate less than in the United States and one with a tax rate higher. It would seem that the firm should pay additional tax on income earned in the low-tax country and not on the other income. The firm should, in effect, calculate a separate foreign tax credit for each country and then use the sum. This type of structure is known as a foreign tax credit with a "per country limitation." The United States structure uses, instead, an "overall limitation" for most firms.[7] A firm with operations in two or more countries adds its income earned and taxes paid abroad. If total foreign taxes are less than 46% of total foreign income, then the difference is owed to the United States government. Only 46% of foreign income can be claimed as a credit if total foreign taxes are greater than this amount.

An example illustrates how the presence of the overall limitation complicates the foreign tax structure. A firm may be operating in a country with a 40% tax rate. The firm would then owe an additional 6% to the United States on income earned there, so that its final rate of tax on this income would be 46%. Now the firm opens up an operation of equal size in a country with a 54% tax rate. The overall foreign tax rate is now 47%, so that the firm now owes no tax to the United States on any foreign income. The effective tax rate on income from the first country thus falls from 46% to 40%, for reasons unrelated to anything happening in that country. It is clear that incentives are different under the per-country limitation versus the overall limitation. For this reason, imposition of the per-country limitation is one of the reforms analyzed in this study.

Note that this analysis makes use of the availability of data by country. Data aggregated up to the industry level already have the overall limitation built into them, in effect. Therefore analysis of the per-country limitation would be impossible with it.

The second departure from a pure foreign tax credit is the issue of "deferral." Simply put, not all income from foreign operations is subjected to the foreign tax credit mechanism. Profits earned abroad by

6. Feldstein and Hartman (1977), Horst (1980), and Dutton (1980) are examples of works that consider welfare implications.

7. Oil-related activities must now use the per-country limitation; note that no oil-related industries are included in the simulations. In 1972, firms could choose the per-country limitation, but few did so.

foreign subsidiaries of United States firms are included only if they are repatriated to the parent as dividends. If retained abroad, they are left out of the United States' definition of worldwide income until and unless the subsidiary is dissolved. In 1972, foreign subsidiaries as a whole repatriated 40.9% of their income. Since pretax profits were $15.356 billion, $9.075 billion were "deferred."United States firms earned another $9.983 billion overseas from operations not separately incorporated ("branch" operations) and from receipts of interest, royalties, and other fees. This income is not affected by deferral in any way. Thus repealing deferral would have increased taxable foreign source income of United States firms by 56%.[8]

It is not clear, of course, how much additional tax revenue would have been raised. For example, if all countries in the world had tax rates greater than the United States rate, no extra revenue would accrue. It is therefore worthwhile to include plans that end deferral in the reforms to be studied.

There are two approaches to ending deferral that should be mentioned. One would tax United States firms as if their subsidiaries repatriate 100% of their profits. The second would treat subsidiaries like branches; in other words, this method would consolidate foreign subsidiaries for tax purposes much as domestic subsidiaries are consolidated. One difference between them would arise from foreign subsidiaries with losses. Under the first method, they would be ignored, since dividends cannot be negative. Under the second, their losses would be allowed to decrease the firm's worldwide income. Both methods are considered in this study. However, data limitations will force the difference between them to be understated. Subsidiaries with losses cannot be treated separately if they appear in the same industry-country cell as subsidiaries with positive profits. Since some cells do show losses, however, the two methods for ending deferral do show different results.

Two more reforms to the basic foreign tax structure are considered. They are the major alternatives to the foreign tax credit mechanism. The first is the "territorial" system. Under it, basically no attempt would be made to collect taxes on income from activities abroad. The tax systems of France and the Netherlands are closest to this approach.

The second alternative would replace the foreign tax credit with a deduction for foreign taxes paid. This approach was contained in the Burke-Hartke Bill, debated by Congress in 1971. Just as a foreign tax credit is supposed to help attain "capital export neutrality," a deduction system is supposed to attain "national neutrality." This is the situation under which United States firms are led to equalize social rates of return

8. The numbers are computed from IRS, *Statistics of Income, 1968–1977, Controlled Foreign Corporations*, p. 93, and IRS, *Statistics of Income, 1968–1972, Foreign Tax Credit, Corporations*, p. 77.

on capital used at home and abroad, where social rates of return are defined from the United States perspective. Let

r = rate of return to capital in the United States;
t = tax rate in the United States;
r^* = rate of return abroad, and
t^* = tax rate abroad.

Then social rates of return, defined as income accruing to either United States shareholders or the United States government, are equal to r for capital used at home and $r^*(1 - t^*)$ for capital used abroad. Private rates of return are equal to $r(1 - t)$ for domestically used capital and $r^*(1 - t^*)(1 - t)$ for foreign capital when a deduction system applies. Since the firms equate private rates of return,

$$r(1 - t) = r^*(1 - t^*)(1 - t).$$

Thus $r = r^*(1 - t^*)$ so that social rates of return are also equalized. As Feldstein and Hartman (1977), Horst (1980), and Dutton (1980) show, this reasoning is far from a satisfactory welfare analysis of the deduction system. Still, the claims made for it render it an interesting addition to the list of reforms to be studied.

9.1.2   Methods for Allocating Income

It is useful at this point to summarize some of the tax structures described so far. Total taxes paid by a United States firm operating in one other country are, in general,

(1) $$T_{TOTAL} = T + T^*.$$

Taxes paid to the foreign government, T^*, are, in general,

(2) $$T^* = t^* Y^*,$$

where Y^* is the foreign country's measure of taxable income from the firm's activities there and t^* is the foreign tax rate. Under a foreign tax credit mechanism, United States taxes are

(3) $$T = t(Y + zY^*) - C,$$

where Y is the United States government's measure of taxable income of domestic operations; t is the corporate tax rate; z is the payout ratio for the firm's foreign subsidiary, the ratio of dividends paid over total after-tax earnings of the subsidiary;[9] and C is the foreign tax credit. It equals

(4) $$C = \text{Min} \begin{bmatrix} zt^* & Y^* \\ zt & Y^* \end{bmatrix}.$$

9. Note that zY^* is greater than actual dividends paid. It equals actual dividends "grossed up" to reflect pretax profits of the subsidiaries. In 1972, United States firms did not have to "gross up" dividends received from less developed countries; the formulas are slightly different for this income.

It is easy to see how the reforms mentioned so far could be incorporated into this structure. For example, ending deferral could be modeled as setting z to unity (with possibly an adjustment for subsidiaries with losses). A territorial system would set z to zero. A deduction system, with deferral left intact, would replace (3) with

$$(5) \qquad\qquad T = t(Y + zY^* - zt^*Y^*).$$

More countries would have to be added to these simple equations before the per-country limitation could be modeled.

The remaining questions all concern Y and Y^*, the measures of taxable income. It is useful first to specify their sum, the worldwide income of the firm, in a simple way:

$$(6) \qquad\qquad Y_{TOTAL} = Y + Y^* = P(S + S^*) - D_{TOTAL},$$

where P is the world price of the firm's one product, and S and S^* are quantities sold to customers at home and abroad; $P(S + S^*)$ thus equals worldwide sales revenues. D_{TOTAL} are worldwide deductions, and include cost of materials, payments to factors, depreciation allowances, and the like. Except for issues concerning exchange rates, defining Y_{TOTAL} is conceptually neither easier nor harder than defining taxable income for a purely domestic firm; all the same issues appear. For this reason, problems in defining Y_{TOTAL} are neglected and a measure of it is assumed known and constant.

How should Y_{TOTAL} be split up between Y and Y^*? Most governments have agreed to use the "arm's length" system.[10] The fundamental idea is to ask how market forces would make the split. This rule asks the firm to pretend, for tax purposes, that its domestic and overseas operations are independent economic entities, operating at arm's length from each other. Profits of each entity would be naturally defined as its sales minus deductions.

Intrafirm flows of goods must be measured when defining sales revenues of each part. Let E (for exports) represent sales of the home office to foreigners, the net of sales of the foreign operation in the home market. Alternatively, one may assume that each entity carries on all sales to local customers. Then E represents net intrafirm flows of the product between the United States firm and its foreign subsidiary. Since there is a single world price for all transactions, sales revenue of the domestic part of the firm would be $P(S + E)$, which equals its revenue from sales to local customers and from exports. "Net" revenues of the foreign part would be $P(S^* - E)$, which equals its sales to its local customers minus what it had to pay for imports from the domestic part.

How should total deductions of the firm be split up? In the market, each producer has to pay for the factors it uses. Therefore each part of the

10. McDaniel and Ault (1977, chapter 8), Musgrave (1973), Surrey (1978). As an example, see Treas. Reg. 1.482-1(b)(1), T.D. 6952, 1968-7, C.B. 218.

firm should deduct the cost of factors used for what is produced locally. Let D be the cost of factors (and related deductions) used in the United States, and D^* be the cost of factors used abroad. If factors can be used in only one place, then $D + D^*$ will equal D_{TOTAL}. The incomes of domestic and foreign operations may then be defined as

(7) $$Y = P(S + E) - D,$$

(8) $$Y^* = P(S^* - E) - D^*.$$

These two equations represent the simplest form of the arm's length rule for allocation of incomes. Note that $Y + Y^* = Y_{TOTAL}$, as required.

Although the basic conception seems simple, the above description of the arm's length approach may leave the reader somewhat uneasy. There are many heroic assumptions and loose ends. What if intrafirm flows take more complicated forms than exports of a single final good, with its easily observable world price? What if a factor of production acts like a "public good" within the firm, so that all parts of the firm benefit if one part hires it? These problems have of course occurred to other experts in this field, and the response has been the suggestion of an entirely different approach.[11]

This approach begins by recognizing that measuring Y_{TOTAL} directly avoids many of the problems with measuring Y and Y^* using the arm's length rule. Why not, then, just split up Y_{TOTAL} on some sort of reasonable basis to get Y and Y^*? If domestic operations seem to account for 75% of the firm's total activities, then Y should be set to 75% of Y_{TOTAL}. Similarly, Y^* should be set to 25% of Y_{TOTAL}. Of course, a rule must be formulated to decide for what share each part of the firm accounts. The prime requirement for this rule that sets the shares is that it depends on something easy to measure. In symbols, this "shares allocation" approach would set

(9) $$Y = sY_{TOTAL} \text{ and}$$

(10) $$Y^* = (1 - s)Y_{TOTAL}, \text{ with}$$

(11) $$s = X/(X + X^*),$$

where X and X^* are attributes of the firm that are easily observable in both countries.

Domestic and foreign taxable income may be recomputed in this way in order to simulate the effects of adopting a shares allocation approach. Note that such a simulation does not necessitate any change in the foreign tax credit mechanism. Once the new taxable income measures are defined, the original mechanism, described in equations (1)–(4), may be applied to them.

11. Musgrave (1973), Surrey (1978).

United States states that levy a corporate income tax face the same problems in taxing national firms as national governments do in taxing multinational ones. Although the arm's length approach is the rule among national governments, the shares allocation approach is typically used by the states. They usually use a weighted average of three attributes, sales, assets, and employment, to define the shares of taxable incomes.[12]

The data to be used in this study do not contain information on employment. Therefore the following definition of s will be used in the simulation of the shares allocation system:

$$(12) \qquad s = a\left(\frac{S}{S + S^*}\right) + (1 - a)\left(\frac{A}{A + A^*}\right).$$

S and S^* are local sales, and A and A^* are local assets. Proxies used to measure them are discussed in section 9.2 below. A value of 0.5 is used for a in the simulations presented in sections 9.3 and 9.4.

It should be noted that z in equations (3) and (4), the fraction of foreign income in the United States tax base, now has a different interpretation. This fraction is, implicitly, the ratio of actual intrafirm dividends to measured foreign taxable income. Up to this point, firms do not change their behavior when tax laws change; in particular, intrafirm dividends do not change. Thus z and Y^* move in precisely offsetting directions and the quantity of foreign income in the United States tax base zY^* does not change. Note that the domestic tax base Y and foreign taxes paid T^* do change.

In sum, there are at least two ways for governments to define Y and Y^*. What happens if different governments adopt different methods? The country that hosts the subsidiaries of United States firms need concern itself only with Y^*. The United States, however, needs to define taxable income both at home and abroad. It is possible for the foreign government's measure of local taxable income and the United States' measure of income in that country to differ. We need to complicate the basic specification of taxes as follows:

$$(1) \qquad T_{\text{TOTAL}} = T + T^*,$$

$$(2) \qquad T^* = t^*Y^*,$$

$$(3') \qquad T = t(Y + z\hat{Y}^*) - C,$$

$$(4') \qquad C = \text{Min}\begin{bmatrix} zt^*\ Y^* \\ zt\ \hat{Y}^*. \end{bmatrix}$$

Equations (1) and (2) are repeated for convenience. Y^* should now be interpreted as the foreign government's measure of taxable income aris-

12. Musgrave (1973), McLure (1980).

ing out of a United States firm's activities in its country. $\hat{Y}^*$ is defined as the United States government's measure of income from the same activities.

Note that the top line of equation (4') contains Y^*; t^*Y^* equals the taxes paid by the firm to the foreign government, an observable quantity. Therefore this actual tax liability is used in the United States foreign tax credit computation. A separate measure of foreign taxable income is needed in the computation of C only to ensure that too much credit is not taken.

Tax treaties between governments usually specify that both signatories will strive to coordinate their treatment of multinational firms.[13] In our symbols, it is deemed desirable that $Y^* = \hat{Y}^*$. However, if one government decides that a shares allocation approach should be substituted for arm's length, there would certainly be a long lag before all other governments concurred. Therefore simulation of both a "coordinated" reform, in which both Y^* and $\hat{Y}^*$ will be altered, and a "noncoordinated" one, in which only $\hat{Y}^*$ will be altered, will be considered.

Another modification must be made to equations (1)–(4) in order to analyze the 861 regulations:

(1) $$T_{\text{TOTAL}} = T + T^*,$$

(2) $$T^* = t^*Y^*,$$

(3') $$T = t(Y + z\hat{Y}^*) - C,$$

(4'') $$C = \text{Min} \begin{bmatrix} zt^* & Y^* \\ zt & \tilde{Y}^* \end{bmatrix}.$$

The only change is the appearance of a new measure of taxable income abroad, $\tilde{Y}^*$, in the bottom line of the credit computation. It is needed because this measure need not equal $\hat{Y}^*$ in equation (3'), the measure of taxable income earned abroad that is subjected to the basic United States tax rate t.

$\tilde{Y}^*$ is governed by section 482 of the Internal Revenue Code, which deals with the division of income of related parties. Defining $\tilde{Y}^*$ for purposes of the foreign tax credit is not seen as a matter of dividing income of related parties; rather, it is seen as a matter of defining foreign as opposed to domestic income. This distinction has meaning in situations that are much more complex than those considered in this paper. For example, consider a purely domestic firm which receives income from abroad that is somehow subjected to a foreign tax. Since there is no related party abroad, there is no $\hat{Y}^*$. Yet the firm gets to claim a credit for the foreign taxes; therefore a $\tilde{Y}^*$ must be computed. For this reason, a separate part of the Internal Revenue Code, sections 861–64, governs the definition of income used in the foreign tax credit computation.

13. McDaniel and Ault (1977, chapter 8).

In short, there are administrative reasons why $\hat{Y}^*$ and $\tilde{Y}^*$ need not be identical. As mentioned above, the IRS recently issued a set of regulations that affect the latter concept and not the former. It should be stated at the outset that this study is not intended as an exhaustive analysis of these regulations. They are much too complex to be included fully in the simple model developed here. In particular, they list many alternative solutions for each of the problems they raise. It is not clear that the solutions singled out here are the ones enforced most frequently; indeed, it is not clear they are or ever will be the ones enforced. This study is intended rather as a discussion of the implications of certain principles that seem to underlie the regulations.

The major reason new regulations were issued in 1977 was the problem of accounting for factors of production that operate like public goods within the firm. Many expenses are typically incurred by the head office of a multinational firm, yet benefit all parts of it. Examples cited in the regulation include administrative costs and research and development expenses. Perhaps a little harder to see as a public good is the renting of capital. Yet interest expenses are also included. This reasoning

> is based on the approach that money is fungible and that interest expense is attributable to all activities and property regardless of any specific purposes for incurring an obligation on which interest is paid.[14]

If these head office charges benefit all parts of the firm, then a fair share should be charged to foreign source income. The effect is to reduce $\tilde{Y}^*$ in the bottom line of equation (4″) and, if this line applies, reduce the foreign tax credit and raise the United States tax liability.

How should $\tilde{Y}^*$ be computed according to the 861 regulations? Arm's length, since it is the basic principle, should be used for most aspects of revenue and costs. Yet for the factors singled out as head office charges, an additional allocation must be done. The regulations suggest as one alternative that the shares allocation approach be used to compute this additional piece.

This option would split D, domestic deduction in equation (7), into ordinary deductions, D_{NHO}, and head office deductions, D_{HO}:

(13) $$D = D_{\text{NHO}} + D_{\text{HO}}.$$

Income for the purpose of computing the credit limitation is then

(14) $$\tilde{Y}^* = P(S^* - E) - D^* - (1 - s')D_{\text{HO}},$$

(15) $$s' = a'\left(\frac{S}{S + S^*}\right) + (1 - a')\left(\frac{A}{A + A^*}\right),$$

where s' and a' are the weights that perform the special shares allocation of D_{HO}.

---

14. Treas. Reg. 1-861-8(e)(2), T.D. 7456, 1977-6, I.R.B. 6.

The baseline for the study is the tax law as of 1972, which did not include these regulations. Therefore this computation may be considered a reform package which may be simulated. Two simulations are performed. The first sets a' equal to 0.5, the same value used for a in the shares allocation reforms. The second sets a' equal to zero, so that only assets are used to perform the allocation of the head office deductions.

To summarize, nine simulations are to be performed. They are: (1) Imposition of the per-country limitation. (2) Repeal of the deferral, complete payout method. (3) Repeal of the deferral, consolidation method. (4) Territorial treatment of all foreign source income. (5) Substitution of deduction for foreign taxes paid for foreign tax credit. (6) Substitution of shares allocation for arm's length method, by all countries. (7) Substitution of shares allocation for arm's length method, by United States only. (8) Allocation of 861 regulations with $a' = 0.5$. (9) Allocation of 861 regulations with $a' = 0$.

9.2   Data and Techniques

9.2.1   Data

The basic source of data is a file of 1972 tax returns of United States multinational companies maintained by the Treasury Department. Specifically, each firm files an "information return" (Form 2952) for each of its "controlled foreign corporations." The Office of International Tax Affairs at the Treasury kindly made information from these forms available to me.

In order to preserve the confidentiality of the tax returns, the Treasury had to cross-tabulate the data before releasing them. Fifteen manufacturing industry groups and seventeen countries were chosen (see table 9.1). Cells with information drawn from fewer than three tax returns were suppressed, and the amounts were placed in the seventeenth country column ("other countries"); 246 cells of data resulted.

The variables included in the data set are subsidiaries' assets, business receipts (the measure of sales), earnings and profits, dividends, payments of interest and royalties to the parents, and income taxes paid to foreign governments. Taxes are divided into ordinary corporate income taxes and so-called withholding taxes paid on flows of dividends, interest, and royalties to the parents. The firms are required to calculate all quantities according to United States tax definitions, except that accelerated depreciation may not be used. Note that assets are therefore based on historic costs.[15] Tables 9.2, 9.3, and 9.4 present foreign subsidiaries' assets, taxable income, and tax paid to foreign governments, respectively.

---

15. For more information on these data, see Frisch (1980) and IRS, *Statistics of Income, 1968–1972, U.S. Corporations and Their Controlled Foreign Corporations*, section 2, "Explanation of Terms."

Table 9.1   **Industry Groups and Countries**

Industry Groups

1. Food and kindred products
2. Textile and apparel products
3. Lumber and paper products
4. Printing and publishing
5. Chemicals and allied products
6. Rubber and miscellaneous plastics products
7. Stone, clay, and glass products
8. Primary metal industries
9. Fabricated metal products, except machinery
10. Machinery, except electrical
11. Electrical machinery
12. Motor vehicles and equipment
13. Transportation equipment, except motor vehicles
14. Scientific instruments, photographic equipment, watches, and clocks
15. Other, including tobacco, furniture, leather, and miscellaneous products

Countries

1. Canada
2. Mexico
3. Argentina
4. Brazil
5. Venezuela
6. Belgium
7. France
8. Italy
9. Netherlands
10. West Germany
12. Switzerland
13. United Kingdom
14. South Africa
15. Japan
16. Australia
17. Other countries

Supplementary data, taken from IRS *Statistics of Income, 1968–1972, Foreign Tax Credit, Corporations*, provide information about the domestic activities of the fifteen industries and are used to calibrate the simulation program. This volume contains data on various intermediate quantities calculated as part of the foreign tax credit structure. An example is worldwide taxable income, corresponding to equation (3) of the last section. Only industry totals are given.

The simulator can calculate the same concepts from the basic data and aggregate across countries. When these figures do not agree, a residual variable is created and spread out over the countries in proportion to

Table 9.2   Foreign Subsidiaries' Assets

	Canada	Mexico	Argentina	Brazil
Food prods.	.1400E+10	.2990E+09	.1305E+09	.2225E+09
Textiles	.3842E+09	.1483E+09	.5301E+08	.3902E+08
Lmbr., paper	.1855E+10	.6701E+08	0.	.9440E+08
Print, publ.	.4378E+09	.4411E+08	.1438E+07	.1060E+08
Chemicals	.3246E+10	.6280E+09	.2692E+09	.6490E+09
Rubber prods.	.4558E+09	.1000E+09	.6347E+08	.1785E+09
Stone, clay	.6774E+09	.3420E+08	.3025E+08	.8651E+08
Prim. metal	.1636E+10	.2273E+09	.6627E+08	.1155E+09
Fabr. metal	.7868E+09	.8387E+08	.1378E+08	.4865E+08
Machinery	.2311E+10	.3254E+09	.1145E+09	.5652E+09
Elec. mach.	.1787E+10	.2213E+09	.4987E+09	.2892E+09
Motor veh.	.4302E+10	.3194E+09	.4237E+09	.7352E+09
Aircraft	.1575E+10	.2486E+08	.1346E+08	.4373E+08
Scientific	.3575E+09	.5648E+08	.2479E+08	.9757E+08
Other manu.	.4647E+09	.2853E+08	.2064E+08	.1515E+08
Tot. cntry.	.2168E+11	.2608E+10	.1724E+10	.3191E+10

	W. Ger.	Spain	Switz.	UK
Food prods.	.4479E+09	.7984E+08	.1350E+09	.1249E+10
Textiles	.1001E+09	0.	.6434E+08	.1489E+09
Lmbr., paper	.1173E+09	.4704E+08	.2349E+08	.3202E+09
Print, publ.	.2954E+08	.1159E+08	.2470E+08	.1560E+09
Chemicals	.1163E+10	.3202E+09	.1309E+10	.1742E+10
Rubber prods.	.1640E+09	0.	.1321E+09	.3403E+09
Stone, clay	.2458E+09	.1344E+08	.3028E+08	.1340E+09
Prim. metal	.2345E+09	0.	.4689E+08	.3790E+09
Fabr. metal	.4064E+09	.2127E+08	.8608E+08	.3212E+09
Machinery	.2088E+10	.2763E+09	.8444E+09	.2718E+10
Elec. mach.	.1750E+10	.4519E+09	.5485E+09	.2103E+10
Motor veh.	.2612E+10	.2540E+09	.3099E+09	.1366E+10
Aircraft	.2085E+09	.1224E+08	.5964E+08	.5318E+09
Scientific	.3992E+09	.4868E+08	.1570E+09	.7910E+09
Other manu.	.1544E+09	.1610E+08	.2689E+09	.1436E+09
Tot. cntry.	.1012E+11	.1553E+10	.4040E+10	.1244E+11

Note: Results from INTERSIM computer simulation package. All quantities are in 1972 dollars. 15 February 1981.

income. In this way, the basic data are not changed, but industry totals from the simulator can be brought into conformity with the published numbers.

An example of the ways in which the numbers can diverge is carry-overs of foreign tax credits. Firms that operate in high-tax countries are allowed to carry over excess foreign tax credits. These quantities are included in the *Statistics of Income* volume and not in the basic data. The simulator spreads them out over countries as it does the residuals, but in

Venezuela	Belgium	France	Italy	Neth.
.1699E + 09	.1204E + 09	.5787E + 09	.2379E + 09	.2657E + 09
.5800E + 08	.7101E + 08	.6705E + 08	.5647E + 08	.1678E + 08
.1598E + 08	.1630E + 09	.2063E + 09	.2160E + 09	.1184E + 09
.1150E + 08	.5117E + 07	.3881E + 08	.6576E + 08	.2953E + 08
.3025E + 09	.7077E + 09	.1033E + 10	.1093E + 10	.8891E + 09
.7901E + 08	.2123E + 09	.2486E + 09	.1127E + 09	.1026E + 09
.5140E + 08	.4164E + 08	.9225E + 08	.5339E + 08	.8625E + 07
.1052E + 09	.6750E + 08	.6361E + 08	.9775E + 08	.3462E + 09
.4322E + 08	.1427E + 09	.1857E + 09	.1677E + 09	.1611E + 09
.1699E + 09	.5913E + 09	.1932E + 10	.1077E + 10	.7810E + 09
.1086E + 09	.6683E + 09	.7547E + 09	.7917E + 09	.3477E + 09
.1967E + 09	.1203E + 09	.1093E + 10	.2826E + 09	.3093E + 09
.3426E + 07	.1501E + 08	.2752E + 09	.7053E + 08	.3641E + 08
.1198E + 08	.8217E + 08	.7760E + 09	.3047E + 09	.2305E + 09
.8153E + 08	.4295E + 08	.3385E + 08	.2225E + 08	.3806E + 08
.1409E + 10	.3051E + 10	.7379E + 10	.4649E + 10	.3681E + 10

S. Africa	Japan	Australia	All Other	Tot. Indus.
.6633E + 08	.1667E + 09	.4572E + 09	.1506E + 10	.7533E + 10
.3885E + 07	0.	.2783E + 08	.2681E + 09	.1507E + 10
.1969E + 08	0.	.1181E + 09	.6081E + 09	.3990E + 10
.8805E + 07	.2811E + 08	.4761E + 08	.6798E + 08	.1019E + 10
.1452E + 09	.2619E + 09	.6771E + 09	.3494E + 10	.1793E + 11
.5793E + 08	0.	.1184E + 09	.8473E + 09	.3213E + 10
0.	.7733E + 07	.2252E + 08	.2576E + 09	.1787E + 10
.1230E + 08	.3879E + 08	.1199E + 10	.1105E + 10	.5741E + 10
.1758E + 08	.5107E + 07	.9047E + 08	.3844E + 09	.2966E + 10
.2301E + 09	.8812E + 09	.6608E + 09	.1854E + 10	.1742E + 11
.1028E + 09	.8487E + 08	.2764E + 09	.1805E + 10	.1259E + 11
.3118E + 09	.2393E + 08	.1146E + 10	.1154E + 10	.1496E + 11
.3451E + 07	.4480E + 06	.2138E + 09	.4515E + 09	.3539E + 10
.2956E + 08	.3331E + 08	.1504E + 09	.4542E + 09	.4005E + 10
0.	.2380E + 08	.2020E + 09	.4995E + 09	.2056E + 10
.1009E + 10	.1556E + 10	.5408E + 10	.1476E + 11	.1003E + 12

proportion to excess credits generated in 1972. Since excess credits in prior years generated the carry-overs, this seems the most reasonable way.

Head office deductions are needed for the simulations involving the 861 regulations. Data were collected on the two major types, interest deductions and research and development expenses. The former are taken from IRS, *Statistics of Income, 1972, Corporations.* The National Science Foundation's measure of "funds for R & D" is used for the latter

Table 9.3   Foreign Subsidiaries' Taxable Income

	Canada	Mexico	Argentina	Brazil
Food prods.	.2041E+09	.1233E+08	.3400E+07	.2641E+08
Textiles	.2307E+08	.4732E+07	.5622E+07	−.2316E+07
Lmbr., paper	.1304E+09	.1267E+08	0.	.1963E+08
Print, publ.	.3709E+08	.2556E+07	−.1243E+06	.3545E+07
Chemicals	.2775E+09	.1026E+09	.2068E+08	.4805E+08
Rubber prods.	.4566E+08	.1840E+08	.1559E+08	.3757E+08
Stone, clay	.7880E+08	.1931E+07	.3706E+07	.6237E+07
Prim. metal	.5290E+08	.6055E+07	.1611E+07	.7656E+06
Fabr. metal	.9178E+08	.5619E+07	.1160E+07	.8957E+07
Machinery	.3004E+09	.2243E+08	.7216E+07	.5571E+08
Elec. mach.	.1705E+09	.3250E+08	.6915E+07	.1981E+08
Motor veh.	.5551E+09	.1487E+08	−.3361E+06	.6694E+08
Aircraft	.1169E+09	.2741E+07	.6593E+06	.9861E+07
Scientific	.1052E+09	.1597E+08	.2304E+07	.9663E+08
Other manu.	.3925E+08	.2223E+07	.3751E+06	−.7129E+06
Tot. cntry.	.2229E+10	.2576E+09	.6878E+08	.3971E+09

	W. Ger.	Spain	Switz.	UK
Food prods.	.9248E+08	.1022E+08	.5111E+07	.1039E+09
Textiles	.1556E+07	0.	−.5397E+06	.1104E+08
Lmbr., paper	.2644E+08	.9609E+07	.5694E+07	.5941E+08
Print, publ.	.3604E+07	.1600E+07	.4412E+07	.2120E+08
Chemicals	.1826E+09	.4928E+08	.7914E+08	.1966E+09
Rubber prods.	−.8280E+07	0.	.2139E+07	.7820E+07
Stone, clay	.1987E+08	.8368E+06	.4324E+07	.5842E+09
Prim. metal	.5715E+07	0.	.2469E+07	.2090E+08
Fabr. metal	.5045E+08	.4030E+07	.5212E+07	.2839E+08
Machinery	.4874E+09	.5118E+08	.1295E+09	.2948E+09
Elec. mach.	.2017E+09	.5092E+08	.3571E+08	.1456E+09
Motor veh.	.3281E+09	−.1144E+07	.2308E+08	.3322E+08
Aircraft	.9606E+07	.1415E+07	.5128E+07	.1329E+08
Scientific	.7005E+08	.9157E+07	.1960E+08	.1213E+09
Other manu.	.1087E+08	.1635E+07	.4984E+08	.1837E+08
Tot. cntry.	.1482E+10	.1887E+09	.3708E+09	.1660E+10

Note: Results from INTERSIM computer simulation package. All quantities are in 1972 dollars. 15 February 1981.

(see NSF 1978, table B–3). Since these sources include all United States firms in the industries, these two variables are scaled down by the ratio of domestic income of the MNCs to total domestic income. These ratios are computed from the IRS volumes.

9.2.2   Techniques and Assumptions

The presence of the overall credit limitation creates a problem in calculating foreign tax credits using aggregated data. Firms operating in

Venezuela	Belgium	France	Italy	Neth.
.1586E+08	.1291E+08	.3679E+08	.1730E+08	.3400E+08
.1179E+07	.8080E+07	.8636E+07	.8586E+06	.3152E+07
.4751E+07	.4142E+07	.5518E+08	.3037E+07	.1207E+08
−.5149E+05	.1149E+07	.7228E+07	.2160E+07	.4400E+07
.3169E+08	.7225E+08	.1436E+09	.1546E+09	.8678E+08
.1181E+08	.4217E+08	.7595E+07	.4328E+07	.4683E+07
.8226E+07	.6291E+07	.1067E+08	.2312E+07	−.8146E+05
.3228E+07	.9249E+06	.6223E+07	.3853E+07	.1308E+08
.1170E+07	.6140E+07	.2184E+08	.8265E+07	.1399E+08
.2870E+08	.6741E+08	.3290E+09	.1420E+09	.1141E+09
.1524E+08	.4208E+08	.5535E+08	.3380E+08	.1365E+08
.1093E+08	.1164E+08	.5973E+08	.1658E+08	.4260E+08
.1995E+06	.8147E+06	.2333E+08	.5279E+07	−.2550E+06
.5929E+07	.9916E+08	.5547E+08	.5222E+08	.4393E+08
.1125E+08	.3116E+07	.1094E+07	.2325E+06	.1821E+07
.1501E+09	.3403E+09	.8217E+09	.4468E+09	.3879E+09

S. Africa	Japan	Australia	All Other	Tot. Indus.
.5944E+07	.7369E+08	.3565E+08	.9630E+08	.7864E+09
−.1822E+06	0.	.4274E+07	.1905E+08	.8821E+08
.2805E+07	0.	.3668E+08	.3868E+08	.4212E+09
.1122E+07	.1952E+06	.4607E+07	−.1232E+07	.9346E+08
.2274E+08	.4829E+08	.7609E+08	.2365E+09	.1829E+10
.1141E+08	0.	.4944E+07	.7161E+08	.2395E+09
0.	.4900E+06	.1819E+07	.9667E+07	.7393E+09
.1906E+07	.6511E+07	.8663E+08	.6203E+08	.2748E+09
.3024E+07	.5105E+06	.9619E+07	.2264E+08	.2828E+09
.2067E+08	.2242E+09	.7013E+08	.2202E+09	.2565E+10
.3554E+07	.2099E+08	.2258E+08	.1411E+09	.1012E+10
−.1366E+08	.1575E+07	.7946E+08	.4831E+08	.1277E+10
.4960E+06	.1192E+05	.2375E+08	.2117E+08	.2344E+09
.1036E+08	.7855E+07	.4958E+08	.5688E+08	.8216E+09
0.	.2437E+07	.3740E+08	.1120E+08	.1904E+09
.7019E+08	.3868E+09	.5432E+09	.1054E+10	.1086E+11

one country may or may not be operating in other countries simultaneously. The more countries they operate in, the more advantage they can take of the overall limitation. The United States would collect more tax if every firm operated in only one other country than if every firm operated in every country, for given amounts of income. Without microdata, there is no way to tell how completely the present structure of United States firms takes advantage of the overall limitation. Therefore there is no way to calculate credits after limitation precisely.

Table 9.4   **Taxes Paid to Foreign Governments by Subsidiaries**

	Canada	Mexico	Argentina	Brazil
Food prods.	.9605E + 08	.1705E + 08	.3732E + 07	.8179E + 07
Textiles	.1209E + 08	.2800E + 07	.1900E + 07	.3696E + 06
Lmbr., paper	.5273E + 08	.7037E + 07	0.	.4924E + 07
Print, publ.	.1840E + 08	.1437E + 07	.1090E + 05	.6403E + 05
Chemicals	.1333E + 09	.5950E + 08	.1154E + 08	.1858E + 08
Rubber prods.	.2371E + 08	.9887E + 07	.6272E + 07	.1402E + 08
Stone, clay	.3074E + 08	.1681E + 07	.1849E + 07	.1232E + 07
Prim. metal	.3122E + 08	.3177E + 07	.1242E + 07	.1703E + 07
Fabr. metal	.4489E + 08	.4225E + 07	.6715E + 06	.3188E + 07
Machinery	.1543E + 09	.1457E + 08	.4085E + 07	.1700E + 08
Elec. mach.	.7914E + 08	.2002E + 08	.3829E + 07	.3883E + 07
Motor veh.	.2690E + 09	.9107E + 07	.3801E + 07	.2639E + 07
Aircraft	.4795E + 08	.1636E + 07	.5086E + 06	.3744E + 07
Scientific	.8016E + 08	.1321E + 08	.1895E + 07	.8973E + 08
Other manu.	.1701E + 08	.1413E + 07	.4384E + 06	.5073E + 05
Tot. cntry.	.1091E + 10	.1667E + 09	.4178E + 08	.1693E + 09

	W. Ger.	Spain	Switz.	UK
Food prods.	.3907E + 08	.4387E + 07	.5550E + 07	.4112E + 08
Textiles	.1069E + 07	0.	.3118E + 06	.5036E + 07
Lmbr., paper	.1552E + 08	.3017E + 07	.1306E + 07	.1893E + 08
Print, publ.	.2265E + 07	.5923E + 06	.1396E + 07	.9820E + 07
Chemicals	.7713E + 08	.1510E + 08	.2350E + 08	.7471E + 08
Rubber prods.	.2004E + 06	0.	.6934E + 06	.3345E + 07
Stone, clay	.1007E + 08	4462.	.9838E + 06	.2946E + 09
Prim. metal	.2166E + 07	0.	.6109E + 06	.8205E + 07
Fabr. metal	.2393E + 08	.9798E + 06	.7971E + 06	.1332E + 08
Machinery	.2430E + 09	.1945E + 08	.3583E + 08	.1550E + 09
Elec. mach.	.7497E + 08	.1869E + 08	.1118E + 08	.6629E + 08
Motor veh.	.1796E + 09	.1747E + 07	.6758E + 07	.1514E + 08
Aircraft	.3144E + 07	.5811E + 06	.1455E + 07	.8548E + 07
Scientific	.4225E + 08	.2697E + 07	.7287E + 07	.8915E + 08
Other manu.	.5559E + 07	.9103E + 06	.1696E + 08	.7870E + 07
Tot. cntry.	.7199E + 09	.6815E + 08	.1146E + 09	.8111E + 09

Note: Results from INTERSIM computer simulation package. All quantities are in 1972 dollars. 15 February 1981.

The *Statistics of Income* book presents the actual level of credits allowed after limitation in 1972, by industry. The following procedure allows one to use this information to skirt this problem.

It is assumed that there are only eighteen (types of) firms in each industry. Seventeen operate in the United States and one other country only; they are called "binational" firms. The last firm in each industry is assumed to operate in every country; it is an "omninational" firm. The last assumption is that the omninational firm accounts for a constant

Venezuela	Belgium	France	Italy	Neth.
.6586E + 07	.4267E + 07	.1719E + 08	.1159E + 08	.1369E + 08
.1759E + 07	.4262E + 07	.4230E + 07	.1667E + 07	.1295E + 07
.1280E + 07	.1507E + 07	.1122E + 08	.1986E + 07	.4436E + 07
7354.	.4425E + 06	.3240E + 07	.1597E + 07	.1337E + 07
.1322E + 08	.2814E + 08	.6749E + 08	.4792E + 08	.4005E + 08
.5808E + 07	.1045E + 07	.3283E + 07	.1613E + 07	.2393E + 07
.3322E + 07	.2417E + 07	.4883E + 07	.1088E + 07	.3686E + 06
.1201E + 07	.9536E + 06	.3083E + 07	.2344E + 07	.3540E + 07
.1345E + 06	.2006E + 07	.7597E + 07	.3842E + 07	.8103E + 07
.1251E + 08	.2405E + 08	.1484E + 09	.8025E + 08	.5737E + 08
.7438E + 07	.1808E + 08	.2145E + 08	.2515E + 08	.9882E + 07
.6813E + 07	.5492E + 07	.2700E + 08	.9740E + 07	.1524E + 08
.1771E + 06	.5290E + 06	.7937E + 07	.2759E + 07	.1694E + 06
.4647E + 07	.8320E + 08	.3122E + 08	.2640E + 08	.2018E + 08
.4806E + 07	.1824E + 07	.9920E + 06	.2827E + 06	.2614E + 06
.6971E + 08	.1782E + 09	.3592E + 09	.2182E + 09	.1783E + 09

S. Africa	Japan	Australia	All Other	Tot. Indus.
.3072E + 07	.3344E + 08	.1913E + 08	.3340E + 08	.3575E + 09
.4445E + 05	0.	.1957E + 07	.4318E + 07	.4311E + 08
.1927E + 07	0.	.1077E + 08	.1924E + 08	.1558E + 09
.3474E + 06	.1841E + 06	.1357E + 07	.1021E + 07	.4351E + 08
.1054E + 08	.2475E + 08	.3743E + 08	.9485E + 08	.7777E + 09
.5065E + 07	0.	.2540E + 07	.3042E + 08	.1103E + 09
0.	.3358E + 06	.8647E + 06	.2771E + 07	.3572E + 09
.8846E + 06	.3122E + 07	.1805E + 08	.2271E + 08	.1042E + 09
.1487E + 07	.2258E + 06	.4543E + 07	.8301E + 07	.1282E + 09
.1173E + 08	.9675E + 08	.4080E + 08	.9594E + 08	.1211E + 10
.1834E + 07	.1035E + 08	.1081E + 08	.4097E + 08	.4240E + 09
.5151E + 06	.1571E + 06	.3680E + 08	.2583E + 08	.6153E + 09
.2241E + 06	7870.	.5270E + 07	.8123E + 07	.9276E + 08
.8898E + 07	.3726E + 07	.3991E + 08	.3722E + 08	.5818E + 09
0.	.1881E + 06	.2201E + 08	.4430E + 07	.8500E + 08
.4656E + 08	.1732E + 09	.2522E + 09	.4295E + 09	.5087E + 10

proportion of the industry's activities in each country. This proportion may be called α_1 for the first industry, and so forth through α_{15}.

Given the α_i's, the simulator can calculate final credits. Foreign income taxes are split in two in each industry-country cell; α_i go to the omninational and $(1 - \alpha_i)$ to the binational. The limitation is immediately calculated for the binational, and its final credit computed. The sum of credits for all binationals is then computed by adding over countries. First, the omninational's credit is computed by adding its shares of income and taxes over the countries; then, its limitation is computed and imposed. The total credits for the industry are then the sum of the binational's credits and the omninational's.

The larger is α_i, the larger is the total credit for the industry. This is so because the overall credit limitation does more "good" the closer the industry is to complete omninationality. There will be one value of α_i, for each industry, that causes credits computed by the calulator to match credits reported in *Statistics of Income*. Once they are known, calibration of the simulator is complete. They may be used whenever limitations need to be calculated.

The α_i that satisfy this condition are as follows:

1)	Food products	.6680
2)	Textiles and apparels	.2118
3)	Lumber and paper	.4908
4)	Printing and publishing	.5000
5)	Chemicals	.4544
6)	Rubber products	.9593
7)	Stone, clay, and glass	.7152
8)	Primary metal products	.1929
9)	Fabricated metal products	.0023
10)	Machinery, except electrical	.2520
11)	Electrical machinery	.1291
12)	Motor vehicles	.4199
13)	Aircraft and other transportation equipment	.8989
14)	Scientific instruments, etc.	.6924
15)	Other manufacturing	.7196

Two adjustments were made. First, there never are excess credits in the fourth industry, printing and publishing. Thus the problem of how to compute the limitation never arises. All values of α_4 would yield the same answer for this industry; therefore a value of 0.5 is arbitrarily chosen. The simulator calculated credits of $24.17 million, the published number of $24.00 million. These are off by less than 1%. A residual equal to the difference will be subtracted from credits for the seventeenth country class in all runs.

The other problem concerns industry 9, fabricated metal products. Even when α_9 is set to zero, calculated credits exceed reported credits. There may be an error in the data or method. Or the aggregation done to compute the seventeenth country group may not allow a strict enough limitation to be imposed. With α_9 set to 0.0023, computed credits are $61.73 million. Reported credits are $61.29 million; the computation is off by 0.72%. Again, a residual equal to the difference will be subtracted from the seventeenth country class in all runs.

9.3 Simulation Results

With the calculation of the proper α_i, the calibration stage is complete. The simulation package, INTERSIM, is therefore able to analyze the tax issues discussed in section 9.1.

In order to facilitate comparisons among the reform proposals, a baseline proposal is defined first. It simulates the effect of two minor changes in actual 1972 experience. These changes are also included in the simulation of each reform proposal, and the final results from each are expressed relative to the baseline. The first of these changes is that carry-overs of excess foreign tax credits from prior years are neglected. Without a series of years of data, there would be no way to simulate how the carry-overs would change when the laws were changed. By dropping them in the baseline, the analysis may consistently neglect them for the whole analysis. Second, dividends received from less-developed countries were taxed in a special way until 1976; this "no gross up" provision is taken out in the baseline and all other simulations.

The data show that total assets of foreign subsidiaries of United States manufacturing firms were equal to $100.250 billion in 1972. Total United States corporate income tax paid by these firms was $11.810 billion. Note that only taxes paid by United States multinational companies are included in this number; also, it is the net of foreign tax credits and investment tax credits. These firms and their subsidiaries paid $5.087 billion in taxes to foreign governments. Thus their total tax liabilities were $16.897 billion.

Table 9.5, row 1, displays the changes caused by the baseline simulation. United States tax revenues increase by $96 million, in 1972 dollars. Foreign tax revenues are not affected. Thus, except for rounding errors, the change in total tax liabilities equals the United States change. The possibility that assets of the firm could change is considered in the next section.

The results of imposing the per-country limitations are presented in row 2. This reform would seem to have little effect. Foreign tax credits are reduced, and thus United States taxes increased, by $70 million over the baseline. Again, except for rounding, this change equals the increase in total tax liabilities, since foreign taxes are unaffected.

The two proposals that eliminate deferral show more of an effect. The consolidation method causes an increase in United States tax revenues of $344 million over the baseline. For the reasons described above, the complete payout method causes a slightly larger increase in tax, $354 million.

Eliminating all United States taxation of income earned abroad, the territorial approach, would reduce United States taxes by $815 million relative to the baseline. Row 6 shows that substituting a deduction for the

Table 9.5   Simulation Results Including No Behavioral Response

	Change in Assets of Foreign Subsidiaries	Change in U.S. Tax Liabilities	Change in Foreign Tax Liabilities	Change in Total Tax Liabilities
Changes from 1972 data				
1. Baseline simulation	…	+96	…	+97
Changes from baseline simulation				
2. Per-country limitation	…	+70	…	+69
3. Repeal deferral, complete payout	…	+344	…	+344
4. Repeal deferral, consolidation	…	+354	…	+354
5. Territorial treatment	…	−815	…	−815
6. Deduction for foreign taxes	…	+1,366	…	+1,365
7. Shares allocation, worldwide	…	+2,387	−1,842	+544
8. Shares allocation, by U.S. only	…	+2,059	…	+2,058
9. 861 allocation, sales and assets used	…	+888	…	+888
10. 861 allocation, assets only used	…	+922	…	+921

Note: In millions of 1972 dollars.

foreign tax credit would raise United States tax revenues by $1.366 billion. Dismantling the foreign tax credit system in favor of a deduction would be an important change in United States tax policy toward international income.

A coordinated worldwide move to a shares allocation approach would also have major repercussions. The firms' overall tax liabilities would increase by $544 million. This is the net effect of increasing United States taxes by $2.387 billion and decreasing taxes paid to foreign governments by $1.842 billion (except for rounding errors). The current arm's length approach allocates more income to the foreign subsidiaries than would an approach based on shares of sales and especially assets. Substantial redistributions of worldwide tax revenues are implied.

Countries that show especially large ratios of income to sales and assets suffer the largest decreases in tax revenues. Since the INTERSIM package is able to calculate results by industry and country, it is possible to break down the aggregate change in foreign tax revenues shown in the third column, row 7, of table 9.5. Table 9.6 displays foreign tax liabilities by country, before and after worldwide adoption of a shares allocation approach.

Undoubtedly, many foreign governments would balk at a move to a shares allocation system. Row 8 of table 9.5 presents the results if only the United States used the shares allocation approach in computing taxable incomes. Foreign tax revenues are preserved. United States, and thus total, tax liabilities rise by approximately $2.059 billion. This rise is smaller than the one for United States taxes in the worldwide reform because higher levels of foreign tax imply higher foreign tax credits. Still, the rise in United States revenues is substantial. Now, however, instead of foreign governments bearing the cost, the firms do. In fact, this reform would cause a larger change in total tax liabilities of the firms than any other reform simulated.

The last two rows of table 9.5 present the results of simulating the special allocation mentioned in the 861 regulations. They imply that foreign tax credits will decline, since the foreign tax base used in computing the credit limitation must be reduced. When sales and assets are used in the required allocation, credits decline, and total taxes rise, by $888 million. Using assets alone causes a slightly larger allocation of head office deductions; therefore taxes rise slightly more, by $921 million, approximately.

To summarize, the largest changes in tax revenues would be produced by the deduction for foreign taxes paid and by the shares allocation approach. If a shares allocation system were instituted worldwide simultaneously, it would affect the distribution of tax revenues more than the total burden on the firms. The territorial system would also produce a large change in United States and total taxes, in the opposite direction.

Table 9.6   Foreign Tax Revenues

	From 1972 Data	With Shares Allocation	Change
Canada	1,091	737.1	− 353.9
Mexico	166.7	127.3	− 39.4
Argentina	41.38	38.55	− 2.83
Brazil	169.3	68.06	− 101.24
Venezuela	69.71	50.86	− 18.85
Belgium	178.2	86.87	− 91.33
France	359.2	247.5	− 111.7
Italy	218.2	142.3	− 75.9
Netherlands	178.3	113.8	− 64.5
West Germany	719.9	389.9	− 333.0
Spain	68.15	44.27	− 23.88
Switzerland	114.6	79.77	− 34.83
United Kingdom	811.1	409.8	− 401.3
South Africa	46.56	36.94	− 9.62
Japan	173.2	61.23	− 111.97
Australia	252.2	181.7	− 70.5
Other	429.5	434.5	+ 5.0

Note: In millions of 1972 dollars.

Finally, the aspects of the 861 regulations that are simulated produce sizable changes in tax liabilities.

9.4 Behavioral Responses

The simulation results presented so far assume that the firms' decisions are fixed. This assumption is unwarranted; the firms may respond to the tax reform proposals in ways that could affect the results substantially. This section considers two sets of responses the firms might make and ways to include them in the simulations.

9.4.1 Responses in Financial Decisions

Accounting for changes in intrafirm financial flows can have substantial impacts on the simulation results. Bergsten, Horst, and Moran (1978) present a model aimed at dealing in considerable detail with this issue. Partly because their analysis is so complete, this question is handled in a much more cursory fashion here.

The deferral provision of United States law emphasizes the importance of financial variables. If all firms made full use of deferral, by having their subsidiaries retain all profits, they could avoid paying any tax to the United States. Note that this policy would not place substantial limits on the firms' movements of capital. They could use intrafirm loans and changes in the subsidiaries' equity structure to reallocate retained funds for investment purposes.

Of course, full use of deferral would place some restrictions on the firms. If all funds are retained abroad, they do not show up in the parent corporations' incomes. Since dividends paid out by the parents cannot exceed their profits, it is possible that complete deferral could restrict payouts by the corporations to their ultimate shareholders. It seems that in order to understand why the firms do not use intrafirm flows to minimize taxes, one must answer the question, Why do the United States firms pay dividends? The difficulty others have had in answering this question is the second reason financial responses are given cursory treatment here.[16]

The simplest treatment for intrafirm dividends is to assume that the subsidiaries keep their payout rates constant. This is done, with two adjustments. In the simulation of shares allocation with coordination, dividends are assumed proportional to net income as measured by the present, arm's length, method. In other words, dividends do not change just because the way of measuring net income for tax purposes changes.

The second adjustment concerns measuring payout rates with the cross-tabulated data. Cells containing subsidiaries with both positive and negative profits could pose problems. The cells may show positive dividends, since the firms with losses will not pay dividends and the others may, but total profits could easily be negative. Spurious negative payout rates would result. The Treasury computed a special tabulation, which excluded firms with losses, in order to solve this problem. Payout rates are computed from the dividends and profits reported by this tabulation.

Interest, royalties, and other fees also flow between the subsidiaries and parents. It is assumed that the ratios of these variables to gross income are kept constant.

9.4.2 Responses in Investment Decisions

The focus of concern with behavioral responses is the firms' investment decisions. Frisch (1981) presents evidence about the sensitivity of location of investment to rate of return and tax rates. Using much the same data as are used here, it relates changes in assets between 1968 and 1972 to gross and net rates of return. A significant relation seems to exist. Specifically, a 1% decrease in rate of return, accounting for taxes, in one country seems to cause a decrease in assets there of between 0.1 and 0.2% over the next four years.

The partial equilibrium nature of this approach should be stressed. Some of the tax reform proposals raise effective tax rates, and thus

---

16. For examples, see King (1977), Bradford and Gordon (1980), and Feldstein and Green (1979).

reduce net rates of return, in almost every situation. The empirical results in Frisch (1981) imply that these reforms would reduce assets of United States firms in almost every country. Where would this capital go? Some might be invested by the firms in the United States, some might be bid away by local firms in the countries, and some might be consumed in the long run as investment opportunities are worsened. Of course, all of these mechanisms would have repercussions, and a complete analysis would have to include these general equilibrium effects. Unfortunately they are beyond the scope of this paper, since they require the construction of a general equilibrium model of the world economy.

The basic approach, in short, is to assume that firms change their overseas assets in response to net rates of return, which change as tax rates change. The reform proposals thus influence behavior through their effects on tax rates on investment. The computation of these tax rates and the effects that the reforms would have on them are discussed below and in more detail in the next section.

Applying an elasticity to changes in net rates of return yields changes in assets. A set of assumptions is needed to translate these changes into changes in income flows and tax liabilities. The simplest assumption is that gross income is proportional to assets, in other words, that gross rates of return are constant. The special tabulation mentioned above allows one improvement. Presumably, a firm losing money in a country is not likely to expand assets there in the expectation that it will lose even more money. Only positive gross rates of return should be used. Thus ratios of gross income to assets are computed from the tabulation that includes only profitable subsidiaries. Intercept terms are added to account for losses. For example, consider a small reduction in a tax rate, thus a small increase in net rate of return, and a small increase in assets. If gross income was positive before, it will increase in proportion; if negative, it will be a little less so.

Interest, royalties, and other fees are then computed from gross income as discussed above. Foreign taxable income is then equal to gross income minus these fees (except in the worldwide shares allocation regime). Foreign tax liability equals taxable income times the effective foreign tax rate. These tax rates are computed from the special tabulation in order to avoid spurious negative tax rates. Dividends are then computed from net income, as described above. The INTERSIM package is then ready to compute all other parts of total tax liabilities and display the results as desired.

The remaining issue is the computation of tax rates on investment. Needed are changes in total tax that would result from changes in investment, on the margin, under each tax regime. The INTERSIM package is able to compute these marginal effective tax rates directly. It perturbs assets, traces the effects on income flows and tax liabilities, and computes the resulting changes in total tax. Likely values of the marginal tax rates under each regime are discussed in detail below.[17]

In the first set of results presented, a value of 0.15 is used for the elasticity of assets with respect to net rate of return. This value is chosen because it is in the middle of the range of findings in Frisch (1981). The tentative nature of this paper suggests, however, that a sensitivity analysis on this parameter is appropriate. For example, the paper is able to capture only four-year responses; therefore the true long-run elasticity may be larger. For this reason, further results are presented which use elasticities that range from 0.05 to 1.00.

9.5 Results Including Behavioral Responses

Table 9.7 presents simulation results with behavioral responses included. The elasticity of assets with respect to net rate of return is set to 0.15. The two changes in the baseline simulation cause a slight decrease in overseas investments. Assets decline by $100 million, or 0.099%, from actual 1972 levels. As a result, foreign income and taxes decline slightly. The baseline simulation now shows an increase of only $91 million in the total tax liabilities of the firms.

Imposition of the per-country limitation either raises marginal tax rates or leaves them unaffected. Consider an omninational firm that, for simplicity, does not use deferral. Say its foreign taxes are only 40% of its foreign income. Then its effective tax rate on all foreign income, after the United States credit mechanism, becomes 48%, the basic United States rate in 1972. Now impose the per-country limitation. The effective tax rate in low-tax countries is still 48%. However, the firm might have some operations in a country with a 50% tax rate; the effective tax rate for this country would go from 48% to 50%.

The opposite case is an omninational firm with an average foreign tax rate over 48% but with some operations in a low-tax country. Now the tax rates in high-tax jurisdictions are unaffected, but the effective tax rate in the low-tax country is raised to the United States level.

In short, the "typical" operations of the omninational firms are unaffected. Tax rates that are on the other side of 48% from the firms' average rate will go up, either to 48% or to the foreign rate, whichever is higher. Income that is deferred or attributed to the binational firms is unaffected.

---

17. This process for computing marginal tax rates embodies all of the assumptions made up to this point. Frisch (1981), containing the empirical work, makes different assumptions about financial decisions and therefore uses different measures of the marginal tax rates. It would be interesting to rerun the empirical analysis using marginal tax rates as computed here; before this could be done, however, INTERSIM would have to be extended to include 1968 tax law and data.

Table 9.7   **Simulation Results, Elasticity = 0.15**

	Change in Assets of Foreign Subsidiaries	Change in U.S. Tax Liabilities	Change in Foreign Tax Liabilities	Change in Total Tax Liabilities
Changes from 1972 data				
1. Baseline simulation	−100	+96	−4	+91
Changes from baseline simulation				
2. Per-country limitation	−30	+69	−2	+68
3. Repeal deferral, complete payout	−1,594	+314	−66	+249
4. Repeal deferral, consolidation	−1,594	+322	−66	+257
5. Territorial treatment	+800	−815	+40	−774
6. Deduction for foreign taxes	−2,221	+1,314	−169	+1,146
7. Shares allocation, worldwide	−852	+2,353	−1,845	+509
8. Shares allocation, by U.S. only	−4,351	+1,777	−408	+1,370
9. 861 allocation, sales and assets used	−1,644	+860	−106	+755
10. 861 allocation, assets only used	−1,650	+895	−103	+793

Note: In millions of 1972 dollars.

Row 2 of table 9.7 illustrates these effects on investment incentives. Assets decrease slightly compared to the baseline results. Detailed results (available from the author) show that some industries are totally unaffected. Total foreign assets of United States firms decrease by $30 million more than the baseline; this change causes a small reduction in foreign tax revenues. Imposition of the per-country limitation, taking behavioral responses into account, would increase total tax liabilities of the firms by $68 million relative to the baseline.

Inferring the direction of movements in marginal tax rates is easier for this reform plan than for most of the ones to follow. Per-country limitation is one of only two reforms in which movements can occur in only one direction. In the others, some marginal tax rates increase and others decline. The reason is the overall limitation, together with omninational firms whose average tax rate flips from one side of 48% to the other.

Consider the plans that end deferral. If subsidiaries in low-tax countries retain more than average, ending deferral will lower averaged foreign tax rates. An omninational firm could find itself pushed from above 48% to below. Effective tax rates on all its income will go from being equal to local levels to 48%, the United States rate. This means that effective rates decline for high-tax countries and increase for low-tax countries. Another industry might have its omninational in exactly the opposite position: below 48% at first and above 48% after deferral is ended. Then marginal tax rates in the same countries would move in exactly the opposite directions. The overall limitation can lead to some exceedingly complex patterns in marginal tax rates and investment incentives.

Although anything can happen to marginal tax rates in specific circumstances, typical trends are clearer. Movements for the binational firms and for more typical circumstances for the omninationals are usually unambiguous. For example, ending deferral can only raise marginal tax rates for the binational firms. If the deferred income is taxed more than 48% abroad, then there is no effect; if the tax rate is lower abroad, the marginal tax rate has to increase.

The first column in rows 3 and 4 of table 9.7 shows that ending deferral would cause sizable reductions in investments abroad. Assets decline by $1.594 billion relative to the baseline. The plans have exactly the same effect on investment since they differ only in the treatment of losses and, by assumption, subsidiaries with losses do not respond.

These changes in investment decisions are large enough to affect United States as well as foreign tax revenues. Foreign income is reduced; therefore repatriations to the parents fall. As a result, United States revenues fall by $30 to $32 million compared to the simulations that neglect behavioral responses. In addition, foreign tax revenues fall by $66 million. The result is that total tax payments by the firms are only $249 million larger than the baseline for the complete payout method, and $257 million larger for the consolidation method.

Territorial treatment reduces marginal tax rates in typical situations. The credit mechanism, in general, sets the effective tax rate on repatriated income to the higher of the local rate or 48%. Since the territorial system suspends this mechanism entirely, marginal tax rates in low-tax countries decline. Some marginal tax rates could still increase. An omninational firm that is low-tax on average has marginal tax rates of 48% on all nondeferred income, including income from high-tax countries, if any. Suspending the credit system causes the marginal tax rates for this high-tax income to go up to the local rate. In this atypical case, to reset marginal tax rates to local levels is to raise them.

Row 5 of table 9.7 shows that the typical situations rule. Territorial treatment lowers investment disincentives and causes assets abroad to increase by $800 million. Foreign tax payments rise by $40 million as a result. Note that the change in United States tax revenues is not affected by the inclusion of behavioral responses. Since basically no attempt is made to tax foreign operations, United States revenues are insulated from changes in the firms' overseas investment decisions.

Substituting a deduction for the foreign tax credit raises marginal tax rates in every instance. In the simplest case, the marginal tax rate under the credit system is the higher of the foreign tax rate and the United States tax rate. Under the deduction regime,

(16) $$MTR = t^* + (1 - t^*)t.$$

As long as t^*, the foreign tax rate, is between zero and one, MTR exceeds both t^* and t, the United States rate. Therefore the marginal tax rate under the deduction is greater than either of the values it could take under the credit. Inclusion of deferral, overall limitation, and the other aspects of actual law does not change the conclusion that marginal taxes on investment must increase.

The result is that assets abroad fall by $2.221 billion. The firms end up paying an additional $1.314 billion to the United States and $1.146 billion overall.

The remaining four simulations involve some form of the shares allocation approach to defining tax bases. This approach can have some fascinating effects on marginal tax rates and investment incentives. For example, marginal tax rates on domestic activities can be affected directly, since domestic assets and income appear in the allocation formulas. The question of incentives for domestic investment is beyond the scope of this paper; however, some simple examples are presented in an appendix.

Marginal tax rates on foreign investment can increase or decrease, no matter what the credit situation, and can even become negative. Consider a coordinated shares allocation with only assets used to define the shares. Furthermore, consider, for simplicity, a firm that does not use deferral and that operates in only the United States and one other country, which has a higher tax rate than the United States. Equations (1)–(4) and (9)–(11) would then imply that total taxes paid by the firm are

$$(17) \qquad T_{\text{TOTAL}} = t^* \left(\frac{A^*}{A + A^*} \right) Y_{\text{TOTAL}} + t \left(1 - \frac{A^*}{A + A^*} \right) Y_{\text{TOTAL}}.$$

Note that the credit mechanism ensures that the tax rate on foreign income is t^*, since it is higher than t. This equation may be reexpressed

$$(18) \qquad T_{\text{TOTAL}} = \bar{t}\, Y_{\text{TOTAL}},$$

$$(19) \qquad \bar{t} = \frac{t^* A^* + tA}{A^* + A},$$

where $\bar{t}$ is the appropriate weighted average of tax rates applied to total income. The marginal tax rate on overseas investment is

$$(20) \qquad \frac{\partial T_{\text{TOTAL}}}{\partial A^*} = \bar{t}\, \frac{\partial Y_{\text{TOTAL}}}{\partial A^*} + Y_{\text{TOTAL}}\, \frac{\partial \bar{t}}{\partial A^*}.$$

There are now two channels by which a marginal investment abroad can affect taxes. First, the usual one: more assets imply more income to be taxed. Second, assets affect the average tax rate because they affect the weighting scheme. Evaluating the derivative in the second term,

$$(21) \qquad \frac{\partial T_{\text{TOTAL}}}{\partial A^*} = \bar{t}\, \frac{\partial Y_{\text{TOTAL}}}{\partial A^*} + Y_{\text{TOTAL}} (t^* - t)\, \frac{A}{(A^* + A)^2}.$$

If t^* is less than t, the second term is negative; increasing assets abroad reduces taxes because the smaller tax rate becomes more important in the average.

The first term is always positive. It will be small, however, if the gross rate of return in the foreign country is small. In fact, if the gross rate of return abroad is extremely small and the tax rate there is low, the whole expression can be negative. Note that baseline marginal tax rates should be small in such a situation, since not much income is produced on margin and it is lightly taxed. In sum, it is possible for low-baseline marginal tax rates to be pushed through zero by the shares allocation schemes.

This occurs in 5 out of the 246 cells in the data. The cells and the marginal tax rates for the baseline and shares allocation scheme with coordination are

		Marginal Tax Rate	
Industry	Country	Baseline	Shares
Printing, etc. (4)	Venezuela (5)	.0008	− .0157
Stone, etc. (7)	Spain (11)	.0003	− .0122
Fabricated metals (9)	Venezuela (5)	.0026	− .0025
Motor vehicles (12)	South Africa (14)	.0057	− .0044
Other (15)	Japan (15)	.0096	− .0104

In these cases, interactions among tax rates in the various countries actually result in subsidies to investment.

Such sharp declines in marginal tax rates are not typical for the shares allocation regimes. On average, in fact, marginal tax rates rise moderately. Assets and sales are distributed in the data in a way that shifts income into the relatively high-tax countries. The net result is to discourage investment abroad by United States firms. As table 9.7 shows, assets fall by $852 million under the coordinated shares allocation regime.

Total tax liabilities rise by $509 million when behavioral responses are included. Foreign taxes fall by $1.845 billion, and tax collected by the United States rises by $2.353 billion. Again, this regime implies a particularly large redistribution of tax revenues away from foreign governments and toward the United States. (Disaggregated results, analogous to table 9.6, are available from the author.)

Marginal tax rates for the shares allocation scheme without coordination are more complex. First, income is taxed at the basic foreign rate; then United States law adds aspects that work through the two channels outlined above. In effect, foreign income is potentially double-taxed, once by the ordinary foreign rate and again by the shares allocation mechanism. To the extent that income is deferred, this double taxation is avoided.

The effect is to cause greater increases in the marginal tax rates. In three cases, they rise by enough to force the net rate of return negative. This fact poses a problem for the routine that calculates behavioral responses. Since a constant elasticity form is used, a negative net rate of return would call for an infinitely large reduction in assets. It is clear that the simple functional form chosen is inadequate for some of the large changes that can result from this reform. Rather than investigate more realistic, but more complex, functional forms, this study resets the three negative net rates of return to 25% of their pre-reform levels. This procedure ensures that behavioral responses in these three cells are proportionately larger than in any other cell, but not so large as to skew the whole analysis. The three cells are all in industry 14, scientific instruments. The countries and the net rates of return under the baseline, under this reform before adjustment, and after adjustment are

		Net Rate of Return	
Country	Baseline	Not Adjusted	Adjusted
Brazil (4)	.0993	− .2027	.0248
Venezuela (5)	.1176	− .0079	.0294
Belgium (6)	.1986	− .1390	.0496

Overall, adoption of a shares allocation approach by the United States alone would cause assets abroad to decrease by $4.351 billion (see row 8 of table 9.7), the largest response in assets of any of the simulations. This result agrees with the fact that, when behavioral responses are neglected, this same regime causes the largest change in taxes. With responses included, taxes increase by $1.370 billion. Inclusion of behavioral responses causes the change in total tax liabilities to be only two-thirds as large as before.

The final two simulations involve the aspects of the 861 regulations. Under these regimes, a share of certain domestic deductions is allocated to the measure of income used to compute the foreign tax credit limitation. The result is to reduce credits and raise United States taxes.

Since taxes must increase, it should not be too surprising that marginal tax rates increase on average. None increase by enough to cause the net rate of return to go negative. On the other hand, it is probably not surprising by now to discover that some rates go down. In fact, the third of the five cells that experience a negative tax rate under shares allocation again shows a tax rate that falls through zero. The marginal tax rate in this cell is -0.000002.

How can a marginal tax rate fall so sharply in this regime? Remember that the tax rate in this cell is very low; therefore the foreign tax credit never approaches the limitation. So an allocation that reduces this limitation does no damage. But head office deductions allocated into this country cannot do damage elsewhere. In short, the firms have the incentive to increase operations in this country so that the special deductions are allocated away from where they matter into a situation where they do not.

The average effect, however, is to increase disincentives for investment abroad. Row 9 of table 9.7 presents the results when both assets and sales are used in the 861 allocations. Assets abroad decline by $1.644 billion. Total taxes increase by $755 million. Finally, the last row presents the results when only assets are used as the basis of the allocations. The decline in assets is slightly larger, $1.650 billion. The change in total taxes is still slightly higher, $793 million.

In summary, the nine reform proposals can change investment incentives in complex ways. The result is that overseas investments of United States firms can respond by large amounts. Substituting a deduction for the foreign tax credit and instituting a shares allocation scheme without coordination would have the largest effects. Changes in total tax liabilities are smaller than when behavioral responses are neglected. It is clear, however, that changes in tax revenues are not the only important aspect for evaluating the reforms.

Tables 9.8, 9.9, and 9.10 present the results of the sensitivity analysis on the basic response elasticity. Perhaps the most interesting changes show up in table 9.10, when the elasticity is set equal to 1.00. Assets now change by as much as $-$23.963 billion; again, the shares allocation regime instituted by the United States only shows the largest response.

Table 9.8   **Simulation Results, Elasticity = 0.05**

	Change in Assets of Foreign Subsidiaries	Change in U.S. Tax Liabilities	Change in Foreign Tax Liabilities	Change in Total Tax Liabilities
Changes from 1972 data				
1. Baseline simulation	−30	+96	−1	+95
Changes from baseline simulation				
2. Per-country limitation	−10	+70	−1	+69
3. Repeal deferral, complete payout	−537	+334	−22	+312
4. Repeal deferral, consolidation	−537	+343	−22	+321
5. Territorial treatment	+270	−815	+13	−802
6. Deduction for foreign taxes	−749	+1,348	−57	+1,291
7. Shares allocation, worldwide	−289	+2,375	−1,844	+531
8. Shares allocation, by U.S. only	−1,484	+1,964	−143	+1,821
9. 861 allocation, sales and assets used	−554	+879	−36	+843
10. 861 allocation, assets only used	−556	+913	−35	+878

Note: In millions of 1972 dollars.

Table 9.9   **Simulation Results, Elasticity = 0.50**

	Change in Assets of Foreign Subsidiaries	Change in U.S. Tax Liabilities	Change in Foreign Tax Liabilities	Change in Total Tax Liabilities
Changes from 1972 data				
1. Baseline simulation	−332	+94	−15	+79
Changes from baseline simulation				
2. Per-country limitation	−125	+69	−6	+63
3. Repeal deferral, complete payout	−5,122	+248	−213	+35
4. Repeal deferral, consolidation	−5,122	+258	−213	+45
5. Territorial treatment	+2,692	−813	+136	−677
6. Deduction for foreign taxes	−7,126	+1,202	−536	+688
7. Shares allocation, worldwide	−2,656	+2,302	−1,823	+479
8. Shares allocation, by U.S. only	−13,395	+1,249	−1,190	+59
9. 861 allocation, sales and assets used	−5,282	+801	−338	+462
10. 861 allocation, assets only used	−5,311	+838	−330	+508

Note: In millions of 1972 dollars.

Table 9.10   Simulation Results, Elasticity = 1.00

	Change in Assets of Foreign Subsidiaries	Change in U.S. Tax Liabilities	Change in Foreign Tax Liabilities	Change in Total Tax Liabilities
Changes from 1972 data				
1. Baseline simulation	−662	+92	−30	+62
Changes from baseline simulation				
2. Per-country limitation	−247	+68	−12	+56
3. Repeal deferral, complete payout	−9,707	+163	−406	−243
4. Repeal deferral, consolidation	−9,707	+176	−406	−230
5. Territorial treatment	+5,492	−811	+278	−533
6. Deduction for foreign taxes	−13,489	+1,062	−1,008	+54
7. Shares allocation, worldwide	−4,671	+2,330	−1,667	+663
8. Shares allocation, by U.S. only	−23,936	+682	−2,348	−1,318
9. 861 allocation, sales and assets used	−10,016	+723	−639	+84
10. 861 allocation, assets only used	−10,092	+763	−626	+137

Note: In millions of 1972 dollars.

This reduction in overseas investment causes large reductions in tax revenues in the United States and abroad. In fact, these changes are large enough to reverse the direction of change in total tax revenues; total tax payments now fall. Note that United States revenues still increase, although the change is smaller than with no or more modest response elasticities. Similar results hold for the simulations that repeal deferral.

In sum, the effects on investments now appear to swamp, or nearly swamp, the effects on total tax revenues. One implication is that the reforms do more to redistribute revenues from the foreign governments to the United States than they do to increase total tax payments.

This implication does not apply, of course, to the territorial treatment simulation, which reduces United States tax revenues. Note that changes in overseas investments are so large that United States revenues are affected even for this reform. Comparing row 5 of table 9.10 to the same line in tables 9.5 or 9.7 shows that the United States collects an extra $4 million as the result of the response in assets. This increase comes from the small flows of interest payments, royalties, and other fees paid by the subsidiaries to the parents. These flows are still part of the income of the parents and thus are taxed by the United States, even though the subsidiaries' profits are not taxed by the United States under this regime.

9.6 Conclusions

This paper looks at some aspects of United States tax policy toward multinational corporations. Six basic issues and nine specific reforms are formulated. The INTERSIM computer simulation package is used to estimate the effects of these reforms on investment decisions and tax liabilities.

It is important to emphasize the limitations of the analysis. First, it is necessary to work with cross-tabulated data rather than with data from individual firms. This fact makes dealing with the overall credit limitation somewhat difficult. Perhaps simulation of the per-country limitation, which is closely related, is inaccurate as a result. Further, the difference between the two plans for ending deferral is probably understated, since some of the subsidiaries with losses are hidden in the cross-tabulation process.

One could wish for better data, also, on quantities that are not now involved in the tax calculations but are important to the analysis. The prime example is assets of foreign subsidiaries. This number is required on the information returns filed by the corporations; however, since it does not affect tax liabilities, it is possible that neither the firms nor the IRS takes it very seriously. Biases may result in the simulations involving shares allocations, since they depend on assets to set the shares. The simulation of behavioral responses also relies on assets and may also be faulty. Of course, it is impossible to measure these biases with the current data.

Similar problems arise in measuring the special deductions needed for the 861 regulations regimes. Only a proxy could be used, since research and development expenses of the United States firms are not separately listed in the data or in published IRS statistics.

As discussed above, the analysis of behavioral responses by the firms is certainly not complete. Responses in financial decisions are given only summary treatment. Only partial equilibrium analysis of responses in investment decisions is attempted.

In sum, this paper extends previous analyses of United States taxation of international income in some ways. It uses data that afford an improvement since they provide information by industry and by country. A wider set of issues is examined, particularly in connection with allocation of income among national tax jurisdictions. Treatment of responses to tax changes in the investment decision of the firms is begun. However, it is clear that many extensions need to be done before analysis of these issues can be considered complete.

Appendix

Marginal Tax Rates on Domestic Activities: Two Examples

This appendix points out that international aspects of United States law may affect purely domestic activities of United States multinational corporations. Specifically, the marginal corporate tax rate on debt-financed capital is examined. It is well known that this tax rate is zero for a completely domestic firm.[18] Two simple examples are presented to show that this rate can differ from zero for a multinational firm even on its domestic activities.[19]

Consider a firm with investments as listed in rows 1–4, column 1, of table 9.A.1. Total investment in the United States is $2,000, of which half is debt financed. Investment abroad, which for simplicity involves only one foreign country, equals $1,000 and is all equity financed. What happens if the firm undertakes a new investment project at home and uses debt to finance it? Column 2 displays the results after a $1,000 project of this type is undertaken (the size is immaterial for the conclusions that follow).

18. See Stiglitz (1973).
19. For a more formal analysis of similar issues, see Frisch (1981).

Table 9.A.1   Example of Shares Allocation

	1	2
Capital stocks		
1. Domestic, equity financed	1,000	1,000
2. Domestic, debt financed	1,000	2,000
3. Foreign (equity financed)	1,000	1,000
4. Total capital	3,000	4,000
Taxable income		
5. Return to capital, (4) × .10*	300	400
6. Interest expense, (2) × .10	100	200
7. Taxable income, (5) − (6)	200	200
Taxes paid		
8. Allocation share, (3) ÷ (4)	.33	.25
9. Foreign taxable income, (7) × (8)	66	50
10. Tax paid to foreign gov., (9) × .60	39.6	30.0
11. U.S. tax before credit, (7) × .46	92	92
12. Potential foreign tax credit, (10)	39.6	30.0
13. Credit limitation, (9) × .46	30.4	23.0
14. Foreign tax credit, lesser of (12), (13)	30.4	23.0
15. Tax paid to U.S., (11) − (14)	61.6	69.0
16. Total taxes paid, (10) + (15)	101.2	99.0
Marginal tax rate on return to capital		
17. Change in tax, from (16)		−2.2
18. Change in return to capital, from (5)		100
19. Marginal tax (subsidy) rate, (16) ÷ (17)		−2.2%

*Row 4 times .10.

Assume that the return to capital equals 10% worldwide. Also, the worldwide interest rate is set equal to this rate by competition. Then the extra return to capital (in row 5) will be offset by the extra interest expenses (in row 6). If these expenses are deductible, taxable income is unchanged (in row 7). A purely domestic firm would therefore find its tax liability unchanged. The project would engender no increase in taxes; thus debt-financed capital would be untaxed at the corporate level. A similar result would hold for a multinational company facing a pure foreign tax credit mechanism based on arm's length principles.

Injection of shares allocation principles can alter this result, however. To see this, consider the simplest form of a shares allocation regime, with complete coordination worldwide and with only one factor, assets, used in the allocation formula.

The allocation share (in row 8) changes as the structure of assets changes. The result is that less income is allocated to the foreign government (in row 9) and, implicitly, more to the United States. The first effect is that taxes paid to the foreign government (row 10) fall.

This fall in taxes abroad is partially made up by a rise in taxes in the United States. Note that it is assumed, for simplicity, that the firm does not defer any foreign income. In this example, the foreign tax rate, 60%, exceeds the United States rate, 46%. Therefore the extra taxes at home do not fully offset the drop in taxes abroad. Rows 11–15 show this. Tax paid to the United States equals total income times 46% (row 11) minus foreign income times 46% (line 13), since the credit limitation applies. Since foreign income is lower, taxes paid to the United States (row 15) increase. However, row 16 shows that total taxes paid by the firm decrease.

In sum, total taxes paid by the firm fall by $2.20. Since return to capital rises by $100, there is an implied subsidy rate to capital of 2.2%. Although this result is highly sensitive to the assumptions, particularly relative United States and foreign tax rates, it is clear that the marginal tax rate on a purely debt-financed, purely domestic project is not identically zero.

The 861 regulations issued in 1977 incorporate some aspects of the shares allocation approach, as is discussed in the present paper. Table 9.A.2 presents a simple example of how these aspects can affect the marginal tax rate on the same type of project. Rows 1–7 of this table reintroduce the experiment.

The first difference between the tables is in computation of foreign taxable income, in rows 8 and 9. The arm's length approach is to be used for the basic allocation of incomes in this tax regime. Thus foreign gross income and deductions are computed separately, and foreign taxable income derived from them. Given the competitive assumptions made here and the assumption that no debt is used for foreign capital, foreign taxable income is simply equal to the marginal product of foreign capital. Since this capital does not change, neither foreign taxable income (in row 9) nor tax paid abroad (in row 10) changes.

The only aspect of taxes that is affected by the project is the foreign tax credit, computed in rows 13–17. Specifically, a special allocation of interest expenses, which are part of head office charges, is required. Row 13 displays the allocation share; as in table 9.A.1, it declines from 0.33 to 0.25. Interest expenses, however, increase as a result of the project. Therefore the required allocation (in row 14) rises. The foreign tax base to be used in the credit limitation (row 15) falls, and thus the limitation (row 16) falls. Since the limitation applies in this example, foreign tax credits (row 17) fall, and taxes paid to the United States (row 18) rise.

In sum, the project affects total taxes paid, even though neither domestic nor foreign taxable income is affected. As long as the firm is in a situation where the credit limitation applies, requiring the allocation of

Table 9.A.2   **Example of Aspects of 861 Regulations**

	1	2
Capital stocks		
1. Domestic, equity financed	1,000	1,000
2. Domestic, debt financed	1,000	2,000
3. Foreign (equity financed)	1,000	1,000
4. Total capital	3,000	4,000
Taxable income		
5. Return to capital, (4) × .10*	300	400
6. Interest expense, (2) × .10	100	200
7. Taxable income, (5) − (6)	200	200
Taxes paid		
8. Foreign return to equity, (3) × .10	100	100
9. Foreign taxable income, (8)	100	100
10. Tax paid to foreign gov., (9) × .60	60	60
11. U.S. tax before credit, (7) × .46	92	92
12. Potential foreign tax credit, (10)	60	60
13. Allocation share, (3) ÷ (4)	.33	.25
14. Allocation of head office charges, (6) × (13)	33	50
15. Foreign base for limitation, (9) − (14)	67	50
16. Credit limitation, (15) × .46	30.8	23.0
17. Foreign tax credit, lesser of (12), (16)	30.8	23.0
18. Tax paid to U.S., (11) − (17)	61.2	69.0
19. Total taxes paid, (10) + (18)	121.2	129.0
Marginal tax rate on return to capital		
20. Change in tax, from (19)		7.8
21. Change in return to capital, from (5)		100
22. Marginal tax rate, (20) ÷ (21)		7.8%

*Row 4 times .10.

interest deductions will reduce foreign tax credits and raise total taxes paid. Thus United States multinational corporations in this situation will face a positive marginal tax rate on purely domestic, purely debt-financed investments. In this example, total tax rises by $7.80, so that the marginal tax rate on a project of this type is 7.8%.

References

Bergsten, C. F.; T. Horst; and T. H. Moran. 1978. *American multinationals and American interests*. Washington: Brookings Institution.
Bradford, D., and R. Gordon. 1980. Taxation and corporate finance. Princeton University Financial Research Center Memo 31, January.

Dutton, J. 1980. Optimal taxation of international investment income. North Carolina State University Working Paper.

Feldstein, M., and J. Green. 1979. Why do companies pay dividends? NBER Working Paper no. 413.

Feldstein, M., and D. Hartman. 1977. The optimal taxation of foreign source investment income. Harvard Institute of Economic Research Discussion Paper no. 563.

Frisch, D. 1981. Issues in the taxation of multinational corporations. Ph.D. dissertation, Harvard University.

Horst, T. 1980. A note on the optimal taxation of international investment income. *Quarterly Journal of Economics* 94: 793–98.

Hufbauer, G., and D. Foster. 1976. U.S. taxation of undistributed income of controlled foreign corporations. In United States Department of Treasury, *Essays in international taxations: 1976.* Washington: Government Printing Office.

Internal Revenue Service. 1977. *Statistics of income, 1972, corporations.* Washington: Government Printing Office.

———. 1979. *Statistics of income, 1968–1972, foreign tax credit, corporations.* Washington: Government Printing Office.

———. 1979. *Statistics of income, 1968–1972, U.S. corporations and their controlled foreign corporations.* Washington: Government Printing Office.

King, M. 1977. *Public policy and the corporation.* New York: Halstead Press.

McDaniel, P. R., and H. J. Ault. 1977. *Introduction to U.S. international taxation.* Deventer, Netherlands: Kluwer.

McLure, C. E. 1980. The state income tax: Lambs in wolves' clothing. In H. J. Aaron and M. J. Boskin, eds., *Economics of taxation.* Washington: Brookings Institution.

Musgrave, P. B. 1973. International tax base division and the multinational corporation. *Public Finance,* pp. 394–411.

National Science Foundation. 1978. *Research and development in industry, 1975.* Survey of Science Resources Series. Washington: Government Printing Office.

Stiglitz, J. E. 1973. Taxation, corporate financial policy, and the cost of capital. *Journal of Public Economics* 2, no. 1: 1–34.

Surrey, S. S. 1978. Reflections on the allocation of income and expenses among national tax jurisdictions. *Law and Policy in International Business* 10, no. 2: 409–60.

Comment   Thomas Horst

Dan Frisch's paper represents a significant step forward in the economic analysis of United States taxation of the foreign income of United States–based multinational firms. The paper is particularly valuable in providing a precise description of the various and differing measures of foreign income relevant to the computation of taxable income. Although certain key issues are not dealt with—foreign currency translation being the most notable—the author is to be commended for incorporating systematically as many issues as he did.

The paper is also to be commended for examining a wide range of important policy issues. Surely the alternatives of exempting foreign source income, changing the limitation on the foreign tax credit to a per-country method, eliminating deferral, and replacing the foreign tax credit with a deduction from taxable income span the range of economically interesting changes and politically relevant possibilities. A particularly striking result is the high revenue cost to the corporations of a "shares allocation" system. The reason why the "unitary apportionment" method employed by California and certain other states has stirred such debate is easier to understand.

There are two aspects of the analysis which leave me somewhat uneasy. First, the seventeen-binational, one-multinational method of determining the potential for tax credit "averaging" is very clever, but unlikely in my view to yield reasonable results. Binational firms, apart from those with a Canadian subsidiary, are statistical freaks. The common pattern of foreign expansion is to establish operations first in Canada, then in one or more subsidiaries in Europe, next in the larger developed countries (Brazil, Mexico, etc.). The probable consequence of Frisch's assumption is to understate the extent to which foreign taxes are "averaged" under the overall limitation and thus the significance of requiring the per-country limitation.

A second and more fundamental criticism relates to the assumption that real investment varies inversely with the marginal tax rates but that financial parameters (e.g. the dividend payout rate) are fixed. Having often made the same or similar assumptions myself, I am reluctant to cast the first stone. But from my experience at the Treasury Department, I would conclude that financial behavior is most sensitive to tax consequences, the choice of legal form (branch versus subsidiary, selling versus licensing) is somewhat less so, and the location of real investment is the least sensitive. The differing degrees of sensitivity to tax consequences probably reflects the economic costs of modifying behavior and, perhaps, the organizational structure of corporations (tax, financial, and legal

Thomas Horst is a partner of Taxecon Associates.

expertise are often closely grouped within a corporation, but somewhat separate from operations). The point is important because the more a corporation can mitigate or avoid the impact of a tax change by modifying its financial behavior and/or its legal form, the less the pressure to relocate real investment. Although more difficult to model than real investment behavior, financial accommodation and legal accommodation of tax changes deserve more attention than they have yet received.

10 Domestic Tax Policy and the Foreign Sector: The Importance of Alternative Foreign Sector Formulations to Results from a General Equilibrium Tax Analysis Model

Lawrence H. Goulder, John B. Shoven, and John Whalley

10.1 Introduction

There is a growing recognition among public finance economists of the inappropriateness of closed economy models for analyzing alternative United States tax policies. Foreign trade has increased fairly sharply as a fraction of GNP and capital markets have become more international in scope since the early 1960s. United States investors participate in foreign capital markets both directly and indirectly through multinational corporations, and foreign direct investment in the United States has grown enormously since the early 1970s. In this paper we report on some alternative treatments of the external sector within an empirical general equilibrium model of the United States economy and tax system. This general equilibrium model has been described elsewhere (Fullerton, Shoven, and Whalley 1978; Fullerton, King, Shoven, and Whalley 1981). The new specifications of the external sector are motivated by the twin concerns of developing a general equilibrium analysis of tax policy where foreign trade issues enter, and of assessing the sensitivity of earlier results concerning alternative domestic tax policies to the specification of the external sector.

In previous analyses employing this general equilibrium model, we have given little emphasis to foreign trade. The external or foreign sector

Lawrence H. Goulder is with the Department of Economics, Harvard University. John B. Shoven is with the Department of Economics, Stanford University, and the National Bureau of Economic Research. John Whalley is with the Department of Economics, University of Western Ontario.

The research reported in this paper was supported by the Office of Tax Analysis, United States Treasury Department. The views are those of the authors and not of any organization. The authors are very grateful to Charles Ballard of Stanford University for outstanding research assistance.

was modeled quite simply, and relatively little attention was given to how the foreign sector might influence the United States economy. One simplifying assumption employed in previous versions of the model was that for each commodity the value of net trades between the United States and the rest of the world remained unchanged as prices changed. This assumption provided us with a convenient way of closing the model but was difficult to reconcile with utility maximization. Our alternative specifications are somewhat more complex but more plausible.

The first alternative we explore is the use of constant-elasticity excess demand functions (a constant-elasticity offer curve in the two-good case) to describe foreigners' merchandise trade behavior. We also consider a variant of this formulation in which certain imports are treated as imperfect rather than perfect substitutes for comparable domestic products. For both of these formulations, we consider several different elasticity parameters to evaluate model sensitivity. We then present two formulations which model capital mobility between the United States and the rest of the world. The first of these formulations introduces flows of capital services between the United States and abroad which depend on the difference between domestic and foreign rental rates. An elasticity parameter controls the sensitivity of capital service flows to differences in rental rates. The second of these formulations is similar but involves capital goods rather than capital services. These last two formulations permit us to model the United States as a taker of the rental prices of foreign capital. We were motivated to introduce these formulations partly by the belief that treating the United States in this way might significantly affect the model's evaluation of alternative tax policies.

In order to evaluate the sensitivity of the model to these different specifications, we analyze the integration of corporate and personal income taxes (Fullerton, King, Shoven, and Whalley 1981) and the elimination of savings distortions in the United States income tax (Fullerton, Shoven, and Whalley 1982) under each of these alternative formulations. We also consider the effects of adopting alternative forms of value-added tax (VAT) in the United States. We consider VATs of both the income and consumption type, and on both destination and origin bases.

The plan of the paper is as follows. First, we outline the structure of the basic tax model before any of the modifications we describe are incorporated. Then, we present our alternative foreign sector formulations and discuss the linkage between foreign trade issues and tax policy design. A final section of the paper presents results and major findings.

10.2   Main Characteristics of the Fullerton-Shoven-Whalley General Equilibrium Tax Model

The Fullerton-Shoven-Whalley general equilibrium tax model of the United States can be regarded as a higher-dimensional extension of traditional Edgeworth box analysis, with particular functions and parameter values used to represent preferences and production possibilities.[1] Taxes enter as ad valorem distortions of factor use, production decisions, and consumer purchases. The model generates sequences of equilibria through time. The equilibria are connected through savings decisions that imply different augmentations to the capital service endowment passed between periods. The model is calibrated to 1973 benchmark data assumed to lie on a balanced growth path for the economy.

The production side of the model includes nineteen profit-maximizing industries which use labor and capital according to constant elasticity of substitution (CES) or Cobb-Douglas production functions. Substitution elasticities are chosen for each industry as the central figures in Caddy's (1976) survey of the literature and range from 0.6 to one. We use data from the *Survey of Current Business* and unpublished data from the Commerce Department's National Income Division to obtain each industry's payments for labor and capital.[2] Base year quantities are derived according to the convention that a unit of each primary factor is that amount which earns one dollar net of taxes in the 1973 benchmark year. A fixed coefficient input-output matrix is derived from Bureau of Economic Analysis tables.

The ad valorem tax on each industry's use of capital comprises the corporation income tax, state corporate franchise taxes, and local property taxes. The social security tax and contributions to workmen's compensation are modeled as an ad valorem tax on industry's use of labor. Various federal excise taxes and indirect business taxes are modeled as output taxes; a different tax rate applies to each of the nineteen industries. State and local sales taxes apply to each of the fifteen consumer goods in the model.

The nineteen producer goods can be used directly by government, for export, or for investment. These producer goods can also be translated into the fifteen consumer goods which enter consumer demand functions. This translation is made possible by a fixed-coefficient G matrix.[3] The G matrix is necessary because the Commerce Department production side data include industries such as mining, electrical manufacturing, and trade, while the Labor Department's *Survey of Consumer Expenditures* provides data on purchases of goods like furniture, appliances, and recreation.

---

1. The model description given in the present paper draws heavily from section 2 in Fullerton (1980).

2. Labor compensation includes all wages, salaries, commissions, and tips, while capital earnings include net interest paid, net rent paid, and corporate profits with capital consumption adjustments and inventory valuation adjustments. Noncorporate profits were divided between labor and capital on the basis of full-time-equivalent hours and average wage for each industry. Some industries were averaged over several years to avoid recording transitory effects.

3. The G matrix derives from data in the February 1974 *Survey of Current Business*.

Industry and government payments to buy labor and capital services are exactly matched by total household receipts from the supply of each factor. The Treasury Department's Merged Tax File provides information on labor and capital income for each of our twelve consumer classes, as well as tax payments and an estimate of the average marginal income tax rate τ_j for each group. These range from a 1% average marginal rate for the first income class to a 40% rate for the highest income class. A progressive income tax system is then modeled as a series of linear schedules, one for each group. Pensions, IRA plans, and Keogh plans are modeled as a 30% saving subsidy to capture the proportion of saving that now has such tax-sheltered treatment.

We also model a "personal factor tax," a construct designed to capture discrimination among industries by the personal income tax. Each industry is assigned a fraction f_i representing the proportion of capital income from industry i which is fully taxable at the personal level. This fraction is determined from proportions of capital income paid as noncorporate income, dividends, capital gains, interest, and rent.[4] Taxable capital income is subject to τ, the overall capital-weighted average marginal personal income tax rate. At the consumer level, rebates are given to groups with a τ_j less than τ, while additional tax is collected from others. The personal factor tax acts as a withholding tax at the industry level, and corrections at the consumer level sum to zero. The model thus captures the favorable tax treatment given to industries with noncorporate investment tax credit and to the housing industry.

The expanded income of each consumer group is given by transfer income plus capital and labor endowments.[5] The latter is defined as 7/4 of labor income. The figure 7/4 results from our estimate that in the benchmark, forty hours are worked out of a possible seventy hours. Consumer demands are based on budget-constrained maximization of the nested CES utility function:

$$(2.1) \qquad U = U\left[H\left(\sum_{i=1}^{15} X_i^{\lambda_i}, l \right), C_f \right].$$

In the first stage, consumers save some income for future consumption C_f and allocate the rest to a subutility function H over present consumption goods X_i and leisure l. The elasticity of substitution between C_f and H is based on Boskin's (1978) estimate of 0.4 for the elasticity of saving with

4. All dividends are 96% taxable, because of the 4% that fell under the $100 exclusion in 1973. All retained earnings are 73% taxable. This results from the value tax deferral and rate advantages for capital gains, as well as the taxation of purely nominal gains. Interest and rents are fully taxable except for the imputed net rent of owner-occupied homes, while the noncorporate investment tax credit also appears as a personal tax reduction varying by industry.

5. Portfolio effects are ignored because dividends, capital gains, interest, rent, and other types of capital income are summed to obtain capital endowments.

respect to the net-of-tax rate of return. Saving in the model derives from consumer demands for future consumption under the expectation that all present prices, including the price of capital, will prevail in all future periods. Then income for H is divided between the purchase of leisure l and the purchase of a bundle of fifteen consumer goods. The composition of the consumer-good bundle derives from the maximization of a Cobb-Douglas function. The elasticity of substitution between leisure and consumer goods is based on an estimate of 0.15 for the elasticity of labor supply with respect to the net-of-tax wage.

Consumer decisions regarding factor supplies are thus made jointly with consumption decisions. Demands for leisure and for saving will depend on all relative prices, whether for factor endowments or for commodity purchases. Saving is converted immediately into investment demand for producer goods, with proportions based on national accounting data for fixed private investment and inventories.

In previous versions of the model, the foreign trade sector has been modeled such that the net value of exports less imports is constant for each producer good. This simple treatment closed the model, maintained zero trade balance, and allowed easy calculation of trade quantities, given prices. As we shall see in the next section, however, this specification was hard to reconcile with traditional trade theory; hence the alternative external sector formulations.

The specification of the government sector completes the model. Revenues from the various taxes described above are used for transfers, labor, capital, and producer goods. Lump-sum transfers to each consumer group are based on Treasury Department data for social security, welfare, government retirement, food stamps, and similar programs. Government demands for factors and commodities are represented by a linear expenditure system derived from a Stone-Geary utility function. In equilibrium the government budget is balanced.

Because the benchmark data required for this model are so comprehensive, the sources are necessarily divergent. The two sides of a single account are often collected by different agencies with different procedures, and thus do not match. In order to use all of these data together, there must be adjustments to ensure that each part is consistent with the rest. To do this we accept some data as superior and other data are adjusted to match. All industry and government uses of factors are taken to be fixed, so consumers' factor incomes and expenditures must be scaled. Tax receipts, transfers, and government endowments are fixed, so government expenditures must be scaled to balance their budget. Similar adjustments ensure that supply equals demand for all goods and factors.[6]

6. In particular, the input-output matrix does not conform to the requirement that gross output of each good can be measured by the column sum plus value added, or the row sum plus final demand. An iterative row and column scaling method is employed to generate a consistent matrix, and similar scaling satisfies similar conditions for the expenditure matrix.

The fully consistent data set then represents a benchmark equilibrium, where values are separated into prices and quantities by assuming that a physical unit of each good and factor is the amount that sells for one dollar. Certain elasticity parameters are imposed exogenously, and the model's equilibrium conditions are used to generate remaining behavioral equation parameters which are consistent with the data set. Factor employments by industry are used to derive production function weights, and household expenditures are used to derive utility function and demand function weights. We can use the resulting tax rates, function parameters, and endowments to solve the model, perfectly replicating the benchmark equilibriunm. This calibration allows for a test of the solution procedure and ensures that the various agents' behaviors are mutually consistent in our benchmark data set.

We use the Merrill (1971) variant of Scarf's (1973) algorithm to solve in each period for a competitive equilibrium in which profits are zero and supply equals demand for each good or factor. Simplex dimensions are required only for labor, capital, and government revenue, since a knowledge of these three "prices" is sufficient to evaluate all agent behavior. Producer-good prices are calculated on the basis of factor prices and the zero-profits condition, while consumer-good prices derive from producer-good prices through the G transition matrix. A complete set of prices, quantities, incomes, and allocations is calculated for every equilibrium. Since it is not based on differential calculus, the computational model can accommodate discrete changes in any tax or distortion without linearity assumptions and without ignoring income effects. There can be any number of sectors and agents, and any specifications of demand, so long as Walras's law holds.

The dynamic sequencing of single-period equilibria in the model first assumes that the 1973 consistent data set or benchmark equilibrium lies on a steady-state growth path. Observed saving behavior and the capital endowment are translated into an annual growth rate for capital (approximately 2.75%), and this growth is also attributed to effective labor units. This exogenous growth rate for labor is split evenly between population growth and Harrod-neutral technical progress. The benchmark sequence of equilibria is then calculated by maintaining all tax rates and preferences, increasing labor exogenously, and allowing saving to augment capital endowments over time.[7] By construction, this sequence will have constant factor ratios and constant prices all equal to one.

Policy change simulations are performed by altering tax rates while retaining preference parameters and the exogenous labor growth rate.

---

7. We convert a dollar of saving into capital service rental units through multiplication by γ, the real after-tax rate of return. The model assumes that twenty-five dollars of saving can purchase a capital asset that will earn one dollar per period net of depreciation and taxes. That is, a value of 0.04 is used for γ.

Saving and other behavior then conform to the specified elasticities, growth of capital diverges from the steady-state rate, and the economy begins to approach a new steady-state path with a new capital/labor ratio. Sequences are compared by discounting the H composites of instantaneous consumption through time with appropriate terminal conditions. Only leisure and present consumption are included in this welfare measure because saving is reflected in later consumption of the sequence. The sequence is discounted at a 4% rate and includes only the initial population. Otherwise, the importance of future periods would be sensitive to population growth.

The welfare gain or loss of a tax change is the aggregate compensating variation, defined as the number of dollars at new prices that would be required for each consumer to attain the old sequence of consumption values. The model thus incorporates both interindustry and intertemporal tax distortions and efficiency changes.

10.3   Different External Sector Formulations

In this section we outline alternative ways of modeling external sector behavior in the general equilibrium tax model of the United States. In section 10.4 we explore the sensitivity of results from various policy simulations to the external sector specifications.

10.3.1   The Existing Foreign Sector Specification

The external sector modeling currently used in the United States general equilibrium tax model focuses solely on commodity trade and ignores all capital transactions. Exports and imports are classified into three categories of producer goods: those for which there are net imports (seven commodities); those for which there are net exports (seven commodities); and those which are not traded (five commodities). The benchmark data set for 1973 is adjusted to guarantee that the value of total exports equals the value of total imports. The model then assumes that the value of net exports remains constant for each export commodity and the value of net imports remains constant for those commodities which are imported. For each of the import commodities we have

$$(3.1) \qquad P_i M_i = M_i^0,$$

and for the export commodities we have

$$(3.2) \qquad P_j E_j = E_j^0,$$

where M_i^0 and E_j^0 are the benchmark net import and export quantities, respectively. Recall that the benchmark prices are unity, by the units assumptions. P_i, M_i, P_j, and E_j are the current prices and quantities for imports and exports. Since initially

(3.3) $$\sum_j E_j^0 = \sum_i M_i^0,$$

we always have the condition that

(3.4) $$\sum P_j E_j = \sum P_i M_i,$$

or the value of exports equals the value of imports. This trade balance condition is necessary in a general equilibrium model that does not allow for international capital flows.

This modeling has several drawbacks. First, commodities cannot switch between being imported and being exported. Far more serious is the feature that import supply by foreigners reacts perversely to changes in commodity prices: this specification has import supplies negatively related to prices with an elasticity of -1.

A related problem with this treatment is that in the two-good analogue it implies an offer curve which is different from those usually found in traditional trade theory. This difficulty is transparent if we plot, for the two-good case, the foreign offer curve the United States economy is assumed to face. Suppose E and M each now refer to scalars rather than vectors; the constant-value net trade formulation implies

(3.5) $$E = E^0 P_E^{-1},$$

(3.6) $$M = M^0 P_M^{-1},$$

where E^0 and M^0 are base year exports and imports, and P_E and P_M are export and import prices, respectively. When superimposed on a diagram incorporating the usual form of home country offer curve (figure 10.2), this is seen to violate traditional trade theory on two counts: (a) the foreign offer curve does not go through the origin; and (b) the foreign offer curve is concave rather than convex to the M axis.

Clearly this simple formulation contains some major departures from traditional trade theory; consequently, we consider a number of alternative external sector formulations.

10.3.2   General Constant Elasticity Specification

The first alternative specification differs from the simple specification above in two main ways.[8] First, import supply functions are modeled so as to have a positive price elasticity. Second, the restrictive Cobb-Douglas type assumption of the previous specification—the assumption that the value of net exports remains constant for each commodity—is no longer employed.

---

8. This section relies on material presented in Whalley and Yeung (1980), which analyzes the external sector equation system discussed in Boadway and Treddenick (1978).

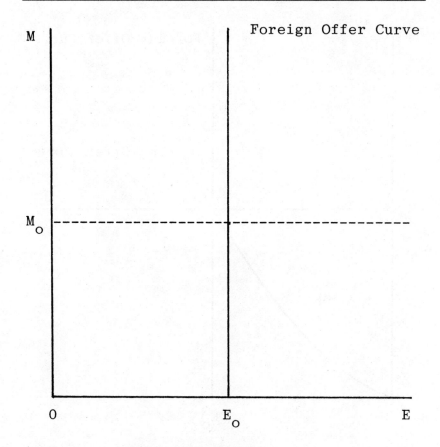

Fig. 10.1   Diagram of foreign offer curve.

In this formulation, the relative prices of traded goods are endogenously determined in the model. Trade balance is assured since foreigners' excess demand functions (export demand and import supply) satisfy budget balance.

This specification operates as follows. For each of the n producer goods (in the case of our model, $n = 19$), we specify an import supply function and an export demand function, with parameters μ and η as price elasticities of import supply and export demand, respectively:

$$(3.7) \qquad M_i = M_i^0 \left(\frac{P_{M_i}}{e}\right)^{\mu} \quad \begin{aligned} & 0 < \mu < \infty, \\ & i = 1, \ldots, n \end{aligned}$$

$$E_i = E_i^0 \left(\frac{P_{E_i}}{e}\right)^{\eta} \quad \begin{aligned} & -\infty < \eta < 0, \\ & i = 1, \ldots, n \end{aligned}$$

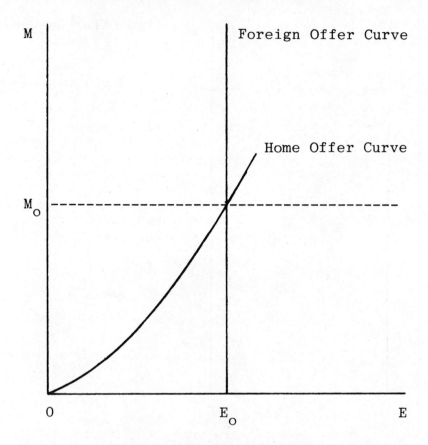

Fig. 10.2   Diagram of foreign offer curve with superimposition of traditional home offer curve.

where P_{M_i} is the domestic price of imports and P_{E_i} is the domestic price of United States exports (cost-covering price received by United States producers). The variable e can be interpreted as an exchange rate between domestic and foreign prices although we will show below how e can be removed by a simple substitution into the trade balance equation. As in all classical general equilibrium models which focus solely on relative goods prices, this exchange rate is a purely financial magnitude with no significance for real behavior in long-run equilibrium, although it is helpful for our exposition if we use this terminology.[9] P_{M_i}/e is the price the foreign exporter receives, and P_{E_i}/e is the price foreign purchasers must

9. No well-defined financial sectors are specified in our model; there is no domestic or foreign demand-for-money function which determines the relative prices of domestic and foreign monies (the exchange rate) in a purely monetary sense.

pay for United States exports. The sign restrictions on μ and η are discussed below.

In order to close the system and solve the general equilibrium model, we add the trade balance constraint that

$$(3.8) \qquad \sum_{i=1}^{n} P_{M_i} M_i = \sum_{i=1}^{n} P_{E_i} E_i.$$

If we substitute for M_i and E_i from equation (3.7), we have

$$(3.9) \qquad \sum_{i=1}^{n} P_{Mi} M_i^0 \left(\frac{P_{M_i}}{e}\right)^{\mu} = \sum_{i=1}^{n} P_{E_i} E_i^0 \left(\frac{P_{E_i}}{e}\right)^{\eta}$$

If we now define

$$(3.10) \qquad \begin{aligned} \alpha_1 &= \sum_{i=1}^{n} (P_{M_i})^{\mu+1} M_i^0, \\[2mm] \alpha_2 &= \sum_{i=1}^{n} (P_{E_i})^{\eta+1} E_i^0, \end{aligned}$$

equation (3.9) can be solved for the exchange rate parameter

$$(3.11) \qquad e = \left(\frac{\alpha_2}{\alpha_1}\right)^{1/(\eta-\mu)}.$$

Finally, substituting this result in (3.7) gives

$$(3.12) \qquad M_i = M_i^0 P_{M_i}^{\mu} \left(\frac{\alpha_2}{\alpha_1}\right)^{\mu/(\mu-\eta)},$$

$$(3.13) \qquad E_i = E_i^0 P_{E_i}^{\eta} \left(\frac{\alpha_2}{\alpha_1}\right)^{\eta/(\mu-\eta)}$$

Note that α_1 and α_2 are themselves functions of import and export prices, respectively. Equations (3.12) and (3.13) can be thought of as reduced-form import supply and export demand equations. Another interpretation is that they are the external sector behavior equations compensated for zero trade balance. They reflect the fact that one cannot simply specify an import supply elasticity and an export demand elasticity, and simultaneously assume zero trade balance. The trade balance condition provides a cross-equation restriction implicit in our solution procedure for equations (3.12) and (3.13).

Another thing to note about the reduced-form import supply and export demand equations is that they depend only on domestic prices: the exchange rate has been eliminated by substitution. Thus equations (3.12) and (3.13) depend only upon the real terms of trade given by the (α_2/α_1) term.

In the case where only two commodities are involved, the equation system (3.7) specifies an offer curve of constant elasticity which describes the excess demand functions for the foreign sector. The elasticity of the offer curve is

$$(3.14) \qquad \epsilon^{OC} = \frac{\eta}{1 + \eta} \frac{1 + \mu}{\mu},$$

and this parameter ϵ^{OC} is related to the price elasticity of both foreign export demand and foreign import supply through the equation (see Johnson 1953, chapter 2, appendix)

$$(3.15) \qquad \epsilon^{OC} = \frac{\epsilon_E^{FD}}{\epsilon_E^{FD} + 1} = \frac{\epsilon_M^{FS} + 1}{\epsilon^{FS}},$$

where ϵ_E^{FD} and ϵ_M^{FS} define the foreign price elasticities of export demand and import supply.

This implies that in terms of the reduced-form equations characterizing the system,

$$(3.16) \qquad \epsilon_E^{FD} = \frac{\eta(1 + \mu)}{\mu - \eta},$$

which for $\eta \leq -1$, $\mu > 0$ implies $\epsilon_E^{FD} \leq 0$. Also,

$$(3.17) \qquad \epsilon_M^{FS} = \frac{-\mu(1 + \eta)}{\mu - \eta}$$

and for $\mu \geq 0$, $\eta \leq -1$, $\epsilon_M^{FS} > 0$.

These elasticities imply that the true price elasticities of the system of foreign excess demand functions are not in fact given by η and μ as the equations (3.7) might seem to suggest, but by the more complicated forms described above. Furthermore, μ and η are not independent parameters but jointly imply an elasticity for the offer surfaces we use. To have the appropriate sign for the value of ϵ_M^{FS}, η must be less than -1 rather than simply negative as stated above.

Because of the form properties of this system, we describe this specification of the external sector as one where the United States is a taker of a foreign offer surface (satisfying a foreign economy version of Walras's law) of constant-elasticity form. The form of utility functions necessary to generate such surfaces is discussed more fully in Johnson (1953), and Gorman (1957). In the section in which we present our results, we discuss further our choice of μ and η.

When we analyze trade in homogeneous products, it is natural to assume that a country will not import and export the same good. This assumption can be expressed as

$$(3.18) \qquad E_i^0 M_i^0 = 0 \quad i = 1, \ldots, n.$$

However, the assumption is violated by empirical data: there are a number of commodities which are both exported and imported by the United States. This phenomenon of "cross-hauling" is evident from trade statistics, even with finely aggregated data, and underlies much of the recent literature on intraindustry trade (see Grubel and Lloyd 1975 and the subsequent literature).

There are many reasons for this phenomenon. In some cases, cross-hauling is dictated by explicitly noncompetitive behavior, such as that mandated by the United States–Canada automobile manufacturing agreement. However, it is also possible to reconcile cross-hauling with competitive behavior. One explanation asserts that foreign commodities are qualitatively different from domestic goods. This assumption of qualitative difference by country (e.g. United States and foreign cars being treated as close but not perfect substitutes) is referred to as the "Armington assumption," following Armington (1969). Cross-hauling can also be explained by reference to geography and transportation costs. For example, it may be perfectly sensible for the United States to export Alaskan oil to Japan and at the same time import oil through ports on the East Coast and the Gulf of Mexico, given the cost of delivering Alaskan oil to the eastern United States.

Previous versions of the model dealt only with net trade flows, as if trade occurred only in one direction for each commodity and there were no cross-hauling. In each of the new formulations, it is possible to deal only with net trades, as before, or alternatively to allow for cross-hauling. When cross-hauling is specified, it is necessary to substitute gross trade flows for net trade flows in the export demand and import supply equations. (For example, E_i^0 and M_i^0 would represent gross magnitudes in the base year in the previous equations in this section.) Although our formulations can incorporate cross-hauling, the reasons for the cross-hauling are not explicitly provided by the model.

10.3.3 Trade Modeling with Imperfectly Substitutable Imports

Our second external sector specification separates imports into two broad categories, depending on whether they are perfect or imperfect substitutes in production for domestically produced intermediate goods. We treat all of the imports discussed in previous subsections as perfect substitutes in production for United States producer goods. We then represent these imports as a negative component of final demand; as a consequence, every additional unit of import of producer good i reduces the gross output requirement of industry i in the model. Industries demanding intermediate goods from industry i are assumed to be indifferent as to whether those goods are produced at home or imported.

We now consider a model specification which allows some imports to be imperfect substitutes for domestic goods in production. Under this specification, we introduce a single new aggregated import commodity which enters the production structure as an imperfectly substitutable input.[10] This specification invokes the Armington assumption, since it assumes that there is a qualitative difference between the imported input and any domestic inputs used in production (Armington 1969).

The foreign excess demand equations are now

(3.19) $$M_i = M_i^0 \left(\frac{P_{M_i}}{e}\right)^\mu \quad 0 < \mu < \infty,$$
$$i = 1, \ldots, n,$$

(3.20) $$E_i = E_i^0 \left(\frac{P_{E_i}}{e}\right)^\eta \quad -\infty < \eta < -1,$$
$$i = 1, \ldots, n,$$

and

(3.21) $$R = R^0 \left(\frac{P_R}{e}\right)^\mu \quad 0 < \mu < \infty,$$

where (3.21) is the supply function for the import commodity ("resource") which enters the production structure. This commodity is different from all domestically available goods. The demand for imported resources is a derived demand based on production requirements (as with the other factors of production, labor and capital). M_i^0 and E_i^0 may represent either gross or net magnitudes as desired.

The trade balance condition is now

(3.22) $$P_R R + \sum_{i=1}^{n} P_{M_i} M_i = \sum_{i=1}^{n} P_{E_i} E_i.$$

Let

(3.23) $$\gamma_1 = R^0 (P_R)^{\mu+1} + \sum_{i=1}^{n} (P_{M_i})^{\mu+1} M_i^0$$

and

(3.24) $$\gamma_2 = \sum_{i=1}^{n} (P_{E_i})^{\eta+1} E_i^0.$$

Then, substituting (3.19), (3.20), and (3.21) into (3.22) and using the above notation, we get

(3.25) $$e = \left(\frac{\gamma_2}{\gamma_1}\right)^{1/(\eta-\mu)}$$

and

10. The quantities of this imperfectly substitutable import into each industry were based on rows 80A and 80B of the 1971 United States input-output matrix published by the Bureau of Economic Analysis of the Department of Commerce.

$$(3.26) \qquad M_i = M_i^0 P_{M_i}^\mu \left(\frac{\gamma_2}{\gamma_1}\right)^{-\mu/(\mu-\eta)},$$

$$(3.27) \qquad E_i = E_i^0 P_{E_i}^\eta \left(\frac{\gamma_2}{\gamma_1}\right)^{-\eta/(\mu-\eta)},$$

$$(3.28) \qquad R = R^0 P_R^\mu \left(\frac{\gamma_2}{\gamma_1}\right)^{-\eta/(\mu-\eta)}.$$

As in the previous section, these are the reduced-form or (trade balance) compensated import supply and export demand equations. They provide a constant elasticity set of excess demand functions to describe foreign behavior.

With this formulation, the production structure has also been modified to incorporate the imported resource. In the previous version of the model, the production function for each sector could be written as

$$(3.29) \qquad Q_j = \min\left[\frac{1}{a_{0j}}\mathrm{VA}(K_j, L_j), \frac{x_{1j}}{a_{1j}}, \ldots, \frac{x_{nj}}{a_{nj}}\right],$$

where the a_{ij} ($i = 1,\ldots,n$) are the fixed per unit intermediate input requirements, x_{ij} are the available intermediate inputs, $\mathrm{VA}(\cdot,\cdot)$ is a CES value added function with capital (K_j) and labor (L_j) as inputs, and a_{0j} is the requirement of value added per unit of output.

Under this new specification, the production function is

$$(3.30) \qquad Q_j = \min\left\{\frac{1}{a_{0j}}J[\mathrm{VA}(K_j, L_j), R], \frac{x_{1j}}{a_{1j}}, \ldots, \frac{x_{nj}}{a_{nj}}\right\},$$

where J is a CES or Cobb-Douglas function for each sector, and a_{0j} now represents the requirements of the resource/value added composite per unit of output. A critical parameter in this formulation is the value chosen for the elasticity of substitution between R and $\mathrm{VA}(K_j, L_j)$ for each sector. We denote these elasticities by σ_{VA}^R. We will return to the choice of values for σ_{VA}^R.

The solution procedure takes advantage of the separability of the production structure, as in the original Fullerton-Shoven-Whalley model. Each producer first calculates the optimal factor proportions to use in his value added function, given the minimum factor costs of production. From this information, the optimal combination of domestic factor value added and imported resources can be determined by minimizing the per unit cost of the J function. From this solution, we can compute all domestic producer prices using the Samuelson nonsubstitution theorem. These prices can be used to determine the government's demand for producer products, the foreign demand for producer goods (exports), and the supply of both producer-good imports and resource imports. The producer-good prices determine consumer-good prices, while the factor prices and the government revenue determine consumer incomes. Consumer demands are evaluated, and the derived demands for producer goods necessary to meet consumer demand for consumption and investment goods are computed. With these components, we can obtain the demand for domestically supplied producer goods, from which the derived demand for labor, capital, and imported resources is determined. Further, from all the transactions in the model, government tax receipts can be calculated. The excess demand for labor, capital, resources, and government revenue is then computed, and the model proceeds as in earlier versions, until an equilibrium set of prices and tax revenue is found where all markets clear.

This specification presents two additional data requirements. We use a modified version of the 1970 United States input-output table underlying our 1973 benchmark data, to separately identify a row of factor imports by industry in our input-output data. We also need to specify a substitution elasticity between United States value added and R. For these, we use estimates of the aggregate import price elasticity of import demand for the United States. In the central case we take the value (from Stern, Francis, and Schumacher 1977) of 1.7 to represent the pure substitution effect between domestic value added and imported resources, and take 0.5, 1.0, and 3.0 as sensitivity cases.

10.3.4   A Simple Modeling of International Capital Flows

To this point, our model formulations have not accounted for international capital flows. From a modeling perspective, however, it is very important whether a single international capital market or separate national capital market is considered, since this choice may significantly affect the perceived impact of a tax change. In this subsection, we present a simple formulation of international capital flows which allows foreign rental rates on capital to affect rental rates in the United States.

Here we add one consumer to the model—a "foreigner" endowed with large quantities of those commodities which the United States imports or exports, and with a large amount of capital services. In the benchmark year, the foreigner's endowment of each import or export commodity is usually set at five times the benchmark level of imports of that commodity by the United States, while the foreigner's capital services endowment is five times the United States capital services endowment in the benchmark. As part of a sensitivity analysis we have varied the magnitudes of the foreigner's endowments of goods and capital services. The foreigner "consumes" most of his endowments; that is, most of these import goods and capital services are used by the foreign economy rather than sold or rented to the United States. In the benchmark, in particular, the foreigner sells just the observed amount of import commodities (a fifth of his endowment) to the United States economy and purchases the observed quantity of export commodities (also a fifth of his endowment) from the United States. The foreigner rents no capital services to the United States in the benchmark; he thus consumes his entire endowment of capital services. A loose interpretation would be that these capital services are foreign resources which provide directly consumable output to the foreigner.

As United States prices change with a tax change, however, the foreigner alters his behavior. If the United States rental price of capital increases above the foreign rental price (exogenously fixed in real terms), the foreigner will "rent" some of his endowment to be used in United States production (i.e. there will be a capital inflow from the perspective of the United States). On the other hand, should the United States rental price of capital fall below the foreign rental price, the foreigner may "rent" United States capital for his foreign consumption (i.e. a capital outflow from the United States perspective).

This behavior is specified as

$$(3.31) \qquad W_K - X_K = W_K (P_K/P_{KF})^{E_K},$$

where W_K is the capital service endowment of the foreigner, X_K are capital services rented to the United States by the foreigner (or rented from the United States if X_K is negative), and E_K is an elasticity parameter controlling capital flow responses in the model. P_K and P_{KF} are the rental rates of capital in the United States and abroad, respectively. Since $P_K = P_{KF} = 1$ in the benchmark, the benchmark value of X_K is zero.

The critical parameters in this formulation are the ratio of W_K to the United States capital service endowment (five in our central case analysis) and E_K. E_K should be negative to give the capital service flow responses we require. In our central case E_K is -1.0. For sensitivity analysis, we use values for E_K ranging from zero to -10.0.

Equation (3.31) thus determines capital service flows in the model, once factor prices are known. A two-stage procedure is thus involved in determining foreign behavior. We first determine X_K, and from this we calculate income remaining to be spent on all other goods. For simplicity, the expenditure on other goods follows a Cobb-Douglas specification, with weights determined from benchmark data. A point worth noting is that equation (3.31) is not explicitly derived from utility-maximizing behavior of the foreigner. We focus on welfare evaluations for the United States only, and treat our model of the foreign sector as a model closure system which satisfies external sector balance and has the qualitative properties we desire.

Our motivation for this formulation incorporating capital service flows relates to the recent debate between Feldstein (see Feldstein and Horioka 1980) and Harberger (1980) about the degree to which the United States operates in a relatively competitive world capital market.

Feldstein, observing a high correlation between the savings of countries and their investment, argues that there are severe restrictions on the operation of a world capital market. Harberger asserts that this correlation is not so large and that this statistic is not sufficient evidence for concluding the malfunctioning of the world capital market.

This issue is important because of its implications for policy evaluation from general equilibrium tax models. In a world with a perfect, frictionless international capital market, the domestic choice between an income and consumption tax would not affect the aggregate employment of capital in the United States. Despite the fact that an income tax discourages saving by United States consumers and thus tends to discourage capital formation, the rest of the world would provide United States industry with capital until its rate of return was equal to the world level. However, an origin-based tax such as the United States corporation income tax would still be distortionary, affecting both the amount of capital in the economy and its allocation across industrial sectors. In their most recent exchange, Feldstein and Harberger seemed to be converging to the view that, while there is some pressure toward equalizing the rates of return to capital across world markets, this equilibrium is incomplete and even the partial movements observed take substantial amounts of time. We can capture the key aspects of this debate by altering E_K, the elasticity parameter for the demand for capital services by foreigners.

10.3.5 An Extension of the Capital Flows Modeling

The previous subsection has the rest of the world endowed with a large amount of capital services which it "rents" to the United States if the United States offers a higher rental price. If the rental price in the United States falls, the foreigner rents capital from the United States. While this is a step toward including world capital markets in our model, it fails to capture important aspects of foreign investment. Under this specification, a capital inflow involves a financial outflow (the United States must make the rental payments). In fact, the principal response to high United States rates of return is more likely to be direct foreign investment in the United States rather than the rental to the United States of foreign-owned capital. The rest of the world would *purchase* United States capital goods, providing an immediate financial inflow. Foreigners would then accumulate a claim on the future earnings of their acquired capital rather than receive immediate financial compensation.

This behavior can be incorporated in our model using a somewhat different representation of the "foreigner." The initial United States capital endowment of the foreigner is taken as zero. The foreigner, however, can acquire United States capital by purchasing the savings good (the 16th consumer good, which is a fixed proportion portfolio of real investment goods). He will do this if the expected rate of return on

United States investments rises above the expected rate of return on foreign investments. This will generate a capital and monetary flow. He is interested in the rate of return net of the corporation income tax, the corporation franchise tax, and property taxes. Should the United States rate of return fall relative to the foreign rate, he may sell foreign capital to domestic savers. Once again, we do not model the production structure of the rest of the world; rather, the foreigner simply "consumes" foreign capital as in the previous subsection.

This formulation is reasonably complex in terms of modeling. There now are two kinds of capital goods, foreign and domestic, offering separate (although conceivably identical) rates of return. Initially, domestic consumers own only domestic capital and the foreigner owns only foreign capital. The demand functions are structured such that the foreigners will save in the United States only if the United States rate of return rises above the foreign rate, whereas the United States consumers will purchase foreign capital service endowments only if the United States rate of return falls below the foreign rate. While the United States rate of return is endogenous in the model, the foreign rate is usually set at the benchmark rate, although it can be influenced by certain tax policies of the United States.[11]

Savings behavior in the United States stems from the same demand functions as in the Fullerton-Shoven-Whalley model, except that it involves not just a domestic savings good but a composite savings good aggregated over domestic and foreign savings goods. For each household,

(3.32)
$$S^D = \beta S,$$
$$S^F = (1 - \beta)S,$$

where S is total savings, and S^D and S^F are domestic and foreign savings goods acquired. β is a distribution parameter which depends on the relation between domestic and foreign rates of return (r^F, r^{US}):

(3.33)
$$\beta = 1 \qquad\qquad\qquad\qquad\quad \text{if } r^{US} \geq r^F,$$
$$\beta = \exp\left[-Z_1\left(r^F - r^{US}\right)\right] \quad \text{if } r^{US} < r^F.$$

Here r^F and r^{US} are expected rates of return to United States consumers. Because of differences in marginal tax rates, r^F and r^{US} each will differ across the twelve household classes distinguished by the model. We account for these differences in the model, although for convenience we speak of a single r^F and r^{US} in this discussion.

---

11. For example, in this model the foreign rate of return would be affected by a United States policy changing the percentage of United States consumers' savings which can be deducted from taxable income. Such a policy alters the after-tax price of savings to United States consumers, whether the savings are at home or abroad. Consequently, the policy affects the foreign rate of return to United States consumers of saving abroad.

In the benchmark $r^F = r^{US} = 1$ and $\beta = 1$ (United States households buy no foreign capital goods). In the solution of the model, β for each household is used to form a composite price for savings goods which enters household budget constraints. Household utility functions only have an interpretation over composite goods since we do not investigate real characteristics of assets (such as risk) which would account for a diversified portfolio by savers. We set Z_1, the elasticity parameter in equation (3.33), at 250 in our central case. We consider this figure to be roughly comparable to the E_K value of -1.0 in the previous specification.

The foreigner's savings in the United States, S^F_{US}, are given by

$$(3.34) \qquad S^F_{US} = 0 \qquad\qquad\qquad \text{if } r^{US}_F \leq r^F_F,$$
$$S^F_{US} = Z_2\left(r^{US}_F - r^F_F\right)^{Z_3} \quad \text{if } r^{US}_F > r^F_F.$$

Here r^{US}_F and r^F_F are United States and foreign rates of return expected *by the foreigner*. Because United States consumers and foreigners are not treated identically in the tax system, r^{US} generally differs from r^{US}_F, and r^F from r^F_F.

A two-stage procedure similar to that in subsection 10.3.4 applies here. First, we determine the foreigner's investment behavior abroad, with remaining expenditures allocated in a Cobb-Douglas fashion. In our central case analysis, we take Z_2 to equal 50,000 and Z_3 to equal 0.5. In this specification, our dynamic sequencing of equilibria takes account of previous investments abroad in determining capital service endowments in each country in each period. Investments abroad in a given period imply international capital service flows in subsequent periods.

In the following section, we investigate how the model's findings are affected by the four formulations we have just described.

10.4   Policy Analyses under Alternative External Sector Formulations

In this section we examine results from a number of policy analyses, using the various formulations of external sector behavior presented in the preceding section. We consider the introduction of an 80% savings deduction in the United States income tax (as considered by Fullerton, Shoven, and Whalley 1982). We also consider corporate tax integration in the United States (as considered by Fullerton, King, Shoven, and Whalley 1981), and the introduction of alternative forms of value-added tax in the United States.

We use the same dynamic sequence of equilibria approach used in the earlier papers by Fullerton et al. and compute sequences of equilibria linked through household savings decisions, as described earlier. In the base case, the economy is assumed to lie on a balance growth path. Under different policies, the economy is initially displaced from balanced growth and asymptotically returns to a new balanced growth path with a different ratio of capital service to labor endowment in each period. Our welfare analysis of gain or loss to the economy involves a calculation of the Hicksian compensating variation in each period for each household group. We first discount into present value terms, using the real net of return to capital as the discount rate, and then we sum over households.

Our analyses involve the same numerical specification used by Fullerton et al. We analyze six periods, each of ten years' duration, using the same values for all parameters which do not deal with the external sector. The various external sector formulations are incorporated as separate model extensions.

We refer to the four formulations as follows:

1. CONS ELAS NO ARM   Foreigners' behavior involves constant-elasticity demand functions (constant-elasticity offer curve in two-good case); no Armington product heterogeneity enters; no capital service or capital good flows are considered.

2. CONS ELAS WITH ARM   As in (1) except that we also consider Armington product heterogeneity for certain imported inputs.

3. CAP SERV FLOW   Flows of capital services take place between the United States and the rest of the world.

4. CAP GOOD FLOW   Flows of capital goods take place between the United States and the rest of the world.

These formulations were described above in subsections 10.3.2, 10.3.3, 10.3.4, and 10.3.5, respectively.

These formulations are listed in table 10.1 along with the values we have specified for the more critical parameters. In the case of the first formulation, the parameters μ and η imply an export price elasticity which the United States faces. We use an export price elasticity for the foreigner's demands of -1.4. This is approximately the central case value reported in the recent compendium of Stern, Francis, and Schumacher (1977). We use values for μ of 0.465 and η of -10. These jointly imply the -1.4 export price elasticity; the implied elasticity of the foreigner's import supply function is approximately 0.4.

For sensitivity analyses in this case, we consider μ and η set first at 10 and -10 and then at 1 and -1. For the 10, -10 case the export price elasticity is approximately -5. In the two-good case, as η and μ both become large (in absolute value), the elasticity of the offer curve approaches unity and this specification for the foreigner's behavior would imply that the United States is a small, open, price-taking economy. For

Table 10.1   Characteristics of Alternative External Sector Specifications

Specification	CONS ELAS NO ARM	CONS ELAS WITH ARM	CAP SERV FLOW	CAP GOOD FLOW
Section where described	10.3.2	10.3.3	10.3.4	10.3.5
Brief description	Constant-elasticity excess demands, no product heterogeneity, no capital flows, gross trade flows	Constant-elasticity excess demands, product heterogeneity for intermediate imports, no capital flows, gross trade flows	Capital service flows, no product heterogeneity, Cobb-Douglas commodity demands, gross trade flows	Capital good flows, no product heterogeneity, Cobb-Douglas commodity demands, gross trade flows
Critical parameters	μ, η	μ, η, σ_{VA}^{R}	E_K, RATIO*	Z_1, Z_2, Z_3, RATIO*
Values in central case	$\mu = .465$ $\eta = -10$ (jointly imply U.S. faces export price elasticity of -1.4)	$\mu = .465$ $\eta = -10$ $\sigma_{VA}^{R} = 1.7$	$E_K = -1$ RATIO = 5	$Z_1 = 250$ $Z_2 = 50,000$ $Z_3 = 0.5$ RATIO = 5
Sensitivity cases	$\mu = 10$, $\eta = -10$ $\mu = 1$, $\eta = -1$ Net rather than gross trade flows used	$\sigma_{VA}^{R} = 0.5, 1.0, 3.0$	$E_K = 0, -0.1, -10.0$ RATIO = 2, 10 Gross-of-tax rather than net-of-tax return to capital used	$Z_1 = 1,000, 100, 10$ $Z_2 = 100,000$ $Z_3 = .25, 1.0$ RATIO = 2, 10

*RATIO represents the ratio of the foreigner's benchmark endowments of capital services, input commodities, and export commodities to the United States benchmark endowments of capital services, level of imports, and level of exports, respectively.

the case of 1, -1 the export price elasticity is -1, and in the two-good case the elasticity of the offer curve is ∞. We also consider cases where net trade flows rather than the gross flows enter the benchmark calculation.

For the second formulation, the critical parameters are μ, η, and σ_{VA}^R. We take the same μ and η values as for the central case in our first formulation. σ_{VA}^R is set at 1.7. In our sensitivity runs, σ_{VA}^R is set at 0.5, 1.0, and 3.0.

For the capital service flow formulation, a critical parameter is E_K, which expresses the sensitivity of the foreigner's behavior to differences between the rental rates on capital employed in the United States and abroad. In our central case under this formulation, we set E_K at -1.0; in sensitivity runs we consider values of 0, -0.1, and -10.0 for E_K.

Another key parameter in this formulation is RATIO, the ratio of the foreigner's benchmark endowments of capital services, import commodities, and export commodities to the United States endowment of capital services, level of imports, and level of exports in the benchmark. RATIO is a rough indicator of the "size" of the rest of the world relative to the United States. In our central case, we set RATIO equal to 5; in sensitivity runs, we consider values of 2 and 10 for RATIO.

A final and important sensitivity analysis in this case involves the return to capital. In the central case, when foreigners rent to the United States, they receive P_K, the real net-of-tax rental price of, or return to, capital. P_{KF} is paid to the United States when Americans rent to foreigners. Because of the tax system in the United States, a differential exists between the marginal product of capital (the gross of tax price) and the net-of-tax return to capital. Thus the United States gains if it rents capital services from abroad, since the United States collects the marginal product of capital but pays the net-of-tax return to capital. Conversely, if the United States rents capital to the foreigner, the United States suffers a loss for the same reason. To correct for this, we calculate a tax rate which applies to international capital service transactions and use this new rate in one of our sensitivity cases.

For the capital good formulation, the critical parameters are Z_1, Z_2, and Z_3. These parameters determine the sensitivity of domestic households and of the foreigner to differences between domestic and foreign rates of return. We use values of 250 for Z_1, 50,000 for Z_2, and 0.5 for Z_3 in our central case. In sensitivity cases we consider values of 1,000, 100, and 10 for Z_1, 100,000 for Z_2, and 0.25 and 1.0 for Z_3.

10.4.1 Savings Deduction

In table 10.2 we show model results for a single tax policy—an 80% savings deduction—under the different external sector formulations. This policy, described in detail in Fullerton, Shoven, and Whalley (1982), represents a move from the current income tax system toward an expend-

Table 10.2   **Further Analysis of 80% Savings Deduction in United States Income Tax (dynamic welfare effects in present value of compensating variations over time)**

	Welfare Effect*	
1. Original Fullerton-Shoven-Whalley type of formulation	538	(1.10)
2. CONS ELAS NO ARM (central case)	511	(1.04)
3. CONS ELAS WITH ARM (central case)	479	(0.98)
4. CAP SERV FLOW (central case)	−476	(−.97)
5. CAP GOOD FLOW (central case)	−33	(−.07)

Note: All results are from runs including six equilibria spaced ten years apart. An "additive" method of tax replacement (see subsection 10.4.1) was employed in every case.

*In billions of 1973 dollars. The numbers in parentheses represent the welfare gain or loss as a percentage of the present discounted value of consumption plus leisure in the base sequence ($49 trillion).

iture or consumption tax system. The deduction is only 80% since roughly 20% of savings is used for new housing construction, which does not incur the "double" taxation of the income tax system. Thus an 80% deduction would closely approximate a full consumption tax system. We "additively" adjust marginal income tax rates (increasing or decreasing all rates by a certain number of percentage points) so that the total revenue raised by the government is not altered in any period by the policy change. We consider six equilibria spaced ten years apart.

The original analysis suggests a present value gain to the United States of $538 billion (1973 prices) from the tax change. It is useful to compare this number with the discounted present value of consumption plus leisure in the base sequence of $49 trillion (1973 prices). The gain thus amounts to 1.10% of this discounted present value of the economy. Put another way, after allowing for the change in the timing of consumption, and spreading the gain involved over a number of years, an 80% savings deduction increases total consumer welfare by 1.10% per year.

The first two external sector formulations do not change this broad picture very much. In the constant-elasticity case with no Armington good, the gain falls to $511 billion. With the Armington good, the gain falls further, to $479 billion. This result indicates that the terms of trade effects of the tax change are weak, a finding which contrasts with the papers by Boadway and Treddenick (1978) and Whalley (1980); these studies find significant terms of trade effects associated with changes in factor taxes. These two papers both incorporate a complete Armington specification which leads to stronger terms of trade effects. In addition, in the present formulation there are not substantial differences in factor intensities of export and import competing industries; as a consequence, the offer surfaces for the United States have only limited bowness.

The major changes in results occur with the capital service and capital good flow formulations. In the service flow case, the $538 billion gain changes to a $476 billion loss. The main reason for this has already been indicated above: the United States incurs substantial capital service outflows as a result of the policy change so that the United States foregoes the gross-of-tax return to capital (capital's marginal product), but only receives the net-of-tax return. In effect, the foreign tax authority gains at the expense of the United States Treasury, as a United States tax credit is given for foreign taxes paid. The cumulative capital service outflow in this case over fifty years is approximately $1.7 trillion. In the sensitivity analysis, we note that the efficiency loss is reduced and even reversed as the E_K parameter is reduced toward zero. An interesting policy prescription from this case is that the United States should either have additional taxes on capital income received from abroad or revoke the foreign tax credit. The additional tax rates, if used, should equal United States capital factor tax rates. This prescription ignores possible retaliatory consequences of such action. The capital good flow case reveals a similar result, although the effect is quantitatively weaker.

10.4.2 Sensitivity Analysis

In table 10.3 we report our sensitivity analyses for our two constant-elasticity formulations. Given that the central case results of these two forms do not differ significantly from each other or from those of the original specification, it may not be surprising that a similar conclusion applies for sensitivity cases. The choice of the μ and η combination, or whether gross or net trade flows are specified, makes very little difference in the cases with no Armington good. In the Armington cases, the results

Table 10.3	Sensitivity Analysis of 80% Savings Deduction in United States Income Tax for Constant-Elasticity Formulations (dynamic welfare effects in present value of compensating variations over time)

	Welfare Effect*
1. Original formulation (table 10.2, case 1)	538
2. CONS ELAS NO ARM	
Central case ($\mu = .465, \eta = -10$)	511
$\mu = 10, \eta = -10$	502
$\mu = 1, \eta = -1$	538
Net rather than gross trade flows	529
3. CONS ELAS WITH ARM	
Central case ($\mu = .465, \eta = -10, \sigma^R_{VA}\ 1.7$)	479
$\sigma^R_{VA} = .5$	446
$\sigma^R_{VA} = 1.0$	467
$\sigma^R_{VA} = 3.0$	487

*In billions of 1973 dollars.

are relatively robust with respect to changes in σ^R_{VA}. Gains fall from \$487 billion to \$446 billion as σ^R_{VA} is lowered from 3.0 to 0.5.

In table 10.4 we report our sensitivity analysis of the 80% savings deduction cases from table 10.2 for our capital service and capital good flow formulations. For the capital service flow formulation, a most dramatic result appears when the gross-of-tax rental price is employed instead of the net-of-tax price in international capital service transactions. In this case the large loss of \$476 billion in the central case changes to a gain of \$562 billion. This gain is even larger than in the cases without capital flows. The reason is that with a closed capital market the additional saving caused by the adoption of a consumption tax depresses the marginal product of capital more than with an international capital market. This demonstrates clearly the significance in the model of the United States instituting a compensatory tax on capital income received from abroad.

Sensitivity analysis for the capital service flow formulation also included changing E_K from -1.0 to 0.0, -0.1, and -10.0 and varying RATIO, the goods and service endowment ratio, between 2 and 10. As expected, the welfare loss is larger for higher absolute values of E_K. With $E_K = 0$, we get results essentially equivalent to the formulations without capital flows.

Table 10.4   **Sensitivity Analysis of 80% Savings Deduction in United States Income Tax for Capital Service and Capital Good Flow Formulations (dynamic welfare effects in present value of compensating variations over time)**

	Welfare Effect*
A. Capital service flow formulation	
1. Central case (table 10.2, case 4)	-476
2. Gross of tax rental price used in place of net tax price	562
3. $E_K = .0$ (changed from -1)	525
4. $E_K = -.1$ (changed from -1)	192
5. $E_K = -10.0$ (changed from -1)	-730
6. RATIO = 2 (changed from 5)	-221
7. RATIO = 10 (changed from 5)	-601
B. Capital good flow formulation	
1. Central case (table 10.2, case 5)	-33
2. $Z_1 = 1,000$ (changed from 250)	-337
3. $Z_1 = 100$ (changed from 250)	122
4. $Z_1 = 10$ (changed from 250)	441
5. RATIO = 2 (changed from 5)	-38
6. RATIO = 10 (changed from 5)	-26

*In billions of 1973 dollars.

Table 10.5   **Further Analysis of United States Corporate and Personal Tax Integration (dynamic welfare effects in present value of compensating variations over time)**

	Welfare Effect*	
1. Original formulation	265	(.54)
2. CONS ELAS NO ARM (central case)	287	(.59)
3. CONS ELAS WITH ARM (central case)	321	(.66)
4. CAP SERV FLOW (central case)	1,031	(2.10)
5. CAP GOOD FLOW (central case)	497	(1.01)
6. CAP GOOD FLOW (central cases)		
$Z_2 = 100,000$ (changed from 50,000)	666	(1.36)
$Z_3 = .25$ (changed from .5)	927	(1.89)
$Z_3 = 1.0$ (changed from .5)	326	(.67)

Note: All results are from runs involving six equilibria spaced ten years apart. An "additive" method of tax replacement (see subsection 10.4.1) was employed in every case.

*In billions of 1973 dollars. The numbers in parentheses represent the welfare gain or loss as a percentage of the present discounted value of consumption plus leisure in the base sequence ($49 trillion).

For our capital good formulation we only report sensitivity on Z_1 and the endowment ratio in table 10.4, because with an 80% savings case the United States saves abroad with no foreign savings in the United States.[12] Z_2 and Z_3 are immaterial in this case but have an effect in the integration cases reported below, where the capital good flow is in the opposite direction. We thus report Z_2 and Z_3 sensitivity later. Table 10.4 reveals significant sensitivity to Z_1 values; there is relatively little sensitivity to the values for RATIO.

10.4.3   Tax Integration

In table 10.5 we present further analyses of corporate and personal tax integration in the United States using the alternative external sector formulations presented earlier. Here we evaluate a policy of "full integration" as described in Fullerton, King, Shoven, and Whalley (1981). Such a policy involves the elimination of the corporate income tax accompanied by increases in personal taxes on capital income. The corporate income tax is eliminated for both domestic- and foreign-owned firms situated in the United States. Individuals are taxed on the basis of their total capital income, whether that income is realized (as dividends, rents, etc.) or accrues (e.g. as retained earnings).

As with table 10.2, the two constant-elasticity formulations do not make very much difference to results although gains increase rather than

12. For domestic consumers and more importantly for foreigners, this policy change lowers the United States rate of return relative to the foreign rate. Under these circumstances foreigners do not save in the United States (see subsection 10.3.5).

fall in comparison to the original. The capital service and capital good flow formulations, however, yield gains which are significantly higher than those under the original formulation. In these cases the gains are $1,031 and $497 billion, respectively. Tax integration induces a reallocation of capital from noncorporate to corporate sectors, since the latter experience a larger tax reduction from a policy of tax integration. This leads to an increase in the net-of-tax rental price of capital in the United States; the rental price and rate of return to capital rise in the United States relative to the rest of the world. Under the capital service flow formulation, this induces foreigners to rent their capital to the United States, while in the capital good flow formulation, this leads to foreign saving in the United States. In both cases, the United States experiences a substantial efficiency gain since it pays the net-of-tax return as its marginal product. We report sensitivity analyses on Z_2 and Z_3 for the capital good flow case; they have an impact in this situation as the foreigner saves in the United States (unlike the 80% savings deduction case).

10.4.4   Value Added Tax

In table 10.6 we present results from our simulations of introducing four alternative forms of value added tax (VAT) in the United States. Much of the recent discussion of value added taxation in the United States has been prompted by the VAT systems introduced in Europe over the last fifteen to twenty years. The destination-based VAT in Europe is seen in some quarters in the United States as a trade-restricting measure since exports leave Europe tax-free but imports are taxed as they enter. While this view is criticized by many academic economists who stress the

Table 10.6   **Welfare Impacts of Introducing 10% VAT of Differing Types (dynamic welfare effects in present value of compensating variations over time)**

	Income-Type VAT		Consumption-Type VAT	
	Origin Basis	Destination Basis	Origin Basis	Destination Basis
1. Original formulation	−42	−47	265	261
2. CONS ELAS NO ARM	−39	−39	256	256
3. CONS ELAS WITH ARM	−47	−47	213	213
4. CAP SERV FLOW	261	236	91	106
5. CAP GOOD FLOW	−529	−467	128	127

Note: All results are central case results for runs involving six equilibria spaced ten years apart. An "additive" method of tax replacement (see subsection 10.4.1) was employed in every case. Welfare effects are measured in billions of 1973 dollars.

neutrality of either tax base for a broadly based tax, it has nonetheless been influential in policy debate.

We model an origin-based VAT as an equal rate factor tax on both primary factors and a destination-based tax as an equal rate final sales tax on expenditures in the United States. Under the income-type VAT all goods are taxed; under the consumption-type only current consumption goods are taxed. We model the latter feature through a savings deduction for the origin-based VAT of the consumption type. We impose equal yield through an additive replacement in the income tax; income tax collections fall through a linear income tax reduction applied to all household income tax rates. These tax changes are thus regressive.

The VAT is constructed to be a nondistorting tax save for impacts on labor supply and savings. The introduction of this tax alternative therefore implies a scaling down of existing distorting taxes, which produces welfare gains. Consumption-type VAT gains are due primarily to the reduction in the intertemporal distortion of the income tax. In the consumption-type runs the VAT compounds multiplicatively with other taxes, and neutrality between origin and destination bases holds exactly for the Armington and capital service flow cases and nearly so for the other cases.

The welfare gains in the income-type VAT runs are generally smaller than in the corresponding consumption-type VAT runs. The gains are smaller because the income-type VAT inefficiently distorts individuals' consumption-saving decisions more than the consumption-type VAT, since the former tax applies to investment goods (as well as consumption goods) and in effect taxes savings. There is one exception to this general result: in the capital service flow case, the gains under an income-type VAT are larger than under the consumption-type VAT. The domestic rental price of capital eventually rises (relative to the foreign rental price) under the income-type VAT but falls (relative to the foreign price) under the consumption-type VAT. As a result, capital is rented to the United States under the former tax and from the United States under the latter, in the capital service flow formulation. Since, as discussed earlier, those offering capital overseas receive only the net-of-tax price of capital as compensation, the direction of the capital service flow is favorable to the United States under the income-type VAT and unfavorable to the United States under the consumption-type VAT. The favorable effect under the income-type tax more than compensates for any adverse impact related to the tax's distortion of consumption-saving decisions.

The policy prescriptions from these runs are that foreign trade concerns regarding destination- versus origin-based taxes do not provide a legitimate reason for the United States to introduce a VAT, but a broadly based VAT which replaces existing distorting taxes may be an efficiency-gaining tax change.

10.5 Conclusion

In this paper we have described four alternative external sector formulations which can be used to represent external sector behavior in the Fullerton-Shoven-Whalley tax model for the United States. Our motivations are twofold: to assess the impact of alternative formulations on model findings, and to provide an enhanced capability for the analysis of tax policies (such as a VAT) which connect closely with foreign trade issues. We consider two formulations of merchandise trade behavior using constant-elasticity excess demand functions for foreigners' behavior. We also consider internationally mobile capital services and capital goods.

Under these different formulations, we reinvestigate two policy alternatives considered earlier by Fullerton, King, Shoven, and Whalley (1981) and Fullerton, Shoven, and Whalley (1982): an 80% savings deduction in the income tax, and personal and corporate tax integration. We also examine the effects of introducing a 10% value added tax, of the income type or consumption type, on either an origin or a destination basis.

Results indicate that the different external sector formulations can substantially affect the model's findings. The allowance for capital service flows can either greatly increase the efficiency gain of a tax policy (as in the case of corporate tax integration) or turn a significant gain into a large loss (as in moving to a consumption tax). Each of the policies we investigated appears to have the potential to generate substantial capital service flows between the United States and abroad. When the net flow is from the United States to foreigners, the United States is adversely affected since those offering capital receive only the net-of-tax rental price. The specification of merchandise and service trade appears to affect our results far less than the capital flow modeling.

This paper indicates that the evaluation of domestic tax policy is very sensitive to the functioning of international capital markets. Therefore further research which reveals more precisely the operation of these markets would be most useful for future analyses.

References

Armington, P. S. 1969. A theory of demand for products distinguished by place of production. *I.M.F. Staff Papers*, pp. 159–76.

Boadway, R., and J. M. Treddenick. 1978. A general equilibrium computation of the effects of the Canadian tariff structure. *Canadian Journal of Economics*, August, pp. 424–46.

Boskin, M. J. 1978. Taxation, saving, and the rate of interest. *Journal of Political Economy*, vol. 68, no. 2, part 2.

Caddy, V. 1976. Empirical estimation of the elasticity of substitution: A review. Preliminary Working Paper OP-09, IMPACT Project, Industrial Assistance Commission, Melbourne, Australia, November.

Deardoff, A., and R. M. Stern. 1979. An economic analysis of the effects of the Tokyo round of Multilateral Trade Negotiations on the United States and the other major industrialized countries. MTN Studies no. 5, prepared for Subcommittee on International Trade, Committee on Finance, United States Senate, 96th Congress, Washington.

Feldstein, M., and C. Horioka. 1980. Domestic savings and international capital flows. Forthcoming in *Economic Journal*.

Fullerton, D. 1980. Transition losses of partially mobile industry specific capital. NBER Working Paper no. 520.

Fullerton, D.; A. T. King; J. B. Shoven; and J. Whalley. 1981. Corporate tax integration in the U.S.: A general equilibrium approach. *American Economic Review* 71: 677–91.

Fullerton, D.; J. B. Shoven; and J. Whalley. 1978. General equilibrium analysis of U.S. taxation policy. *1978 Compendium of Tax Research*. Washington: Office of Tax Analysis, United States Treasury Department.

———. 1982. Replacing the U.S. income tax with a progressive consumption tax: A sequenced general equilibrium approach. NBER Working Paper no. 892, May. Forthcoming in *Journal of Public Economics*.

Gorman, W. M. 1957. Tariffs, retaliation, and the elasticity of demand for imports. *Review of Economic Studies* 25: 133–62.

Grubel, H. C., and P. J. Lloyd. 1975. *The theory and measurement of international trade in differentiated products*. New York: Wiley, Halsted Press.

Harberger, A. C. 1980. Vignettes on the world capital market. *American Economic Review*, May.

Johnson, H. G. 1953. Optimum tariffs and retaliation. *Review of Economic Studies* 21: 142–53. Reprinted with amendments in H. G. Johnson, *International trade and economic growth*. George Allen & Unwin, 1961.

Merrill, O. H. 1971. Applications and extensions of an algorithm that computes fixed points of certain upper semi-continuous mappings. Ph.D. thesis, University of Michigan.

Scarf, H. E., with the collaboration of T. Hansen. 1973. *The computation of economic equilibria*. New Haven: Yale University Press.

Stern, R. M.; J. Francis; and B. Schumacher. 1977. *Price elasticities in international trade: An annotated bibliography*. Macmillan Publishers for the Trade Policy Research Center.

Whalley, J. 1980. Discriminatory features of domestic factor tax systems in a goods mobile, factors immobile trade model: An empirical general equilibrium approach. *Journal of Political Economy*, December.

Whalley, J., and B. Yeung. 1980. External sector "closing" rules in applied general equilibrium models. Mimeo, University of Western Ontario, April.

Comment   David G. Hartman

The analysis of domestic saving or investment incentives has nearly always ignored the role of international trade and investment. Because of the increasing importance of international transactions, this paper, which "opens" the economy previously modeled by Fullerton, Shoven, and Whalley, is particularly welcome.

The main contributions of the paper are in the warnings it gives to users of general equilibrium models which do not include a sophisticated foreign sector. Its lessons should include not only the potential importance of foreign influences for domestic policy analysis but also the unfortunate nonneutrality of the simple "model closure" conditions usually used to describe the foreign sector.

In particular, previous versions of the Fullerton, Shoven, and Whalley model had a very simple foreign sector in which the value of net imports for each imported good was taken as constant, as was the value of net exports for each exported good. The authors assert here that the previous specification was unfortunate since foreigners were assumed to respond "perversely" to price changes, i.e. with their export supply having a price elasticity of -1.

In fact, since only relative prices matter, a negative foreign supply elasticity, at least locally, is not as perverse as is alleged. Such an elasticity is indicative only of an inelastic foreign demand for United States export goods. That is, there is no reason why the foreign offer curve could not be as shown in figure 10.1 over some range. What is important is that far from the previous trade specification representing a neutral model closure condition, it guarantees that extreme terms of trade effects will result from United States policy changes. So, included in all of the "original formulation" results could be important welfare effects arising from the international trade sector. If not literally perverse, the implied foreign behavior is at least extreme. This fact not only casts doubt on the reliability of previous results but also explains some apparent anomalies

David G. Hartman is with the National Bureau of Economic Research and Harvard University.

in the conclusions one reaches when comparing the authors' new results to the original formulation.

The new trade sector specification developed in this paper is carefully done and attractive in allowing for a range of possible foreign responses to United States policy changes. Unfortunately, the industry detail of the original model is lost at this point, presumably because of the lack of reliable estimates of foreign demand and supply elasticities for individual goods. Since the trade balance condition links aggregate foreign export supply and import demand, only one parameter is required to completely describe foreign behavior: it is determined by the authors' choices of μ and η, as shown in equation (3.14). With the qualification that one cannot tell how sensitive the analysis is to this aggregation, the results are striking and quite reassuring, in that the welfare effects of domestic tax policies are not sensitive to the foreign elasticities. That domestic policies directed toward savings and investment would not produce major terms of trade effects should not be surprising in light of the international trade literature, which provides contradictory evidence on whether United States import or export goods are relatively more capital intensive.

In fact, the results in this paper are weakly supportive of the notion that United States imports are relatively capital intensive (the Leontief paradox). For example, a savings deduction provides greater welfare gains when foreign demand for United States exports is highly inelastic ($\mu = 1$ and $\eta = -1$) than when the United States is virtually a price-taker ($\mu = 10$ and $\eta = -10$). That is, increased investment results in the expansion of United States production of its import good. Similarly, the "original formulation" estimate of the welfare gain, which was implicitly based on highly inelastic foreign demand, was an overestimate if the "central case" is taken as the most plausible. Fortunately, the results in general show that the welfare effects of these domestic policy changes do not depend significantly on the values of unknown foreign parameters.

This standard welfare analysis neglects both the costs of short-run dislocations and the changes in distribution which accompany policy change. One lesson of simple trade models is that massive changes in production patterns, and hence relatively major adjustment costs, could result from changes in factor proportions in an open economy. Also, a sizable effect on the distribution of income among factors of production can be produced by smaller changes in the terms of trade. Thus, along with the increased openness of the United States economy comes the greater importance to policymakers of factors other than aggregate equilibrium welfare changes. While these issues are not explored in this paper, the authors' methodology would allow them to be considered in a sophisticated fashion.

While the aggregate welfare effects of policy are found to be insensitive to the traded goods sector specification, a more disturbing result emerges with respect to international capital flows. The conclusion that the usual analysis can be quite misleading in a world of highly elastic capital flows provides an important warning to researchers.

That capital flows could play a crucial role in determining the welfare effects of a policy to increase savings or investment should come as no surprise in the light of the arguments advanced by Peggy Musgrave (1969). Musgrave argued that United States investors will view foreign investment as attractive when after-tax returns abroad exceed those available at home. However, since a portion of the taxes paid on the foreign investment income accrue to the foreign government, the United States would earn a greater total return on its capital stock if foreign investment took place only when the after-foreign-tax return exceeded the gross return available at home. Allowing only a deduction for foreign tax payments, rather than the existing tax credit, would induce firms to follow a decision rule consistent with maximization of the total capital return, as the authors note here.

The qualitative results of this paper follow directly. Any change in domestic policy which stimulates saving produces a reduction in the domestic capital return, a capital outflow, and hence a tendency toward a loss in welfare. A simulus to investment, on the other hand, produces a capital inflow and a tendency toward a welfare gain, as the United States government collects a portion of the return to the foreign-owned capital.

Whether these welfare effects are sufficiently important to change the evaluation of a given policy depends on the elasticity of international capital flows. Since the size of this elasticity is highly controversial, the range of alternative results is crucial.

The range of results produced by different elasticity assumptions is very wide, but it is important to note that all the alternatives considered here are extreme by most standards. For example, under the central case of E_K equal to -1.0 (see table 10.4), only a 10% decline in the United States rental price of capital is required to cause half the United States capital stock to move overseas. The smallest alternative value of E_K considered is -0.1, which still implies a movement abroad of 5% of the United States capital stock in response to such a change in the capital return. This criticism should not detract from the clear thrust of the paper, which is methodological; but one should not be misled into believing that the broad range of results reported in this paper are produced by comparing the situation of no capital flows to cases of modest elasticity.

A further caution is that domestic policy measures which are straightforward to describe in a closed economy can become quite complex in a world of mobile capital. The very simple type of corporate and personal tax integration considered here represents only one of a wide variety of possible methods, which are discussed by McLure (1979). For example, foreigners could be denied relief from the tax, producing a reduction rather than an increase in foreign investment in the United States.

Obviously, very different outcomes could be expected from the various treatments of international investment under integration, so caution must be exercised in applying the authors' results.

This example also highlights the need to recognize the considerable stock of the United States capital currently invested abroad. While United States investment would not become more attractive to foreigners, it would become more attractive to United States investors under an integration scheme such as that just described. The welfare gain from inducing United States investors to repatriate capital, which is neglected here, is the subject of Griffin's (1974) analysis of integration. Even under the form of integration considered by Fullerton, Shoven, and Whalley, any welfare gains from capital repatriation should exceed those arising from foreigners' investment in the United States of the same amount, by the Musgrave argument. Thus the assumption that the original situation is one of no United States capital abroad tends to bias the results.

Finally, capital flows are assumed in the model to have no impact on the foreign demand and supply relations for goods. That assumption is, of course, not theoretically justified (see Jones 1967), but is very attractive compared to constructing a complete model of the rest of the world. This simplification would seem quite reasonable, except that direct investment, which is of particular concern in this paper, tends to be highly sector-specific. Foreign investment therefore can produce very direct terms of trade effects, the nature of which depend on such controversial factors as whether production abroad is a substitute for or complement to United States exports. Given the lack of evidence on these issues, the authors' specification seems sensible. Even more important, the basic domestic model, with its sectoral detail, does hold the potential for incorporating a more sophisticated description of foreign investment.

In general, the results reported here serve as a graphic reminder of how carefully tax policy must be conducted in a world of highly mobile capital. Unfortunately, it is with respect to capital flows that the least evidence is available. The authors have developed a powerful tool which requires much more information before its potential will be realized.

References

Griffin, J. A. 1974. The effect on U.S. foreign direct investment of the integration of the corporate and personal income taxes. Office of Tax Analysis Paper 22, United States Treasury Department.

Jones, R. W. 1967. International capital movements and the theory of tariffs and trade. *Quarterly Journal of Economics* 81: 1–38.

McLure, C. E. 1979. *Must corporate income be taxed twice?* Washington: Brookings Institution.

Musgrave, P. 1969. *United States taxation of foreign investment income.* Cambridge: Harvard Law School International Tax Program.

11   A Reexamination of Tax Distortions in General Equilibrium Models

Don Fullerton and Roger H. Gordon

General equilibrium models of the United States economy have grown much more realistic in the last few years (the late 1970s and early 1980s), becoming more disaggregated and using more recent and extensive data on differences in behavior among individual consumers and producers. Serious attempts have been made using these models to simulate the effects of several proposed tax changes, including integration of the corporate with the personal income tax and replacement of the income tax with a consumption tax. However, in attempting to capture the effects of the government on the economy, these models have generally assumed for simplicity that marginal tax rates equal the observed average tax rates and that marginal benefit rates are zero.

The main purpose of this paper is to derive improved estimates of various marginal tax rates and to take into account certain offsetting marginal benefits. We use the general equilibrium tax model of Fullerton, Shoven, and Whalley (1978, 1980, hereafter FSW) as a starting point for this remodeling effort. Most important, we include in the model recent theories developed in Gordon (1980) concerning the effects of combined corporate and personal taxes on firms' financial and capital intensity decisions. We also apply the same theoretical approach to the modeling

Don Fullerton is with the National Bureau of Economic Research and the Woodrow Wilson School of Princeton University. Roger H. Gordon is with the National Bureau of Economic Research and Bell Laboratories.

The authors thank Yolanda Kodrzycki Henderson for careful assistance throughout the course of this research. They also thank Tom Kronmiller, who helped with some of the programming, and Daniel Feenberg and Burton Malkiel, who helped obtain needed data. They are grateful to Charles McLure for thorough comments on a draft of the paper as well as helpful discussion throughout the course of the project. Finally, they thank the participants in the NBER preconference at Sturbridge, particularly David Bradford, for helpful comments on an earlier draft.

of governmental financial and capital intensity decisions. This approach takes explicit account of uncertainty, the flexibility of corporate financial policy, and inflation. In addition, we briefly reexamine the modeling of the property tax, unemployment insurance, workmen's compensation, and social security.

To test the importance of the above changes in the modeling of government-induced distortions, we resimulate the effects of the integration of corporate with personal income taxes. We find, contrary to FSW, that the welfare gains of lessening tax distortions through integration are more than offset by the welfare losses resulting from raising tax rates on labor income in order to replace lost revenue. This result is particularly strong because FSW included only intertemporal and interindustry allocation welfare gains, whereas we allow further welfare gains from eliminating the tax distortion which favors debt finance.

The organization of the paper is as follows. In section 11.1 we reexamine some of the marginal distortions created by the various taxes on labor. In section 11.2 we describe our modeling of the effects of corporate and personal taxes on firms' financial and investment decisions. We also describe here the construction of the data needed to calculate the new industry-specific marginal costs of capital. Section 11.3 describes a few other adjustments in the model made necessary by the change in the modeling of taxes on capital income. Finally, section 11.4 describes the simulation procedure and the results from our resimulation of corporate tax integration using our revised general equilibrium model.

11.1   Changes in the Modeling of Tax Distortions on Labor Income

While FSW carefully measure the size of the various taxes that apply to labor income, they ignore the fact that higher tax payments are often associated with larger transfer receipts. In particular, benefits are closely associated with tax payments in the social security program, in unemployment insurance, and in workmen's compensation. The taxes from these programs are distorting only to the degree that marginal taxes differ from marginal benefits. We discuss each of these programs in turn.

We do not attempt to take into account in this paper other transfer programs, such as food stamps, public housing, and AFDC, where benefits also create an implicit tax on labor income. We model these transfers as though they are paid in a lump-sum fashion, as did FSW. As a result, we may underestimate the welfare costs of increases in tax rates on labor income.[1]

---

1. This underestimation of welfare losses from the replacement tax serves to strengthen our result that this welfare loss more than offsets welfare gains from integration, as discussed below.

11.1.1 Social Security

The effect of current labor supply on future social security benefits is very complicated, as described in Blinder, Gordon, and Wise (1980). The present value of marginal benefits arising from further work will exceed marginal taxes for older men (at least as old as sixty-five) but will probably fall short of marginal taxes for the very elderly, for younger workers, and for most women. However, we have insufficient information to capture this diversity of net distortions. We would need to know the sex composition and age of workers in each industry as well as individuals in each consumer group. Instead, in the simulations below, we assume that the average net distortion from social security is zero, on the assumption that those facing a net subsidy come close to counterbalancing those who face a net tax. Since we therefore omit from the model the diverse distortions on individual labor supply created by social security, we may further underestimate the welfare costs of tax increases on labor income.

11.1.2 Unemployment Insurance

Most state unemployment insurance programs use a reserve ratio formula to set the firm's tax rate. This formula tries to ensure that the tax payments made by the firm just match the benefits received by its former workers. When this happens, workers anticipate future benefits equal in value to the taxes they currently pay, so the program should not distort labor supply decisions. For a discussion of the law and some remaining distortions, see Brown (1980).

However, state unemployment insurance programs also set a maximum and minimum tax rate on each firm. When a firm is at such a constraint, its workers should anticipate receiving either more or less in benefits, on average, than they currently pay in taxes, implying a net tax or subsidy. The degree to which this happens does differ systematically by industry. Becker (1972) examined the net transfers among industries in several states during the 1950s and 1960s and calculated a net tax or subsidy rate for many industries.[2] The appendix describes how we obtain labor tax rates for our industry classification from Becker's classification. Table 11.1, column 1, reports the resulting net unemployment insurance tax rates by industry.

11.1.3 Workmen's Compensation

The final change we made was to assume that workmen's compensation programs are nondistorting. While such programs are normally mandated by the government, the cost of the program to each firm is typically

---

2. For a discussion of the interindustry labor misallocations and general equilibrium incidence effects caused by this tax/subsidy system, see McLure (1977).

Table 11.1   Data Used in Calculating Tax Rates

	Labor Tax Rate	t_p^*	γ	δ_c	k	d	d_x
All Industries	.002	.005	.399	.079	.021	.036	.004
(1) Agriculture, forestry, and fisheries	−.035	.020	.159	.168	.039	.058	.020
(2) Mining	−.006	.010	.258	.096	.021	.054	.016
(3) Crude petroleum and gas	−.006	.021	.173	.107	.012	.013	−.010
(4) Construction	−.023	.009	.080	.110	.020	.094	.056
(5) Food and tobacco	−.004	.008	.253	.073	.061	.057	.020
(6) Textile, apparel, and leather	−.008	.015	.435	.092	.005	.213	.167
(7) Paper and printing	.009	.010	.268	.096	.043	.106	.059
(8) Petroleum refining	.008	.002	.194	.081	.037	.005	−.019
(9) Chemicals and rubber	.007	.006	.169	.079	.038	.081	.040
(10) Lumber, furniture, stone, clay, and glass	−.005	.007	.273	.111	.094	.081	.042
(11) Metals and machinery	.008	.009	.160	.095	.035	.064	.026
(12) Transportation equipment	.011	.050	.433	.108	.057	.117	.078
(13) Motor vehicles	.006	.003	.255	.092	.046	.039	.005
(14) Transportation, communication, and utilities	.006	.010	.497	.058	.035	.051	.013
(15) Trade	.007	.012	.313	.098	.025	.053	.015
(16) Finance and insurance	.012	.005	.605	.067	.049	.079	.041
(17) Real estate	.004	0	.787	.057	.001	.009	−.016
(18) Services	.008	.013	.503	.102	.011	.042	.006

*Note that t_p is half of the average property tax payment rate in each industry except real estate.

negotiated with a private insurance company. Competition among insurance companies implies that expected taxes and benefits ought to be equal for each firm. There are a few public programs, but these correspond closely in form to the private programs, and should therefore be nearly nondistorting as well.

11.2 Tax Distortions Affecting Firms' Financial and Investment Decisions

In the FSW model, corporate financial policy is exogenous, while capital intensity decisions are distorted by a marginal tax rate set equal to the observed average tax rate on capital income, calculated separately by industry. The average tax rate in each industry is set equal to the ratio of corporate, personal, and property tax payments in 1973 to capital income in that year. Capital is then allocated such that the rate of return to capital net of taxes and depreciation is equated in all industries.

This approach conveniently abstracts from the many detailed provisions of the United States tax law. However, it has many problems. Most immediately, the measured average tax rate depends critically on the measure for true earnings to capital. This latter number is difficult to calculate appropriately in any year and varies greatly from year to year. This variation implies that there is substantial measurement error in the calculated tax rates. In this paper, we instead model the tax law directly and calculate the cost of capital implied by the prevailing market interest rate and the existing tax law. While this procedure requires many new data in order to characterize the tax law by industry, it does not require capital income and tax payment figures, which can fluctuate sharply from year to year.

A more important reason for our remodeling, however, is that the explicit model of the effect of taxes on capital intensity decisions implies that marginal tax distortions differ dramatically from average tax rates, even if all figures can be measured without error. In this model, the government shares in the risk in the return to capital since its tax revenue is stochastic. The benefits to the firm of transferring to the government some of the risk in the return to its capital is not taken into account when calculating an average tax rate. This offsetting benefit turns out to be very important.

In addition to explicitly modeling a firm's capital intensity decisions, we model simultaneously how taxes affect the firm's optimal financial policy.[3] We assume that firms choose a debt-equity ratio which minimizes their cost of capital, trading off the tax advantages of debt against bankruptcy or other leverage-related costs. These leverage-related costs

---

3. For an earlier introduction of an endogenous debt-equity decision into a Harberger (1962) style general equilibrium model, see Ballentine and McLure (1981).

are real costs which profit-maximizing firms will choose to bear in order to save taxes and are part of the distortion costs created by the existing taxes on capital income.

In our model of both financial and capital intensity decisions, we explicitly model both uncertainty and inflation. The basic model, a generalization of the capital asset pricing model, is developed in Gordon and Bradford (1980).[4] It is further analyzed in Gordon and Malkiel (1980) and in Gordon (1980). In the next two sections, we briefly describe how in this model corporate financial and capital intensity decisions depend on the tax law.

11.2.1   Modeling of Corporate Financial Decisions

The tax law treats the returns to bonds and equity differently. First, only payments to bondholders are deductible from the corporate tax base. Counterbalancing this, however, the personal income tax is generally higher on income from bonds, since much of the income from equity is in the form of capital gains, which are taxed more lightly. Let $(1 - \alpha)$ represent the effective personal tax rate on nominal income earned from stocks, $(1 - \alpha_b)$ the effective personal tax rate on interest income from bonds, τ the corporate tax rate, and r the nominal interest rate paid on bonds. Then if the firm were to issue another dollar of debt and use the proceeds to repurchase a dollar of equity (holding the capital stock unchanged), the change in after-tax income to investors would be $\alpha_b r - \alpha r(1 - \tau)$. The new bondholder receives $\alpha_b r$ after taxes while the remaining equityholders lose only $\alpha r(1 - \tau)$ after both corporate and personal income taxes (when they pay the interest on the extra debt). Gordon and Malkiel (1980) show that for plausible values of α and α_b, the expression $r(\alpha_b - \alpha(1 - \tau))$ is positive, which implies that investors as a group can save on taxes by any and all increases in the firm's debt-capital ratio.

While replacing equity with debt is advantageous for tax reasons, a higher debt-capital ratio also implies a higher probability of default.

---

4. This version of the capital asset pricing model allows for an arbitrary variation in tax rates across investors and across types of return (e.g. interest payments versus capital gains). The key assumptions underlying the model are: (1) investors care only about the mean and the variance in the return on their portfolio, (2) only returns taxed at capital gains rates are stochastic, (3) capital gains are taxed at accrual, (4) there are no short sales constraints, and (5) the tax law allows for full loss offset. The latter assumption, as stated, is clearly false. A firm with tax losses has the ability, however, to carry losses backward and forward to other tax years, and it has the option to merge with a firm with taxable profits. Moreover, we are concerned with the marginal investment and not necessarily the marginal firm. Most of these marginal investments will be undertaken by preexisting firms that are, on average, profitable. Any loss on such a marginal investment would only serve to reduce the taxable profits of such a firm. We assume that, given these possibilities, full loss offset is a reasonable first approximation.

Bankruptcy and the threat of bankruptcy create real costs.[5] The firm's debt-capital ratio is in equilibrium when the increase in expected leverage-related costs resulting from replacing a dollar of equity with a dollar of debt just offsets the tax savings from using a dollar of debt instead of equity. Let γ represent the firm's debt-capital ratio, and let $c(\gamma)$ represent the increase in expected leverage-related costs borne by investors as a group from having an extra dollar of debt when the initial debt-capital ratio is γ.[6] Then in equilibrium γ is chosen such that $r(\alpha_b - \alpha(1 - \tau)) = c(\gamma)$. One would expect that $c(0) \approx 0$ and $\partial c/\partial \gamma > 0$. If there were no tax distortion favoring debt, this formula implies that the firm would use only equity finance and thus avoid all bankruptcy risk.

Leverage-related costs include more than just direct litigation costs in bankruptcy. As Warner (1977) and Gordon and Malkiel (1980) show, litigation costs themselves are very small. When the firm faces the possibility of bankruptcy, however, it also faces distorted investment incentives, as described in Myers (1977). When considering a risky investment, equityholders ignore the higher probability of losses to existing debtholders. Since equityholders receive any gains but pass large enough losses onto bondholders, they face distorted investment decisions. Though debtholders would presumably charge for these costs ex ante, distorted investment incentives would remain and equityholders would bear the costs of this inefficiency. In addition, labor costs can rise, since employees would be reluctant to remain in a job with an uncertain future. The function $c(\gamma)$ is intended to capture all such leverage-related costs.

Let D^* represent the amount of debt chosen to finance the capital stock K, and let $\gamma^* = D^*/K$. Then, since $c(\gamma)$ measures the marginal leverage costs of using a dollar more debt, $\int_0^{D^*} c(D/K)dD$ measures the total leverage cost borne by the firm's investors. If we assume that $c(\gamma)$ has the functional form $c(\gamma) = a\gamma^e$, then in equilibrium the total costs from having D^* of debt would be

$$(1) \qquad \frac{a\gamma^{*e}D^*}{e+1} = \frac{rD^*(\alpha_b - \alpha(1 - \tau))}{e+1}.$$

This expression provides a measure of the privately borne costs resulting from the tax distortion favoring debt finance.[7]

However, any extra expenses arising from a higher debt-capital ratio, e.g. resources spent negotiating and monitoring an agreement, would be deductible from the corporate tax base. These net of corporate tax costs

---

5. If there were no bankruptcy costs but merely a transfer of risk to bondholders, then the firm still would have the incentive to move to all debt finance, as shown in Modigliani and Miller (1963).

6. The form of the function $c(\gamma)$, and so the optimal value of γ, will vary by firm.

7. To the extent that others are hurt but cannot charge the firm for their costs, even ex ante, this measure is an underestimate of the private costs of leverage.

would then also reduce the individual's personal tax base. Therefore the expression for private leverage costs $c(\gamma)$ represents only $\alpha(1 - \tau)$ percent of the total (social) extra leverage-related costs resulting from replacing a dollar of equity with a dollar of debt. Total before-tax leverage-related costs can then be approximated by

$$\frac{rD^*(\alpha_b - \alpha(1 - \tau))}{\alpha(1 - \tau)(e + 1)}.$$

In the simulations of proposed tax changes, we will calculate the change in this estimate of leverage-related costs. This change represents an efficiency gain (or loss) resulting from changing the tax distortion which presently favors debt finance.

11.2.2   Modeling of Capital Intensity Decisions

✔ Corporate capital intensity decisions will depend on the cost of finance when the firm is using this optimal debt-capital ratio. We assume that the capital stock of a corporation is in equilibrium when investors are willing to pay just a dollar for the returns from an additional dollar of capital. Consider a type of investment where the returns are nonstochastic. Then the investment would be pursued using debt finance (with the capital as security), since there would be no leverage-related costs offsetting the tax advantage of debt. When the return to an investment is risky, however, the optimal percent of debt, γ^*, used in financing it will be lower because the firm will trade off the tax advantages of debt against the costs arising from the higher risk of default. If the return from new investment is just as risky as the return from existing capital, we would expect that the appropriate γ^* for the new capital would equal the existing γ for the firm as a whole. We will assume that these conditions hold, so that the marginal γ equals the average γ.

To be willing to finance a project, equity- and debtholders must receive at least the risk-free return after taxes, plus enough to compensate them for the risk that they bear. Define δ_c as the total after-tax risk premium required by corporate equity- and debtholders together on the return from each dollar they invest in the project. By definition, δ_c includes any leverage-related costs. Also, let r_z be the before-tax risk-free interest rate, and let ρ_c be the project's expected rate of return gross of both taxes and depreciation. Then, in equilibrium, the marginal investment ought to earn a ρ_c such that

$$(2) \qquad \alpha(1 - \tau)(\rho_c - \gamma r) + \alpha_b \gamma r = \alpha_b r_z + \delta_c.$$

The first term on the left-hand side measures the return to equityholders after taxes, and the second term measures the after-tax return to debtholders. This implies that

(3)
$$\rho_c = r_z \frac{\alpha_b}{\alpha(1-\tau)} - \gamma r \frac{\alpha_b - \alpha(1-\tau)}{\alpha(1-\tau)} + \frac{\delta_c}{\alpha(1-\tau)}.$$

The right-hand side of this equation in effect measures the before-tax rate of return to the investment required by the market. Note that, at the optimal debt-capital ratio, this expression is minimized.[8]

This derivation ignores many complications, however. Suppose that, for each industry, d is the geometric rate of economic depreciation of capital, and d_x is the constant geometric rate of depreciation for tax purposes that implies the same discounted present value of tax deductions as the more complicated tax law. Suppose that k is the effective rate of the investment tax credit, and t_p is the effective rate of state and local property tax (net of benefits) on the capital stock. Suppose also that π is the expected inflation rate. When all these additional factors are introduced, the equilibrium value of ρ_c will satisfy[9]

(4)
$$\rho_c = d + t_p + (1-k)r_z \frac{\alpha_b}{\alpha(1-\tau)} + \frac{\delta_c(1-k)}{\alpha(1-\tau)}$$

$$- \gamma r \left[\frac{\alpha_b - \alpha(1-\tau)}{\alpha(1-\tau)} \right] + \frac{\tau(d - d_x)}{1-\tau} - \frac{\pi}{(1-\tau)}.$$

Here, ρ_c is a *real* rate of return, while r and r_z are *nominal* risky and risk-free interest rates, respectively.

This formula is basically a generalization of the well-known formula for the cost of capital in Hall and Jorgenson (1967). If uncertainty is ignored (so $\delta_c = 0$ and $r = r_z$), if personal and property taxes are ignored (so $\alpha = \alpha_b = 1$ and $t_p = 0$), if inflation is ignored (so $\pi = 0$), and finally, if the possibility of debt finance is ignored (so $\gamma = 0$), the above formula simplifies to

(5)
$$\rho_c = \frac{d + r(1-k) - \tau d_x}{1-\tau}.$$

This formula now differs from that in Hall-Jorgenson only because the decision under consideration here is to invest a dollar now and then maintain a dollar of capital in place through later investments to offset depreciation. Hall-Jorgenson, in contrast, consider only whether to invest a dollar now.[10] Each of the generalizations included here changes the degree to which taxes affect the equilibrium marginal product of capital. In some cases they change it greatly.

---

8. Differentiating the right-hand side with respect to γ and equating to zero implies that $r(\alpha_b - \alpha(1-\tau)) = d\delta_c/d\gamma$. This equation is just the equilibrium condition for an optimal debt-capital ratio derived above, where $d\delta_c/d\gamma$ corresponds to $c(\gamma)$.

9. See Gordon (1980) for a derivation.

10. Hall-Jorgenson also describe tax depreciation allowances in terms of their present value Z rather than the equivalent constant flow d_x.

Now consider the capital stock of a noncorporate firm in the same setting. It will be in equilibrium when the nominal return (after depreciation and taxes) equals the after-tax return on a risk-free asset plus enough to compensate for the risk. Define δ_{nc} as the after-tax risk premium required by noncorporate proprietors in each industry on the return from each dollar they invest, and define m as the proprietor's personal marginal tax rate. Then, ρ_{nc} will satisfy

$$(6) \qquad \frac{1}{1-k}(\rho_{nc} + \pi - t_p - d) - \frac{m}{1-k}(\rho_{nc} - d_x - t_p)$$

$$= r_z(1 - m) + \delta_{nc}.$$

Solving for ρ_{nc}, we find

$$(7) \qquad \rho_{nc} = d + t_p + (1-k)r_z + \frac{\delta_{nc}(1-k)}{1-m}$$

$$+ \frac{m}{1-m}(d - d_x) - \frac{\pi}{1-m}.$$

In these equations, we have assumed that the proprietor finances the capital himself. If he obtains extra funds from another party with the same marginal tax rate, then the equation continues to hold, whether the proprietor borrows from the other individual or makes him a partner in the business. Since there is no tax advantage to debt finance here, debt will only be used when it creates no leverage-related costs. Also, since the proprietor's personal assets, as well as the business's assets, can be put up as collateral, debt can be kept riskless, and presumably free of leverage costs, much more easily here than in the corporate sector.

We modified equation (6) slightly for the real estate industry, which includes both rental and owner-occupied housing. For owner-occupied housing, there is basically no personal income tax on the returns to the investment, though t_p continues to be deductible, implying that in equilibrium

$$(8) \qquad \frac{1}{1-k}(\rho_{nc} + \pi - d - t_p(1-m)) = r_z(1-m) + \delta_{nc}.$$

The above analysis of noncorporate investment is also not quite appropriate for rental housing. We ignore any taxation of inflationary capital gains in other noncorporate business on the presumption that the gains would be realized sufficiently rarely, except at death when they would be tax free. In rental housing, however, gains are realized much more frequently. If g equals the effective capital gains tax rate, then the equilibrium condition becomes

(9)
$$\frac{1}{1-k}\,(\rho_{nc} + \pi - d - t_p) - \frac{m}{1-k}\,(\rho_{nc} - d_x - t_p)$$

$$-\frac{g\pi}{1-k} = r_z(1-m) + \delta_{nc}.$$

To obtain ρ_{nc} for the real estate industry as a whole, we took a weighted average of the equilibrium values for rental and owner-occupied housing. For weights, we used the sizes of the capital stock in each sector.[11]

In order to apply the above theory to the FSW general equilibrium model, several further assumptions must be made. Each industry will be characterized by its own values for d, d_x, k, and δ_{nc}, the risk premium when there are no leverage costs. In effect, the inherent riskiness and durability of capital assets used by each industry will be taken to be exogenous. The corporate sector in each industry will also be characterized by its observed values for γ and δ_c. However, corporate financial policy (γ) will be endogenous in the model, as will be the size of the leverage cost component of δ_c. A later section derives expressions for the inherent risk component of δ_c, which will remain constant, and the leverage cost component of δ_c, which varies with γ. When tax changes are simulated, these parameters γ and δ_c will vary systematically from their observed values.

The values for these industry-specific parameters, together with the market parameters r_z, r, π, τ, α, and α_b, determine a value of ρ_c for each industry. The same industry and market parameters are used along with a proprietor's tax rate m to determine a value of ρ_{nc} in each industry. We then take a weighted average of ρ_c and ρ_{nc}, using as weights the relative sizes of the corporate and noncorporate capital stocks in that industry. The percent of capital in each industry used by incorporated firms is assumed to be exogenous.[12] The resulting industry-wide value for the marginal product of capital we denote by ρ.

Given the market interest rates r and r_z, we have a separate value of ρ for each industry. Given the rest of the model, these values for ρ imply a desired capital stock for each industry. The sum over all industries of these desired capital stocks equal the total demand for capital. In each equilibrium simulation, the solution algorithm finds an r_z such that this

11. There are no explicit estimates for the proportion of housing capital that is owner-occupied. Using numbers from the *Statistical Abstract*, we multiplied the number of homeowners by the median value of owner-occupied homes, and then divided by the value of the total housing stock. These figures reveal that, although approximately 65% of households own their own homes, 85% of the value of housing stock is owner-occupied.

12. Too little is known about the responsiveness to tax parameters of the decision to incorporate to model this decision explicitly.

total demand for capital just equals the available supply of capital.[13] The supply of capital in each period is fixed, but the endogenous savings response of one period is used to appropriately augment the capital stock for the next equilibrium in the sequence. This process is described in more detail below.

11.2.3   Derivation of Data Required to Calculate ρ

In order to use the above procedure to calculate the equilibrium marginal product in each industry, many new data are needed. In this section, we describe how we calculate each of the needed variables. We calculate data values for 1973 in order to be comparable with the FSW model.

Property Tax Rates (t_p)

In FSW, the property tax is modeled as a distorting proportional income tax on capital. The benchmark tax rate on any industry is set equal to the observed property tax payments relative to net capital income in that industry. Since owner-occupied housing is included in the housing industry, this modeling applies to household as well as commercial and industrial payers of property taxes.

In the above derivation, the property tax was modeled instead as a proportional tax on the value of the capital stock. However, the appropriate value of t_p is not clear. The average tax rate can readily be calculated by taking the ratio of property tax payments to the value of the capital stock in each industry. However, local public expenditures financed by the property tax provide some offsetting benefits. Tiebout (1956), McGuire (1974), and Hamilton (1976) take both benefits and taxes into account and develop a set of assumptions under which the property tax on residential property is nondistorting. It is just a price at which households can purchase local public goods. The assumptions underlying this conclusion are strong. For example, they rule out any spillover of benefits across community lines. They also require a large number of communities, yet the population of each community must be sufficiently large that further expansion entails congestion costs which just offset the gains from sharing the costs of public expenditures with more people. In this paper, however, we will accept the Tiebout hypothesis for households as a first approximation. Specifically, we assume that the effective property tax rate in the housing industry is zero.[14] However, we do report briefly below

13. We assume that the bond risk premium $r - r_z$ equals a given preset value in all contexts. It would have been preferable to allow it to vary by industry and across simulations. Lacking the information necessary to do this seriously, we did not attempt to do it at all. Fortunately, sensitivity analysis indicates that the value of the risk premium $r - r_z$ has very little effect on the value of ρ.

14. The application of the Tiebout model to the property tax depends critically on the availability of zoning regulations (see Hamilton 1976). The argument does not apply to state and local income (wage) taxes, where zoning is not available to enforce the creation of

on a simulation where half of property taxes on housing are treated as distorting.

Application of the Tiebout hypothesis to commercial and industrial property seems less convincing. A defense of this application is developed in Fischel (1975) and White (1975). The essence of the argument is that if communities compete to obtain commercial and industrial property, then the property tax payments and the benefits will, in equilibrium, be set such that the community is indifferent to whether or not a new firm enters. As a result, a profit-maximizing firm will choose the most efficient location. Its tax payments may go not only to finance the benefits it receives but also to compensate the community for the noise, pollution, or congestion that it creates. In this setting it seems plausible to assume that the tax is nondistorting.

However, once a firm has located and is considering additional investment, it has lost its bargaining position with the community. To relocate, the firm would incur large fixed costs. The community may have some inhibition about exploiting captive firms. Some firms may indeed leave, and certainly new firms would as a result be more reluctant to enter. Yet in this context there is certainly less competitive pressure to equate additional taxes with additional benefits.

Because of the ambiguity of the theory, we ran two sets of simulations. In one simulation, all property tax payments were exactly offset by benefits. In the other simulation, half of nonresidential tax payments were assumed to be offset by benefits while all of residential tax payments were assumed to be offset by benefits. Together the two simulations provide a sensitivity test of the importance of the treatment of the property tax. The effective tax rates t_p used in the second case are reported in column 2 of table 11.1. These parameters equal half of the observed property tax divided by the capital stock in that industry.

Corporate Debt-Capital Ratios (γ)

Gordon and Malkiel (1980) used data from the COMPUSTAT[15] tape to estimate the ratio of the market value of debt to the market value of debt plus equity. This calculation included firms with securities traded on the New York Stock Exchange, on the American Stock Exchange, and over the counter. Only economy-wide figures were reported in that paper. Here, we used the same procedure to calculate the ratio separately for each of our eighteen private industries.[16] The resulting figures for 1973 are reported in column 3 of table 11.1.[17]

communities with homogeneous income as well as homogeneous tastes for public services. We therefore continue to treat state and local income taxes as distorting taxes.

15. COMPUSTAT is a data set compiled by Standard and Poor Corporation containing balance sheet information on many publicly traded corporations.

16. Only the book value of debt is reported on the COMPUSTAT tape. We used figures from von Furstenburg, Malkiel, and Watson (1980) on each industry's average ratio of

Risk Premiums (δ_c and δ_{nc})

Consider a particular security s, with an expected after-tax return $\bar{r}_s$, where the overbar indicates expectations. The capital asset pricing model implies that the risk premium $\bar{r}_s - \alpha_b r_z$ ought to equal $\beta_s(\bar{r}_m - \alpha_b r_z)$, where $\bar{r}_m$ is the expected after-tax return on the market portfolio, and β_s is the covariance of r_s and r_m, divided by the variance of r_m. The risk premium can be measured either directly, by using $\bar{r}_s - \alpha_b r_z$, or it can be measured indirectly, by estimating β_s for that security and multiplying by the expected risk premium on the market portfolio

Here, in estimating δ_c, we have chosen the indirect method to measure the risk premium on equity in each industry and the direct method to measure the risk premium on bonds. The risk premium δ_c appropriate for a dollar invested in corporate capital in each industry is then the sum of the risk premium on γ dollars of debt and the risk premium on $(1 - \gamma)$ dollars of equity.

To calculate each industry's risk premium on equity, we proceeded by first estimating the β for a value-weighted portfolio of the equity from all firms in the industry which were traded publicly on the New York Stock Exchange. The estimation was done over the period 1969–73 using the Center for Research in Securities Prices monthly returns data. The market portfolio was taken to be a value-weighted portfolio of the equity from *all* firms traded on the New York Stock Exchange. The risk premium on the equity in each industry is then this estimate of β times the expected excess return on the market portfolio, which Merton (1980) estimates to be 0.1075.[18]

Lacking information about how the risk premium on bonds varied by industry, we assumed a common risk premium of $\alpha_b(r - r_z)$, which equals 0.0246 using the parameter values discussed below. The value of δ_c was then set equal to $0.1075(1 - \gamma)\beta + 0.0246\gamma$ in each industry. Implicitly we assume here that the potential new capital in an industry is equally as risky as the existing capital. The resulting values for δ_c by industry are reported in column 4 of table 11.1.

The value of δ_{nc} ought to differ from that for δ_c for two major reasons. First, given present tax law, investment will be riskier in the corporate sector where tax incentives favor debt. For noncorporate investment, no taxes are saved through debt rather than "equity" finance, so there is no

market value to book value of debt to construct figures for the market value of debt for each firm on the tape. When the ratio of the market value of debt to the book value of debt was not available for a specific industry, we applied the economy-wide ratio to the firms of that industry.

17. The debt-value ratio, as calculated here, will differ slightly from the debt-capital ratio used in the theory, however. In particular, a dollar raised in the market is sufficient to purchase $1/(1 - k)$ dollars of capital yet is valued in the market at a dollar. Therefore the calculated debt-value ratio would equal $\gamma/(1 - k)$, where γ is the debt-capital ratio.

18. We used the estimates from Merton's model 3, estimated over the time period 1962–78.

tax incentive to accept real leverage-related costs.[19] Therefore the risk premium on a noncorporate investment ought to be smaller than that on an otherwise equivalent corporate investment since it ought to be free of leverage-related costs.

To estimate the additional leverage cost arising from investment in one more dollar of corporate capital, assume that leverage costs are proportional to the size of the capital stock for any firm, holding γ constant. The marginal leverage costs would then equal the expression for privately borne leverage costs derived earlier, divided by the size of the capital stock, or

$$\frac{\gamma r(\alpha_b - \alpha(1 - \tau))}{e + 1}.$$

Without the tax distortion favoring debt, the corporate risk premium would be smaller by this amount.

A second reason for δ_{nc} to differ from δ_c is that the government absorbs a different percent of the risk from investment in each sector. The risk borne by investors on a dollar investment would differ between the sectors, even if the inherent[20] riskiness of the investment were the same, because the tax rates differ. Because of taxes, the risk borne by corporate investors is only $\alpha(1 - \tau)$ percent of the total risk in the return to corporate capital. Similarly, noncorporate investors bear only $(1 - m)$ percent of the total risk in the return on their capital.

We assume that these are the only two reasons why δ_{nc} differs from δ_c. In particular, we assume that noncorporate capital is just as risky as corporate capital, leverage costs aside, and that noncorporate investors charge the same risk premium per unit risk that they bear as do corporate investors.[21] We then conclude that

$$(10) \qquad \delta_{nc} = \frac{1 - m}{\alpha(1 - \tau)} \left(\delta_c - \frac{\gamma r(\alpha_b - \alpha(1 - \tau))}{e + 1} \right).$$

In the simulations, we will assign to the investment in each industry a constant inherent risk premium δ equal to $\delta_{nc}/(1 - m)$. (This measure corrects for the fact that only $(1 - m)$ percent of noncorporate risk is borne privately and does not include any leverage costs.) The risk premium appropriate for privately borne risk in the noncorporate sector will then be simply $(1 - m)\delta$. Only if the proprietor's tax rate changes in a

---

19. There may be other reasons besides taxes to prefer debt finance, however.

20. By "inherent risk," we refer to risk associated with the capital asset, regardless of financing and regardless of taxes.

21. Noncorporate investors may not have the same ability to spread risk, however, since their securities are not publicly traded, so they may require a larger risk premium. The tax system may discourage incorporation where risk bearing is more efficient, but we ignore this tax distortion and assume that the risk premium required per unit risk is indeed the same.

simulation would the noncorporate risk premium change. Similarly, the corporate risk premium for privately borne risk will be set equal to

$$(11) \qquad \delta_c = \alpha(1 - \tau)\delta + \frac{\gamma r(\alpha_b - \alpha(1 - \tau))}{e + 1}.$$

Thus, if the tax incentive favoring debt is reduced, the leverage cost component of δ_c will decline.

Investment Tax Credit Rates (k)

After an April 1969 repeal, the investment tax credit (ITC) was reintroduced in 1971. It allowed any corporate or noncorporate business to subtract from its tax bill 7% (4% for public utilities) of its eligible investment expenditures, defined as equipment with at least a seven year useful life. One-third credit was allowed for assets with three to five year lives and two-thirds credit for five to seven year lives. The 7% statutory rate was increased to 10% in 1975 and subsequently made permanent. The parameter k in above formulas, however, refers to an effective ITC rate on all investment (including inventories and plant as well as equipment). It ought to take into account all limitations, carry-forward, and carry-back provisions. Because the proportion of investments which are eligible for the credit, or for different fractions of the credit, will vary by industry, the effective ITC rate k will also vary by industry.

In order to estimate this effective ITC rate in each industry, we looked at the dollar value of credit taken in a particular year relative to that year's total investment. Because the credit taken in 1973 may not reflect the credit which eventually accrued to 1973 investments, we took the average of the effective rates in 1973 and 1974.[22] We thus tried to obtain a "steady state" rate which accounts for carry-forwards and carry-backs. The appendix provides details concerning how the data were obtained. The resulting figures for the effective ITC rates appear for each industry in table 11.1, column 5.

Economic Depreciation Rates (d)

The above formulas require eighteen annualized rates of depreciation for the industries defined in this model. Several other studies[23] have estimated rates of depreciation using various assumptions and various investment disaggregates, but none is immediately applicable for our purposes. Some studies, however, provide dollar values of economic depreciation for industry definitions similar to ours. Using time series on investment by industry, we can estimate geometric annual rates of depreciation for use in this model.

22. These are the two years for which the best data were available. The same 7% credit rate applied from 1971 to 1975.
23. See, for example, Christensen and Jorgenson (1969) and Hulten and Wykoff (1980).

Looking at a particular industry, suppose that ED_i is the dollar figure for economic depreciation in the ith year during the period 1972 to 1974. The sources for data on ED are described in the appendix. We then tried to find that geometric depreciation rate on all prior investments in that industry which would be most consistent with the observed values ED_i. Let I_t^R represent gross real investment undertaken in year t, in year i dollars. Then, if there were geometric depreciation at rate d, economic depreciation in year i would equal

$$ED_i^{pr} = \sum_{t=0}^{\infty} d(1-d)^t I_{i-t}^R.$$

Here, the superscript "pr" indicates the predicted, in contrast to the actual, ED_i.

One problem, of course, is that investment data by industry were not available prior to 1947. The small effect of pre-1947 investment can be approximated by assuming that investment in all years before 1947 grew at the same rate μ. We estimated μ to be 0.027 for all nonresidential investment and 0.021 for residential investment from aggregate data available over the period 1929 to 1947. If these two categories of real investments did grow at these rates before 1947 and if the same depreciation rate applied in all years before 1947, then the depreciation on pre-1947 investments in 1972 would be

$$(12) \qquad d\int_{26}^{\infty} I_{1947}^R e^{-\mu(t-26)} e^{-dt} dt = \frac{dI_{1947}^R e^{-26d}}{\mu + d},$$

where 26 is the number of years between 1946 and 1972. In general, then, we approximated ED_i^{pr} by

$$(13) \qquad ED_i^{pr} = \frac{dI_{1947}^R e^{-d(i-1947+1)}}{\mu + d} + \sum_{t=0}^{i-1947} dI_{i-t}^R (1-d)^t.$$

We then chose that value of d for each industry which minimized the sum of squared differences between the observed and predicted ED_i during the period 1972–74. The appendix provides information about the sources of the data and further details about the procedure. The eighteen resulting economic depreciation rates d are reported in table 11.1, column 6.

Tax Depreciation Rates (d_x)

Above formulas used d_x as the effective constant nominal depreciation allowance for tax purposes per dollar of maintained capital. We estimated this concept by starting with the assumption that the tax law allows exponential depreciation at an annual rate d' based on historical cost. (Derivation of the value of d' which best approximates the actual tax code is described below.)

In the situation of equation (4), we consider an additional dollar of investment which is maintained in nominal terms through subsequent replacement investment at the rate $(d - \pi)$. Exponential depreciation for tax purposes at rate d' on this maintained investment will generally not result in a constant stream of allowances. Though d' may remain constant, the remaining basis for tax purposes does not. In particular, the basis in the first year is one dollar, while the basis in the second year is $(1 - d') + (d - \pi)$. The second year basis will not equal one dollar if $d \neq d' + \pi$. The inflation rate enters here since tax depreciation is based on historical cost. Since the basis is nonconstant, depreciation allowances of d' times the bases are also nonconstant.

As shown in Gordon (1980), the value of d_x, which is constant over time and which implies the same present value of deductions for corporations as the nonconstant d' stream, would satisfy

$$(14) \qquad d_x = d' \frac{(d - \pi) + r_z(1 - \tau)}{d' + r_z(1 - \tau)}.$$

(For noncorporate firms, the same expression applies, except that τ is replaced by m.) We therefore can solve for d_x on the basis of figures for d' and other data.[24]

Analogous to the economic depreciation rates d, the tax depreciation rates d' are estimated from IRS depreciation data and time series on investment. Looking at a particular industry, suppose that TD_i is the dollar figure for tax depreciation in the ith year between 1972 and 1976. We then solved for the geometric depreciation rate d' that best approximates the observed tax depreciation allowances TD_i, using a procedure similar to that used in solving for d. If I_t measures the nominal investment in a given industry which occurred in year t, then d' was chosen so as to minimize

$$(15) \qquad \sum_{i=1972}^{1976} (TD_i - TD_i^{pr})^2,$$

where

$$TD_i^{pr} = \sum_{t=0}^{i-1947} d'_{i-t} I_{i-t} (1 - d'_{i-t})^t$$

$$+ \frac{d'_{1947} I_{1947} \exp(-d'_{1947}(i - 1947 + 1))}{\mu + d'_{1947}}.$$

Here, d'_t is a function of time since the relevant tax law changed several times during the period. Also, μ here refers to the growth rate for nominal investment prior to 1947, estimated to be 0.057 for nonresidential investment and 0.059 for residential investment. In the appendix, we

---

24. In the simulations, d' is kept constant while d_x varies due to changes in r_z, τ, or m.

describe how I_t and d'_t were obtained. The eighteen resulting effective constant tax depreciation rates d_x for 1973 appear in column 7 of table 11.1.

Proprietors' Marginal Tax Rates (m, g)

The parameter m represents the average personal marginal tax rate paid by proprietors in the noncorporate sector. In principle, this marginal tax rate should vary by industry, but we found no data capable of providing such information. Instead, we used the NBER TAXSIM programs to calculate economy-wide average marginal tax rates for business income, supplemental schedule income, partnership income, and small business corporation profits. We then set m equal to 0.365, the weighted average of the average marginal tax rates for each category of income.[25]

The parameter g represents the effective capital gains tax rate on rental housing. By 1973 tax law, only half of capital gains is taxable. We assumed in addition that the postponement of the tax payment until realization halves the effective tax rate. We therefore assumed that $g = 0.25m = 0.091$.

Other Parameter Values (r_z, e, α, α_b, r, π, τ)

There remain several economy-wide parameters that need to be estimated for 1973. For r_z, the nominal before-tax risk-free interest rate, many economists have used the Treasury bill rate, which equaled 0.07 in 1973. While Treasury bills are not risky in nominal terms, they are risky in real terms. Lacking any better estimate, we assumed the risk premium in the Treasury bill interest rate was 0.02, implying a risk-free interest rate of 0.05. As a sensitivity test, we also report results for a 0.07 risk-free rate.

We estimated e using time series data for γ and the market interest rate. According to the theory developed in section 11.1, the debt-capital ratio will be in equilibrium when $c(\gamma) = a\gamma^e = r(\alpha_b - \alpha(1 - \tau))$. This implies that

$$(16) \qquad \log(\gamma) = \frac{1}{e}\log\left(\frac{\alpha_b - \alpha(1 - \tau)}{a}\right) + \frac{1}{e}\log(r).$$

If a, e, α_b, α, and τ are all constant across time, e can be estimated by regressing $\log(\gamma)$ on $\log(r)$ and a constant term using time series data, and taking the inverse of the estimated coefficient of $\log(r)$. Gordon and Malkiel (1980) provide yearly data on γ for the period 1958–78. For r, we

---

25. In calculating capital income in each category to use as weights, we followed the Treasury Department procedure of assuming that only 30% of business income, partnership income, and small business corporation income is really return to capital, the rest being return to labor. We would like to thank Daniel Feenberg for performing these calculations for us.

used a yearly commercial paper rate. When we regressed log (γ) on log (r), we obtained

$$\log(\gamma) = -2.44 + 0.557 \log(r),$$
$$(0.19) \quad (0.116)$$

where standard errors are in parentheses under the coefficient estimates.[26] We therefore used $1/0.557 = 1.79$ as an estimate for e.

Next, consider α and α_b, the personal tax parameters for equity and bonds. There is no need to estimate each parameter separately since it is only their ratio α_b/α which matters in any of the computations.[27]

Let us consider then the problem of measuring the ratio α_b/α. The first problem faced is that the tax treatment of the returns to equity depends on whether the returns take the form of dividends or capital gains. It is not clear how to proceed since economists do not yet have a good explanation for why dividends are paid, given their unfavorable tax treatment (see Black 1976). By repurchasing shares, a firm can create a dollar in capital gains in lieu of paying a dollar in dividends, and presumably would do so if capital gains were valued more highly by the market. Since firms do pay dividends, we assume that the market does value dividends and capital gains equally. In fact, Gordon and Bradford (1980) estimate the value in the market of dividends versus capital gains and find that the market value of a dollar of dividends does not differ systematically from the market value of a dollar of capital gains. That is, dividends must provide some other advantage which offsets their tax disadvantage. We therefore assume that the effective tax rate on equity is the capital gains tax rate.

The ratio α_b/α thus measures the value in the market of a dollar of interest payments relative to a dollar in either dividends or capital gains. According to the derivation in Gordon and Bradford (1980), this ratio is a weighted average of the valuation each investor gives to interest relative to capital gains.[28] The weights are proportional to the investor's wealth and inversely proportional to a measure of his risk aversion. We there-

26. Of course, if any of the terms assumed to be constant had varied significantly over time, then the estimate of e could be biased. Probably the most important problem is that any increase in the riskiness in the economy during the period would have caused the function $c(\gamma)$ to shift upward, raising the parameter a. If this had occurred, our estimate of e should be too high, implying that our estimate of leverage costs may be too small.

27. The only place where α appears alone is in the term $\delta_c/[\alpha(1 - \tau)]$. However, δ_c, while defined to be the after-tax risk premium, is estimated in this paper as in others by using before-personal-tax data. The resulting estimate therefore equals δ_c/α directly, avoiding any need for a separate estimate of α.

28. Some authors, e.g. Miller (1977), have constructed models with sharp clientele effects, where α_b/α would equal the marginal tax rate of the marginal individual investing in bonds rather than stocks. All other individuals specialize in either bonds or stocks. However, in a model with uncertainty and no short sales constraints, as in Gordon and Bradford (1980), all investors will hold some amount (positive or negative) of both types of investment, so that everyone is a marginal investor.

fore calculated an estimate for α_b/α directly from the twelve consumer groups of the FSW model by taking a weighted average of their relative valuations of interest and capital gains. In doing so, we made the following assumptions: (1) risk preferences do not vary across consumers, (2) the effective tax rate on capital gains is one-eighth of the tax rate on interest,[29] and (3) only 70% of an individual's investments are taxable. According to 1973 *Flow of Funds* data, approximately 30% of savings were in pensions, IRA accounts, or other tax-free vehicles. The implied value of α_b/α was 0.82.

The remaining parameters r, π, and τ were directly observable. We set $r = 0.08$ and $\pi = 0.05$,[30] on the basis of the data for 1973 appearing in the *Economic Report of the President*. We set $\tau = 0.48$, the statutory tax rate in 1973.

11.3   Other Changes to the Fullerton, Shoven, and Whalley Model

11.3.1   Modeling of Government Enterprises and General Government

The FSW model includes not only the eighteen private sectors described above but two government sectors as well. One, government enterprises, includes government-run business activities, mainly the post office and TVA. This sector was modeled like the other private industries except that it received a large output subsidy from general government. The other sector, general government, captures the remaining activities of government. We need to calculate equilibrium values for ρ for these two "industries" comparable to those which characterize the other eighteen industries to help determine the demand for capital. Unfortunately, we do not have available the same quality of information for these two sectors.

We assume that government enterprises are cost-minimizing industries which meet all demand at the output prices dictated to them by higher levels of government. We assume therefore that they invest until the real marginal product of their capital is just high enough to cover depreciation, the real risk-free interest rate, and a suitable risk premium δ_G. Formally, we assume that $\rho = r_z - \pi + d + \delta_G$.[31] Lacking any independent information about d in this industry, we assume that it equals the weighted average of the values in the eighteen private industries, where

29. Only one-half of capital gains was taxable in 1973. In addition, the effective tax rate is approximately halved due to the postponement of tax payments until realization. We assume it is about halved again due to the markup of the basis at death and due to the selective realization of capital losses sooner than capital gains.

30. While π represents the expected inflation rate, we set it equal to the observed rate on the assumption of myopic expectations.

31. This equation can be derived from equation (7) by setting $\delta_{nc}/(1 - m)$ equal to δ_G, and setting k, t_p and m equal to zero.

the weights are the sizes of the capital stock in each industry. To construct an estimate for δ_G, we first calculate for each private industry the value of the risk premium on a dollar of capital that would prevail if there were no leverage costs (as with noncorporate investments) and if all risk were borne by the private sector. This risk premium would equal $\delta_{nc}[(1 - k)/(1 - m)]$.[32] We then took the weighted average of these values over the eighteen private industries.

General government includes all remaining activities of government. It receives revenue from the various taxes and from selling its endowment of capital on the market. Part of the total revenue is earmarked for lump-sum transfers to each consumer group. The benchmark transfers are based on data for welfare, government retirement, food stamps, and similar programs.[33] As prices change in a simulation, government maintains the same real payments in transfers to each group.

General government also purchases each of the nineteen producer goods (eighteen private industry outputs and government enterprises output), plus capital and labor. In doing so, it is assumed to maximize a Cobb-Douglas utility function whose arguments are these nineteen producer goods plus capital and labor.

The question here is the appropriate measure for the cost of capital to government. Since most of the capital used in general government is used in state and local governments,[34] we model capital intensity decisions in this sector as if they were entirely local public decisions.

The capital intensity of a community's public sector is in equilibrium when the (assumed) homogeneous residents in that community are indifferent to adding an extra dollar of capital. The community must also decide whether it is cheaper to finance its capital stock directly through property taxes or indirectly through the municipal bond market. The key tax factors in determining the equilibrium ρ here are: (1) property tax payments are deductible from taxable personal income if the residents itemize, (2) the interest rate paid on debt is the municipal bond rate, and (3) there is no tax on the "profits" of the sector.

In calculating the equilibrium marginal product of capital in the local public sector, let us assume that γ percent of an additional dollar of capital investment under consideration would be financed by debt. Let n equal the effective personal marginal tax rate at which residents deduct

---

32. The extra term $(1 - k)$ enters because $\delta_{nc}/(1 - m)$ measures the risk premium required for all the risk resulting from a dollar invested in a firm. But this investment buys $1/(1 - k)$ dollars of new capital.

33. While the former (FSW) model includes social security and unemployment compensation payments as part of the government's lump-sum transfers, our model assumes these net out at the industry level.

34. According to the figures in Musgrave (1980), 72% of the capital stock in this sector is owned by state and local governments.

property taxes.[35] Then the community must put up $1 - \gamma$ through taxes to finance the nondebt part of the one dollar investment, at an after-tax cost of $(1 - n)(1 - \gamma)$.

Let ρ represent the dollar value in each period to residents in the community of the marginal product of this dollar investment. Also, let r_f be the nominal (tax-free) municipal bond interest rate at which the community borrows. Then, as a result of this investment, residents receive an implicit net nominal return equal to $\rho - \gamma r_f(1 - n) - (d - \pi)r_f/r$.[36] Bondholders receive γr_f before and after taxes.

Together the community and the bondholders have invested $(1 - n)(1 - \gamma) + \gamma$ dollars and must absorb together the risk in the return from the investment. Because of this risk, they demand a suitable risk premium δ_G which we assume equals the risk premium for government enterprises. Bondholders would require a risk-free return of r_{fz}, the risk-free municipal bond rate, while members of the community would require an after-tax risk-free return of $\alpha_b r_z$. Together they therefore would require a return on their investment of $(1 - n)(1 - \gamma)\alpha_b r_z + \gamma r_{fz} + \delta_G$.

Therefore in equilibrium

(17)
$$\rho - \gamma r_f(1 - n) - (d - \pi)r_f/r + \gamma r_f$$
$$= (1 - n)(1 - \gamma)\alpha_b r_z + \gamma r_{fz} + \delta_G.$$

We find solving for ρ that

(18)
$$\rho = (d - \pi)r_f/r + (1 - n)\alpha_b r_z$$
$$- \gamma((1 - n)\alpha_b r_z + nr_f - r_{fz}) + \delta_G.$$

The required value for ρ is lower when γ is larger. Therefore the community would use only debt finance unless marginal leverage costs are sufficiently large. We will assume that $\gamma = 1$, implying that $\rho = (d - \pi)r_f/r + r_{fz} - nr_f + \delta_G$. The equilibrium ρ here is lower than that for government enterprises because of both the income tax deductibility of property tax payments and the availability of municipal bond interest rates.

---

35. This rate n is equal to the personal marginal tax rate if (homogeneous) residents in the community itemize and is equal to zero if they do not itemize. In the calculations, we use a weighted average value for n, as described below.

36. This expression captures the annual flows to community residents when they make a municipal investment, maintained in nominal terms through the reinvestment of $(d - \pi)$ each year. This subsequent capital loss and reinvestment is also assumed to be financed by issuing municipal bonds, generating an after-tax interest expense in each future year of $(d - \pi)r_f(1 - n)$. We then need the present value of these costs in the year the capital loss takes place. Because individuals could have made nonmunicipal investments with an after-tax return $r(1 - n)$, their relevant discount rate is $r(1 - n)$. The present value of the stream of interest payments $(d - \pi)r_f(1 - n)$, in the year of the capital loss itself, is $(d - \pi)r_f/r$.

Similarly, property taxes paid to cover other local government expenses are deductible from the federal personal income tax. In particular, the after-tax cost of hiring one more dollar of labor services is only $(1 - n)$ dollars. We therefore include an n percent factor subsidy to labor in this industry. Current expenditures on any of the nineteen commodities also cost $(1 - n)$ percent of the market price.[37]

In order to calculate values for ρ and the labor factor subsidy in this industry, we need values for d, δ_G, r_f, r_{fz}, and n. We set d and δ_G equal to the same weighted averages used for government enterprises.

We also assumed that municipal bond interest rates are a given fraction θ of the interest rates on taxable bonds, so that $r_f = \theta r$ and $r_{fz} = \theta r_z$. Gordon and Malkiel (1980) measure θ to be 0.75.

In calculating a value for n, several steps were involved. First, according to the NBER TAXSIM file, the weighted average marginal tax rate in 1975 for those who itemized and deducted property tax payments was 0.260. In making this calculation, an individual's tax rate was weighted by the size of his property tax payments.[38] We assume that the same rate applied in 1973. However, not all property owners itemize. Using unpublished data from the National Income Division of the Commerce Department along with the figures from the TAXSIM file, we infer that only 44.8% of property taxes paid on residential property was in fact deducted from taxable income. This implies that the average marginal value of n equals $(0.448)(0.260) = 0.117$.

This calculation, however, ignores the possibility that industrial and commercial property may pay part of the costs of additional local public services. In fact, only two-thirds of property tax receipts come from residential property. When considering the effective property tax rate on business investment in earlier sections, we decided to explore the two alternative assumptions that (1) benefits completely offset taxes at the margin, and (2) firms (except in real estate) receive benefits which offset half of their property taxes. In the first scenario, we set $n = 0.117$ because households are subsidized in their local public good "purchases" by the deductibility of their property taxes. Households receive no further subsidy or benefits from taxing businesses, because competitive pressure prevents communities from collecting any tax from firms without paying for commensurate benefits to them.

In the second scenario, however, half of industrial property taxes are left for services to residential property. (The other half of the revenues from business property are used to provide services to the firms.) Con-

---

37. One might argue, however, that these implicit subsidies to local public expenditures are to a degree Pigovian subsidies which correct for the spillover of benefits to other communities. To that degree, they are nondistorting. In this paper, however, we assume that these subsidies are distorting.

38. We would like to thank Daniel Feenberg for performing these calculations for us.

sider, for the moment, $1.20 of local property tax revenue. One-third, or $0.40, on average would be paid by businesses. They would receive $0.20 in benefits, which leaves exactly $1.00 for residential benefits. Residents then would pay only $0.80 for a dollar of benefits, at a cost of $0.80 $(1 - 0.117) = 0.707 after taxes. We therefore use $(1 - 0.707) = 0.293$ for n when simulating the second scenario.

11.3.2   Measurement of Initial Capital Stocks

In the FSW model, net corporate earnings (NCE) after taxes and after depreciation were assumed to be proportional to the true capital stock (i.e. to equal rK, where r is the same for all industries). Therefore NCE/r provided a measure of the capital stock in each industry.[39]

According to the model in this paper, the size of corporate earnings relative to the underlying capital stock will depend on many factors such as the risk premium, tax versus true depreciation rates, etc. However, expected gross corporate earnings (GCE) before taxes and before depreciation ought to equal $\rho_c K$. In section 11.2.2 ρ_c was defined as the cost of capital gross of taxes and depreciation; it varies by industry. We therefore used GCE/ρ_c as a measure of the corporate capital stock in each industry.

Here, GCE was defined to equal the sum of

1. corporate profits, from the *Survey of Current Business (SCB)* corrected for the inventory valuation adjustment,
2. corporate capital consumption allowances, from the *SCB*,
3. corporate interest payments, from unpublished data of the Commerce Department's National Income Division (NID), and
4. corporate rental payments. Rents paid by industry were available from NID, and we divided these into corporate and noncorporate payments in the same proportions that the sums of other earnings were divided in each industry.

The same procedure will not work for the noncorporate sector since earnings there are also in part labor income of the proprietors. Instead we assumed that within any industry capital consumption allowances are proportional to the capital stock. We then multiplied our estimate of the corporate capital stock in each industry by the ratio of noncorporate to corporate capital consumption allowances in that industry to produce an estimate of the noncorporate capital stock. This logic helps provide estimates of initial (1973) labor income in the noncorporate sector. If $K_{nc}\rho_{nc}$ is equal to before-tax earnings of capital and GPE is gross proprietor's earnings, then GPE $- K_{nc}\rho_{nc}$ equals imputed labor income. Here, GPE is defined to equal the sum of noncorporate profits (from the *SCB*), noncorporate capital consumption allowances (from NID), in-

---

39. Interest payments and rental payments are included in NCE so as to capture the return to bond- and landowners as well as equityowners.

terest paid (from NID), and rents paid. Noncorporate rents were imputed by the above procedure. If this residual for labor in 1973 turned out to be negative, we assumed there was measurement error and used zero for the initial noncorporate labor in that industry.

For the two government sectors, we used estimates from Musgrave (1980) for the size of the 1973 capital stocks.

11.3.3   Measurement of Capital Income before and after Taxes

The FSW model defined total capital income net of tax and depreciation to equal the sum of corporate profits, capital consumption adjustment, net interest paid, net rents paid, and noncorporate returns to capital. In the new model, we set total capital income equal to $K(\rho - d)$. The major differences from the old procedure are: (1) depreciation is measured by the calculated dK rather than by reported capital consumption allowances with capital consumption adjustment, and (2) noncorporate capital income is in effect measured by $K_{nc}(\rho_{nc} - d)$ rather than by the reported data for noncorporate capital income.[40]

Let t_k equal the average capital tax rate. We initially set t_k equal to the ratio of observed 1973 capital taxes to before-tax capital income $K(\rho - d)$. In simulations, net capital income then equals $K(\rho - d)(1 - t_k)$ and capital tax revenue equals $K(\rho - d)t_k$. Calculation of the benchmark equilibrium replicates observed capital taxes in 1973, while appropriate changes in t_k (together with changes in τ, k, d', etc.) allow simulation of counterfactual equilibria.

11.3.4   Savings Incentives

While the procedure described above provides estimates for the capital stock in the initial equilibrium, the capital stock in the next period will equal this initial capital stock plus net savings undertaken during the initial period by the twelve separate consumer groups. The capital stock in later periods will follow in a similar fashion. While we devoted much effort in this paper to improving the modeling of investment decisions (by taking account of uncertainty and the optimal form of finance), we made few changes to the assumptions about individual savings decisions found in the earlier model.

In the FSW model, individuals in each consumer group $j = 1,12$ choose to save some income to finance future consumption C_f. They allocate the rest to a subutility function H which is defined over fifteen consumption goods X_i and leisure l. The fifteen X_i consumption goods enter a Cobb-

---

40. Data are available only for total noncorporate income I and for the number of noncorporate workers L. FSW set the noncorporate wage rate w equal to the observed average wage rate from the corporate part of that industry, then set initial (1973) noncorporate capital income equal to $I - wL$. In this paper, we instead calculate a net rate of return to capital $\rho_{nc} - d$, then set initial noncorporate labor income equal to $I - K_{nc}(\rho_{nc} - d)$.

Douglas function with preference parameters λ_i as exponents. Specifically, each of the twelve consumer groups will be characterized by a nested CES utility function

$$(19) \qquad U_j = U_j\left[H\left(\prod_{i=1}^{15} X_i^{\lambda_i}, l\right), C_f\right].$$

As in the FSW model, we use 0.15 for the uncompensated labor supply elasticity of each group with respect to its net of tax wage. This parameter is used to set the elasticity of substitution for the inner nest, between consumption goods and leisure. Unlike the FSW model, however, we cannot use a savings elasticity with respect to the real after-tax interest rate. In our model, this rate will normally be negative. Instead, we use 12.3 as the uncompensated savings elasticity with respect to one plus the real after-tax interest rate. This parameter is used to set the elasticity of substitution for the outer nest, between present and future consumption. The 12.3 figure was derived from Boskin's (1978) equation (2). Boskin estimated that $\log C = A - 1.07R$, where C is consumption, R is the real net of tax interest rate, and A represents other variables in his equation. But therefore $\log C \approx A - 1.07 \log (1 + R)$. It then follows that

$$\frac{1 + R}{S} \frac{\partial S}{\partial(1 + R)} = 1.07 \frac{C}{S}.$$

In 1973, the ratio of total consumption to net savings was 11.5, from the *Economic Report of the President*. We then used $(1.07)(11.5) = 12.3$ for the elasticity of S with respect to $1 + R$ in all periods for all consumer groups. In spite of many objections to Boskin's estimation procedure, we felt there was no good alternative. Saving is then converted immediately into investment demand for producer goods.

A remaining issue is the determination of the net of tax real market interest rate faced by each group. As in the FSW model, we assume that individuals put a fixed fraction of their (marginal) savings into pensions, Keogh and IRA accounts, and life insurance. We assume that such savings earn the market rate of return free of taxes. On the basis of *Flow of Funds* data for 1973, we set this fraction equal to 0.3. The remaining 70% of their savings is then invested either in taxable bonds or in tax-free municipal bonds. The return on taxable bonds is taxed at a constant personal tax rate m_j which ranges from 0.01 to 0.40 across the twelve consumer groups. Each individual can therefore earn a real net of tax risk-free[41] rate of return on his savings equal to $0.3r_z + 0.7 \max(r_{fz}, (1 - m_j)r_z) - \pi$. In this expression r_{fz} represents the risk-free

---

41. We assume that savers respond to the real net of tax risk-free rate of return. Although they can obtain a higher real after-tax return by accepting risk, this premium is not inherently part of the return to savings. It is a return to accepting risk.

municipal bond rate. In the initial simulations, we set $r_{fz} = 0.75r_z$, on the basis of the results in Gordon and Malkiel (1980).

11.3.5   The Benchmark Equilibrium

The FSW model, as used here, consists of eighteen producer industries, fifteen consumer goods, twelve consumer groups, plus the two government sectors. Before the model can be simulated, production and utility functions and their parameters must be specified. The overall strategy is to choose remaining parameters such that the model will calculate an equilibrium that exactly replicates the consistent benchmark data set.

Each industry in the FSW model is characterized by either a constant elasticity of substitution or a Cobb-Douglas production function. Substitution elasticities are chosen from the best estimates in the available literature. The size of each industry's capital stock is calculated as described in section 11.3.2. The size of the benchmark demand for labor in the corporate sector is measured by the size of the labor payments in that industry in 1973, as reported in the *SCB*. The demand for labor in the noncorporate sector is measured as gross income of the industry minus our estimate for the gross return to capital, $\rho_{nc}K_{nc}$.

As in the FSW model, the parameters in the production function were then selected such that the optimal capital-labor ratio would equal the ratio which was in fact chosen, and such that the output produced using these factors would equal the observed 1973 output. In doing so, the rental cost of capital was set equal to the calculated equilibrium rate $\rho - d$ for that industry. The cost of a standardized unit of labor was set equal to one plus the effective unemployment compensation tax rate reported in column 1 of table 11.1. Various federal excise taxes and indirect business taxes were modeled as output taxes for each of the eighteen industries.

As in equation (19) above, each consumer group has a nested utility function over future consumption, leisure, and fifteen commodities. The innermost nest is a Cobb-Douglas utility function over the fifteen consumer goods. The λ_i coefficients were chosen so as to replicate observed relative expenditures on these commodities. In doing so, expenditures were measured gross of state and local sales taxes. In the next nest, there is a CES function by which the consumer chooses between these commodities and leisure. Weights were chosen such that individuals will choose to work forty hours out of a potential seventy hours at their net of tax wage rate. In the outer nest of equation (19), individuals choose between current and future consumption.

Similarly, general government has a Cobb-Douglas utility function over the nineteen producer goods plus capital and labor.[42] The param-

---

42. We use this aggregate function to capture the utility created by government expenditures, rather than having government expenditures enter directly into production functions

eters in this function were selected such that optimal demands for goods, given market prices, would equal actual demands in 1973.

Finally, the foreign sector is modeled by the assumption that the net value of exports less imports for each producer good is constant. This simple treatment closes the model, maintains zero trade balance, and allows easy calculation of trade quantities given prices.[43]

Because the data set for this model comes from many different sources, the figures are often inconsistent. For example, Treasury data on various forms of capital income of consumers differs from Commerce Department data on industry payments for capital. In such cases, the data on one side of the account were judged to be of superior quality and the other data were adjusted to match. All reported industry and government uses of factors were accepted, so consumers' factor incomes and expenditures were scaled to match. Reported tax receipts and transfers were accepted, so government expenditures were scaled to balance the budget. The nearly balanced actual budget of 1973 luckily makes this treatment more reasonable. Similar adjustments ensure that supply equals demand for all goods and factors.

The above assumptions guarantee that the model simulation in the initial period will replicate the 1973 figures. The dynamic model is derived assuming that the 1973 benchmark equilibrium lies on a steady state growth path. Observed saving behavior and the capital endowment are translated into an annual growth rate for capital, and this growth rate is also attributed to effective labor units. The benchmark sequence of equilibria is then calculated by maintaining all tax rates and preferences fixed, increasing labor exogenously, and allowing saving to augment capital endowments over time.[44] By construction, this sequence will have constant factor ratios and constant prices. In simulations of revised tax policies, labor growth is exogenous while capital growth depends on the savings response to new tax rates and interest rates.

11.4 Model Simulations

11.4.1 Simulation Procedure

A variant of Scarf's (1973) algorithm is used to solve for each equilibrium. A new dynamic sequence of the economy results from a change in

or each consumer group's utility function. Because we always hold government utility constant in the simulations described below, this treatment will not affect our estimates of changes in consumer welfare attributable to tax policy changes.

43. Goulder, Shoven, and Whalley (chapter 10 of the present volume) suggest that the results may be sensitive to this assumption.

44. We assume that the relative wealth of the twelve consumer groups remains unchanged over time. While the groups save different proportions of income, the unmodeled movement of individuals across our twelve groups over time ought to maintain the initial wealth distribution.

initial conditions, such as a change in the tax law. In each equilibrium period of the sequence, demand will equal supply for all producer goods and factors, and each industry will have zero profits. Both capital and labor are assumed to be homogeneous and freely mobile across industries. In addition, as described below, we adjust personal income tax rates so as to produce a government revenue at each date which provides the same utility to government given the new market prices as it had in the same period of the benchmark equilibrium sequence. We make this assumption so that in the simulations we can focus on the changes in utility that individuals derive from private activities, holding constant the utility that individuals implicitly derive from public activities.

Simplex dimensions are required only for w, r_z, and the additive surtax rate on the personal income tax. Knowledge of these values is sufficient to evaluate the behavior of all agents. Producer-good prices are based on factor prices and zero profits, while consumer-good prices are based on producer-good prices.

A complete set of prices, quantities, incomes, and allocations is calculated for every equilibrium. A revised tax equilibrium can be compared to the benchmark equilibrium to provide a direct examination of the effects of the proposed tax changes.

In describing the effects of any proposed tax change, we also calculate the equivalent variation in each period. This is the lump-sum dollar amount that would have to be transferred to individuals in the benchmark equilibrium so as to give each consumer group the utility that they would have in the revised tax equilibrium. One complication in calculating this equivalent variation is that tax changes cause a change in the amount of risk and leverage costs, yet these costs do not appear explicitly in the model:[45] our individual utility functions implicitly include the utility provided from spending the risk premiums but do not explicitly subtract for the disutility of bearing risk.

However, by assumption, the risk premiums δ_c or δ_{nc} measure the cost to the individuals of bearing what risk is left after taxes from their investments. In addition, the government bears risk since its tax revenue is uncertain, yet costs of risk bearing do not appear in the government utility function either. We assume in this paper that individuals ultimately bear this risk in proportion to their wealth and find it just as costly to bear as risk they receive directly.[46] In each simulation, we then measure the

45. Corporations take account of leverage costs when making investment decisions at the margin, but these costs are never actually subtracted from firms' profits.

46. Diamond (1967) provides a formal argument for this assumption. Also, we assume that individuals view the risk they bear indirectly as a lump-sum tax, even though we apply this "tax" in proportion to their (initial) wealth. We could have distributed the lump-sum tax in proportion to (initial) income, but the results would be very similar. The difference between these two procedures is only a lump-sum redistribution, which has general equilibrium effects only to the degree that individual preferences for commodities differ.

time pattern of consumption that each consumer group would have had, everything else equal, if it did not receive the risk premium appropriate for all the risk in the return on its capital (including that borne by the government) but also bore no risk. Since we have then standardized utility at the point where there is no risk, we can directly compare utilities across simulations. The reported values for the equivalent variation refer to this standardized measure for utility.[47]

11.4.2 Tax Distortions on Capital in the Initial Equilibrium

In our initial simulations with the model, we left all tax rates at their observed values in 1973, thereby replicating the historical equilibrium. The results from this simulation provide us with a benchmark from which we can examine the welfare effects of several proposed tax changes.

The key element that characterizes each of the simulations that we undertake is the function relating the market interest rate r_z to the equilibrium marginal product of capital ρ in each industry. The formula used in calculating ρ in the initial equilibrium was derived in section 11.2. The equilibrium ρ is a weighted average of the values of ρ_c and ρ_{nc} characterizing corporate and noncorporate investment.

In the first three columns of table 11.2, we report the equilibrium values by industry for

$$(20) \qquad s_c \equiv \rho_c + \pi - d - \frac{\delta_c(1-k)}{\alpha(1-\tau)},$$

$$s_{nc} \equiv \rho_{nc} + \pi - d - \frac{\delta_{nc}(1-k)}{1-m},$$

and their weighted average by industry, defined as s. Here, we assume that the property tax is nondistorting. Each of these figures represents the nominal return required by investors in that industry before any taxes but after depreciation. These returns are measured net of compensation for the riskiness in the return and net of any leverage costs. As such, they also represent the nominal social marginal product of the investment, net of the social costs from depreciation, risk, and leverage costs.[48]

Were there no corporation tax, the risk-free nominal return on corporate capital s_c ought to equal the risk-free nominal market interest rate

---

47. The FSW model calculated the discounted sum of this stream of equivalent variations to obtain a present value of welfare gains. The proper discount rate, however, is the real after-tax interest rate, which in our model is negative. The present value of any stream of gains or losses would then be infinite. Instead, we report the stream directly.

48. We assume that risk borne by the government has the same social cost as risk remaining in the private sector, as would be implied by efficient risk spreading. The risk terms in equation (20) then do indeed correct for the social costs of the risk created by the marginal investment. We also assume that the measure of leverage costs included in δ_c captures the social costs of leverage. If the government bears risk more cheaply, then there is a social benefit from taxes on capital income because of the resulting redistribution of risk.

Table 11.2   Nominal Risk-free Returns to Capital Net of Depreciation

	No Property Tax				With Property Tax	
	Base			Revise	Base	Revise
	s_c	s_{nc}	s	s_c	s_c	s_c
All Industries*	.036	.032	.034	.040	.044	.048
(1) Agriculture, forestry, and fisheries	.049	.033	.035	.041	.069	.061
(2) Mining	.045	.034	.041	.041	.055	.051
(3) Crude petroleum and gas	.036	.026	.035	.039	.057	.060
(4) Construction	.053	.034	.047	.041	.062	.049
(5) Food and tobacco	.042	.031	.042	.039	.050	.047
(6) Textile, apparel, and leather	.046	.040	.046	.045	.061	.060
(7) Paper and printing	.051	.039	.051	.043	.061	.053
(8) Petroleum refining	.035	.025	.035	.037	.037	.039
(9) Chemicals and rubber	.051	.036	.051	.042	.057	.048
(10) Lumber, furniture, stone, clay, and glass	.041	.031	.040	.038	.048	.045
(11) Metals and machinery	.049	.033	.048	.040	.058	.049
(12) Transportation equipment	.036	.033	.036	.040	.086	.089
(13) Motor vehicles	.040	.030	.040	.038	.043	.041
(14) Transportation, communication, and utilities	.033	.033	.033	.041	.043	.051
(15) Trade	.042	.034	.040	.041	.054	.053
(16) Finance and insurance	.028	.032	.028	.040	.033	.044
(17) Real estate	.010	.032	.030	.039	.010	.039
(18) Services	.033	.034	.033	.042	.046	.055
(19) Government enterprises†	.050	.050	.050	.050	.050	.050
(20) General government	.037	.037	.037	.037	.026	.026

*Averages are calculated over eighteen private industries. All s_c use benchmark corporate capital as weights. The s_{nc} column uses benchmark noncorporate capital as weights, and s uses benchmark total capital as weights.

†Government sectors are neither corporate nor noncorporate. We show their s values for purposes of comparison.

$r_z = 0.05$. This equivalence would hold even if there were a (comprehensive) personal income tax on the nominal return from all forms of saving. Had we just used the simplified modeling of the corporate tax as a flat tax rate on the nominal return to corporate capital, as did Harberger (1962), then s_c would equal $r_z/(1 - \tau)$ or 0.096 with our parameters. In sharp contrast, the equilibrium values of s_c reported in table 11.2 are not only well below 0.096 but also mostly below 0.05. In fact, the weighted average value of s_c over all industries is only 0.036. Using the formula for ρ_c in equation (4), we can reexpress s_c (without the property tax) as

$$(21) \qquad s_c = r_z\left(\gamma + (1 - k - \gamma)\frac{\alpha_b}{\alpha(1 - \tau)}\right)$$

$$- \gamma(r - r_z)\left(\frac{\alpha_b}{\alpha(1 - \tau)} - 1\right)$$

$$- \frac{\tau\pi}{1 - \tau} + \frac{\tau(d - d_x)}{1 - \tau}.$$

The following factors, identifiable in this formula, account for the surprisingly low value for s_c.

1. Equityholders require an after-corporate-tax return of only $\alpha_b r_z/\alpha$, not r_z, since the personal income tax on the alternative risk-free asset earning r_z exceeds the personal tax rate on corporate equity. This lowers s_c from $r_z/(1 - \tau)$ to $\alpha_b r_z/[\alpha(1 - \tau)]$, which equals 0.079.

2. The use of debt finance has multiple effects. First, the required nominal risk-free rate of return on debt before corporate taxes is only $r_z = 0.05$. Since on average 40% of capital is financed by debt, s_c is thereby lowered to $(0.079)(0.6) + (0.05)(0.4) = 0.067$.[49] Second, α_b percent of the risk premium on bonds is received by bondholders after tax, while only $\alpha(1 - \tau)$ percent of the risk remains on the investment after taxes. This exchange is favorable to investors, lowering s_c by another 0.007.

3. The inflationary capital gains component of the nominal return s_c is not subject to the corporate tax. This lowers the equilibrium value of s_c by $\tau\pi/(1 - \tau) = 0.055$.

4. Partially offsetting this, the effective tax depreciation rate d_x is below the economic depreciation rate d due to depreciation at historical cost in the tax law. This raises s_c on average by 0.033.

5. Finally, the availability of the investment tax credit lowers the equilibrium s_c by 0.002.

The equilibrium values of the noncorporate s_{nc} are also normally below r_z because of the above explanations 3 and 5, more than offsetting

---

49. Also, leverage costs per unit capital are raised to 0.007, as implied by equation (11), though this does not show up in equation (21) since s_c is net of leverage costs.

explanation 4. The nominal equilibrium return to all capital s is on average only 0.034 (in column 3 of table 11.2).

The equilibrium marginal time preference rate of individuals will also be well below r_z because of the personal income tax. The weighted average marginal time preference rate[50] for our twelve consumer groups turns out to be 0.043. Therefore, while individuals require a return of 0.043 on their savings, the resulting investment produces a net return of only 0.034. An implicit government subsidy of 0.009 makes up the difference. Tax distortions therefore result in an inefficiently large amount of savings and investment. (When we assume that the property tax is half distorting in industries other than real estate, there will still be a small net subsidy to savings and investment.)

If this distortion is negative, though small, why is so much tax revenue collected on the return to capital from both the corporate and personal income taxes? The explanation for this apparent puzzle is that most (in fact more than all according to our figures) of the taxable expected return is the risk premium. Yet while a significant percent of the risk premium is taxed away, the same percent of the risk (standard deviation) is absorbed by the government through risky tax revenues. According to the capital asset pricing model, investors demand a risk premium proportional to the amount of risk that they bear. Investors are therefore indifferent when they lose to the government a given percent of both the risk premium and the risk, so their behavior is undistorted. The government is just charging the market price for the risk that it absorbs. Since the risk premium is positive, however, expected tax revenues will be positive.

Even if the saving-investment distortion is small, however, other tax distortions remain. First, the variation of the numbers in column 3 of table 11.2 implies an intersectoral misallocation of capital across industries, as emphasized in Harberger (1962). In addition, saving is misallocated across individuals because of the variation in after-tax rates of return across investors. (Efficiency requires the same marginal time preference rate for each investor, and thus the same available after-tax rate of return). Also, as always, labor supply decisions are distorted because of the personal tax. Finally, in our initial simulation, yearly leverage-related costs are estimated to equal 0.7% of the value of the corporate capital stock, or 0.6% of GNP. This is hardly an insignificant figure.

11.4.3   Modeling of the Proposed Tax Revision

The model in this paper is used to evaluate the general equilibrium effects of integrating corporate and personal taxes. Detailed descriptions

---

50. The marginal time preference rate for consumer group j was assumed to equal $(0.3r_z + 0.7 \max(r_{fz}, (1 - m_j)r_z))$, the risk-free after-tax return to savings. Thirty percent of (marginal or average) savings are assumed here to be untaxed.

of such proposals can be found in McLure (1975, 1979). Under the full integration proposal, as modeled in Fullerton, King, Shoven, and Whalley (1980, 1981), the corporate tax would be eliminated. Instead, corporate earnings would be included in the personal income tax base of each of the shareholders in proportion to their holdings and would be taxed at ordinary personal income tax rates.[51]

Several changes must be made in the model to capture the effects of this tax change. First, equation (4) relating ρ_c and r_z changes substantially. Corporate profits would now be taxed at each investor's ordinary tax rate, regardless of corporate financial decisions. Since the tax distortion favoring debt finance is thereby eliminated, γ goes to zero. There is now no offsetting advantage to counterbalance the leverage costs arising from debt finance. As a result, leverage-related costs go to zero as well.

After integration, the corporation would be treated for tax purposes as if it were a partnership. The only reason why ρ_c now differs from ρ_{nc} is that the average marginal tax rates of corporate and noncorporate investors differ.[52] We previously estimated that the marginal tax rate of noncorporate investors equaled 0.365. Let m_c equal the average marginal tax rate of corporate investors after integration. We set

$$m_c = 0.7 \sum_{j=1}^{12} w_j m_j ,$$

which equals 0.1948. Here, the m_j are the marginal tax rates of the twelve consumer groups and the w_j are the proportions of consumer wealth held by each group.[53] We continue to assume that only 70% of capital income is taxable.

The s_c after corporate tax integration can therefore be obtained from the s_{nc} formula in equation (20), with $m = 0.365$ replaced by $m_c = 0.1948$.[54] The resulting figures, reported in column 4 of table 11.2, are calculated under the assumption that r_z remains unchanged at 0.05, to ensure comparability with the other figures in table 11.2. (In the simulations, as r_z changes, all the s will change in response.) Note that tax integration will not affect the equilibrium value of s_{nc}, holding r_z constant.

51. The major purpose of this paper is to investigate, for integration of corporate and personal taxes, the sensitivity of estimates to different model specifications. Rather than look at several types of integration (including partial plans or dividend relief) under one model specification, we find it more useful to look at one type of integration under several model specifications. For more discussion of partial integration plans, see McLure (1979) or Fullerton, King, Shoven, and Whalley (1981).

52. These marginal tax rates differ if individuals who choose to form their own businesses differ systematically from those who invest in financial securities.

53. This formula for m_c follows from the derivation of the Gordon and Bradford (1980) model on the assumption that individuals are equally risk averse at the margin.

54. An equivalent procedure, actually used in our calculations, uses equation (4) for ρ_c, sets τ to 0.1948, and sets α_b to $1. - 0.1948 = 0.8052$. Together, these changes imply that $\gamma = 0$ and that leverage costs go to zero.

We find that the new values for s_c exceed the (new and old) values for s_{nc}. Investing in real capital is advantageous during inflation since inflationary capital gains escape full taxation. This advantage is greater in the non-corporate sector, where the marginal tax rate is greater. (Use of historical cost depreciation is more of a disadvantage when marginal tax rates are greater, but this effect is not as important.)

The relation between the values for s_c before and after integration is more complicated. The advantage to investing in real capital, where inflationary capital gains escape full taxation, declines with integration since the ordinary marginal tax rate on the return to capital declines. Offsetting this, however, the required before-tax risk-free nominal return on equity-financed capital was $(\alpha_b r_z)/[\alpha(1-\tau)]$ before integration, while the required return declines to r_z after integration, regardless of the form of finance.

When we assume that property taxes are half distorting in all industries except housing, the equilibrium values for s_c, s_{nc}, and s, with or without integration, all go up by the values for t_p reported in column 2 of table 11.1. In columns 5 and 6 of table 11.2 we report explicitly the resulting values for s_c before and after corporate tax integration.

In addition to recalculating the values for s, we need to calculate how government revenues change each period as a result of corporate tax integration. Clearly, corporate tax revenues go to zero. However, corporate earnings, whether retained or paid out as dividends, become fully taxable under the personal income tax.[55] The new average tax rate on capital income t_k' is set equal to the ratio of these revised capital taxes to the capital income $K(\rho - d)$ in the benchmark equilibrium. These new taxes include only property tax payments (when relevant) and personal income tax payments as they would be with no corporate tax but with full personal taxation of all corporate earnings. (These personal income tax payments will be referred to as the personal factor tax.) Tax revenue from taxation of capital income in the revised equilibrium will then equal $t_k' K'(\rho' - d)$, where primes denote the values in the revised equilibrium.

We simulated corporate tax integration under several sets of assumptions in order to test the sensitivity of the results to the different specifications. Table 11.3 summarizes the parameter values assumed in each of the simulations. The basic simulation, summarized as case 1 in the table,

---

55. For income effects of taxation in this model, we use features from the FSW model. In the benchmark equilibrium, only 96% of dividends are taxable, to account for the $100 dividend exclusion in 1973. Retained earnings were assumed to generate equivalent accrued capital gains, but these are taxed on a deferred basis at preferential rates. Accounting for taxation of purely nominal capital gains, however, FSW use 73% as the proportion of retained earnings subject to full personal rates. Integration changes both of these latter proportions to one. Also in the benchmark, individuals reduce their personal tax base by 30% of savings, the amount contributed to pensions, Keogh accounts, and IRA accounts. This remained unchanged under integration.

Table 11.3   Summary Information for the Different Cases Considered

	Benchmark	Case 1	Case 2	Case 3	Case 4
Identifier	...	Central	No property tax	$r_z = .07$	Lump-sum equal yield
Tax changes					
α_b	.8222	.8052	.8052	.8052	.8052
τ	.48	.1948	.1948	.1948	.1948
t_k^*	$\dfrac{\text{CIT} + \text{PFT}(+\text{PT})}{\text{capital income}}$	$\dfrac{\text{PFT}' + \text{PT}}{\text{capital income}}$	$\dfrac{\text{PFT}'}{\text{capital income}}$	$\dfrac{\text{PFT}' + \text{PT}}{\text{capital income}}$	$\dfrac{\text{PFT}' + \text{PT}}{\text{capital income}}$
Sensitivity analysis					
t_p	As appropriate for comparison	Real estate: nondistorting others: half	All non-distorting	Real estate: nondistorting others: half	Real estate: nondistorting others: half
r_z	As appropriate for comparison	.05	.05	.07	.05
Extra tax for equal yield[†]	...	Add scalar to personal rates	Add scalar to personal rates	Add scalar to personal rates	Lump-sum tax on individuals

*CIT = corporate income tax, PFT = personal factor tax (explained in the text), PT = property tax. Only the distorting parts of observed 1973 property tax revenues are added to the numerator. For case 2, no PT is in the numerator of either base or revised average tax rates. PFT' indicates a changed PFT (see text).

†See text for descriptions.

assumes that half of the property tax was distorting in all industries except real estate, where it was assumed to be nondistorting.

In order to make up for lost tax revenue in this simulation, we assumed that all personal tax rates would be raised by a uniform scalar amount. This scalar increase in tax rates was chosen in each period so that government had just enough revenue to attain the utility level that it had in the same period of the benchmark sequence. In particular, we added the same scalar to the following tax rates: m_j, the personal tax rates of the twelve consumer groups ($j = 1,12$); m, the personal tax rate of proprietors; m_c, the personal tax rate of corporate owners with integration; n, the implicit rate of subsidy for purchase of local public goods; and $1 - r_{fz}/r_z$, the implicit tax rate on municipal bonds.

Each of the other simulations represents a slight variation from this central case simulation. In the second simulation, we assumed that the property tax was nondistorting in all industries. In this case property tax revenues are deleted from government revenues in both base and revised simulations. Property taxes are implicitly treated as benefit payments for public "consumer goods" or intermediate inputs in production.

In the third simulation, we set the risk-free rate to 0.07, the Treasury bill rate in 1973. This change affected the parameterization of the benchmark equilibrium, which was carried through to the new revised equilibrium.

Finally, in the fourth simulation, we assumed that any extra tax revenue needed to maintain government utility is raised through a lump-sum tax on individuals. The amount of extra tax paid by each group is proportional to its original after-tax income, but the extra tax has no price effects. While this case is unrealistic, it allows us to isolate the effects of changing the tax distortions on capital income. (With additions to personal income tax rates, there are further distortions in labor-leisure choices.)

11.4.4   Simulation Results

Tables 11.4–11.6 present some of the information from our simulations of corporate and personal tax integration. As a basis of comparison, we extended the consistent 1973 benchmark economy to a sequence of seven equilibria spaced five years apart. Each equilibrium is proportionately larger than the previous one, with all values growing at the steady state rate. For a revised case, the first period has the same total capital as in the benchmark. The endogenous savings response determines capital stock in the six subsequent periods, again spaced five years apart. With disproportionate growth, however, we need to interpolate values for intervening years. For each variable, we calculate the annual growth rate implied by its values from two successive periods. This rate is applied to

Table 11.4   **Equivalent Variations Relative to National Income for**
Each Year from Integration of Corporate and Personal Taxes

		(EV/NI)		
Year	Central Case (1)	No Property Tax Case (2)	$r_z = .07$ Case (3)	Lump-sum Equal Yield Case (4)
1	− .0001	− .0003	− .0025	.0040
2	− .0002	− .0003	− .0025	.0041
3	− .0003	− .0003	− .0025	.0041
4	− .0004	− .0004	− .0024	.0042
5	− .0005	− .0004	− .0024	.0043
6	− .0006	− .0005	− .0024	.0043
7	− .0006	− .0005	− .0024	.0044
8	− .0006	− .0005	− .0023	.0044
9	− .0006	− .0005	− .0023	.0044
10	− .0007	− .0005	− .0023	.0044
11	− .0007	− .0005	− .0023	.0044
12	− .0007	− .0005	− .0023	.0044
13	− .0007	− .0005	− .0023	.0044
14	− .0007	− .0005	− .0023	.0044
15	− .0007	− .0005	− .0023	.0044
16	− .0007	− .0005	− .0023	.0044
17	− .0007	− .0005	− .0023	.0044
18	− .0007	− .0005	− .0023	.0044
19	− .0007	− .0005	− .0023	.0044
20	− .0007	− .0006	− .0023	.0044
21	− .0007	− .0006	− .0023	.0044
22	− .0007	− .0006	− .0023	.0044
23	− .0007	− .0006	− .0023	.0044
24	− .0007	− .0006	− .0023	.0044
25	− .0007	− .0006	− .0022	.0044
26	− .0007	− .0006	− .0022	.0044
27	− .0007	− .0006	− .0022	.0044
28	− .0007	− .0006	− .0022	.0044
29	− .0007	− .0006	− .0023	.0044
30	− .0007	− .0006	− .0023	.0044
31	− .0007	− .0006	− .0023	.0044

the value from the first of those periods to obtain values for each year
between them.

Table 11.4 presents equivalent variations for all thirty-one years, each
measured relative to national income in the corresponding year of the
benchmark simulation. The seven actual equilibrium calculations are
reflected in years 1, 6, 11, 16, 21, 26, and 31, while other years' values are
obtained using interpolated data.

Table 11.5   Key Variables Relative to the Benchmark, Over Five Year Periods, for Integration of Corporate and Personal Taxes (revise value/base value)

	Time Period	Con- sumption	Saving	Capital Stock	Risk-free Interest Rate
1. Central case	1	1.0016	.9657	1.0000	.9745
	2	.9982	.9798	.9924	1.0039
	3	.9974	.9831	.9906	1.0110
	4	.9972	.9839	.9902	1.0126
	5	.9972	.9841	.9901	1.0130
	6	.9972	.9841	.9901	1.0131
	7	.9972	.9841	.9901	1.0131
2. No property tax case	1	1.0009	.9750	1.0000	.9870
	2	.9985	.9847	.9945	1.0071
	3	.9980	.9871	.9931	1.0121
	4	.9978	.9877	.9928	1.0133
	5	.9978	.9878	.9927	1.0135
	6	.9978	.9879	.9927	1.0136
	7	.9978	.9879	.9927	1.0136
3. $r_z = .07$ case	1	.9983	1.0078	1.0000	1.0320
	2	.9991	1.0050	1.0018	1.0275
	3	.9993	1.0043	1.0023	1.0263
	4	.9993	1.0041	1.0024	1.0259
	5	.9993	1.0039	1.0025	1.0259
	6	.9994	1.0044	1.0025	1.0261
	7	.9994	1.0039	1.0026	1.0256
4. Lump-sum equal yield case	1	.9994	1.0189	1.0000	1.0111
	2	1.0013	1.0110	1.0042	.9952
	3	1.0017	1.0092	1.0052	.9917
	4	1.0018	1.0088	1.0054	.9909
	5	1.0018	1.0087	1.0054	.9907
	6	1.0018	1.0087	1.0054	.9907
	7	1.0018	1.0087	1.0054	.9907

Table 11.5 summarizes results by looking at just a few key variables in each of the seven periods. Each entry is the ratio of the revise-case value to the base-case value of the same period. A capital stock ratio less than one, for example, does not imply reduced capital stock over time; it only implies less capital than in the growing benchmark sequence.

Table 11.6 shows the reallocation of the fixed total capital stock in the first period. The entry for each industry is the percent change in capital used in the first period of the revised sequence from the first period of the base sequence.

Integration of the corporate income tax with the personal income tax may seem like a dramatic change in the tax law. Indeed, Fullerton, King, Shoven, and Whalley (1980, 1981) find significant welfare gains from

Table 11.6 Reallocation of Capital with Corporate and Personal Tax Integration: Percent Change from the Benchmark Use of Capital for Each Sector

Industry	Central Case (1)	No Property Tax Case (2)	$r_z = .07$ Case (3)	Lump-sum Equal Yield Case (4)
(1) Agriculture, forestry, and fisheries	−.282	−.311	−.549	.364
(2) Mining	1.492	1.710	3.479	2.648
(3) Crude petroleum and gas	−.844	−.814	.445	.314
(4) Construction	3.551	3.928	6.610	5.390
(5) Food and tobacco	3.747	3.833	4.712	3.439
(6) Textile, apparel, and leather	3.955	4.151	6.151	4.009
(7) Paper and printing	5.169	5.348	7.105	5.446
(8) Petroleum refining	−.538	−.579	.210	.343
(9) Chemicals and rubber	6.889	7.027	8.687	6.854
(10) Lumber, furniture, stone, clay, and glass	1.752	1.946	4.265	3.162
(11) Metals and machinery	3.173	3.511	5.635	4.573
(12) Transportation equipment	1.316	1.681	3.688	1.683
(13) Motor vehicles	2.217	2.270	4.246	3.187
(14) Transportation, communication, and utilities	1.249	1.055	4.537	.336
(15) Trade	2.526	2.577	3.981	2.610
(16) Finance and insurance	−1.075	−1.573	2.012	−2.212
(17) Real estate	−.934	−1.298	−2.206	−1.763
(18) Services	.156	−.078	1.228	−.178
(19) Government enterprises	−.453	−.700	−1.581	−.104
(20) General government	−1.009	−.537	−1.897	−.271

integration. However, the results here indicate that the effects on the economy would be very modest. Except when revenues are replaced by a lump-sum tax, table 11.4 shows that the tax change results in a very slight *drop* in the utility from current consumption of commodities and leisure during at least the first thirty years after the tax change.

Net welfare losses occur with integration when the revenue is replaced by raising personal tax rates, because the labor-leisure distortion is exacerbated.[56] This overall loss occurs in spite of welfare improvements on three other margins.

First, integration eliminates the distortion favoring debt finance, removing the leverage costs that were 0.6% of benchmark national income.

Second, interindustry welfare gains follow along the lines of previous Harberger-type analyses, as indicated in the last two columns of table 11.2. The generally high required rates of return in manufacturing are lowered, while the low required rates of return in real estate and petroleum refining are raised.

Third, there are welfare effects on the intertemporal allocation of consumption. Table 11.2 shows that the average s_c is a bit higher with integration, whether or not the property tax was modeled as distorting. Integration reduces the small net subsidy to the risk-free return on savings, discussed in an earlier section. These three welfare effects are summarized in the fourth simulation of table 11.4, where revenue losses with integration are recovered through lump-sum taxes. Together they imply a slight welfare gain from integration alone. Without changing personal tax rates, labor supply remains basically unchanged. If personal tax rates have to rise, however, the first three columns of table 11.4 indicate a net welfare loss from integration. We find that the resulting drop in labor supply creates the largest welfare effect. We probably underestimate the welfare cost of this drop in labor supply because we ignore some existing distortions to labor supply created by various transfer programs such as food stamps and AFDC. In the first period of the central case, labor supply drops by 1.4% in response to the 0.026 rise in marginal tax rates. The figures for the second and third cases are very similar.

In the third case, where $r_z = 0.07$ in the benchmark equilibrium, the equivalent variation figures are even less favorable. It turns out that the benchmark intersectoral misallocation of capital and the intertemporal savings-investment distortion are slightly smaller in this case. The smaller gains from integration on those margins are offset by the same size loss from raising personal tax rates, for a larger net loss overall.

Because of the drop in labor supply with a fixed initial supply of capital, capital-labor ratios rise in the first period in all sectors except general

---

56. When personal income tax rates are raised, the interpersonal allocation of savings is further distorted, as are local public goods decisions.

government. In order to encourage this increase in capital-labor ratios, the cost of capital must fall. The last two columns of table 11.2 show that with no change in interest rates, integration would imply a higher cost of capital on average. Therefore the market interest rate must fall initially, as seen in table 11.5. The lower interest rate causes a fall in savings. The resulting reduction in the growth rate of the capital stock allows r_z to rise back up slightly above 0.05.

When $r_z = 0.07$, however, the tax change tends to increase the cost of capital relatively less (since lowering $(\alpha_b r_z)/[\alpha(1 - \tau)]$ to r_z becomes more important). In this simulation, interest rates have to rise to offset the stronger investment incentive resulting from the tax change. Note also that when labor supply does not fall, as when lump-sum taxes are used to replace lost tax revenue, the story is reversed. Interest rates initially rise in order to maintain an unchanged capital-labor ratio. The resulting savings rate is sufficiently high, however, that interest rates must fall later to create demand for all the resulting capital.

Capital-labor ratios do not rise uniformly, however. Capital is reallocated slightly across sectors in response to the tax change, as shown for the first period in table 11.6. Capital tends to leave the industries that are little affected by the tax changes: government,[57] the primarily noncorporate industries (1 and 17), and, to a lesser degree, industries which are heavily debt financed initially (16, 17, and 18). The major impetus for this reallocation of capital is the change in s_c resulting from the tax change, but many other factors are also involved. Included among these other factors are the relative size of the corporate sector, the relative size of the drop in leverage costs, and varying factor substitution elasticities in each industry.

We also see from table 11.5 that current consumption (of both commodities and leisure) falls eventually except when lump-sum taxes are used to replace lost revenue. In cases 1 and 2, this fall in consumption results mainly from the fall in potential output caused by the fall in the capital stock. In case 3 it results from the rise in interest rates which shifts income into savings. These current consumption figures are less interesting than the eqivalent variation figures, however, since they do not control for the amount of risk bearing. Note that risk bearing increases initially (in spite of the elimination of leverage costs) because of the reallocation of capital toward riskier industries.

In addition to these four simulations, we ran several others, not reported here, which produced very similar results. In particular, the assumption that property taxes on housing are also half distorting made almost no difference to the results. Also, raising extra tax revenues

---

57. Capital tends to leave general government in part because as personal income tax rates rise, its relative prices for labor and commodities (which are proportional to $(1 - n)$) fall more than does the cost of capital.

through a proportional rather than an additive increase in all personal tax rates made little difference.

11.5 Conclusions

Previous versions of the FSW model have assumed that marginal tax rates equal average tax rates and that government expenditures are nondistorting. In this paper we have reexamined the modeling of many of these marginal tax and benefit distortions. Particular attention was paid to the modeling of the effect of taxes on financial and investment decisions of corporations and local public governments.

We found that average tax rates provide a poor characterization of government-created distortions. In the cases of the social security, unemployment insurance, and workmen's compensation programs, we have argued that individuals receive extra government benefits which would come close to offsetting any extra taxes they pay on the margin, as well as on average. We also argued that recipients of capital income receive benefits which largely compensate them for the taxes they pay and often more than compensate them. However, this compensation comes in a subtle form: these recipients are able to reduce some of the risk in the return on their investments by transferring it to the government through risky tax revenue. We also found that the tax distortion favoring corporate use of debt rather than equity finance is quite costly from a social point of view.

Our results also emphasize the importance of using a general equilibrium model to evaluate welfare effects in a second-best world. The current model simultaneously accounts for tax distortions in corporate financial decisions, in the interindustry (and private versus government) allocations of labor and capital, in the intertemporal allocation of consumption, and in the labor/leisure choice of individuals. Concentration on only some of these distortions can give a very misleading view of the effects of integrating the corporate income tax with the personal income tax. In particular, we find that the extra distortion costs caused by raising personal income tax rates to restore government revenue more than offset the efficiency gains from changing the method of taxing income from corporate capital through corporate tax integration.

Appendix
Construction of Industry-specific Data
Yolanda Kodrzycki Henderson

This appendix describes the procedures for obtaining four data series: unemployment insurance tax rates, investment tax credit rates, economic depreciation rates, and tax depreciation rates.

Unemployment Insurance Tax Rates

In the above simulations, we required the net (of benefit) unemployment insurance tax rates for 1973 for eighteen private industries. These industries are for the most part aggregations of two to three SIC two-digit industries in manufacturing, and broader classifications (e.g. wholesale and retail trade) outside of manufacturing. Becker's (1972) data for unemployment insurance benefit and tax rates, on the other hand, came from sixteen state employment security agencies for various combinations of years and industries (see his tables A.5 to A.9). He has provided information for 1961, 1967, and the 1957–67 average. Industry detail included broad classifications such as "manufacturing" and "wholesale and retail trade," selected two-digit industries, and selected three-digit industries. Typically, data for a particular industry were available for only a few states and not all time periods.

In view of the discrepancies between required and available data, we computed the net tax rate for each industry from the 1957–67 sample and the 1967 sample. The unweighted average from the two samples was taken as the estimate for the industry. If the FSW industry consisted of several two-digit industries, this procedure was applied to each two-digit industry, and the average of these tax rates was used as the FSW industry tax rate. There were two exceptions to this general procedure caused by lack of industry information. For the two mining industries, petroleum and natural gas and other mining, we used the same estimate, the one available for their total. For petroleum refining, we averaged estimates for two other nondurable industries, chemicals and rubber and paper and printing.

Effective Investment Tax Credit Rates

To compute the investment tax credit rates, we divided the dollar amount of the credit taken in each industry by the level of investment in that industry. Because we were calculating effective rates, investment included purchases of structures and the change in inventories, even though these types of investment are not eligible for the ITC. We were

Yolanda Kodrzycki Henderson is with the Department of Economics, Amherst College.

forced to aggregate corporate and noncorporate data because there was no separate information about investment in these two sectors. This procedure is appropriate in that the same statutory rates apply to both sectors, but may be inaccurate if the type of investment differs between the corporate and noncorporate sectors of an industry.

Tables on the investment tax credit by industry appear in the Internal Revenue Service *Statistics of Income, Corporation Income Tax Returns*, but the ITC for sole proprietors and partners does not appear in the *Statistics of Income* publications for these returns. Unpublished data on the 1973 noncorporate ITC were made available by the Treasury Department, and we used the assumption of a constant ratio of noncorporate to corporate ITC in each industry to estimate the noncorporate ITC for 1974. These data were then aggregated to our industry definitions for each of the two years.

Our principal source for data on fixed investment by industry was the Commerce Department's survey of expenditures for new plant and equipment by United States business, as reported in the *Survey of Current Business (SCB)*. Supplementary unpublished data were provided by the Bureau of Economic Analysis (BEA) of the Commerce Department. The coverage of this survey was satisfactory for our manufacturing industries and for transportation, communications, and utilities. Information on other industries was inadequate for various reasons: agricultural business and housing are excluded entirely from the survey, some service industries are omitted, and investment in mining is underreported because capital expenditures for unsuccessful mineral explorations are expensed rather than being included as an investment on company books. As a result, we used several different procedures for obtaining investment in these remaining industries. For real estate, we used the National Income and Product Accounts (NIPA) figures for residential investment. This omits the relatively small nonresidential investment by this industry (brokers' offices), but we were not able to find information on this component. For agriculture, we used NIPA data on investment in agricultural machinery and nonresidential farm structures. Agricultural machinery is only part of the equipment purchased by farmers, and the rest (tractors, trucks, automobiles, etc.) is not broken down between agricultural and nonagricultural uses on an annual basis. We scaled up our estimate of equipment spending to total agricultural equipment in both years using information from the 1972 capital flow table (CFT) of BEA. For the remaining industries, we used the CFT data for 1972, multiplied by growth rates for the closest corresponding category from the 1973 and 1974 investment surveys.

Inventory investment estimates for agriculture and trade came directly from the *SCB* (tables 1.1 and 5.8, respectively). For other industries, we added together the book value change in inventories and the inventory valuation adjustment (IVA). BEA provided unpublished data for the IVA (consistent with table 6.16 of the *SCB*) for each of our industries for 1973. The 1974 IVAs were estimated using growth rates in the IVA for broad industry classifications (such as "durable manufacturing") from table 5.8 of the *SCB*.[58] The change in the book value of inventories came from the Census Bureau's monthly report on Manufacturers' Shipments, Inventories, and Orders, available from Data Resources, Inc. In some cases, it was necessary to impute data for two-digit manufacturing industries and nonmanufacturing industries. This was done using information on the size of the industry as measured by investment in the 1972 CFT, as well as information on inventory change in table 5.8 of the *SCB*.

Economic Depreciation Rates

As described in section 11.2.3 above, economic depreciation rates were found for each industry by calculating the rate that was most consistent with the dollar value of economic depreciation for the period 1972 to 1974 and the stream of investment through 1974.

For economic depreciation in twelve two-digit and three-digit manufacturing industries, we used the "variant *C*" estimates of Coen (1980), which are provided through 1974. For agriculture and real estate we used the Commerce Department's capital consumption allowances with capital consumption adjustment from the *SCB*, tables 1.13, 6.15, and 6.24. Estimates of economic depreciation rates were not available for more than these fourteen industries, but a procedure to extend depreciation rates to other industries is described below.

The data for nominal fixed investment described in the previous section (on investment tax credit rates) were extended back to 1947, and the price deflator for fixed investment from the National Income Accounts was used to convert those figures to constant dollars for the appropriate year ($i = 1972, 1973, 1974$). This was not possible for all industries, however. The investment survey data described in the previous section were available from Data Resources, Inc., for sixteen two-digit industries since 1947 (including the twelve manufacturing industries). For the real estate industry, we were able to use the NIPA data discussed in the previous section. For agriculture, we had investment in agricultural machinery since 1947, but information on nonfarm structures was available only back to 1958. We extended the latter to 1947 by assuming that it was 0.77 of the former, a figure based on the ratios for 1958, 1959, and 1960.

We still had to account for the (small) amount of the capital stock in

---

58. Both tables 5.8 and 6.16 of the *SCB* provide data on the inventory valuation adjustment, but are taken from different sources. Table 5.8 estimates are used in the product side of the GNP accounts, while table 6.16 estimates are used for the income side. See the *SCB* for further detail on the concepts.

1972 to 1974 that was the result of investment prior to 1947. Using NIPA data, we estimated that real nonresidential fixed investment increased at a 2.7% rate between 1929 and 1947, and real residential investment at a 2.1% rate, and applied these aggregate growth rates as described in the text.

Using the above information, we computed economic depreciation rates for fourteen industries. Some of the eighteen FSW industries correspond exactly to these industries. Some are aggregates of these available industries, and we computed economic depreciation rates for these aggregates.

For industries for which we had no depreciation data, we inferred information on the durability of their capital stock from data on their relative purchases of structures and equipment, as reported in the 1972 BEA CFT, which was available for all of our disaggregated industries. We used our estimated depreciation rates for available two-digit and three-digit industries, agriculture, and real estate in a regression on the ratios of equipment to total plant and equipment (and the square of that ratio). This regression gave us a predictive equation for depreciation rates of other two-digit industries based on *their* ratios of equipment to total plant and equipment. If one of the model's industries was entirely unrepresented in the available depreciation rate estimates, we used the predicted rate based on its 1972 CFT data. If part of an industry was represented in the available depreciation rate estimates, we used that estimate in combination with a prediction for the other part, weighting by the value of the capital stock in 1972 in each section of the industry.

Since a published estimate of the capital stock was not available for each two-digit industry, we estimated each capital stock ourselves. In particular, if d is our estimate for the economic depreciation rate in a particular industry, if μ is the estimated growth rate in real investment in that industry during the period 1947 to 1972, and if I^R is the real gross fixed investment in the industry in 1972, then the capital stock in the industry in 1972 is approximated by

$$K = \int_0^\infty I^R e^{-\mu t} e^{-dt} dt = \frac{I^R}{\mu + d}.$$

Where an industry's growth rate of investment was unavailable, we used a growth rate based on more aggregated data (e.g. manufacturing).

Tax Depreciation Rates

The methodology for computing tax depreciation rates was similar to the methodology for economic depreciation: we searched for the rate in each industry that was consistent with observed depreciation allowances and investment streams. The data for depreciation allowances came from the IRS *Statistics of Income* for both corporate and noncorporate enterprises, by industry. For real estate and agriculture, we used *SCB* tables 6.15 and 6.24. The rates for industries for which investment data were missing were derived in a manner similar to the economic depreciation rates, by regressions using the ratio of equipment to total investment.

The main difference in the methodology from that for economic depreciation rates was that we accounted for major changes in tax laws regarding depreciation allowances. In particular, prior to 1954, firms could use straight-line depreciation based on Bulletin F lifetimes. In 1954, double declining balance or sum of the years' digits methods of tax depreciation were introduced, and in 1971, tax lifetimes were reduced by 20% through the asset depreciation range (ADR) system. In each of these periods, therefore, the tax depreciation rate was different. We proceeded by calculating how the effective geometric depreciation rates would differ among these periods for a representative asset with a fourteen year tax lifetime prior to ADR. Suppose investment in this asset had been growing continuously at the nominal rate $\mu = 0.07$ (calculated by regressing the log of the NIPA total fixed nonresidential investment from 1947 to 1976 on time). Then under the double declining balance formula, tax depreciation deductions in year i would be

$$\text{TD}_i = \int_0^{T/2} \frac{2}{T} I_i e^{-2t/T} e^{-\mu t} dt$$
$$+ \int_{T/2}^T \frac{2}{T} I_i e^{-(2/T)(T/2)} e^{-\mu t} dt,$$

where I_i is nominal investment in year i. The equivalent geometric depreciation rate would be that rate d' which would have implied the same size of tax deductions. With geometric depreciation, tax deductions would have been

$$\text{TD}_i = \int_0^\infty d' I_i e^{-d't} e^{-\mu t} dt.$$

When we equate these two formulas and use $T = 14$ and $\mu = 0.07$, the only remaining unknown is d'. We therefore conclude that the effective depreciation rate for this representative asset would have been 0.162 for the period 1954–70. After 1971, when T was reduced by 20%, the effective rate implied by the above formulas increased to 0.205.

In contrast, with straight-line depreciation, tax deductions would have been

$$\text{TD}_i = \int_0^T \frac{1}{T} I_i e^{-\mu t} dt.$$

Therefore the effective geometric depreciation rate for this representative asset prior to 1954 would have been 0.123.

On the basis of these results, we assumed in our calculations that if the effective geometric depreciation rate d' was available on investments made since 1971, then the rate $0.789d'$ was available during the period 1954–70, and the rate $0.600d'$ during the period prior to 1954.[59] We recognize that our procedure omits the effects of many other revisions during the period both in Treasury Department rulings and in the degree to which firms took advantage of the available rulings. A more thorough procedure, for example, might use information from Vasquez (1974) on the proportion of investment that was depreciated by the faster methods allowed following the 1954 and 1971 changes in the law. Our procedure should effectively capture the basic differences in the tax treatment of depreciation among the various industries, which is what we needed.

References

Ballentine, J. G., and C. E. McLure, Jr. 1981. Taxation and corporate financial policy. *Quarterly Journal of Economics* 94: 351–72.

Becker, J. M. 1972. *Experience rating in unemployment insurance*. Baltimore: Johns Hopkins University Press.

Black, F. 1976. The dividend puzzle. *Journal of Portfolio Management* 2: 5–8.

Blinder, A. S.; R. H. Gordon; and D. E. Wise. 1980. Reconsidering the work disincentive effects of social security. *National Tax Journal* 33: 431–42.

Boskin, M. J. 1978. Taxation, saving, and the rate of interest. *Journal of Political Economy* 86: S3–S27.

Brown, E. 1980. Experience rating for unemployment insurance taxes. Ph.D. thesis, Princeton University.

Christensen, L. R., and D. W. Jorgenson. 1969. The measurement of U.S. real capital input, 1929–1967. *Review of Income and Wealth* 15: 293–320.

Coen, R. M. 1980. Alternative measures of capital and its rate of return in U.S. manufacturing. In D. Usher, ed., *The measurement of capital*. Chicago: University of Chicago Press.

Diamond, P. A. 1967. The role of a stock market in a general equilibrium model with technological uncertainty. *American Economic Review* 57: 759–76.

Feldstein, M. S., and L. Summers. 1979. Inflation and the taxation of capital income in the corporate sector. *National Tax Journal* 32: 445–70.

---

59. Note that 0.162/0.205 equals 0.789, while 0.123/0.205 equals 0.600.

Fischel, W. A. 1975. Fiscal and environmental considerations in the location of firms in suburban communities. In E. S. Mills and W. E. Oates, eds., *Fiscal zoning and land use controls*. Lexington, Massachusetts: Lexington Books.

Fullerton, D.; A. T. King; J. B. Shoven; and J. Whalley. 1980. Corporate and personal tax integration in the United States: Some preliminary findings. In R. H. Haveman and K. Hollenbeck, eds., *Microeconomic simulation models for public policy analysis*. New York: Academic Press.

———. 1981. Corporate tax integration in the United States: A general equilibrium approach. *American Economic Review* 71: 677–91.

Fullerton, D.; J. B. Shoven; and J. Whalley. 1978. General equilibrium analysis of U.S. taxation policy. In United States Office of Tax Analysis, Department of Treasury, *1978 compendium of tax research*. Washington: Government Printing Office.

———. 1980. Dynamic general equilibrium impacts of replacing the U.S. income tax with a progressive consumption tax. NBER Conference Paper no. 55.

Gordon, R. H. 1980. Inflation, taxation, and corporate behavior. NBER Working Paper no. 588.

Gordon, R. H., and D. F. Bradford. 1980. Taxation and the stock market valuation of capital gains and dividends. *Journal of Public Economics* 14: 277–308.

Gordon, R. H., and B. G. Malkiel. 1980. Taxation and corporation finance. NBER Working Paper no. 576.

Hall, R. E., and D. W. Jorgenson. 1967. Tax policy and investment behavior. *American Economic Review* 57: 391–414.

Hamilton, B. W. 1976. Capitalization of intrajurisdictional differences in local tax prices. *American Economic Review* 66: 743–53.

Harberger, A. 1962. The incidence of the corporation income tax. *Journal of Political Economy* 70: 215–40.

Hulten, C. R., and F. C. Wykoff. 1980. The estimation of economic depreciation using vintage asset prices. Urban Institute Working Paper no. 1390-01.

Kendrick, J. W. 1976. *The national wealth of the United States*. New York: Conference Board.

King, M. A. 1974. Taxation and the cost of capital. *Review of Economic Studies* 41: 21–36.

McGuire, M. 1974. Group segregation and optimal jurisdictions. *Journal of Political Economy* 82: 112–32.

McLure, C. E., Jr. 1975. Integration of the personal and corporate taxes: The missing element in recent tax reform proposals. *Harvard Law Review* 88: 532–82.

———. 1977. The incidence of the financing of unemployment insurance. *Industrial and Labor Relations Review* 30: 469–79.

————. 1979. *Must corporate income be taxed twice?* Washington: Brookings Institution.

Merton, R. C. 1980. On estimating the expected return on the market. NBER Working Paper no. 444.

Miller, M. H. 1977. Debt and taxes. *Journal of Finance* 32: 261–75.

Modigliani, F., and M. H. Miller. 1963. Corporate income taxes and the cost of capital: A correction. *American Economic Review* 53: 433–43.

Musgrave, J. C. 1980. Government owned fixed capital in the United States, 1925–79. *Survey of Current Business*. Washington: Government Printing Office.

Myers, S. C. 1977. Determinants of corporate borrowing. *Journal of Financial Economics* 5: 147–75.

Scarf, H. E., with the collaboration of T. Hansen. 1973. *The computation of economic equilibria*. New Haven: Yale University Press.

Shoven, J. B. 1976. Incidence and efficiency effects of taxes on income from capital. *Journal of Political Economy* 84: 1261–83.

Stiglitz, J. E. 1973. Taxation, corporate financial policy, and the cost of capital. *Journal of Public Economics* 2: 1–34.

Tiebout, C. 1956. A pure theory of local expenditures. *Journal of Political Economy* 64: 416–24.

United States, Bureau of Economic Analysis, Department of Commerce. *Survey of Current Business*. Washington: Government Printing Office.

United States, Internal Revenue Service, Department of Treasury. *Statistics of Income*. Washington: Government Printing Office.

Vasquez, T. 1974. The effects of the asset depreciation range system on depreciation practices. United States Treasury Department Office of Tax Analysis, paper no. 1.

von Furstenburg, G. M.; B. G. Malkiel; and H. S. Watson. 1980. The distribution of investment between industries. In G. M. von Furstenburg, ed., *Capital, efficiency, and growth*. Washington: American Council of Life Insurance.

Warner, J. 1977. Bankruptcy costs, absolute priority, and the pricing of risky debt claims. *Journal of Financial Economics* 4: 239–76.

White, M. 1975. Firm location in a zoned metropolitan area. In E. S. Mills and W. E. Oates, eds., *Fiscal zoning and land use controls*. Lexington, Massachusetts: Lexington Books.

Comment   Charles E. McLure, Jr.

Fullerton and Gordon's objective in this paper is to develop a descendent of the Fullerton-Shoven-Whalley (FSW) general equilibrium model and use it to simulate the effects of integration of the income taxes. Their primary contribution lies in the attempt to incorporate in the model an improved description of corporate and noncorporate financial policy. A more realistic description of corporate financial policy is, of course, necessary if one is to analyze adequately the effects of integration, one primary benefit of which is neutrality toward corporate financial policy. This modification allows the authors to incorporate in their analysis the government's sharing in risk initially taken in the private sector. By comparison, most of the previous empirical attempts to implement the Harberger model, such as those by FSW, have examined a riskless world. Fullerton and Gordon also employ the same basic theoretical framework to analyze the financial decisions of government enterprises and of general government. A distinctly subsidiary effort involves consideration of marginal benefits of public spending as potential offsets to marginal taxes.

One must be impressed with the ambitiousness of what Fullerton and Gordon have attempted in the analysis reported here. To some extent they have "only" brought together and included in their model disparate threads of literature in public and corporate finance. Of course, this is a major undertaking in itself. But in other cases—especially in the analysis of government activities—they have had to attempt entirely new analyses of largely unexplored problems in order to flesh out their model.

While one must commend Fullerton and Gordon for their daring, it is not clear that they have been uniformly successful in all their pioneering efforts, or even in their eclecticism. Most of my remarks will focus on what I perceive to be shortcomings of Fullerton and Gordon's analysis rather than on the many manifest contributions of this paper.

Tax-induced Leverage

Fullerton and Gordon go well beyond earlier attempts to incorporate the financial decisions of firms in general equilibrium models. In particular, much is made—and properly so—of the public's sharing of risk, including that of bankruptcy, through the tax system. It is here that Fullerton and Gordon's major contribution lies. Yet one must note several deficiencies in their analysis.

First, the authors choose to illustrate the capability of their model by

Charles E. McLure, Jr., is a senior fellow at the Hoover Institution and a research associate of the National Bureau of Economic Research. At the time these comments were prepared he was vice-president of the NBER. The views expressed here are his own and not those of any organization.

examining full integration under the partnership approach. This is a useful exercise; since so much has been made of the potential welfare gains from eliminating the distortions of corporate financial structures induced by the unintegrated taxation of corporate equity income, it is good to know that these gains would be roughly offset if revenues lost in integration were made up by raising taxes that further distort the labor-leisure choice. But one must wish that the authors had also examined the effects of providing only relief from double taxation of dividends, since complete integration is commonly agreed to be administratively difficult, if not impossible, and very unlikely to occur. That would, of course, be much more complicated to model, since it would necessitate addressing head-on the crucial question of the treatment of tax preferences.

Second, one cannot adequately model tax effects on decisions in the important petroleum industry without considering (a) tax preferences peculiar to that industry, such as the depletion allowance and the expensing of intangible drilling costs, and (b) the foreign tax credit. (See McLure 1979, chapters 4 and 6.) The effect of the preferences in reducing average tax rates in this industry is well known; but what is the effect at the margin? (Harberger 1966 included petroleum in the noncorporate sector in his two-sector analysis of the efficiency effects of capital taxes.)

One cannot fault Fullerton and Gordon for choosing not to consider foreign tax issues in detail. But in the petroleum industry the existence of surplus foreign tax credits (FTC) implies that domestic activities in this industry effectively carry a marginal tax rate near zero. These omissions become especially important when one considers integration of the income taxes. Would integration, if complete, involve passing the preferences and the foreign tax credit through to individual shareholders, or would the preferences and FTC be eliminated? If dividend relief were at stake, how would these tax preferences and the FTC be treated?

A number of minor points must be noted about Fullerton and Gordon's treatment of leverage costs and risk:

The calculation of industry-specific risk premiums on equity seems inconsistent with the use of a common risk premium for debt. One wonders how likely it is that risk premiums on the two types of securities issued in the same industry would not be highly correlated. I am disappointed that the authors felt it necessary to use a common risk premium for the bonds of all industries.

Fullerton and Gordon go to great lengths to tell elaborate stories about leverage in the corporate and government sectors. By comparison, they assume only equity finance in the noncorporate sector. Their brief discussion of this in a footnote leaves the reader wanting a more complete explanation.

Fullerton and Gordon assume that capital is just as risky at the margin as is existing capital, so that the optimal debt-capital ratio is the same for marginal investment as for prior investments. But this seems quite unlikely.

Through their assumption of uncertainty and no constraint on short sales the authors reject various theories that imply clientele effects and justify the repeated use of weighted averages of tax rates. Given the existence of constraints on short sales one must wonder whether much of the paper should not be recast in terms of (for example) marginal tax rates of marginal investors rather than averages of marginal tax rates. This is especially relevant since their approach forces Fullerton and Gordon to assume that the marginal personal tax rates of investors in the corporate and noncorporate sectors are not affected by integration. It is thought by some that existing patterns of ownership of assets reflect current taxation and that they—and related marginal tax rates—would change in response to integration.

Tax-exempt organizations play no role in this analysis, except as conduits for the saving of individuals. Is that appropriate, or should these organizations be assumed to have investment objectives of their own? Does the answer differ, depending on whether pension funds, universities, or foundations are concerned?

Benefit Taxation

Fullerton and Gordon claim that they model the distorting effects of government activity more accurately than do FSW by considering marginal increases in benefits that may offset marginal increases in taxes. This is clearly a worthwhile objective, since little is to be gained from treating taxes that are linked directly to benefits as distortionary levies. However, I find part of their discussion of which taxes are offset by benefits at the margin inadequate and some of their decisions on the matter arbitrary and questionable.

Fullerton and Gordon treat personal and corporate income taxes and various indirect taxes as "real" taxes. By comparison, they assume that the residential property tax only reflects benefits of public services. Thus they do not treat it as a distortionary tax. Though I would argue that this conclusion is not totally accurate, it is probably closer to the truth than the polar opposite assumption that residential property taxes buy nothing. Whether it can be said that nonresidential property taxes are also benefit taxes is unclear. Personally, I doubt it. But the authors' argument that once investment has been made nonresidential capital can be taxed by local governments with relative impunity seems oddly inconsistent with the instantaneous equilibration implicit in their formal model of capital allocation. On the other hand, since property taxes are deductible in calculating federal income tax liability, the pressure on local governments to provide a quid pro quo for property taxes paid is less than in the absence of deductibility.

Fullerton and Gordon argue that competition between states and localities will assure that property taxes merely reflect benefits. But I am not sure that they should limit the argument to property taxes, especially since the apportionment formulas used in state corporate income taxes to allocate total income among states ordinarily give a weight of one-third to property in the state. Similarly, why are all state and local indirect taxes and personal income taxes treated as unrequited levies rather than benefit taxes? Though the formal conditions required for an assumption of benefit taxation are less fully met in these instances than in the case of property taxes, I believe that some of the same economic forces that lead to classification of residential property taxes as benefit taxes would probably also lead to qualitatively similar results for general sales taxes and income taxes. Finally, Fullerton and Gordon treat all excises as taxes that increase production costs, even though the most important of these, the levies on motor fuels, are arguably benefit taxes levied for the construction and maintenance of highways.

In short, what Fullerton and Gordon have done to extend the FSW model by incorporating recent work on taxes and corporate financial policy is impressive and important. By comparison, their treatment of the benefit offsets to taxation is more debatable. This is especially unfortunate, since they tend to give these more questionable assumptions equal billing with their important work on tax-induced effects on financial policy and the public sharing of private risk.

Having said all that, one wonders whether it really matters. After all, the conceptual experiment being simulated is the replacement of one tax with another. Since the tax change under examination would almost certainly affect corporate financial policy, incorporating the financial decision in the model is crucial. But the taxes involved in the experiments in differential analysis are not said to be benefit taxes. Thus it appears on a priori grounds that it would make very little difference for tax incidence how the taxes that may be benefit taxes are treated. On the other hand, since welfare effects are proportional to squares of distortions, the same cannot necessarily be said of them. At several points the authors provide useful sensitivity analysis of how welfare effects depend on their treatment of property taxes.

The Government Sector

Fullerton and Gordon are forced by their desire for completeness, as well as by methodological necessity, to consider explicitly two components of the public sector, government enterprises and general government. There are, however, questionable aspects of both treatments.

The Fullerton and Gordon treatment of government enterprise does not involve including in their model standard results from the literature on government enterprises. Rather, it is simply a mechanical adaptation of their private-sector modeling of risk taking and investment. While one cannot necessarily expect a full-blown theory of public enterprise, one must be a bit uneasy about casually assuming that public firms follow so closely in the assumed footprints of private firms. Particularly trouble-some is the modeling of leverage costs; though public enterprises rarely founder, the risk of bankruptcy in the public sector may not be negligible, and it may be different in kind from that in the private sector. Thus it seems unlikely that correcting the average private risk premium to ab-stract from risk of bankruptcy gives an accurate estimate of the appropri-ate risk premium to use for either government enterprises or general government.

The Fullerton and Gordon treatment of general government is even more questionable. First, it may be true that 72% of all government capital occurs in the state and local area. But through its budget deficits and the need to refinance the national debt the federal government generates enormous demands for financial capital. Beyond that, the treatment of governmental demand for labor in the model is sketchy, at best.

Second, Fullerton and Gordon assume, without adequate justification, that government revenues adjust so that government utility, given by a Cobb-Douglas function, remains constant, despite tax-induced changes in relative prices. This approach is questionable on several grounds. Most basically, the notion that government derives utility directly, rather than meeting the demands of consumers and producers for public services, is quite extreme. Moreover, it is inconsistent to treat much of general government (especially local government financed by property taxes) as supplying goods and services in response to benefit-related taxes, without including those goods and services in the utility functions of households or in the production functions of firms. Finally, except under very special assumptions, the assumption that government's utility remains constant when taxes are changed is not a satisfactory shortcut to assuming that the utility individuals receive from government services remains constant.

A final extreme assumption that deserves attention is the fixing of the real value of transfers in the face of tax-induced changes in consumer prices. As Browning (1978; Browning and Johnson 1979) has shown, this assumption can have dramatic effects on results of incidence analysis. But whether it is defensible is another issue. One must wonder whether this assumption is significantly more innocuous in the present context of analysis of the welfare costs of taxation.

Other Matters

The treatment of personal saving behavior seems rather odd. Fullerton and Gordon seem to be saying that individuals allocate a given percent-age of saving to pensions, Keogh plans, and related tax preferred savings vehicles and then allocate the rest of saving between taxable and tax-exempt securities on the basis of the rate of return. This description of behavior is suspect on several counts. First, why do they choose this partioning between fixed allocations and allocations that depend on rates of return? Is the first split really independent of tax considerations?

Fullerton and Gordon employ a standard 70–30 split between taxable and exempt forms of saving. But some forms of exempt saving, such as IRAs, have statutory dollar limits. Thus one wonders if this split is appropriate at the margin. If it is not, the use of weights of 70% and 30% in calculating the average of marginal tax rates of investors is inappropriate. Finally, does it matter whether "pensions" are defined benefit plans or defined contribution plans? I can imagine that the individual may have considerable discretion over whether to invest in the latter. But I doubt that the same discretion exists so far as defined benefit plans are concerned.

Fullerton and Gordon deal quite summarily with what appears to be a major problem, cases in which their calculation of the demand for labor in the noncorporate sector produces a negative number. They apparently get around this by aggregating corporate and noncorporate labor and capital in each industry before inserting their values into the production function. Such an approach does, of course, imply a rather strange theory of production at the firm level.

It is surprising that after making so much fuss over the difference between average and marginal tax rates Fullerton and Gordon do not provide more information about differences in these rates. It would be interesting, for example, to know (a) how average and marginal tax rates differ, for each industry, (b) the primary sources of the differences, and (c) how much the difference makes for the effects of the tax changes under examination.

References

Browning, E. K. 1978. The burden of taxation. *Journal of Political Economy* 86: 649–71.

Browning, E. K., and W. R. Johnson. 1979. *The distribution of the tax burden*. Washington: American Enterprise Institute.

Harberger, A. C. 1966. Efficiency effects of taxes on income from capital. In M. Krzyzankiak, ed., *Effects of corporation income tax*, pp. 107–17. Detroit: Wayne State University Press.

McLure, C. E., Jr. 1979. *Must corporate income be taxed twice?* Washington: Brookings Institution.

12   A General Equilibrium Model of Taxation with Endogenous Financial Behavior

Joel Slemrod

12.1   Introduction

This paper presents and utilizes a new general equilibrium simulation model of capital income taxation. Its chief advantage over existing models of taxation is that it recognizes that agents may adjust their financial behavior in response to changes in the way that capital income is taxed. The model can trace the general equilibrium impact of these financial adjustments and calculate the tax-induced changes in the allocation of factors and production as well as the distributional effects of any tax change.

The paper is organized as follows. Section 12.2 provides as background a brief review of the important antecedent literature. In section 12.3, I describe the structure of the model, while in section 12.4, the parameterization and control solution of the model are detailed. Section 12.5 uses the model to simulate the general equilibrium impact of changing the present system of taxing capital income under inflation to a perfectly indexed tax system. Some concluding remarks are made in section 12.6.

12.2   Review of the Literature

General equilibrium analysis of the effects of taxation began with the static, two-sector, two-factors-of-production model of Harberger (1959, 1962, 1966).[1] In the original version of the model, two competitive

Joel Slemrod is with the Department of Economics, University of Minnesota.

The author acknowledges helpful comments on an earlier draft from Daniel Frisch and Don Fullerton, and able research assistance from Richard Rogerson. Financial assistance was provided by the National Bureau of Economic Research and a University of Minnesota Faculty Research Grant.

1. For earlier uses of this type of model, see Meade (1955) and Johnson (1956).

427

industries employ two factors which are perfectly mobile between the sectors, but are fixed in total supply; the factors are paid a return which, including taxes paid, is equal to their respective marginal products. All consumers (and the government by implication) have identical homothetic preference functions as to the two goods. This formulation allows one to account directly for the interdependence among all product and factor markets.[2]

The Harberger model is especially suited for the analysis of differential taxation of either final outputs or factors. The effect of a differential tax on factor returns and the commodity price ratio is shown to depend on the relative factor intensity of production in the two sectors, the substitutability of factors in production, and the extent of demand substitutability. If all consumers and the government do not have identical homothetic preference functions, then any shifting of income among these groups would also have repercussions for relative prices since the composition of aggregate demand would change. The personal incidence of a differential tax depends on the personal distribution of factor endowments and consumption preferences. If all individuals have identical factor endowments, then any changes in factor returns have no income distributional effect from the sources of income side. If consumption preferences do not vary, then relative price variations do not have any distributional implications from the uses of income side.

Harberger's methodology was to solve the general equilibrium system analytically, making the problem tractable by assuming linearity or using a local approximation, and by limiting the dimensions of the problem. Shoven and Whalley (1972) showed that such a general equilibrium system could be solved explicitly without simplifications, using an appropriate solution algorithm. A variety of functional forms for production and demand functions could then be specified. The comparative static effects of a tax change are found by simply comparing the pre- and postchange equilibria. The flexibility of this method of solution allowed Shoven and Whalley to disaggregate the general equilibrium model more extensively than had been previously attempted. Disaggregation of production allows a more detailed calculation of the intersectoral misallocation caused by, for example, differential factor tax application. Disaggregation of consumer groups permits a detailed assessment of changes in the personal distribution of income.

In the most recent use of this technique, sixteen consumer goods (counting savings as one such good) are distinguished. Using input-output information, a vector of consumer goods is translated into a vector of nineteen produced goods, which in turn are produced by labor and capital. Twelve consumer classes are distinguished on the basis of differ-

2. For a discussion of the relative merits of general versus partial equilibrium analyses of taxation, see McLure (1975).

ing marginal personal tax rates, factor endowments, and consumption preferences. Although it is larger, the Fullerton-Shoven-Whalley[3] model has the same basic structure as the simple Harberger model.

Some recent research, though, has focused on a number of potentially important aspects of the capital income tax environment which are outside the scope of a Harberger-type model. For example, one characteristic of the Harberger-type models is that in an equilibrium situation all individuals face the same relative rates of tax on capital placed in the various sectors. The pattern of marginal products of capital is such that the after-tax rates of return on capital in all sectors are equal for all individuals; each individual can be thought of as owning a proportionate share of all the economy's capital goods. Note that this kind of equilibrium would be impossible if the relative rates of tax on capital goods differed for different individuals. Feldstein and Slemrod (1980) point out that this is in fact the case in the United States, where there is (i) progressive personal taxation with marginal rates ranging from below the corporate rate to above the corporate rate, and (ii) the opportunity to substantially reduce personal taxation through corporate retained earnings. In this situation corporate-source capital income may be taxed more or less heavily than noncorporate capital income depending on one's tax bracket. If corporate equity and other capital income sources were perfect substitutes for other than tax reasons, then we would expect to observe that in equilibrium any individual would invest entirely in corporate equity or entirely in the alternative asset, but never both; this specialization will occur whenever the relative tax on two types of investment differs for different groups. In order to explain the observed tendency for investors to hold diversified portfolios, an explicit portfolio balance relation is required.

Ideally, a model should specify the sources of risk in the economy, individuals' attitude toward risk bearing (expressed in the form of cardinal utility functions), and the opportunities for portfolio diversification. In such a model, portfolios will differ by consumer class. Therefore, for certain problems it may be incorrect to assume that all capital owners bear the burden of tax changes identically.

The work of Stiglitz (1973) and King (1974), building on the classic paper of Modigliani and Miller (1958), made clear that any analysis of corporation taxation must consider the financial flexibility that corporations have. Interest paid on debt is deductible from corporate taxable income, and dividends are taxed differently than retained earnings so that the effective tax on equity earnings depends on the capital structure and the payout policy of the corporation. When Harberger and Shoven-Whalley calculate the total effective tax on corporate-source capital income, they consider the financial structure of the sector, but when the

---

3. The later versions of the model are the work of Fullerton, Shoven, and Whalley.

effects of a tax change are simulated, financial policy is assumed to be unaffected.[4] Papers by Ballentine and McLure (1978) and Feldstein, Green, and Sheshinski (1979) have investigated the effects of corporation income tax in a world of flexible corporate financial policy, but neither posed the question in a general equilibrium model with differentially taxed wealth owners and several production sectors.

This concludes the overview of the important antecedent literature. The research since Harberger may, it seems, be divided into two categories. The first category features highly stylized, usually partial equilibrium, models that focus on one aspect of capital income taxation, such as the implications of a progressive tax system or the role of corporate financial decisions. In the second category is the work of Shoven and his collaborators, where a large general equilibrium model is constructed as a framework for the analysis of a wide range of taxation issues. However, the Shoven model, being fundamentally identical to the smaller Harberger model, inadequately treats several of the important issues raised in the first group of papers. The remainder of this paper is devoted to the development of a new model which is general equilibrium in the tradition of the second category of research, but can also offer insight into the issues raised by the first categroy of the recent literature.

12.3   Description of the Model

12.3.1   Distinguishing Characteristics

In this section, the structure of the general equilibrium model with financial behavior (to be referred to hereafter as GEFB) is presented. Before proceeding to a more detailed discussion of its features, its distinguishing characteristics are briefly noted here.

1. Explicit treatment of riskiness. Income from capital is not certain, and individuals are risk-averse. Individuals allocate their wealth among the available asset types on the basis of optimal portfolio considerations.

2. Portfolio choice under progressive taxation. Since different agents face different tax rates, they will hold different portfolios.[5] Thus, for incidence results, it is not generally true that all capital owners will be identically affected to the extent that they own capital.

3. Endogenous tax rates. An individual's marginal tax rate is not fixed, but rather depends on the amount of his or her taxable income. This is an important consideration in the decision of how much financial leverage to

---

4. In Fullerton, King, Shoven, and Whalley (1979), corporations can adjust their dividend policy in environments where dividends get preferential tax treatment, but only the extreme alternative of 100% payout is considered.

5. Compare this to the result of standard general equilibrium models that all individuals hold exactly the same mix of capital goods, which is clearly counterfactual.

acquire, since the marginal tax saving from borrowing declines with greater borrowing in a progressive tax system.

4. Tax-exempt bonds. These securities are a potentially significant outlet for the wealth of high-tax-bracket individuals and are included in the available asset menu.

5. Rental and owned housing. The capital income from these two ways of consuming housing are subject to very different taxation schemes. In this model the two types of housing are treated separately.

6. Corporate financial policy. The importance of the ability to alter corporate financial decisions in response to the tax environment has already been noted. The GEFB model can accommodate endogenous corporate decisions in a number of ways.

12.3.2   Risk, Risk Aversion, and Portfolio Choice

Each agent in the economy is endowed with a fixed amount of capital goods and a fixed amount of labor in efficiency units. The capital goods may be used in the production of goods for sale or in the production of housing services to be consumed by the owner. Labor is inelastically supplied to firms in return for a wage.

The production functions of all goods other than owner-occupied housing are stochastic. The stochastic element, though, refers only to the contribution to production of the capital input; thus the marginal product of labor is certain.[6]

In the standard Harberger model, the individual implicitly faces a two-stage decision process. In the first stage, his endowment of factors is allocated in order to maximize the flow of income or, equivalently, wealth at some point in time. In the second stage, the income flow is allocated among consumption goods in order to maximize utility. In the GEFB model, a similar but modified two-stage decision process is envisioned. In the first stage, the individual constructs a portfolio to maximize the expected utility of the stream of income or, equivalently, the expected utility of some future period's wealth. Once the uncertainty is resolved and actual income is revealed, the income is allocated among consumption goods to maximize the utility obtained.

The following special form of the first-stage maximand will be considered:

$$\bar{y} - \beta \frac{V}{K},$$

where $\bar{y}$ is the expected flow of after-tax income, β is a trade-off coefficient, V is the variance of after-tax income, and K is the capital endowment. This formulation has the desirable feature that the portfolio de-

---

6. An example of such a production function is $Q = K^{\gamma}L^{1-\gamma} + \theta K$, where θ is stochastic.

mand functions implied by its maximization are identical to the optimal rules for an individual who has only capital income and is faced with a frictionless capital market and an infinitesimal planning horizon.[7]

In the second stage, realized income is allocated among the consumption goods. Since only homothetic utility functions are considered, maximizing the expected utility of income in the first stage also maximizes the expected utility of consumption.

12.3.3   Model Structure

In this section, the overall structure of the model will be laid out. In subsequent sections, more detailed attention will be paid to certain sectors of the model and their parameterization.

The economy's agents are considered to consist of nine stylized types, each representing a different income class. The agents vary in their (fixed) endowment of capital and labor as well as their preferences for consumption goods. All individuals are assumed to have the same coefficient of risk aversion. Because there is a progressive tax system, the different categories of individuals, called "income groups" for convenience, will have different marginal tax rates and the after-tax riskiness of assets will also differ among individuals.

The model has production functions for each of four goods: food, rental housing, owner-occupied housing, and a composite good produced by corporations. Each income class has a demand function for each good, which depends on real income, relative prices, and the tastes of the income group.

There are asset demand functions of each class for each of six assets: food-sector capital, rental housing, owner-occupied housing, corporate equity, taxable debt, which is assumed to be riskless, and tax-exempt debt, which has some uncertainty of return. These functions are derived from the first-order conditions for the maximization of expected utility, and include as arguments the capital endowment, the after-tax expected real rate of returns on the available assets, the after-tax variance-covariance structure, and the degree of risk aversion. The tax system is assumed to regard net losses symmetrically with net gains, and the marginal tax rate is assumed constant in the calculation of after-tax variances and covariances.

There are market-clearing equations for all assets and all goods. The supply equations of different assets have different characteristics. For housing and food-sector capital, the supply simply equals the capital stock used in production. For corporate equity, asset supply is the equity-

---

7. In the case of a portfolio choice between one risky and one riskless asset, the demand for the risky asset is given by $K_E = K(r_E - r_B)/2\beta V_E$, where E refers to the risky asset and β to the riskless asset. The coefficient β is proportional to Pratt's measure of relative risk aversion. The generalization to many assets is straightforward. See Friend and Blume (1975).

capital ratio, which is endogenous, multiplied by the corporate capital stock. The supply of tax-exempt debt is fixed by state and local governments, and is exogenous to the model. The supply of taxable debt is the sum of the exogenously given supply of federal government debt and the amount of corporate debt, which is equal to the corporate debt-capital ratio times the corporate capital stock. Since both the debt-capital ratio and the corporate capital stock may be endogenous, the total supply of taxable debt also may be endogenous. The market-clearing equations for goods simply state that demand equals production.

The model also includes equations for the allocation of labor to sectors (equalization of marginal revenue product), factor supply identities, and determination of real income and taxable income by income group. There is also a corporate earnings exhaustion equation, which ensures that total corporate earnings net of corporation income tax accrue either to corporate debtholders or to equityholders.

The basic structure of the model is thus similar to the standard general equilibrium model of taxation, except that the simple capital allocation equations are replaced by explicit portfolio demand equations and market-clearing equations for each of several financial assets. Other distinguishing aspects of the model are discussed further below.

12.3.4   Endogenous Tax Rates

The total tax liability and marginal tax rates in the various kinds of income are calculated by appropriately reducing the income flows of the group to a per-tax-return basis, calculating taxable income, and applying the actual pattern of tax brackets and rates that were applicable in 1977.[8] Taxable income differs from real income in a number of significant ways. First of all, certain deductions and exemptions are allowed. The average value of all such deductions and exemptions other than for interest and property tax payments is considered to be fixed and is entered as a subtraction from income. The amount of allowable deductions for interest and property tax paid is endogenously determined using the simulated portfolios.[9] Second, nominal interest received rather than real interest received (and paid) is included in taxable income. Third, the imputed income from owned housing is not included in taxable income, though a small fraction of the nominal rise in housing values due to inflation is included in order to reflect the partial taxation of capital gains on residences. Similarly, a fraction of the inflation-induced capital gains

8. Since the discontinuous marginal tax rates of the actual tax system cause problems for the solution algorithm, a smooth approximation of the tax table is used.

9. Of course not all taxpayers itemize deductions. To reflect this fact, the average exogenous deduction amount is calculated including the standard deduction for itemizers, and only a percentage of property tax and interest payments are allowed as additional deductions. The percentage is chosen to approximate the fraction of such payments which are made by itemizers, and varies by income class.

on other assets is included.[10] The income from equity, after the corporation tax, is only partially included in taxable income to reflect the fact that retained earnings are virtually exempt from personal taxation. The fraction included in taxable income is equal to $d + (1 - d)c$, where d is the payout ratio and c is the ratio of the effective tax on capital gains to the tax on dividends. The value of c will be less than one because of the exclusion of one-half of long-term capital gains, the value of the deferral of tax payments until realization of the gain, and the opportunity to avoid tax by bequeathing appreciated stock. For present purposes the value of c is taken to be 0.125. The income from state and local securities is not part of the taxable income. Finally, there is an addition to individual taxable income (for rental housing and food-sector capital owned) and to corporation taxable income (for corporate capital) to reflect the mismeasurement of capital income that is due to historical cost depreciation and certain inventory accounting methods. Since depreciation on owner-occupied housing is not deductible from taxable income, inflation does not thereby cause any additional tax to be paid due to consuming owned housing services.

Once the total taxable income is determined, the marginal tax rate on a dollar of taxable income (call it t) is calculated by referring to the tax tables. The real after-tax rate of return earned by the ith asset is then equal to $r_i - t(r_i^\tau)$, where r_i is the before-tax real rate of return and r_i^τ is the addition to taxable income from holding one dollar of the ith asset. For all the reasons mentioned above, r_i^τ may differ from r_i. For example, the after-tax real rate of return to holding a nominal debt security is $r_B - t(r_B + \pi)$, since a dollar of debt yields $r_B + \pi$ (the nominal interest rate) of taxable income.

12.3.5   Tax-exempt Bonds

In the model there is a fixed supply of debt issued by state and local governments, the interest from which is exempt from federal income taxation. They are presumed here to be risky assets, though they are significantly less risky than corporate equity, rental housing, or food-sector capital.

Individuals cannot borrow at the tax-exempt interest rate; that is, they must hold a nonnegative quantity of these securities. An important question is whether individuals can simultaneously hold tax-exempt bonds and receive a tax deduction for interest paid on their outstanding borrowing. The tax law states that individuals cannot borrow for the express purpose of buying tax-exempt bonds and still claim the interest expense as a deduction. However, it is possible for an individual to

---

10. Nominal capital gains on all assets other than corporate equity are assumed to be equal to the rate of inflation. The real value of corporate stock also increases to the extent that earnings are retained within the corporation.

deduct interest payments while at the same time holding tax-exempt debt. The Internal Revenue Service position is apparently that whenever an outstanding obligation is not directly connected with a personal or business loan, it will be inferred that its purpose is to carry tax-exempt assets, and therefore its interest expense will be disallowed as a tax deduction. However, the Tax Court and other courts have ruled that in order to be disallowed the debt and the tax-exempt property must somehow be related in purpose.[11]

For present purposes what is needed is an operational rule which approximately captures the regulations' effective limitation on interest expense deductions when a portfolio includes tax-exempt bonds. We have chosen the rule that the IRS will disallow that fraction of any individual's interest deductions equal to the ratio of the value of tax-exempt bonds to total net wealth. Under this rule, the net cost of borrowing depends on the amount of wealth invested in tax-exempt bonds; also, the after-tax return of tax-exempt bonds depends on how leveraged one's portfolio is.

12.3.6   Housing

It is assumed that the housing sector produces housing services from capital with no labor input. Though the omission of labor is certainly a stylization of the production process, it is not an unwarranted exaggeration. Aaron (1972) notes that housing services require the combination of more capital per unit of labor than does any major category of consumer or investment goods. Using a detailed input-output matrix, Fullerton, King, Shoven, and Whalley (1979) calculate the capital-labor ratio of producing housing services to be approximately twenty times higher than the economy-wide capital-labor ratio and fifteen times higher than any other major sector.[12]

It is further assumed that the services from rented housing and the services from owner-occupied housing are considered by consumers to be distinct commodities. In actuality, though their characteristics tend to differ, the distinction is not absolute. Which type of housing will be chosen by a given family unit (they may in many cases effectively be mutually exclusive commodities), and the quantity consumed given that choice, will depend on tastes as well as the relative price of rented versus owner-occupied housing. If all the individuals within an income group are aggregated, the aggregate relative consumption of the two types of

11. See Internal Revenue Service Proceedings 72-18 and James (1979).
12. Aaron and others have pointed out that although the production of housing services is capital-intensive, production of the housing stock itself is relatively labor-intensive; of all the major private sectors of the economy, only finance and insurance had as high a fraction of direct labor requirements. Analysis of this issue would require expanding the model to include the demand for and production of capital goods; this looms beyond the scope of current research aims.

housing services may be represented as a smooth function of the relative price of the two goods and the distribution of tastes within the class (see Rosen and Rosen 1980).

The set of available assets includes rented and owner-occupied housing. It is assumed that the production of services from rental housing capital is subject to stochastic influences, and the production of services from owner-occupied housing is not stochastic. In expected-value terms, the two production functions are identical. The model then has a market-clearing equation for rental housing, where the sum of the nine income groups' demand for it as an asset must equal the stock necessary to supply the rental services demanded by consumers at the equilibrium relative prices. For owner-occupied housing, the situation is somewhat different. For each income class, there is an additional constraint that the desired stock must produce a flow of services equal to the amount of services demanded *by that class*. Thus there is implicitly a separate market for each class in which each individual rents the housing services from himself. For each class, there is a shadow price of consuming housing. This price has three components: (i) the pecuniary income foregone through holding capital in housing rather than another asset, (ii) the cost of maintenance and depreciation, and (iii) any attendant tax liabilities or rebates.

12.3.7   The Government Sector

One function of the government is relative price stabilization. In the absence of government intervention, the market-clearing pattern of relative prices would depend on the state of the world that obtains. In this economy, though, the government maintains stocks of all commodities, and pledges to defend a particular relative price structure by buying all production at these prices and selling that amount of each commodity such that these announced prices support markets that clear. The relative price structure that the government supports is the one that would obtain if realized production was equal to the expected value of production in each sector. Of course which prices are supported depends on the allocation of capital and labor by sector. This arrangement leads to market clearing with no intervention necessary if the expected values of all sectors' production obtain, and with some use of the government's commodity stocks possibly required if they do not. Note that by doing this the government does not insulate agents from the production uncertainty, but rather confines the effects of the uncertainty to incomes while making relative prices nonstochastic.[13]

---

13. Two considerations motivate the introduction of this role for government. The first is that in the absence of such a role, the individual must consider the covariation between asset returns and relative prices in making his or her portfolio decision. This is a significant complication that the assumption of no relative price uncertainty avoids. Second, and

The government must also collect taxes to finance its expenditure, which has three components. The first is spending on goods and services, which is fixed. The second component is interest payments, which vary according to the equilibrium interest rates on government debt. The third component is the cost of the price supports discussed above. Since uncertain capital income constitutes part of the tax base, total tax revenue is also uncertain. The government constructs its tax schedules so that the expected value of its tax revenues equals its expenditure commitments. Any divergence of actual tax revenues from this expected value is made up by a special tax levied in proportion to the value of each agent's tax liability.

When the economic environment changes so that expected revenues no longer equal desired expenditure, the government alters the tax rate schedules to reestablish the equality. Thus the expected value of the stochastic tax transfers will always be zero.

12.3.8 Corporate Financial Policy

Corporate financial policy represents another dimension of possible behavioral response to changes in the tax environment. Modigliani and Miller (1958) demonstrated the irrelevance to firm market value of corporate financial decisions in the absence of taxes, and speculated that financial flexibility would allow firms to avoid any corporation income tax by issuing debt instead of equity and to avoid any tax on dividends by retaining earnings within the corporation. Much recent work, some of which was referred to earlier, has reexamined the interaction between capital income taxation and corporate finance taking into account, among other things, the personal taxation of debt interest, the effective capital gains tax on retained earnings, and progressive taxation.

In Slemrod (1980)[14] I discuss several methods of introducing the financial flexibility of corporations into a GEFB model. Because of the lack of a consensus about just what characterizes a capital market equilibrium in the environment described above, no simple procedure will be completely satisfactory. Nevertheless, in that work I utilized a procedure which is in the spirit of several theoretical treatments of corporate financial behavior in the presence of taxes and is consistent with the econometric evidence concerning financial policy behavior. I will briefly describe

---

related, in the presence of price uncertainty there is some ambiguity about how "risky" an asset is. As Stiglitz (1969) has pointed out, even if the real output from an investment were perfectly certain, fluctuations in outputs of other commodities would still make the given investment risky, since both its relative price and the marginal utility of income would vary. Under certain conditions a sector with no technological uncertainty may experience greater uncertainty in return than an industry which does have a stochastic production function. Assuming no price uncertainty avoids this ambiguity.

14. See pp. 69–97 for a more detailed treatment of the issues raised in this section and for alternative treatments of financial policy in this model.

in turn the procedure, its theoretical justification, and the relevant econometric evidence.

The suggested procedure is to set both important corporate financial decisions (debt-equity and payout) to be functions of critical "tax cost" values. Behind this procedure is a theory which envisions the corporation maximizing its value by balancing the net tax advantages of its financial structure with the other costs and benefits of the policy. For debt-equity policy, the costs that offset the tax advantages of debt may be real bankruptcy costs or agency costs. For dividend policy, the tax advantages of retained earnings must be balanced against the transactions cost of receiving income in the form of capital gains, the signaling value of dividends, constraints on firm growth, and the law which inhibits the unwarrranted accumulation of funds within the corporation.

One common element of these nontax factors is the difficulty of quantifying them and explicitly relating their magnitude to the financial policies chosen. Rather than arbitrarily constructing such measures, I instead use econometrically estimated responses of financial policy to the tax cost of the policies involved. The presumption is that these measured responses are the result of an optimal balancing of tax considerations with the other implications of the financial decision.

The estimated responsiveness of the debt-equity ratio comes from King (1978), where he finds an elasticity of 0.8 with respect to the tax cost variable $t_c(1 - t_\beta)^A$, where t_c is the rate of corporation income tax and $(1 - t_\beta)^A$ is a weighted average of (one minus) the marginal tax rate of equityholders. This value measures the cost of raising new capital through debt versus new share issue. The estimated responsiveness of the payout ratio is taken from Slemrod (1980), where the work of Brittain (1966) was updated. The estimated elasticity of the payout ratio with respect to the tax cost of dividends $(t_D - t_{RE})^A$ (the weighted average of the difference in the tax rate on dividends minus the effective tax rate on retained earnings) was found there to be -0.79.

12.4   Parameterization and the Control Solution

12.4.1   Parameterizing the Model

The model is parameterized to represent a stylized United States economy of the year 1977. That year is chosen because it is the most recent year for which detailed tax return information is available. Unfortunately, though, the best information available about certain key values refers to earlier years. Thus it is often necessary to update and adjust data to represent the 1977 situation.

One crucial set of values for which the best data available are severely outdated is the distribution of wealth. The most accurate source for this as well as for the structure of portfolios by income and wealth class remains the Federal Reserve Board's *Survey of Financial Characteristics of Consumers* (*SFCC*), which refers to year-end 1962. The *SFCC* disaggregates the wealth and portfolio information into nine income classes. In order to obtain a wealth distribution for 1977, it is assumed here that the relative distribution of wealth by real income class has not changed since 1962. The *SFCC* income classes are thus inflated by a factor of three, which is approximately the factor by which per capita disposable personal income rose between 1962 and 1977.[15] The resulting nine income classes for the 1977 model are as follows: $0–$9,000, $9,000–$15,000, $15,000–$22,500, $22,500–$30,000, $30,000–$45,000, $45,000–$75,000, $75,000–$150,000, $150,000–$300,000, and over $300,000. The nine stylized individuals in the economy represent average individuals of each of these income classes. The relative distribution of wealth among these classes is assumed to be the same as the relative distribution among the equivalent 1962 classes.[16]

Under the model's assumptions the relative gross remuneration of labor will equal the relative endowment of labor in efficiency units. To approximate this distribution, I use the 1977 *Statistics of Income* measure of wages and salaries received by taxpaying units in each income class, supplemented by adding one-half of the net return to business, profession, farm, and partnership as an approximation to the labor input share in self-employment.[17] The resulting distribution of labor is given in table 12.A.1 of the appendix.

In order to obtain the value of total private wealth, the ratio of private wealth to labor units as of 1962 was calculated and then applied to the total labor endowment in 1977. That procedure yielded 4.24 billion units, or $4.24 billion worth, of private wealth.[18] As mentioned above, the

15. The exact factor of increase is 2.92.

16. In Harberger's original treatment and in the subsequent Shoven et al. papers, the unit of capital was defined as that amount which (in the assumed equilibrium) earned one dollar of income net of all taxes. This procedure is perfectly consistent with their model that ignores the differential riskiness of capital, since then it is a condition of equilibrium that the net return of each unit of capital be equalized. However, when risk (and any other) differences in particular forms of capital are recognized, this procedure is no longer valid. For example, the quantity of risky capital which produces a given expected net return will be less than the required quantity of riskless capital.

The long-run equilibrium condition that would be observed in a world with differential riskiness of capital is that each unit of capital be valued the same. Since capital can move between sectors, any difference in value would be incompatible with equilibrium. Thus I have chosen to represent a unit of capital as that quantity which in 1977 was valued at one dollar.

17. This is an imperfect measure of the appropriate return to labor since it does not include employer contributions for social insurance programs.

18. A more direct method of calculating private wealth yields a similar figure. The 1977 net stock of fixed nonresidential capital was valued by the Bureau of Economic Analysis at $1.616 billion, residential capital at $1.713 billion, and inventories at $0.506 billion, for a total of $3.835 billion. The value of federal, state, and local securities held by households

distribution of that wealth is determined according to the relative ownership of wealth from *SFCC*. The resulting wealth distribution is also shown in table 12.A.1 of the appendix.

Because the utility function of each class is assumed to be Cobb-Douglas, knowing the share of consumption that goes to each good is sufficient for parameterizing the function. The source for spending shares is the Bureau of Labor Statistics' *Consumer Expenditure Interview Survey, 1972–73*. The income classes delineated in the survey are inflated to refer to 1977.[19] The food share is computed as the ratio of expenditure on food at home to current consumption expenditures; the rental housing share is the ratio of expenditure on rented dwellings to current consumption expenditures. The appropriate share for owner-occupied housing cannot be straightforwardly obtained from the expenditure survey, since the true cost of this behavior is not correctly measured. To obtain the true cost of owner-occupied housing, I apply a conversion factor to the reported spending equal to the ratio of actual spending to reported spending.[20] The highest income bracket for which results are reported in the expenditure survey is $50,000 and over ($75,000 and over in 1977 dollars). This blurs any possible distinction in the consumption preferences of the top three income classes. Rather than use the reported expenditure shares of the over $75,000 group for all of the top three classes (and implicitly assume an income elasticity of one in this range), the shares of spending of the top three classes are found by extrapolating the share of the sixth income class to higher incomes using estimated income elasticities.[21] The resulting shares for food, rental housing, and owned housing, and, as a residual, the corporate good, are displayed in table 12.A.2 of the appendix.

The effective corporation income tax is calculated by dividing 1977 corporate profits without inventory valuation or capital consumption adjustment into the total 1977 corporate profits tax liability; this yields a value of 0.41.

---

was reported by the Federal Reserve Board to be $0.234 billion, while the amount held by private domestic nongovernment agents was $0.680 billion.

Since the procedure for precisely calculating private wealth in our stylized model without financial institutions is not obvious, it must suffice to show that a synthetic calculation using these figures will yield a number not far from the $4.24 billion used in the model.

19. The brackets used in the Consumer Expenditure Interview Survey are inflated by a factor of 1.5, which is approximately the factor of increase in per capita disposable personal income between 1977 and the end of 1972. (The figure for 1977 is $6,017, and the average of 1972 and 1973 is $4,061.)

20. Details of how this conversion factor is calculated are available from the author.

21. The income elasticity of food is taken to be 0.51, as estimated by Houtthaker and Taylor (1966). The income elasticities of rental and owner-occupied housing in the upper income classes are assumed to be 0.70 and 1, respectively. These numbers are compatible with the findings of Rosen (1978) that the income elasticities of rental and owned housing were both 0.76, given tenure choice, but that the probability of being an owner increased with income.

The property tax rate of 0.0154 is calculated by dividing total property tax payments in 1975 ($51.49 billion) by total assessed value of property in that year ($1,063.9 billion) and applying an estimated percentage of assessed value to market value (0.327).[22]

The aggregate corporate debt-equity ratio of 0.721 is calculated by dividing the flow of funds estimate of the 1977 value of corporate debt by the value of corporate equity ($749.7 billion divided by $1,039.5 billion).

The payout ratio of 0.544 is found by dividing dividend payments in 1977 by corporate profits after inventory valuation and capital consumption adjustment ($42.1 billion divided by $77.3 billion).

The anticipated rate of inflation is taken to be 6%, which was the average annual increase in the Consumer Price Index between 1975 and 1977.

The mismeasurement of corporate taxable income due to inflation is calculated to be $0.00515 of additional taxable income per dollar of corporate capital for each percentage point of inflation. For example, a 6% rate of inflation will cause a $46.35 billion ($0.00515 \times 6 \times 1.5 \times 10^{12}$) overstatement of corporate profits on a corporate capital stock valued at $1.5 trillion. This coefficient was calculated using estimates of the overstatement of taxable profits taken from Feldstein and Summers (1979) and values of corporate fixed capital and inventories. The desired coefficient, call it d, should make the equation $E = d\pi K_c$ correct, where E is the profit overstatement, π is the inflation rate, and K_c is the value of corporate capital. Solving for d, $E/\pi K_c$ comes to 0.00512 for 1977, and as an average over the period 1970 to 1977 comes to 0.00519. I therefore use 0.00515 to represent d for corporate capital as well as food-sector capital and rental housing capital.

Since most government securities are not directly held by households, the appropriate value of these stocks in a model with no financial institutions is problematic. I have chosen values of $100 billion of state and local securities, and $200 billion of federal government securities. These values are approximately 1.25 times the reported household holdings of these assets in 1977.

The measure of risk aversion β is taken to be 3 for all income groups. This value was chosen since equilibria calculated using this value yielded simulated risk premiums consistent with observed magnitudes and because it is compatible with some recent research.[23] There is little empirical basis for choosing the variance-covariance structure of the assets. For these simulations I will assume all covariances to be zero, and the average

22. The source for the property tax payments and total assessed value is *Facts and Figures on Government Finance* (Washington: Tax Foundation, 1977). The assessment ratio is from the 1972 Census of Governments.

23. A value for β of 3 is comparable to a coefficient of relative risk aversion of 6. This is consistent with the recent findings of Friend and Hasbrouck (1980), although earlier research (see Friend and Blume 1975) found values on the order of 2.

after-tax variances of the assets to be 0.07 for corporate equity, 0.05 for rental housing, 0.12 for food-sector capital, and 0.02 for tax-exempt bonds. Of course the methodology can handle any variance-covariance structure, including one with nonzero off-diagonal elements.

The exponents on capital input in the Cobb-Douglas production functions are set at 0.207 for the corporate sector and 0.111 for the food-related sector.

12.4.2 The Control Solution

With this parameterization, the model is solved for an equilibrium solution using a modified Gauss-Seidel algorithm. The equilibrium values of some of the key variables are presented in table 12.1. Note that the expected returns given in the table are net of any corporation income and property tax payments, but are before personal tax payments. The choice of simple function specifications and realistic parameters makes it impossible to reproduce exactly all the actual 1977 prices and allocations. It is reassuring, though, that the model solution yields an allocation of factors, production, and relative prices which is close to what the actual 1977 economy looked like.

The calculated expected rates of return are compatible with actual observations. The actual 1977 nominal interest rate on corporate debt was 0.080 for Aaa bonds and 0.090 for Baa-rated bonds, compared to the model result of 0.104. The difference may be attributed to the model's anticipated inflation rate of 6%, which may be an overestimate of actual long-term inflation expectations in that year. The predicted nominal rate on tax-exempt bonds is 0.061, compared to Standard and Poor's yield index in 1977 of 0.056, again a slight overestimate. The expected real rate of return to equity that the model calculates in 0.106. That is somewhat higher than the average annual rate of return on the Standard and Poor's composite index of New York Stock Exchange equities over the period 1926–77, which is 0.081.[24] However, 0.106 is substantially higher than the realized real rate of return on equities in the decade preceding 1977. All in all, 0.106 seems a not too unreasonable though perhaps optimistic reading of the expected return on equity in 1977.

The equilibrium solution includes the portfolio holdings of each income class. This information is not reproduced in detail here, though some characteristics deserve note. As expected, the ownership of equity is skewed toward the higher income classes. The top three income classes (over $75,000 income), which are presumed to account for 27% of private wealth, own 43.9% of the equity. This is consistent with available data on dividends received, which indicate that these classes get approximately

24. This calculation is derived by updating the average nominal rate of return for 1926–71 presented in Friend and Blume (1975), and subtracting the average annual increase in the consumer price index over the period.

Table 12.1   Equilibrium Values of Key Variables in Simulated 1977 Economy

Expected real rate of return on corporate equity	.106
Expected real rate of return on food-sector capital	.082
Expected real rate of return on rental housing	.090
Expected real rate of return on taxable debt	.044
Expected real rate of return on tax-exempt debt	.001
Corporate capital stock	1,489.8
Corporate equity	865.6
Food-sector capital stock	260.0
Rental housing stock	770.5
Owner-occupied housing stock	1,418.1

Note: All rates of return are net of any corporation income tax and property tax payments, but are before payment of any individual income tax liability.

37% of all dividends.[25] Owner-occupied housing is much less concentrated among the higher income classes, with 79.5% of the stock owned by taxpaying units of $45,000 or less in income. The ownership of tax-exempt securities is limited to the top two classes. The lower seven classes own positive amounts of riskless debt, while the top two classes are net borrowers of funds. In fact, these highly taxed classes have a debt position amounting to 26.2% of their net wealth.

12.5   An Indexed Tax System—Simulation Results

12.5.1   With Constant Corporate Financial Policy

As is well known by now, the United States system of taxing capital income is decidedly nonneutral with respect to inflation. The problem arises because in the presence of inflation real capital income is mismeasured. Nominal interest received is treated as income with no deduction for the real loss in the value of the principal. Similarly, nominal interest payments are fully deductible. Increases in nominal asset value that do not correspond to real value increases are subject to the capital gains tax if and when these gains are realized. Also, historical cost depreciation rules and certain inventory accounting methods lead to an overestimate of real net earnings.[26]

The mismeasurement of capital income does not uniformly apply to all assets. Thus inflation alters the pattern of real after-tax rates of return available. This is turn causes a readjustment of portfolios and a shift in the allocation of capital to production sectors, which affects the pretax

25. Since the higher income brackets tend to own lower dividend-yielding stocks, 37% of dividends received is certainly compatible with owning (at least) 43.9% of all stock.

26. As time passes, inflation also pushes taxpayers into higher personal tax brackets, increasing both marginal and average tax rates. This dynamic aspect of an unindexed tax system is not treated in this exercise in comparative statics.

return on assets. The tax penalty (or benefit) from the mismeasurement of capital also varies depending on the marginal tax rate of the agents involved. Extra corporate taxable income due to inflation is subject to the corporation income tax rate, as are the extra deductions of nominal interest payments. For individuals, the tax cost varies with their tax bracket. Thus the overall impact of inflation depends on the tax-induced distortion of rates of return and agents' financial response to these distortions. Clearly a general equilibrium analysis is well suited to this type of problem.

An indexed tax system would eliminate the distortionary effects of inflation by correctly measuring real capital income.[27] In order to simulate the effects of indexing, the GEFB model is re-solved for the equilibrium that would obtain in the presence of a zero rate of inflation. This effectively eliminates any mismeasurement of capital income. Since the equilibrium under an indexed tax system will be identical to the equilibrium under an unindexed tax system which has a zero rate of inflation, the simulation results can be interpreted in either of two ways. The difference between the two equilibria can be seen as either the effect of an indexed tax system or the effect of 6% inflation under an unindexed tax system.

With no adjustment in tax rates, the total federal tax revenue declines as a result of indexation by $28.2 billion, from $228.3 billion to $199.1 billion.[28] This decrease consists almost entirely of a $27.8 billion decrease in individual income tax liability. The other component is a surprisingly small $0.4 billion reduction in corporation income tax paid. This small change is the net result of a few offsetting factors. First, the elimination of the excess tax that is due to historical cost depreciation and inventory accounting methods outweighs the elimination of the deductibility of the inflation premium in nominal interest deductions, amounting to a $3.7 billion tax saving. The increase in the amount of corporate capital is approximately offset by the decrease in the marginal product of capital. What largely offsets the $3.7 billion tax saving is a large decline in the real riskless interest rate. The reduced value of interest deductions owing to this change causes the corporate tax bill to increase by over $2 billion. The combination of these factors yields the small increase in corporate income tax liability.

In order to compare two tax systems with equal total yield, tax rates must be raised under indexation. In the results reported below, all individual income tax rates were multiplied by an identical factor; brackets were unchanged as was the corporation income tax rate. This procedure required a 21.1% increase in all personal tax rates, raising the first marginal tax rate to 0.170 and the highest marginal rate to 0.848. This

27. The details of an indexing system need not concern us here.
28. For this exercise the shortfall in revenue is made up by a levy on individuals that is proportional to their federal tax payments and is assumed to have no substitution effects.

equal-yield procedure is a crucial element in the simulation results reported below, since alternative rate adjustments to make up the lost revenue would undoubtedly change the distributional impact of indexing and could also affect its allocational implications.

The equilibrium solution under an indexed tax system is partially characterized in table 12.2. There is a substantial change in the pattern of rates of return in the economy. First of all, there is a large decline in the real rate of return on riskless debt, from 0.044 to 0.035. Since inflation in an unindexed tax system increases the personal taxation of debt relative to equity, indexation relieves this excess taxation and thereby increases the positive demand for riskless debt by the lower-taxed classes, and also decreases the desired leverage of the high income, high-tax-rate classes. Since the excess supply of riskless debt by agents other than individuals is virtually fixed (government borrows a fixed amount, and corporations borrow a fixed proportion of a slightly changing total capital stock), the real rate of return on riskless debt must fall in order to clear its market. The real rate of return on equity rises from 0.106 to 0.114, indicating that the net effect of indexation is to render equity a relatively less attractive investment, requiring a higher rate of return in equilibrium. That the extra tax burden due to inflation is greater for debt than for equity is clearly evidenced by the fact that the premium equity earns over debt is 0.062 without indexing, and increases to 0.079 under indexation or, equivalently, in the absence of inflation.

Another striking shift in the pattern of rates of return is the sharp increase in the equilibrium yield on tax-exempt securities, which earn a real rate of return of 0.0012 in the unindexed inflationary economy but whose real return would be 0.0236 in the indexed, or noninflationary, equilibrium. The differential between the real return on taxable and tax-exempt debt increases from 0.0428 to only 0.0102 in the indexed

Table 12.2   Equilibrium Values of Key Variables in Indexed Economy

		Change from Unindexed Equilibrium
Expected real rate of return on corporate equity	.114	+ .008
Expected real rate of return on food-sector capital	.082	.000
Expected real rate of return on rental housing	.088	− .002
Expected real rate of return on taxable debt	.035	− .009
Expected real rate of return on tax-exempt debt	.025	+ .024
Corporate capital stock	1,490.2	+ .4
Corporate equity	865.8	+ .2
Food-sector capital stock	259.2	− .8
Rental housing stock	775.4	+ 4.9
Owner-occupied housing stock	1,413.7	− 4.4

equilibrium. The explanation here is quite straightforward. The issuers of tax-exempt debt benefit from the mismeasurement and subsequent over-taxation of the real return on taxable debt; this enables them to sell debt to high-tax-bracket individuals while offering nearly a zero real return. When this mismeasurement is eliminated, state and local governments must increase their real interest payments by more than 2% in order to have their outstanding debt willingly held.

These changes in the pattern of real returns are accompanied by substantial shifts in the portfolios of the income groups. Since the tax advantages to the highly taxed groups of equity relative to debt diminish under indexing, the concentration of equity holdings might be expected to decline. This does in fact occur, with the proportion of equity held by the top three income classes falling from 43.9% to 37.5%. Another striking change in the portfolios of the high income groups is the sharp decline in the amount of owner-occupied housing held. Remember, with nominal interest payments fully deductible from taxable income, the opportunity cost of housing becomes very low under inflation in an unindexed system. Individuals in high tax brackets respond by holding large amounts of owner-occupied housing. Under indexing, even though the real rate of interest declines, the opportunity cost of owned housing services increases significantly for individuals in high tax brackets. In response, the amount of wealth put into owner-occupied housing under indexing is just 69% of what it would be under an unindexed system for the highest two income groups. On the other hand, the low income groups experience a decline in the cost of owned housing services, since the decline in the real interest rate more than compensates for the reduced value of interest paid tax deductions. In response, they increase the amount that they hold.

The decline in the high income groups' holdings of equity and owner-occupied housing is offset primarily by a decline in their indebtedness and slightly by increases in their ownership of the other risky assets. As noted above, in the unindexed 6% inflation equilibrium, the top two income classes borrowed an amount equal to 26.2% of their net wealth; in the equilibrium under indexing the borrowing is reduced to 9.9% of net wealth.

According to this simulation, the allocational impact of indexing would be minimal, causing a slight decrease in the amount of capital in the owner-occupied housing, largely at the expense of rental housing. This aspect of the simulation results is especially sensitive to the specification of the model; in fact, in earlier versions of this model (see Slemrod 1980) indexing caused a much larger shift of capital away from owner-occupied housing. This earlier result seems consistent with intuition, since indexing eliminates the deductibility of nominal interest payments and thus apparently raises the cost of housing. Although in a model of this complexity it is difficult to trace a result to a particular aspect of the model, the absence of such a shift in the present version seems due to the following facts. First of all, the substantially lower real rate of interest under indexation means that, for the lower-taxed groups who make up the bulk of owner-occupied housing demand, the opportunity cost of owned housing declines. In fact, a comparison of the two equilibria shows that the five lowest income groups find owned housing less expensive in the indexed equilibrium; these five groups own about 85% of all owned housing. Thus the ownership of housing shifts from high-income to low-income individuals, but the total does not significantly decrease. A second reason is the fact that the increased tax rates under indexation tend to lower the cost of owned housing to all individuals, especially the highly taxed groups who experience the greatest absolute tax rate increase. Since this increases the value of deducting interest payments from taxable income, the effect is to increase the demand for owned housing.

The welfare effects of indexing are presented in table 12.3. The numbers in the first column refer to the dollar compensation that must be paid before the resolution of the uncertainty in order to make the nonindexed inflationary situation indifferent to the indexed situation. The usual index number problem applies here, since the value of the required compensation depends on whether it is to be paid (or received) in the preindexing or postindexing situation. The values presented in table 12.3 are the simple average of these two compensation figures.

The simulation results indicate that a system of indexation, with lost revenue made up by adjusting all personal tax rates upward by a multiplicative factor, would cause an increase in welfare for the highest five income groups and a decrease in welfare for the lowest four income groups, with the dividing income level being approximately $30,000 in annual income. Without an explicit social welfare function to balance the

Table 12.3   Simulated Welfare Effects Due to Indexing

Income Class (× $1,000)	Welfare Change ($ billions)	Welfare Change as a Percentage of Pre-Indexing Income
0–9	−.38	−.15
9–15	−1.48	−.60
15–22.5	−3.35	−1.06
22.5–30	−2.09	−.90
30–45	+.10	+.08
45–75	+.93	+1.24
75–150	+3.71	+8.02
150–300	+6.82	+42.78
More than 300	+2.13	+28.93
Total	+6.39	+.48

gains and losses, it is impossible to say whether this would be a desirable change to make. However, the sum of the compensation values is clearly positive ($6.4 billion, or about one-half of 1% of national income adjusted for the disutility of risk), indicating that a compensation system could be arranged so that indexation would be a Pareto-optimal improvement. In that sense, indexation would reduce the distortionary cost of the tax system. Note that this result does not consider any dynamic efficiency effects of indexation.

There are several aspects to this increase in efficiency. First, there is a small efficiency gain from the slight shift of capital away from owner-occupied housing, which is oversupplied because of the tax advantages it receives even in the absence of inflation. Second, indexation tends to reduce the dispersion in the cost of owner-occupied housing and thus reduces the inefficiency that results from individuals facing different prices for the same good. In the unindexed inflationary economy, the total cost of owner-occupied housing ranged from $0.094 per unit of housing service (where one unit of service is produced by one unit of capital) for the lowest income group to $0.029 for the highest taxed group. In the indexed equilibrium, the range of prices is $0.085 to $0.047. Thus the owner-occupied housing stock is more efficiently distributed under indexation, as there is less incentive for the high income groups to borrow in order to hold housing.

A third source of the efficiency gain under indexation is the improved allocation of risk-bearing. Since after-tax risk premiums are not the same for all individuals, risk is not borne optimally. Inflation in an unindexed system exacerbates this problem since it widens the dispersion of risk premiums because of its differential impact on risky and riskless assets. Thus, under indexing, this dispersion is reduced and risk is borne more efficiently.

The pattern of the distributional impact of inflation also has several sources. First, indexation tends to reduce the total taxation of capital income. In order to make up the lost revenue, all personal tax rates were increased. Since labor income constitutes the bulk of personal taxable income, the indexing scheme is accompanied by a not insignificant shift in the tax burden from the high income classes to the low income classes, who have a much higher relative endowment of labor versus capital. Thus the lowest four income classes, the ones who apparently suffer under indexation, find their federal tax burden increased by $6.44 billion under the indexed system, or an increase of 8.8%

The highest two income classes of course face the highest increase in tax rates under the general tax increase scheme, but their reduced taxable income under indexation almost entirely cancels out this effect so that in the end they pay only $0.93 billion more in federal taxes, just 3.1% of their initial tax payments. However, it is important to keep in mind that the increased tax rates also serve to reduce the after-tax variance of their risky capital investments. This plus the fact that under indexation these two classes hold a much less levered portfolio implies that the disutility from risky income is substantially lower in their optimal portfolios under indexation. These individuals also substitute income-earning assets for a large chunk of their owner-occupied housing, the marginal utility of which was very low. Finally, the top two classes benefit greatly from the increased real return earned by tax-exempt securities, which are held almost exclusively by these individuals. The increase in their real yield from 0.001 to 0.025 provides a transfer of approximately $2.4 billion from the general public to these two classes.

At this point it is important to alert the reader that the results of these simulations are meant to be illustrative of the kind of analysis this kind of model can provide. The results are not seen as the final word on the effects of indexation on the United States economy, owing to our lack of knowledge about certain of the parameters and functional forms of the model, and also to the sensitivity of the results to certain aspects of the model itself. For example, sensitivity analysis not reported here indicates that the allocational impact of indexation is sensitive to the modeling of the housing sector and the distributional implications depend on the kind of equal-yield tax adjustment that is assumed to be used as well as the relation of the after-tax variance of assets to the marginal tax rate. This model has a multitude of dimensions to which sensitivity analysis could conceivably be applied. This warning is meant to serve as a less cumbersome substitute to reporting these results.

12.5.2   With Responsive Corporate Financial Policy

Now the simulation of an indexed tax system is repeated, this time allowing corporations to adjust their financial policy in response to the changing tax environment. An earlier section discussed the methodology to be used in calculating the corporate behavioral response. Note that the optimal financial policy on which this methodology is based is independent of the rate of inflation and is therefore unaffected by indexing.[29] Nevertheless, although the indexing (or inflation) itself does not matter,

29. King (1978), pp. 111–12, shows that, in models with one type of investor, no bankruptcy costs, and no constraints on individual portfolios, the conditions determining whether a firm should prefer debt or equity are unaffected by the rate of inflation. However, this formulation is not compatible with the existence of an optimal debt-equity ratio, either for the firm or for the economy as a whole. In models of capital market equilibrium which feature optimal nonextreme financial policies, the rate of inflation may have a direct impact on the equilibrium financial structure of the firm and/or economy. (See for instance Auerbach and King 1980 and Gordon 1980). However, at the moment there is no econometric evidence on the relation between inflation and financial structure that can be invoked in this simulation model, and explicitly modeling the conditions which lead to an interior equilibrium, such as constraints on borrowing or the existence of bankruptcy costs, is beyond the scope of this present study.

certain changes in the economy caused by the indexation scheme may cause corporations to alter their financial decisions. Changes in the ownership of equity by income class will alter the tax cost of a given financial policy; indexation tends to reduce the concentration of equity ownership among the higher income classes, and thus reduce the tax advantage of debt and retentions. Other relevant factors are any changes in the marginal tax rates on dividends, debt interest, and capital gains. These changes may result either from changes in the taxable income of the individuals or from changes in the tax rate schedule needed to keep total tax revenues unchanged. The net effect of these influences will determine the direction and magnitude of the corporate financial response.

The simulation results indicate that there would be very little adjustment in corporate financial policy. The ownership of equity shifts toward individuals with lower marginal tax rates, but the upward adjustment of all tax rates to maintain equal yield offsets that to a large extent. In the indexed equilibrium, the aggregate corporate debt-capital ratio falls from 0.419 to 0.378 and the payout ratio does not change at all.

The equilibrium looks very similar to that which is depicted in table 12.2. The only significant difference is that the real rate of return on equity is 0.108 instead of 0.114. This difference is due to the fact that with a reduced debt-equity ratio equity shares are less risky and therefore earn a lower risk premium in equilibrium.

The distributional implications of indexing are also not substantially changed by allowing corporations financial flexibility. The shift toward equity and away from debt would be expected to benefit the higher-taxed individuals, for whom the retention of earnings at the corporate level has a sheltering effect, at the expense of the lower-taxed individuals. This is exactly the pattern that the simulation results reveal. The top two income classes benefit even more from indexing than table 12.3 indicates, and the lower seven classes fare slightly less well than that table suggests. In all cases, since the corporate financial adjustment is not large, the difference in results is not great; for that reason the detailed results are not presented here.

12.6 Concluding Remarks

This research demonstrates the feasibility of integrating a structural treatment of portfolio choice and financial markets with the standard multisector general equilibrium model of taxation. The model developed here takes account of the unsurprising fact that when there are changes in the taxation of capital income, individuals will adjust their financial behavior in response. A correct understanding of the effects of a tax change, including its implications for total tax revenue, the allocation of production, and the distributional impact, requires consideration of the general equilibrium impact of this financial behavioral response.

The model is used to simulate the impact of a completely indexed tax system. Owing to uncertainty about the values of several parameters and the relatively simple formulations of the determinants of portfolio choice and the United States financial structure, the simulation results should not be regarded as disposing of the policy questions involved. Nevertheless, the simulation results point to significant financial adjustment in response to indexation or, conversely, to inflation in an unindexed economy. A significant shifting of the location of private risk bearing accompanies a slight reallocation of the capital stock away from owner-occupied housing toward its other uses and a substantial change in the ownership of this stock by income class. All in all, indexing the tax system of an economy like the United States in 1977 seems to lead to an efficiency gain, slightly hurts the lowest income classes, and substantially improves the welfare of the highest income groups.

Further research is needed for a more complete understanding of the relation between taxation on the one hand and financial behavior and markets on the other hand. The role and behavior of financial institutions should be integrated into the modeling of individuals' behavior presented here.[30] The dynamic implications of introducing financial behavior into tax models is also a promising topic for future investigation.

Appendix

Table 12.A.1   Endowment of Capital and Labor by Income Class, 1977

Income Class (× $1,000)	Capital (billions)	Labor (billions)
0–9	440.3	140.2
9–15	405.8	186.7
15–22.5	572.0	259.6
22.5–30	611.4	187.0
30–45	615.7	111.7
45–75	447.0	63.1
75–150	517.3	35.5
150–300	463.7	11.4
More than 300	162.7	6.2
Total	4,238.5	1,001.4

30. A first step toward a model with financial institutions is made in Slemrod (1980, pp. 165–204).

Table 12.A.2   Shares of Spending on Food, Rental Housing, and Owned Housing

Income Class (× $1,000)	Food	Rental Housing	Owned Housing
0–9	.206	.152	.070
9–15	.176	.114	.059
15–22.5	.167	.070	.081
22.5–30	.159	.044	.095
30–45	.145	.028	.091
45–75	.128	.023	.085
75–150	.101	.020	.085
150–300	.076	.018	.085
More than 300	.058	.016	.085

References

Aaron, H. 1972. Shelter and subsidies. Washington: Brookings Institution.

Auerbach, A. 1979a. Wealth maximization and the cost of capital. *Quarterly Journal of Economics* 93 (August): 433–66.

———. 1979b. Share valuation and corporate equity policy. *Journal of Public Economics* 8 (June): 291–305.

Auerbach, A., and M. King. 1980. Taxation, portfolio choice, and debt-equity ratios: A general equilibrium analysis. NBER Working Paper no. 546.

Ballentine, J. G., and C. McLure, Jr. 1978. Corporate tax integration: Incidence and effects on financial structure. In *1978 Compendium of Tax Research*. Washington: Department of the Treasury.

Board of Governors of the Federal Reserve System. 1978. *Flow of Funds accounts: Assets and liabilities outstanding, 1967–1977*. Washington. August.

Bradford, D. F. 1979. The incidence and allocation effects of a tax on corporate distributions. NBER Working Paper no. 349.

Brittain, J. A. 1966. *Corporate dividend policy*. Washington: Brookings Institution.

Feldstein, M. S. 1976. Inflation, taxes, and the rate of interest: A theoretical analysis. *American Economic Review* 66 (December): 809–20.

Feldstein, M. S.; J. Green; and E. Sheshinski. 1978. Inflation and taxes in a growing economy with debt and equity finance. *Journal of Political Economy* 86 (April, part 2): 553–70.

———. 1979. Corporate financial policy and taxation in a growing economy. *Quarterly Journal of Economics* 93 (August): 411–32.

Feldstein, M. S., and J. Slemrod. 1980. Personal taxation, portfolio choice, and the corporation income tax. *Journal of Political Economy.* 88 (October): 854–66.

Feldstein, M. S., and L. Summers. 1979. Inflation and the taxation of capital income in the corporate sector. *National Tax Journal* 32 (December): 445–70.

Friend, I., and M. E. Blume. 1975. The demand for risky assets. *American Economic Review* 65 (December): 900–922.

Friend, I., and J. Hasbrouck. 1980. Effect of inflation on the profitability and valuation of U.S. corporations. University of Pennsylvania. Mimeo.

Fullerton, D.; J. B. Shoven; and J. Whalley. 1978. Dynamic general equilibrium impacts of replacing the U.S. income tax with a progressive consumption tax. NBER Conference Paper no. 55.

Fullerton, D.; A. T. King; J. B. Shoven; and J. Whalley. 1979. Static and dynamic resource allocation effects of corporate and personal tax integration in the U.S.: A general equilibrium approach. NBER Working Paper no. 337.

Gordon, R. 1980. Inflation, taxation, and corporate behavior. NBER Working Paper no. 588.

Harberger, A. C. 1959. The corporation income tax: An empirical appraisal. In House Committee on Ways and Means, *Tax Revision Compendium*, pp. 231–50.

———. 1962. The incidence of the corporation income tax. *Journal of Political Economy* 70 (June): 215–40.

———. 1966. Efficiency effects of taxes on income from capital. In M. Krzyzaniak, ed., *Effects of corporation income tax.* Detroit: Wayne State University Press.

Houtthaker, H. S., and L. Taylor. 1966. *Consumer demand in the United States, 1929–1970: Analyses and projections.* Cambridge, Massachusetts: Harvard University Press.

James, B. C. 1979. Ownership of tax-exempt assets may endanger deduction for otherwise allowable items. *Taxation for Accountants*, vol. 23 (November).

Johnson, H. G. 1956. General equilibrium analysis of excise taxes: Comment. *American Economic Review* 46 (March): 151–56.

King, M. A. 1974. Taxation and the cost of capital. *Reveiw of Economic Studies* 41 (January): 21–35.

———. 1978. *Public policy and the corporation.* London: Chapman & Hall.

McLure, C. E., Jr. 1975. General equilibrium analysis: The Harberger model after ten years. *Journal of Public Economics* 4 (February): 125–62.

Meade, J. E. 1955. Mathematical supplement to *Trade and welfare.* Oxford: Oxford University Press.

Mieszkowski, P. 1967. On the theory of tax incidence. *Journal of Political Economy* 75 (June): 250–62.

Modigliani, F., and M. Miller. 1958. The cost of capital, corporation finance, and the theory of investment. *American Economic Review* 48 (June): 261–97.

Projector, D. S., and G. S. Weiss. 1966. *Survey of financial characteristics of consumers*. Washington: Board of Governors of the Federal Reserve System.

Rosen, H. 1978. Housing decisions and the U.S. income tax: An econometric analysis. Hebrew University of Jerusalem, Institute for Advanced Studies Report no. 20/78.

———. 1979. Owner-occupied housing and the federal income tax: Estimates and simulations. *Journal of Urban Economics* 6 (April): 247–66.

Rosen, H. S., and K. T. Rosen. 1980. Federal taxes and homeownership: Evidence from time series. *Journal of Political Economy* 88 (February): 59–74.

Shoven, J. B. 1976. The incidence and efficiency effects of taxes on income from capital. *Journal of Political Economy* 84 (November/December): 1261–83.

Shoven, J. B., and J. Whalley. 1972. A general equilibrium calculation of the effects of differential taxation of income and from capital in the U.S. *Journal of Public Economics* 1 (November): 281–321.

———. 1977. Equal yield tax alternatives: General equilibrium computational techniques. *Journal of Public Economics* 8 (October): 211–24.

Slemrod, J. 1980. A general equilibrium model of capital income taxation. Ph.D. thesis, Harvard University.

Stiglitz, J. 1969. Taxation, risk taking, and the allocation of investment in a competitive economy. In M. Jensen, ed., *Studies in the theory of capital markets*. New York.

———. 1973. Taxation, corporate financial policy, and the cost of capital. *Journal of Public Economics* 2 (February): 1–34.

Tobin, J. 1969. A general equilibrium approach to monetary theory. *Journal of Money, Credit, and Banking* 1 (February): 15–29.

United States Bureau of Labor Statistics. 1978. *Consumer expenditure interview survey, 1972–1973*. BLS Bulletin 1985. Washington.

United States Department of the Treasury. 1980. *Statistics of income—1977, individual income tax returns*. Washington.

Comment   Peter Mieszkowski

In this paper and in the longer version of his work (1980), Joel Slemrod has made a very significant contribution to our understanding of the taxation of capital income and the effects of inflation in a unindexed tax system.

The work is notable in a number of respects. Slemrod integrates a structural model of portfolio choice and financial markets with the multisector general equilibrium model of taxation developed by Harberger and Shoven-Whalley. Nine income groups are recognized, and asset demand equations for corporate equity, taxable and nontaxable debt, rental and owner-occupied housing are specified. The different income groups face different tax rates, and they hold different portfolios. High-income groups hold most of the tax-exempt (municipal) debt and a large portion of corporate equity. Some of the most interesting results of the paper relate to the varying impact of tax policy changes on different income groups. For example, Slemrod concludes that a decrease in the rate of inflation or the indexation of the tax system for inflation will increase the cost of housing to high-income groups and decrease its cost to low-income groups.

The asset demand equations are quite general and account for changes in the tax-induced changes in risk (variance of return) as well as changes in after-tax rates of return. All rates of return are endogenous, and the analysis allows for changes in corporate financial policy. The analysis is comparative statics. The overall stocks of wealth and labor are taken as given, and changes in equilibrium stocks of capital in various industries and changes in the rates of return on various investments are calculated by means of simulation techniques. The long-run equilibrium nature of the analysis should be kept in mind in relating Slemrod's results to other work on the effects of inflation which emphasizes changes in inflationary expectations.

Slemrod has performed two simulation experiments. One is on the effects of integrating the corporate and personal income taxes. The second experiment, which is reported in this paper, is on the effects of indexing the existing tax system for inflation. This is equivalent to analyzing the change resulting from changes in the rate of inflation in a tax system that is not indexed, and we shall adopt this interpretation.

Before turning to the specific results, let us take note of the following, which should be very helpful to the understanding of most of the results.

Suppose that in the absence of inflation the nominal and real before-tax rate of return on taxable debt is 6%. Taxpayers in the 50% marginal rate bracket will earn a 3% rate after taxes. If the expected rate of inflation

Peter Mieszkowski is with the Department of Economics, Rice University, and the National Bureau of Economic Research.

increases to 10% and the nominal rate increases to 16%, the real yield for households in low tax brackets (say zero) remains unchanged at 6% while for taxpayers in the 50% bracket the real after-tax yield is $16(1 - t_y) - 10: -2\%$.

This example has a number of more general implications. (1) It is possible for the real before-tax yield on debt to rise as the result of inflation but for the after-tax real yield to decrease (become negative) for high income groups. This implies changes in the composition of portfolios for different income groups as the result of inflation. (2) Inflation makes taxable debt a less (more) attractive asset for high (low) income groups. The real yield on nontaxable municipal debt will fall as will the return on equity. (3) As inflation may make the real after-tax yield on bonds negative to high income groups, these groups will find it very profitable to borrow under inflationary conditions as they deduct nominal interest. Investment in housing and other durables will be profitable for high income groups.

I present these results as if they are self-evident, but they are clear only as the result of Slemrod's work.

In his analysis the move to an indexed tax system is equivalent to moving from a 6% rate of inflation to a zero rate of inflation. The principal result is that the before-tax real rate of return on taxable debt decreases significantly as taxes are imposed on real, rather than nominal, interest. Also, as a result of indexation high income groups find taxable debt a more attractive investment, and the returns to equity and tax-exempt municipals must rise to maintain portfolio balance. Thus Slemrod's long-run equilibrium model does *not* provide indirect evidence for the view that the low level of stock prices during the recent inflationary experience can be explained by tax considerations. It illustrates how state and local governments can benefit from inflation at the expense of high income groups that hold the tax-exempt debt.

Another result is that indexation of the tax system leads to a decrease in the demand for owner-occupied housing and an increase in rental housing. This confirms the familiar point that inflation increases the demand for owner-occupied housing as nominal mortgage payments are deducted under the income tax. But the adjustment in the aggregate is quite small. The owner-occupied housing stock falls by only 3% as the result of indexation.

But the small change in the aggregate is apparently the net result of two offsetting tendencies. Inflation without indexation reduces the real borrowing rates for the wealthy and significantly increases the borrowing of high income groups to hold equity and owner-occupied housing. On the other hand inflation also increases the real before-tax borrowing rate for lower and moderate income groups, who are less likely to itemize and whose marginal tax rate is relatively low. So we have the interesting result that indexation, by decreasing the before-tax borrowing rate, decreases the cost of owner-occupied housing to lower income groups and increases the cost of housing to the rich.

A related point that is presented in Slemrod's thesis is that inflation, by decreasing the cost of rental housing relative to corporate goods, may make low income groups better off, at least with respect to this consumption effect.

The main result of the indexation experiment is that indexation will decrease the welfare of households whose income is less than $30,000 a year and increase the welfare of the wealthy. The welfare change as a percentage of preindexed income for the two wealthiest groups is very large.

There are a number of aspects to the change in the distribution of real income. These include the efficiency gains of indexation, the increase in the return to equity and tax-exempt debt. The main effect is the decrease in the overall rate of taxation on capital income and the increase in wage taxation to maintain budget balance. Slemrod calculates that with no adjustment in tax rates total federal tax revenues decline by about 12% as the result of indexation. This increase is due almost entirely to a decrease in individual tax liability, implying that the tax saving correcting for historical cost depreciation and inventory accounting methods is largely offset by the lower deductions for lower nominal interest.

These results are in rough accordance with earlier work (see Feldstein and Summers 1979). But unfortunately they are not consistent with Slemrod's earlier results presented in his dissertation (1980) that indexation would actually increase federal revenues, since indexation would significantly decrease the borrowing of the wealthy and since the decrease in the deduction of interest would increase tax collections.

Obviously the reader should rely on the latest version of the model, which is calibrated for a more recent year. But without knowing the details it is difficult not to be skeptical, given the wide range of results, about the accuracy of the model's predictions.

It is certainly not my intention to end on a sour note. Slemrod has done a great deal to integrate the financial and real sides of tax analysis.

He has assembled the empirical facts with care, and the work is sufficiently general that virtually every partial story that has been told about the effects of inflation on resource allocation and effective taxation can be fitted into his framework. The real contribution of his work is that most of the issues involved are much more transparent from a qualitative standpoint. The quantitative ambiguities need to be investigated further, but they are minor detractions from Joel Slemrod's overall contribution.

References

Feldstein, M. S., and L. Summers. 1979. Inflation and the taxation of capital income in the corporate sector. *National Tax Journal* 32 (December): 445–70.

Slemrod, J. 1980. A general equilibrium model of capital income taxation. Ph.D. thesis, Harvard University.

13 National Savings, Economic Welfare, and the Structure of Taxation

Alan J. Auerbach and Laurence J. Kotlikoff

13.1 Introduction

In the course of the last century, the United States rate of net national savings as conventionally defined declined dramatically from over 20% in the 1880s to less than 8% in the 1970s. Over this same period, government expenditure rose from 7% to 22% of GNP, the size of the federal debt measured at book value excluding social security varied enormously from under 10% to over 90% of GNP in particular years, and the level and structure of taxes changed significantly. While economic theory provides qualitative predictions of the effects of these changes in government policy on national savings, the quantitative importance of these changes is little understood. This paper develops a perfect foresight general equilibrium simulation model of life-cycle savings that may be used to investigate the potential impact of a wide range of government policies on national savings and economic welfare. While the strict life-cycle model of savings has been questioned at both the theoretical (Barro 1974) and empirical (Kotlikoff and Summers 1981) levels, the strict (no bequests) life-cycle model provides an important benchmark to consider the range of savings and welfare responses to government policy in general and deficit policy in particular.

The simulation model can provide quantitative answers to a number of long-standing questions concerning the government's influence on capital formation. These include the degree of crowding out of private invest-

Alan J. Auerbach is with the Department of Economics, Harvard University, and the National Bureau of Economic Research. Laurence J. Kotlikoff is with the Department of Economics, Yale University, and the National Bureau of Economic Research.

The authors are grateful to Jon Skinner, Christophe Chamley, and Lawrence Summers for helpful comments, to Maxim Engers, David Reitman, Jon Skinner, and Thomas Seal for excellent research assistance, and to the NBER for financial support.

ment by debt-financed increases in government expenditure, the differential effect on consumption of temporary versus more permanent tax cuts, the announcement effects of future changes in tax and expenditure policy, and the response to structural changes in the tax system, including both the choice of the tax base and the degree of progressivity. The model tracks the values of all economic variables along the transition path from the initial steady-state growth path to the new steady-state growth path. Hence the model can be used to compute the exact welfare gains or losses for each age cohort associated with tax reform proposals. Finally, the simulation experiments can usefully instruct the specification of time series consumption regression models that purport to estimate how government policy alters national savings.

This paper describes the technical structure of the simulation model and the solution algorithm used to compute perfect foresight life-cycle growth paths. Four examples of potential applications of the model are briefly examined. These are an analysis of the welfare costs of capital income taxation, the incidence of the progressive income tax, the effect of fiscal policy on national savings, and the savings response of the private sector to early announcements of future tax policy changes.

The principal findings from these applications of the model are:

1. The excess burden associated with the taxation of capital income provides some limited scope for improving the welfare of all current and future cohorts when lump-sum taxes and transfers are available. However, given that lump-sum taxes and transfers are not available policy tools, "tax reform" proposals are likely to significantly reduce the welfare of some cohorts and significantly raise the welfare of others unless annual tax rates and their associated deficit levels are chosen with extreme care.

2. The intercohort allocation of the tax burden of government expenditure is a significantly more important determinant of national savings than is the structure of taxation.

3. The long-run effect on the capital output ratio of switching from a progressive to a proportional income tax with no change in the stock of government debt is roughly 13%.

4. Short-run crowding out of private investment by balanced budget increases in government expenditure is on the order of 50 cents per dollar, while long-run crowding out is 20 cents per dollar of government expenditure.

5. Temporary as well as more permanent tax cuts can lead to increases rather than decreases in national savings in the first few years following the enactment of the tax cut. This depends both on which taxes are cut and on which taxes are subsequently raised to finance interest payments on the associated deficit.

6. Early announcement of future tax policy changes can significantly

affect the national savings rate in periods prior to implementation of the legislation.

The welfare costs of capital income taxation, the effects of government deficit policy on capital formation, and the long-run incidence of alternative tax instruments are the focus of a growing body of economic literature. While understanding of these issues has been greatly enhanced in recent years, the literature remains seriously deficient with respect to a number of theoretical and empirical concerns. The next section of this paper provides a selected and brief review of this literature and points out those deficiencies that can be addressed with the model developed here. Section 13.3 develops life-cycle optimization conditions for both proportional and progressive wage, interest income, and consumption tax structures. The simulation methodology is described in this section as well. Section 13.4 examines the welfare costs of capital income taxation, distinguishing pure efficiency issues associated with the structure of taxation from the issue of intercohort redistribution. Section 13.5 discusses the effect of progressive taxation on national savings and describes the economic transition from a progressive income tax to a progressive consumption tax. Section 13.6 investigates the long- and short-run savings impact of alternative government fiscal policies including temporary and more permanent tax cuts, changes in the level of government expenditure, and early announcements of future changes in tax policy. Section 13.7 summarizes the paper and suggests areas for future research.

13.2 Selected Literature Review

The long-run welfare implications of deficit policy and the choice of the tax base have been the focus of numerous recent articles (Feldstein 1974; Boskin 1978; Auerbach 1979; Kotlikoff 1979; Summers 1981; and Bradford 1980). These analyses have emphasized the welfare of cohorts living in the new steady state that results from alterations in government policy; little attention has been paid to the welfare of generations alive during the transition to the new steady state. This long-run focus has obscured the true scope for Pareto-efficient tax reform; to the unwary reader it may also convey the incorrect impression that deficit policy by itself is inefficient rather than simply redistributive. As this paper demonstrates, changes in government tax and expenditure policies may entail significant redistribution between cohorts alive today and in the indefinite future. The incidence of these policies can be understood only by examining changes in the welfare of all cohorts—transition cohorts as well as cohorts living in the distant future when the economy converges to a new steady state. The pure efficiency gains from "tax reform" cannot be isolated by looking at changes in the welfare of only a selected group of cohorts, since welfare changes may reflect redistribution from other cohorts as opposed to the elimination of excess burdens in the tax system.

Summers's stimulating study represents the sole attempt to explicitly examine the welfare of transition cohorts. His simulation analysis suggested that proportional wage and consumption taxation can have markedly different long-run impacts despite the fact that the long-run structure of these two tax systems are identical. Summers demonstrated that the requirement that the government's budget be balanced at each point in time implied a quite different intercohort distribution of the tax burden of financing government expenditure under the wage versus the consumption tax. While the long-run tax structures are identical under the two tax systems, the actual long-run tax rates are not.

Summers's analysis, while suggestive of many of the findings presented here, is based on the assumption of myopic rather than rational expectations; the transition path of myopic life-cycle economies with respect to the size of the capital stock and the level of utility is likely to differ significantly from the perfect foresight rational expectations paths analyzed here. In general, myopic expectation paths will exhibit too rapid a convergence to the new steady state since future general equilibrium changes in gross wage rates and rates of return are not taken into account in today's consumption decisions; these future expected general equilibrium changes tend to dampen initial behavioral responses to exogenous changes in government policy parameters.

In addition to explicit steady state modeling, there have been a number of recent calculations of the efficiency costs of capital income taxation (Feldstein 1978; Boskin 1978; Green and Sheshinski 1979; and King 1980). While pointing out a number of the key determinants of the potential inefficiencies associated with the taxation of capital income, these analyses are deficient in four respects:

1. The calculations are partial equilibrium, assuming that gross factor returns are not affected by compensated changes in the structure of taxation; this may be a convenient expositional device but gives incorrect estimates of excess burden.

2. Very simple models of life-cycle behavior are used, in which individuals live and consume for two periods, working in the first period only. Once again, this simplification may be useful for some purposes but is certainly a poor description of actual life-cycle behavior. One problem is that the first-period labor supply assumption implies that changes in the interest rate have no impact on the present value of resources. Summers (1981) found that the size of the uncompensated elasticity of savings with respect to the interest rate depends critically on the magnitude of future labor earnings. The compensated elasticity of consumption is presumably also quite sensitive to the inclusion of future labor earnings.

3. These "triangle" calculations ignore the fact that any actual transition from one tax system to another must begin when some individuals are partway through life. While these calculations make some sense under the assumption that cohort-specific tax schedules could be introduced in switching from one tax regime to another, they make little sense under the realistic assumption that cohort-specific tax instruments are not available. The scope for Pareto-efficient tax reform may be greatly reduced when the set of alternative tax instruments is restricted to realistic, noncohort specific tax schedules.

4. These analyses study transitions between systems of proportional taxation, while both current and prospective tax systems are in fact progressive. It is not clear that a switch from a progressive income tax to a progressive tax on annual consumption would improve efficiency, even if such were the case for a switch from a proportional income tax to a proportional consumption tax. If individual consumption profiles rise with age, a progressive consumption tax implies rising marginal rates of tax on future relative to current consumption, thus mimicking a tax on capital income. Moreover, if the progressivity of each tax is chosen according to a desire to maintain a certain degree of equality in society, tax rates may be substantially more progressive under an annual consumption tax than under an income tax.

Each of these deficiencies may have an important effect on the measurement of the potential gains to society in switching from the current tax system to one that fully exempts capital income from taxation.

Empirical investigations of the effects of government policy on capital formation have relied primarily on time series regression models. Feldstein's (1974) and Barro's (1978) analyses of the effects of social security on savings and Boskin's (1978) estimation of the "interest elasticity of saving" provide examples of standard time series procedures. Variables over which the government has some control such as the level of social security benefits or the current net rate of return are used in a regression explaining aggregate consumption. In addition to social security variables and the net interest rate, the candidates for "exogenous" variables have included current disposable income, the stock of private wealth, the level of the government deficit, and the level of government expenditure.

As tests of the effects of government policy on savings in a life-cycle model, these regressions are subject to a number of criticisms.

1. The theoretical coefficients of the variables included in these regressions are functions not only of preferences but also of current and future values of capital income and consumption tax rates as well as current and future gross rates of return. Hence, even if government policy remains constant over the period of estimation, the coefficients cannot be expected to remain stable since values of the gross rate of return as well as

tax rates will vary over time as the economy proceeds along its general equilibrium growth path toward a steady state.

2. Since the coefficients incorporate current and future tax rates as well as underlying intertemporal consumption preferences, the estimated coefficients cannot be used to analyze changes in government policy that will necessarily alter the time path of future tax rates and gross rates of return. This is the Lucas critique and is particularly applicable to Boskin's (1978) study, which contemplates switching from our income tax regime to a completely different tax regime, namely a consumption tax.

3. Total consumption is the aggregate of consumption of cohorts of different ages. Since in a life-cycle model the marginal propensity of cohorts to consume out of their total net future resources differs by age, the coefficients in the aggregate consumption regression will be unstable if the distribution of future resources changes over time. This is clearly the case for the private net worth variable in the social security regressions.

4. The regressions use proxy variables such as disposable income instead of the present value of net human wealth in the actual estimation. Since disposable income is correlated with each of the other variables in the regressions this problem of errors in the variables is likely to impart bias in each coefficient of the regression.

5. Despite the fact that some variables included in the regression do not affect aggregate consumption linearly, linearity is forced on the data. Each of these critiques can be explored with the simulation model developed here. We intend to simulate particular policy alternatives and thereby produce "simulated" data. These data will then be used in regressions following the specifications found in the literature. The estimated coefficients will provide an indication of what economic theory actually predicts about these coefficients in a truly controlled experiment. For example, the estimated coefficients on social security wealth obtained from these regressions might well prove to be negative, while the data were obtained from a model in which social security dramatically lowers the capital stock.

13.3 The Model and Its Solution

We model the evolution over time of an economy composed of government, household, and production sectors. The household sector is, at any given time, made up of fifty-five overlapping generations of individuals. Each person lives for fifty-five years, supplying labor inelastically for the first forty-five of these years and then entering retirement.[2] Members of a

---

1. Chamley (1980, 1981) provides a careful and extensive discussion of the welfare implications of the tax structure and public debt in an intertemporal model of altruistic behavior.

2. This is intended to model a typical household that "appears" at age twenty, retires at sixty-five, and dies at seventy-five.

given generation may differ in their endowments of human capital but are assumed to be identical in all other respects. To reflect observed wage profiles, the human capital endowment of each individual grows at a fixed rate h. The population as a whole grows at rate n.

As stated above, each household is a self-contained unit, engaging in life-cycle consumption behavior with no bequests. Because labor is supplied inelastically, the labor-leisure choice is not considered. We assume the lifetime utility of each household takes the form

$$
(1) \qquad u(C) = \begin{cases} \displaystyle\sum_{t=1}^{55} (1+\rho)^{-(t-1)}\dfrac{C_t^{1-\gamma}}{1-\gamma} & \gamma > 0, \neq 1 \\[2ex] \displaystyle\sum_{t=1}^{55} (1+\rho)^{-(t-1)} \log C_t & \gamma = 1, \end{cases}
$$

where C_t is the household's consumption at the end of its tth year, and ρ and γ are, respectively, taste parameters characterizing its pure rate of time preference (degree of "impatience") and the inverse of the partial elasticity of substitution between any two years' consumption. A large value of ρ indicates that the individual will consume a greater fraction of lifetime resources in the early years of life and would lead to a lower aggregate rate of savings. A large value of γ indicates a strong desire to smooth consumption in different periods. In the extreme, when γ equals infinity, the household possesses Leontief indifference curves and there is no substitution effect on consumption behavior.

The individual maximizes lifetime utility (1) subject to a budget constraint, the exact specification of which depends on the particular tax system in force. For a progressive income tax, the individual's lifetime budget constraint is

$$
(2) \qquad \sum_{t=1}^{55} \left[\prod_{s=2}^{t} (1 + r_s(1 - \bar{\tau}_{ys})) \right]^{-1} (1 - \bar{\tau}_{yt}) w_t \ell_t
$$

$$
\geq \sum_{t=1}^{55} \left[\prod_{s=2}^{t} (1 + r_s(1 - \bar{\tau}_{ys})) \right]^{-1} C_t,
$$

where r_t and w_t are the gross payments to capital and labor at the end of year t, ℓ_t is the labor supplied in year t, and $\bar{\tau}_{yt}$ is the *average* tax rate on income faced by the household in year t.

By constructing a Lagrangean from expressions (1) and (2), and differentiating with respect to each C_t, we obtain the first-order conditions:

$$
(3) \qquad (1+\rho)^{-t} C_t^{-\gamma} = \lambda \left[\prod_{s=2}^{t} (1 + r_s(1 - \bar{\tau}_{ys})) \right]^{-1} \theta_t \quad \forall t,
$$

where λ is the Lagrange multiplier of the lifetime budget constraint,

$$
(4) \qquad \theta_t = \prod_{s=t+1}^{55} \frac{1 + r_s(1 - \tau_{ys})}{1 + r_s(1 - \bar{\tau}_{ys})},
$$

and τ_{yt} is the *marginal* income tax rate in year t. To understand these first-order conditions, consider first the proportional tax case, where marginal and average tax rates are the same. In this case, $\theta_t = 1$, and (3) dictates that the marginal utility of consumption in year t should equal the marginal utility of lifetime resources λ times the implicit price of a dollar of year t consumption in year one dollars. With progressive taxes, θ_t is less than one and represents a reduction in the implicit price of year t consumption. This additional term reflects the fact that an increase in consumption in year t will reduce income from assets in all future years and thus reduce all future average tax rates.[3]

Combination of condition (3) for successive values of t implies

$$(5) \qquad C_t = \left[\frac{1 + r_t(1 - \tau_{yt})}{1 + \rho}\right]^{1/\gamma} C_{t-1}.$$

This "transition equation" indicates how preferences and the tax structure interact to determine the shape of life-cycle consumption patterns. First, note that, as γ grows, time preference and tax factors play a smaller role in determining the ratio of C_t to C_{t-1}; at $\gamma = \infty$, $C_t \equiv C_{t-1}$ regardless of other parameter values. For finite values of γ, the rate of consumption growth increases with an increase in the net interest rate and decreases with an increase in the rate of pure time preference.

It is important to remember that equation (5) determines only the *shape* of the consumption growth path, not its *level*. To obtain the latter, we apply (5) recursively to relate C_t to C_1 for all t, then substitute the resulting expression for C_t into the budget constraint (2) to obtain the following expression for C_1 in terms of lifetime resources:

$$(6) \qquad C_1 = x_y \sum_{t=1}^{55} \left[\prod_{s=2}^{t}(1 + r_s(1 - \bar{\tau}_{ys}))\right]^{-1}(1 - \bar{\tau}_{yt})w_t\ell_t,$$

where

$$x_y = \left\{\sum_{t=1}^{55}(1 + \rho)^{-((t-1)/\gamma)}\left[\prod_{s=2}^{t}(1 + r_s(1 - \bar{\tau}_{ys}))\right]^{-1}\right.$$
$$\left. \times \left[\prod_{s=2}^{t}(1 + r_s(1 - \tau_{ys}))\right]^{1/\gamma}\right\}^{-1}$$

is the proportion of lifetime resources consumed in the first year.

For a progressive consumption tax, the budget constraint corresponding to (2) is

$$(2') \qquad \sum_{t=1}^{55}\left[\prod_{s=2}^{t}(1 + r_s)\right]^{-1}w_t\ell_t$$
$$\geq \sum_{t=1}^{55}\left[\prod_{s=2}^{t}(1 + r_s)\right]^{-1}(1 + \bar{\tau}_{ct})C_t,$$

---

3. The term θ_t corrects for the present-value change in taxes assessed on the stream of income arising from a change in average tax rates. In a one-period setting, letting t stand for taxes and y for income, $y\Delta(T/y) = (\Delta T/\Delta y - T/y)\Delta y$.

where $\bar{\tau}_{ct}$ is the *average* tax rate on consumption in year t. The conditions corresponding to (5) and (6) are

(5')
$$C_t = \left[\left(\frac{1+r_t}{1+\rho}\right)\left(\frac{1+\tau_{ct-1}}{1+\tau_{ct}}\right)\right]^{1-\gamma} C_{t-1}$$

and

(6')
$$C_1 = x_c \sum_{t=1}^{55}\left[\prod_{s=2}^{t}(1+r_s)\right]^{-1} w_t \ell_t,$$

where

$$x_c = \left\{(1+\tau_{c1})^{1/\gamma}\sum_{t=1}^{55}(1+\rho)^{-((t-1)/\gamma)}\right.$$

$$\left[\prod_{s=2}^{t}(1+r_s)\right]^{-(1-(1/\gamma))}$$

$$\left. \times (1+\bar{\tau}_{ct})(1+\tau_{ct})^{-1/\gamma}\right\}^{-1}$$

(τ_{ct} is the *marginal* tax rate on consumption in year t). A comparison of (5) and (5') indicates that, in its influence on the consumption path, a progressive consumption tax with marginal rates increasing over time has a similar influence on the shape of the consumption path as a progressive income tax. If the progressive consumption tax is levied on annual rather than lifetime consumption, then τ_{ct} is a function of C_t. From (5') it is clear that $\tau_{ct} \geq \tau_{ct-1}$ as $r_t \geq \rho$. Hence the steeper the growth of consumption in the absence of taxes, the greater will be the relative taxation of future consumption under an annual progressive consumption tax.

Explicit presentation of the optimizing behavior of households under other tax systems is omitted since the derivation of these results from those just presented follows in a straightforward manner.

The economy's single production sector is characterized by the Cobb-Douglas production function:

(7)
$$Y_t = AK_t^\epsilon((1+g)^t L_t)^{1-\epsilon},$$

where Y_t, K_t, and L_t are output, capital, and labor at time t, A is a scaling constant, g is an exogenous productivity growth rate, and ϵ is the capital share of output, assumed throughout the paper to equal 0.25. L_t is simply equal to the sum of labor endowments of all individuals in the work force. K_t is generated by a recursive equation that dictates that the change in the capital stock equals private plus public savings. Competitive behavior on the part of producers ensures that the gross factor returns r_t and w_t are equated to the marginal products of capital and labor at time t:

(8a)
$$r_t = \epsilon A(K_t/(1+g)^t L_t)^{-(1-\epsilon)},$$

(8b)
$$w_t = (1-\epsilon)A(1+g)^t(K_t/(1+g)^t L_t)^\epsilon.$$

The assumption that the return to capital equals its marginal product implies that the market value of capital goods always equals their reproduction cost; i.e. adjustment of capital to the desired levels is instantaneous.

The government in our model needs to finance a stream of consumption expenditures, labeled G_t, that grows at the same rate as population plus productivity. For simplicity, the impact of government expenditures on individual utility is not considered in the analysis. Aside from various taxes, the government has at its disposal one-period debt which is a perfect substitute for capital in household portfolios. This enables the government to save (run surpluses) and dissave (run deficits) without investing directly. If Ag_t is defined as the value of government's assets (taking a negative value if there is a national debt), government tax revenue at the end of period t is

$$(9) \qquad R_t = \bar{\bar{\tau}}_{yt}[w_t L_t + r_t(K_t - Ag_t)] + \bar{\bar{\tau}}_{ct}C_t,$$

where $\bar{\bar{\tau}}_{yt}$ and $\bar{\bar{\tau}}_{ct}$ are the aggregate average tax rates on income and consumption, respectively, calculated as weighted averages of individual average tax rates. Given the government's ability to issue and retire debt, its budget constraint relates the present value of its expenditures to the present value of its tax receipts plus the value of its initial assets:

$$(10) \qquad Ag_0 + \sum_{t=0}^{\infty}\left[\prod_{s=0}^{t}(1+r_s)\right]^{-1}R_t$$
$$= \sum_{t=0}^{\infty}\left[\prod_{s=0}^{t}(1+r_s)\right]^{-1}G_t.$$

(Note that G_t corresponds to a different concept from that reported in the National Income Accounts, which includes government purchase of capital goods.)

The solution method used to compute the perfect foresight general equilibrium path of the economy depends on the type of policy change being examined. In general, one may distinguish two cases. In the first, the ultimate characteristics of the economy are known, and the final steady state to which the economy converges after the policy change is enacted may be described without reference to the economy's transition path. An example of such a policy change is the replacement of a system of income taxation with a tax on consumption, subject to year-by-year budget balance. The configuration of taxes and the government debt in the final steady state is known here. Thus it is possible to solve for the final steady state and then use our knowledge of the initial and final steady states to solve for the economy's transition path.

The second class of problems is one where a policy involves specific actions during the transition and the final steady state cannot be identified independently from the actual transition path. For example, under a policy which specifies a ten year cut in income taxes, compensated for by concurrent increases in the national debt, with the debt per capita held constant thereafter and a new constant rate of income tax ultimately established, it is impossible to solve for this new rate without also knowing the level of per capita debt which is established in the transition. Here, it is necessary to solve for the final steady state and transition path simultaneously.

The actual solution for the economy's behavior over time always begins with a characterization of the initial steady state, given initial tax structure and government debt. We assume that individuals of different generations alive during this steady state correctly perceive the tax schedule and factor prices they will face over time, and behave optimally with respect to these conditions. We utilize a Gauss-Seidel iteration technique to solve for this equilibrium, starting with an initial guess of the capital-labor ratio (K/L), deriving from each iteration a new estimate used to update our guess and continuing the procedure until a fixed point is reached. Given the method of deriving new estimates of K/L, such a fixed point corresponds to a steady-state equilibrium.

The iteration step is slightly different for each type of tax system, but the following description of how it proceeds for a progressive income tax should be instructive. (In this example, we assume each generation is composed of one representative individual. In the actual simulations, we sometimes allow cohorts to have heterogeneous members.) A schematic representation is provided in figure 13.1. In the first stage, a guess is made of the capital-labor ratio (equivalent to a guess of the capital stock, since labor supply is fixed). Given the marginal productivity equations (8a) and (8b), this yields values for the wage w and interest rate r. Combining these values with initial guesses for the paths of marginal and average tax rates over the life cycle, we apply equations (3) and (6) to obtain the life-cycle consumption plan of the representative individual C. From the definition of savings, this yields the age-asset profile A, which may be aggregated (subtracting any national debt assumed to exist) to provide a new value of the capital stock and capital-labor ratio. The age-asset profile, along with the estimates of w and r, also provides a solution for the age-income profile, which, in turn, dictates the general level at which taxes must be set (typically one parameter is varied in the tax function) to satisfy the government budget constraint and hence the new values of marginal and average tax rates faced over the life cycle, τ_y and $\bar{\tau}_y$, respectively. When the initial and final values of K/L and the tax rates are the same, this implies that the steady state has been reached.

Solution for the final steady state, when this may be done separately (the first case discussed above), proceeds in a similar manner. In such a case, the transition is solved for in the following way. We assume the transition to the new steady state takes 150 years, then solve simul-

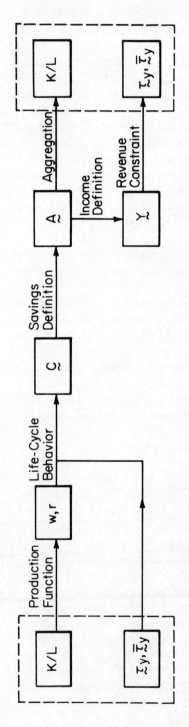

Fig. 13.1   Iteration procedure: progressive income tax.

taneously for equilibrium in each of the 150 years of the transition period under the assumption that everyone believes that after year 150 the new steady state will obtain. This solution method is necessary because each household is assumed to take the path of future prices into account in determining its behavior. Hence the equilibrium that results in later years will affect the equilibrium in earlier years. Specifically, we assume that individuals born after the transition begins know the transition path immediately and that those born before the beginning of the transition behaved up to the time of the change in government policy as if the old steady state would continue forever. At the time of the announcement of a new policy to be instituted either immediately or in the near future, existing cohorts are "born again"; they behave like members of the new generation except that their horizon is less than fifty-five years, and they possess initial assets as a result of prior accumulation. An iteration technique is used again, but here we must begin with a *vector* of capital stocks (one value for each year) and two *matrices* of tax rates (two vectors for each year). Further, we cannot simply solve for the behavior of a representative cohort, but rather must calculate the behavior of each cohort alive during the transition. This procedure, while conceptually no more difficult than that used to find the steady states, requires considerably more computation. As the ultimate paths converge to the final steady state well before year 150, the assumption about conditions after year 150 does not influence our results.

When the final steady state may not be calculated independently from the transition path, the two stages are combined. Rather than calculate the final steady state, we simply calculate an "augmented" transition path lasting 205 years, where the final 55 years are constrained to have the characteristics of a steady state.

13.4 The Welfare Costs of Capital Income Taxation

The ultimate impact on the economy of a change in government policy depends on three key factors. First, the intercohort allocation of the total tax burden of financing government expenditures will determine the level of tax rates and have important income effects on the consumption of particular cohorts. Second, the tax structure (choice of tax base) offers the vector of prices each generation faces. Third, preferences determine each household's response to a change in incentives. In the case of a heterogeneous population, the intragenerational distribution of the tax burden may also be an important determinant of the growth path of the economy.

Typically, the impact of tax policy has been studied most closely in partial equilibrium, static models in which the welfare of a representative individual is evaluated under alternative tax regimes. As discussed above, this approach does not permit a study of the inefficiency involved during the transition from one steady state to another, nor does it tell us about the intergenerational transfers that may accompany the transition. For such issues to be studied, one must use a model in which overlapping generations exist and the change in tax regime is not considered as an exercise in comparative statics but rather as an explicit policy change that evolves over time.

The classic study of the static type just discussed is that of Feldstein (1978), who examines the welfare gain from switching to a consumption tax or a tax on labor income alone from one on labor and interest income. As Feldstein points out, the choice between taxing labor income and taxing consumption at a constant rate sufficient to produce an equal present-value revenue yield has no effect on the path of individual behavior. Thus, if government uses debt finance to undo any differences in the timing of tax collections, there is no difference in national savings either, since both private and public consumption are identical under the two systems. All that differs is the distribution of savings between the household and government sectors, with the government saving more under a wage tax because of the earlier receipt of tax revenues.

When there is only one generation under study, it is impossible to imagine a change in individual lifetime tax burden without a concomitant change in government expenditures. However, once several generations are considered simultaneously, it is possible to allow tax burdens to be shifted across generations as the structure of taxation changes. For example, a switch from wage taxation to consumption taxation which requires not equal present-value yield per generation but rather year-by-year budget balance will change the tax burden of each generation in the transition to the new long-run steady state. To see why this is so, consider a simple model in which there is no growth in population or government expenditures and each individual lives for two periods, working only in the first and consuming only in the second. In the long run, if there is no government debt or deficit, the tax paid on consumption by each individual in his second year must equal the amount which would be paid in the first year under a wage tax. As long as the interest rate is positive, this involves a lower present value of taxes and, because relative prices are the same under the two systems, a gain in long-run utility. This result carries through to a more general model, with individuals living, working, and consuming for several years, as long as wages occur earlier in life, on average, than does consumption. Thus Summers (1981) found that, holding government revenue per year fixed, steady-state utility is substantially higher under a consumption tax than under a wage tax.

But this gain is not due to increased efficiency, since by such a criterion the two systems are equal (and completely nondistortionary with a fixed labor supply). What is occurring is a transfer from transitional generations to those in the steady state. In the simple example used above, if there were an immediate switch to a consumption tax, all generations would be better off *except* the first, which would pay its taxes twice and therefore be worse off. As long as the economy is not on a path which is "dynamically inefficient" in the sense that conducting such a chain transfer in reverse would make all generations better off (as would be true if the growth rate of annual tax revenues exceeded the interest rate), such steady-state differences do not provide a fair comparison, because implicit in them is an intergenerational realignment of the tax burden.

One could respond to this problem by requiring that government debt policy be used to neutralize any such intergenerational transfers, but this may still fall short of equating the effect of consumption and wage taxation on all generations. Consider again a simple example with individuals laboring in their first period and consuming in their second, and suppose the economy initially faces a wage tax. A complete neutralization of a switch to a consumption tax would require an exemption of the first generation from consumption taxation (they have already paid the wage tax under the old system) with revenues in that year being paid for by deficit finance. Thereafter, each period's consumption tax receipts would redeem the previous period's debt.

However, if, for example, we extended the model to allow individuals to consume in both periods, this policy would no longer suffice, for exempting the older generation from consumption taxes would exempt the younger generation's first-period consumption as well. Thus a complete separation of tax structure from intergenerational transfers would appear to require not only an unconstrained use of debt policy but the ability to assess age-specific tax rates as well. In the absence of such instruments, it may be impossible to go from one tax system to an "equivalent" one without having real effects on the welfare of individuals in the transition.

Constraints on the set of tax instruments limit our ability not only to move between structurally equivalent tax systems without changing the distribution of cohort welfare but also to move to a priori less distortionary tax structures in a Pareto-efficient manner. Indeed, use of the limited set of tax instruments themselves may generate distortions along the transition path. One example here is transition to a consumption tax, to the extent that annual consumption tax rates change during the transition. These tax rate changes will introduce distortions in the intertemporal consumption choice of affected cohorts. In such a case, it may be possible to improve the welfare of all generations, but it is not obvious what the appropriate government policy is to accomplish this, given the limitation on generation-specific tax rates. In this case, requiring that the present value of taxes be unaffected by the change in tax structure does not provide a guide to choosing a Pareto-efficient tax transaction since interest rates will be changing over the transition and there is no "correct" interest rate to use in the present value calculations.

We turn now to the results of some simple simulations to demonstrate some of the points just made.

In the following example, we consider the transition paths of an economy that starts at an initial steady state with a proportional wage tax of 0.2 and a proportional interest income tax of 0.4 and switches to either a pure consumption tax or a pure wage tax. The government's budget is assumed to be balanced each year; hence annual revenues are the same in both transitions. Individual utility parameters ρ and γ are set at 0.02 and 1, respectively. The population grows at a rate $n = 0.01$, while individual human capital is assumed to grow at an annual rate of $h = 0.007$. In addition, we assume a constant productivity growth rate of $g = 0.02$. The tax rates on capital and labor and the parameters n, h, and g are chosen to accord with empirically observed magnitudes, while ρ and γ provide reasonable results for the age-consumption profile and capital-output ratio in the initial steady state. Nevertheless, the results should be seen as illustrative and specific magnitudes viewed with some care.

Some steady-state results of the simulation are summarized in table 13.1. From a capital-output ratio of 2.92 and a savings rate of 10% under the income tax, the economy goes to a moderately higher value of each under a wage tax (3.97 and 13.5%, respectively), but the shift to a consumption tax goes much further: the capital-output ratio is more than double under a consumption tax. It appears from these results that the change in efficiency of a tax structure may be less important in determining the characteristics of the ultimate steady state than the coincident intergenerational transfers. To see the effect of such transfers, consider figure 13.2, which presents the change in welfare for each generation between each of the two new systems and the status quo in which the income tax is kept in place. The welfare change is measured by the percentage increase or decrease in the vector of household consumption chosen under the initial tax system necessary to reach the level of utility attained under the new tax system. VC represents the gain in welfare under a consumption tax, and VW the gain under a wage tax. The

Table 13.1   **Income, Wage, and Consumption Taxes: Steady States**
$(\rho = .02, \gamma = 1)$

	Tax System		
	Income	Wage	Consumption
Capital-output ratio	2.92	3.97	7.16
Gross interest rate	.086	.063	.035
Aggregate savings rate	.100	.135	.244
Tax rate	.40/.20	.30	.32

horizontal axis indexes the individual generations, with generation 1 being born at the beginning of the period in which the changes are enacted. As is clear from the graph, though steady-state welfare is improved under each tax change, there are losing generations along the way. Moreover, the identity of such generations, as well as the size of the ultimate steady-state welfare gain, is very different under the two regimes.

For a switch to wage taxation, retired generations, as well as those soon to retire, gain because the bulk of their remaining income and tax liability under the income tax would be in the form of interest income and taxes on such income. Individuals born soon before or soon after the tax change are hurt. To understand why, it helps to consider the path of capital stock growth under the wage tax, relative to the baseline economy, depicted in figure 13.3 as KW. (The corresponding path for the consumption tax is labeled KC.) Note that while the capital stock is eventually 50% larger, this higher level is not reached for several years. Thus, while the added capital will eventually lead to an increase in real wages, this rise will not

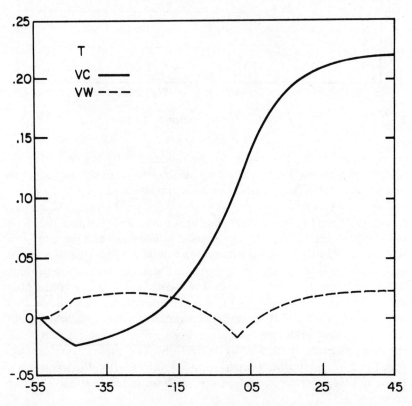

Fig. 13.2   Welfare paths: consumption and wage taxes.

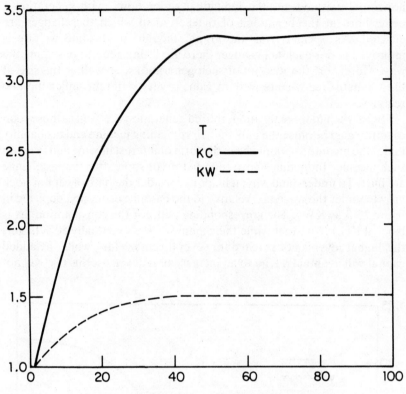

Fig. 13.3   Capital for wage and consumption taxes.

occur immediately. Moreover, as the revenue lost from removing the interest income tax must be made up by an increase in the wage tax, net real wages decline substantially in early transition years.

The move to a consumption tax has very different effects. All generations older than twenty at the time of enactment lose, because they have paid labor income taxes when young and will now have to pay consumption taxes when old. The maximum loss of about 2.5% of lifetime resources for individuals ages forty-five at the time of enactment represents a very large loss during this cohort's *remaining* years—consumption taxes are on the order of 40% in the earliest transition years, more than doubling the tax liability for such individuals relative to the old system. These losses are greater in total than those under a wage tax, but so are the eventual gains for succeeding generations. The implicit transfers from the old allow generations born as soon as five years into the transition to enjoy a 12% increase in real wealth, with an ultimate steady-state increase of 22%.

A response to these findings concerning welfare changes under a consumption tax might be to accept the prospect that some generations will lose and that, for any plausible discount rate applied to the gains of succeeding generations, the social gain must be quite positive. This is the argument made by Summers (1981). On the other hand, such an approach would also appear to favor a consumption tax over a wage tax, judging by the welfare comparison in figure 13.2, so it is questionable what role, if any, is being played by pure efficiency gains.

Following Phelps and Riley (1978), another way of attacking this problem is to require that other measures accompany the tax change to ensure that no generation be harmed. Without lump-sum transfers, such a policy probably requires a combination of deficit policy and the use of wage as well as consumption taxes. In figure 13.4, the welfare path of one such policy, labeled VPARETO, is presented, along with the paths VC and VW from figure 13.2. Figure 13.5 presents the corresponding capital growth paths. The policy depicted involves starting with a wage tax of 23% and a consumption tax of 9%, gradually lowering the wage tax over fifty years to 15% while raising the consumption tax to 18%, and running

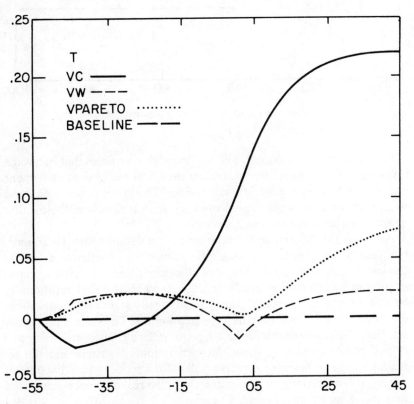

Fig. 13.4   A Pareto-superior welfare path.

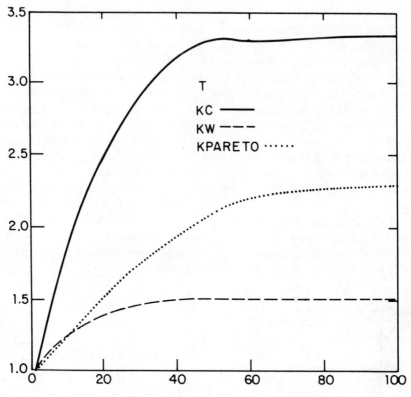

Fig. 13.5   Capital stock under a Pareto-superior plan.

deficits over the same period. The welfare path resembles that of a wage tax, except that generations older than twenty at the time of enactment gain less and all other generations do better. The use of deficit policy and wage taxation causes the capital stock to reach a value well below that attained under a pure consumption tax.

Although this "Pareto path" is not unique, it demonstrates two important results. First, even without a full complement of instruments at the disposal of government, the long-run efficiency gains of exempting capital income from taxation are large enough to allow all generations to benefit. Of equal importance, the ultimate steady-state gain is only about one-third the gain under a pure consumption tax. Thus one may loosely attribute about two-thirds of the long-run welfare gains of switching to a consumption tax to coincident intergenerational transfers and the remainder to tax efficiency. As this result is for a model with a fixed labor supply, it is if anything an overstatement of the real efficiency gains to be had under such a change in tax regime.

13.5 Progressive Taxation

The previous section of the paper focused on the transition from a system of proportional income taxation to alternative systems of proportional taxation. In reality, the United States tax system is progressive (at least as measured by statutory tax rates) and it is likely that any new tax system would possess this characteristic as well.

In considering the additional influence of tax progressivity, we alter our existing model in a number of ways. To facilitate the more complicated simulations necessary we ignore growth of human capital or productivity. (These parameters were found to have minor effects on the nature of transitions under proportional taxation.) As progressive taxes exist in part to mitigate the inequality of resource distribution in society, it is important to allow for the existence of heterogeneous individuals. This is accommodated in a simple manner, by assuming that each cohort has three representative individuals, with equal tastes but unequal incomes. Letting the median individual have an annual labor endowment of 1.0, the poor household is assumed to possess an endowment of 0.5, and the wealthy one an endowment of 1.5. Our final change is in the tax system itself. We replace the different systems of proportional taxation with two-parameter progressive taxes; that is, if z is the relevant tax base, we choose two parameters, labeled α and β, and set the *marginal* tax rate equal to $\alpha + \beta z$ for all values of z. It follows that the corresponding *average* tax rate is $\alpha + \frac{1}{2}\beta z$. Setting $\beta = 0$ amounts to proportional taxation. Highly progressive tax systems are represented by low values of α and high values of β. For the simulations of this section, the parameters from the basic proportional tax simulations above are maintained ($\gamma = 1$, $\rho = 0.02$, $n = 0.01$); α and β are set equal to 0.12 and 0.14, respectively, for the progressive income tax. These values of α and β were obtained from a least squares regression of the marginal tax rates contained in the United States tax code, with income normalized to correspond to the levels in our simulations.

Table 13.2 gives the marginal and average tax rates which result in the steady state under progressive income taxation. For the poor person, marginal tax rates rise from 0.19 to 0.24, then dropping to 0.17 upon retirement and to 0.13 in the last year of life. The corresponding values for the median and wealthy households are (0.26, 0.34, 0.20, 0.13) and (0.33, 0.43, 0.22, 0.13), respectively. This tax structure would be expected to reduce the inequality in society, but changing marginal rates might cause inefficiencies in excess of the tax wedges introduced by equal-revenue proportional taxes. These two propositions are verified by examining the results of a switch from progressive to proportional income taxation. The poor in the long run have their real wealth (as measured above) reduced by 7.00%; the rich gain in wealth by 6.37%, and the

Table 13.2   **Simulated Tax Rates under Progressive Income Taxation**

	Poor		Median		Wealthy	
Age	MTR	ATR	MTR	ATR	MTR	ATR
1	.190	.155	.260	.190	.330	.225
2	.191	.156	.262	.191	.333	.226
3	.193	.156	.264	.192	.335	.228
4	.194	.157	.267	.193	.338	.229
5	.195	.158	.269	.194	.341	.230
6	.196	.158	.271	.195	.344	.232
7	.198	.159	.273	.197	.346	.233
8	.199	.160	.275	.198	.349	.234
9	.200	.160	.277	.199	.352	.236
10	.202	.161	.280	.200	.354	.237
11	.203	.162	.282	.201	.357	.238
12	.204	.162	.284	.202	.360	.240
13	.206	.163	.286	.203	.362	.241
14	.207	.164	.288	.204	.365	.242
15	.208	.164	.291	.205	.367	.244
16	.210	.165	.293	.206	.370	.245
17	.211	.166	.295	.207	.372	.246
18	.212	.166	.297	.208	.375	.247
19	.214	.167	.299	.209	.377	.249
20	.215	.168	.301	.211	.380	.250
21	.216	.168	.303	.212	.382	.251
22	.218	.169	.305	.213	.385	.252
23	.219	.169	.307	.214	.387	.254
24	.220	.170	.309	.215	.389	.255
25	.221	.171	.311	.215	.392	.256
26	.223	.171	.313	.216	.394	.257
27	.224	.172	.315	.217	.396	.258
28	.225	.172	.317	.218	.398	.259
29	.226	.173	.318	.219	.401	.260
30	.227	.174	.320	.220	.403	.261
31	.228	.174	.322	.221	.405	.262
32	.229	.175	.323	.222	.407	.263
33	.230	.175	.325	.222	.409	.264
34	.231	.175	.326	.223	.411	.265
35	.232	.176	.328	.224	.412	.266
36	.233	.176	.329	.225	.414	.267
37	.233	.177	.330	.225	.416	.268
38	.234	.177	.332	.226	.418	.269
39	.235	.177	.333	.226	.419	.270
40	.235	.178	.334	.227	.421	.270
41	.236	.178	.335	.227	.422	.271
42	.236	.178	.335	.228	.424	.272
43	.236	.178	.336	.228	.425	.272
44	.237	.178	.337	.228	.426	.273
45	.237	.178	.337	.229	.427	.274
46	.167	.143	.198	.159	.219	.170
47	.164	.142	.193	.156	.212	.166

Table 13.2 (cont.)

Age	Poor		Median		Wealthy	
	MTR	ATR	MTR	ATR	MTR	ATR
48	.160	.140	.187	.153	.205	.162
49	.156	.138	.181	.150	.197	.158
50	.152	.136	.174	.147	.188	.154
51	.148	.134	.166	.143	.179	.149
52	.143	.132	.158	.139	.168	.144
53	.138	.129	.150	.135	.157	.139
54	.132	.126	.140	.130	.146	.133
55	.126	.123	.130	.125	.133	.126

median group ia virtually unaffected (their wealth loss is 0.45%). This may very well represent a large loss in social welfare, taking distribution into account. However, it is clearly a gain in efficiency, since the proportional wealth gain of the rich is calculated on a much larger base than the proportional loss of the poor. This is corroborated by the fact that the long-run capital stock under progressive income taxation is 11% lower than under proportional income taxation.

Turning next to consider a switch from progressive income to progressive consumption taxes, we may ask two additional questions. First, how progressive does the consumption tax have to be to maintain the same degree of wealth inequality, measured by the Lorenz curve, as exists under a progressive income tax? Second, how is the change in steady-state utility and capital intensity between the two systems affected by the introduction of progressivity?

In answer to our first question, we find that the values of α and β which must be applied under a consumption tax to provide an identical Lorenz curve in the long run to that of the income tax are 0.104 and 0.432, respectively. These translate into the marginal and average tax rates listed in table 13.3. As consumption profiles rise over time, so do the tax rates of all three groups. The marginal tax rates applied to the poor person's consumption range between 0.30 and 0.34. As these rates are fractions of consumption, it is helpful in comparing them to income tax rates to translate them into fractions of resources used for consumption (consumption plus taxes paid on such consumption). The corresponding values are 0.23 and 0.25 respectively. For median-income households, the range is 0.48 to 0.54 (0.32 to 0.35 gross); for wealthy individuals, the range is 0.63 to 0.71 (0.39 to 0.42, gross). Interestingly, the top (gross) marginal rax rates for the three groups are almost identical to the top rates for each under an income tax (0.25, 0.35, and 0.42 versus 0.24, 0.34, and 0.43).

Table 13.3   **Simulated Tax Rates under Progressive Consumption Taxation**

Age	Poor MTR	Poor ATR	Median MTR	Median ATR	Wealthy MTR	Wealthy ATR
1	.302	.203	.475	.289	.629	.366
2	.303	.203	.476	.290	.630	.367
3	.303	.204	.477	.290	.632	.368
4	.304	.204	.478	.291	.633	.369
5	.305	.204	.479	.292	.635	.369
6	.305	.205	.480	.292	.636	.370
7	.306	.205	.481	.293	.638	.371
8	.307	.205	.482	.293	.639	.372
9	.307	.206	.483	.294	.641	.372
10	.308	.206	.484	.294	.642	.373
11	.309	.206	.486	.295	.644	.374
12	.309	.207	.487	.295	.645	.375
13	.310	.207	.488	.296	.647	.375
14	.311	.207	.489	.297	.648	.376
15	.311	.208	.490	.297	.650	.377
16	.312	.208	.491	.298	.651	.378
17	.313	.208	.492	.298	.653	.378
18	.313	.209	.493	.299	.654	.379
19	.314	.209	.495	.299	.656	.380
20	.315	.209	.496	.300	.657	.381
21	.315	.210	.497	.301	.659	.381
22	.316	.210	.498	.301	.660	.382
23	.317	.210	.499	.302	.662	.383
24	.317	.211	.500	.302	.663	.384
25	.318	.211	.502	.303	.665	.385
26	.319	.211	.503	.303	.667	.385
27	.319	.212	.504	.304	.668	.386
28	.320	.212	.505	.305	.670	.387
29	.321	.212	.506	.305	.671	.388
30	.321	.213	.507	.306	.673	.388
31	.322	.213	.509	.306	.674	.389
32	.323	.213	.510	.307	.676	.390
33	.323	.214	.511	.307	.677	.391
34	.324	.214	.512	.308	.679	.392
35	.325	.214	.513	.309	.681	.392
36	.326	.215	.514	.309	.682	.393
37	.326	.215	.516	.310	.684	.394
38	.327	.216	.517	.310	.685	.395
39	.328	.216	.518	.311	.687	.396
40	.328	.216	.519	.312	.689	.396
41	.329	.217	.520	.312	.690	.397
42	.330	.217	.522	.313	.692	.398
43	.330	.217	.523	.313	.693	.399
44	.331	.218	.524	.314	.695	.400
45	.332	.218	.525	.315	.697	.400
46	.333	.218	.527	.315	.698	.401
47	.333	.219	.528	.316	.700	.402

Table 13.3 (cont.)

Age	Poor		Median		Wealthy	
	MTR	ATR	MTR	ATR	MTR	ATR
48	.334	.219	.529	.317	.702	.403
49	.335	.219	.530	.317	.703	.404
50	.335	.220	.531	.318	.705	.404
51	.336	.220	.533	.318	.706	.405
52	.337	.221	.534	.319	.708	.406
53	.338	.221	.535	.320	.710	.407
54	.338	.221	.536	.320	.711	.408
55	.339	.222	.538	.321	.713	.409

In comparison to the change in capital stock under proportional taxes, a switch to consumption taxes under progressive taxation leads to a lower capital stock increase, with the capital stock going up by a factor of 3.06 in the current simulation relative to the 3.32 found above under proportional taxes. Similarly, the welfare gain is smaller. Each group in the steady state obtains a 16% increase in real wealth relative to the 22% gain under proportional taxes. These differences result because as emphasized above under progressive consumption taxes there remains an intertemporal distortion in the choice of consumption. With consumption rising over time, each household's net rate of return is less than the gross interest rate. Our results suggest that efficiency gains of a switch may still be possible, even with the requirement that no generation be harmed, but the scope for such gains is clearly reduced by the need for tax progressivity to address the important problem of societal inequality.

13.6 The Effects of Tax Cuts, Government Expenditure, and Policy Announcements on Capital Formation

In this section, we consider the general equilibrium effects of selected fiscal policies and also examine how a switch from income taxation to the taxation of either consumption or wages would be affected by a prior announcement of such a policy.

By assumption, the government is rational and recognizes that its tax rate and expenditure paths will affect the economy's path of labor earnings, interest income, and consumption. Hence changes in announced tax rates and expenditure levels must satisfy the government budget constraint (9) consistent with the general equilibrium changes in income and consumption such government policy choices induce.

This suggests the following important points about government policy:
Temporary or permanent increases in government expenditures necessitate changes in the path of tax rates. The choice of which tax rates to

increase and when to increase those tax rates will determine the short-run and long-run impact of increases in government expenditure on national savings.

Temporary cuts in tax rates holding expenditures constant must be made up by increases in tax rates in the future.[4] Again the timing and choice of future tax rate increases will influence the economic reaction to temporary tax cuts.

Balanced budget changes in the choice of tax bases will require annual adjustments in tax rates until the economy converges to a new steady state. These annual tax changes during the transition are likely to be both inefficient in the sense of generating excess burdens and capricious in their cohort allocation of the tax burden of financing government expenditure.

Announcement today of future changes in tax rates can have important implications for current revenue since the current stream of income and consumption may be affected by future tax rate policy.

13.6.1   Temporary Tax Cuts

Table 13.4 presents the effect of cuts in tax rates lasting five, ten, and twenty years on transition and long-run values of the economy's consumption and capital output ratio. Two types of tax cuts are considered: a reduction in the proportional rate of income taxation and a reduction in the tax rate on wage income alone, holding the tax rate on capital income constant. As mentioned, temporary tax rate cuts require future tax rate increases. The simulations presented are based on the assumption that following the period of tax rate cuts the per capita debt resulting from these tax cuts is permitted from that point on to grow at the economy's 2% rate of productivity growth. The base case with which to compare these results assumes $\rho = 0.02$ and $\gamma = 1$, and a 30% proportional rate of income taxation with no initial government debt. For cuts in the proportional income tax, tax rates are reduced to 25% for the period in question. In the case of wage tax reductions, this tax rate is lowered to 23.33% for either five, ten, or twenty years; a 23.33% wage tax rate provides the same first year tax revenue reduction that is generated by cutting both wage and capital income tax rates to 25%.

Although taxes are cut initially by over 15%, table 13.4 indicates fairly small responses of aggregate consumption to tax cuts of short duration. A five year cut in the wage tax rate leads to only a 0.5% increase in consumption in the first year of the cut. The reason is simply that the majority of cohorts will end up paying for these current tax cuts in terms of higher tax rates and lower future wages after the five year period. The deficit created by this short-term tax reduction has a limited wealth effect on the economy.

---

4. This rules out the possibility that tax rates are so high initially that lowering them increases tax receipts.

Table 13.4   Temporary Tax Cuts

| | Base Case | | 5 Year Tax Cut | | | | 10 Year Tax Cut | | | | 20 Year Tax Cut | | | |
| | | | Income Tax | | Wage Tax | | Income Tax | | Wage Tax | | Income Tax | | Wage Tax | |
Year	K/Y	C	K/Y	C	K/Y	C	K/Y	C	K/Y	C	K/Y	C	K/Y	C
1	3.11	34.77	3.11	34.77	3.11	34.95	3.11	34.79	3.11	35.12	3.11	34.69	3.11	35.37
5	3.11	37.64	3.10	37.98	3.10	37.80	3.11	37.99	3.09	37.97	3.11	37.90	3.08	38.22
10	3.11	41.55	3.08	41.78	3.09	41.69	3.06	42.33	3.07	41.84	3.08	42.25	3.03	42.10
20	3.11	50.65	3.05	50.55	3.07	50.59	2.98	50.67	3.01	50.60	2.93	52.09	2.93	50.76
50	3.11	91.74	3.01	90.81	3.03	91.07	2.87	89.52	2.93	90.19	2.52	86.44	2.69	88.31
100	3.11	246.93	3.01	244.06	3.03	244.76	2.85	239.56	2.92	241.52	2.41	225.94	2.62	232.11
150	3.11	664.63	3.01	656.90	3.03	658.80	2.85	644.77	2.92	650.08	2.41	604.87	2.62	624.46

Tax cuts of longer duration have more significant effects on national savings. A twenty year wage tax cut increases aggregate consumption in the first year of the transition by 1.73% and lowers the national savings rate in year 2 from 9.40% to 8.34%. There is a 15% long-run reduction in the capital output ratio from 3.11 to 2.62; the gross wage rate falls by 5.56% in the long run, while the wage tax rate levied on this lower tax base must rise to 39% to finance interest payments on the debt as well as future government expenditures. The net wage falls therefore by 15% relative to its value in the no tax cut case.

For each of the wage tax cut simulations the long run crowding out of private capital by one dollar of government debt is approximately 52 cents. The long-run ratios of debt to capital are respectively 0.07, 0.17, and .50 for wage tax cuts of five, ten, and twenty years. The 52 cent figure reflects two facts. First, holding gross factor returns fixed, switching government tax receipts from the present to the future leads to a reduction in government savings but an increase in private savings to pay for the higher future taxes. Second, the reduction in the long-run capital stock lowers gross wages and raises gross and net interest rates; both of these factors induce greater savings.

Deficits resulting from capital as well as wage tax cuts can generate a quite different impact on capital formation in the initial phase of the tax cut. Rather than increase consumption, income tax cuts can lead to more national savings in the short run. In the twenty year income tax cut example, the first year national savings rate rises from 9.40% to 9.52%, although the long-run savings rate falls from 9.40 to 7.28%. Apparently the temporarily higher net rate of return induces a sufficiently strong savings response that the government deficit actually "crowds in" private capital. The incentives to savings are, however, only temporary. As the end of the period of tax cuts approaches, the impending higher tax rates on capital income reduce savings incentives and the income effects of the tax cut take hold. In the long run there is a smaller capital stock for deficits arising from changes in the proportional income tax rate; the long-run higher tax rate on capital income generates a permanent savings disencentive. The long-run degree of crowding out is approximately 70 cents on a dollar for each of these three cases.

13.6.2 Government Expenditures and Capital Formation

Increases in government expenditures affect capital formation directly by raising the government's contribution to total national consumption and indirectly by altering the expected path of future tax rates. Table 13.5 describes the effect on capital formation of a 5% permanent increase in expenditures under a number of different financing scenarios. The first scenario is that the government balances its budget on an annual basis and therefore immediately raises tax rates to accommodate the increased

Table 13.5   **Balanced Budget and Deficit Financed 5% Permanent Increases in Government Expenditure—the Crowding Out of National Investment by Permanent Increases in Government Expenditures**

Financing	$\Delta I/\Delta G_2$	$\Delta I/\Delta G_{10}$	$\Delta I/\Delta G_{50}$	$\Delta I/\Delta G_{150}$
Balanced budget	−.519	−.387	−.214	−.210
5 year constant tax rates	−.530	−.527	−.336	−.320
10 year constant tax rates	−.520	−.743	−.495	−.451
20 year constant tax rates	−.504	−.690	−.939	−.800

level of expenditures. Alternatively, the government is assumed to keep tax rates constant for five, ten, or twenty years, i.e. use deficit financing for these lengths of time. At the end of the constant tax rate interval, the government is assumed to maintain the current level or per capita debt adjusted for growth. In each case the tax rate that is adjusted is the proportional income tax rate.

Table 13.5 indicates that short-run crowding out of private investment is roughly 50 cents per dollar of government expenditure. Under the balanced budget regime, crowding out is 52 cents in the first year of the transition, it is 53 cents under the assumption of constant tax rates for five years, but it is only 50 cents for the case of constant tax rates for twenty years. In the last case, the extended period during which capital income is taxed at a lower rate promotes savings and "crowds in" an additional 2 cents of investment in the first year of the transition.

Short-run crowding out exceeds long-run crowding out in the balanced budget example for two reasons. First, even in partial equilibrium permanently increasing the rate of proportional income taxation will alter the economy's path of wealth accumulation; existing cohorts at the time of the tax increase hold assets that were accumulated on the basis of the previously low capital income tax rate. The initial set of elderly in particular find that at the lower net interest rate their assets are large relative to their new desired levels of future consumption. They proceed to rapidly adjust their consumption levels upward. In the long run this consumption of "excess assets" does not occur; all long-run cohorts hold assets that were accumulated from birth on the basis of the lower net return to capital. The second reason is that crowding out leads to lower long-run capital labor ratios and, in general equilibrium, higher gross and net rates of return. These higher long-run gross interest rates dampen the savings response to the higher tax rates. Although tax rates increase in the transition from 0.315 in the first year to 0.318 in year 150, the net interest rate starts out at 0.055 and rises to 0.056 because the gross interest rate increases from 0.080 to 0.082.

In the example of a twenty year, deficit-financed permanent increase in government expenditure, long-run crowding out is 80 cents, which exceeds short-run crowding out by 30 cents. The failure to make early elderly transition cohorts pay for any of the higher level of government expenditure leaves the economy with a lower long-run capital stock. Although consumption in year 1 is lower in the twenty year deficit case than in the balanced budget example, consumption in the twenty year deficit economy is higher in succeeding years than in the balanced budget case, and this lowers long-run capital intensity.

13.6.3 Effects of Early Announcement of Future Policy on National Savings

Early announcement of future policy changes can significantly alter economic behavior in periods prior to the actual implementation of the new policy. Given the time required to formulate and enact new tax legislation, announcement effects are a serious issue of concern. Indeed, the simulation results suggest that the very process of formulating tax

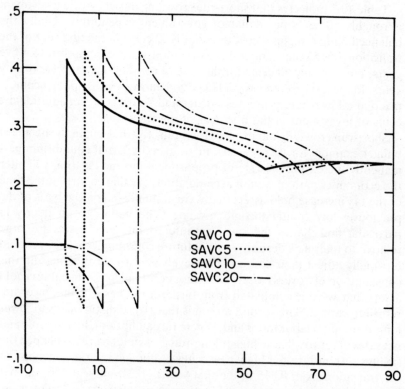

Fig. 13.6   Savings rates with varying announcement policies: consumption tax.

incentives to stimulate national savings can itself dramatically reduce national savings in the short run depending on the particular type of tax incentives proposed.

Figures 13.6 and 13.7 depict the effect of announcements in year 0 of a complete switch to either consumption or wage taxation starting either immediately, in five years, in ten years, or in twenty years. While the national savings rate jumps from 10% to over 40% if the consumption tax is immediately enacted, the short-run savings rate actually becomes negative in response to information that the consumption tax switch will occur in the near future. Obviously the anticipated high tax rates on future consumption dramatically lower the price of consumption today relative to tomorrow producing a consumption frenzy in the short term.

Announcements of future wage taxation have the opposite effect on short-term savings rates. Here the promise of lower rates of capital income taxation in the near future reduces the relative price of future consumption and immediately stimulates savings. Both diagrams indicate that economic behavior changes less in the short term the further in the

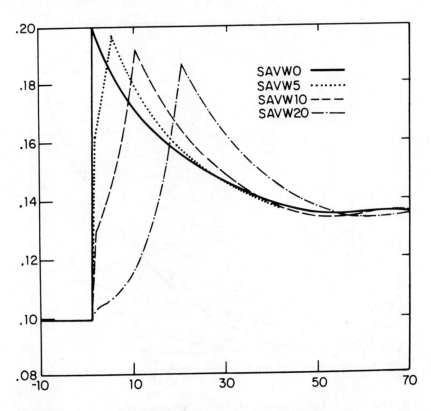

Fig. 13.7   Savings rates with varying announcement policies: wage tax.

future is the date of policy implementation. Yet policy changes that will not occur for ten years can still change savings rates in year 0 by over 25%.

Figures 13.8 and 13.9 graph the utility paths associated with these announced changes in the future tax structure. More distant implementation of the consumption tax relieves initial elderly cohorts of the heavy taxation of their retirement consumption. Initial young cohorts are, in contrast, hit hard by a delay in the switch to a consumption tax. Early announcement reduces somewhat the loss in utility of that cohort unfortunate enough to retire immediately prior to the tax switch. The reason is that the induced consumption frenzy lowers the capital stock and raises the rate of return these retirees receive on their savings, providing a small offset to the additional substantial tax burden these cohorts are forced to shoulder.

A similar situation arises in the wage tax case. Here immediate implementation significantly lowers the utility of initial young cohorts because these cohorts face higher wage tax rates during their working years and

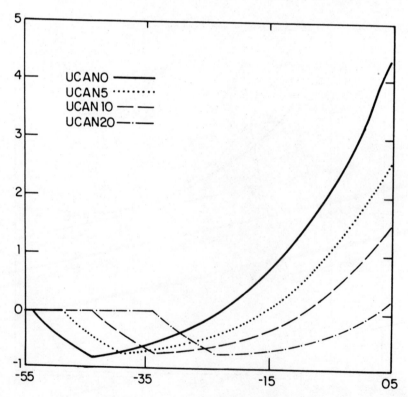

Fig. 13.8   Utility paths with varying announcement policies: consumption tax.

lower gross interest rates during their retirement. Delaying the wage tax implementation causes capital accumulation to increase immediately, providing a higher gross wage for initial young cohorts who now face a shorter period of high wage tax rates. The short-run increases in capital lower somewhat the utility of initial elderly cohorts by lowering the gross and therefore net return available on their savings. For announcements of wage tax adoption ten and twenty years in the future, only initial cohorts of the elderly are adversely affected. The induced short-run capital accumulation raises the gross wage enough to compensate workers for higher wage tax rates when the switch takes place.

13.7   Summary and Suggestions for Future Research

This paper has developed an equilibrium simulation model that can evaluate the effects of a variety of government policies on national savings and the inter- and intracohort distribution of welfare. The simulations described in the paper indicate that the long-run welfare gains of

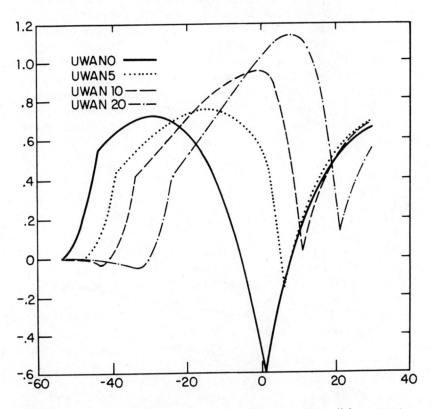

Fig. 13.9   Utility paths with varying announcement policies: wage tax.

alleged "tax reform" policies arise to a considerable degree as a result of redistribution from earlier cohorts. Pareto-efficient tax reform policies do exist, but involve careful use of our limited set of tax instruments. The current impact of current tax and expenditure policy depends critically on the nature and timing of associated future tax rate changes. A corollary of this is that questions such as "what is the effect of government deficit on current savings?" or "what is the effect on savings of capital income taxation?" are sorely underidentified. Informed discussion of policy alternatives requires a full description of the entire future paths of policy choice variables.

The simulation model can be modified in a number of different ways to conform more closely with economic reality and to investigate additional savings policy questions. First, preferences can be extended to include utility from the actual level of bequests rather than the utility of descendents per se. This feature will limit the wealth effects of deficit policies but permit more realistic modeling of the United States economy (see Kotlikoff and Summers 1981). Second, the model can be altered to allow for costs of quickly adjusting the capital stock. Summers (1980) and Lipton and Sachs (1980) have analyzed such q models in altruistic intertemporal settings, but the transition effects of adding investment adjustment costs in selfish life-cycle models may be quite different because of the real effects on savings of intercohort wealth transfers (Feldstein 1977). In addition to distinguishing new capital goods from capital goods in place, the introduction of other assets into the economy including land, money, and housing will improve the predictive capacity of the model and permit an analysis of the effect of inflation on the allocation of the capital stock between housing and industrial capital goods.

References

Auerbach, A. J. 1979. The optimal taxation of heterogeneous capital. *Quarterly Journal of Economics*, November, pp. 589–612.

Barro, R. J. 1974. Are government bonds net wealth? *Journal of Political Economy*, November/December, pp. 1095–17.

———. 1978. The impact of social security on private saving. *American Enterprise Institute Studies*, no. 199.

Boskin, M. J. 1978. Taxation, saving, and the rate of interest. *Journal of Political Economy*, April, pp. S3–S27.

Bradford, D. 1980. Economics of tax policy towards savings. In G. von Furstenburg, ed., *Government and capital formation*. Cambridge, Massachusetts: Ballinger Press.

Chamley, C. 1980. Optimal taxation and the public debt. Cowles Foundation Paper no. 554, April.

―――. 1981. The welfare cost of capital income taxation in a growing economy. *Journal of Political Economy*, June, pp. 468–96.

Feldstein, M. S. 1974. Social security, induced retirement, and aggregate capital accumulation. *Journal of Political Economy*, September/October, pp. 905–26.

―――. 1977. The surprising incidence of a tax on pure rent: A new answer to an old question. *Journal of Political Economy*, April, pp. 349–60.

―――. 1978. The welfare cost of capital income taxation. *Journal of Political Economy*, April, pp. S29–S51.

Green, J. R., and E. Sheshinski. 1979. Approximating the efficiency gains of tax reforms. *Journal of Public Economics*, April, pp. 179–96.

King, M. A. 1980. Savings and taxation. In G. A. Hughes and G. M. Heal, eds., *Essays in public policy*. London: Chapman & Hall.

Kotlikoff, L. J. 1979. Social security and equilibrium capital intensity. *Quarterly Journal of Economics*, May, pp. 233–54.

Kotlikoff, L. J., and L. H. Summers. 1981. The role of intergenerational transfers in aggregate capital accumulation. *Journal of Political Economy*, August, pp. 706–32.

Lipton, D., and J. Sachs. 1980. Accumulation and growth in a two country model. NBER Working Paper no. 572.

Phelps, E. S., and J. G. Riley. 1978. Rawlsian growth: Dynamic programming of capital and wealth for intergenerational "Maximin" justice. *Review of Economic Studies*, February, pp. 103–20.

Summers, L. H. 1980. Capital taxation in a general equilibrium perfect foresight growth model. Mimeo, MIT.

―――. 1981. Capital taxation and accumulation in a life-cycle growth model. *American Economic Review*, September, pp. 533–44.

Comment   Joseph E. Stiglitz

The Auerbach and Kotlikoff paper is a tour de force. The authors present a simulation model of an economy in which individuals live for fifty-five years and determine their savings by maximizing intertemporal utility with perfect foresight concerning future interest rates and wage rates. The dynamic path of the economy is traced out over an extended period

Joseph E. Stiglitz is with the Department of Economics, Princeton University, and the National Bureau of Economic Research.

of time; a number of alternative tax proposals are considered, and the consequences for each cohort are examined in detail. The analysis is thus an order of magnitude more difficult than that involved in solving a conventional one-period general equilibrium problem (which is often difficult enough). It is an impressive piece of work.

Obviously, to undertake a project of this ambitiousness requires some simplifying assumptions; as always in economics, there are trade-offs: the advantages of complexity and generality in some directions are partially offset by the simplifications and idealizations made in others. The simplifications and idealizations they employed were, I think, mainly dictated by the difficulty of the problem they faced: they have chosen a set of assumptions which makes what would have seemed an impossibly difficult problem into one which is apparently tractable. But the consequence of this is that the results need to be treated with considerable caution. This is particularly true because the authors have not yet had the chance to run the sensitivity tests which would allow us to judge how robust the various results are. What particularly disturbs me about some of the assumptions employed is that earlier theoretical work on the questions at hand has identified a number of parameters that are important in determining the magnitude of the consequences (and welfare losses) associated with various tax changes. The parameterizations employed in the study include several that have some very special properties which seriously bias the results obtained.

There are several critical assumptions employed in the analysis. First, they use a Cobb-Douglas production function. Many results on tax incidence are very sensitive to what happens to the distribution of income as the capital-labor ratio changes. Hence it seems questionable to begin one's analysis with a model where constant shares are assumed.

A second assumption, which is in fact common to almost all the models that have been talked about in this conference, is that capital is perfectly malleable, and capital constructed at different dates is identical (all capital is homogeneous). For a long-run model I find that perfectly acceptable. But the authors are concerned about dynamic transition paths, and one of the lessons that those of us who worked in growth theory a number of years ago learned was that these assumptions concerning capital may make a significant difference. Although the steady states may not be much affected by whether a vintage or nonvintage capital model is employed, transition paths can be very dependent on which assumption is made.

A third property of the technology which I think is restrictive (although I don't know how restrictive it is) is that there are no public capital goods. This limits the ability of the model to discuss a number of interesting questions. These are the three critical assumptions on the technology side.

On the consumer side, the authors employ a life-cycle model. First, they have explicitly left out bequest savings (in spite of the importance which at least one of the authors has elsewhere ascribed to bequests).

Second, there is no social security. Given the importance of the effect that the social security program has on savings, the absence of social security is something with which one should be concerned. I will come back to the effect this has on some of the conclusions that the authors reach.

A third assumption concerning consumers is that they all have additive utility functions with constant elasticity. On other occasions these assumptions have been shown to lead to peculiar and implausible savings behavior.

A fourth assumption, that the elasticity of the labor supply is zero, means that a tax on labor is nondistortionary; this combined with the assumption of a positive elasticity of savings means that a consumption tax is preferred to an income tax: the simulation exercises simply confirm the result which has been built into the model.

Finally, there is the assumption that money and capital are perfect substitutes, that government bonds are perfect substitutes for equities. This is clearly a critical assumption in any analysis of the extent to which public debt crowds out private investment.

The authors ask a number of interesting questions, and they obtain a number of interesting results. I have the uneasy feeling in reading these results (a feeling that I'm sure some other people must occasionally experience) of finally becoming an old man: most of the results which are presented as if they are new were included in what we taught our graduate students in the late sixties; many are standard results in growth theory. Some of them are in the literature in articles that I'm sure are long since forgotten. Tony Atkinson and I, in our book,[1] have tried to keep some of these "old" results alive, but evidently with only partial success. To summarize my overall reaction to the results: at the qualitative level, I don't think there were any results that I found surprising or that I didn't know. On the other hand, one of the things that theory doesn't tell us is how important some of these qualitative propositions are. The contribution of the paper is to provide a quantitative estimate of the importance of these qualitative effects. But because the authors haven't yet done much sensitivity analysis, I don't know how much to believe the quantitative results they present. I just don't know at this juncture how much significance to attach to their results.

The first proposition is that a switch from one tax regime to another may have significant intergenerational effects. In particular one of the

1. A. B. Atkinson and J. E. Stiglitz, *Lectures in Public Economics* (New York and London: McGraw-Hill, 1980).

important cautions of the paper is that one should not evaluate alternatives on the basis of what happens to the steady states. If we know that the initial situation is Pareto efficient, then moving from one steady state to another obviously is going to involve some amount of redistribution. Indeed there are cases where the initial situation was not even Pareto efficient, but still steady-state consumption levels decrease with what would seem to be a desirable policy change (say, with the opening of free trade). One of the major subjects of discussion in the growth theory of the late sixties was how bad the earlier growth theory literature that just looked at steady states was and how misleading it could be. In that sense I welcome the emphasis here on the transition paths.

One of the interesting points that the authors raise is that it may be very difficult, even if you know that you're in a Pareto-inefficient state, to generate a transition that will make everyone better off. For instance, if you believe that the consumption tax is Pareto superior to the present income tax in some static sense, to go from the present tax system to a consumption tax involves a transition. To make the compensations to make sure that everybody is better off may be very difficult. In fact, they say it may be impossible. In the model they present, their conclusion is correct because, as they point out, to do it in their model would require having cohort-specific tax structures, and in general we do not allow cohort-specific tax structures. But in a model with social security, it is easy to make social security payments effectively vary with the cohort. We allow the benefits to change over time: there is a change in the benefits of social security security over time which is equivalent to a cohort-specific lump-sum redistribution. We are thus able to engineer a Pareto improvement, making sure that everybody along the transition path is better off.

A second point they raise is that temporary increases in taxes have effects outside the period in which the tax is imposed. Early announcements can have significant effects prior to the imposition of the tax. This observation is hardly new. Indeed there was considerable literature in the late sixties providing rigorous analysis of the dynamic consequences of the temporary imposition of taxes (anticipated and unanticipated). The contribution of this paper is to provide some quantitative estimates of the magnitudes involved.

One of the other points the authors raise is that a consumption tax and a wage tax are not equivalent. This appears to contradict the widely held view that they are equivalent; the difference, of course, is the effect on savings. But there exists the Modigliani-Miller theorem for consumption versus wage taxes, which says that a consumption tax and a wage tax are equivalent when the government deficit policy changes in the appropriate way. Now the assumptions in this paper, that private debt and public debt are perfect substitutes for one another in an individual's portfolio, are precisely the assumptions under which this generalized Modigliani-Miller theorem is relevant. I can see no reason why, in switching from a wage to a consumption tax, the government would not make the compensating changes in deficit policy. Thus the only reason the authors obtain a difference between a consumption and a wage tax is that they accompany the switch with a change in deficit policy which is not the appropriate change. Thus there is a confusion between the effects of a change in tax policy with a change in deficit policy. (In their paper they have a particular set of rules by which the government changes deficits over time. What the authors thus do is to show us the consequences of a change in tax policy if the government doesn't alter its debt policy.) Their analysis tells us more about the importance of deficit policy than about tax policy.

Similar questions can be raised concerning their interesting results on the magnitude of crowding out. As they point out, these results seem particularly sensitive to the implicit assumptions relating to the particular pattern of debt policy they assume the government is going to pursue (as well as to the particular assumptions about the substitutibility of debt and capital).

Another interesting numerical result that they obtain is that in the switch to the consumption tax, two-thirds of the steady-state gain represent a redistribution from earlier generations and only one-third represents efficiency gains. One again knows from the literature precisely what conditions will determine the magnitude of the efficiency gain associated with switching from an income tax to a consumption tax. That is to say, one knows that a consumption tax is optimal (a) if the labor supply is inelastic or (b) even if it is elastic, if the marginal rates of substitution between consumption at different dates are independent of the amount of labor that individuals consume. These conditions are both satisfied in their model. Their assumptions thus clearly bias the results they obtain. Again, because of the lack of sensitivity analysis, one cannot tell how important quantitatively these biases are. But it is important in their future work that the authors focus on parameterizations which at least allow the possibility that the consumption tax is not optimal. Unfortunately, this requires that they employ utility functions in which leisure and consumption are not separable.

Let me conclude by mentioning two other points. First, a progressive consumption tax is distortionary, unless you have lifetime averaging; consumption at different dates will be subjected to different marginal tax rates. Second, one of the important results of the earlier theoretical literature is that one can get very close to a utilitarian optimum with a linear income tax or a linear consumption tax, and that the deviation from the welfare optimum will be a function of the degree of nonconstancy in the elasticity of the relevant consumption functions. That is, if you have a constant-elasticity utility function you can get very close to the utilitarian solution by a linear tax structure. Thus the model they employ, with a constant-elasticity utility function, biases the analyses, perhaps strongly, in favor of a linear tax structure. (This would greatly simplify the tax structure and solve a lot of the problems presently facing tax authorities.)

Thus, while the authors have accomplished a tour de force in providing us with a dynamic, life-cycle simulation model within which the effects of certain tax policies may be analyzed, tractability has forced them to employ a number of assumptions which seriously bias the results obtained. In their future work, I hope the authors can extend the model by testing the sensitivity of their model and the robustness of the results. In doing so, let me encourage them in particular to focus their efforts on investigating the effect of altering those parameters which theoretical analysis has shown to be critical in determining, for instance, the desirability of consumption versus income taxation.

Contributors

Henry Aaron
Brookings Institution
1775 Massachusetts Avenue, N.W.
Washington, DC 20036

Alan J. Auerbach
National Bureau of Economic
  Research
1050 Massachusetts Avenue
Cambridge, MA 02138

Marcy Avrin
4010 Dunster Way
Sacramento, CA 95825

Martin J. Bailey
Department of Economics
University of Maryland
College Park, MD 20742

Michael J. Boskin
National Bureau of Economic
  Research
104 Junipero Serra Boulevard
Stanford, CA 94305

Kenneth Cone
National Bureau of Economic
  Research
104 Junipero Serra Boulevard
Stanford, CA 94305

Daniel R. Feenberg
National Bureau of Economic
  Research
1050 Massachusetts Avenue
Cambridge, MA 02138

Martin Feldstein
Council of Economic Advisers
Old Executive Office Building
Seventeenth and Pennsylvania
  Avenue, N.W.
Washington, DC 20506

Daniel J. Frisch
Department of Economics
University of Washington
301 Savery Hall
Seattle, WA 98195

Don Fullerton
Woodrow Wilson School
Princeton University
Princeton, NJ 08544

Harvey Galper
Brookings Institution
1775 Massachusetts Avenue, N.W.
Washington, DC 20036

Roger H. Gordon
Bell Laboratories
600 Mountain Avenue
Murray Hill, NJ 07974

Lawrence H. Goulder
Department of Economics
Littauer Center 236
Harvard University
Cambridge, MA 02138

David G. Hartman
National Bureau of Economic
    Research
1050 Massachusetts Avenue
Cambridge, MA 02138

Jerry A. Hausman
Department of Economics
Massachusetts Institute of Technology
Cambridge, MA 02139

James J. Heckman
Economics Research Center/NORC
University of Chicago
6030 South Ellis
Chicago, IL 60637

Patric H. Hendershott
Department of Economics
Ohio State University
1775 South College Road
Columbus, OH 43210

Thomas Horst
Taxecon Associates
11708 Ibsen Drive
Rockville, MD 20852

Mervyn A. King
University of Birmingham
Department of Economics
Faculty of Commerce and
    Social Science
P.O. Box 363
Birmingham B15 2TT
England

Laurence J. Kotlikoff
Council of Economic Advisers
Old Executive Office Building
Washington, DC 20506

Lawrence B. Lindsey
Council of Economic Advisers
Old Executive Office Building
Washington, DC 20506

Charles E. McLure, Jr.
Hoover Institution
Stanford University
Stanford, CA 94305

Peter Mieszkowski
Department of Economics
University of Houston
Houston, TX 77004

Joseph J. Minarik
Deputy Assistant Director
Congressional Budget Office
Second and D Streets
Washington, DC 20515

Harvey S. Rosen
Department of Economics
Princeton University
Princeton, NJ 08544

Michael A. Salinger
Graduate School of Business
Uris Hall, Room 605B
Columbia University
New York, NY 10027

Robert J. Shiller
Cowles Foundation
Yale University
2125 Yale Station
New Haven, CT 06520

John B. Shoven
Department of Economics
Fourth Floor, Encina Hall
Stanford University
Stanford, CA 94305

Joel Slemrod
Department of Economics
University of Minnesota
Minneapolis, MN 55455

Joseph E. Stiglitz
Department of Economics
Princeton University
Princeton, NJ 08544

Lawrence H. Summers
National Bureau of Economic
    Research
1050 Massachusetts Avenue
Cambridge, MA 02138

John Whalley
Department of Economics
University of Western Ontario
London, Ontario
Canada

David A. Wise
John F. Kennedy School of
    Government
Harvard University
79 Boylston Street
Cambridge, MA 02138

Author Index

Subject Index